BENCHMARK SERIES

MICROSOFT
POWERPOINT®
2013

NITA RUTKOSKY
Pierce College at Puyallup
Puyallup, Washington

AUDREY ROGGENKAMP
Pierce College at Puyallup
Puyallup, Washington

IAN RUTKOSKY
Pierce College at Puyallup
Puyallup, Washington

Paradigm
PUBLISHING

St. Paul

Managing Editor	Christine Hurney
Director of Production	Timothy W. Larson
Production Editor	Sarah Kearin
Cover and Text Designers	Leslie Anderson and Jaana Bykonich
Copy Editor	Nan Brooks, Abshier House
Desktop Production	Jaana Bykonich, Julie Johnston, Valerie King, Timothy W. Larson, Jack Ross, and Sara Schmidt Boldon
Indexer	Terry Casey
VP & Director of Digital Projects	Chuck Bratton
Digital Projects Manager	Tom Modl

Acknowledgements: The authors, editors, and publisher thank the following instructors for their helpful suggestions during the planning and development of the books in the Benchmark Office 2013 Series: Olugbemiga Adekunle, Blue Ridge Community College, Harrisonburg, VA; Letty Barnes, Lake WA Institute of Technology, Kirkland, WA; Erika Nadas, Wilbur Wright College, Chicago, IL; Carolyn Walker, Greenville Technical College, Greenville, SC; Carla Anderson, National College, Lynchburg, VA; Judy A. McLaney, Lurleen B. Wallace Community College, Opp, AL; Sue Canter, Guilford Technical Community College, Jamestown, NC; Reuel Sample, National College, Knoxville, TN; Regina Young, Wiregrass Georgia Technical College, Valdosta, GA; William Roxbury, National College, Stow, OH; Charles Adams, II, Danville Community College, Danville, VA; Karen Spray, Northeast Community College, Norfolk, NE; Deborah Miller, Augusta Technical College, Augusta, GA; Wanda Stuparits, Lanier Technical College, Cumming, GA; Gale Wilson, Brookhaven College, Farmers Branch, TX; Jocelyn S. Pinkard, Arlington Career Institute, Grand Prairie, TX; Ann Blackman, Parkland College, Champaign, IL; Fathia Williams, Fletcher Technical Community College, Houma, LA; Leslie Martin, Gaston College, Dallas, NC; Tom Rose, Kellogg Community College, Battle Creek, MI; Casey Thompson, Wiregrass Georgia Technical College, Douglas, GA; Larry Bush, University of Cincinnati, Clermont College, Amelia, OH; Tim Ellis, Schoolcraft College, Liconia, MI; Miles Cannon, Lanier Technical College, Oakwood, GA; Irvin LaFleur, Lanier Technical College, Cumming, GA; Patricia Partyka, Schoolcraft College, Prudenville, MI.

The authors and publishing team also thanks the following individuals for their contributions to this project: checking the accuracy of the instruction and exercises—Brienna McWade, Traci Post, and Janet Blum, Fanshawe College, London, Ontario; creating annotated model answers and developing lesson plans—Ann Mills, Ivy Tech Community College, Evansville, Indiana; developing rubrics—Marjory Wooten, Laneir Techncial College, Cumming, Georgia.

Trademarks: Access, Excel, Internet Explorer, Microsoft, PowerPoint, and Windows are trademarks or registered trademarks of Microsoft Corporation in the United States and/or other countries. Some of the product names and company names included in this book have been used for identification purposes only and may be trademarks or registered trade names of their respective manufacturers and sellers. The authors, editors, and publisher disclaim any affiliation, association, or connection with, or sponsorship or endorsement by, such owners.

We have made every effort to trace the ownership of all copyrighted material and to secure permission from copyright holders. In the event of any question arising as to the use of any material, we will be pleased to make the necessary corrections in future printings. Thanks are due to the aforementioned authors, publishers, and agents for permission to use the materials indicated.

Paradigm Publishing is independent from Microsoft Corporation, and not affiliated with Microsoft in any manner. While this publication may be used in assisting individuals to prepare for a Microsoft Office Specialist certification exam, Microsoft, its designated program administrator, and Paradigm Publishing do not warrant that use of this publication will ensure passing a Microsoft Office Specialist certification exam.

ISBN 978-0-76385-352-5 (Text)
ISBN 978-0-76385-395-2 (Text + CD)
ISBN 978-0-76385-374-7 (ebook via email);
ISBN 978-0-76385-417-1 (ebook via mail)

Contents

Microsoft PowerPoint 2013

Benchmark Series Microsoft PowerPoint 2013 teaches students how to build eye-catching presentations that communicate key information to audiences in business, academic, and organization settings. No prior knowledge of presentation software is required. After successfully completing a course using this textbook, students will be able to

- Plan, create, and revise presentations, including executing basic skills such as opening, editing, running, saving, and closing a presentation
- Format slides using design templates, slide and title masters, styles, bullets and numbering, headers and footers, and speaker notes
- Create visual appeal with images, SmartArt, charts, animation effects, and sound and video effects
- Share presentations for collaboration and review with others
- Given a workplace scenario requiring a presentation solution, assess the information requirements and then prepare the materials that achieve the goal efficiently and effectively

In addition to mastering PowerPoint skills, students will learn the essential features and functions of computer hardware, the Windows 8 operating system, and Internet Explorer 10. Upon completing the text, they can expect to be proficient in using PowerPoint to organize, analyze, and present information.

Well-designed textbook pedagogy is important, but students learn technology skills from practice and problem solving. Technology provides opportunities for interactive learning as well as excellent ways to quickly and accurately assess student performance. To this end, this textbook is supported with SNAP, Paradigm Publishing's web-based training and assessment learning management system. Details about SNAP as well as additional student courseware and instructor resources can be found on page xiv.

Achieving Proficiency in PowerPoint 2013 ■■■■■

Since its inception several Office versions ago, the Benchmark Series has served as a standard of excellence in software instruction. Elements of the book function individually and collectively to create an inviting, comprehensive learning environment that produces successful computer users. The following visual tour highlights the text's features.

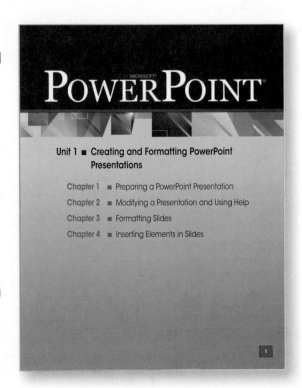

UNIT OPENERS display the unit's four chapter titles. Each unit concludes with a comprehensive unit performance assessment emphasizing the use of program features plus analytical, writing, and research skills.

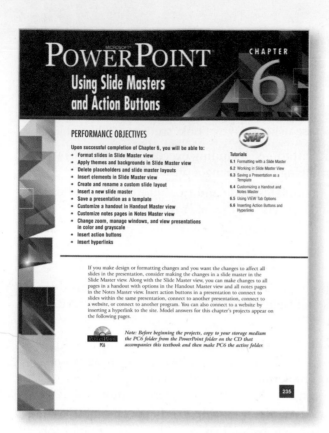

CHAPTER OPENERS present the performance objectives and an overview of the skills taught.

SNAP interactive tutorials are available to support chapter-specific skills at snap2013.emcp.com.

DATA FILES are provided for each chapter. A prominent note reminds students to copy the appropriate chapter data folder and make it active.

PROJECT APPROACH: Builds Skill Mastery within Realistic Context

MODEL ANSWERS provide a preview of the finished chapter projects and allow students to confirm they have created them accurately.

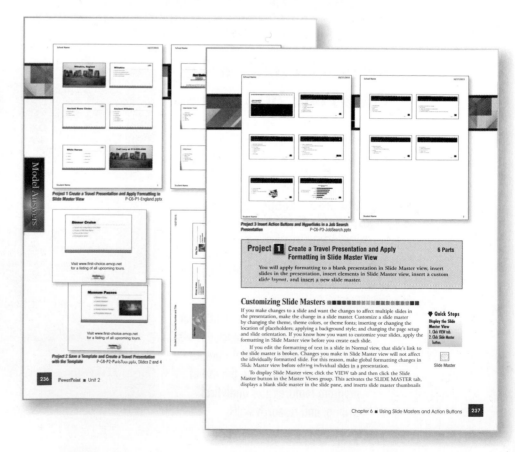

Project 4 Create and Apply Custom Themes to Presentations
4 Parts

You will create custom theme colors and custom theme fonts and then save the changes as a custom theme. You will then apply the custom theme to a job search presentation and a resume writing presentation.

Creating Custom Themes ■■■■■■■■■■■■■■■■■■■■■■

If the default themes, theme colors, and theme fonts do not provide the formatting you desire for your presentation, you can create your own custom theme colors, custom theme fonts, and a custom theme. A theme you create will display in the *Custom* section of the Themes drop-down gallery. To create a custom theme, change the theme colors, theme fonts, and/or theme effects.

Click the More button in the Variants group on the DESIGN tab and the options at the drop-down list display a visual representation of the current theme. If you change the theme colors, the colors are reflected in the small color squares on the *Colors* option. If you change the theme fonts, the *A* on the *Fonts* option reflects the change.

Creating Custom Theme Colors

To create custom theme colors, click the DESIGN tab, click the More button located to the right of the Variants group, point to the *Colors* option at the drop-down list, and then click *Customize Colors* at the side menu. This displays the Create New Theme Colors dialog box, similar to the one shown in Figure 3.10. Theme colors contain four text and background colors, six accent colors, and two hyperlink colors, as shown in the *Themes color* section of the dialog box. Change a color in the option box by clicking the color button at the right side of the color option and then clicking the desired color at the color palette.

▼ **Quick Steps**

Create Custom Theme Colors
1. Click DESIGN tab.
2. Click More button in Variants group.
3. Point to Colors.
4. Click Customize Colors.
5. Change to desired background, accent, and hyperlink colors.
6. Type name for custom theme colors.
7. Click Save button.

Figure 3.10 Create New Theme Colors Dialog Box

Change a theme color by clicking the color button and then clicking the desired color at the drop-down palette.

Click the Reset button to reset color back to the default.

MULTIPART PROJECTS provide a framework for instruction and practice on software features. A project overview identifies tasks to accomplish and key features to use in completing the work.

Between project parts, the text presents instruction on the features and skills necessary to accomplish the next section of the project.

QUICK STEPS provide feature summaries for reference and review.

STEP-BY-STEP INSTRUCTIONS guide students to the desired outcome for each project part. Screen captures illustrate what the student's screen should look like at key points.

Creating Custom Theme Fonts

To create custom theme fonts, click the DESIGN tab, click the More button in the Variants group, point to the *Fonts* option, and then click *Customize Fonts* at the side menu. This displays the Create New Theme Fonts dialog box similar to the one shown in Figure 3.11. At this dialog box, choose a heading font and body font. Type the name of the custom theme fonts in the *Name* box and then click the Save button.

▼ **Quick Steps**

Create Custom Fonts
1. Click DESIGN tab.
2. Click More button in Variants group.
3. Point to Fonts.
4. Click Customize Fonts.
5. Choose desired fonts.
6. Type name for custom theme fonts.
7. Click Save button.

Figure 3.11 Create New Theme Fonts Dialog Box

Choose a heading font and body font, type a new name for the theme in the *Name* text box, and then click Save.

Project 4b Creating Custom Theme Fonts
Part 2 of 4

1. With **P-C3-P4-CustomTheme.pptx** open, create custom theme fonts by completing the following steps:
   a. If necessary, click the DESIGN tab.
   b. Click the More button in the Variants group, point to the *Fonts* option, and then click the *Customize Fonts* option at the drop-down gallery.
   c. At the Create New Theme Fonts dialog box, click the down-pointing arrow at the right side of the *Heading font* option box, scroll up the drop-down list, and then click *Candara*.
   d. Click the down-pointing arrow at the right side of the *Body font* option box, scroll down the drop-down list, and then click *Constantia*.
2. Save the custom theme fonts by completing the following steps:
   a. Select the current text in the *Name* text box.
   b. Type your first and last names.
   c. Click the Save button.
3. Save **P-C3-P4-CustomTheme.pptx**.

Step 1c

Step 1d

Step 2h

Step 2n

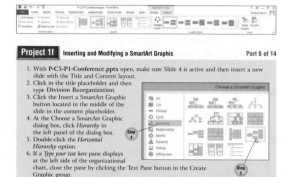

Modifying SmartArt

Predesigned graphics display in the middle panel of the Choose a SmartArt Graphic dialog box. Use the scroll bar at the right side of the middle panel to scroll down the list of graphic choices. Click a graphic in the middle panel and the name of the graphic displays in the right panel along with a description of the graphic type. SmartArt includes graphics for presenting a list of data; showing data processes, cycles, and relationships; and presenting data in a matrix or pyramid. Double-click a graphic in the middle panel of the dialog box and the graphic is inserted in the slide.

When you double-click a graphic at the dialog box, the graphic is inserted in the slide and a text pane may display at the left side of the graphic. You can type text in the text pane or directly in the graphic. Apply design formatting to a graphic with options on the SMARTART TOOLS DESIGN tab, shown in Figure 5.5. This tab is active when the graphic is inserted and selected in the slide. With options and buttons in this tab you add objects, change the graphic layout, apply a style to the graphic, and reset the graphic back to the original formatting.

Figure 5.5 SMARTART TOOLS DESIGN Tab

HINT
Use SmartArt to communicate your message and ideas in a visual manner.

HINT
Limit the number of shapes and the amount of text to key points in a slide.

Project 1f   Inserting and Modifying a SmartArt Graphic   Part 6 of 14

1. With **P-C5-P1-Conference.pptx** open, make sure Slide 4 is active and then insert a new slide with the Title and Content layout.
2. Click in the title placeholder and then type **Division Reorganization**.
3. Click the Insert a SmartArt Graphic button located in the middle of the slide in the content placeholder.
4. At the Choose a SmartArt Graphic dialog box, click *Hierarchy* in the left panel of the dialog box.
5. Double-click the *Horizontal Hierarchy* option.
6. If a *Type your text here* pane displays at the left side of the organizational chart, close the pane by clicking the Text Pane button in the Create Graphic group.
7. Delete one of the boxes in the organizational chart by clicking the border of the top box at the right side of the slide (the top box of the three stacked boxes) and then pressing the Delete key. (Make sure that the selection border that surrounds the box is a solid line and not a dashed line. If a dashed line displays, click the box border again. This should change it to a solid line.)

---

b. Click the left mouse button to advance slides.
c. Click the Custom Slide Show button, click *FijiTourCustom* at the drop-down list, and then view the presentation. (Click the left mouse button to advance slides.)
4. Edit the FijiTourCustom custom slide show by completing the following steps:
   a. Click the Custom Slide Show button on the SLIDE SHOW tab and then click *Custom Shows* at the drop-down list.
   b. At the Custom Shows dialog box, click *FijiTourCustom* in the *Custom shows* list box and then click the Edit button.
   c. At the Define Custom Show dialog box, click Slide 2 in the *Slides in custom show* list box and then click the Down button at the right side of the list box three times. (This moves the slide to the bottom of the list.)
   d. Click OK to close the dialog box.
   e. Click the Close button to close the Custom Shows dialog box.
5. Run the FijiTourCustom custom show.
6. Print the FijiTourCustom custom show by completing the following steps:
   a. Click the FILE tab and then click the *Print* option.
   b. At the Print backstage area, click the first gallery in the *Settings* category and then click *FijiTourCustom* in the *Custom Shows* section.
   c. Click the second gallery in the *Settings* category and then click *6 Slides Horizontal* at the drop-down list.
   d. Click the Print button.
7. Save and then close **P-C7-P3-AdvTours-Custom.pptx**.

Project 4   Insert Audio and Video Files in a Presentation   4 Parts

You will open a presentation and then insert an audio file, video file, and clip art image with motion. You will also customize the audio and video files to play automatically when running the presentation.

Inserting Audio and Video Files ■■■■■■■■■■■■■■■

Adding audio and/or video files to a presentation will turn a slide show into a true multimedia experience for your audience. Including a variety of elements in a presentation will stimulate interest in your presentation and keep the audience motivated.

Inserting an Audio File

To add an audio file to your presentation, click the INSERT tab, click the Audio button in the Media group, and then click *Audio on My PC* at the drop-down list. At the Insert Audio dialog box, navigate to the desired folder and then double-click the audio file.

HINTS provide useful tips on how to use features efficiently and effectively.

MAGENTA TEXT identifies material to type.

At the end of the project, students save, print, and then close the file.

CHAPTER REVIEW ACTIVITIES: A Hierarchy of Learning Assessments

Chapter Summary

- With the Table button in the Tables group on the INSERT tab, you can create a table, insert an Excel spreadsheet, and draw a table in a slide.
- Change the table design with options and buttons on the TABLE TOOLS DESIGN tab. Change the table layout with options and buttons in the TABLE TOOLS LAYOUT tab.
- Use the SmartArt feature to insert predesigned graphics such as diagrams and organizational charts in a slide.
- Use options and buttons in the SMARTART TOOLS DESIGN tab to change the graphic layout, apply a style to the graphic, and reset the graphic back to the original formatting.
- Use options and buttons in the SMARTART TOOLS FORMAT tab to change the size and shapes of objects in the graphic; apply shape styles; change the shape fill, outline, and effects; and arrange and size the graphic.
- Insert text directly into a SmartArt graphic shape or at the Text pane. Display this pane by clicking the Text Pane button in the Create Graphic group on the SMARTART TOOLS DESIGN tab.
- You can convert text or WordArt to a SmartArt graphic and convert a SmartArt graphic to text or shapes.
- A chart is a visual presentation of data. Y... described in Table 5.2.
- To create a chart, display the Insert Char... Chart button in a content placeholder or... Illustrations group on the INSERT tab.
- Enter chart data in an Excel worksheet. Y... the next cell active, press Shift + Tab to... Enter to make the cell below active.
- Modify a chart design with options and... DESIGN tab.
- Cells in the Excel worksheet used to crea... the slide. To edit chart data, click the Ed... DESIGN tab and then make changes to...
- Customize the format of a chart and char... on the CHART TOOLS FORMAT tab. Y... element, apply a style to a shape, apply a... size the chart.
- Use the Photo Album feature in the Ima... a presentation containing pictures and th...
- At the Photo Album dialog box (or the E... pictures and then use options to customi...
- Use options on the DRAWING TOOLS... TOOLS FORMAT tab to format pictures...

CHAPTER SUMMARY captures the purpose and execution of key features.

- Type text in a slide in the slide pane or in the outline pane. Display the outline pane by clicking the VIEW tab and then clicking the Outline View button.
- Enhance a presentation by adding transitions (how one slide is removed from the screen and replaced with the next slide) and sound. Add transitions and sound to a presentation with options on the TRANSITIONS tab.
- Advance slides automatically in a slide show by removing the check mark from the *On Mouse Click* check box on the TRANSITIONS tab, inserting a check mark in the *After* check box, and then specifying the desired time in the time measurement box.
- Click the Apply To All button to apply transitions, sounds, and/or time settings to all slides in a presentation.

Commands Review

FEATURE	RIBBON TAB, GROUP	BUTTON, OPTION	KEYBOARD SHORTCUT
close presentation	FILE	*Close*	Ctrl + F4
design theme	DESIGN, Themes		
New backstage area	FILE	*New*	
new slide	HOME, Slides		Ctrl + M
Normal view	VIEW, Presentation Vie...		
Notes Page view	VIEW, Presentation Vie...		
Open backstage area	FILE		
Outline view	VIEW, Presentation Vie...		
Print backstage area	FILE		
run presentation	SLIDE SHOW, Start Sli... OR Quick Access Toolbar		
Save As backstage area	FILE		
slide layout	HOME, Slides		
Slide Sorter view	VIEW, Presentation Vie...		
sound	TRANSITIONS, Timing		
transition	TRANSITIONS, Transiti...		
transition duration	Transitions, Timing		

COMMANDS REVIEW summarizes visually the major features and alternative methods of access.

Concepts Check Test Your Knowledge

Completion: In the space provided at the right, indicate the correct term, command, or number.

1. Click this tab to display options for working with and managing presentations.
2. This toolbar contains buttons for commonly used commands.
3. This area contains the tabs and commands divided into groups.
4. This is the keyboard shortcut to close a presentation.
5. Display theme templates in this backstage area.
6. Insert a new slide by clicking the New Slide button in this group on the HOME tab.
7. Change to this view to view all slides in the presentation as slide thumbnails.
8. This is the default view and displays two panes.
9. Click this button on the VIEW tab to display the outline pane.
10. The Previous Slide and Next Slide buttons display in this location.
11. To run a presentation beginning with Slide 1, click this button on the Quick Access toolbar.
12. Apply a theme to a presentation by clicking this tab and then clicking the desired theme in the Themes group.
13. To add a transition, click a transition thumbnail in the Transition to This Slide group on this tab.
14. When you apply a transition to slides in a presentation, these display below the slides in the slide thumbnails pane.
15. To advance slides automatically, remove the check mark from the *On Mouse Click* option, insert a check mark in this option, and then insert the desired number of seconds.

CONCEPTS CHECK questions assess knowledge recall. Students enrolled in SNAP can complete the Concepts Check online. SNAP automatically scores student work.

Skills Check   Assess Your Performance

Assessment

1   CREATE, FORMAT, AND MODIFY A BENEFITS PRESENTATION

1. At a blank presentation, create the slides shown in Figure 3.12.
2. Apply the Facet design theme and then apply the blue variant.
3. Make Slide 1 active and then make the following changes:
    a. Select the title *BENEFITS PROGRAM*, change the font to Candara and the font size to 60 points, apply the Turquoise, Accent 1, Darker 50% font color, and apply italic formatting.
    b. Select the subtitle *Changes to Plans*, cha[...] size to 32 points, apply the Turquoise, [...] and shadow formatting.
    c. Click the title placeholder and then clic[...] Paragraph group.
    d. Center the subtitle in the placeholder.
4. Make Slide 2 active and then make the f[...]
    a. Select the title *INTRODUCTION*, cha[...] size to 44 points, apply the Turquoise, [...] and apply shadow formatting.
    b. Using Format Painter, apply the title fo[...] remaining slides.
5. Center-align and middle-align the titles in[...]
6. Make Slide 2 active, select the bulleted te[...] to double spacing (2.0).
7. Make Slide 3 active, select the bulleted te[...] to double spacing (2.0).
8. Make Slide 4 active, select the bulleted te[...] to 1.5.
9. Make Slide 5 active, select the bulleted te[...] paragraphs to *18 pt. Hint: Do this at the[...]*
10. Make Slide 2 active and then select the t[...] Display the Bullets and Numbering dialog[...] selected, choose the *1. 2. 3.* option, chang[...] Turquoise, Accent 1, Darker 50% color, a[...]
11. Make Slide 3 active and then select the t[...] Display the Bullets and Numbering dialog[...] selected, choose the *1. 2. 3.* option, chang[...] Turquoise, Accent 1, Darker 50% color, c[...] and then close the dialog box.
12. Make Slide 4 active, select the text in th[...] change the bullets to *Hollow Square Bullets[...]*
13. Make Slide 5 active, select the text in the[...] change the bullets to *Hollow Square Bullets[...]*
14. Save the presentation and name it **P-C3-[...]**
15. Print the presentation as a handout with s[...]
16. Apply the Organic design theme.
17. Apply a transition and sound of your cho[...]
18. Run the presentation.

Visual Benchmark   Demonstrate Your Proficiency

FORMAT A PRESENTATION ON HOME SAFETY

1. Open **HomeSafety.pptx** and then save the presentation with Save As and name it **P-C3-VB-HomeSafety**.
2. Format the presentation so the slides appear as shown in Figure 3.13 with the following specifications.
    a. Apply the Facet design theme and the blue variant color.
    b. Delete and rearrange slides as shown in the figure.
    c. Apply the Parchment texture slide background and change the slide background transparency to 50% for all slides in the presentation. *Hint: Apply these options using the Format Background task pane.*
    d. Change the font size of the title in Slide 1 to 60 points, apply bold formatting, apply the Blue, Accent 2, Darker 25% font color, and center-align the title.
    e. Change the font size of the subtitle in Slide 1 to 28 points, apply italics, change the font color to Turquoise, Accent 1, Darker 25%, and center-align the subtitle.
    f. Change the font size of the titles in Slides 2 through 6 to 48 points and the font color to Turquoise, Accent 1, Darker 50%.
    g. Change the line spacing, spacing after, column formatting, and bullet styles so your slides display in a manner similar to the slides in Figure 3.13.
    h. Select the bulleted text placeholder in Slide 6, display the Format Shape task pane, select the *Solid fill* option, and then change the color to Turquoise, Accent 1, Lighter 80%. Display the Format Shape task pane with the TEXT OPTIONS tab selected and the Textbox icon selected, then change the left margin to 1 inch and th[...]
3. Print the presentation as a handout with s[...] page.
4. Save and then close the presentation.

Figure 3.13 Visual Benchmark

Safety at Home

Stairs

Kitchen

Bathroom

Outdoor

Safety Supplies

Case Study   Apply Your Skills

Part 1

You are the office manager at the Career Finders agency. One of your responsibilities is to conduct workshops to prepare individuals for the job search process. A coworker has given you a presentation for the workshop but the presentation needs some editing and modifying. Open **JobAnalysis.pptx** and then save the presentation with Save As and name it **P-C2-CS-JobAnalysis**. Check each slide in the presentation and then make modifications to maintain consistency in the size and location of placeholders (consider using the Reset button to reset the formatting and size of the placeholders), maintain consistency in heading text, move text from an overcrowded slide to a new slide, complete a spelling check, apply a design theme, and make any other modifications to improve the presentation. Save **P-C2-CS-JobAnalysis.pptx**.

Part 2

After reviewing the presentation, you realize that you need to include slides on resumes. Open the **ResumePres.pptx** presentation and then copy Slides 2 and 3 into the **P-C2-CS-JobAnalysis.pptx** presentation (at the end of the presentation). You want to add additional information on resume writing tips and decide to use the Internet to find information. Search for tips on writing a resume and then create a slide (or two) with the information you find. Add a transition and sound to all slides in the presentation. Save **P-C2-CS-JobAnalysis.pptx**.

Part 3

You know that Microsoft Word offers a number of resume templates you can download from the Office.com website. You decide to include information in the presentation on how to find and download resumes. Open Microsoft Word and then click the *Blank document* template at the Word 2013 opening screen. At the blank document, click the FILE tab and then click the *New* option. At the New backstage area, click in the search text box, type **resume**, and then press Enter. Scroll through the list of resume templates that displays and then experiment with downloading a template. With the **P-C2-CS-JobAnalysis.pptx** presentation open, add an additional slide to the end of the presentation that provides steps on how to download a resume in Microsoft Word. Print the presentation as a handout with nine slides printed horizontally per page. Save, run, and then close the presentation.

UNIT PERFORMANCE ASSESSMENT: Cross-Disciplinary, Comprehensive Evaluation

UNIT 2

PowerPoint Performance Assessment

ASSESSING PROFICIENCY checks mastery of features.

Note: Before beginning unit assessments, copy to your storage medium the PU2 folder from the PowerPoint folder on the CD that accompanies this textbook and then make PU2 the active folder.

Assessing Proficiency

In this unit you have learned to add visual elements to presentations such as tables, charts, and SmartArt graphics; create a photo album; apply formatting in Slide Master view; insert action buttons; apply custom animation effects; and set up slide shows. You also learned how to copy, embed, and link data between programs; how to insert comments; and how to protect and prepare a presentation.

Assessment 1 Save a Slide in JPEG Format and Copy and Link Objects in a Presentation

1. Open **GreenDesignLogo.pptx**, save the only slide in the presentation as a JPEG graphic image, and then close **GreenDesignLogo.pptx**.
2. Open **GreenDesignPres.pptx** and then save the presentation with the name **P-U2-A1-GreenDesignPres**.
3. Display the presentation in Slide Master view and then make the following changes:
   a. Click the top slide master thumbnail.
   b. Select the text *Click to edit Master text styles* (in the bulleted section), change the font color to Tan, Background 2, Darker 75% (third column, fifth row), and change the font size to 28 points.
   c. Select the text *Second level*, apply the Green, Accent 1 font color (fifth column, first row), and then change the font size to 24 points.
   d. Close Slide Master view.
4. Make Slide 1 active and then make the following changes:
   a. Insert the **GreenDesignLogo.jpg** graphic image.
   b. Set transparent color for the logo background (the white background). (Do this with the *Set Transparent Color* option at the Color button drop-down gallery on the PICTURE TOOLS FORMAT tab.)
   c. Reduce the size of the logo and position it in the white space in the upper right corner of the slide above the water image.
5. Make Slide 6 active and then insert the following data in a table. You determine the formatting and positioning of the table and its data (next page):

6. Open **P-U2-A5-GreenDesignPres.pptx** and then save the presentation as a PDF document.
7. View the presentation in Adobe Reader.
8. After viewing all of the slides, close Adobe Reader.
9. Close **P-U2-A5-GreenDesignPres.pptx** without saving the changes.
10. Capture an image of the Open dialog box and insert the image in a PowerPoint slide by completing the following steps:
    a. Press Ctrl + N to display a new blank presentation.
    b. Click the Layout button in the Slides group on the HOME tab and then click the *Blank* layout at the drop-down list.
    c. Press Ctrl + F12 to display the Open dialog box.
    d. At the Open dialog box, click the option button that displays to the right of the *File name* text box (option button that contains the text *All Power-Point Presentations*) and then click *All Files (*.*)* at the drop-down list.
    e. Scroll down the Open dialog box list box to display your assessment files.
    f. Hold down the Alt key and then press the Print Screen button on your keyboard. (This captures an image of your Open dialog box.)
    g. Click the Cancel button to close the Open dialog box.
    h. Click the Paste button. (This inserts the image of your Open dialog box into the slide.)
11. Print the slide as a full page slide.
12. Close the presentation without saving it.

Writing Activities

The following activities give you the opportunity to practice your writing skills along with demonstrating an understanding of some of the important PowerPoint features you have mastered in this unit. Use correct grammar, appropriate word choices, and clear sentence structure.

WRITING ACTIVITIES involve applying program skills in a communication context.

Activity 2 Prepare and Format a Presentation on Media Files

Using PowerPoint's Help feature, learn more about audio and video file formats compatible with PowerPoint 2013. (Use the search terms *video and audio file formats*.) Using the information you find in the Help files, create a presentation with *at least* the following specifications:

- A slide containing the title of the presentation and your name.
- Two slides that each contain information on compatible audio file formats, including the file extension
- Two slides that each contain information on compatible video file formats, including the file extensions
- Optional: If you are connected to the Internet, search for websites where you can download free audio clips and then include this information in a slide with a hyperlink to the site.

Save the completed presentation and name it **P-U2-Act2-AudioVideo**. Run the presentation and then print the presentation as a handout with six slides printed horizontally per page. Close **P-U2-Act2-AudioVideo.pptx**.

Internet Research

INTERNET RESEARCH project reinforces research and presentation development skills.

Presenting Office 2013

Make sure you are connected to the Internet and then explore the Microsoft website at www.microsoft.com. Browse the various categories and links on the website to familiarize yourself with how information is organized.

Create a PowerPoint presentation to deliver to someone who has just purchased Office 2013 and wants to know how to find more information about the software on the Microsoft website. Include tips on where to find product release information and technical support, as well as hyperlinks to other important pages. Add formatting and enhancements to make the presentation as dynamic as possible. Save the presentation and name it **P-U2-Int-Office2013**. Run the presentation and then print the presentation as a handout with six slides printed per page. Close **P-U2-Int-Office2013.pptx**.

Job Study

JOB STUDY at the end of Unit 2 presents a capstone assessment requiring critical thinking and problem solving.

Creating a Skills Presentation

You are preparing a presentation to give at your local job fair. Open the Word document **JobDescriptions.docx**, print the document, and then close the document and close Word. Use the information in the document to prepare slides that describe each job (do not include the starting salary). Using the Internet, locate information on two other jobs that interest you and then create a slide about the responsibilities of each job. Determine the starting salary for the two jobs and then use that information along with the starting salary information for the jobs in the Word document to create a chart that displays the salary amounts. Locate at least two online job search websites and then include their names in your presentation along with hyperlinks to the sites. Save the presentation and name it **P-U2-JobStudy**. Run the presentation and then print the presentation as a handout with six slides printed horizontally per page. Close **P-U2-JobStudy.pptx**.

Student Courseware

Student Resources CD Each Benchmark Series textbook is packaged with a Student Resources CD containing the data files required for completing the projects and assessments. A CD icon and folder name displayed on the opening page of chapters reminds students to copy a folder of files from the CD to the desired storage medium before beginning the project exercises. Directions for copying folders are printed on the inside back cover.

Internet Resource Center Additional learning tools and reference materials are available at the book-specific website at www.paradigmcollege.net/BenchmarkPowerPoint13. Students can access the same files that are on the Student Resources CD along with study tools, study quizzes, web links, and tips for using computers effectively in academic and workplace settings.

SNAP Training and Assessment Available at snap2013.emcp.com, SNAP is a web-based program offering an interactive venue for learning Microsoft Office 2013, Windows 8, and Internet Explorer 10. Along with a web-based learning management system, SNAP provides multimedia tutorials, performance skill items, Concepts Check matching activities, Grade It Skills Check Assessment activities, comprehensive performance evaluations, a concepts test bank, an online grade book, and a set of course planning tools. A CD of tutorials teaching the basics of Office, Windows, and Internet Explorer is also available if instructors wish to assign additional SNAP tutorial work without using the web-based SNAP program.

eBook For students who prefer studying with an eBook, the texts in the Benchmark Series are available in an electronic form. The web-based, password-protected eBooks feature dynamic navigation tools, including bookmarking, a linked table of contents, and the ability to jump to a specific page. The eBook format also supports helpful study tools, such as highlighting and note taking.

Instructor Resources

Instructor's Guide and Disc Instructor support for the Benchmark Series includes an *Instructor's Guide* and Instructor Resources Disc package. This resource includes course planning resources, such as Lesson Blueprints, teaching hints, and sample course syllabi; presentation resources, such as PowerPoint slide shows with lecture notes; and assessment resources, including an overview of available assessment venues, live model answers for chapter projects, and live and annotated PDF model answers for end-of-chapter exercises. Contents of the *Instructor's Guide* and Instructor Resources Disc package are also available on the password-protected section of the Internet Resource Center for this title at www.paradigmcollege.net/BenchmarkPowerPoint13.

Computerized Test Generator Instructors can use the ExamView® Assessment Suite and test banks of multiple-choice items to create customized web-based or print tests.

Blackboard Cartridge This set of files allows instructors to create a personalized Blackboard website for their course and provides course content, tests, and the mechanisms for establishing communication via e-discussions and online group conferences. Available content includes a syllabus, test banks, PowerPoint presentations, and supplementary course materials. Upon request, the files can be available within 24–48 hours. Hosting the site is the responsibility of the educational institution.

System Requirements ■■■■■■■■■■■■■■■■■■■■■■■■

This text is designed for the student to complete projects and assessments on a computer running a standard installation of Microsoft Office Professional Plus 2013 and the Microsoft Windows 8 operating system. To effectively run this suite and operating system, your computer should be outfitted with the following:

- 1 gigahertz (GHz) processor or higher; 1 gigabyte (GB) of RAM (32 bit) or 2 GB of RAM (64 bit)
- 3 GB of available hard-disk space
- .NET version 3.5, 4.0, or 4.5
- DirectX 10 graphics card
- Minimum 1024 × 576 resolution (or 1366 × 768 to use Windows Snap feature)
- Computer mouse, multi-touch device, or other compatible pointing device

Office 2013 will also operate on computers running the Windows 7 operating system.

Screen captures in this book were created using a screen resolution display setting of 1600 × 900. Refer to the *Customizing Settings* section of *Getting Started in Office 2013* following this preface for instructions on changing your monitor's resolution. Figure G.9 on page 10 shows the Microsoft Office Word ribbon at three resolutions for comparison purposes. Choose the resolution that best matches your computer; however, be aware that using a resolution other than 1600 × 900 means that your screens may not match the illustrations in this book.

About the Authors ■■■■■■■■■■■■■■■■■■■■■■■■

Nita Rutkosky began teaching business education courses at Pierce College in Puyallup, Washington, in 1978. Since then she has taught a variety of software applications to students in postsecondary Information Technology certificate and degree programs. In addition to *Benchmark Office 2013,* she has co-authored *Marquee Series: Microsoft Office 2013, 2010, 2007,* and *2003; Signature Series: Microsoft Word 2013, 2010, 2007,* and *2003; Using Computers in the Medical Office: Microsoft Word, Excel, and PowerPoint 2010, 2007* and *2003;* and *Computer and Internet Essentials: Preparing for IC³.* She has also authored textbooks on keyboarding, WordPerfect, desktop publishing, and voice recognition for Paradigm Publishing, Inc.

Audrey Roggenkamp has been teaching courses in the Business Information Technology department at Pierce College in Puyallup since 2005. Her courses have included keyboarding, skill building, and Microsoft Office programs. In addition to this title, she has co-authored *Marquee Series: Microsoft Office 2013, 2010,* and *2007; Signature Series: Microsoft Word 2013, 2010,* and *2007; Using Computers in the Medical Office: Microsoft Word, Excel, and PowerPoint 2010, 2007,* and *2003;* and *Computer and Internet Essentials: Preparing for IC³* for Paradigm Publishing, Inc.

Ian Rutkosky teaches Business Technology courses at Pierce College in Puyallup, Washington. In addition to this title, he has coauthored *Computer and Internet Essentials: Preparing for IC³, Marquee Series: Microsoft Office 2013,* and *Using Computers in the Medical Office: Microsoft Word, Excel, and PowerPoint 2010.* He is also a co-author and consultant for Paradigm's SNAP training and assessment software.

Getting Started in Office 2013

In this textbook, you will learn to operate several computer programs that combine to make the Microsoft Office 2013 application suite. The programs you will learn are known as *software*, and they contain instructions that tell the computer what to do. Some of the application programs in the suite include Word, a word processing program; Excel, a spreadsheet program; Access, a database program; and PowerPoint, a presentation program.

Identifying Computer Hardware ■■■■■■■■■■■■■■■■■

The computer equipment you will use to operate the Microsoft Office suite is referred to as *hardware*. You will need access to a computer system that includes a CPU, monitor, keyboard, printer, drives, and mouse. If you are not sure what equipment you will be operating, check with your instructor. The computer system shown in Figure G.1 consists of six components. Each component is discussed separately in the material that follows.

Figure G.1 Computer System

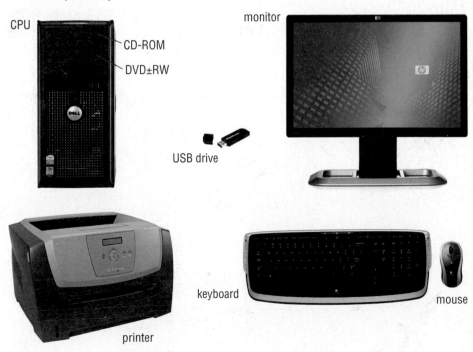

CPU

The *central processing unit (CPU)* is the brain of the computer and is where all processing occurs. Silicon chips, which contain miniaturized circuitry, are placed on boards that are plugged into slots within the CPU. Whenever an instruction is given to the computer, it is processed through the circuitry in the CPU.

Monitor

A computer *monitor* looks like a television screen. It displays the information in a program and the text you input using the keyboard. The quality of display for monitors varies depending on the type of monitor and the level of resolution. Monitors can also vary in size—generally from 13 inches to 26 inches or larger.

Keyboard

The *keyboard* is used to input information into the computer. The number and location of the keys on a keyboard can vary. In addition to letters, numbers, and symbols, most computer keyboards contain function keys, arrow keys, and a numeric keypad. Figure G.2 shows an enhanced keyboard.

The 12 keys at the top of the keyboard, labeled with the letter F followed by a number, are called *function keys*. Use these keys to perform functions within each of the Office programs. To the right of the regular keys is a group of *special* or *dedicated keys*. These keys are labeled with specific functions that will be performed when you press the key. Below the special keys are arrow keys. Use these keys to move the insertion point in the document screen.

Some keyboards include mode indicator lights. When you select certain modes, a light appears on the keyboard. For example, if you press the Caps Lock key, which disables the lowercase alphabet, a light appears next to Caps Lock. Similarly, pressing the Num Lock key will disable the special functions on the numeric keypad, which is located at the right side of the keyboard.

Figure G.2 Keyboard

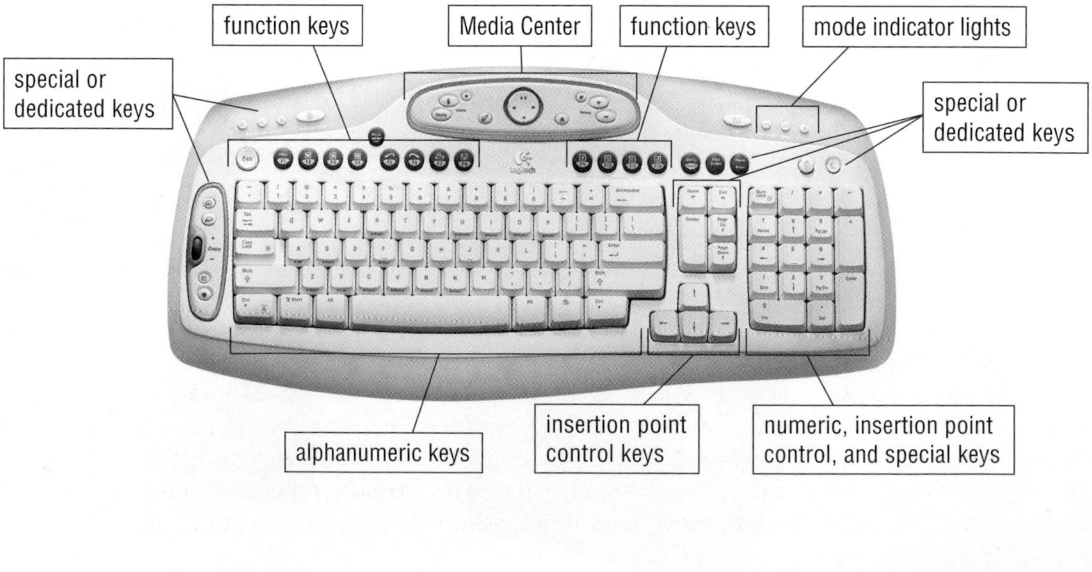

function keys   Media Center   function keys   mode indicator lights

special or dedicated keys

special or dedicated keys

alphanumeric keys   insertion point control keys   numeric, insertion point control, and special keys

Drives and Ports

Depending on the computer system you are using, Microsoft Office 2013 is installed on a hard drive or as part of a network system. Either way, you will need to have a CD or DVD drive to complete the projects and assessments in this book. If you plan to use a USB drive as your storage medium, you will also need a USB port. You will insert the CD that accompanies this textbook into the CD or DVD drive and then copy folders from the disc to your storage medium. You will also save documents you create to folders on your storage medium.

Printer

An electronic version of a file is known as a *soft copy*. If you want to create a *hard copy* of a file, you need to print it. To print documents you will need to access a printer, which will probably be either a laser printer or an ink-jet printer. A *laser printer* uses a laser beam combined with heat and pressure to print documents, while an *ink-jet printer* prints a document by spraying a fine mist of ink on the page.

Mouse or Touchpad

Most functions and commands in the Microsoft Office suite are designed to be performed using a mouse or a similar pointing device. A *mouse* is an input device that sits on a flat surface next to the computer. You can operate a mouse with your left or right hand. Moving the mouse on the flat surface causes a corresponding pointer to move on the screen, and clicking the left or right mouse buttons allows you to select various objects and commands. Figure G.1 contains an image of a mouse.

If you are working on a laptop computer, you may use a touchpad instead of a mouse. A *touchpad* allows you to move the mouse pointer by moving your finger across a surface at the base of the keyboard. You click by using your thumb to press the button located at the bottom of the touchpad.

Using the Mouse

The programs in the Microsoft Office suite can be operated with the keyboard and a mouse. The mouse generally has two buttons on top, which you press to execute specific functions and commands. A mouse may also contain a wheel, which can be used to scroll in a window or as a third button. To use the mouse, rest it on a flat surface or a mouse pad. Put your hand over it with your palm resting on top of the mouse, your wrist resting on the table surface, and your index finger resting on the left mouse button. As you move your hand, and thus the mouse, a corresponding pointer moves on the screen.

When using the mouse, you should understand four terms — point, click, double-click, and drag. When operating the mouse, you may need to point to a specific command, button, or icon. To *point* means to position the mouse pointer on the desired item. With the mouse pointer positioned on the desired item, you may need to click a button on the mouse to select the item. To *click* means to quickly tap a button on the mouse once. To complete two steps at one time, such as choosing and then executing a function, double-click the mouse button. To *double-click* means to tap the left mouse button twice in quick succession. The term *drag* means to press and hold the left mouse button, move the mouse pointer to a specific location, and then release the button.

Using the Mouse Pointer

The mouse pointer will look different depending on where you have positioned it and what function you are performing. The following are some of the ways the mouse pointer can appear when you are working in the Office suite:

- The mouse pointer appears as an I-beam (called the *I-beam pointer*) when you are inserting text in a file. The I-beam pointer can be used to move the insertion point or to select text.
- The mouse pointer appears as an arrow pointing up and to the left (called the *arrow pointer*) when it is moved to the Title bar, Quick Access toolbar, ribbon, or an option in a dialog box, among other locations.

- The mouse pointer becomes a double-headed arrow (either pointing left and right, pointing up and down, or pointing diagonally) when you perform certain functions such as changing the size of an object.
- In certain situations, such as when you move an object or image, the mouse pointer displays with a four-headed arrow attached. The four-headed arrow means that you can move the object left, right, up, or down.
- When a request is being processed or when a program is being loaded, the mouse pointer may appear as a moving circle. The moving circle means "please wait." When the process is completed, the circle is replaced with a normal arrow pointer.
- When the mouse pointer displays as a hand with a pointing index finger, it indicates that more information is available about an item. The mouse pointer also displays as a hand with a pointing index finger when you hover the mouse over a hyperlink.

Choosing Commands ■■■■■■■■■■■■■■■■■■■■■■■■■

Once a program is open, you can use several methods in the program to choose commands. A *command* is an instruction that tells the program to do something. You can choose a command using the mouse or the keyboard. When a program such as Word or PowerPoint is open, the ribbon contains buttons and options for completing tasks, as well as tabs you can click to display additional buttons and options. To choose a button on the Quick Access toolbar or on the ribbon, position the tip of the mouse arrow pointer on the button and then click the left mouse button.

The Office suite provides *accelerator keys* you can press to use a command in a program. Press the Alt key on the keyboard to display KeyTips that identify the accelerator key you can press to execute a command. For example, if you press the Alt key in a Word document with the HOME tab active, KeyTips display as shown in Figure G.3. Continue pressing accelerator keys until you execute the desired command. For example, to begin spell checking a document, press the Alt key, press the R key on the keyboard to display the REVIEW tab, and then press the letter S on the keyboard.

Figure G.3 Word HOME Tab KeyTips

Choosing Commands from Drop-Down Lists

To choose a command from a drop-down list with the mouse, position the mouse pointer on the desired option and then click the left mouse button. To make a selection from a drop-down list with the keyboard, type the underlined letter in the desired option.

Some options at a drop-down list may appear in gray (dimmed), indicating that the option is currently unavailable. If an option at a drop-down list displays preceded by a check mark, it means the option is currently active. If an option at a drop-down list displays followed by an ellipsis (…), clicking that option will display a dialog box.

Choosing Options from a Dialog Box

A *dialog box* contains options for applying formatting or otherwise modifying a file or data within a file. Some dialog boxes display with tabs along the top that provide additional options. For example, the Font dialog box shown in Figure G.4 contains two tabs — the Font tab and the Advanced tab. The tab that displays in the front is the active tab. To make a tab active using the mouse, position the arrow pointer on the desired tab and then click the left mouse button. If you are using the keyboard, press Ctrl + Tab or press Alt + the underlined letter on the desired tab.

Figure G.4 Word Font Dialog Box

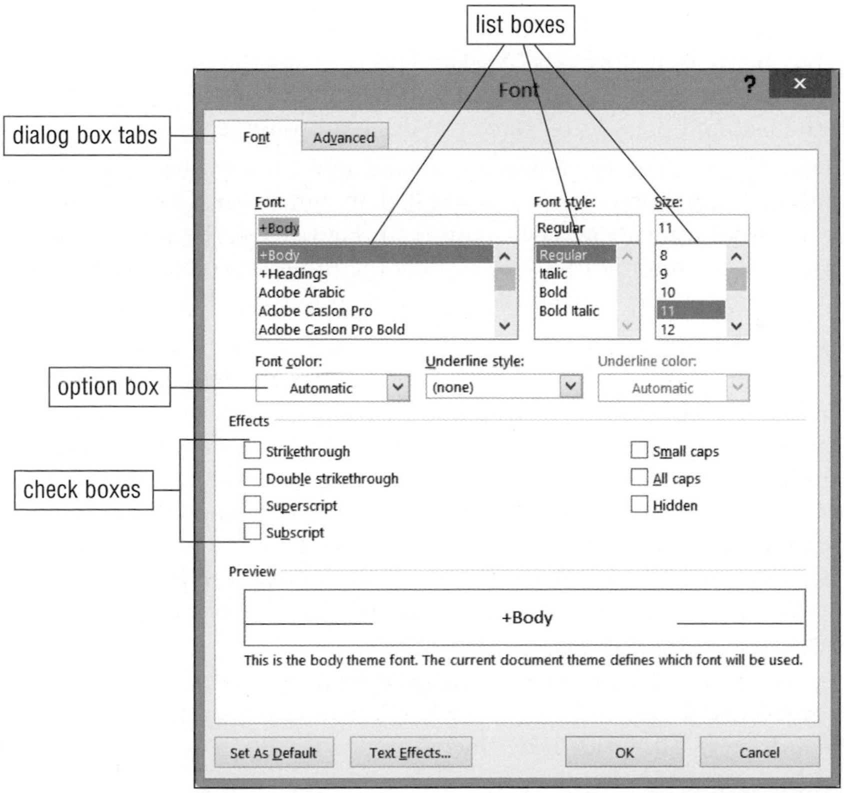

To choose options from a dialog box with the mouse, position the arrow pointer on the desired option and then click the left mouse button. If you are using the keyboard, press the Tab key to move the insertion point forward from option to option. Press Shift + Tab to move the insertion point backward from option to option. You can also hold down the Alt key and then press the underlined letter of the desired option. When an option is selected, it displays with a blue background or surrounded by a dashed box called a *marquee*. A dialog box contains one or more of the following elements: list boxes, option boxes, check boxes, text boxes, option buttons, measurement boxes, and command buttons.

List Boxes and Option Boxes

The fonts below the *Font* option in the Font dialog box in Figure G.4 are contained in a *list box*. To make a selection from a list box with the mouse, move the arrow pointer to the desired option and then click the left mouse button.

Some list boxes may contain a scroll bar. This scroll bar will display at the right side of the list box (a vertical scroll bar) or at the bottom of the list box (a horizontal scroll bar). Use a vertical scroll bar or a horizontal scroll bar to move through the list if the list is longer (or wider) than the box. To move down a list using a vertical scroll bar, position the arrow pointer on the down-pointing arrow and hold down the left mouse button. To scroll up through the list, position the arrow pointer on the up-pointing arrow and hold down the left mouse button. You can also move the arrow pointer above the scroll box and click the left mouse button to scroll up the list or move the arrow pointer below the scroll box and click the left mouse button to move down the list. To navigate a list with a horizontal scroll bar, click the left-pointing arrow to scroll to the left of the list or click the right-pointing arrow to scroll to the right of the list.

To use the keyboard to make a selection from a list box, move the insertion point into the box by holding down the Alt key and pressing the underlined letter of the desired option. Press the Up and/or Down Arrow keys on the keyboard to move through the list, and press Enter once the desired option is selected.

In some dialog boxes where there is not enough room for a list box, lists of options are contained in a drop-down list box called an *option box*. Option boxes display with a down-pointing arrow. For example, in Figure G.4, the font color options are contained in an option box. To display the different color options, click the down-pointing arrow at the right of the *Font color* option box. If you are using the keyboard, press Alt + C.

Check Boxes

Some dialog boxes contain options preceded by a box. A check mark may or may not appear in the box. The Word Font dialog box shown in Figure G.4 displays a variety of check boxes within the *Effects* section. If a check mark appears in the box, the option is active (turned on). If the check box does not contain a check mark, the option is inactive (turned off). Any number of check boxes can be active. For example, in the Word Font dialog box, you can insert a check mark in several of the boxes in the *Effects* section to activate the options.

To make a check box active or inactive with the mouse, position the tip of the arrow pointer in the check box and then click the left mouse button. If you are using the keyboard, press Alt + the underlined letter of the desired option.

Text Boxes

Some options in a dialog box require you to enter text. For example, the boxes below the *Find what* and *Replace with* options at the Excel Find and Replace dialog box shown in Figure G.5 are text boxes. In a text box, you type text or edit existing text. Edit text in a text box in the same manner as normal text. Use the Left and Right Arrow keys on the keyboard to move the insertion point without deleting text and use the Delete key or Backspace key to delete text.

Option Buttons

The Word Insert Table dialog box shown in Figure G.6 contains options in the *AutoFit behavior* section preceded by **option button**s. Only one option button can be selected at any time. When an option button is selected, a blue or black circle displays in the button. To select an option button with the mouse, position the tip of the arrow pointer inside the option button or on the option and then click the left mouse button. To make a selection with the keyboard, hold down the Alt key and then press the underlined letter of the desired option.

Measurement Boxes

Some options in a dialog box contain measurements or amounts you can increase or decrease. These options are generally located in a **measurement box**. For example, the Word Insert Table dialog box shown in Figure G.6 contains the *Number of columns* and *Number of rows* measurement boxes. To increase a number in a measurement box, position the tip of the arrow pointer on the up-pointing arrow at the right of the desired option and then click the left mouse button. To decrease the number, click the down-pointing arrow. If you are using the keyboard, press and hold down Alt + the underlined letter of the desired option and then press the Up Arrow key to increase the number or the Down Arrow key to decrease the number.

Command Buttons

The buttons at the bottom of the Excel Find and Replace dialog box shown in Figure G.5 are called **command buttons**. Use a command button to execute or cancel a command. Some command buttons display with an ellipsis (...), which means another dialog box will open if you click that button. To choose a command button with the mouse, position the arrow pointer on the desired button and then click the left mouse button. To choose a command button with the keyboard, press the Tab key until the desired command button is surrounded by a marquee and then press the Enter key.

Figure G.5 Excel Find and Replace Dialog Box

Choosing Commands with Keyboard Shortcuts

Applications in the Office suite offer a variety of keyboard shortcuts you can use to execute specific commands. Keyboard shortcuts generally require two or more keys. For example, the keyboard shortcut to display the Open dialog box in an application is Ctrl + F12. To use this keyboard shortcut, hold down the Ctrl key, press the F12 function on the keyboard, and then release the Ctrl key. For a list of keyboard shortcuts, refer to the Help files.

Choosing Commands with Shortcut Menus

The software programs in the Office suite include shortcut menus that contain commands related to different items. To display a shortcut menu, position the mouse pointer over the item for which you want to view more options, and then click the right mouse button or press Shift + F10. The shortcut menu will appear wherever the insertion point is positioned. For example, if the insertion point is positioned in a paragraph of text in a Word document, clicking the right mouse button or pressing Shift + F10 will cause the shortcut menu shown in Figure G.7 to display in the document screen (along with the Mini toolbar).

To select an option from a shortcut menu with the mouse, click the desired option. If you are using the keyboard, press the Up or Down Arrow key until the desired option is selected and then press the Enter key. To close a shortcut menu without choosing an option, click anywhere outside the shortcut menu or press the Esc key.

Figure G.6 Word Insert Table Dialog Box

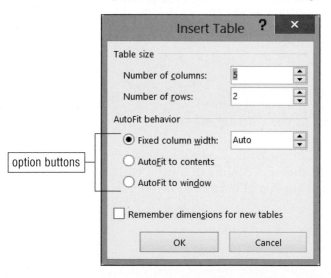

Figure G.7 Word Shortcut Menu

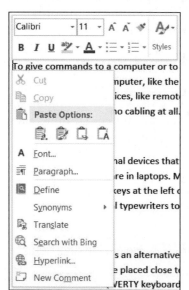

Working with Multiple Programs ■■■■■■■■■■■■■■■■

As you learn the various programs in the Microsoft Office suite, you will notice many similarities between them. For example, the steps to save, close, and print are virtually the same whether you are working in Word, Excel, or PowerPoint. This consistency between programs greatly enhances a user's ability to transfer knowledge learned in one program to another within the suite. Another benefit to using Microsoft Office is the ability to have more than one program open at the same time and to integrate content from one program with another. For example, you can open Word and create a document, open Excel and create a spreadsheet, and then copy the Excel spreadsheet into Word.

When you open a program, a button containing an icon representing the program displays on the Taskbar. If you open another program, a button containing an icon representing that program displays to the right of the first program button on the Taskbar. Figure G.8 on the next page, shows the Taskbar with Word, Excel, Access, and PowerPoint open. To move from one program to another, click the Taskbar button representing the desired program.

Figure G.8 Taskbar with Word, Excel, Access, and PowerPoint Open

Customizing Settings ■■■■■■■■■■■■■■■■■■■■■■■■■■

Before beginning computer projects in this textbook, you may need to customize your monitor's settings and turn on the display of file extensions. Projects in the chapters in this textbook assume that the monitor display is set at 1600 x 900 pixels and that the display of file extensions is turned on.

Before you begin learning the applications in the Microsoft Office 2013 suite, take a moment to check the display settings on the computer you are using. Your monitor's display settings are important because the ribbon in the Microsoft Office suite adjusts to the screen resolution setting of your computer monitor. A computer monitor set at a high resolution will have the ability to show more buttons in the ribbon than will a monitor set to a low resolution. The illustrations in this textbook were created with a screen resolution display set at 1600 × 900 pixels. In Figure G.9 on the next page, the Word ribbon is shown three ways: at a lower screen resolution (1366 × 768 pixels), at the screen resolution featured throughout this textbook, and at a higher screen resolution (1920 × 1080 pixels). Note the variances in the ribbon in all three examples. If possible, set your display to 1600 × 900 pixels to match the illustrations you will see in this textbook.

Figure G.9 Monitor Resolution

1366 × 768 screen resolution

1600 × 900 screen resolution

1920 × 1080 screen resolution

Project 1   Setting Monitor Display to 1600 by 900

1. At the Windows 8 desktop, right-click a blank area of the screen.
2. At the shortcut menu, click the *Screen resolution* option.
3. At the Screen Resolution window, click the *Resolution* option box. (This displays a slider bar. Your slider bar may display differently than what you see in the image at the right.)
4. Drag the button on the slider bar until *1600 × 900* displays to the right of the slider bar.
5. Click in the Screen Resolution window to remove the slider bar.
6. Click the Apply button.
7. Click the Keep Changes button.
8. Click the OK button.

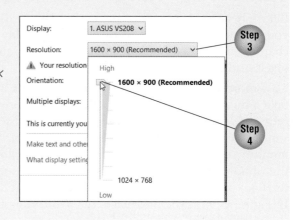

Displaying File Extensions

1. At the Windows 8 desktop, position the mouse pointer in the lower left corner of the Taskbar until the Start screen thumbnail displays and then click the right mouse button.
2. At the pop-up list, click the *File Explorer* option.
3. At the Computer window, click the View tab on the ribbon and then click the *File name extensions* check box in the Show/hide group to insert a check mark.
4. Close the Computer window.

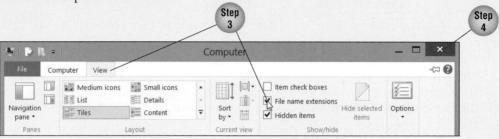

Completing Computer Projects ■■■■■■■■■■■■■■■■■■

Some projects in this textbook require that you open an existing file. Project files are saved on the Student Resources CD in individual chapter folders. Before beginning a chapter, copy the necessary folder from the CD to your storage medium (such as a USB flash drive or your SkyDrive) using the Computer window. To maximize storage capacity, delete previous chapter folders before copying a new chapter folder onto your storage medium.

Copying a Folder from the Student Resources CD to a USB Flash Drive

1. Insert the CD that accompanies this textbook into your computer's CD/DVD drive.
2. Insert your USB flash drive into an available USB port.
3. At the Windows 8 Start screen, click the Desktop tile.
4. Open File Explorer by clicking the File Explorer button on the Taskbar.
5. Click *Computer* in the Navigation pane at the left side of the File Explorer window.
6. Double-click the CD/DVD drive that displays with the name *BM13StudentResources* preceded by the drive letter.
7. Double-click **StudentDataFiles** in the Content pane.
8. Double-click the desired program folder name (and level number, if appropriate) in the Content pane.
9. Click once on the desired chapter (or unit performance assessment) folder name to select it.
10. Click the Home tab and then click the Copy button in the Clipboard group.
11. Click your USB flash drive that displays in the Navigation pane at the left side of the window.
12. Click the Home tab and then click the Paste button in the Clipboard group.
13. Close the File Explorer window by clicking the Close button located in the upper right corner of the window.

Project 4 | Copying a Folder from the Student Resources CD to your SkyDrive Account

Note: SkyDrive is updated periodically, so the steps to create folders and upload files may vary from the steps below.

1. Insert the CD that accompanies this textbook into your computer's CD/DVD drive.
2. At the Windows 8 Start screen, click the Desktop tile.
3. Open Internet Explorer by clicking the Internet Explorer button on the Taskbar.
4. At the Internet Explorer home page, click in the Address bar, type **www.skydrive.com**, and then press Enter.
5. At the Microsoft SkyDrive login page, type your Windows Live ID (such as your email address).
6. Press the Tab key, type your password, and then press Enter.
7. Click the Documents tile in your SkyDrive.
8. Click the Create option on the SkyDrive menu bar and then click *Folder* at the drop-down list.
9. Type the name of the folder that you want to copy from the Student Resources CD and then press the Enter key.
10. Click the folder tile you created in the previous step.
11. Click the Upload option on the menu bar.
12. Click the CD/DVD drive that displays in the Navigation pane at the left side of the Choose File to Upload dialog box.
13. Open the chapter folder on the CD that contains the required student data files.
14. Select all of the files in the folder by pressing Ctrl + A and then click the Open button.

Project 5 | Deleting a Folder

Note: Check with your instructor before deleting a folder.

1. Insert your storage medium (such as a USB flash drive) into your computer's USB port.
2. At the Windows desktop, open File Explorer by right-clicking the Start screen thumbnail and then clicking *File Explorer* at the shortcut menu.
3. Double-click the drive letter for your storage medium (the drive containing your USB flash drive, such as *Removable Disk (F:)*).
4. Click the chapter folder in the Content pane.
5. Click the Home tab and then click the Delete button in the Organize group.
6. At the message asking if you want to delete the folder, click the Yes button.
7. Close the Computer window by clicking the Close button located in the upper right corner of the window.

Using Windows 8

A computer requires an operating system to provide necessary instructions on a multitude of processes including loading programs, managing data, directing the flow of information to peripheral equipment, and displaying information. Windows 8 is an operating system that provides functions of this type (along with much more) in a graphical environment. Windows is referred to as a *graphical user interface* (GUI—pronounced *gooey*) that provides a visual display of information with features such as icons (pictures) and buttons. In this introduction, you will learn these basic features of Windows 8:

- Use the Start screen to launch programs
- Use desktop icons and the Taskbar to launch programs and open files or folders
- Organize and manage data, including copying, moving, creating, and deleting files and folders; and create a shortcut
- Explore the Control Panel and personalize the desktop
- Use the Windows Help and Support features
- Use search tools
- Customize monitor settings

Before using the software programs in the Microsoft Office suite, you will need to start the Windows 8 operating system. To do this, turn on the computer. Depending on your computer equipment configuration, you may also need to turn on the monitor and printer. If you are using a computer that is part of a network system or if your computer is set up for multiple users, a screen will display showing the user accounts defined for your computer system. At this screen, click your user account name; if necessary, type your password; and then press the Enter key. The Windows 8 operating system will start and, after a few moments, the Windows 8 Start screen will display as shown in Figure W.1. (Your Windows 8 Start screen may vary from what you see in Figure W.1.)

Exploring the Start Screen and Desktop ▪▪▪▪▪▪▪▪▪▪▪▪

When Windows is loaded, the Windows 8 Start screen displays. This screen contains tiles that open various applications. Open an application by clicking an application's tile or display the Windows 8 desktop by clicking the Desktop tile. Click the Desktop tile and the screen displays as shown in Figure W.2. Think of the desktop in Windows as the top of a desk in an office. A businessperson places necessary tools—such as pencils, pens, paper, files, calculator—on the desktop to perform functions. Like the tools that are located on a desk, the Windows 8 desktop contains tools for operating the computer. These tools are logically grouped and placed in dialog boxes or panels that you can display using icons on the desktop. The desktop contains a variety of features for using your computer and applications installed on the computer.

Figure W.1 Windows 8 Start Screen

current user

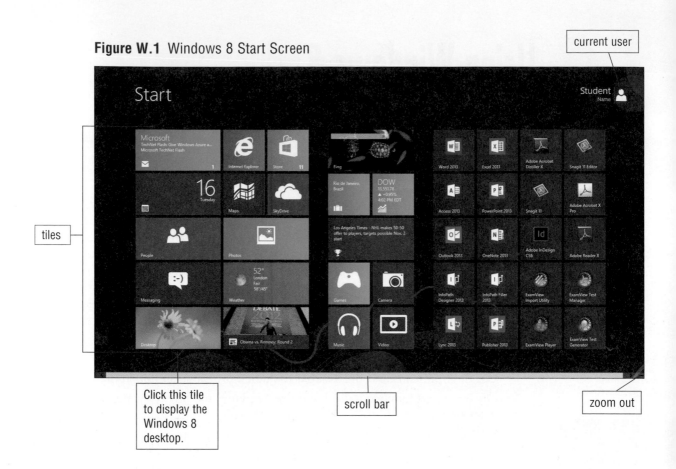

tiles

Click this tile to display the Windows 8 desktop.

scroll bar

zoom out

Figure W.2 Windows 8 Desktop

Recycle Bin icon

Position the mouse pointer here to access the Start screen.

Taskbar

Using Icons

Icons are visual symbols that represent programs, files, or folders. Figure W.2 identifies the Recycle Bin icon on the Windows desktop. The Windows desktop on your computer may contain additional icons. Applications that have been installed on your computer may be represented by an icon on the desktop. Icons that represent files or folders may also display on your desktop. Double-click an icon and the application, file, or folder it represents opens on the desktop.

Using the Taskbar

The bar that displays at the bottom of the desktop (see Figure W.2) is called the *Taskbar*. The Taskbar, shown in Figure W.3, contains the Start screen area (a spot where you point to access the Start screen), pinned items, a section that displays task buttons representing active tasks, the notification area, and the Show desktop button.

Position the mouse pointer in the lower left corner of the Taskbar to display the Start screen thumbnail. When the Start screen thumbnail displays, click the left mouse button to access the Windows 8 Start screen, shown in Figure W.1. (Your Start screen may look different.) You can also display the Start screen by pressing the Windows key on your keyboard or by pressing Ctrl + Esc. The left side of the Start menu contains tiles you can click to access the most frequently used applications. The name of the active user (the person who is currently logged on) displays in the upper right corner of the Start screen.

To open an application from the Start screen, drag the arrow pointer to the desired tile (referred to as *pointing*) and then click the left mouse button. When a program is open, a task button representing the program appears on the Taskbar. If multiple programs are open, each program will appear as a task button on the Taskbar (a few specialized tools may not).

Figure W.3 Windows 8 Taskbar

Manipulating Windows ■■■■■■■■■■■■■■■■■■■■■■■■

When you open a program, a defined work area known as a *window* displays on the screen. A Title bar displays at the top of the window and contains buttons at the right side for minimizing, maximizing, and restoring the size of the window, as well as for closing it. You can open more than one window at a time and the open windows can be cascaded or stacked. Windows 8 contains a Snap feature that causes a window to "stick" to the edge of the screen when the window is moved to the left or right side of the screen. Move a window to the top of the screen and the window is automatically maximized. If you drag down a maximized window, the window is automatically restored down (returned to its previous smaller size).

In addition to moving and sizing a window, you can change the display of all open windows. To do this, position the mouse pointer on the Taskbar and then click the right mouse button. At the pop-up menu that displays, you can choose to cascade all open windows, stack all open windows, or display all open windows side by side.

Project 1 — Opening Programs, Switching between Programs, and Manipulating Windows

1. Open Windows 8. (To do this, turn on the computer and, if necessary, turn on the monitor and/or printer. If you are using a computer that is part of a network system or if your computer is set up for multiple users, you may need to click your user account name, type your password, and then press the Enter key. Check with your instructor to determine if you need to complete any additional steps.)
2. When the Windows 8 Start screen displays, open Microsoft Word by positioning the mouse pointer on the *Word 2013* tile and then clicking the left mouse button. (You may need to scroll to the right to display the Word 2013 tile.)
3. When the Microsoft Word program is open, notice that a task button representing Word displays on the Taskbar.
4. Open Microsoft Excel by completing the following steps:
   a. Position the arrow pointer in the lower left corner of the Taskbar until the Start screen thumbnail displays and then click the left mouse button.
   b. At the Start screen, position the mouse pointer on the *Excel 2013* tile and then click the left mouse button.
5. When the Microsoft Excel program is open, notice that a task button representing Excel displays on the Taskbar to the right of the task button representing Word.
6. Switch to the Word program by clicking the Word task button on the Taskbar.
7. Switch to the Excel program by clicking the Excel task button on the Taskbar.
8. Restore down the Excel window by clicking the Restore Down button that displays immediately left of the Close button in the upper right corner of the screen. (This reduces the Excel window so it displays along the bottom half of the screen.)
9. Restore down the Word window by clicking the Restore Down button located immediately left of the Close button in the upper right corner of the screen.

Step 3

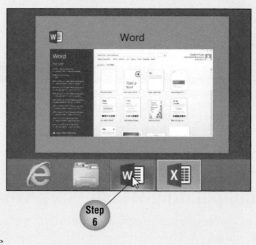

Step 6

Step 8

10. Position the mouse pointer at the top of the Word window screen, hold down the left mouse button, drag to the left side of the screen until an outline of the window displays in the left half of the screen, and then release the mouse button. (This "sticks" the window to the left side of the screen.)

11. Position the mouse pointer at the top of the Excel window screen, hold down the left mouse button, drag to the right until an outline of the window displays in the right half of the screen, and then release the mouse button.

12. Minimize the Excel window by clicking the Minimize button that displays in the upper right corner of the Excel window screen.

13. Hover your mouse over the Excel button on the Taskbar and then click the Excel window thumbnail that displays. (This displays the Excel window at the right side of the screen.)

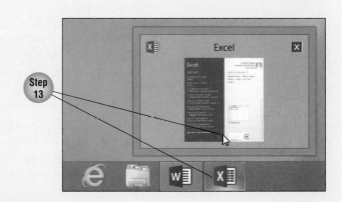

14. Cascade the Word and Excel windows by positioning the arrow pointer in an empty area of the Taskbar, clicking the right mouse button, and then clicking *Cascade windows* at the shortcut menu.

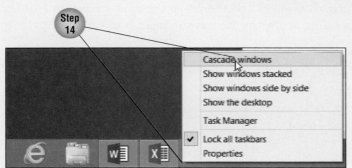

15. After viewing the windows cascaded, display them stacked by right-clicking an empty area of the Taskbar and then clicking *Show windows stacked* at the shortcut menu.

16. Display the desktop by right-clicking an empty area of the Taskbar and then clicking *Show the desktop* at the shortcut menu.

17. Display the windows stacked by right-clicking an empty area of the Taskbar and then clicking *Show open windows* at the shortcut menu.

18. Position the mouse pointer at the top of the Word window screen, hold down the left mouse button, drag the window to the top of the screen, and then release the mouse button. This maximizes the Word window so it fills the screen.

19. Close the Word window by clicking the Close button located in the upper right corner of the window.

20. At the Excel window, click the Maximize button located immediately left of the Close button in the upper right corner of the Excel window.

21. Close the Excel window by clicking the Close button located in the upper right corner of the window.

Using the Pinned Area

The icons that display immediately right of the Start screen area represent *pinned applications*. Clicking an icon opens the application associated with the icon. Click the first icon to open the Internet Explorer web browser and click the second icon to open a File Explorer window containing Libraries.

Exploring the Notification Area

The notification area is located at the right side of the Taskbar and contains icons that show the status of certain system functions such as a network connection or battery power. The notification area contains icons for managing certain programs and Windows 8 features, as well as the system clock and date. Click the time or date in the notification area and a window displays with a clock and a calendar of the current month. Click the <u>Change date and time settings</u> hyperlink that displays at the bottom of the window and the Date and Time dialog box displays. To change the date and/or time, click the Change date and time button and the Date and Time Settings dialog box displays, similar to the dialog box shown in Figure W.4. (If a dialog box displays telling you that Windows needs your permission to continue, click the Continue button.)

Change the month and year by clicking the left-pointing or right-pointing arrow at the top of the calendar. Click the left-pointing arrow to display the previous month(s) and click the right-pointing arrow to display the next month(s).

To change the day, click the desired day in the monthly calendar that displays in the dialog box. To change the time, double-click either the hour, minute, or seconds number and then type the appropriate time or use the up- and down-pointing arrows in the measurement boxes to adjust the time.

Figure W.4 Date and Time Settings Dialog Box

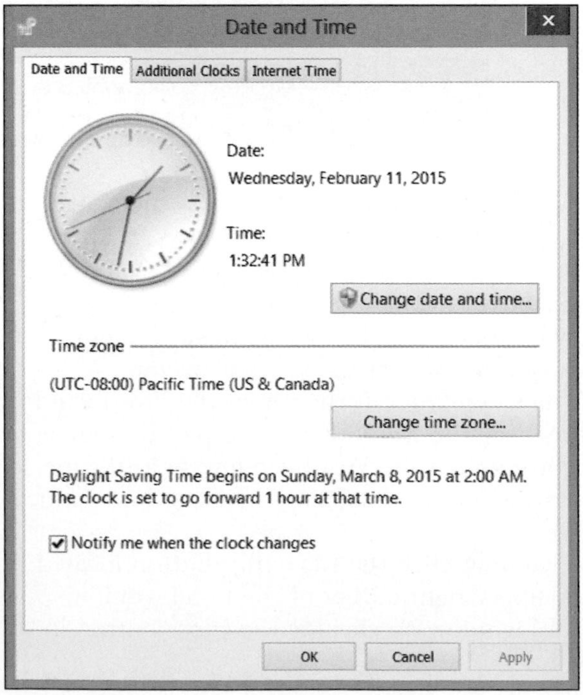

Some applications, when installed, will add an icon to the notification area of the Taskbar. To determine the name of an icon, position the mouse pointer on the icon and, after approximately one second, its label will display. If more icons have been inserted in the notification area than can be viewed at one time, an up-pointing arrow button displays at the left side of the notification area. Click this up-pointing arrow to display the remaining icons.

Setting Taskbar Properties

Customize the Taskbar with options at the Taskbar shortcut menu. Display this menu by right-clicking in an empty portion of the Taskbar. The Taskbar shortcut menu contains options for turning on or off the display of specific toolbars, specifying the display of multiple windows, displaying the Start Task Manager dialog box, locking or unlocking the Taskbar, and displaying the Taskbar Properties dialog box.

With options in the Taskbar Properties dialog box, shown in Figure W.5, you can change settings for the Taskbar. Display this dialog box by right-clicking an empty area on the Taskbar and then clicking *Properties* at the shortcut menu.

Each Taskbar property is controlled by a check box or an option box. If a property's check box contains a check mark, that property is active. Click the check box to remove the check mark and make the option inactive. If an option is inactive, clicking the check box will insert a check mark and turn on the option (make it active). A property option box displays the name of the currently active option. Click the option box to select a different option from the drop-down list.

Figure W.5 Taskbar Properties Dialog Box

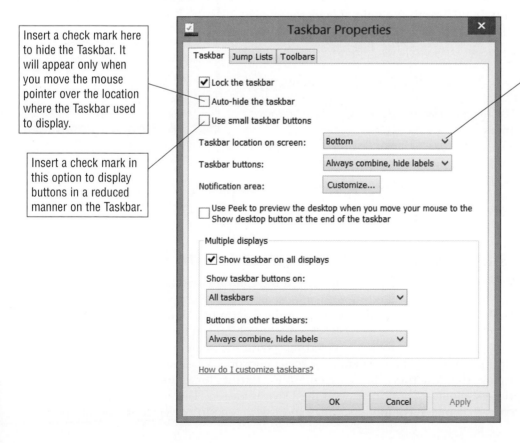

Insert a check mark here to hide the Taskbar. It will appear only when you move the mouse pointer over the location where the Taskbar used to display.

Insert a check mark in this option to display buttons in a reduced manner on the Taskbar.

Use this option box to change the location of the Taskbar from the bottom of the desktop to the left side, right side, or top of the desktop.

1. Make sure the Windows 8 desktop displays.
2. Change the Taskbar properties by completing the following steps:
   a. Position the arrow pointer in an empty area of the Taskbar and then click the right mouse button.
   b. At the shortcut menu that displays, click *Properties*.
   c. At the Taskbar Properties dialog box, click the *Auto-hide the taskbar* check box to insert a check mark.
   d. Click the *Use small taskbar buttons* check box to insert a check mark.
   e. Click the option box (contains the word *Bottom*) that displays at the right side of the *Taskbar location on screen:* option and then click *Right* at the drop-down list.
   f. Click OK to close the dialog box.

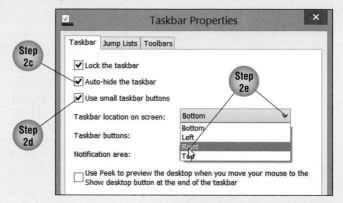

3. Since the *Auto-hide the taskbar* check box contains a check mark, the Taskbar does not display. Display the Taskbar by moving the mouse pointer to the right side of the screen. Notice that the buttons on the Taskbar are smaller than they were before.
4. Return to the default Taskbar properties by completing the following steps:
   a. Move the mouse pointer to the right side of the screen to display the Taskbar.
   b. Right-click an empty area of the Taskbar and then click *Properties* at the shortcut menu.
   c. Click the *Auto-hide the taskbar* check box to remove the check mark.
   d. Click the *Use small taskbar buttons* check box to remove the check mark.
   e. Click the *Taskbar location on screen* option box (displays with the word *Right*) and then click *Bottom* at the drop-down list.
   f. Click OK to close the dialog box.

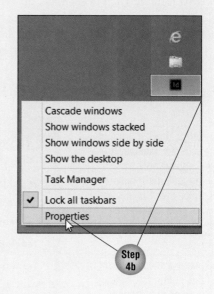

Using the Charm Bar ■■■■■■■■■■■■■■■■■■■■■■■■

Windows 8 contains a new feature called the *Charm bar*. The Charm bar is a bar that displays when you position the mouse pointer in the upper or lower right corner of the screen. Use the buttons on the Charm bar, shown in Figure W.6, to access certain features or tools. Use the Search button to search the computer for applications, files, folders and settings. With the Share button, you can share information with others via email or social networks. Clicking the Start button displays the Windows 8 Start screen. Access settings for various devices such as printers, monitors, and so on with the Devices button. The Settings button gives you access to common computer settings and is also used to power down the computer.

Figure W.6 Charm Bar

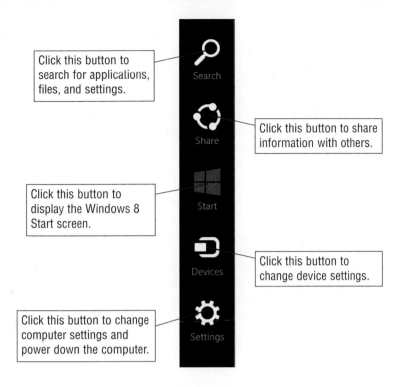

Click this button to search for applications, files, and settings.

Click this button to share information with others.

Click this button to display the Windows 8 Start screen.

Click this button to change device settings.

Click this button to change computer settings and power down the computer.

Powering Down the Computer

If you want to shut down Windows, first close any open programs and then display the Charm bar. Click the Settings button on the Charm bar, click the Power tile, and then click the *Shut down* option. The Power tile also contains options for restarting the computer or putting the computer to sleep. Restarting the computer may be useful when installing new applications or if Windows 8 stops working properly. In sleep mode, Windows saves files and information about applications and then powers down the computer to a low-power state. To "wake up" the computer, press the computer's power button.

In a multi-user environment, you can sign out of or lock your account so that no one can tamper with your work. To access these features, display the Windows 8 Start screen and then click your user account tile in the upper right corner. This displays a shortcut menu with three options. The *Lock* option locks the computer, which means that it is still powered on but requires a user password in order to access any applications or files that were previously opened. (To unlock the computer, click the icon on the login screen representing your account, type your password, and then press Enter.) Use the *Sign out* option to sign out of your user account while still keeping the computer turned on so that others may log on to it. Click the *Change account picture* option if you want to change the picture associated with your user account.

Managing Files and Folders ■■■■■■■■■■■■■■■■■■■■■■■■■■

As you begin working with programs in Windows 8, you will create files in which data (information) is saved. A file might be a Word document, an Excel workbook, an Access database, or a PowerPoint presentation. As you begin creating files, consider creating folders in which to store these files. Complete file management tasks such as creating a folder or moving a file at the Computer window. To display the Computer window, shown in Figure W.7, position your mouse pointer in the lower left corner of the screen to display the Start screen thumbnail, click the right mouse button, and then click *File Explorer* at the shortcut menu. The various components of the Computer window are identified in Figure W.7.

In the Content pane of the Computer window, icons display representing each hard disk drive and removable storage medium (such as a CD, DVD, or USB device) connected to your computer. Next to each storage device icon, Windows displays the amount of storage space available as well as a bar with the amount of used space shaded with color. This visual cue allows you to see at a glance the amount of space available relative to the capacity of the device. Double-click a device icon in the Content pane to change the display to show the contents stored on the device. Display contents from another device or folder using the Navigation pane or the Address bar on the Computer window.

Figure W.7 Computer Window

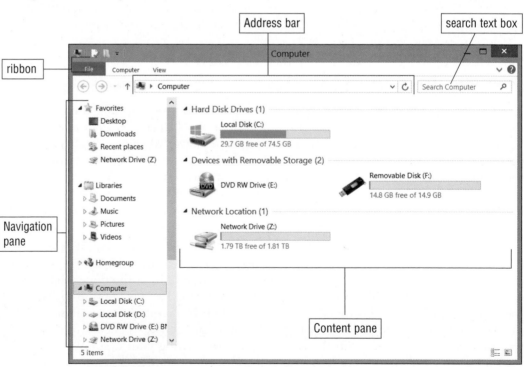

Copying, Moving, and Deleting Files and Folders

File and folder management activities include copying and moving files and folders from one folder or drive to another, as well as deleting files and folders. The Computer window offers a variety of methods for performing these actions. This section will provide you with steps for copying, moving, and deleting files and folders using options from the Home tab (shown in Figure W.8) and the shortcut menu (shown in Figure W.9).

To copy a file to another folder or drive, first display the file in the Content pane. If the file is located in the Documents folder, click the *Documents* folder in the *Libraries* section of the Navigation pane and then, in the Content pane, click the name of the file you want to copy. Click the Home tab on the ribbon and then click the Copy button in the Clipboard group. Use the Navigation pane to navigate to the location where you want to paste the file. Click the Home tab and then click the Paste button in the Clipboard group. Complete similar steps to copy and paste a folder to another location.

If the desired file is located on a storage medium such as a CD, DVD, or USB device, double-click the device in the section of the Content pane labeled *Devices with Removable Storage*. (Each removable device is assigned an alphabetic drive letter by Windows, usually starting at E or F and continuing through the alphabet depending on the number of removable devices that are currently in use.) After double-clicking the storage medium in the Content pane, navigate to the desired folder and then click the file to select it. Click the Home tab on the ribbon and then click the Copy button in the Clipboard group. Navigate to the desired folder, click the Home tab, and then click the Paste button in the Clipboard group.

To move a file, click the desired file in the Content pane, click the Home tab on the ribbon, and then click the Cut button in the Clipboard group. Navigate to the desired location, click the Home tab, and then click the Paste button in the Clipboard group.

To delete a file or folder, click the file or folder in the Content pane in the Computer window. Click the Home tab and then click the Delete button in the Organize group. At the message asking if you want to move the file or folder to the Recycle Bin, click the Yes button.

Figure W.8 File Explorer Home tab

Figure W.9 Shortcut Menu

Project 3 · Copying a File and Folder and Deleting a File

1. Insert the CD that accompanies this textbook into the appropriate drive.
2. Insert your storage medium (such as a USB flash drive) into the appropriate drive.
3. At the Windows 8 desktop, position the mouse pointer in the lower left corner of the Taskbar to display the Start screen thumbnail, click the right mouse button, and then click *File Explorer* at the shortcut menu.
4. Copy a file from the CD that accompanies this textbook to the drive containing your storage medium by completing the following steps:

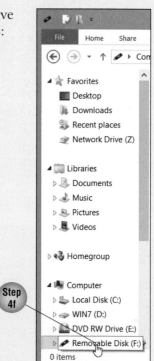

   a. In the Content pane, double-click the drive into which you inserted the CD that accompanies this textbook.
   b. Double-click the *StudentDataFiles* folder in the Content pane.
   c. Double-click the *Windows8* folder in the Content pane.
   d. Click **WordDocument01.docx** in the Content pane.
   e. Click the Home tab and then click *Copy* in the Clipboard group.

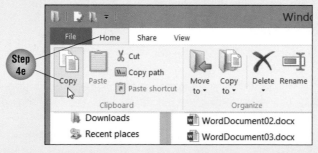

   f. In the Computer section in the Navigation pane, click the drive containing your storage medium. (You may need to scroll down the Navigation pane.)
   g. Click the Home tab and then click the Paste button in the Clipboard group.
5. Delete **WordDocument01.docx** from your storage medium by completing the following steps:
   a. Make sure the contents of your storage medium display in the Content pane in the Computer window.

b. Click *WordDocument01.docx* in the Content pane to select it.

c. Click the Home tab and then click the Delete button in the Organize group.

d. At the message asking if you want to permanently delete the file, click the Yes button.

6. Copy the Windows8 folder from the CD to your storage medium by completing the following steps:

a. With the Computer window open, click the drive in the *Computer* section in the Navigation pane that contains the CD that accompanies this book.

b. Double-click *StudentDataFiles* in the Content pane.

c. Click the *Windows8* folder in the Content pane.

d. Click the Home tab and then click the Copy button in the Clipboard group.

e. In the *Computer* section in the Navigation pane, click the drive containing your storage medium.

f. Click the Home tab and then click the Paste button in the Clipboard group.

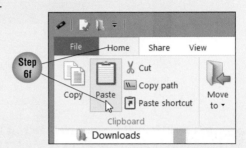

7. Close the Computer window by clicking the Close button located in the upper right corner of the window.

In addition to options on the Home tab, you can use options in a shortcut menu to copy, move, and delete files or folders. To use a shortcut menu, select the desired file(s) or folder(s), position the mouse pointer on the selected item, and then click the right mouse button. At the shortcut menu that displays, click the desired option, such as *Copy*, *Cut*, or *Delete*.

Selecting Files and Folders

You can move, copy, or delete more than one file or folder at the same time. Before moving, copying, or deleting files or folders, select the desired files or folders. To make selecting easier, consider displaying the files in the Content pane in a list or detailed list format. To change the display, click the View tab on the ribbon and then click *List* or *Details* in the Layout group.

To select adjacent files or folders, click the first file or folder, hold down the Shift key, and then click the last file or folder. To select nonadjacent files or folders, click the first file or folder, hold down the Ctrl key, and then click the other files or folders you wish to select.

Project 4 Copying and Deleting Files

1. At the Windows 8 desktop, position the mouse pointer in the lower left corner of the Taskbar to display the Start screen thumbnail, click the right mouse button, and then click *File Explorer* at the shortcut menu.

2. Copy files from the CD that accompanies this textbook to the drive containing your storage medium by completing the following steps:

a. Make sure the CD that accompanies this textbook and your storage medium are inserted in the appropriate drives.

b. Double-click the CD drive in the Content pane in the Computer window.

c. Double-click the *StudentDataFiles* folder in the Content pane.

d. Double-click the *Windows8* folder in the Content pane.

e. Change the display to List by clicking the View tab and then clicking *List* in the Layout group list box.

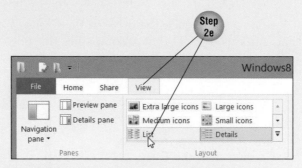

f. Click **WordDocument01.docx** in the Content pane.

g. Hold down the Shift key, click **WordDocument05.docx**, and then release the Shift key. (This selects five documents.)

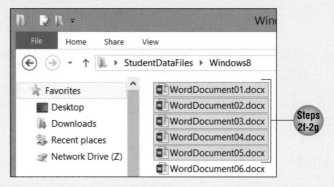

h. Click the Home tab and then click the Copy button in the Clipboard group.

i. In the *Computer* section of the Navigation pane, click the drive containing your storage medium.

j. Click the Home tab and then click the Paste button in the Clipboard group.

3. Delete the files you just copied to your storage medium by completing the following steps:

a. Change the display by clicking the View tab and then clicking *List* in the Layout group.

b. Click **WordDocument01.docx** in the Content pane.

c. Hold down the Shift key, click **WordDocument05.docx**, and then release the Shift key.

d. Position the mouse pointer on any selected file, click the right mouse button, and then click *Delete* at the shortcut menu.

e. At the message asking if you are sure you want to permanently delete the files, click Yes.

4. Close the Computer window by clicking the Close button located in the upper right corner of the window.

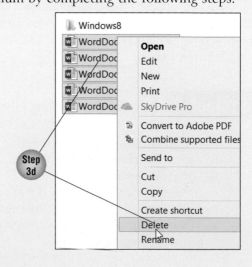

Manipulating and Creating Folders

As you begin working with and creating multiple files, consider creating folders in which you can logically group and store the files. To create a folder, display the Computer window and then display the drive or folder where you want to create the folder in the Content pane. To create the new folder, click the New folder button in the New group on the Home tab; click the New folder button on the Quick Access toolbar; or click in a blank area in the Content pane, click the right mouse button, point to *New* in the shortcut menu, and then click *Folder* at the side menu. Any of the three methods inserts a folder icon in the Content pane and names the folder *New folder*. Type the desired name for the new folder and then press Enter.

Project 5 Creating a New Folder

1. At the Windows 8 desktop, open the Computer window.
2. Create a new folder by completing the following steps:
   a. In the Content pane, double-click the drive that contains your storage medium.
   b. Double-click the *Windows8* folder in the Content pane. (This opens the folder.)
   c. Click the View tab and then click *List* in the Layout group.
   d. Click the Home tab and then click the New folder button in the New group.
   e. Type **SpellCheckFiles** and then press Enter. (This changes the name from *New folder* to *SpellCheckFiles*.)

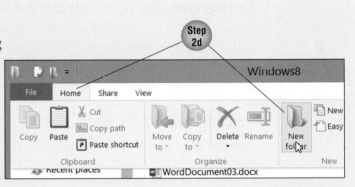

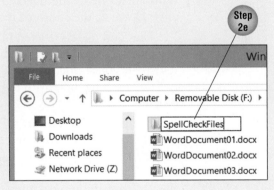

3. Copy **WordSpellCheck01.docx**, **WordSpellCheck02.docx**, and **WordSpellCheck03.docx** into the SpellCheckFiles folder you just created by completing the following steps:
   a. Click the View tab and then click *List* in the Layout group. (Skip this step if *List* is already selected.)
   b. Click *WordSpellCheck01.docx* in the Content pane.
   c. Hold down the Shift key, click *WordSpellCheck03.docx*, and then release the Shift key. (This selects three documents.)
   d. Click the Home tab and then click the Copy button in the Clipboard group.
   e. Double-click the *SpellCheckFiles* folder in the Content pane.
   f. Click the Home tab and then click the Paste button in the Clipboard group.

4. Delete the SpellCheckFiles folder and its contents by completing the following steps:
   a. Click the Back button (contains a left-pointing arrow) located at the left side of the Address bar.
   b. With the SpellCheckFiles folder selected in the Content pane, click the Home tab and then click the Delete button in the Organize group.
   c. At the message asking you to confirm the deletion, click Yes.
5. Close the window by clicking the Close button located in the upper right corner of the window.

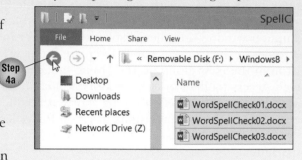

Step 4a

Using the Recycle Bin

Deleting the wrong file can be a disaster, but Windows 8 helps protect your work with the *Recycle Bin*. The Recycle Bin acts just like an office wastepaper basket; you can "throw away" (delete) unwanted files, but you can also "reach in" to the Recycle Bin and take out (restore) a file if you threw it away by accident.

Deleting Files to the Recycle Bin

Files and folders you delete from the hard drive are sent automatically to the Recycle Bin. If you want to permanently delete files or folders from the hard drive without first sending them to the Recycle Bin, select the desired file(s) or folder(s), right-click one of the selected files or folders, hold down the Shift key, and then click *Delete* at the shortcut menu.

Files and folders deleted from a USB flash drive or disc are deleted permanently. (Recovery programs are available, however, that will help you recover deleted files or folders. If you accidentally delete a file or folder from a USB flash drive or disc, do not do anything more with the USB flash drive or disc until you can run a recovery program.)

You can delete files in the manner described earlier in this section and you can also delete a file by dragging the file icon to the Recycle Bin. To do this, click the desired file in the Content pane in the Computer window, drag the file icon to the Recycle Bin icon on the desktop until the text *Move to Recycle Bin* displays, and then release the mouse button.

Restoring Files from the Recycle Bin

To restore a file from the Recycle Bin, double-click the Recycle Bin icon on the desktop. This opens the Recycle Bin window, shown in Figure W.10. (The contents of the Recycle Bin will vary.) To restore a file, click the file you want restored, click the Recycle Bin Tools Manage tab and then click the Restore the selected items button in the Restore group. This removes the file from the Recycle Bin and returns it to its original location. You can also restore a file by positioning the mouse pointer on the file, clicking the right mouse button, and then clicking *Restore* at the shortcut menu.

Figure W.10 Recycle Bin Window

ribbon

Navigation pane

Content pane

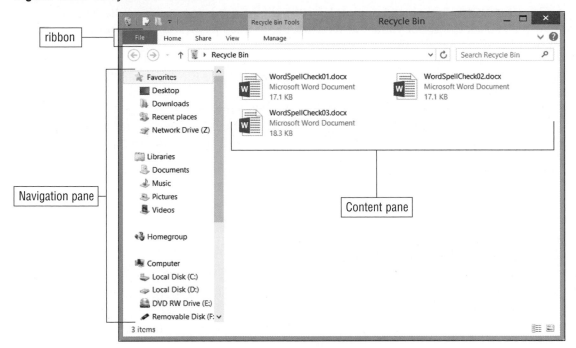

Project 6 Deleting Files to and Restoring Files from the Recycle Bin

Before beginning this project, check with your instructor to determine if you can copy files to the hard drive.

1. At the Windows 8 desktop, open the Computer window.
2. Copy files from your storage medium to the Documents folder on your hard drive by completing the following steps:
   a. In the Content pane, double-click the drive containing your storage medium.
   b. Double-click the *Windows8* folder in the Content pane.
   c. Click the View tab and then click *List* in the Layout group. (Skip this step if *List* is already selected.)
   d. Click *WordSpellCheck01.docx* in the Content pane.
   e. Hold down the Shift key, click *WordSpellCheck03.docx*, and then release the Shift key.
   f. Click the Home tab and then click the Copy button in the Clipboard group.
   g. Click the *Documents* folder in the *Libraries* section of the Navigation pane.
   h. Click the Home tab and then click the Paste button in the Clipboard group.

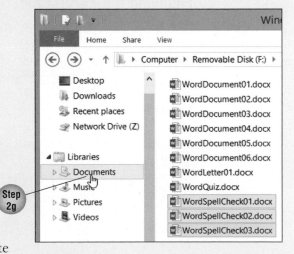

3. With **WordSpellCheck01.docx** through **WordSpellCheck03.docx** selected in the Content pane, click the Home tab and then click the Delete button in the Organize group to delete the files to the Recycle Bin.
4. Close the Computer window.
5. At the Windows 8 desktop, display the contents of the Recycle Bin by double-clicking the Recycle Bin icon.
6. Restore the files you just deleted by completing the following steps:
   a. Select **WordSpellCheck01.docx** through **WordSpellCheck03.docx** in the Recycle Bin Content pane. (If these files are not visible, you will need to scroll down the list of files in the Content pane.)
   b. Click the Recycle Bin Tools Manage tab and then click the Restore the selected items button in the Restore group.

7. Close the Recycle Bin by clicking the Close button located in the upper right corner of the window.
8. Display the Computer window.
9. Click the *Documents* folder in the *Libraries* section of the Navigation pane.
10. Delete the files you restored.
11. Close the Computer window.

Emptying the Recycle Bin

Just like a wastepaper basket, the Recycle Bin can get full. To empty the Recycle Bin, position the arrow pointer on the Recycle Bin icon on the desktop and then click the right mouse button. At the shortcut menu that displays, click the *Empty Recycle Bin* option. At the message asking if you want to permanently delete the items, click Yes. You can also empty the Recycle Bin by displaying the Recycle Bin window and then clicking the Empty Recycle Bin button in the Manage group on the Recycle Bin Tools Manage tab. At the message asking if you want to permanently delete the items, click Yes. To delete a specific file from the Recycle Bin window, click the desired file in the Recycle Bin window, click the Home tab, and then click the Delete button in the Organize group. At the message asking if you want to permanently delete the file, click Yes. When you empty the Recycle Bin, the files cannot be recovered by the Recycle Bin or by Windows 8. If you have to recover a file, you will need to use a file recovery program.

Note: Before beginning this project, check with your instructor to determine if you can delete files/folders from the Recycle Bin.

1. At the Windows 8 desktop, double-click the Recycle Bin icon.
2. At the Recycle Bin window, empty the contents by clicking the Empty Recycle Bin button in the Manage group on the Recycle Bin Tools Manage tab.
3. At the message asking you if you want to permanently delete the items, click Yes.
4. Close the Recycle Bin by clicking the Close button located in the upper right corner of the window.

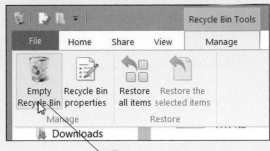

Step 2

Creating a Shortcut ■■■■■■■■■■■ ■■■■■■■■■■■■■■■■

If you use a file or application on a consistent basis, consider creating a shortcut to the file or application. A *shortcut* is a specialized icon that points the operating system to an actual file, folder, or application. If you create a shortcut to a Word document, the shortcut icon is not the actual document but a very small file that contains the path to the document. Double-click the shortcut icon and Windows 8 opens the document in Word.

One method for creating a shortcut is to display the Computer window and then make active the drive or folder where the file is located. Right-click the desired file, point to *Send to*, and then click *Desktop (create shortcut)*. You can easily delete a shortcut icon from the desktop by dragging the shortcut icon to the Recycle Bin icon. This deletes the shortcut icon but does not delete the file to which the shortcut pointed.

1. At the Windows 8 desktop, display the Computer window.
2. Double-click the drive containing your storage medium.
3. Double-click the *Windows8* folder in the Content pane.
4. Change the display of files to a list by clicking the View tab and then clicking *List* in the Layout group. (Skip this step if *List* is already selected.)
5. Create a shortcut to the file named **WordQuiz.docx** by right-clicking **WordQuiz.docx**, pointing to *Send to*, and then clicking *Desktop (create shortcut)*.
6. Close the Computer window.

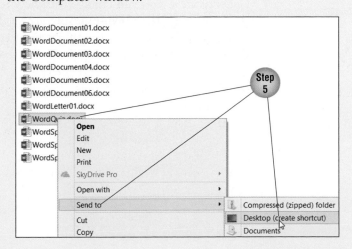

Step 5

7. Open Word and **WordQuiz.docx** by double-clicking the *WordQuiz.docx* shortcut icon on the desktop.
8. After viewing the file in Word, close Word by clicking the Close button that displays in the upper right corner of the window.
9. Delete the *WordQuiz.docx* shortcut icon by completing the following steps:
   a. At the desktop, position the mouse pointer on the *WordQuiz.docx* shortcut icon.
   b. Hold down the left mouse button, drag the icon on top of the Recycle Bin icon, and then release the mouse button.

Exploring the Control Panel ▮▮▮▮▮▮▮▮▮▮▮▮▮▮▮▮▮▮

The Control Panel, shown in Figure W.11, contains a variety of icons for customizing the appearance and functionality of your computer as well as accessing and changing system settings. Display the Control Panel by right-clicking the Start screen thumbnail and then clicking *Control Panel* at the shortcut menu. The Control Panel organizes settings into categories to make them easier to find. Click a category icon and the Control Panel displays lower-level categories and tasks within each of them.

Hover your mouse over a category icon in the Control Panel and a ScreenTip displays with an explanation of what options are available. For example, if you hover the mouse over the Appearance and Personalization icon, a ScreenTip displays with information about the tasks available in the category, such as changing the appearance of desktop items, applying a theme or screen saver to your computer, or customizing the Taskbar.

If you click a category icon in the Control Panel, the Control Panel displays all of the available subcategories and tasks in the category. Also, the categories display in text form at the left side of the Control Panel. For example, if you click the Appearance and Personalization icon, the Control Panel displays as shown in Figure W.12. Notice how the Control Panel categories display at the left side of the Control Panel and options for changing the appearance and personalizing your computer display in the middle of the Control Panel.

By default, the Control Panel displays categories of tasks in what is called *Category* view. You can change this view to display large or small icons. To change the view, click the down-pointing arrow that displays at the right side of the text *View by* that displays in the upper right corner of the Control Panel, and then click the desired view at the drop-down list (see Figure W.11).

Figure W.11 The Control Panel

Click a category icon or hyperlink to display all of the category's options.

Use this option to change views.

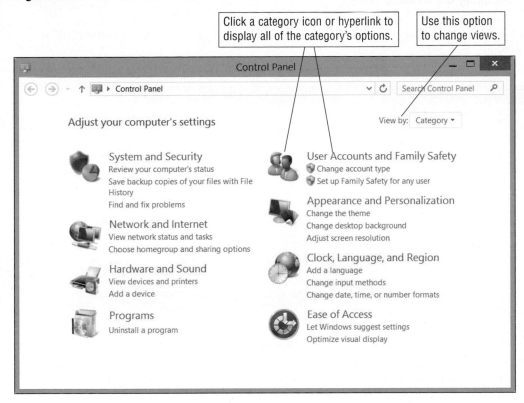

Figure W.12 Appearance and Personalization Window

Click this option to return to the main Control Panel.

lower-level categories

task hyperlinks

Click a category to display category options.

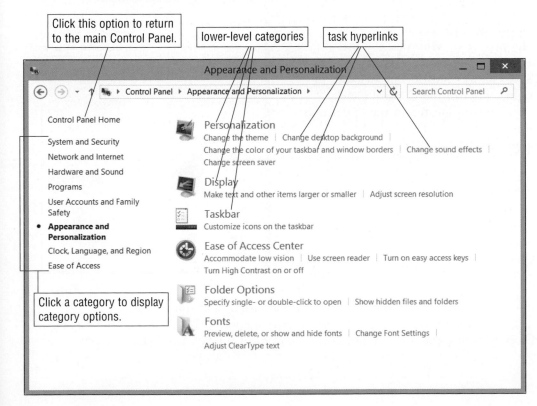

Project 9   **Changing the Desktop Theme**

1. At the Windows 8 desktop, right-click the Start screen thumbnail and then click *Control Panel* at the shortcut menu.
2. At the Control Panel, click the Appearance and Personalization icon.

3. Click the <u>Change the theme</u> hyperlink that displays below *Personalization* in the panel at the right in the Control Panel.
4. At the window that displays with options for changing visuals and sounds on your computer, click *Earth* in the *Windows Default Themes* section.

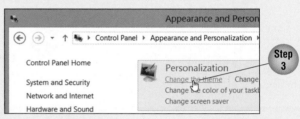

5. Click the <u>Desktop Background</u> hyperlink that displays in the lower left corner of the panel.
6. Click the button that displays below the text *Change picture every* and then click *10 Seconds* at the drop-down list. (This tells Windows to change the picture on your desktop every 10 seconds.)
7. Click the Save changes button that displays in the lower right corner of the Control Panel.
8. Click the Close button located in the upper right corner to close the Control Panel.
9. Look at the picture that displays as the desktop background. Wait for 10 seconds and then look at the second picture that displays.
10. Right-click the Start screen thumbnail and then click *Control Panel* at the shortcut menu.
11. At the Control Panel, click the Appearance and Personalization icon.
12. Click the <u>Change the theme</u> hyperlink that displays below *Personalization* in the panel at the right.

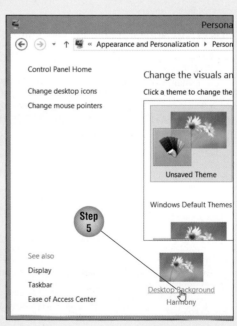

13. At the window that displays with options for changing visuals and sounds on your computer, click *Windows* in the *Windows Default Themes* section. (This is the default theme.)
14. Click the Close button located in the upper right corner of the Control Panel.

Searching in the Control Panel

The Control Panel contains a large number of options for customizing the appearance and functionality of your computer. If you want to customize a feature and are not sure where the options for the feature are located, search for the feature. To do this, display the Control Panel and then type the name of the desired feature. By default, the insertion point is positioned in the *Search Control Panel* text box. When you type the feature name in the text box, options related to the feature display in the Control Panel.

Project 10 | Customizing the Mouse

1. Right-click the Start screen thumbnail and then click *Control Panel*.
2. At the Control Panel, type **mouse**. (The insertion point is automatically located in the *Search Control Panel* text box when you open the Control Panel. When you type *mouse*, features for customizing the mouse display in the Control Panel.)
3. Click the Mouse icon that displays in the Control Panel.
4. At the Mouse Properties dialog box, notice the options that display. (The *Switch primary and secondary buttons* option might be useful, for example, if you are left-handed and want to switch the buttons on the mouse.)
5. Click the Cancel button to close the dialog box.
6. At the Control Panel, click the <u>Change the mouse pointer display or speed</u> hyperlink.

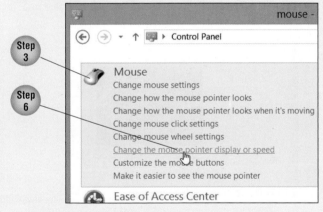

7. At the Mouse Properties dialog box with the Pointer Options tab selected, click the *Display pointer trails* check box in the *Visibility* section to insert a check mark.
8. Drag the button on the slider bar (located below the *Display pointer trails* check box) approximately to the middle of the bar.
9. Click OK to close the dialog box.
10. Close the Control Panel.
11. Move the mouse pointer around the screen to see the pointer trails.

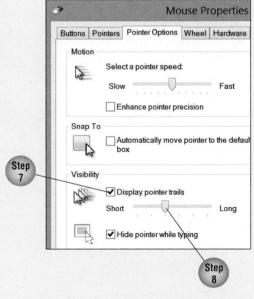

Displaying Personalize Options with a Shortcut Command

In addition to the Control Panel, display customization options with a command from a shortcut menu. Display a shortcut menu by positioning the mouse pointer in the desired position and then clicking the right mouse button. For example, display a shortcut menu with options for customizing the desktop by positioning the mouse pointer in an empty area of the desktop and then clicking the right mouse button. At the shortcut menu that displays, click the desired shortcut command.

Project 11   Customizing with a Shortcut Command

1. At the Windows 8 desktop, position the mouse pointer in an empty area on the desktop, click the right mouse button, and then click *Personalize* at the shortcut menu.
2. At the Control Panel Appearance and Personalization window that displays, click the <u>Change mouse pointers</u> hyperlink that displays at the left side of the window.
3. At the Mouse Properties dialog box, click the Pointer Options tab.
4. Click in the *Display pointer trails* check box to remove the check mark.
5. Click OK to close the dialog box.
6. At the Control Panel Appearance and Personalization window, click the <u>Screen Saver</u> hyperlink that displays in the lower right corner of the window.
7. At the Screen Saver Settings dialog box, click the option button below the *Screen saver* option and then click *Ribbons* at the drop-down list.
8. Check the number in the *Wait* measurement box. If a number other than *1* displays, click the down-pointing arrow at the right side of the measurement box until *1* displays. (This tells Windows to display the screen saver after one minute of inactivity.)
9. Click OK to close the dialog box.
10. Close the Control Panel by clicking the Close button located in the upper right corner of the window.

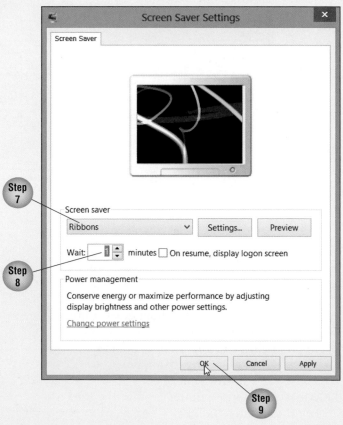

11. Do not touch the mouse or keyboard and wait over one minute for the screen saver to display. After watching the screen saver, move the mouse. (This redisplays the desktop.)
12. Right-click in an empty area of the desktop and then click *Personalize* at the shortcut menu.
13. At the Control Panel Appearance and Personalization window, click the <u>Screen Saver</u> hyperlink.
14. At the Screen Saver Settings dialog box, click the option button below the *Screen saver* option and then click *(None)* at the drop-down list.
15. Click OK to close the dialog box.
16. Close the Control Panel Appearance and Personalization window.

Exploring Windows Help and Support

Windows 8 includes an on-screen reference guide providing information, explanations, and interactive help on learning Windows features. Get help at the Windows Help and Support window, shown in Figure W.13. Display this window by clicking the Start screen thumbnail to display the Windows 8 Start screen. Right-click a blank area of the Start screen, click the All apps button, and then click the *Help and Support* tile in the Windows System group. Use options in the Windows Help and Support window to search for help on a specific feature; display the opening Windows Help and Support window; print the current information; and display information on getting started with Windows 8, setting up a network, and protecting your computer.

Figure W.13 Windows Help and Support Window

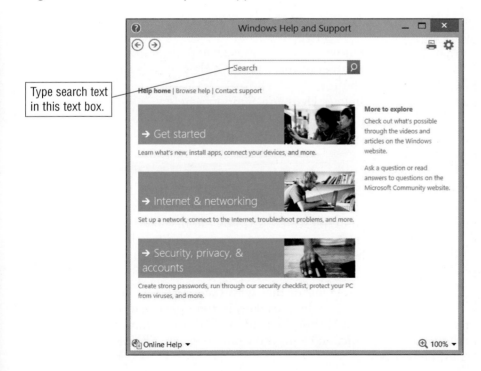

Type search text in this text box.

1. Display the Windows 8 Help and Support window by following these steps:
   a. At the Windows 8 desktop, position the mouse pointer in the lower left corner of the screen and then click the Start screen thumbnail.
   b. Position the mouse in a blank area of the Windows 8 Start screen and then click the right mouse button.
   c. Click the All apps button that appears in the lower right corner of the Start screen and then scroll to the right of the Start screen.
   d. Click the *Help and Support* tile located in the *Windows System* category.

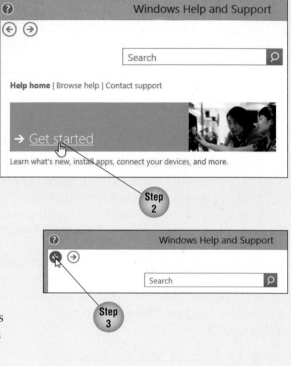

2. At the Windows Help and Support window, click the Get started hyperlink.
3. Click a hyperlink that interests you, read the information, and then click the Back button. (The Back button is located in the upper left corner of the window.)
4. Click another hyperlink that interests you and then read the information.
5. Click the Help home hyperlink that displays below the search text box. (This returns you to the opening Windows Help and Support window.)
6. Click in the search text box, type **delete files**, and then press Enter.
7. Click the How to work with files and folders hyperlink that displays in the window.
8. Read the information that displays about working with files or folders and then click the Print button located in the upper right corner of the Windows Help and Support window.
9. At the Print dialog box, click the Print button.
10. Click the Close button to close the Windows Help and Support window.

Using Search Tools ■■■■■■■■■■■■■■■■■■■■■■■■■■

The Charm bar contains a search tool you can use to quickly find an application or file on your computer. To use the search tool, display the Charm bar, click the Search button and then type in the search text box the first few characters of the application or file for which you are searching. As you type characters in the text box, a list displays with application names or file names that begin with the characters. As you continue typing characters, the search tool refines the list.

You can also search for programs or files with the search text box in the Computer window. The search text box displays in the upper right corner of the Computer window at the right side of the Address bar. If you want to search a specific folder, make that folder active in the Content pane and then type the search text in the text box.

When conducting a search, you can use the asterisk (*) as a wildcard character in place of any letters, numbers, or symbols within a file name. For example, in the following project you will search for file names containing *check* by typing **check** in the search text box. The asterisk indicates that the file name can start with any letter but it must contain the letters *check* somewhere in the file name.

Project 13   Searching for Programs and Files

1. At the Windows 8 desktop, display the Charm bar and then click the Search button.
2. With the insertion point positioned in the search text box, type **paint**. (Notice as you type the letters that Windows displays applications that begin with the same letters you are typing or that are associated with the same letters in a keyword. Notice that the Paint program displays below the heading *Apps* at the top of the list. Depending on the contents stored in the computer you are using, additional items may display below Paint.)

Step 2

3. Click *Paint* that displays below the *Apps* heading.
4. Close the Paint window.
5. Right-click the Start screen thumbnail and then click *File Explorer*.
6. At the Computer window, double-click the icon representing your storage medium.
7. Double-click the *Windows8* folder.
8. Click in the search text box located at the right of the Address bar and then type **document**. (As you begin typing the letters, Windows filters the list of files in the Content pane to those that contain the letters you type. Notice that the Address bar displays *Search Results in Windows8* to indicate that the files that display matching your criteria are limited to the current folder.)

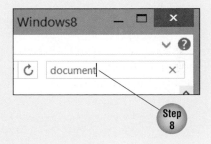

Step 8

9. Select the text *document* that displays in the search text box and then type **check**. (Notice that the Content pane displays file names containing the letters *check* no matter how the file name begins.)
10. Double-click ***WordSpellCheck02 .docx*** to open the document in Word.
11. Close the document and then close Word by clicking the Close button located in the upper right corner of the window.
12. Close the Computer window.

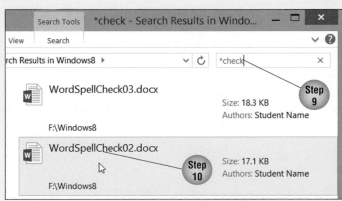

Browsing the Internet Using Internet Explorer 10

Microsoft Internet Explorer 10 is a web browser with options and features for displaying sites as well as navigating and searching for information on the Internet. The *Internet* is a network of computers connected around the world. Users access the Internet for several purposes: to communicate using instant messaging and/or email, to subscribe to newsgroups, to transfer files, to socialize with other users around the globe on social websites, and to access virtually any kind of information imaginable.

Using the Internet, people can find a phenomenal amount of information for private or public use. To use the Internet, three things are generally required: an *Internet Service Provider (ISP)*, software to browse the Web (called a *web browser*), and a *search engine*. In this section, you will learn how to:

- Navigate the Internet using URLs and hyperlinks
- Use search engines to locate information
- Download web pages and images

You will use the Microsoft Internet Explorer web browser to locate information on the Internet. A *Uniform Resource Locator*, referred to as a *URL*, identifies a location on the Internet. The steps for browsing the Internet vary but generally include opening Internet Explorer, typing the URL for the desired site, navigating the various pages of the site, navigating to other sites using links, and then closing Internet Explorer.

To launch Internet Explorer 10, click the Internet Explorer icon on the Taskbar at the Windows desktop. Figure IE.1 identifies the elements of the Internet Explorer 10 window. The web page that displays in your Internet Explorer window may vary from what you see in Figure IE.1.

If you know the URL for a desired website, click in the Address bar, type the URL, and then press Enter. The website's home page displays in a tab within the Internet Explorer window. The format of a URL is *http://server-name.path*. The first part of the URL, *http*, stands for HyperText Transfer Protocol, which is the protocol or language used to transfer data within the World Wide Web. The colon and slashes separate the protocol from the server name. The server name is the second component of the URL. For example, in the URL http://www.microsoft.com, the server name is *microsoft*. The last part of the URL specifies the domain to which the server belongs. For example, *.com* refers to "commercial" and establishes that the URL is a commercial company. Examples of other domains include *.edu* for "educational," *.gov* for "government," and *.mil* for "military."

Internet Explorer 10 has been streamlined to provide users with more browsing space and reduced clutter. By default, Microsoft has turned off many features in Internet Explorer 10 such as the Menu bar, Command bar, and Status bar. You can turn these features on by right-clicking the empty space above the Address bar and to the right of the new tab button (see Figure IE.1) and then clicking the desired option at the drop-down list that displays. For example, if you want to turn on the Menu bar (the bar that contains File, Edit, and so on), right-click the empty space above the Address bar and then click *Menu bar* at the drop-down list. (This inserts a check mark next to *Menu bar*.)

Figure IE.1 Internet Explorer Window

Project 1 Browsing the Internet Using URLs

1. Make sure you are connected to the Internet through an Internet Service Provider and that the Windows 8 desktop displays. (Check with your instructor to determine if you need to complete steps for accessing the Internet such as typing a user name and password to log on.)
2. Launch Microsoft Internet Explorer by clicking the Internet Explorer icon located at the left side of the Windows Taskbar, which is located at the bottom of the Windows desktop.
3. Turn on the Command bar by right-clicking the empty space above the Address bar or to the right of the new tab button (see Figure IE.1) and then clicking *Command bar* at the drop-down list.
4. At the Internet Explorer window, explore the website for Yosemite National Park by completing the following steps:
   a. Click in the Address bar, type **www.nps.gov/yose**, and then press Enter.
   b. Scroll down the home page for Yosemite National Park by clicking the down-pointing arrow on the vertical scroll bar located at the right side of the Internet Explorer window.

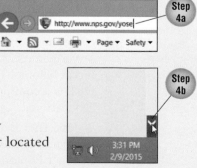

c. Print the home page by clicking the Print button located on the Command bar. (Note that some websites have a printer-friendly button you can click to print the page.)

5. Explore the website for Glacier National Park by completing the following steps:
   a. Click in the Address bar, type **www.nps.gov/glac**, and then press Enter.
   b. Print the home page by clicking the Print button located on the Command bar.

6. Close Internet Explorer by clicking the Close button (contains an X) located in the upper right corner of the Internet Explorer window.

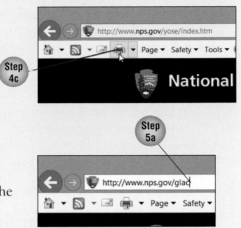

Navigating Using Hyperlinks ▪▪▪▪▪▪▪▪▪▪▪▪▪▪▪▪▪▪▪▪▪▪▪▪▪▪

Most web pages contain *hyperlinks* that you click to connect to another page within the website or to another site on the Internet. Hyperlinks may display in a web page as underlined text in a specific color or as images or icons. To use a hyperlink, position the mouse pointer on the desired hyperlink until the mouse pointer turns into a hand and then click the left mouse button. Use hyperlinks to navigate within and between sites on the Internet. The Internet Explorer window contains a Back button (see Figure IE.1) that, when clicked, takes you to the previous web page viewed. If you click the Back button and then want to return to the previous page, click the Forward button. You can continue clicking the Back button to back your way out of several linked pages in reverse order since Internet Explorer maintains a history of the websites you visit.

Project 2 | Navigating Using Hyperlinks

1. Make sure you are connected to the Internet and then click the Internet Explorer icon on the Windows Taskbar.
2. At the Internet Explorer window, display the White House web page and navigate in the page by completing the following steps:
   a. Click in the Address bar, type **whitehouse.gov**, and then press Enter.
   b. At the White House home page, position the mouse pointer on a hyperlink that interests you until the pointer turns into a hand and then click the left mouse button.
   c. At the linked web page, click the Back button. (This returns you to the White House home page.)
   d. At the White House home page, click the Forward button to return to the previous web page viewed.
   e. Print the web page by clicking the Print button on the Command bar.

3. Display the website for Amazon.com and navigate in the site by completing the following steps:

a. Click in the Address bar, type **www.amazon.com**, and then press Enter.

b. At the Amazon.com home page, click a hyperlink related to books.

c. When a book web page displays, click the Print button on the Command bar.

4. Close Internet Explorer by clicking the Close button (contains an X) located in the upper right corner of the Internet Explorer window.

Searching for Specific Sites ▪■■■■■■■■■■■■■■■■■■■■■

If you do not know the URL for a specific site or you want to find information on the Internet but do not know what site to visit, complete a search with a search engine. A *search engine* is software created to search quickly and easily for desired information. A variety of search engines are available on the Internet, each offering the opportunity to search for specific information. One method for searching for information is to click in the Address bar, type a keyword or phrase related to your search, and then press Enter. Another method for completing a search is to visit the website for a search engine and use options at the site.

Bing is Microsoft's online search portal and is the default search engine used by Internet Explorer. Bing organizes search results by topic category and provides related search suggestions.

Project 3 Searching for Information by Topic

1. Start Internet Explorer.
2. At the Internet Explorer window, search for sites on bluegrass music by completing the following steps:

a. Click in the Address bar.

b. Type **bluegrass music** and then press Enter.

c. When a list of sites displays in the Bing results window, click a site that interests you.

d. When the page displays, click the Print button.

3. Use the Yahoo! search engine to find sites on bluegrass music by completing the following steps:

a. Click in the Address bar, type **www.yahoo.com**, and then press Enter.

b. At the Yahoo! website, with the insertion point positioned in the search text box, type **bluegrass music** and then press Enter. (Notice that the sites displayed vary from sites displayed in the earlier search.)

c. Click hyperlinks until a website displays that interests you.
d. Print the page.
4. Use the Google search engine to find sites on jazz music by completing the following steps:
   a. Click in the Address bar, type **www.google.com**, and then press Enter.
   b. At the Google website, with the insertion point positioned in the search text box, type **jazz music** and then press Enter.
   c. Click a site that interests you.
   d. Print the page.
5. Close Internet Explorer.

Using a Metasearch Engine

Bing, Yahoo!, and Google are search engines that search the Web for content and display search results. In addition to individual search engines, you can use a metasearch engine, such as Dogpile, that sends your search text to other search engines and then compiles the results in one list. With a metasearch engine, you type the search text once and then access results from a wider group of search engines. The Dogpile metasearch engine provides search results from Google, Yahoo!, and Yandex.

Project 4   **Searching with a Metasearch Search Engine**

1. Start Internet Explorer.
2. Click in the Address bar.
3. Type **www.dogpile.com** and then press Enter.
4. At the Dogpile website, type **jazz music** in the search text box and then press Enter.
5. Click a hyperlink that interests you.
6. Close the Internet Explorer window. If a message displays asking if you want to close all tabs, click the Close all tabs button.

Completing Advanced Searches for Specific Sites

The Internet contains an enormous amount of information. Depending on what you are searching for on the Internet and the search engine you use, some searches can result in several thousand "hits" (sites). Wading through a large number of sites can be very time-consuming and counterproductive. Narrowing a search to very specific criteria can greatly reduce the number of hits for a search. To narrow a search, use the advanced search options offered by the search engine.

Project 5 — Narrowing a Search

1. Start Internet Explorer.
2. Search for sites on skydiving in Oregon by completing the following steps:
   a. Click in the Address bar, type **www.yahoo.com**, and then press Enter.
   b. At the Yahoo! home page, click the Search button next to the search text box.
   c. Click the More hyperlink located above the search text box and then click *Advanced Search* at the drop-down list.

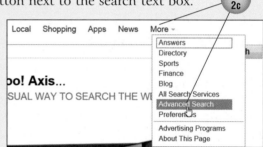

   d. At the Advanced Web Search page, click in the search text box next to *all of these words*.
   e. Type **skydiving Oregon tandem static line**. (This limits the search to web pages containing all of the words typed in the search text box.)
   f. Click the Yahoo! Search button.
   g. When the list of websites displays, click a hyperlink that interests you.
   h. Click the Back button until the Yahoo! Advanced Web Search page displays.

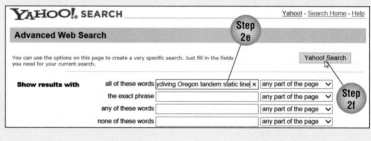

   i. Click in the *the exact phrase* text box and then type **skydiving in Oregon**.
   j. Click the *Only .com domains* option in the *Site/Domain* section.
   k. Click the Yahoo! Search button.
   l. When the list of websites displays, click a hyperlink that interests you.
   m. Print the page.

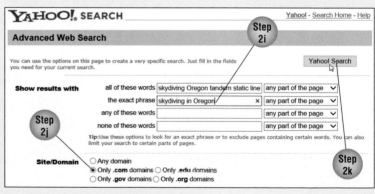

3. Close Internet Explorer.

Downloading Images, Text, and Web Pages
from the Internet ■■■■■■■■■■■■■■■■■■■■■■

The image(s) and/or text that display when you open a web page, as well as the web page itself, can be saved as a separate file. This separate file can be viewed, printed, or inserted in another file. The information you want to save in a separate file is downloaded from the Internet by Internet Explorer and saved in a folder of your choosing with the name you specify. Copyright laws protect much of the information on the Internet. Before using information downloaded from the Internet, check the site for restrictions. If you do use information, make sure you properly cite the source.

Project 6 — Downloading Images and Web Pages

1. Start Internet Explorer.
2. Download a web page and image from Banff National Park by completing the following steps:
   a. Search for websites related to Banff National Park.
   b. From the list of sites that displays, choose a site that contains information about Banff National Park and at least one image of the park.
   c. Make sure the Command bar is turned on. (If the Command bar is turned off, turn it on by right-clicking the empty space above the Address bar or to the right of the new tab button and then clicking *Command bar* at the drop-down list.)
   d. Save the web page as a separate file by clicking the Page button on the Command bar and then clicking *Save as* at the drop-down list.
   e. At the Save Webpage dialog box, type **BanffWebPage**.
   f. Click the down-pointing arrow for the *Save as type* option and then click *Web Archive, single file (*.mht)*.
   g. Navigate to the drive containing your storage medium and then click the Save button.

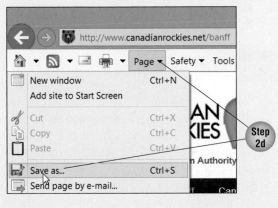

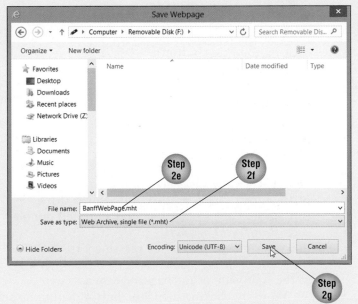

3. Save an image file by completing the following steps:
   a. Right-click an image that displays at the website.
   b. At the shortcut menu that displays, click *Save picture as*.

 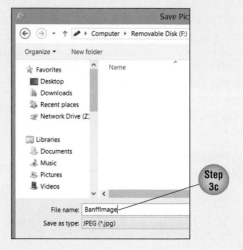

Step 3b

Step 3c

   c. At the Save Picture dialog box, type **BanffImage** in the *File name* text box.
   d. Navigate to the drive containing your storage medium and then click the Save button.
4. Close Internet Explorer.

Project 7   Opening the Saved Web Page and Image in a Word Document

1. Open Microsoft Word by positioning the mouse pointer in the lower left corner of the Taskbar, clicking the Start screen thumbnail, and then clicking the *Word 2013* tile in the Windows 8 Start screen. At the Word opening screen, click the *Blank document* template.
2. With Microsoft Word open, insert the image in a document by completing the following steps:
   a. Click the INSERT tab and then click the Pictures button in the Illustrations group.
   b. At the Insert Picture dialog box, navigate to the drive containing your storage medium and then double-click **BanffImage.jpg**.

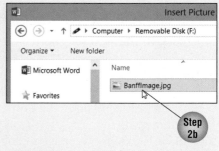

Step 2b

   c. When the image displays in the Word document, print the document by pressing Ctrl + P and then clicking the Print button.
   d. Close the document by clicking the FILE tab and then clicking the *Close* option. At the message asking if you want to save the changes, click the Don't Save button.
3. Open the **BanffWebPage.mht** file by completing the following steps:
   a. Click the FILE tab and then click the *Open* option.
   b. Double-click the *Computer* option.
   c. At the Open dialog box, navigate to the drive containing your storage medium and then double-click **BanffWebPage.mht**.

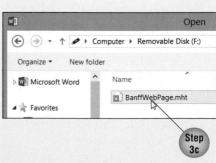

Step 3c

   d. Preview the web page(s) by pressing Ctrl + P. At the Print backstage area, preview the page shown at the right side of the backstage area.
4. Close Word by clicking the Close button (contains an X) that displays in the upper right corner of the screen.

MICROSOFT® POWERPOINT®

Unit 1 ■ Creating and Formatting PowerPoint Presentations

1

MICROSOFT®

POWERPOINT®

Preparing a PowerPoint Presentation

CHAPTER

PERFORMANCE OBJECTIVES

Upon successful completion of Chapter 1, you will be able to:

- Open, save, run, print, close, and delete a presentation
- Pin a presentation to a recent list
- Plan a presentation
- Create a presentation using a theme template
- Insert slides, insert text in slides, and choose slide layouts
- Change presentation views
- Navigate and edit slides
- Preview and print a presentation
- Apply a design theme and variant to a presentation
- Prepare a presentation from a blank presentation
- Prepare a presentation in Outline view
- Add transitions, sounds, and timings to a presentation

Tutorials

1.1 Opening, Running, and Closing a Presentation

1.2 Creating and Saving a Presentation

1.3 Navigating and Inserting Slides in a Presentation

1.4 Changing Views and Slide Layout

1.5 Previewing Slides and Printing a Presentation

1.6 Running a Presentation

1.7 Adding Transition and Sound

During a presentation, the person doing the presenting may use visual aids to strengthen the impact of the message as well as help organize the presented information. Visual aids may include transparencies, slides, photographs, or an on-screen presentation. With Microsoft's PowerPoint program, you can easily create visual aids for a presentation and then print copies of the aids as well as run the presentation. PowerPoint is a presentation graphics program that you can use to organize and present information. Model answers for this chapter's projects appear on the following page.

PC1

Note: Before beginning the projects, copy to your storage medium the PC1 subfolder from the PowerPoint folder on the CD that accompanies this textbook. Steps on how to copy a folder are presented on the inside of the back cover of this textbook. Do this every time you start a chapter's projects.

3

Project 2 Create an Internet Presentation Using a Theme Template
P-C1-P2-Resumes.pptx

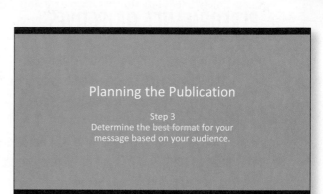

Project 3 Create a Planning Presentation from an Existing Presentation
P-C1-P3-PlanningPres-Ink.pptx

P-C1-P3-PlanningPres.pptx

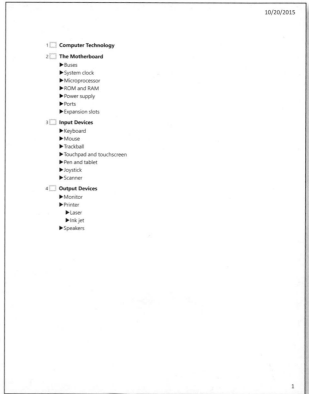

Project 4 Create a Technology Presentation in Outline View
P-C1-P4-Computers.pptx

Project **1** **Open and Run a Presentation**   **1 Part**

You will open a presentation, run the presentation, and then close the presentation.

Creating a PowerPoint Presentation ■■■■■■■■■■■■■■

PowerPoint provides several methods for creating a presentation. You can create a presentation using a theme template or starting with a blank slide. The steps you follow to create a presentation will vary depending on the method you choose, but will often follow these basic steps:

1. Open PowerPoint.
2. Choose the desired theme template or start with a blank presentation.
3. Type the text for each slide, adding additional elements, such as graphic images, as needed.
4. If necessary, apply a design theme.
5. Save the presentation.
6. Print the presentation as slides, handouts, notes pages, or an outline.
7. Run the presentation.
8. Close the presentation.
9. Close PowerPoint.

After you choose the specific type of presentation you want to create, you are presented with the PowerPoint window in the Normal view. What displays in the window will vary depending on the type of presentation you are creating. However, the PowerPoint window contains some consistent elements, as shown in Figure 1.1 on the next page. The PowerPoint window contains many elements similar to those in other Microsoft Office programs such as Word and Excel. For example, the PowerPoint window, like the Word window, contains a FILE tab, Quick Access toolbar, tabs, ribbon, vertical and horizontal scroll bars, and Status bar. The PowerPoint window elements are described in Table 1.1 on the next page.

PowerPoint, like other Microsoft Office programs, provides enhanced ScreenTips for buttons and options. Hover the mouse pointer over a button or option and, after approximately one second, an enhanced ScreenTip will display near the button or option. The enhanced ScreenTip displays the name of the button or option, any shortcut command if one is available, and a description of the button or option.

Figure 1.1 PowerPoint Window

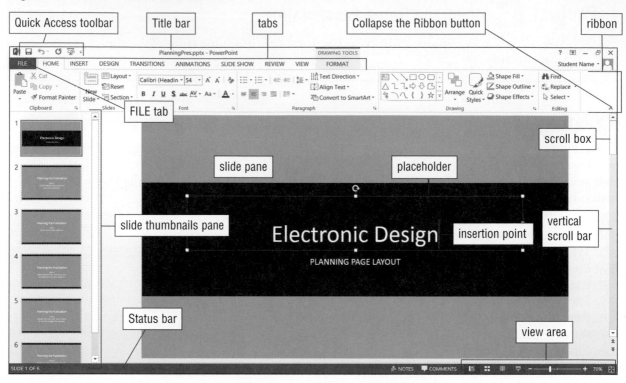

Table 1.1 PowerPoint Window Elements

Feature	Description
Collapse the Ribbon button	When clicked, removes the ribbon from the screen.
FILE tab	Click the FILE tab and the backstage area displays containing options for working with and managing presentations.
horizontal scroll bar	Shift text left or right in the slide pane.
I-beam pointer	Used to move the insertion point or to select text.
insertion point	Indicates the location of the next character entered at the keyboard.
placeholder	Location on a slide that holds text or objects.
Quick Access toolbar	Contains buttons for commonly used commands.
ribbon	Area containing the tabs and commands divided into groups.
slide pane	Displays the slide and slide contents.
slide thumbnails pane	The left side of the screen that displays slide thumbnails.
Status bar	Displays the slide number and number of slides, buttons for inserting notes and comments, view buttons, and the Zoom slider bar.
tabs	Contain commands and features organized into groups.
Title bar	Displays presentation name followed by the program name.
vertical scroll bar	Display specific slides using this scroll bar.
view area	Located toward the right side of the Status bar and contains buttons for changing the presentation view.

Opening a Presentation

When you create, save, and then close a presentation, you can open the presentation at the Open dialog box. To display this dialog box, click the FILE tab and then click the *Open* option. This displays the Open backstage area, as shown in Figure 1.2. You can also display the Open backstage area by clicking the <u>Open Other Presentations</u> hyperlink that displays in the lower left corner of the PowerPoint 2013 opening screen or with the keyboard shortcut Ctrl + O. Another method for displaying the Open backstage area is to insert an Open button on the Quick Access toolbar and then click the button.

At the Open backstage area, click the desired location, such as your SkyDrive or the *Computer* option, and then click the Browse button. (If you are opening a presentation from your computer's hard drive or removable drive, you can double-click the *Computer* option.) When you click the Browse button (or double-click the *Computer* option), the Open dialog box displays. At this dialog box, open a presentation by double-clicking the presentation name in the Content pane. You can go directly to the Open dialog box without displaying the Open backstage area by pressing the keyboard shortcut Ctrl + F12.

At the Open backstage area with your SkyDrive or the *Computer* option selected, the most recently accessed folder names display in the Recent Folders list. If you open PowerPoint and then access a presentation from a particular folder, that folder name will display above the Recent Folders list below the heading *Current Folder* at the Open backstage area with your SkyDrive or the *Computer* option selected. Click the folder name in the Current Folder list or Recent Folders list if you want to open a presentation from the folder.

▼ Quick Steps

Open a Presentation
1. Click FILE tab.
2. Click *Open* option.
3. Click desired location.
4. Click Browse button.
5. Navigate to desired folder or drive.
6. Double-click presentation.

H I N T

Press Ctrl + F12 to display the Open dialog box without displaying the Open backstage area.

Figure 1.2 Open Backstage Area

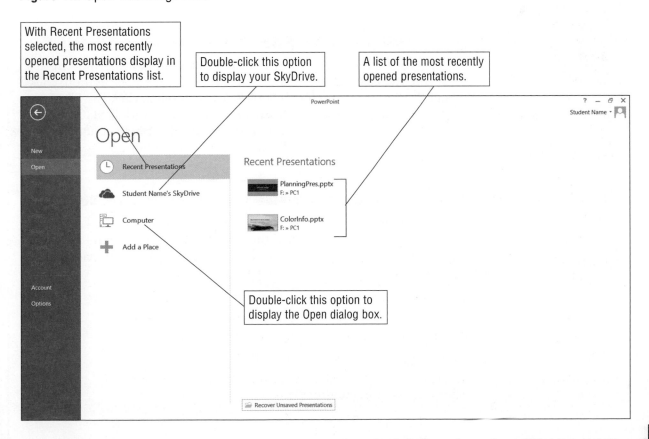

Opening a Presentation from the Recent Presentations List ■■■■■■■■■■■■■■■■■■■■■

At the Open backstage area with Recent Presentations selected, the Recent Presentations list displays up to 25 of the most recently opened presentations. The PowerPoint 2013 opening screen also contains a Recent list with the most recently opened presentations. To open a presentation from the Recent list, open PowerPoint to display the opening screen or display the Open backstage area with Recent Presentations selected and then click the desired presentation in the list.

Start from Beginning

Pinning a Presentation to a Recent List ■■■■■■■■■■■■■

If you want a presentation to remain in the Recent Presentations list at the Open backstage area or the Recent list at the PowerPoint 2013 opening screen, "pin" the presentation to the list. To pin a presentation, position the mouse pointer over the desired presentation name in the Recent Presentations list or Recent list and then click the left-pointing stick pin that displays at the right of the presentation name. This turns the stick pin into a down-pointing stick pin. The next time you open PowerPoint or display the Open backstage area, the presentation you "pinned" displays at the top of the list. To "unpin" a presentation, click the pin to change it from a down-pointing pin to a left-pointing pin. You can pin more than one presentation to the list.

When you click your SkyDrive or the *Computer* option at the Open backstage area, the most recently accessed folders display in the Recent Folders list. You can pin a folder to the Recent Folders list in the same way you pin a presentation. If you access a particular folder on a regular basis, consider pinning it to the list.

Running a Presentation ■■■■■■■■■■■■■■■■■■■■■■■■■■■■

When you open a presentation, the presentation displays in Normal view. In this view, you can edit and customize the presentation. To run the presentation, click the Start From Beginning button on the Quick Access toolbar, click the Slide Show button in the view area on the Status bar, or click the SLIDE SHOW tab and then click the From Beginning button in the Start Slide Show group. Navigate through slides in the presentation by clicking the left mouse button.

Closing a Presentation ■■■■■■■■■■■■■■■■■■■■■■■■■■■■■■

To remove a presentation from the screen, close the presentation. Close a presentation by clicking the FILE tab and then clicking the *Close* option. You can also close a presentation with the keyboard shortcut Ctrl + F4. If you made any changes to the presentation, you will be asked if you want to save the presentation.

1. Open PowerPoint by clicking the PowerPoint 2013 tile at the Windows 8 Start screen. (Depending on your operating system, these steps may vary.)
2. At the PowerPoint 2013 opening screen, click the <u>Open Other Presentations</u> hyperlink that displays in the lower left corner of the screen.
3. At the Open backstage area, click the location where the PC1 folder containing your student data files is located. (For example, click your SkyDrive or click the *Computer* option.)
4. Click the Browse button.
5. At the Open dialog box, navigate to the PC1 folder on your storage medium and then double-click *ColorInfo.pptx*.

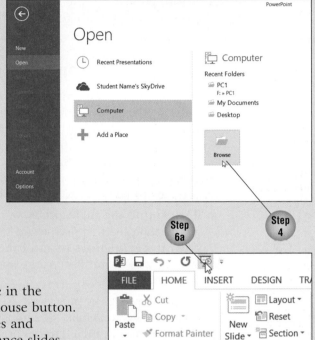

6. Run the presentation by completing the following steps:
   a. Click the Start From Beginning button on the Quick Access toolbar.
   b. Read the information in the first slide in the presentation and then click the left mouse button.
   c. Continue reading information in slides and clicking the left mouse button to advance slides.
   d. At the black screen with the message *End of slide show, click to exit.*, click the left mouse button. (This returns the presentation to Normal view.)
7. Close the presentation by clicking the FILE tab and then clicking the *Close* option.
8. Pin **ColorInfo.pptx** to the Recent Presentations list by completing the following steps:
   a. Click the FILE tab.
   b. At the Open backstage area with Recent Presentations selected, hover your mouse over the **ColorInfo.pptx** presentation name that displays at the top of the Recent Presentations list and then click the stick pin that displays to the right of the presentation name.
   c. Click the Back button to return to the blank presentation screen. (The Back button is located in the upper left corner of the backstage area and displays as a circle with a left-pointing arrow.)
9. Close PowerPoint by clicking the Close button that displays in the upper right corner of the screen.
10. Open PowerPoint by clicking the PowerPoint 2013 tile at the Windows 8 Start screen. (These steps may vary; check with your instructor.)
11. At the PowerPoint 2013 opening screen, notice that **ColorInfo.pptx** is pinned to the Recent list. Open the presentation by clicking *ColorInfo.pptx* at the top of the list.
12. Close **ColorInfo.pptx**.
13. Unpin **ColorInfo.pptx** from the recent list by completing steps 8a through 8c.

Project 2 **Create a Resume Style Presentation Using a** **3 Parts**
Theme Template

You will use a theme template to create a presentation, insert text in slides in the presentation, choose a slide layout, insert new slides, change views, navigate through the presentation, edit text in slides, and then print the presentation.

Planning a Presentation ■■■■■■■■■■■ ■■■■■■■■■■ ■■■■

When planning a presentation, first define the purpose of the presentation. Is the intent to inform? educate? sell? motivate? and/or entertain? In addition, consider the audience who will be listening to and watching the presentation. Determine the content of the presentation and the medium that will be used to convey the message. Will a computer monitor be used to display the presentation or will the presentation be projected onto a screen? Some basic guidelines to consider when preparing the content of a presentation include:

- **Determine the main purpose of the presentation.** Do not try to cover too many topics — this may strain the audience's attention or cause confusion. Identifying the main point of the presentation will help you stay focused and convey a clear message to the audience.

- **Determine the output.** Is the presentation going to be presented on a computer or will the slides be projected? To help determine which type of output to use, consider the availability of equipment, the size of the room where the presentation will be given, and the number of people who will be attending the presentation.

- **Show one idea per slide.** Each slide in a presentation should convey only one main idea. Too many thoughts or ideas on a slide may confuse the audience and cause you to stray from the purpose of the slide. Determine the specific message you want to convey to the audience and then outline the message to organize your ideas.

- **Maintain a consistent layout.** Using a consistent layout and color scheme for slides in a presentation will create continuity and cohesiveness. Do not get carried away by using too many colors, pictures, and/or other graphic elements.

- **Keep slides simple.** Keep slides uncluttered so that they are easy for the audience to read. Keep words and other items, such as bullets, to a minimum.

- **Determine the output needed.** Will you be providing audience members with handouts? If so, will these handouts consist of a printing of each slide? an outline of the presentation? a printing of each slide with space for taking notes?

Creating a Presentation Using a Design Theme Template ■■■■■■■■■■ ■■■■■■■■■ ■■■

▼ Quick Steps
Create a Presentation Using a Design Theme Template
1. Click FILE tab.
2. Click *New* option.
3. Click desired theme template.
4. Click color variant.
5. Click Create button.

PowerPoint provides built-in design theme templates you can use when creating slides for a presentation. These design theme templates include formatting such as color, background, fonts, and so on. Choose a design theme template at the New backstage area, as shown in Figure 1.3. Display the New backstage area by clicking the FILE tab and then clicking the *New* option. At this backstage area, click the desired design theme template or search for a template or theme at Office.com by typing a category in the search text box or clicking one of the categories listed

Figure 1.3 New Backstage Area

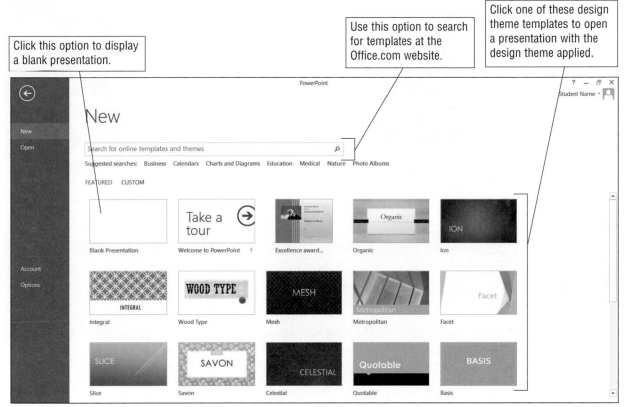

Click this option to display a blank presentation.

Use this option to search for templates at the Office.com website.

Click one of these design theme templates to open a presentation with the design theme applied.

next to *Suggested searches* below the search text box. Microsoft provides a variety of predesigned templates in many different categories at Office.com.

When you click a design theme template at the New backstage area, a window opens containing a slide with the design theme applied as well as theme color variants. The color variants display at the right side of the window and provide color options for the theme. If you want to change the color of the theme, click the desired color variant and then click the Create button. This opens a presentation with the design theme and theme colors applied.

Creating Slides in a Presentation

When you choose a blank presentation template or design theme template at the New backstage area, a slide displays in the slide pane in Normal view. The slide displays with a default Title Slide layout. This layout contains placeholders for entering the slide title and subtitle. To insert text in a placeholder, click the placeholder text. This moves the insertion point inside the placeholder, removes the default placeholder text, and makes the placeholder active. An active placeholder displays surrounded by a dashed border with sizing handles and a white rotation handle, as shown in Figure 1.4.

With the insertion point positioned in a placeholder, type the desired text. Edit text in a placeholder in the same manner as you would edit text in a Word document. Press the Backspace key to delete the character immediately left of the insertion point and press the Delete key to delete the character immediately right of the insertion point. Use the arrow keys on the keyboard to move the insertion point in the desired direction.

Figure 1.4 Slide Placeholders

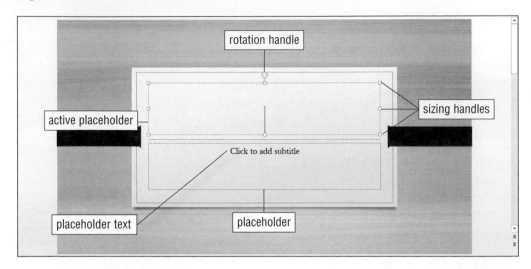

Choosing a Slide Layout

Quick Steps
Choose a Slide Layout
1. Click Layout button.
2. Click desired layout option in drop-down list.

Layout

When you choose a blank presentation template or design theme template to create a presentation, the slide displays in the Title Slide layout. You can change the slide layout with the Layout button in the Slides group on the HOME tab. Click the Layout button and a drop-down list of layouts displays. Click the desired layout at the drop-down list and the layout is applied to the current slide.

HINT
PowerPoint includes nine built-in standard layouts.

Inserting a New Slide

Quick Steps
Insert a New Slide
Click New Slide button.
OR
Press Ctrl + M.

New Slide

Create a new slide in a presentation by clicking the New Slide button in the Slides group on the HOME tab or by pressing Ctrl + M. By default, PowerPoint inserts a new slide with the Title and Content layout. Choose a different slide layout for a new slide by clicking the New Slide button arrow and then clicking the desired layout at the drop-down list. You can also change the slide layout by clicking the Layout button in the Slides group on the HOME tab and then clicking the desired layout at the drop-down list.

Saving a Presentation ■■■■■■■■■■■■■■■■■■■■■■■

Quick Steps
Save a Presentation
1. Click Save button.
2. At Save As backstage area, click desired location.
3. Click Browse button.
4. At Save As dialog box, navigate to desired folder.
5. Type presentation name in *File name* text box.
6. Press Enter or click Save button.

Save

After creating a presentation, save it by clicking the Save button on the Quick Access toolbar, by clicking the FILE tab and then clicking the *Save As* option, or with the keyboard shortcut Ctrl + S. This displays the Save As backstage area. At this backstage area, click the desired location where you want to save the presentation. For example, click your SkyDrive or click the *Computer* option if you are saving to your computer's hard drive or removable drive. After specifying the location, click the Browse button and the Save As dialog box displays. If you are saving the presentation to your computer's hard drive or removable drive, you can double-click the *Computer* option at the Save As backstage area to display the Save As dialog box. At the Save As dialog box, type a name for the presentation in the *File name* text box and then press Enter or click the Save button. You can press the F12 function key to go directly to the Save As dialog box without displaying the Save As backstage area.

When you click your SkyDrive or the *Computer* option at the Save As backstage area, the names of the most recently accessed folders display below the *Recent Folders* heading in the *Computer* section. Open a folder by clicking the folder name.

A presentation file name can contain up to 255 characters, including drive letter and any folder names, and can include spaces. You cannot give a presentation the same name in first uppercase and then lowercase letters. Also, some symbols cannot be used in a file name, including /, ?, \, ", >, :, <, ;, *, and |.

H I N T
Press F12 to display the Save As dialog box without displaying the Save As backstage area.

Project 2a	**Creating a Presentation Using a Design Theme Template**	**Part 1 of 3**

1. With PowerPoint open, click the FILE tab and then click the *New* option.
2. At the New backstage area, click the *Organic* design theme template.
3. At the window that displays, click the Create button.

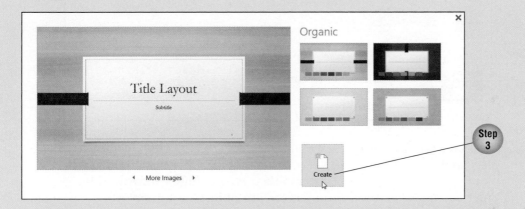

Organic

Title Layout

Subtitle

◄ More Images ►

Create

Step 3

4. Click in the placeholder text *Click to add title* and then type **Career Finders.**
5. Click in the placeholder text *Click to add subtitle* and then type **Resume Writing.**
6. Click the New Slide button in the Slides group on the HOME tab. (This inserts a slide with the Title and Content layout.)

Step 6

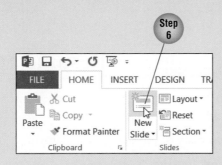

7. Click the placeholder text *Click to add title* and then type **Resume Styles**.
8. Click the placeholder text *Click to add text* and then type **Chronological resume**.
9. Press the Enter key (this moves the insertion point to the next line and inserts a bullet) and then type **Functional resume**.
10. Press the Enter key and then type **Hybrid resume**.

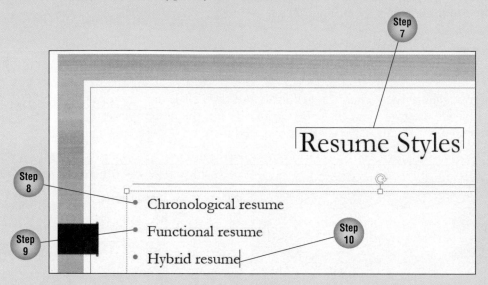

11. Click the New Slide button in the Slides group.
12. Click the placeholder text *Click to add title* and then type **Resume Sections**.
13. Click the placeholder text *Click to add text* and then type **Contact information**.
14. Press the Enter key and then type **Summary or job objective statement**.
15. Press the Enter key and then type **Work history**.
16. Press the Enter key and then type **Education details**.
17. Press the Enter key and then type **References**.

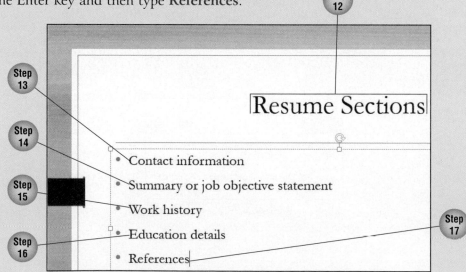

18. Click the New Slide button arrow and then click the *Title Slide* layout option.

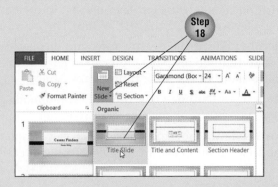

Step
18

19. Click the placeholder text *Click to add title* and then type **Career Finders**.
20. Click the placeholder text *Click to add subtitle* and then type **Contact us by calling 1-800-555-2255**.

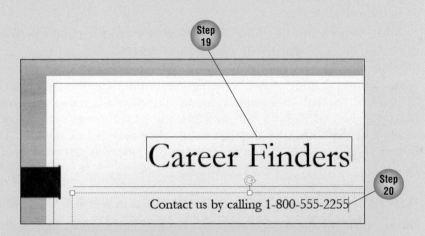

Step
19

Step
20

21. Click in the slide pane but outside the slide. (This deselects the placeholder.)
22. Save the presentation by completing the following steps:
    a. Click the Save button on the Quick Access toolbar.
    b. At the Save As backstage area, click the desired location, such as your SkyDrive or *Computer* option, and then click the Browse button.
    c. At the Save As dialog box, navigate to the PC1 folder on your storage medium.
    d. Select the text in the *File name* text box and then type **P-C1-P2-Resumes** (*P* for PowerPoint, *C1* for Chapter 1, *P2* for Project 2, and *Resumes* because that is topic of the presentation).
    e. Press Enter or click the Save button.

Step
22a

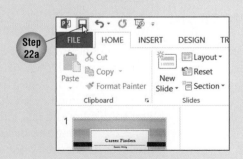

Changing Views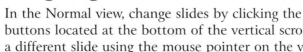

In Normal view, you can increase or decrease the size of the slide thumbnails pane.

PowerPoint provides a variety of viewing options for a presentation. Change the view with buttons in the view area on the Status bar or with options in the Presentation Views group on the VIEW tab. The viewing choices include:

- **Normal view.** This is the default view and displays two panes — the slide pane and the slide thumbnails pane. You can enter text in a slide in the slide pane and manage slides in the slide thumbnails pane.

- **Outline view.** In Outline view, the slide thumbnails pane changes to an outline pane where you can type text for slides.

- **Slide Sorter view.** Choosing Slide Sorter view displays all slides in the presentation as thumbnails. In this view, you can easily add, move, rearrange, and delete slides.

- **Notes Page view.** Change to Notes Page view and an individual slide displays on a page with any added notes displayed below the slide.

- **Reading view.** Use Reading view when you deliver your presentation to someone viewing the presentation on his or her own computer. This view allows you to play the slide show in the PowerPoint window without switching to a full-screen slide show.

- **Slide Show view.** Use Slide Show view to run a presentation. When you choose this view, each slide fills the entire screen.

VIEW tab   **Status bar**

Normal   Normal

Outline View   Slide Sorter

Slide Sorter   Reading View

Page Notes   Slide Show

Reading View

The view area on the Status bar contains four buttons for changing the view — Normal, Slide Sorter, Reading View, and Slide Show. The active button displays with a dark orange background. The Status bar also contains a NOTES button and COMMENTS button. Click the NOTES button and a notes pane displays at the bottom of the slide in the slide pane. Click the COMMENTS button to display the Comments task pane, where you can type a comment.

Navigating in a Presentation ■■■■■■■■■■■■■■■■■■■■

In the Normal view, change slides by clicking the Previous Slide or Next Slide buttons located at the bottom of the vertical scroll bar. You can also change to a different slide using the mouse pointer on the vertical scroll bar. To do this, position the mouse pointer on the scroll box on the vertical scroll bar, hold down the left mouse button, drag up or down until a box displays with the desired slide number, and then release the button.

You can also use the keyboard to display slides in a presentation. In Normal view, press the Down Arrow or Page Down key to display the next slide or press the Up Arrow or Page Up key to display the previous slide in the presentation. Press the Home key to display the first slide in the presentation and press the End key to display the last slide in the presentation. Navigate in the slide thumbnails pane by clicking the desired slide thumbnail. Navigate in Slide Sorter view by clicking the desired slide or using the arrow keys on the keyboard.

Previous Slide

Next Slide

1. With **P-C1-P2-Resumes.pptx** open, navigate in the presentation by completing the following steps:
   a. Make sure no placeholders are selected.
   b. Press the Home key to display Slide 1 in the slide pane.
   c. Click the Next Slide button located toward the bottom of the vertical scroll bar.
   d. Press the End key to display the last slide in the slide pane.
   e. Click the Slide Sorter button in the view area on the Status bar.

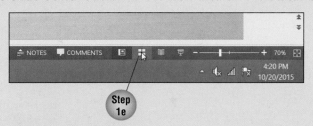

   f. Click Slide 1. (Notice that the active slide displays with an orange border.)
   g. Double-click Slide 3. (This closes Slide Sorter view and displays the presentation in Normal view with Slide 3 active.)
2. Insert text in slides by completing the following steps:
   a. Click any character in the bulleted text. (This positions the insertion point inside the placeholder.)
   b. Move the insertion point so it is positioned immediately right of *Education details*.
   c. Press the Enter key and then type **Professional affiliations**.

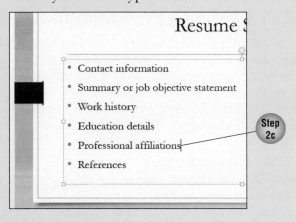

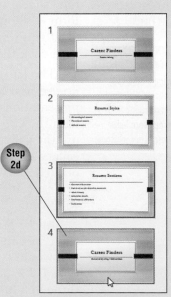

   d. Click Slide 4 in the slide thumbnails pane. (This displays Slide 4 in the slide pane.)
   e. Click in the text containing the telephone number, move the insertion point so it is positioned immediately right of the telephone number, press the spacebar, and then type **or visit our website at www.emcp.net/careerfinders**.
3. Type a note in the notes pane by completing the following steps:
   a. Click Slide 2 in the slide thumbnails pane.
   b. Click the NOTES button on the Status bar.
   c. Click the text *Click to add notes* that displays in the notes pane.

d. Type **Distribute resume examples to the audience.**

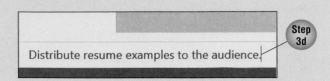

Distribute resume examples to the audience.

Step 3d

e. Display the slide in Notes Page view by clicking the VIEW tab and then clicking the Notes Page button in the Presentation Views group. (Notice the note you typed displays below the slide in this view.)

Step 3e

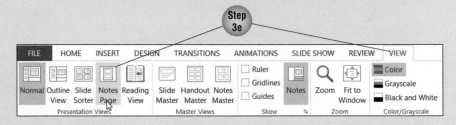

f. Return to Normal view by clicking the Normal button in the view area on the Status bar.
g. Click the NOTES button on the Status bar to close the notes pane.
h. Press the Home key to make Slide 1 the active slide.
4. Save the presentation by clicking the Save button on the Quick Access toolbar.

Printing and Previewing a Presentation ■■■■■■■■■■■

▼ **Quick Steps**

Print a Presentation
1. Click FILE tab.
2. Click *Print* option.
3. Click Print button.

Printing a hard copy of your presentation and distributing it to your audience helps reinforce your message.

You can print a PowerPoint presentation in a variety of formats. You can print each slide on a separate piece of paper; print each slide at the top of the page, leaving the bottom of the page for notes; print a specific number of slides (up to nine slides) on a single piece of paper; or print the slide titles and topics in outline form. Use options in the Print backstage area, shown in Figure 1.5, to specify what you want printed. To display the Print backstage area, click the FILE tab and then click the *Print* option or use the keyboard shortcut Ctrl + P.

The left side of the Print backstage area displays three categories—*Print*, *Printer*, and *Settings*. Click the Print button in the *Print* category to send the presentation to the printer and specify the number of copies you want printed with the *Copies* option. The two other categories contain galleries. For example, use the gallery in the *Printer* category to specify the desired printer. Click the first gallery in the *Settings* category and options display for specifying what you want printed such as all of the presentation or specific slides in the presentation. The *Settings* category also contains a number of galleries that describe how the slides will print.

In the *Settings* category, you can print a range of slides using the hyphen and print specific slides using a comma. For example, to print Slides 2 through 6, you would type *2-6* in the *Slides* text box. To print Slides 1, 3, and 7, you would type *1,3,7*. You can combine a hyphen and comma. For example, to print Slides 1 through 5 and Slide 8, you would type *1-5,8* in the *Slides* text box.

Figure 1.5 Print Backstage Area

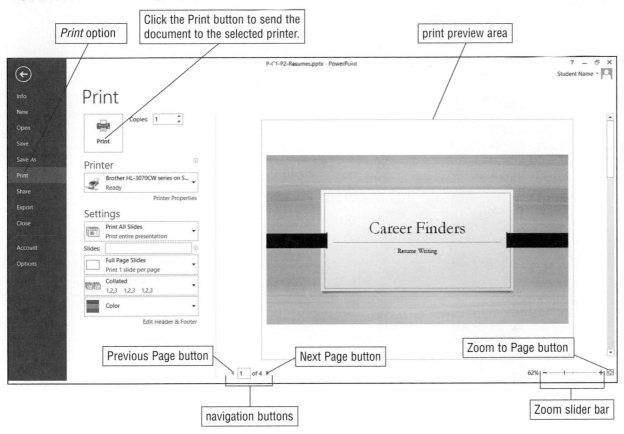

A preview of how a slide or slides will print displays at the right side of the Print backstage area. If you have a color printer selected, the slide or slides that display at the right side of the Print backstage area display in color, and if you have a black-and-white printer selected, the slide or slides will display in grayscale. Use the Next Page button (right-pointing arrow) located below and to the left of the page to view the next slide in the presentation, click the Previous Page button (left-pointing arrow) to display the previous slide in the presentation, use the Zoom slider bar to increase or decrease the size of the slide, and click the Zoom to Page button to fit the slide in the viewing area in the Print backstage area.

You can choose to print a presentation as individual slides, handouts, notes pages, or an outline. If you print a presentation as handouts or an outline, PowerPoint will automatically print the current date in the upper right corner of the page and the page number in the lower right corner. If you print the presentation as notes pages, PowerPoint will automatically print the page number in the lower right corner. PowerPoint does not insert the date or page number when you print individual slides.

1. With **P-C1-P2-Resumes.pptx** open, click the FILE tab and then click the *Print* option.
2. Click the Next Page button (located below and to the left of the slide in the viewing area) twice to display Slide 3 in the print preview area.

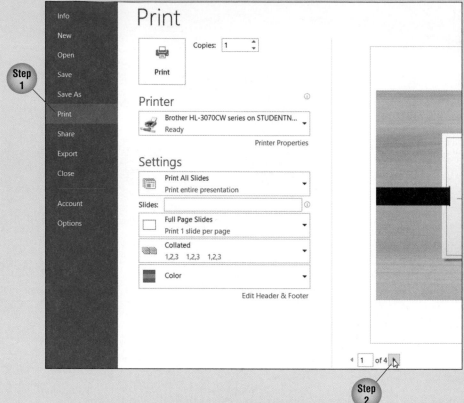

3. Click the Previous Page button twice to display Slide 1.
4. Change the zoom by completing the following steps:
   a. Position the mouse pointer on the Zoom slider bar button (located at the bottom right of the Print backstage area), drag the button to the right to increase the size of the slide in the print preview area of the Print backstage area, and then to the left to decrease the size of the slide.
   b. Click the percentage that displays at the left side of the Zoom slider bar. (This displays the Zoom dialog box.)
   c. Click the *50%* option in the Zoom dialog box and then click OK.
   d. Click the Zoom to Page button located to the right of the Zoom slider bar. (This increases the size of the slide to fill the print preview area.)

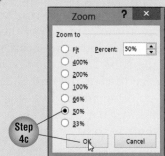

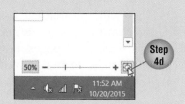

5. Print the presentation as a handout with four slides horizontally on the page by completing the following steps:
   a. At the Print backstage area, click the second gallery (displays with *Full Page Slides*) in the *Settings* category and then click *4 Slides Horizontal* in the *Handouts* section.

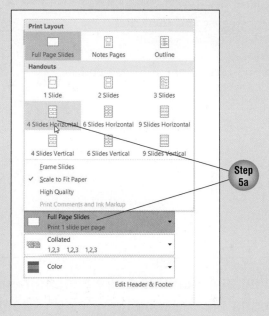

   b. Click the Print button.
6. Print Slide 2 as a notes page by completing the following steps:
   a. Click the FILE tab and then click the *Print* option.
   b. At the Print backstage area, click in the *Slides* text box located in the *Settings* category, and then type **2**.
   c. Click the second gallery (displays with *4 Slides Horizontal*) in the *Settings* category and then click *Notes Pages* in the *Print Layout* section.
   d. Click the Print button.

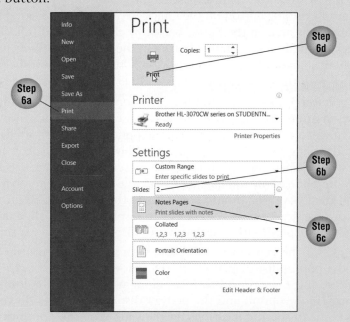

7. Print Slides 1, 2, and 4 by completing the following steps:
   a. Click the FILE tab and then click the *Print* option.
   b. At the Print backstage area, click in the *Slides* text box located in the *Settings* category and then type **1-2,4**.
   c. Click the second gallery (displays with *Notes Pages*) in the *Settings* category and then click *Slides Horizontal* in the *Handouts* section.
   d. Click the Print button.
8. Close the presentation by clicking the FILE tab and then clicking the *Close* option.

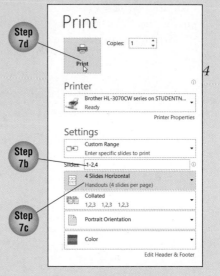

Project ❸   **Opening and Running a Presentation and**   **3 Parts**
                       Changing the Presentation Design Theme

You will open a presentation, run the presentation using buttons on the Slide Show toolbar, apply a different design theme to the presentation, and then delete the presentation.

Running a Slide Show ■■■■■■■■■■■■■■■■■■■■■■■■■■■■■

From Beginning

From Current Slide

As you learned earlier in this chapter, you can run a presentation by clicking the Start From Beginning button on the Quick Access toolbar, clicking the Slide Show button in the view area on the Status bar, or by clicking the SLIDE SHOW tab and then clicking the From Beginning button in the Start Slide Show group. This group also contains a From Current Slide button. Use this button to begin running the slide show with the currently active slide rather than the first slide in the presentation.

PowerPoint offers a number of options for navigating through slides in a presentation. You can click the left mouse button to advance slides in a presentation, right-click in a slide and then choose options from a shortcut menu, or use buttons on the Slide Show toolbar. The Slide Show toolbar displays in the lower left corner of a slide when you are running the presentation. Figure 1.6 identifies the buttons on the Slide Show toolbar. To display the Slide Show toolbar, run the presentation and then hover the mouse pointer over the buttons. Click the Next button (displays with a right arrow) on the toolbar to display the next slide and click the Previous button (displays with a left arrow) to display the previous slide.

Click the Pen button (displays with a pen icon) on the Slide Show toolbar and a pop-up list displays with the following options: *Laser Pointer, Pen, Highlighter, Eraser,* and *Erase All Ink on Slide*, along with a row of color options. Click the *Laser Pointer* option and the pointer displays as a red, glowing circle you can use to point to specific locations on the slide. Use the *Pen* option to draw in the slide

Figure 1.6 Slide Show Toolbar

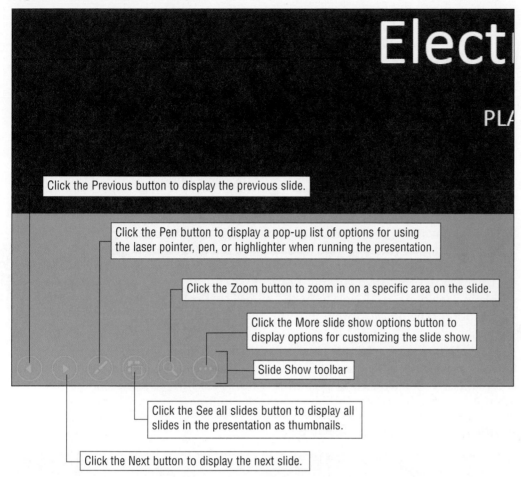

Click the Previous button to display the previous slide.

Click the Pen button to display a pop-up list of options for using the laser pointer, pen, or highlighter when running the presentation.

Click the Zoom button to zoom in on a specific area on the slide.

Click the More slide show options button to display options for customizing the slide show.

Slide Show toolbar

Click the See all slides button to display all slides in the presentation as thumbnails.

Click the Next button to display the next slide.

and use the *Highlighter* option to highlight specific items in the slide. Select the *Pen* or *Highlighter* option and then drag with the mouse in the slide to draw or highlight items. If you draw or highlight in a slide, you can erase the drawing or highlighting by clicking the Pen button on the Slide Show toolbar, clicking the *Eraser* option, and then dragging with the mouse to erase the drawing or highlighting. If you want to erase all drawing or highlighting in the slide, click the Pen button and then click the *Erase All Ink on Slide* option.

Change the pen or highlighter color by clicking the Pen button and then clicking a color option in the color row. If you draw in a slide with the Pen or Highlighter, PowerPoint will ask you at the end of the slide show if you want to keep or discard the ink annotations. At this message, specify what you want to do with the ink annotations. Return the laser pointer, pen, or highlighter option back to the mouse pointer by pressing the Esc key on your keyboard.

Click the See all slides button on the Slide Show toolbar and all slides in the presentation display on the screen. Use this feature if you want to display all of the slides in the presentation and/or move to a different slide by clicking the desired slide.

Zoom in on a portion of a slide by clicking the Zoom button (contains an image of a magnifying glass) on the Slide Show toolbar. Clicking this button creates a magnification area and dims the remainder of the slide. Drag the

▼ **Quick Steps**

Use the Pen or Highlighter During a Presentation
1. Run presentation.
2. Display desired slide.
3. Click Pen button on Slide Show toolbar.
4. Click pen or highlighter option.
5. Drag to draw line or highlight text.

If you use the pen or highlighter on a slide when running a presentation, choose an ink color that the audience can see easily.

magnification area with the mouse to specify what you want magnified and then click the left mouse button. Return to the normal zoom by pressing the Esc key or right-clicking in the slide.

Click the More slide show options button (the last button on the Slide Show toolbar; contains three dots) and a pop-up list displays with a variety of options. The pop-up list contains options for displaying a custom show or switching to Presenter view; changing the screen display, display settings, and arrow options; and pausing or ending the show. Click the *Help* option and the Slide Show Help dialog box displays, as shown in Figure 1.7. This dialog box contains various tabs that describe the keyboard options available when running a presentation.

In addition to the options on the Slide Show toolbar, right-click in a slide and a shortcut menu displays with many of the same options as the options that display when you click the More slide show options button.

When running a presentation, the mouse pointer is set, by default, to be hidden automatically after three seconds of inactivity. The mouse pointer will appear again when you move the mouse. You can change this default setting by clicking the More slide show options button on the Slide Show toolbar, pointing to *Arrow Options*, and then clicking *Visible* if you want the mouse pointer always visible or *Hidden* if you do not want the mouse to display at all as you run the presentation. The *Automatic* option is the default setting.

If you have selected the pen or highlighter and then want to return to the regular mouse pointer, press the Esc key or click the More slide show options button on the Slide Show toolbar, click *Arrow Options* at the pop-up list, and then click *Visible*.

Figure 1.7 Slide Show Help Dialog Box

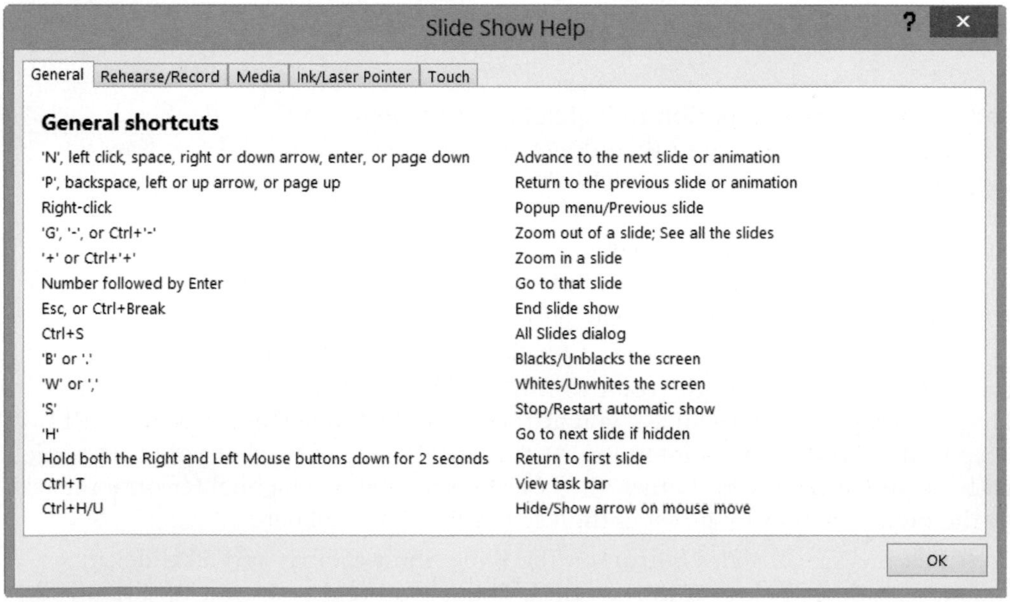

1. Click the FILE tab and then click the *Open* option.
2. At the Open backstage area, click your SkyDrive if you are opening presentations from your SkyDrive or click the *Computer* option if you are opening presentations from the computer's hard drive or a USB flash drive.
3. Click the Browse button.
4. At the Open dialog box, navigate to the PC1 folder on your storage medium and then double-click ***PlanningPres.pptx***.
5. Save the presentation by completing the following steps:
   a. Click the FILE tab and then click the *Save As* option.
   b. At the Save As backstage area, click the *PC1* folder name that displays below the *Current Folder* heading in the *Computer* section of the backstage view. (If this folder name does not display, double-click your SkyDrive or the *Computer* option.)
   c. At the Save As dialog box, make sure the PC1 folder on your storage medium is active and then type **P-C1-P3-PlanningPres** in the *File name* text box.
   d. Press Enter or click the Save button.
6. Run the presentation by completing the following steps:
   a. Click the Slide Show button in the view area on the Status bar.
   b. When Slide 1 fills the screen, move the mouse to display the Slide Show toolbar. (This toolbar displays in a dimmed manner in the lower left corner of the slide.)
   c. Click the Next button (contains a right arrow) to display the next slide.
   d. Continue clicking the Next button until a black screen displays.

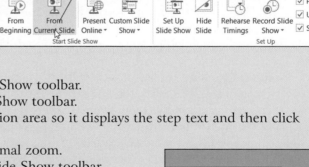

Step 6c

   e. Click the left mouse button. (This displays the presentation in Normal view.)
7. Run the presentation from the current slide by completing the following steps:
   a. Click Slide 4 in the slide thumbnails pane. (This makes Slide 4 active.)
   b. Click the SLIDE SHOW tab.
   c. Click the From Current Slide button in the Start Slide Show group.

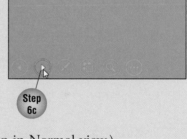

Step 7c   Step 7b

8. With Slide 4 active, zoom in on the step text by completing these steps:
   a. Move the mouse to display the Slide Show toolbar.
   b. Click the Zoom button on the Slide Show toolbar.
   c. Using the mouse, drag the magnification area so it displays the step text and then click the left mouse button.
   d. Press the Esc key to return to the normal zoom.
9. Click the See all slides button on the Slide Show toolbar and then click the Slide 2 thumbnail.
10. With Slide 2 active, use the pen to draw in the slide by completing the following steps:
    a. Move the mouse to display the Slide Show toolbar.
    b. Click the Pen button on the Slide Show toolbar and then click *Pen* at the pop-up list. (This changes the mouse pointer to a small circle.)

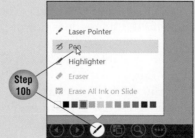

Step 10b

c. Using the mouse, draw a circle around the text *Step 1*.

d. Draw a line below the word *identify*.

e. Press the Esc key to return the mouse pointer to an arrow.

11. Erase the pen markings by clicking the Pen button on the Slide Show toolbar and then clicking *Erase All Ink on Slide* at the pop-up list.

12. Click the Next button to display Slide 3.

13. Click the Pen button and then click *Highlighter*.

14 Click the Pen button and then click the *Light Green* color (sixth option in the bottom row).

15. Drag through the text *Assess your target audience*.

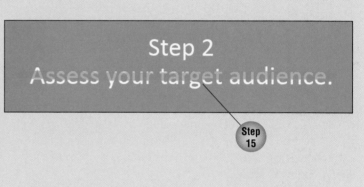

16. Press the Esc key to return the mouse pointer to an arrow.

17. Press the Esc key to end the slide show. Click the Discard button at the message asking if you want to keep or discard the ink annotations.

18. With Slide 3 active, click the Slide Show button on the Status bar to start the slide show.

19. Click the Pen button on the Slide Show toolbar and then click *Laser Pointer* at the pop-up list.

20. Use the laser pointer to point to various locations on the slide.

21. Press the Esc key to return to the mouse pointer to an arrow.

22. Click the Next button on the Slide Show toolbar. (This displays Slide 4.)

23. Turn on the highlighter and then drag through the words *best format* to highlight them.

24. Press the Esc key to return the mouse pointer to an arrow.

25. Continue clicking the left mouse button to move through the presentation.

26. At the black screen, click the left mouse button.

27. At the message asking if you want to keep your ink annotations, click the Keep button.

28. Save the presentation with a new name by completing the following steps:

   a. Click the FILE tab and then click the *Save As* option.

   b. Click the *PC1* folder name that displays below the *Current Folder* heading. (If the PC1 folder name does not display, double-click the *Computer* option.)

   c. At the Save As dialog box, make sure the PC1 folder on your storage medium is the active folder, type **P-C1-P3-PlanningPres-Ink** in the *File name* text box, and then press Enter.

29. Print Slide 4 as a handout.

30. Close **P-C1-P3-PlanningPres-Ink.pptx**.

Applying a Design Theme and Color Variant ■■■■■■■■■

As you have learned, PowerPoint provides a variety of built-in design theme templates you can use when creating slides for a presentation. Choose a design theme template at the New backstage area or with options in the Themes group on the DESIGN tab. Click the DESIGN tab and theme thumbnails display in the Themes group. Click one of these themes to apply it to the current presentation. Click the More button at the right side of the theme thumbnails to display any additional themes. You can also click the up-pointing or down-pointing arrows at the right side of the theme thumbnails to scroll through the list. Hover your mouse pointer over a theme and the active slide in the presentation displays with the theme formatting applied. This is an example of the *live preview* feature, which allows you to see how theme formatting will affect your presentation.

Each design theme contains color variations that display in the Variants group on the DESIGN tab. These are the same theme color variants that display when you apply a theme template at the New backstage area. Click a color variant thumbnail in the Variants group to apply the colors to the slides in the presentation.

Hover the mouse pointer over a theme thumbnail and a ScreenTip displays (after approximately a second) containing the theme name. Theme names in PowerPoint are similar to those in Word, Excel, Access, and Outlook and apply similar formatting. With the availability of the themes across these applications, you can "brand" your business documents, workbooks, and presentations with a consistent, uniform appearance.

▼ Quick Steps

Apply a Design Theme
1. Click DESIGN tab.
2. Click desired theme in Themes group.

More

H I N T

Design themes were designed by professional graphic artists who understand the use of color, space, and design.

Project 3b Applying a Design Theme and Variant   Part 2 of 3

1. Open **P-C1-P3-PlanningPres.pptx**.
2. Make sure Slide 1 is active and that the presentation displays in Normal view.
3. Apply a different design theme to the presentation by completing the following steps:
   a. Click the DESIGN tab.
   b. Hover the mouse pointer over the *Ion* theme thumbnail in the Themes group and notice the theme formatting applied to the slide in the slide pane.
   c. Click the *Ion* theme.

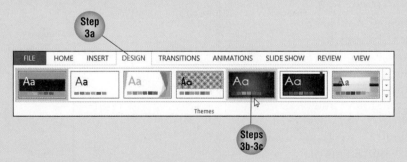

4. Run the presentation and notice the formatting applied by the theme.
5. With the presentation displayed in Normal view, apply a different design theme by clicking the *Facet* theme thumbnail in the Themes group on the DESIGN tab.

6. Apply a color variant by clicking the fourth thumbnail in the Variants group.

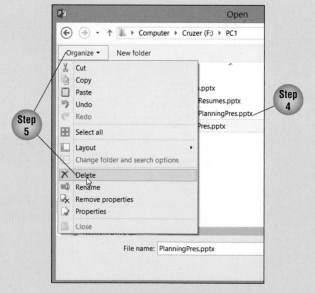

Step 6

Variants

7. Run the presentation.
8. Print the presentation as a handout by completing the following steps:
   a. Click the FILE tab and then click the *Print* option.
   b. At the Print backstage area, click the second gallery (displays with *Full Page Slides*) in the *Settings* category and then click *6 Slides Horizontal* in the *Handouts* section.
   c. Click the Print button.
9. Save and then close **P-C1-P3-PlanningPres.pptx**.

▼ **Quick Steps**
Delete a Presentation
1. Display Open dialog box.
2. Navigate to desired folder or drive.
3. Click the presentation.
4. Click Organize button, *Delete*.
5. Click Yes.

Deleting a Presentation ■■■■■■■■■■■■■■■■■■■■■■■

File management tasks in PowerPoint can be performed at the Open dialog box or Save As dialog box. To delete a PowerPoint presentation, display the Open dialog box, click the presentation you want deleted, click the Organize button on the toolbar, and then click *Delete* at the drop-down list. At the message asking if you are sure you want to delete the presentation, click the Yes button. The presentation file must be closed to be deleted.

Project 3c **Deleting a PowerPoint Presentation** Part 3 of 3

1. Click the FILE tab and then, if necessary, click the *Open* option.
2. At the Open backstage area, click your SkyDrive or the *Computer* option.
3. Click the *PC1* folder name that displays below the *Recent Folder* heading in the *Computer* section of the backstage area. (If this folder name does not display, double-click your SkyDrive or the *Computer* option.)
4. At the Open dialog box, make sure the PC1 folder on your storage medium is the active folder and then click **PlanningPres.pptx** in the Content pane.
5. Click the Organize button on the toolbar and then click *Delete* at the drop-down list.
6. At the message asking if you are sure you want to delete the presentation, click Yes.
7. Click the Cancel button to close the Open dialog box.

Project 4 — Create a Technology Presentation in the Outline Pane

3 Parts

You will create a computer technology presentation in the outline pane, add and remove transitions and sounds to the presentation, and set up the presentation to advance slides automatically after a specified amount of time.

Preparing a Presentation from a Blank Presentation ▪▪▪

If you want to create a presentation without a design theme applied, open a blank presentation. Open a blank presentation at the PowerPoint opening screen or at the New backstage area by clicking the Blank Presentation template. You can also open a blank presentation with the keyboard shortcut Ctrl + N.

Preparing a Presentation in Outline View ▪▪▪▪▪▪▪▪▪▪

You can create slides in a presentation by typing the slide text in the outline pane. Display this pane by clicking the VIEW tab and then clicking the Outline View button in the Presentation Views group. The outline pane replaces the slide thumbnails pane at the left side of the screen. A slide number displays in the pane followed by a small slide icon. When typing text in the outline pane, press the Tab key to move the insertion point to the next tab stop. This moves the insertion point and also changes the formatting. The formatting will vary depending on the theme you chose. Press Shift + Tab to move the insertion point to the previous tab stop. Moving the insertion point back to the left margin will create a new slide.

> **▼ Quick Steps**
>
> **Prepare a Presentation from a Blank Presentation**
> 1. Click FILE tab.
> 2. Click *New* option.
> 3. Click *Blank Presentation*.
> OR
> Press Ctrl + N.

Project 4a — Preparing a Presentation in Outline View

Part 1 of 3

1. At a blank screen, click the FILE tab and then click the *New* option.
2. At the New backstage area, click the *Blank Presentation* template.
3. At the blank presentation, click the VIEW tab and then click the Outline View button in the Presentation Views group.

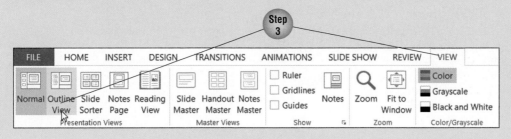

4. Click in the outline pane immediately right of the slide icon.
5. Type the first slide title shown in Figure 1.8 (*Computer Technology*), and then press Enter. (The text you type displays immediately right of the small orange slide icon that displays in the outline pane.)
6. Type the second slide title shown in Figure 1.8 (*The Motherboard*) and then press Enter.
7. Press the Tab key, type the text after the first bullet in Figure 1.8 (*Buses*), and then press Enter.
8. Continue typing the text as it displays in Figure 1.8. Press the Tab key to move the insertion point to the next tab stop or press Shift + Tab to move the insertion point back to a previous tab stop.

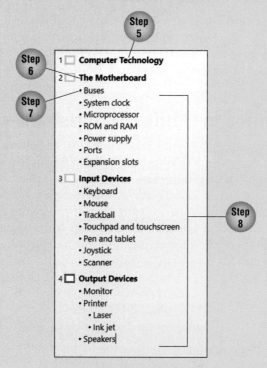

9. After typing all of the information as shown in Figure 1.8, click the Normal button in the Presentation Views group on the VIEW tab.
10. Click Slide 1 in the slide thumbnails pane. (This displays Slide 1 in the slide pane.)
11. Apply a design theme by completing the following steps:
    a. Click the DESIGN tab.
    b. Click the *Ion* thumbnail in the Themes group.
    c. Click the fourth thumbnail in the Variants group (the orange color variant).
12. Save the presentation and name it **P-C1-P4-Computers**.
13. Run the presentation.

Figure 1.8 Project 4a

1 Computer Technology
2 The Motherboard
   - Buses
   - System clock
   - Microprocessor
   - ROM and RAM
   - Power supply
   - Ports
   - Expansion slots
3 Input Devices
   - Keyboard
   - Mouse
   - Trackball
   - Touchpad and touchscreen
   - Pen and tablet
   - Joystick
   - Scanner
4 Output Devices
   - Monitor
   - Printer
     - Laser
     - Ink jet
   - Speakers

Adding Transitions and Sound Effects ■■■■■■■■■■■■■

You can apply interesting transitions and sounds to a presentation. A *transition* is how one slide is removed from the screen during a presentation and the next slide is displayed. You can apply transitions such as cut, fade, push, wipe, split, reveal, and random bars. To add transitions and sounds, open a presentation, and then click the TRANSITIONS tab. This displays transition buttons and options, as shown in Figure 1.9.

Transitions and sounds apply by default to the active slide. If you want transitions and sound to affect all slides, click the Apply To All button in the Timing group. In Slide Sorter view, you can select all slides by pressing Ctrl + A (or by clicking the HOME tab, clicking the Select button, and then clicking *Select All* at the drop-down list) and then apply the desired transition and/or sound.

Apply To All

Figure 1.9 TRANSITIONS Tab

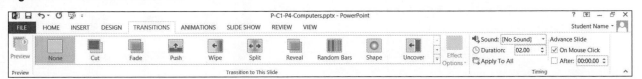

Adding Transitions

▼ Quick Steps

Apply a Transition to Slides
1. Click TRANSITIONS tab.
2. Click desired transition in Transition to This Slide group.
3. Click Apply To All button.

Apply Sound to Slides
1. Click TRANSITIONS tab.
2. Click down-pointing arrow at right of *Sound* option.
3. Click desired sound.
4. Click Apply To All button.

Make a presentation more appealing by adding effects such as transitions and sounds.

To add a transition, click a transition thumbnail in the Transition to This Slide group on the TRANSITIONS tab. When you click a transition thumbnail, the transition displays in the slide in the slide pane. Use the down-pointing and up-pointing arrows at the right side of the transition thumbnails to display additional transitions. Click the More button that displays at the right side of the visible transition thumbnails and a drop-down gallery displays with additional transition options. Use the *Duration* measurement box to specify the duration of slide transitions when running the presentation. Click the up- or down-pointing arrows at the right side of the *Duration* measurement box to change the duration time. You can also select the current time in the measurement box and then type the desired time.

When you apply a transition to slides in a presentation, animation icons display below the slides in the slide thumbnails pane and in Slide Sorter view. Click an animation icon for a particular slide and the slide will display the transition effect.

Adding Sounds

You can also add sounds to your transitions. To add a sound, click the down-pointing arrow at the right side of the *Sound* option box and then click the desired sound at the drop-down list. Preview a transition and or sound applied to a slide by clicking the Preview button located at the left side of the TRANSITIONS tab.

Removing Transitions and Sounds

You can remove a transition and/or sound from specific slides or from all slides in a presentation. To remove a transition, click the *None* transition thumbnail in the Transition to This Slide group. To remove transitions from all slides, click the Apply To All button in the Timing group. To remove sound from a slide, click the down-pointing arrow at the right side of the *Sound* option and then click *[No Sound]* at the drop-down gallery. To remove sound from all slides, click the Apply To All button.

Project 4b Adding Transitions and Sounds to a Presentation Part 2 of 3

1. With **P-C1-P4-Computers.pptx** open, click the TRANSITIONS tab.
2. Apply transitions and sound to all slides in the presentation by completing the following steps:
   a. Click the More button at the right side of the transition thumbnails.
   b. Click the *Fall Over* option in the *Exciting* section.

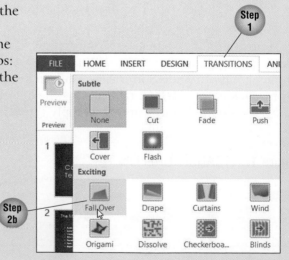

c. Click the Effect Options button in the Transition to This Slide group and then click *Right* at the drop-down list.

d. Click in the *Duration* measurement box in the Timing group, type 1, and then press Enter.

e. Click the down-pointing arrow at the right side of the *Sound* option box in the Timing group and then click *Chime* at the drop-down list.

f. Click the Apply To All button in the Timing group.

3. Run the presentation. (Notice the transitions and sound as you move from slide to slide.)

4. With the presentation in Normal view and the TRANSITIONS tab active, remove the transitions and sound by completing the following steps:

a. Click the More button at the right side of the transition thumbnails in the Transition to This Slide group and then click the *None* thumbnail.

b. Click the down-pointing arrow at the right side of the *Sound* option box and then click *[No Sound]* at the drop-down list.

c. Click the Apply To All button.

5. Apply transitions and sounds to specific slides by completing the following steps:

a. Make sure the presentation displays in Normal view.

b. Click Slide 1 in the slide thumbnails pane.

c. Hold down the Shift key and then click Slide 2. (Slides 1 and 2 will display with orange backgrounds.)

d. Click the More button at the right side of the transition thumbnails and then click the *Ferris Wheel* option in the *Dynamic Content* section.

e. Click the down-pointing arrow at the right side of the *Sound* option box and then click the *Breeze* option.

f. Click Slide 3 in the slide pane.

g. Hold down the Shift key and then click Slide 4.

h. Click the More button at the right side of the transition thumbnails and then click the *Glitter* option in the *Exciting* section.

i. Click the down-pointing arrow at the right side of the *Sound* option box and then click the *Wind* option.

6. Run the presentation from the beginning.

7. Remove the transitions and sounds from all slides. (Refer to Step 4.)

8. Save **P-C1-P4-Computers.pptx**.

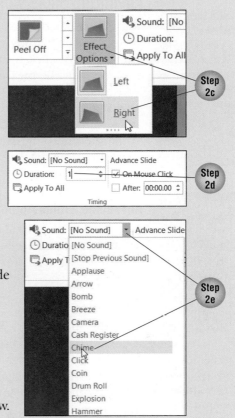

▼ **Quick Steps**

**Advance Slides
Automatically**
1. Click TRANSITIONS tab.
2. Click *After* check box.
3. Insert desired
   number of seconds in
   measurement box.
4. Click *On Mouse Click*
   check box.
5. Click Apply To All
   button.

Advancing Slides Automatically

You can advance slides in a slide show after a specific number of seconds with options in the Timing group on the TRANSITIONS tab. To advance slides automatically, click in the *After* check box and then insert the desired number of seconds in the measurement box. You can select the current time in the measurement box and then type the desired time or click the up- or down-pointing arrows to increase or decrease the time. Click the *On Mouse Click* check box to remove the check mark. If you want the transition time to affect all slides in the presentation, click the Apply To All button. In Slide Sorter view, the transition time displays below each affected slide.

Project 4c   **Advancing Slides Automatically**   **Part 3 of 3**

1. With **P-C1-P4-Computers.pptx** open, make sure the TRANSITIONS tab is active.
2. Click in the *After* check box in the Timing group to insert a check mark.
3. Click the *On Mouse Click* check box to remove the check mark.
4. Click the up-pointing arrow at the right side of the *After* measurement box until *00:04.00* displays in the box.
5. Click the Apply To All button.
6. Run the presentation from the beginning. (Each slide will advance automatically after four seconds.)
7. At the black screen, click the left mouse button.
8. Print the presentation as an outline by completing the following steps:
   a. Click the FILE tab and then click the *Print* option.
   b. At the Print backstage area, click the second gallery (displays with *Full Page Slides*) in the *Settings* category and then click *Outline* in the *Print Layout* section.
   c. Click the Print button.
9. Save and then close **P-C1-P4-Computers.pptx**.

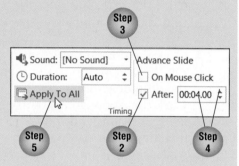

Chapter Summary

- PowerPoint is a presentation graphics program you can use to create slides for an on-screen presentation.
- Open a presentation at the Open dialog box. Display this dialog box by clicking the FILE tab and then clicking the *Open* option. At the Open backstage area, click your SkyDrive or the *Computer* option and then click the Browse button.
- You can pin a presentation to and unpin a presentation from the Recent list at the PowerPoint 2013 opening screen and the Recent Presentations list at the Open backstage area.
- Start running a presentation by clicking the Start From Beginning button on the Quick Access toolbar, clicking the Slide Show button in the view area on the Status bar, or by clicking the VIEW tab and then clicking the From Beginning button.
- Close a presentation by clicking the FILE tab and then clicking the *Close* option or with the keyboard shortcut Ctrl + F4.

- Before creating a presentation in PowerPoint, plan the presentation by defining the purpose and determining the content and medium.

- Build-in presentation design theme templates are available at the New backstage area. Display this backstage area by clicking the FILE tab and then clicking the *New* option.

- To insert text in a slide, click the desired placeholder and then type the text.

- A slide layout provides placeholders for specific data in a slide. Choose a slide layout by clicking the Layout button in the Slides group on the HOME tab.

- Insert a new slide in a presentation with the Title and Content layout by clicking the New Slide button in the Slides group on the HOME tab. Insert a new slide with a specific layout by clicking the New Slide button arrow and then clicking the desired layout at the drop-down list.

- Save a presentation by clicking the Save button on the Quick Access toolbar or clicking the FILE tab and then clicking the *Save As* option. At the Save As backstage area, click your SkyDrive or the *Computer* option and then click the Browse button. At the Save As dialog box, type a name for the presentation.

- View a presentation in one of the following six views: Normal view, which is the default and displays two panes — the slide thumbnails pane and the slide pane; Outline view, which displays the outline pane for typing text in slides; Slide Sorter view, which displays all slides in the presentation in slide thumbnails; Reading view, which delivers a presentation to someone viewing it on his or her own computer; Notes Page view, which displays an individual slide with any added notes displayed below the slide; and Slide Show view, which runs the presentation.

- Navigate to various slides in a presentation using the mouse and/or keyboard. You can use the Previous Slide and Next Slide buttons located at the bottom of the vertical scroll bar, the scroll box on the vertical scroll bar, arrow keys on the keyboard, or the Page Up and Page Down keys on the keyboard.

- Click the FILE tab and the backstage area displays options for working with and managing presentations.

- With options at the Print backstage area, you can print presentations with each slide on a separate piece of paper; each slide at the top of the page, leaving room for notes; all or a specific number of slides on a single piece of paper; or slide titles and topics in outline form.

- When running a presentation, the Slide Show toolbar displays in the lower left corner of the slide. This toolbar contains buttons and options for running a presentation. Use the buttons to navigate to slides, make ink notations on slides, display slide thumbnails, zoom in on a specific location in a slide, and display a Help menu.

- Apply a design theme to a presentation by clicking the DESIGN tab and then clicking the desired theme in the Themes group. Apply a color variation to a theme by clicking the desired thumbnail in the Variants group on the DESIGN tab.

- Delete a presentation at the Open dialog box by clicking the presentation file name, clicking the Organize button on the toolbar, and then clicking *Delete* at the drop-down list.

- Open a blank presentation by displaying the New backstage area and then clicking the *Blank Presentation* template or with the keyboard shortcut Ctrl + N.

- Type text in a slide in the slide pane or in the outline pane. Display the outline pane by clicking the VIEW tab and then clicking the Outline View button.
- Enhance a presentation by adding transitions (how one slide is removed from the screen and replaced with the next slide) and sound. Add transitions and sound to a presentation with options on the TRANSITIONS tab.
- Advance slides automatically in a slide show by removing the check mark from the *On Mouse Click* check box on the TRANSITIONS tab, inserting a check mark in the *After* check box, and then specifying the desired time in the time measurement box.
- Click the Apply To All button to apply transitions, sounds, and/or time settings to all slides in a presentation.

Commands Review

FEATURE	RIBBON TAB, GROUP/OPTION	BUTTON, OPTION	KEYBOARD SHORTCUT
close presentation	FILE, *Close*		Ctrl + F4
design theme	DESIGN, Themes		
New backstage area	FILE, *New*		
new slide	HOME, Slides		Ctrl + M
Normal view	VIEW, Presentation Views		
Notes Page view	VIEW, Presentation Views		
Open backstage area	FILE, *Open*		Ctrl + O
Outline view	VIEW, Presentation Views		
Print backstage area	FILE, *Print*		Ctrl + P
run presentation	SLIDE SHOW, Start Slide Show OR Quick Access Toolbar		F5
Save As backstage area	FILE, *Save* OR *Save As*		Ctrl + S
slide layout	HOME, Slides		
Slide Sorter view	VIEW, Presentation Views		
sound	TRANSITIONS, Timing		
transition	TRANSITIONS, Transition to This Slide		
transition duration	Transitions, Timing		

Concepts Check

Test Your Knowledge

Completion: In the space provided at the right, indicate the correct term, command, or number.

1. Click this tab to display options for working with and managing presentations. _____

2. This toolbar contains buttons for commonly used commands. _____

3. This area contains the tabs and commands divided into groups. _____

4. This is the keyboard shortcut to close a presentation. _____

5. Display design theme templates in this backstage area. _____

6. Insert a new slide by clicking the New Slide button in this group on the HOME tab. _____

7. Change to this view to view all slides in the presentation as slide thumbnails. _____

8. This is the default view and displays two panes. _____

9. Click this button on the VIEW tab to display the outline pane. _____

10. The Previous Slide and Next Slide buttons display in this location. _____

11. To run a presentation beginning with Slide 1, click this button on the Quick Access toolbar. _____

12. Apply a design theme to a presentation by clicking this tab and then clicking the desired theme in the Themes group. _____

13. To add a transition, click a transition thumbnail in the Transition to This Slide group on this tab. _____

14. When you apply a transition to slides in a presentation, these display below the slide numbers in the slide thumbnails pane. _____

15. To advance slides automatically, remove the check mark from the *On Mouse Click* check box, insert a check mark in this check box, and then insert the desired number of seconds. _____

Skills Check   Assess Your Performance

Assessment

1   CREATE A PRESENTATION ON TYPES OF RESUMES

1. Create a presentation with the text shown in Figure 1.10 on the next page by completing the following steps:
   a. With PowerPoint open, click the FILE tab and then click the *New* option.
   b. At the New backstage area, click the *Wood Type* theme, click the variant in the top row in the second column, and then click the Create button.
   c. Create slides with the text shown in Figure 1.10. Use the Title Slide layout for slides 1 and 5 and use the Title and Content layout for slides 2, 3, and 4.
2. Save the completed presentation in the PC1 folder on your storage medium and name the presentation **P-C1-A1-ResumeTypes**.
3. Apply the Push transition (located in the *Subtle* section) with a From Left effect to all slides in the presentation.
4. Change the transition duration to 01.50 seconds.
5. Apply the Wind sound to all slides in the presentation.
6. Run the presentation.
7. Print the presentation as a handout with six slides printed horizontally per page.
8. Save and then close **P-C1-A1-ResumeTypes.pptx**.

Assessment

2   CREATE A PRESENTATION ON PREPARING A COMPANY NEWSLETTER

1. At the blank screen, click the FILE tab and then click the *New* option.
2. At the New backstage area, click the *Blank Presentation* template.
3. Create slides with the text shown in Figure 1.11 on page 40.
4. Apply the Basis design theme and the orange variant (third thumbnail in the Variants group).
5. Run the presentation.
6. Print the presentation as a handout with all six slides printed horizontally on the page.
7. Make the following changes to the presentation:
   a. Apply the Parallax design theme and the red variant (fourth thumbnail in the Variants group).
   b. Add the Switch transition (located in the *Exciting* section) with a Left effect to all slides.
   c. Add the Camera sound to all slides.
   d. Specify that all slides advance automatically after five seconds.
8. Run the presentation.
9. Save the presentation and name it **P-C1-A2-Newsletter**.
10. Close **P-C1-A2-Newsletter.pptx**.

Figure 1.10 Assessment 1

Slide 1	Title	=	Career Finders
	Subtitle	=	Types of Resumes

Slide 2	Title	=	Functional Resume
	Bullets	=	• Emphasizes skills and achievements
			• Used when you lack a formal education
			• Used when you have had many different jobs with no clear pattern or progression

Slide 3	Title	=	Chronological Resume
	Bullets	=	• List more recent training or jobs first and then proceed backwards
			• Components include:
			- personal contact information
			- employment history including employers, employment dates, positions held, and achievements
			- educational qualifications
			- professional development

Slide 4	Title	=	Hybrid Resume
	Bullets	=	• Combines best of chronological and functional resume
			• Contains fixed order of chronological resume
			• More emphasis on skills and achievements

Slide 5	Title	=	Career Finders
	Subtitle	=	Sign up today for Career Finder's resume writing workshop!

Visual Benchmark   Demonstrate Your Proficiency

CREATE A PRESENTATION ON PREPARING A NEWSLETTER

1. Create the presentation shown in Figure 1.12 with the following specifications:
   a. Create the presentation with the Organic design theme template and apply the appropriate variant.
   b. Create the slides as shown in the figure (reading from left to right).
   c. Apply a transition, sound, and transition duration time of your choosing to each slide in the presentation.
2. Save the completed presentation and name it **P-C1-VB-Interview**.
3. Run the presentation.
4. Print the presentation as a handout with all six slides printed horizontally on the page.
5. Close the presentation.

Figure 1.11 Assessment 2

| Slide 1 | Title | = | PREPARING A COMPANY NEWSLETTER |
| | Subtitle | = | Planning and Designing the Layout |

Slide 2	Title	=	Planning a Newsletter
	Bullets	=	• Use pictures of different people from your organization in each issue.
			• Distribute contributor sheets soliciting information from employees.
			• Keep the focus of the newsletter on issues of interest to employees.

Slide 3	Title	=	Planning a Newsletter
	Bullets	=	• Make sure the focus is on various levels of employment; do not focus on top management only.
			• Conduct regular surveys to see if your newsletter provides a needed source of information.

Slide 4	Title	=	Designing a Newsletter
	Bulllets	=	• Maintain consistent elements from issue to issue such as:
			- Column layout
			- Nameplate formatting and location
			- Formatting of headlines
			- Use of color

Slide 5	Title	=	Designing a Newsletter
	Bullets	=	• Consider the following elements when designing a newsletter:
			- Focus
			- Balance
			- White space
			- Directional flow

Slide 6	Title	=	Creating a Newsletter Layout
	Bullets	=	• Choose paper size
			• Choose paper weight
			• Determine margins
			• Specify column layout

Figure 1.12 Visual Benchmark

Interviewing for the Job

Job Interviewing Tips

Company Research

- Gather company background information.
- Review the company's website.
- Ask the employer for company history.
- Search online for information on the company.

Practice

- Practice interviewing with a friend.
- Record interview responses and listen to determine how well you did.
- Prepare answers to commonly-asked interview questions.

Interviewing for the Job

Job Interviewing Strategies

Prepare for the Interview

- Prepare a list of questions for the interviewer.
- Bring extra copies of your resume and list of references.
- Be on time for the interview.
- Know the interviewer's name and use it during the interview.

Maintain Composure

- Ask for clarification on questions.
- Take a moment or two to frame your responses.
- At the end of the interview:
  - Thank the interviewer.
  - Reiterate your interest in the position.
- Send a thank you note restating your interest in the position.

Case Study — Apply Your Skills

Part 1

You work for Citizens for Consumer Safety, a nonprofit organization providing information on household safety. Your supervisor, Melinda Johansson, will be presenting information on smoke detectors at a community meeting and has asked you to prepare a PowerPoint presentation. Open the Word document named **PPSmokeDetectors.docx**. Read over the information and then use the information to prepare a presentation. Consider the information in the *Planning a Presentation* section of this chapter and then prepare at least five slides. Apply an appropriate design theme and add a transition and sound to all slides. Save the presentation and name it **P-C1-CS-PPSmokeDetectors**. Run the presentation and then print the presentation as a handout with all slides on one page.

Part 2

Ms. Johansson has looked at the printout of the presentation and has asked you to print the presentation with two slides per page and in grayscale. Use the Help feature to learn about printing in grayscale and then print the presentation in grayscale with two slides per page.

Part 3

Ms. Johansson would like to provide information to participants at the presentation on online companies that sell smoke detectors. Using the Internet, locate at least three online stores that sell smoke detectors. Insert a new slide in the **P-C1-CS-PPSmokeDetectors.pptx** presentation that includes the names of the stores, web addresses, and any additional information you feel is important. Save the presentation and then print the presentation in Outline view. Close the presentation.

PERFORMANCE OBJECTIVES

Upon successful completion of Chapter 2, you will be able to:

- Check spelling
- Use the Thesaurus
- Insert and delete text in slides
- Find and replace text in slides
- Cut, copy, and paste text in slides
- Rearrange text in the slide thumbnails pane
- Size and rearrange placeholders
- Insert, delete, move, and copy slides
- Copy slides between presentations
- Duplicate slides
- Reuse slides
- Create and manage sections
- Customize the Quick Access toolbar
- Use the Help feature

When preparing a presentation, you may need to modify it by inserting and deleting text in slides or finding and replacing specific text. Improve the quality of your presentation by completing a spelling check to ensure that the words in your presentation are spelled correctly and use the Thesaurus to find synonyms and antonyms for words. Additional modifications you may need to make to a presentation include sizing and rearranging placeholders and rearranging, inserting, deleting, or copying slides. In this chapter, you will learn how to make these modifications to a presentation as well as how to preview a presentation and use the Help feature. Model answers for this chapter's projects appear on the following pages.

PowerPoint
PC2

Note: Before beginning the projects, copy to your storage medium the PC2 subfolder from the PowerPoint folder on the CD that accompanies this textbook and then make PC2 the active folder.

Project 1 Check Spelling and Manage Text in a Design Presentation   P-C2-P1-ElectronicDesign.pptx

Project 2 Cut, Copy, Paste, Rearrange, and Manage Slides in a Network Presentation   P-C2-P2-NetworkSystem.pptx

Project 3 Insert and Manage Slides in an Adventure Tours Presentation   P-C2-P3-AdvTours.pptx

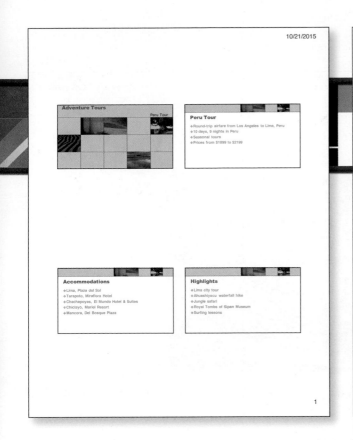

Project 4 Use PowerPoint Help Feature and Create a Presentation   P-C2-P4-Shortcuts.pptx

<table>
<tr><td>**Project**</td><td>**1**</td><td>**Check Spelling, Use the Thesaurus, and Manage Text in a Design Presentation**</td><td>**3 Parts**</td></tr>
</table>

You will open a presentation on steps for planning a design publication, complete a spelling check on the text in the presentation, use the Thesaurus to find synonyms, and find and replace specific text in slides.

Checking Spelling ■■■■■■■■■■■■■■■■■■■■■■■■■■

When preparing a presentation, perform a spelling check on text in slides using PowerPoint's spelling checker feature. The spelling checker feature compares words in slides in a presentation with words in its dictionary. If a match is found, the word is passed over. If a match is not found, the Spelling task pane displays with replacement suggestions. At this task pane, you can choose to change the word or ignore the word and leave it as written. To perform a spelling check, click the REVIEW tab and then click the Spelling button in the Proofing group. You can also start the spelling checker by pressing the F7 function key on the keyboard.

When you begin checking spelling in the presentation in Project 1a, the spelling checker will stop at the misspelled word *Layuot* and display the Spelling task pane as shown in Figure 2.1. The options available in the Spelling task pane are described in Table 2.1 on the next page.

▼ **Quick Steps**

Complete a Spelling Check
1. Click REVIEW tab.
2. Click Spelling button.
3. Change or ignore errors.
4. Click OK.

Spelling

Figure 2.1 Spelling Task Pane

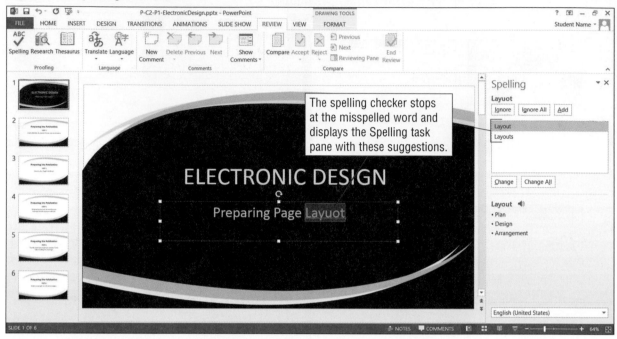

Table 2.1 Spelling Task Pane Options

Button	Function
Add	Adds selected word to the main spelling check dictionary.
Change	Replaces selected word in slide with selected word in the task pane list box.
Change All	Replaces selected word in slide with selected word in the task pane list box and all other occurrences of the word in all slides.
Delete	Deletes the currently selected word(s).
Ignore	Skips that occurrence of the word.
Ignore All	Skips that occurrence of the word and all other occurrences of the word in all slides.

▼ **Quick Steps**

Using the Thesaurus
1. Click desired word.
2. Click REVIEW tab.
3. Click Thesaurus button.
4. Position mouse pointer on desired replacement word in Thesaurus task pane.
5. Click down-pointing arrow at right of word.
6. Click *Insert*.

Thesaurus

Using the Thesaurus ▪▪▪▪▪▪▪▪▪▪▪▪▪▪▪▪▪▪▪▪▪▪▪▪

Use the Thesaurus to find synonyms, antonyms, and related words for a particular word. Synonyms are words that have the same or nearly the same meaning and antonyms are words with opposite meanings. To use the Thesaurus, click the word for which you want to display synonyms and antonyms, click the REVIEW tab, and then click the Thesaurus button in the Proofing group. This displays the Thesaurus task pane with information about the word where the insertion point is positioned. Hover the mouse over the desired synonym or antonym, click the down-pointing arrow that displays at the right of the word, and then click *Insert* at the drop-down list. You can also display and insert synonyms for words by right-clicking the word, pointing to *Synonyms*, and then clicking the desired word at the side menu.

1. Open **ElectronicDesign.pptx** and then save the presentation with Save As and name it **P-C2-P1-ElectronicDesign**.
2. With the presentation in Normal view, run a spelling check by completing the following steps:
   a. Click the REVIEW tab.
   b. Click the Spelling button in the Proofing group.
   c. The spelling checker selects the misspelled word *Layuot* and displays the Spelling task pane. The proper spelling (*Layout*) is selected in the Spelling task pane list box, so click the Change button (or the Change All button).
   d. The spelling checker selects the misspelled word *Clerly*. The correct spelling is selected in the Spelling task pane list box, so click the Change button (or the Change All button).

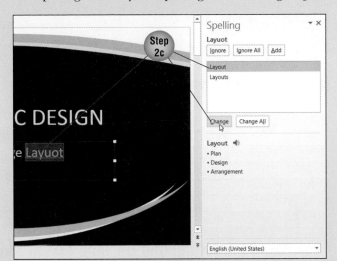

   e. When the spelling checker selects the misspelled word *massege*, click *message* in the Spelling task pane list box and then click the Change button (or the Change All button).

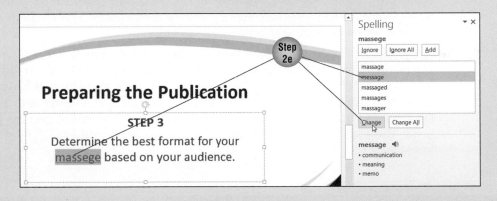

   f. The spelling checker selects the misspelled word *fo*. The correct spelling is selected in the Spelling task pane list box, so click the Change button (or the Change All button).
   g. At the message telling you that the spelling check is complete, click the OK button.
3. Make Slide 2 active and then use the Thesaurus to find a synonym for *point* by completing the following steps:
   a. Click in the word *point*.
   b. Click the REVIEW tab, if necessary, and then click the Thesaurus button.
   c. At the Thesaurus task pane, scroll down the task pane list box to display *purpose* (below *purpose (n.)*).
   d. Hover your mouse pointer over the word *purpose* in the task pane, click the down-pointing arrow, and then click *Insert* at the drop-down list.
   e. Close the Thesaurus task pane.

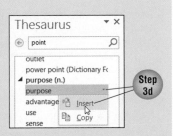

4. Make Slide 6 active and right-click the word *Gather*.
5. Point to *Synonyms* and then click *Collect* at the side menu.
6. Save **P-C2-P1-ElectronicDesign.pptx**.

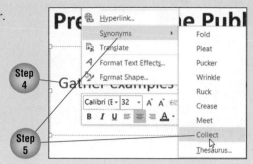

Managing Text in Slides ■■■■■■■■■■ ■■■■■■■■■■■

As you enter text in new slides or manage existing slides, you may need to edit, move, copy, or delete text. You may also want to find specific text in slides and replace it with other text. Text is generally inserted in a slide *placeholder*. Placeholders can be moved, sized, and/or deleted.

Inserting and Deleting Text in Slides

To insert or delete text in an individual slide, open the presentation, edit the text as needed, and then save the presentation. If you want to delete more than one character, consider selecting the text first. This will help reduce the amount of times you have to press the Delete key or Backspace key. Several methods can be used for selecting text, as described in Table 2.2.

Text in a slide is positioned inside a placeholder. Slide layouts provide placeholders for text and generally display with a message suggesting the type of text to be entered in the slide. For example, the Title and Content slide layout contains a placeholder with the text *Click to add title* and another with the text *Click to add text*. Click in the placeholder text and the insertion point is positioned inside the placeholder, the default text is removed, and the placeholder is selected.

Table 2.2 Selecting Text

To select	*Perform this action*
text the mouse pointer passes through	Click and drag the mouse.
an entire word	Double-click the word.
an entire paragraph	Triple-click anywhere in the paragraph.
all text in a selected placeholder	Click Select button in Editing group on HOME tab and then click Select All, or press Ctrl + A.

1. With **P-C2-P1-ElectronicDesign.pptx** open and the presentation in Normal view, click the Previous Slide button or the Next Slide button (located at the bottom of the vertical scroll bar) until Slide 5 displays.
2. Edit Slide 5 by completing the following steps:
   a. Position the I-beam pointer in the sentence below *STEP 4* and then click the left mouse button. (This selects the placeholder.)
   b. Edit the sentence so it reads *Decide what steps you want readers to take after reading the message.* (Use deleting and inserting commands to edit this sentence.)

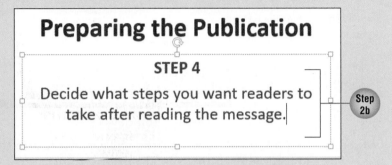

3. Click the Next Slide button to display Slide 6 and then edit Slide 6 in the outline pane by completing the following steps:
   a. Click the VIEW tab and then click the Outline View button in the Presentation Views group.
   b. In the outline pane, click in the sentence below *STEP 5* and then edit the sentence so it reads *Collect and assess examples of effective designs.*
   c. Click the Normal button in the Presentation Views group on the VIEW tab.
   d. Click the NOTES button on the Status bar to close the notes pane.
   e. Click the HOME tab.
4. Save **P-C2-P1-ElectronicDesign.pptx**.

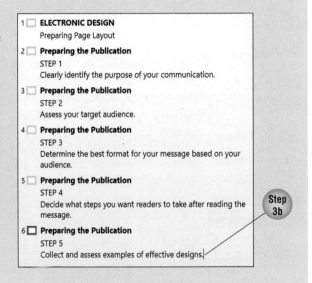

Finding and Replacing Text in Slides

Use the Find feature to look for specific text in slides in a presentation and use the Find and Replace feature to look for specific text in slides in a presentation and replace it with other text. Begin a search by clicking the Find button in the Editing group on the HOME tab. This displays the Find dialog box, as shown in Figure 2.2. In the *Find what* text box, type the text you want to find and then click the Find Next button. Continue clicking this button until a message displays telling you that the search is complete. At this message, click OK.

Use options at the Replace dialog box, shown in Figure 2.3, to search for text and replace it with other text. Display this dialog box by clicking the Replace button on the HOME tab. Type the text you want to find in the *Find what* text

Figure 2.2 Find Dialog Box

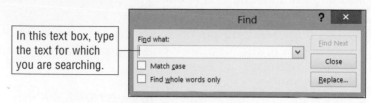

Figure 2.3 Replace Dialog Box

In this text box, type the text for which you are searching.

In this text box, type the replacement text.

▼ **Quick Steps**

Find Text
1. Click Find button.
2. Type text for which you are searching.
3. Click Find Next button.

Replace Text
1. Click Replace button.
2. Type text for which you are searching.
3. Press Tab key.
4. Type replacement text.
5. Click Replace All button.

Find   Replace

box, press the Tab key, and then type the replacement text in the *Replace with* text box. Click the Find Next button to find the next occurrence of the text and then click the Replace button to replace it with the new text, or click the Replace All button to replace all occurrences in the presentation.

Both the Find dialog box and the Replace dialog box contain two additional options. Insert a check mark in the *Match case* check box to specify that the text in the presentation should exactly match the case of the text in the *Find what* text box. For example, if you search for *Planning*, PowerPoint will stop at *Planning* but not *planning* or *PLANNING*. Insert a check mark in the *Find whole words only* check box to specify that the text is a whole word and not part of a word. For example, if you search for *plan* and do not check the *Find whole words only* option, PowerPoint will stop at ex*plan*ation, *plan*ned, *plan*ning, and so on.

Project 1c **Finding and Replacing Text** **Part 3 of 3**

1. With **P-C2-P1-ElectronicDesign.pptx** open, make Slide 1 active.
2. Find all occurrences of *Preparing* in the presentation and replace them with *Planning* by completing the following steps:
   a. With Slide 1 active, click the Replace button in the Editing group on the HOME tab.
   b. At the Replace dialog box, type **Preparing** in the *Find what* text box.
   c. Press the Tab key.
   d. Type **Planning** in the *Replace with* text box.
   e. Click the Replace All button.
   f. At the message telling you that six replacements were made, click OK.
   g. Click the Close button to close the Replace dialog box.
3. Find all occurrences of *Publication* and replace them with *Newsletter* by completing steps similar to those in Step 2.

Step 2b

Step 2d

Step 2e

4. Save the presentation.
5. Apply a transition and sound of your choosing to all slides in the presentation.
6. Run the presentation.
7. Print Slide 1 by completing the following steps:
   a. Click the FILE tab and then click the *Print* option.
   b. At the Print backstage area, click in the *Slides* text box in the *Settings* category and then type 1.
   c. Click the Print button.
8. Print the presentation as a handout with six slides printed horizontally on the page. (Change the second gallery in the *Settings* category to *6 Slides Horizontal* and delete the *1* in the *Slides* text box.)
9. Save and then close **P-C2-P1-ElectronicDesign.pptx**.

Project 2   Cut, Copy, Paste, Rearrange, and Manage   5 Parts
Slides in a Network Presentation

You will open a network evaluation presentation and then cut, copy, and paste text in slides; rearrange text in the slide thumbnails pane; size and rearrange placeholders in slides; and manage slides by inserting, deleting, moving, and copying them. You will also create sections within a presentation and copy slides between presentations.

Cutting, Copying, and Pasting Text in Slides

With buttons in the Clipboard group on the HOME tab and/or shortcut menu options, you can cut, copy, and paste text in slides. For example, to move text in a slide, click once in the placeholder containing the text to be moved, select the text, and then click the Cut button in the Clipboard group. Position the insertion point where you want to insert the text and then click the Paste button in the Clipboard group. To cut and paste with the shortcut menu, select the text you want to move, right-click the text, and then click *Cut* at the shortcut menu. Position the insertion point where you want to insert the text, right-click the location, and then click *Paste* at the shortcut menu. Complete similar steps to copy and paste text, except click the Copy button instead of the Cut button or click the *Copy* option at the shortcut menu instead of the *Cut* option.

 Ctrl + X is the keyboard shortcut to cut selected text, Ctrl + C is the keyboard shortcut to copy selected text, and Ctrl + V is the keyboard shortcut to paste cut or copied text.

 Cut

Copy

 Paste

Project 2a   Cutting, Copying, and Pasting Text in Slides   Part 1 of 5

1. Open **NetworkSystem.pptx**, located in the PC2 folder on your storage medium, and then save the presentation with Save As and name it **P-C2-P2-NetworkSystem**.
2. Insert a new slide by completing the following steps:
   a. Make Slide 4 active.
   b. Click the New Slide button in the Slides group on the HOME tab.
   c. Click in the *Click to add title* placeholder and then type **TIME**.
3. Cut text from Slide 3 and paste it into Slide 5 by completing the following steps:
   a. Make Slide 3 active.
   b. Click any character in the bulleted text in the slide pane.

c. Using the mouse, select the text following the bottom three bullets. (The bullets will not be selected.)

d. With the text selected, click the Cut button in the Clipboard group on the HOME tab.

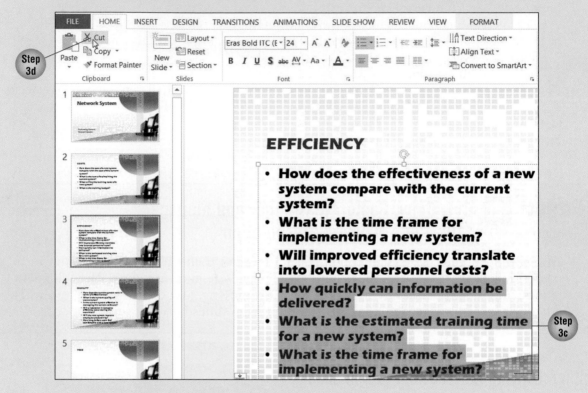

e. Make Slide 5 the active slide (contains the title *TIME*).

f. Click in the *Click to add text* placeholder.

g. Click the Paste button in the Clipboard group.

h. If the insertion point is positioned below the third bulleted item following a bullet, press the Backspace key twice. (This removes the bullet and deletes the blank line below the bullet.)

4. Insert a new slide by completing the following steps:

a. With Slide 5 the active slide, click the New Slide button in the Slides group on the HOME tab.

b. Click in the *Click to add title* placeholder and then type **EASE OF USE**.

5. Cut text from Slide 4 and paste it into Slide 6 by completing the following steps:

a. Make Slide 4 active.

b. Click any character in the bulleted text.

c. Select the text following the bottom three bullets.

d. Click the Cut button in the Clipboard group on the HOME tab.

e. Make Slide 6 active (contains the title *EASE OF USE*).

f. Click in the *Click to add text* placeholder.

g. Click the Paste button in the Clipboard group.

h. If the insertion point is positioned below the third bulleted item following a bullet, press the Backspace key twice.

6. Copy text from Slide 3 to Slide 5 by completing the following steps:

a. Make Slide 3 active.

b. Click any character in the bulleted text.

c. Position the mouse pointer on the last bullet until the pointer turns into a four-headed arrow and then click the left mouse button. (This selects the text following the bullet.)

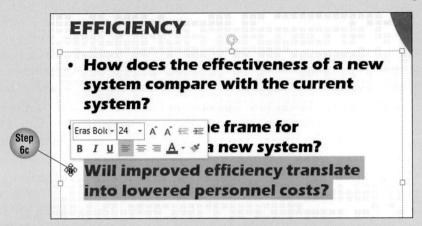

d. Click the Copy button in the Clipboard group.
e. Make Slide 5 active.
f. Click in the bulleted text and then move the insertion point so it is positioned immediately right of the question mark at the end of the second bulleted item.
g. Press the Enter key. (This moves the insertion point down to the next line and inserts another bullet.)
h. Click the Paste button in the Clipboard group.

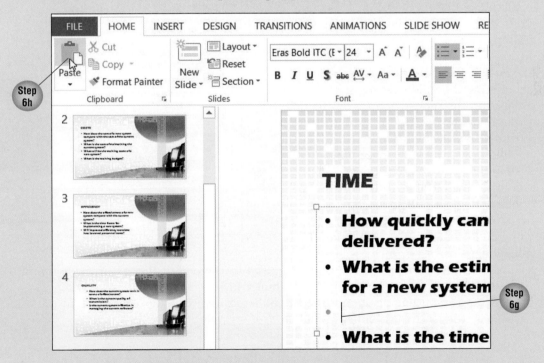

i. If a blank line is inserted between the third and fourth bullets, press the Backspace key twice.

7. Save **P-C2-P2-NetworkSystem.pptx**.

Rearranging Text in the Outline Pane

You can move and copy text in slides in the outline pane. Display the outline pane by clicking the VIEW tab and then clicking the Outline View button in the Presentation Views group or with the keyboard shortcut Ctrl + Shift + Tab. To move text in the outline pane, position the mouse pointer on the slide icon or bullet at the left side of the text until the arrow pointer turns into a four-headed arrow. Hold down the left mouse button, drag the arrow pointer (a thin horizontal line displays) to the desired location, and then release the mouse button.

If you position the arrow pointer on the slide icon and then hold down the left mouse button, all of the text in the slide is selected. If you position the arrow pointer on the bullet and then hold down the left mouse button, all text following that bullet is selected.

Dragging selected text with the mouse moves the selected text to a new location in the presentation. You can also copy selected text. To do this, click the slide icon or click the bullet to select the desired text. Position the arrow pointer in the selected text, hold down the Ctrl key, and then the left mouse button. Drag the arrow pointer (displays with a light gray box and a plus sign attached) to the desired location, release the mouse button, and then release the Ctrl key.

Project 2b **Rearranging Text in the Slide Thumbnails Pane** Part 2 of 5

1. With **P-C2-P2-NetworkSystem.pptx** open, make Slide 1 active.
2. Press Ctrl + Shift + Tab to display the outline pane
3. Move the first bulleted item in Slide 4 in the outline pane to the end of the list by completing the following steps:
   a. Position the mouse pointer on the first bullet below *QUALITY* until it turns into a four-headed arrow.
   b. Hold down the left mouse button, drag the arrow pointer down until a thin horizontal line displays below the last bulleted item, and then release the mouse button.
4. Copy and paste text by completing the following steps:
   a. In the outline pane, move the insertion point to the end of the text in Slide 6 and then press the Enter key. (This inserts a new bullet in the slide.)
   b. Scroll up the outline pane until the last bulleted item in Slide 2 is visible in the outline pane as well as the last bullet in Slide 6.

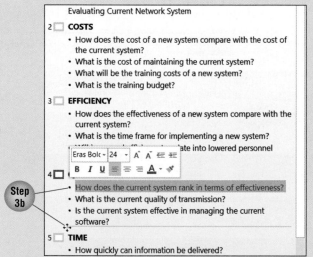

Step 3b

---

c. Position the mouse pointer near the last bulleted item in Slide 2 until it turns into a four-headed arrow and then click the left mouse button. (This selects the text.)

d. Position the mouse pointer in the selected text, hold down the left mouse button, hold down the Ctrl key, and then drag down until the arrow pointer and light gray vertical line display on the blank line below the text in Slide 6.

e. Release the mouse button and then release the Ctrl key.

5. Press Ctrl + Shift + Tab to return to the slide thumbnails pane.

6. Click the NOTES button on the Status bar to close the notes pane.

7. Save **P-C2-P2-NetworkSystem.pptx**.

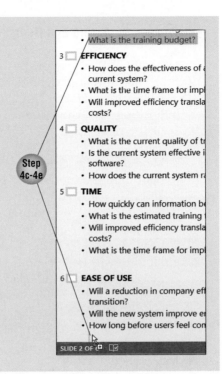

Sizing and Rearranging Placeholders in a Slide

When you click inside a placeholder, the placeholder is selected and white sizing handles and a white rotation handle display around the placeholder border. Use the sizing handles to increase or decrease the size of the placeholder by positioning the arrow pointer on a sizing handle until the pointer turns into a double-headed arrow and then dragging the placeholder border to the desired size. To move a placeholder, position the arrow pointer on the placeholder border until the arrow pointer displays with a four-headed arrow attached. Hold down the left mouse button, drag the placeholder to the desired position, and then release the mouse button.

Dragging a selected placeholder with the mouse moves the placeholder. If you want to copy a placeholder, hold down the Ctrl key while dragging the placeholder. When the placeholder is in the desired position, release the mouse button, and then release the Ctrl key. If you make a change to the size and/or location of a placeholder, click the Reset button in the Slides group on the HOME tab to return the formatting of the placeholder back to the default.

As you drag a placeholder on a slide, guidelines may display. Use these guidelines to help you position placeholders. For example, you can use a guideline to help you align a title placeholder with a subtitle placeholder.

1. With **P-C2-P2-NetworkSystem.pptx** open, make Slide 1 active.
2. Size and move a placeholder by completing the following steps:
   a. Click any character in the subtitle *Evaluating Current Network System*.
   b. Position the arrow pointer on the sizing handle that displays in the middle of the right border until the pointer turns into a left-and-right-pointing arrow.

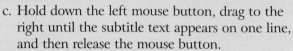

Step 2c

   c. Hold down the left mouse button, drag to the right until the subtitle text appears on one line, and then release the mouse button.
   d. Position the arrow pointer on the border of the placeholder until the pointer turns into a four-headed arrow.

Step 2e

   e. Hold down the left mouse button, drag the placeholder up so the placeholder is positioned as shown at the right, and then release the mouse button. Use the guideline that displays to the left of the title to left-align the subtitle placeholder with the title placeholder.

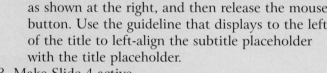

3. Make Slide 4 active.
4. Size and move a placeholder by completing the following steps:
   a. Click any character in the bulleted text.
   b. Position the arrow pointer on the sizing handle that displays in the middle of the right border until the pointer turns into a left-and-right-pointing arrow.
   c. Hold down the left mouse button and then drag to the left until the right border displays just to the right of the question mark in the second bulleted text.
   d. Drag the middle sizing handle on the bottom border up until the bottom border of the placeholder displays just below the last bulleted text.
   e. Position the arrow pointer on the border of the placeholder until the pointer turns into a four-headed arrow.
   f. Hold down the left mouse button and then drag the placeholder to the left until the vertical guideline displays left of the title (see image at the right) and then release the mouse button.
5. Save **P-C2-P2-NetworkSystem.pptx**.

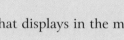

QUALITY

- **What is the current quality of transmission?**
- **Is the current system effective in managing the current software?**
- **How does the current system rank in terms of effectiveness?**

Step 4c

Step 4f

QUALITY

- **What is the current quality of transmission?**
- **Is the current system effective in managing the current software?**
- **How does the current system rank in terms of effectiveness?**

Managing Slides ■■■■■■■■■■■■■■■■■■■■■■■■■■■■■

As you edit a presentation, you may need to reorganize slides, insert new slides, or delete existing slides. Manage slides in the slide thumbnails pane or in Slide Sorter view. Switch to Slide Sorter view by clicking the Slide Sorter button in the view area on the Status bar or by clicking the VIEW tab and then clicking the Slide Sorter button in the Presentation Views group.

Inserting and Deleting Slides

As you learned in Chapter 1, clicking the New Slide button in the Slides group on the HOME tab inserts a new slide in the presentation immediately following the currently active slide. You can also insert a new slide in Slide Sorter view. To do this, click the slide that you want to immediately precede the new slide and then click the New Slide button in the Slides group. Delete a slide in Normal view by clicking the slide thumbnail in the slide thumbnails pane and then pressing the Delete key. You can also delete a slide by switching to Slide Sorter view, clicking the slide thumbnail, and then pressing the Delete key.

Moving Slides

Move slides in a presentation in Normal view or Slide Sorter view. In Normal view, click the desired slide in the slide thumbnails pane and then position the mouse pointer on the selected slide. Hold down the left mouse button, drag up or down until the slide thumbnail is in the desired location, and then release the mouse button. Complete similar steps to move a slide in Slide Sorter view. Click the desired slide, hold down the left mouse button, drag the slide to the desired location, and then release the mouse button.

Copying a Slide

You may want some slides in a presentation to contain similar text, objects, and/or formatting. Rather than creating new slides in these presentations, consider copying an existing slide. To do this, display the presentation in Slide Sorter view, position the mouse on the desired slide, hold down the Ctrl key and then the left mouse button. Drag the copy of the slide thumbnail to the location where you want it inserted, release the mouse button, and then release the Ctrl key.

You can also copy a slide in Normal view or Slide Sorter view with buttons in the Clipboard group on the HOME tab. To copy a slide, click the desired slide and then click the Copy button in the Clipboard group. Make active the slide that you want to precede the copied slide and then click the Paste button in the Clipboard group.

▼ Quick Steps

Insert Slide
Click New Slide button.
OR
Press Ctrl + M.
OR
1. Click Slide Sorter button in view area of Status bar.
2. Click slide that will immediately precede new slide.
3. Click New Slide button.

Delete Slide
1. Click slide thumbnail in slide thumbnails pane.
2. Press Delete key.
OR
1. Click Slide Sorter button in view area of Status bar.
2. Click desired slide thumbnail.
3. Press Delete key.

Slide Sorter

Press Ctrl + X to cut the selected slide and then press Ctrl + V to insert the cut slide.

Press Ctrl + C to copy the selected slide and then press Ctrl + V to insert the copied slide.

1. With **P-C2-P2-NetworkSystem.pptx** open in Normal view, move slides by completing the following steps:
   a. Click Slide 3 (*EFFICIENCY*) in the slide thumbnails pane.
   b. Position the mouse pointer on Slide 3, hold down the left mouse button, drag up until the slide thumbnail displays between Slides 1 and 2, and then release the mouse button.
   c. Click Slide 4 (*QUALITY*) in the slide thumbnails pane.
   d. Position the mouse pointer on Slide 4, hold down the left mouse button, drag down until the slide thumbnail displays below Slide 6, and then release the mouse button.
2. Move and copy slides in Slide Sorter view by completing the following steps:
   a. Click the Slide Sorter button in the view area on the Status bar.
   b. Click Slide 4 to make it the active slide. (The slide thumbnail displays with an orange border.)
   c. Position the mouse pointer on Slide 4, hold down the left mouse button, drag the slide thumbnail between Slides 1 and 2, and then release the mouse button.

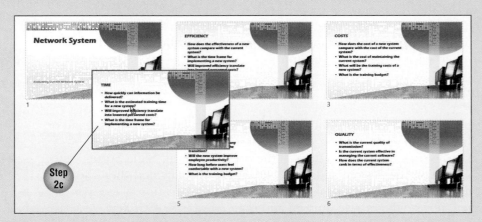

   d. Click Slide 1 to make it the active slide.
   e. Position the mouse pointer on Slide 1, hold down the left mouse button, and then hold down the Ctrl key.
   f. Drag the slide thumbnail down and to the right of Slide 6.
   g. Release the mouse button and then release the Ctrl key.

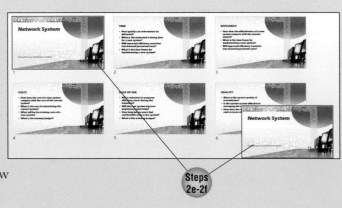

3. Click the Normal button in the view area on the Status bar.
4. Save **P-C2-P2-NetworkSystem.pptx**.

Copying a Slide between Presentations

You can copy slides between presentations as well as within them. To copy a slide, click the slide you want to copy (either in Slide Sorter view or in the slide thumbnails pane in Normal view) and then click the Copy button in the Clipboard group on the HOME tab. Open the presentation into which the slide is to be copied (in either Normal view or Slide Sorter view). Click in the location where you want to position the slide and then click the Paste button. The copied slide will take on the design theme of the presentation into which it is copied.

| **Project 2e** | **Copying Slides between Presentations** | **Part 5 of 5** |

1. With **P-C2-P2-NetworkSystem.pptx** open, open the presentation named **EvalNetwork.pptx** located in the PC2 folder on your storage medium.
2. Copy Slide 2 to the **P-C2-P2-NetworkSystem.pptx** presentation by completing the following steps:
   a. Click Slide 2 in the slide thumbnails pane to make it the active slide.
   b. Click the Copy button in the Clipboard group on the HOME tab.
   c. Click the PowerPoint button on the Taskbar and then click the *P-C2-P2-NetworkSystem.pptx* thumbnail.
   d. Click Slide 4 (*COSTS*) in the slide thumbnails pane.
   e. Click the Paste button in the Clipboard group.
   f. Click the PowerPoint button on the Taskbar and then click the *EvalNetwork.pptx* thumbnail.
3. Copy Slide 3 to the **P-C2-P2-NetworkSystem.pptx** by completing the following steps:
   a. Click Slide 3 in the slide thumbnails pane.
   b. Position the mouse pointer on Slide 3 and then click the right mouse button. (This displays a shortcut menu.)
   c. Click *Copy* at the shortcut menu.
   d. Click the PowerPoint button on the Taskbar and then click the *P-C2-P2-NetworkSystem.pptx* thumbnail.
   e. Right-click Slide 3 in the slide thumbnails pane.
   f. Click the Use Destination Theme button that displays in the *Paste Options* section.

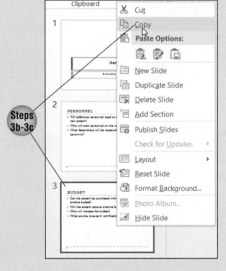

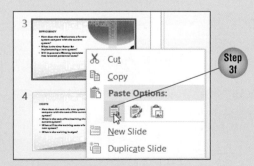

4. Click the PowerPoint button on the Taskbar and then click the **EvalNetwork.pptx** thumbnail.
5. Close the presentation.

6. With **P-C2-P2-NetworkSystem.pptx** open, delete Slide 9 by completing the following steps:
   a. If necessary, scroll down the slide thumbnails pane until Slide 9 is visible.
   b. Click Slide 9 to select it.
   c. Press the Delete key.
7. Save the presentation.
8. Print the presentation as a handout with four slides printed horizontally per page.
9. Close **P-C2-P2-NetworkSystem.pptx**.

Project 3   Insert and Manage Slides in an Adventure   4 Parts
Tours Presentation

You will open a presentation on Adventure Tours and then insert additional slides in the presentation by duplicating existing slides in the presentation and reusing slides from another presentation. You will also divide the presentation into sections and print a section.

Duplicating Slides

▼ **Quick Steps**

Duplicate Slides
1. Select desired slides in slide thumbnails pane.
2. Click New Slide button arrow.
3. Click *Duplicate Selected Slides* at drop-down list.

In Project 2, you used the Copy and Paste buttons in the Clipboard group and options from a shortcut menu to copy slides in a presentation. You can also copy slides in a presentation using the *Duplicate Selected Slides* option from the New Slide button drop-down list or by clicking the Copy button arrow and then clicking *Duplicate* at the drop-down list. In addition to duplicating slides, you can use the *Duplicate* option from the Copy button drop-down list to duplicate a selected object in a slide, such as a placeholder.

You can duplicate a single slide or multiple selected slides. To select adjacent (sequential) slides, click the first slide you want to select in the slide thumbnails pane, hold down the Shift key, and then click the last slide you want to select. To select nonadjacent (nonsequential) slides, hold down the Ctrl key while clicking each desired slide.

Project 3a   Duplicating Selected Slides   Part 1 of 4

1. Open **AdvTours.pptx** and then save the presentation with Save As and name it **P-C2-P3-AdvTours**.
2. Make sure the presentation displays in Normal view.
3. Select and then duplicate slides by completing the following steps:
   a. Click Slide 1 in the slide thumbnails pane.
   b. Hold down the Ctrl key.
   c. Click Slide 3, Slide 4, and Slide 5.
   d. Release the Ctrl key.

e. Click the New Slide button arrow in the Slides group on the HOME tab and then click *Duplicate Selected Slides* at the drop-down list.

4. With Slide 6 active in the slide pane, change *Fiji Tour* to *Costa Rica Tour*.

5. Make Slide 7 active, select *Fiji* and then type **Costa Rica**. Select and delete the existing bulleted text and then type the following bulleted text:
   - **Round-trip airfare from Los Angeles to San Jose, Costa Rica**
   - **8 days and 7 nights in Costa Rica**
   - **Monthly tours**
   - **Prices from $1099 to $1599**

6. Make Slide 8 active, select and delete the existing bulleted text, and then type the following bulleted text:
   - **San Jose, Emerald Suites**
   - **Tortuguero, Plantation Spa and Resort**
   - **Fortuna, Pacific Resort**
   - **Jaco, Monteverde Cabanas**

7. Make Slide 9 active, select and delete the existing bulleted text, and then type the following bulleted text:
   - **San Jose city tour**
   - **Rainforest tram**
   - **Canal cruise**
   - **Forest hike**

8. Save **P-C2-P3-AdvTours.pptx**.

Reusing Slides

PowerPoint provides another method for copying slides from one presentation to another. Click the New Slide button arrow and then click the *Reuse Slides* option at the drop-down list to display the Reuse Slides task pane at the right side of the screen, as shown in Figure 2.4. At this task pane, click the Browse button and then click *Browse File* at the drop-down list and the Browse dialog box displays. At this dialog box, navigate to the desired folder and then double-click the desired presentation. This inserts the presentation slides in the Reuse Slides task pane. Click a slide in the Reuse Slides task pane to insert it in the currently open presentation.

You can also share and reuse slides from a Slide Library on a server running Office SharePoint Server or Microsoft SharePoint Server. You can add slides to a Slide Library and insert slides from a Slide Library into a presentation. Before reusing slides from a Slide Library, the Slide Library must be created. Refer to the SharePoint help files to learn how to create a Slide Library. To reuse slides from a Slide Library in a presentation, click the Open a Slide Library hyperlink located

▼ **Quick Steps**

Reuse Slides
1. Click New Slide button arrow.
2. Click *Reuse Slides*.
3. Click Browse button.
4. Click *Browse File*.
5. Navigate to desired folder.
6. Double-click desired presentation.
7. Click desired slide in Reuse Slides task pane.

Figure 2.4 Reuse Slides Task Pane

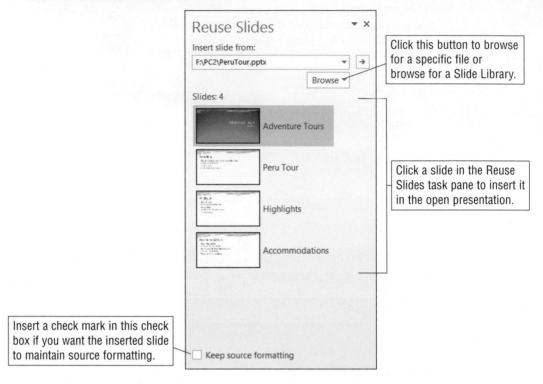

Click this button to browse for a specific file or browse for a Slide Library.

Click a slide in the Reuse Slides task pane to insert it in the open presentation.

Insert a check mark in this check box if you want the inserted slide to maintain source formatting.

in the Reuse Slides task pane. You can also click the Browse button in the Reuse Slides task pane and then click *Browse Slide Library* at the drop-down list. This displays the Select a Slide Library dialog box. At this dialog box, navigate to the location of the desired library and then double-click the library.

By default, the slides you insert from the Reuse Slides task pane into the currently open presentation take on the formatting of the current presentation. If you want the slides to retain their original formatting when inserted in the presentation, insert a check mark in the *Keep source formatting* check box located toward the bottom of the Reuse Slides task pane.

Project 3b   Reusing Slides   **Part 2 of 4**

1. With **P-C2-P3-AdvTours.pptx** open, click the New Slide button arrow in the Slides group on the HOME tab and then click *Reuse Slides* at the drop-down list. (This displays the Reuse Slides task pane at the right side of the screen.)
2. Click the Browse button in the Reuse Slides task pane and then click *Browse File* at the drop-down list.
3. At the Browse dialog box, navigate to the PC2 folder on your storage medium and then double-click *PeruTour.pptx*.
4. In the slide thumbnails pane, scroll down the slide thumbnails until Slide 9 displays and then click below Slide 9. (This inserts a thin, horizontal line below the Slide 9 thumbnail in the slide thumbnails pane.)

5. Click the first slide thumbnail (*Adventure Tours*) in the Reuse Slides task pane. (This inserts the slide in the open presentation immediately below Slide 9.)

6. Click the second slide thumbnail (*Peru Tour*) in the Reuse Slides task pane.
7. Click the fourth slide thumbnail (*Accommodations*) in the Reuse Slides task pane.
8. Click the third slide thumbnail (*Highlights*) in the Reuse Slides task pane.
9. Close the Reuse Slides task pane by clicking the Close button (contains an *X*) located in the upper right corner of the task pane.
10. Save **P-C2-P3-AdvTours.pptx**.

Creating Sections within a Presentation ■■■■■■■■■■■■

If you are working on a presentation with others in a group, or you are working in a presentation containing numerous slides, consider dividing related slides in the presentation into sections. Dividing a presentation into sections allows you to easily navigate and edit slides within a presentation. Create a section by selecting the first slide you want to place in the new section in the slide thumbnails pane, clicking the Section button in the Slides group on the HOME tab, and then clicking *Add Section* at the drop-down list. A section title bar displays in the slide thumbnails pane. By default, the section title is *Untitled Section*. Rename a section by clicking the Section button in the Slides group on the HOME tab and then clicking *Rename Section* at the drop-down list. You can also rename a section by right-clicking the section title bar in the slide thumbnails pane and then clicking *Rename Section* at the shortcut menu. Remove, move, collapse, and expand sections with options in the Section button drop-down list or by right-clicking the section title bar and then clicking the desired option. You can also apply different formatting to an individual section by clicking the section title bar to select the section and then applying the desired formatting.

When you create sections within a presentation, you have the ability to print only certain sections of the presentation. To print a section of a presentation, click the FILE tab, click the *Print* option, click the first gallery in the *Settings* category, click the desired section in the drop-down list, and then click the Print button.

▼ **Quick Steps**
Create Section
1. Select first slide for new section.
2. Click Section button.
3. Click *Add Section*.

Section

1. With **P-C2-P3-AdvTours.pptx** open, create a section for slides about Fiji by completing the following steps:
   a. Click Slide 1 in the slide thumbnails pane.
   b. Click the Section button in the Slides group on the HOME tab and then click *Add Section* at the drop-down list.

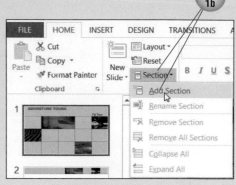

Step 1b

2. Rename the new section by completing the following steps:
   a. Click the Section button and then click *Rename Section* at the drop-down list.
   b. At the Rename Section dialog box, type **Fiji Tour** and then click the Rename button.

3. Create a section for slides about Costa Rica by completing the following steps:
   a. Click Slide 6 in the slide thumbnails pane.
   b. Click the Section button in the Slides group and then click *Add Section* at the drop-down list.
   c. Right-click in the section title bar (contains the text *Untitled Section*) and then click *Rename Section* at the shortcut menu.
   d. At the Rename Section dialog box, type **Costa Rica Tour** and then press Enter.

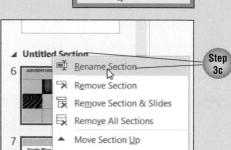

Step 2b

Step 3c

4. Complete steps similar to those in Step 3 to create a section beginning with Slide 10 and rename the section *Peru Tour*.

5. Change the design theme of a section by completing the following steps:
   a. Click the *Fiji Tour* section title bar located at the top of the slide thumbnails pane.
   b. Click the DESIGN tab.
   c. Click the More button located at the right of the themes thumbnails.
   d. Click *Wisp* at the drop-down gallery.
   e. Display Slide 2 in the Slides pane and move the placeholder down so the first line of text is aligned approximately with the orange shape at the left side of the slide.

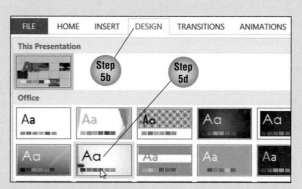

Step 5b

Step 5d

6. Complete steps similar to those in Steps 5a through 5d to apply the Ion design theme to the *Costa Rica Tour* section.

7. Display only slides in the *Costa Rica Tour* section by completing the following steps:
   a. Click the HOME tab, click the Section button in the Slides group, and then click *Collapse All* at the drop-down list.

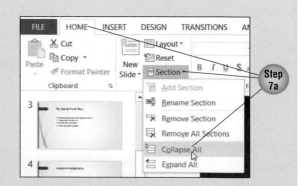

Step 7a

b. Double-click the *Costa Rica Tour* section title bar in the slide thumbnails pane. (Notice that only Slides 6 through 9 display in the slide thumbnails pane and that the slides in the *Fiji Tour* and *Peru Tour* sections are hidden.)

8. Redisplay the *Fiji Tour* section slides by double-clicking the *Fiji Tour* section title bar in the slide thumbnails pane.

9. Display all sections by clicking the Section button in the Slides group and then clicking *Expand All* at the drop-down list.

10. Print only the *Costa Rica Tour* section by completing the following steps:
   a. Click the FILE tab and then click the *Print* option.
   b. At the Print backstage area, click the first gallery in the *Settings* category and then click *Costa Rica Tour* in the *Sections* section (located toward the bottom of the drop-down list).
   c. Click the second gallery (contains the text *Full Page Slides*) in the *Settings* category and then click *4 Slides Horizontal* in the *Handouts* section.
   d. Click the Print button.

11. Complete steps similar to those in Step 10 to print only the *Peru Tour* section.

12. Save **P-C2-P3-AdvTours.pptx**.

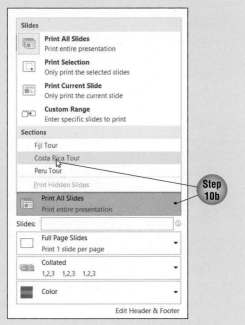

Customizing the Quick Access Toolbar ▪■■■■■■■■■■■■

The Quick Access toolbar contains buttons for some of the most commonly performed tasks. By default, the toolbar contains the Save, Undo, Redo, and Start From Beginning buttons. You can easily add or delete buttons to and from the Quick Access toolbar. To add a button to or delete a button from the Quick Access toolbar, click the Customize Quick Access Toolbar button that displays at the right side of the toolbar. At the drop-down list that displays, insert a check mark next to those buttons you want to display on the toolbar and remove the check mark from those you do not want to appear.

Click the *More Commands* option at the drop-down list and the PowerPoint Options dialog box displays with *Quick Access Toolbar* selected in the left panel. With options at this dialog box, you can choose to add a button from a list of PowerPoint commands. You can also click the Reset button at the dialog box to reset the Quick Access toolbar back to the default.

By default, the Quick Access toolbar displays above the ribbon tabs. You can display the Quick Access toolbar below the ribbon by clicking the Customize Quick Access Toolbar button that displays at the right side of the toolbar and then clicking the *Show Below the Ribbon* option at the drop-down list.

Save

Undo

Redo

Start from Beginning

1. With **P-C2-P3-AdvTours.pptx** open, add a New button to the Quick Access toolbar by clicking the Customize Quick Access Toolbar button that displays at the right side of the Quick Access toolbar and then clicking *New* at the drop-down list.

2. Add an Open button to the Quick Access toolbar by clicking the Customize Quick Access Toolbar button and then clicking *Open* at the drop-down list.

3. Add a Print Preview and Print button to the Quick Access toolbar by clicking the Customize Quick Access Toolbar button and then clicking *Print Preview and Print* at the drop-down list.

4. Move the Quick Access toolbar below the ribbon by clicking the Customize Quick Access Toolbar button and then clicking the *Show Below the Ribbon* option at the drop-down list.

5. Click the Print Preview and Print button on the Quick Access toolbar. (This displays the Print backstage area.)

6. Click the Back button to close the Print backstage area and return to the presentation.

7. Close **P-C2-P3-AdvTours.pptx**.

8. Click the New button to open a new blank presentation.

9. Click the Open button to display the Open backstage area.

10. Press the Esc key to return to the blank presentation and then close the presentation.

11. Move the Quick Access toolbar back to the original position by clicking the Customize Quick Access Toolbar button at the right side of the Quick Access toolbar and then clicking the *Show Above the Ribbon* option at the drop-down list.

12. Remove the New button by clicking the Customize Quick Access Toolbar button and then clicking *New* at the drop-down list.

13. Remove the Open button by right-clicking the button and then clicking *Remove from Quick Access Toolbar* at the drop-down list.

14. Remove the Print Preview and Print button from the Quick Access toolbar.

Project 4 Use PowerPoint Help Feature and Create a Presentation 1 Part

You will use the Help feature to learn more about PowerPoint features. You will also use the Help feature to find information on keyboard shortcuts and then use the information to create a presentation.

Using Help ▪▪▪▪▪▪▪▪▪▪▪▪▪▪▪▪▪▪▪▪▪▪▪▪▪▪▪▪▪▪▪

Microsoft PowerPoint includes a Help feature that contains information about PowerPoint features and commands. This on-screen reference manual is similar to Windows Help and the Help features in Word, Excel, and Access.

Click the Microsoft PowerPoint Help button (the question mark) located in the upper right corner of the screen or press the keyboard shortcut F1 to display the PowerPoint Help window, shown in Figure 2.5. In this window, click in the search text box, type a topic, feature name, or question, and then press the Enter key. Topics related to the search text display in the PowerPoint Help window. Click a topic that interests you. If the topic window contains a <u>Show All</u> hyperlink in the upper right corner, click this hyperlink to expand the topic options to show additional related information. When you click the <u>Show All</u> hyperlink, it becomes the <u>Hide All</u> hyperlink.

Getting Help on a Button

When you position the mouse pointer on a button, a ScreenTip displays with information about the button. Some button ScreenTips display with a Help icon and the text *Tell me more*. Click this hyperlinked text or press F1 and the PowerPoint Help window opens with information about the button feature.

Getting Help in a Dialog Box or Backstage Area

Some dialog boxes and backstage areas contain a help button you can click to display the PowerPoint Help window with specific information about the dialog box or backstage area. After reading and/or printing the information, close a dialog box by clicking the Close button located in the upper right corner of the dialog box or close the backstage area by clicking the Back button or pressing the Esc key.

▼ Quick Steps

Use the Help Feature
1. Click Microsoft PowerPoint Help button.
2. Click in search text box.
3. Type topic or feature name.
4. Press Enter.
5. Click desired topic.

Help

Figure 2.5 PowerPoint Help Window

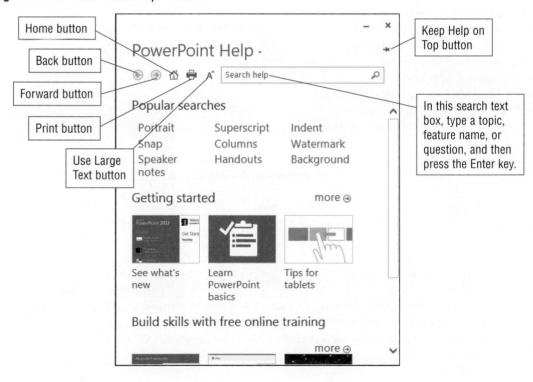

1. At the blank PowerPoint screen, press Ctrl + N to display a blank presentation. (Ctrl + N is the keyboard shortcut to open a blank presentation.)
2. Click the Microsoft PowerPoint Help button located in the upper right corner of the screen.

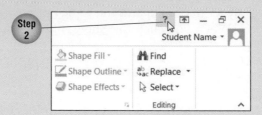

3. At the PowerPoint Help window, click in the search text box, type **create a presentation**, and then press the Enter key.
4. When the list of topics displays, click the <u>Basic tasks for creating a PowerPoint 2013 presentation</u> hyperlink. (If your PowerPoint Help window does not display this hyperlink, click a similar hyperlink.)
5. Read the information in the article. (If you want a hard copy of the information, you can click the Print button that displays to the left of the search text box in the PowerPoint Help window and then click the Print button at the Print dialog box.)
6. Close the PowerPoint Help window by clicking the Close button in the upper right corner of the window.
7. Hover the mouse over the New Slide button in the Slides group on the HOME tab and then click the *Tell me more* text that displays toward the bottom of the ScreenTip.

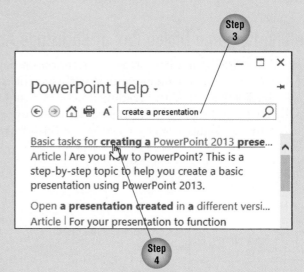

8. At the PowerPoint Help window, read the information on adding, rearranging, and deleting slides and then click the Close button in the upper right corner of the PowerPoint Help window.
9. Click the FILE tab and then click the *Open* option.
10. At the Open backstage area, click the Microsoft PowerPoint Help button that displays in the upper right corner of the backstage area.
11. Read the information that displays in the PowerPoint Help window.
12. Click in the search text box, type **keyboard shortcuts**, and then press the Enter key.
13. When the list of topics displays, click the <u>Keyboard shortcuts for use while creating a presentation in PowerPoint 2013</u> hyperlink. (Not all of the hyperlink text will be visible.)
14. Scroll down the list of topics, display the *Common tasks in PowerPoint* section, and then click the <u>Delete and copy text and objects</u> hyperlink. (This displays a list of keyboard shortcuts for deleting and copying text and objects.)

15. Select the list of keyboard shortcuts for deleting and copying text and objects by positioning the mouse pointer at the left side of the heading *TO DO THIS*, holding down the left mouse button, dragging down to the lower right corner of the list of keyboard shortcuts, and then releasing the mouse button.

16. With the information selected, click the Print button that displays to the left of the search text box in the PowerPoint Help window.

17. At the Print dialog box, click the *Selection* option in the *Page Range* section and then click the Print button.

18. Close the PowerPoint Help window.

19. Press the Esc key to return to the blank presentation.

20. At the blank presentation, click the text *Click to add title* and then type **PowerPoint Help**.

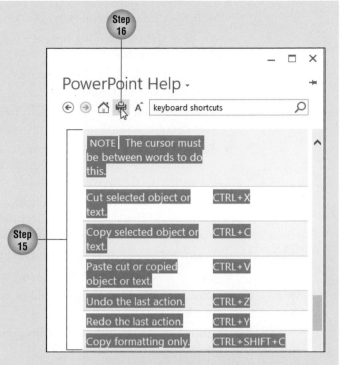

21. Click the text *Click to add subtitle* and then type **Keyboard Shortcuts**.

22. Using the information you printed, create slides with the following information:
    - Slide 2: Insert the text **Delete Text** as the title and then insert the four delete keyboard shortcuts as bulleted text. (For each keyboard shortcut, type the description followed by a colon and then the keyboard shortcut. For example, type **Delete one character to the left: Backspace** as the first bulleted item in the slide.)
    - Slide 3: Insert the text **Cut, Copy, Paste Text** as the title and then insert the three cut, copy, and paste keyboard shortcuts as bulleted text.
    - Slide 4: Insert the text **Undo and Redo** as the title and then insert the two undo and redo keyboard shortcuts as bulleted text.
    - Slide 5: Insert the text **Copy and Paste Formatting** as the title and then insert the three copy and paste formatting keyboard shortcuts as bulleted text.

23. Apply the Facet design theme with the blue variant to the presentation.

24. Apply a transition and sound of your choosing to all slides in the presentation.

25. Print the presentation as a handout with six slides printed horizontally per page.

26. Save and then close **P-C2-P4-Shortcuts.pptx**.

Chapter Summary

- Use the spelling checker feature to check the spelling of the text in a presentation. Begin a spelling check by clicking the REVIEW tab and then clicking the Spelling button in the Proofing group.

- Use the Thesaurus to find synonyms and antonyms for words in a presentation. Display synonyms at the Thesaurus task pane or by right-clicking a word and then pointing to *Synonyms* at the shortcut menu.

- Click in a placeholder to select the placeholder and position the insertion point inside the placeholder.
- Display the Find dialog box by clicking the Find button in the Editing group on the HOME tab.
- Display the Replace dialog box by clicking the Replace button in the Editing group on the HOME tab.
- With buttons in the Clipboard group or with options from a shortcut menu, you can cut and paste or copy and paste text in slides.
- You can use the mouse to move text in the slide thumbnails pane by selecting and then dragging text to a new location. To copy text to a new location, hold down the Ctrl key while dragging.
- Use the sizing handles that display around a selected placeholder to increase or decrease the size of the placeholder. Use the mouse to drag a selected placeholder to a new location in the slide.
- Use the New Slide button on the HOME tab to insert a slide in a presentation.
- Delete a selected slide by pressing the Delete key.
- Move or delete a selected slide in Normal view in the slide thumbnails pane or in Slide Sorter view.
- Copy a selected slide by holding down the Ctrl key while dragging the slide to the desired location.
- Use the Copy and Paste buttons in the Clipboard group on the HOME tab to copy a slide between presentations.
- Select adjacent slides in the slide thumbnails pane or in Slide Sorter view by clicking the first slide, holding down the Shift key, and then clicking the last slide. Select nonadjacent slides by holding down the Ctrl key while clicking each desired slide.
- Duplicate slides in a presentation by selecting the desired slides in the slide thumbnails pane, clicking the New Slide button arrow, and then clicking the *Duplicate Selected Slides* option or clicking the Copy button arrow and then clicking *Duplicate* at the drop-down list.
- Divide a presentation into sections to easily navigate and edit slides in a presentation.
- You can copy slides from a presentation into the open presentation with options at the Reuse Slides task pane. Display this task pane by clicking the New Slide button arrow and then clicking *Reuse Slides* at the drop-down list.
- Customize the Quick Access toolbar by clicking the Customize Quick Access Toolbar button that displays at the right side of the toolbar and then clicking the desired button or option at the drop-down list. You can add buttons to or remove buttons from the Quick Access toolbar and display the toolbar below the ribbon.
- Click the Microsoft PowerPoint Help button or press F1 to display the PowerPoint Help window.
- Some dialog boxes and backstage areas contain a help button you can click to display information specific to the dialog box or backstage area.

Commands Review

FEATURE	RIBBON TAB, GROUP	BUTTON, OPTION	KEYBOARD SHORTCUT
copy text or slide	HOME, Clipboard		Ctrl + C
create section	HOME, Slides		
cut text or slide	HOME, Clipboard		Ctrl + X
duplicate slide	HOME, Slides	, Duplicate Selected Slides	
Find dialog box	HOME, Editing		Ctrl + F
paste text or slide	HOME, Clipboard		Ctrl + V
PowerPoint Help window		?	F1
Replace dialog box	HOME, Editing		Ctrl + H
Reuse Slides task pane	HOME, Slides	, Reuse Slides	
spelling checker	REVIEW, Proofing		F7
Thesaurus task pane	REVIEW, Proofing		Shift + F7

Concepts Check   Test Your Knowledge

Completion: In the space provided at the right, indicate the correct term, symbol, or command.

1. The Spelling button is located in the Proofing group on this tab.   _____

2. This is the keyboard shortcut to select all text in a placeholder.   _____

3. The Find button is located in this group on the HOME tab.   _____

4. To copy text to a new location in the slide thumbnails pane, hold down this key while dragging text.   _____

5. The border of a selected placeholder displays these handles as well as a white rotation handle.   _____

6. You can reorganize slides in a presentation in the slide thumbnails pane or in this view.   _____

7. Copy selected slides in a presentation using this option from the New Slide button drop-down list.   _____

8. To select adjacent slides, click the first slide, hold down this key, and then click the last slide.

9. Click the New Slide button arrow and then click the *Reuse Slides* option at the drop-down list to display this.

10. Divide a presentation into these to easily navigate and edit slides in a presentation.

11. Display the Quick Access toolbar below the ribbon by clicking this button located at the right side of the toolbar and then clicking the *Show Below the Ribbon* option at the drop-down list.

12. This is the keyboard shortcut to display the PowerPoint Help window.

Skills Check Assess Your Performance

Assessment

1 CREATE AN ELECTRONIC DESIGN PRESENTATION

SNAP Grade It

1. Create the presentation shown in Figure 2.6 using the Wisp design theme and the second variant. (When typing bulleted text, press the Tab key to move the insertion point to the desired tab level.)
2. After creating the slides, complete a spelling check on the text in the slides.
3. Save the presentation into the PC2 folder on your storage medium and name the presentation **P-C2-A1-ElecDesign**.
4. Run the presentation.
5. Print the presentation as a handout with four slides printed horizontally per page.
6. Make the following changes to the presentation:
   a. Change to Slide Sorter view and then move Slide 3 between Slides 1 and 2.
   b. Move Slide 4 between Slides 2 and 3.
   c. Change to Normal view.
   d. Search for the word *document* and replace it with the word *brochure*. (After the replacements, make Slide 1 active and, if necessary, capitalize the "b" in *brochure*.)
   e. Add the Uncover transition and Hammer sound to each slide.
7. Save the presentation.
8. Display the Reuse Slides task pane, browse to the PC2 folder on your storage medium, and then double-click *LayoutTips.pptx*.
9. Insert the *Layout Punctuation Tips* slide below Slide 4.
10. Insert the *Layout Tips* slide below Slide 5.
11. Close the Reuse Slides task pane.
12. Find all occurrences of *Layout* and replace with *Design*. (Insert a check mark in the *Match case* check box.)
13. Move Slide 5 between Slides 1 and 2.
14. Move Slide 6 between Slides 2 and 3.

Figure 2.6 Assessment 1

Slide I	Title	=	Electronic Design and Production
	Subtitle	=	Designing a Document

Slide 2 Title = Creating Balance
Bullets =
- Symmetrical balance: Balancing similar elements equally on a page (centered alignment) of the document
- Asymmetrical balance: Balancing contrasting elements on a page of the document

Slide 3 Title = Creating Focus
Bullets =
- Creating focus with titles, headings, and subheads in a document
- Creating focus with graphic elements in a document
  - Clip art
  - Watermarks
  - Illustrations
  - Photographs
  - Charts
  - Graphs

Slide 4 Title = Providing Proportion
Bullets =
- Evaluating proportions in a document
- Sizing graphic elements in a document
- Using white space in a document

15. Change to Normal view and then save the presentation.
16. Print the presentation as a handout with six slides printed horizontally per page.
17. Beginning with Slide 2, create a section named *Design Tips*.
18. Beginning with Slide 4, create a section named *Design Features*.
19. Print only the Design Features section as a handout with four slides printed horizontally per page.
20. Save and then close **P-C2-A1-ElecDesign.pptx**.

Assessment

2 CREATE A NETIQUETTE PRESENTATION

SNAP Grade It

1. Create a presentation with the text shown in Figure 2.7 on the next page. You determine the slide layout. Apply the Organic design theme (in the Themes group) and the fourth variant (in the Variants group).
2. If necessary, size and move placeholders so the text is positioned attractively on the slide.
3. Select Slides 4 through 6 and then duplicate the slides.

Figure 2.7 Assessment 2

Slide l	Title	=	CONNECTING ONLINE
	Subtitle	=	Internet Applications
Slide 2	Title	=	Internet Community
	Bullets	=	• Email
			• Internet voice services
			• Moderated environments
			• Netiquette
Slide 3	Title	=	Netiquette Rule
	Subtitle	=	Remember you are dealing with people.
Slide 4	Title	=	Netiquette Rule
	Subtitle	=	Adhere to the same standards of behavior online that you follow in real life.
Slide 5	Title	=	Netiquette Rule
	Subtitle	=	Respect the privacy of others.
Slide 6	Title	=	Netiquette Rule
	Subtitle	=	Share expert knowledge.

4. Type the following text in place of the existing text in the identified slides:
   a. Slide 7: Select the placeholder netiquette rule text and then type **Do not plagiarize.**
   b. Slide 8: Select the netiquette rule text in the placeholder and then type **Respect and accept people's differences.**
   c. Slide 9: Select the netiquette rule text in the placeholder and then type **Respect others' time.**
5. Complete a spelling check on text in the presentation.
6. Save the presentation and name it **P-C2-A2-InternetApps**.
7. Print the presentation as a handout with six slides printed horizontally per page.
8. Make the following edits to the presentation:
   a. Display the presentation in Slide Sorter view.
   b. Move Slide 3 between Slide 5 and Slide 6.
   c. Move Slide 7 between Slide 3 and Slide 4.
9. Add the Split transition, the Click sound, and change the duration to 01.00 second for all slides in the presentation.
10. Save the presentation.
11. Run the presentation.
12. Print the presentation as a handout with nine slides printed horizontally per page.
13. Close **P-C2-A2-InternetApps.pptx**.

Assessment

3 DOWNLOAD A DESIGN THEME

1. If your computer is connected to the Internet, Office.com provides a number of design themes you can download to your computer. Display the New backstage area, click in the search text box, type **Digital blue tunnel presentation**, and then press Enter.
2. Click the *Digital blue tunnel presentation (widescreen)* template (all of the template name may not be visible) and then click the Create button.
3. When the design theme is downloaded and a presentation is opened with the design theme applied, open **P-C2-A2-InternetApps.pptx**.
4. Select the nine slides in the **P-C2-A2-InternetApps.pptx** presentation and then click the Copy button.
5. Click the PowerPoint button on the Taskbar and then click the thumbnail representing the presentation with the downloaded design theme applied.
6. Click the Paste button to paste the nine slides in the current presentation.
7. Delete Slide 1 and then select and delete Slides 10 through 19.
8. Scroll through and look at each slide and, if necessary, make any changes required so the text is positioned attractively on each slide.
9. Save the presentation and name it **P-C2-A3-InternetApps**.
10. Run the presentation.
11. Print the presentation as a handout with nine slides printed horizontally per page.
12. Close **P-C2-A3-InternetApps.pptx** and then close **P-C2-A2-InternetApps.pptx**.

Visual Benchmark   Demonstrate Your Proficiency

FORMATTING A PRESENTATION ON ONLINE LEARNING

1. Open **OnlineLearning.pptx** in the PC2 folder and then save the presentation with Save As and name it **P-C2-VB-OnlineLearning**.
2. Format the presentation so it appears as shown in Figure 2.8 on the next page with the following specifications:
   a. Apply the Parallax design theme and the fourth variant.
   b. Use the *Reuse Slides* option from the New Slide button drop-down list to insert the last two additional slides from the **Learning.pptx** presentation.
   c. Arrange the slides to match what you see in Figure 2.8. (Read the slides from left to right.)
   d. Size and/or move placeholders so text displays in each slide as shown in Figure 2.8.
3. Add a transition and sound of your choosing to each slide.
4. Run the presentation.
5. Print the presentation as a handout with six slides printed horizontally per page.
6. Save and then close **P-C2-VB-OnlineLearning.pptx**.

Figure 2.8 Visual Benchmark

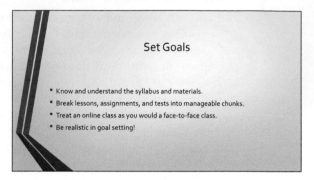

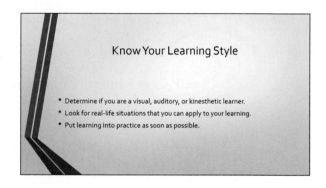

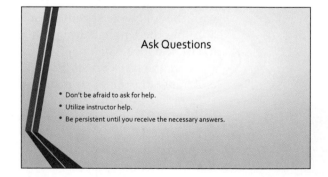

Case Study

Apply Your Skills

Part 1

You are the office manager at the Career Finders agency. One of your responsibilities is to conduct workshops to prepare individuals for the job search process. A coworker has given you a presentation for the workshop but the presentation needs some editing and modifying. Open **JobAnalysis.pptx** and then save the presentation with Save As and name it **P-C2-CS-JobAnalysis**. Check each slide in the presentation and then make modifications to maintain consistency in the size and location of placeholders (consider using the Reset button to reset the formatting and size of the placeholders), maintain consistency in heading text, move text from an overcrowded slide to a new slide, complete a spelling check, apply a design theme, and make any other modifications to improve the presentation. Save **P-C2-CS-JobAnalysis.pptx**.

Part 2

After reviewing the presentation, you realize that you need to include slides on resumes. Open the **ResumePres.pptx** presentation and then copy Slides 2 and 3 into the **P-C2-CS-JobAnalysis.pptx** presentation (at the end of the presentation). You want to add additional information on resume writing tips and decide to use the Internet to find information. Search for tips on writing a resume and then create a slide (or two) with the information you find. Add a transition and sound to all slides in the presentation. Save **P-C2-CS-JobAnalysis.pptx**.

Part 3

You know that Microsoft Word offers a number of resume templates you can download from the Office.com website. You decide to include information in the presentation on how to find and download resumes. Open Microsoft Word and then click the *Blank document* template at the Word 2013 opening screen. At the blank document, click the FILE tab and then click the *New* option. At the New backstage area, click in the search text box, type **resume**, and then press Enter. Scroll through the list of resume templates that displays and then experiment with downloading a template. With the **P-C2-CS-JobAnalysis.pptx** presentation open, add an additional slide to the end of the presentation that provides steps on how to download a resume in Microsoft Word. Print the presentation as a handout with six slides printed horizontally per page. Save, run, and then close the presentation.

PERFORMANCE OBJECTIVES

Upon successful completion of Chapter 3, you will be able to:
- Apply font and paragraph formatting to text in slides
- Apply formatting with the Mini toolbar and Format Painter
- Customize bullets and numbers
- Change page setup
- Customize slide backgrounds
- Create custom themes including custom theme colors and theme fonts
- Delete custom themes

Tutorials

3.1 Applying Formatting Using the Font Group

3.2 Applying Formatting Using the Font Dialog Box

3.3 Formatting with Format Painter

3.4 Changing Paragraph Formatting

3.5 Customizing Bullets and Numbering

3.6 Customizing Placeholders

3.7 Changing Page Setup

3.8 Changing Slide Size, Design Themes, and Background Styles

3.9 Creating and Deleting Custom Themes

The Font and Paragraph groups on the HOME tab contain a number of buttons and options for formatting text in slides. PowerPoint also provides a Mini toolbar and the Format Painter feature to help you format text. You can modify the design theme colors and fonts provided by PowerPoint and create your own custom themes. You will learn to use these features in this chapter along with how to change page setup options. Model answers for this chapter's projects appear on the following pages.

Note: Before beginning the projects, copy to your storage medium the PC3 subfolder from the PowerPoint folder on the CD that accompanies this textbook and then make PC3 the active folder.

Project 1 Format an E-Commerce Presentation

P-C3-P1-E-Commerce.pptx

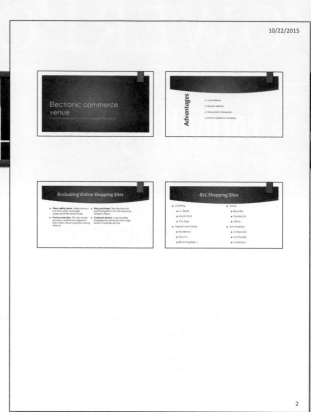

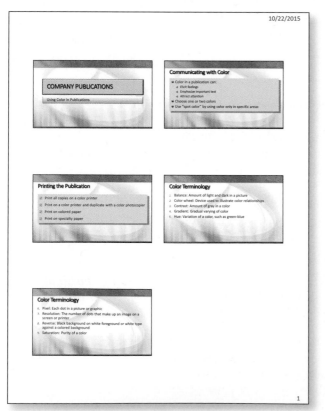

**Project 2 Customize Bullets and Numbers in a
Color Presentation**

P-C3-P2-ColorPres.pptx

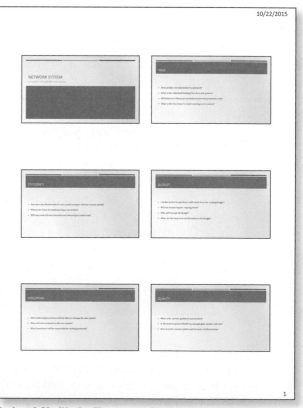

**Project 3 Modify the Theme and Slide Background of a
Network Presentation**

P-C3-P3-NetworkPres.pptx

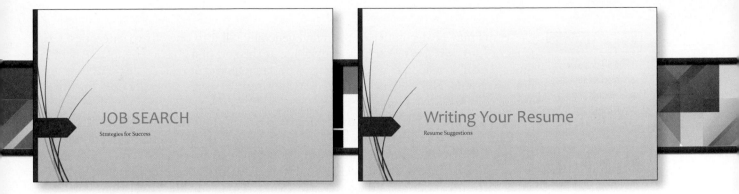

Project 4 Create and Apply Custom Themes to Presentations

P-C3-P4-JobSearch.pptx

P-C3-P4-ResumePres.pptx

Project **1** Format an E-Commerce Presentation   5 Parts

You will open an e-commerce presentation, apply font and paragraph formatting, apply formatting with Format Painter, apply column formatting to text in placeholders, and rotate and vertically align text in placeholders.

Formatting a Presentation ■■■■■■■■■■■■■■■■■■■

PowerPoint provides a variety of design themes you can apply to a presentation. These themes contain formatting such as font, color, and graphics. In some situations, the formatting provided by the theme is appropriate; in other situations, you may want to change or enhance the formatting of a slide in a presentation.

Applying Font Formatting

The Font group on the HOME tab contains a number of buttons for applying font formatting to text in a slide. Use these buttons to change the font, font size, and font color, as well as apply font effects. Table 3.1 describes the buttons in the Font group along with any keyboard shortcuts for applying font formatting.

Changing Fonts

Design themes apply a certain font (or fonts) to text in slides. You may want to change the font to change the mood of a presentation, enhance the visual appearance of slides, or increase the readability of the text. Change the font with the Font and Font Size buttons in the Font group on the HOME tab.

When you select text and then click the Font button arrow, a drop-down gallery displays with font options. Hover your mouse pointer over a font option and the selected text in the slide displays with the font applied. You can continue hovering your mouse pointer over different font options to see how the selected text displays in the specified font. The Font button drop-down gallery is an example of the *live preview* feature, which allows you to see how different formatting options look before you actually apply them. The live preview feature is also available when you click the Font Size button arrow.

Fonts may be decorative or plain and generally fall into one of two categories: *serif fonts* or *sans serif fonts*. A *serif* is a small line at the end of a character stroke. A serif font is easier to read and is generally used for large blocks of text. A sans serif font does not have serifs (*sans* is French for *without*). Sans serif fonts are generally used for titles and headings.

In addition to buttons in the Font group on the HOME tab, you can use options at the Font dialog box, shown in Figure 3.1, to apply character formatting to text. Display the Font dialog box by clicking the Font group dialog box launcher or with the keyboard shortcut Ctrl + Shift + F. (The dialog box launcher is the small button containing a diagonal arrow that displays in the lower right corner of the group.) Use options at the Font dialog box to choose a font, font style, and font size and to apply special effects to text in slides such as superscript, subscript, and double strikethrough.

Table 3.1 PowerPoint HOME Tab Font Group Buttons

Button	Name	Function	Keyboard Shortcut
B	Bold	Adds or removes bold formatting to or from selected text.	Ctrl + B
Aa ▾	Change Case	Changes the case of selected text.	Shift + F3
AV ▾	Character Spacing	Adjusts spacing between characters.	
	Clear All Formatting	Clears all character formatting from selected text.	Ctrl + Spacebar
A▾	Decrease Font Size	Decreases font size of selected text to next available smaller size.	Ctrl + Shift + <
Calibri (Body) ▾	Font	Changes selected text to a different font.	
A ▾	Font Color	Changes the font color for selected text.	
32 ▾	Font Size	Changes selected text to a different font size.	
A▴	Increase Font Size	Increases font size of selected text to next available larger size.	Ctrl + Shift + >
I	Italic	Adds or removes italic formatting to or from selected text.	Ctrl + I
abc	Strikethrough	Inserts or removes a line through the middle of selected text.	
S	Text Shadow	Adds or removes shadow formatting to or from selected text.	
U	Underline	Adds or removes underline formatting to or from selected text.	Ctrl + U

Figure 3.1 Font Dialog Box

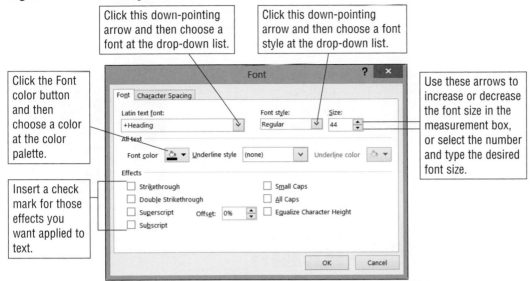

Click this down-pointing arrow and then choose a font at the drop-down list.

Click this down-pointing arrow and then choose a font style at the drop-down list.

Click the Font color button and then choose a color at the color palette.

Use these arrows to increase or decrease the font size in the measurement box, or select the number and type the desired font size.

Insert a check mark for those effects you want applied to text.

Formatting with the Mini Toolbar

When you select text, the Mini toolbar displays above the selected text. Click a button on the Mini toolbar to apply formatting to selected text. If you do not want the Mini toolbar to display when you select text, you can turn it off. To do this, click the FILE tab and then click *Options*. At the PowerPoint Options dialog box with the *General* option selected in the left panel, click the *Show Mini Toolbar on selection* check box to remove the check mark.

Project 1a   Applying Font Formatting to Text   Part 1 of 5

1. Open **E-Commerce.pptx** and then save the presentation with Save As and name it **P-C3-P1-E-Commerce**.
2. Apply the Ion Boardroom design theme with the green variant to the presentation by completing the following steps:
   a. Click the DESIGN tab.
   b. Click the More button located to the right of the theme thumbnails.
   c. Click the *Ion Boardroom* theme thumbnail.
   d. Click the green variant in the Variants group (second thumbnail).
3. Change the font formatting of the Slide 1 subtitle by completing the following steps:
   a. With Slide 1 active, click any character in the subtitle and then select *ONLINE SERVICES*.
   b. Click the HOME tab.
   c. Click the Font button arrow, scroll down the drop-down gallery, and then click *Cambria*.

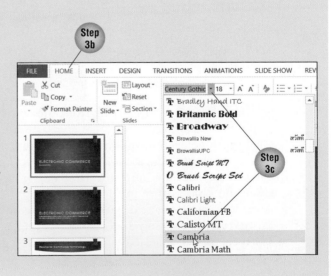

d. Click the Font Size button arrow and then click *40* at the drop-down gallery.
e. Click the Bold button in the Font group.
f. Click the Text Shadow button.
g. Click the Font Color button arrow and then click the *Dark Red, Accent 1, Darker 25%* option (fifth column, fifth row).

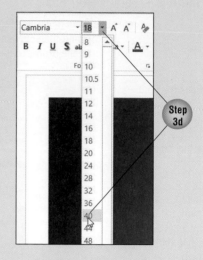

Step 3d

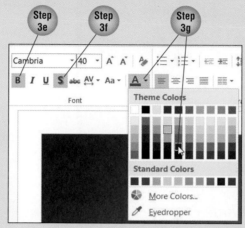

Step 3e Step 3f Step 3g

4. Change the size of the title text by completing the following steps:
   a. Click any character in the title *ELECTRONIC COMMERCE* and then click the placeholder border to change the border line to a solid line.
   b. Click once on the Decrease Font Size button in the Font group.
5. Change the case of the title text by completing the following steps:
   a. Make Slide 2 active.
   b. Click in the title *ELECTRONIC COMMERCE* and then click the placeholder border to change the border line to a solid line.
   c. Click the Change Case button in the Font group and then click *Capitalize Each Word* at the drop-down list.

Step 5c

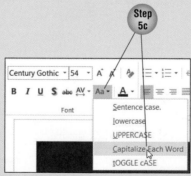

6. Apply and then clear formatting from the content text by completing the following steps:
   a. Make Slide 3 active.
   b. Click in the placeholder containing the bulleted text.
   c. Select *m-commerce* (located in parentheses).
   d. Click the Underline button in the Font group on the HOME tab.
   e. Click the Bold button in the Font group.
   f. After looking at the text with underlining and bold formatting applied, remove the formatting by clicking the Clear All Formatting button in the Font group.
   g. With the text still selected, click the Italic button in the Font group on the HOME tab.

7. Apply italic formatting with the
   Mini toolbar by completing the
   following steps:
   a. Select *B2C* in the second
      bulleted item and then click
      the Italic button on the Mini
      toolbar.
   b. Select *B2B* in the third bulleted
      item and then click the Italic
      button on the Mini toolbar.
8. Save **P-C3-P1-E-Commerce.pptx**.

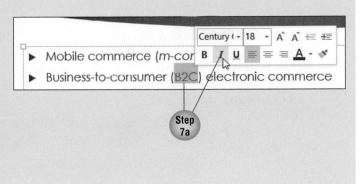

Step
7a

Formatting with Format Painter

If you apply character and/or paragraph formatting to text in a slide and want
to apply the same formatting to additional text in that slide or other slides, use
the Format Painter. With Format Painter, you can apply the same formatting in
more than one location in a slide or slides. To use the Format Painter, apply the
desired formatting to text, position the insertion point anywhere in the formatted
text, and then double-click the Format Painter button in the Clipboard group on
the HOME tab. Using the mouse, select the additional text to which you want to
apply the formatting. After applying the formatting in the desired locations, click
the Format Painter button to deactivate it. If you need to apply formatting in only
one other location, click the Format Painter button once. The first time you select
text, the formatting is applied and the Format Painter is deactivated.

▼ **Quick Steps**

**Format with Format
Painter**
1. Click text containing
   desired formatting.
2. Double-click Format
   Painter button.
3. Select or click on text.
4. Click Format Painter
   button.

Format
Painter

H I N T

You can also turn off
Format Painter by
pressing the Esc key.

Project 1b	**Applying Formatting with Format Painter**	**Part 2 of 5**

1. With **P-C3-P1-E-Commerce.pptx** open, make sure Slide 3 is active.
2. Apply formatting to the title by completing the following steps:
   a. Click in the title text and then click the placeholder border to change the border line to
      a solid line.
   b. Click the Font group dialog box launcher on the HOME tab.

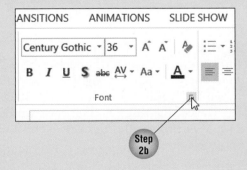

Step
2b

c. At the Font dialog box, click the down-pointing arrow at the right side of the *Latin text font* option box, scroll down the drop-down list, and then click *Candara*.

d. Click the down-pointing arrow at the right side of the *Font style* option box and then click *Bold Italic* at the drop-down list.

e. Select the current number in the *Size* measurement box and then type **40**.

f. Click OK to close the dialog box.

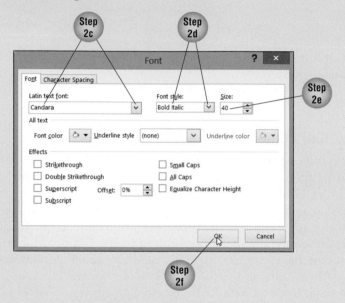

3. Click any character in the title.

4. Double-click the Format Painter button in the Clipboard group on the HOME tab.

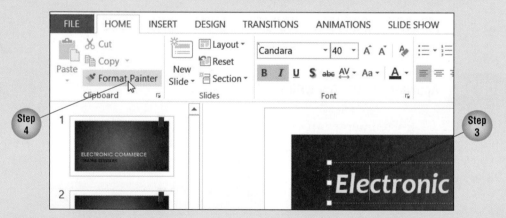

5. Make Slide 8 active.

6. Using the mouse, select the title *Advantages of Online Shopping*. (The mouse pointer displays as an I-beam with a paintbrush attached. Instead of selecting the whole title, you can also click each word in the title to apply the formatting. However, clicking individual words will not format the spaces between the words in multiple-word titles.)

7. Make Slide 9 active and then select the title (or click each word in the title).

8. Make Slide 10 active and then select the title (or click each word in the title).

9. Click the Format Painter button to deactivate it.

10. If necessary, deselect the text.

11. Save **P-C3-P1-E-Commerce.pptx**.

Formatting Paragraphs

The Paragraph group on the HOME tab contains a number of buttons for applying paragraph formatting to text in a slide, such as applying bullets and numbers, increasing and decreasing list levels, changing the horizontal and vertical alignment of text, changing line spacing, and rotating text in a placeholder. Table 3.2 describes the buttons in the Paragraph group along with any keyboard shortcuts.

Fitting Contents in a Placeholder

When text in a placeholder exceeds the size of the placeholder, you can use the AutoFit Options button to decrease the spacing between bulleted items or decrease the font size to ensure that all the text fits in the placeholder. The AutoFit Options button displays in the lower left corner of the placeholder when text no longer fits inside the placeholder. Click the AutoFit Options button to display a list of options such as *Autofit Text to Placeholder, Stop Fitting Text to This Placeholder, Split Between Two Slides, Continue on a New Slide, Change to Two Columns,* and *Control AutoCorrect Options.*

AutoFit Options

Table 3.2 Buttons in the Paragraph group on the HOME tab

Button	Name	Function	Keyboard Shortcut
	Bullets	Adds or removes bullets to or from selected text.	
	Numbering	Adds or removes numbers to or from selected text.	
	Decrease List Level	Moves text to the previous tab stop (level).	Shift + Tab
	Increase List Level	Moves text to the next tab stop (level).	Tab
	Line Spacing	Increases or reduces spacing between lines of text.	
	Align Left	Left-aligns text.	Ctrl + L
	Center	Center-aligns text.	Ctrl + E
	Align Right	Right-aligns text.	Ctrl + R
	Justify	Justifies text.	
	Add or Remove Columns	Splits text into two or more columns.	
	Text Direction	Rotates or stacks text.	
	Align Text	Changes the alignment of text within a text box.	
	Convert to SmartArt Graphic	Converts selected text to a SmartArt graphic.	

1. With **P-C3-P1-E-Commerce.pptx** open, change bullets by completing the following steps:
   a. Make Slide 3 active.
   b. Click any character in the bulleted text.
   c. Select the bulleted text.
   d. Click the Bullets button arrow in the Paragraph group on the HOME tab and then click the *Filled Square Bullets* option at the drop-down gallery.

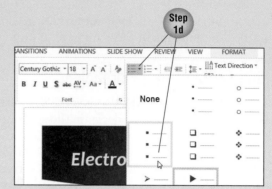

2. Change the bullets to letters by completing the following steps:
   a. Make Slide 8 active.
   b. Click any character in the bulleted text.
   c. Select the bulleted text.
   d. Click the Numbering button arrow in the Paragraph group on the HOME tab and then click the *A. B. C.* option at the drop-down gallery.

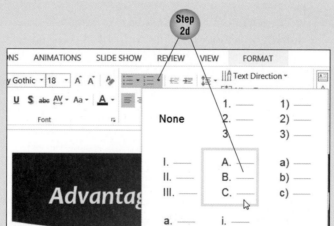

   e. After looking at the letters, change to numbers by clicking the Numbering button arrow and then clicking the *1. 2. 3.* option at the drop-down gallery.
3. Decrease and increase list levels by completing the following steps:
   a. With Slide 8 active and the numbered text selected, click the Increase List Level button in the Paragraph group on the HOME tab.
   b. With the text still selected, click the Font Color button arrow in the Font group on the HOME tab and then click *Teal, Accent 5, Darker 50%* at the drop-down gallery (ninth column, bottom row in the *Theme Colors* section).
   c. Make Slide 10 active.
   d. Click any character in the bulleted text.

e. Move the insertion point so it is positioned immediately left of the *N* in *Nordstrom*.

f. Click the Decrease List Level button in the Paragraph group on the HOME tab.

g. Move the insertion point so it is positioned immediately left of the *M* in *Macy's*.

h. Press Shift + Tab.

i. Move the insertion point so it is positioned immediately left of the first *L.* in *L.L. Bean*.

j. Click the Increase List Level button in the Paragraph group.

k. Move the insertion point so it is positioned immediately left of the *T* in *The Gap*.

l. Press the Tab key.

m. Complete similar steps to those in 3j or 3l to indent *Bloomingdale's, Expedia, Travelocity,* and *Orbitz* to the next level.

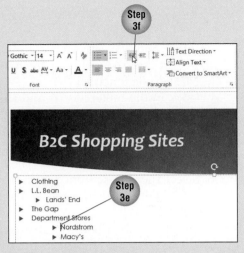

4. Increase the size of the text and make sure the content fits within the Slide 10 placeholder by completing the following steps:

a. With Slide 10 active, select all the bulleted items and then change the font size to 16 points.

b. Click anywhere in the bulleted text to deselect the text.

c. Click the AutoFit Options button that displays in the lower left corner of the placeholder and then click *AutoFit Text to Placeholder* at the drop-down list. (This decreases the spacing between the bulleted items to ensure all items fit in the placeholder.)

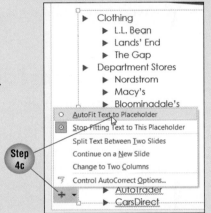

5. Change the line spacing of the text by completing the following steps:

a. Make Slide 3 active.

b. Click in the bulleted text and then select the bulleted text.

c. Click the Line Spacing button in the Paragraph group on the HOME tab and then click *1.5* at the drop-down list.

d. Make Slide 8 active.

e. Click in the numbered text and then select the numbered text.

f. Click the Line Spacing button and then click *2.0* at the drop-down list.

6. Change paragraph alignment by completing the following steps:

a. Make Slide 3 active, click any character in the title, and then click the Center button in the Paragraph group.

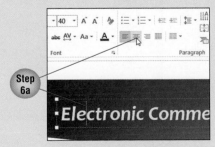

b. Make Slide 8 active, click any character in the title, and then click the Center button.
c. Make Slide 9 active, click any character in the title, and then click the Center button.
d. Make Slide 10 active, click any character in the title, and then click the Center button.
7. Split text into two columns by completing the following steps:
a. Make Slide 9 active.
b. Click in the bulleted text and then select the bulleted text.
c. Click the Add or Remove Columns button in the Paragraph group and then click *Two Columns* at the drop-down list.

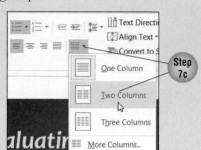

d. Select the first sentence in the first bulleted paragraph (*Clear selling terms.*) and then click the Bold button.
e. Select and then bold the first sentence in each of the remaining bulleted paragraphs in Slide 9.
f. Drag the bottom border of the bulleted text placeholder up until two bulleted items display in each column.
8. Save **P-C3-P1-E-Commerce.pptx**.

Customizing Paragraphs

Line Spacing

If you want more control over paragraph alignment, indenting, and spacing, click the Paragraph group dialog box launcher. This displays the Paragraph dialog box, as shown in Figure 3.2. You can also display this dialog box by clicking the Line Spacing button in the Paragraph group and then clicking *Line Spacing Options* at the drop-down list. Use options at this dialog box to specify text alignment, paragraph indentation, spacing before and after paragraphs, and line spacing.

Figure 3.2 Paragraph Dialog Box

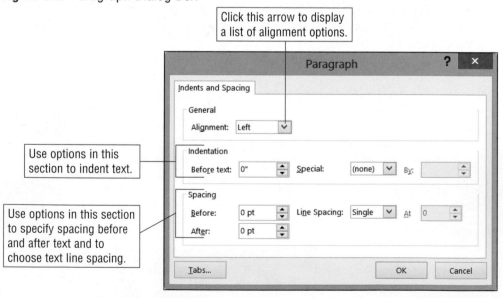

Customizing Columns

Click the Add or Remove Columns button in the Paragraph group to specify one, two, or three columns for your text. If you want to use more than three columns or if you want to control spacing between columns, click the *More Columns* option at the drop-down list. This displays the Columns dialog box, as shown in Figure 3.3. With options in this dialog box, you can specify the number of columns and the amount of spacing between them.

Add or Remove
Columns

Format text into columns to make it attractive and easy to read.

Figure 3.3 Columns Dialog Box

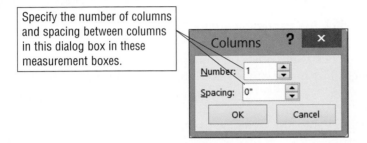

Specify the number of columns and spacing between columns in this dialog box in these measurement boxes.

Project 1d   Customizing Paragraph and Column Formatting   **Part 4 of 5**

1. With **P-C3-P1-E-Commerce.pptx** open, change line and paragraph spacing by completing the following steps:
   a. Make Slide 3 active.
   b. Click in the bulleted text and then select the bulleted text.
   c. Click the Paragraph group dialog box launcher.
   d. At the Paragraph dialog box, click three times on the up-pointing arrow at the right side of the *Before text* measurement box in the *Indentation* section. (This inserts *0.6"* in the measurement box.)
   e. Click twice on the up-pointing arrow at the right side of the *After* measurement box in the *Spacing* section. (This inserts *12 pt* in the box.)
   f. Click the down-pointing arrow at the right side of the *Line Spacing* option box and then click *Multiple* at the drop-down list.
   g. Select the current measurement in the *At* measurement box and then type **1.8**.
   h. Click OK.

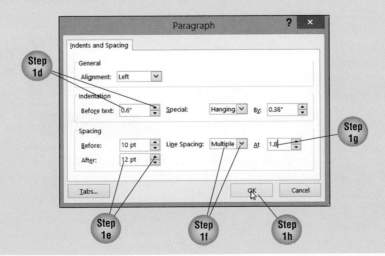

2. Format text in columns by completing the following steps:
   a. Make Slide 10 active.
   b. Click in the bulleted text and then select the text.
   c. Click the Add or Remove Columns button in the Paragraph group and then click *More Columns* at the drop-down list.
   d. At the Columns dialog box, click once on the up-pointing arrow at the right side of the *Number* measurement box. (This inserts a *2* in the measurement box.)

   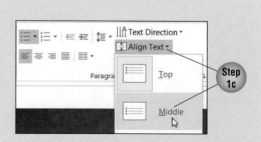

   e. Click the up-pointing arrow at the right side of the *Spacing* measurement box until *0.5"* displays in the measurement box.
   f. Click OK.
   g. With the text still selected, click the Paragraph group dialog box launcher.
   h. At the Paragraph dialog box, click three times on the up-pointing arrow at the right side of the *After* measurement box in the *Spacing* section. (This inserts *18 pt* in the measurement box.)
   i. Click OK.
3. With the bulleted text selected, change the font size to 20 points.
4. Save **P-C3-P1-E-Commerce.pptx**.

Rotating and Vertically Aligning Text

Text Direction

Align Text

If you click the Text Direction button in the Paragraph group on the HOME tab, a drop-down list displays with options for rotating and stacking text. Click the Align Text button in the Paragraph group and a drop-down list displays with options for changing the alignment to the top, middle, or bottom of the placeholder.

Project 1e Rotating and Vertically Aligning Text   Part 5 of 5

1. With **P-C3-P1-E-Commerce.pptx** open, change the vertical alignment of text by completing the following steps:
   a. Make Slide 3 active.
   b. Click any character in the bulleted text.
   c. Click the Align Text button in the Paragraph group on the HOME tab and then click *Middle* at the drop-down list.
2. Make Slide 8 active and then modify the slide so it displays as shown in Figure 3.4 on page 94 by completing the following steps:
   a. Click in the numbered text and then select the numbered text.
   b. Click the Bullets button arrow and then click the *Hollow Square Bullets* option.
   c. Decrease the size of the bulleted text placeholder so the placeholder borders display just outside the text.

d. Drag the placeholder to the middle of the slide until the guideline (a vertical dashed line) displays and then release the mouse button. (Refer to Figure 3.4 for the postion of the placeholder.)

e. Click any character in the title *Advantages of Online Shopping*.

f. Delete the text *of Online Shopping*.

g. Select *Advantages* and then change the font size to 54 points.

h. Drag the right border of the placeholder to the left so it is positioned just outside the text.

i. Click the Text Direction button in the Paragraph group and then click *Rotate all text 270°*.

j. Using the sizing handles that display around the title placeholder, increase the height and decrease the width of the placeholder and then drag the placeholder so the title displays as shown in Figure 3.4. Use the horizontal guideline (a dashed line) to help you vertically center the placeholder on the slide.

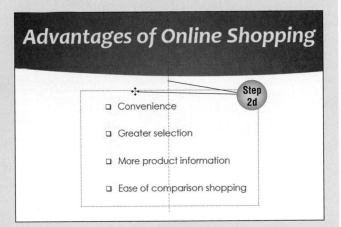

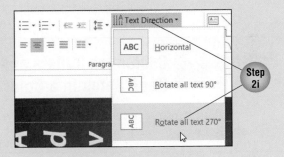

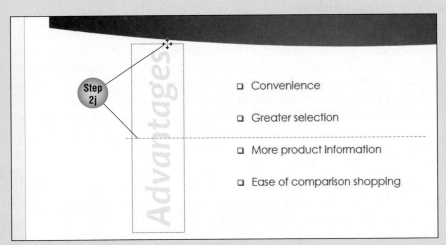

k. With the title placeholder selected, click the Font Color button arrow in the Font group and then click *Dark Red, Accent 1, Darker 25%* at the drop-down gallery (fifth column, fifth row in the *Theme Colors* section).

3. Apply a transition and sound to all slides in the presentation.

4. Print the presentation as a handout with six slides printed horizontally per page.

5. Save and then close **P-C3-P1-E-Commerce.pptx**.

Figure 3.4 Project 1e, Slide 8

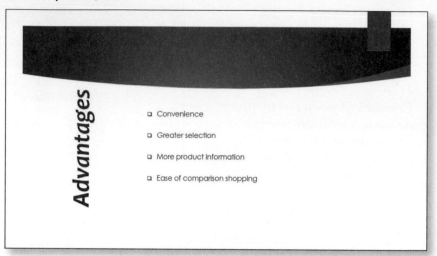

Project 2 Customize Bullets and Numbers and Change   **4 Parts**
Page Setup in a Color Presentation

You will open a presentation on using colors in publications and then create and apply custom bullets and numbering.

Customizing Bullets

Each design theme contains a Title and Content slide layout with bullets. The appearance and formatting of the bullets vary with each design theme. You can choose to use the bullet style provided by the design theme, or you can create custom bullets. Customize bullets with options at the Bullets and Numbering dialog box with the Bulleted tab selected, as shown in Figure 3.5. Display this dialog box by clicking in a placeholder containing a bulleted list, clicking the Bullets button arrow in the Paragraph group on the HOME tab, and then clicking *Bullets and Numbering* at the drop-down gallery.

Figure 3.5 Bullets and Numbering Dialog Box with Bulleted Tab Selected

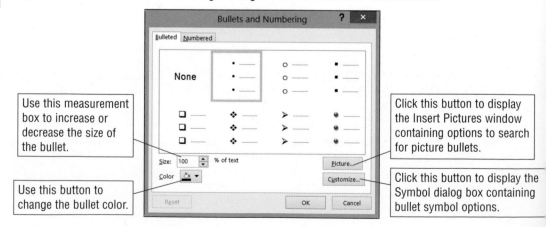

At the Bullets and Numbering dialog box, choose one of the predesigned bullets from the list box, change the size of the bullets (measured by percentage in relation to the size of the text), change the bullet color, and/or specify a picture or symbol to use as a bullet. Click the Picture button located toward the bottom of the dialog box and the Insert Pictures window displays. Click the Browse button to the right of the *From a file* option, navigate to the desired folder in the Insert Picture dialog box, and then double-click the desired picture. You can also search for images online in the Insert Pictures window. Click the Customize button located toward the bottom of the Bullets and Numbering dialog box and the Symbol dialog box displays. Choose a symbol bullet option at the Symbol dialog box and then click OK. Picture or symbol bullets are particularly effective for adding visual interest to a presentation.

To insert a new, blank bullet point in a bulleted list, press Enter. If you want to move the insertion point down to the next line without inserting a new bullet, press Shift + Enter. This inserts a line break without inserting a bullet. A new bullet will be inserted the next time you press Enter.

HINT
Choose a custom bullet that matches the theme or mood of the presentation.

Project 2a　**Customizing Bullets and Numbers**　　　　　　　　**Part 1 of 4**

1. Open **ColorPres.pptx** and then save the presentation with Save As and name it **P-C3-P2-ColorPres**.
2. Increase the list level of text and create custom bullets by completing the following steps:
   a. Make Slide 2 active.
   b. Select the second, third, and fourth bulleted paragraphs.
   c. Click the Increase List Level button in the Paragraph group on the HOME tab.
   d. With the three bulleted paragraphs still selected, click the Bullets button arrow and then click *Bullets and Numbering* at the drop-down list.
   e. At the Bullets and Numbering dialog box with the Bulleted tab selected, select the current number (*100*) in the *Size* measurement box and then type **75**.
   f. Click the Picture button located toward the bottom right corner of the dialog box.
   g. At the Insert Pictures window, click in the search text box to the right of *Office.com Clip Art*, type **colorful bullet icon**, and then press Enter.
   h. When the search results display, double-click the colorful, round bullet, as shown at the right.
3. Insert symbol bullets by completing the following steps:
   a. Make Slide 3 active.
   b. Select all of the bulleted text.
   c. Click the Bullets button arrow and then click *Bullets and Numbering* at the drop-down list.
   d. At the Bullets and Numbering dialog box with the Bulleted tab selected, click the down-pointing arrow at the right side of the *Size* measurement box until *80* displays.
   e. Click the Customize button located toward the bottom right corner of the dialog box.

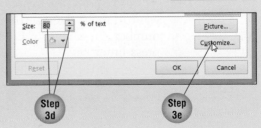

f. At the Symbol dialog box, click the down-pointing arrow at the right side of the *Font* option box, scroll down the drop-down list, and then click *Wingdings*. (This option is located toward the bottom of the list.)

g. Scroll to the bottom of the list box until the last row of symbols displays and then click the second symbol from the right in the bottom row (a check mark inside of a square).

h. Click OK.

i. At the Bullets and Numbering dialog box, click the Color button and then click *Purple, Accent 6* (last column, first row in the *Theme Colors* section).

j. Click OK to close the Bullets and Numbering dialog box. (This applies the purple check mark symbol bullets to the selected text.)

4. Increase the spacing between the bullets and the text by completing these steps:

a. With the bulleted text selected, click the Paragraph group dialog box launcher.

b. At the Paragraph dialog box, select the current measurement in the *By* measurement box (located in the *Indentation* section), type **0.6**, and then press Enter.

5. Save **P-C3-P2-ColorPres.pptx**.

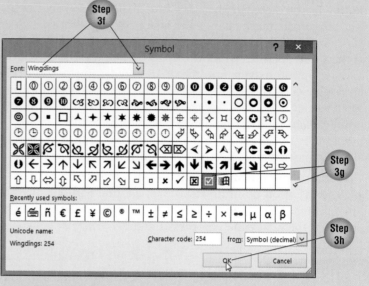

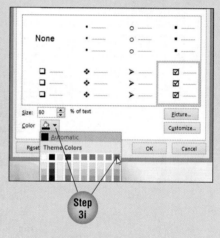

Customizing Numbering

Click the Numbering button arrow in the Paragraph group and several numbering options display in a drop-down gallery. Customize numbering with options at the Bullets and Numbering dialog box with the Numbered tab selected, as shown in Figure 3.6. Display this dialog box by clicking the Numbering button arrow and then clicking *Bullets and Numbering* at the drop-down gallery. Use options at this dialog box to change the size and color of numbers as well as the starting number.

To insert a new, blank numbered item in a numbered list, press Enter. If you want to move the insertion point down to the next line without inserting the next number, press Shift + Enter. The next number will be inserted the next time you press Enter.

Figure 3.6 Bullets and Numbering Dialog Box with Numbered Tab Selected

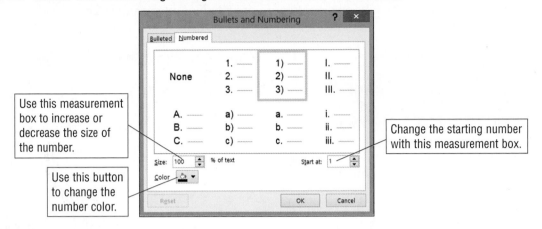

Use this measurement box to increase or decrease the size of the number.

Use this button to change the number color.

Change the starting number with this measurement box.

Project 2b **Customizing Numbers**   Part 2 of 4

1. With **P-C3-P2-ColorPres.pptx** open, make sure the presentation displays in Normal view.
2. Create and insert custom numbers by completing the following steps:
   a. Make Slide 4 active.
   b. Select the bulleted text in the slide.
   c. Click the Numbering button arrow in the Paragraph group on the HOME tab and then click the *Bullets and Numbering* option at the drop-down list.
   d. At the Bullets and Numbering dialog box with the Numbered tab selected, click the *1. 2. 3.* option (second option from the left in the top row).
   e. Select the number in the *Size* measurement box and then type 80.
   f. Click the Color button and then click *Purple, Accent 6* (last column, first row in the *Theme Colors* section).
   g. Click OK.

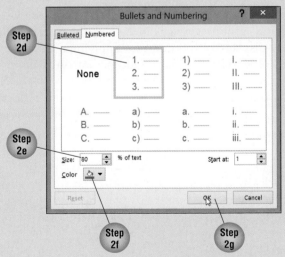

Step 2d

Step 2e

Step 2f

Step 2g

   h. Make Slide 5 active.
   i. Select the bulleted text in the slide.
   j. Click the Numbering button arrow and then click the *Bullets and Numbering* option at the drop-down list.

k. At the Bullets and Numbering dialog box with the Numbered tab selected, click the *1. 2. 3.* option (second option from the left in the top row).

l. Select the number in the *Size* measurement box and then type **80**.

m. Click the Color button and then click *Purple, Accent 6* (last column, first row in the *Theme Colors* section).

n. Click the up-pointing arrow at the right of the *Start at* measurement box until *6* displays.

o. Click OK.

3. Add a transition and sound of your choosing to all slides in the presentation.

4. Run the presentation.

5. Save **P-C3-P2-ColorPres.pptx**.

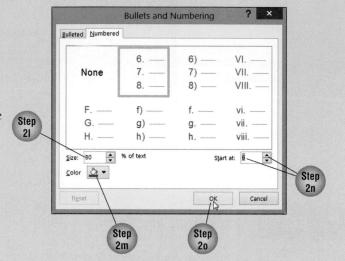

Customizing Placeholders

HINT

You can also use options on the DRAWING TOOLS FORMAT tab to customize a placeholder.

Quick Styles

Arrange

Shape Fill

Shape Outline

Shape Effects

▼ **Quick Steps**

Apply Color with the Eyedropper
1. Click desired object.
2. Click Shape Fill button.
3. Click *Eyedropper*.
4. Click desired color.

Customize a placeholder in a slide with buttons in the Drawing group on the HOME tab. Use options in the Drawing group to choose a shape, arrange the placeholder, apply a quick style, change the shape fill and outline colors, and apply a shape effect.

Click the Quick Styles button in the Drawing group and a drop-down gallery of styles displays. Choose a quick style from this gallery or click the *Other Theme Fills* option to display a side menu with additional fills. Arrange, align, and rotate a placeholder with options at the Arrange button drop-down list. Use the Shape Fill button to apply a fill to a placeholder. Click the Shape Fill button arrow and a drop-down gallery displays with options for applying a color, picture, gradient, or texture to the placeholder. Use the Shape Outline button to apply an outline to a placeholder and specify the outline color, weight, and style. With the Shape Effects button, you can choose from a variety of effects such as shadow, reflection, glow, and soft edges.

Both the Shape Fill and Shape Outline buttons in the Drawing group contain drop-down galleries with the *Eyedropper* option. Use the eyedropper to capture an exact color from one object and apply it to another object in the slide. To use the eyedropper to apply a fill color, click the object to which you want to apply fill color, click the Shape Fill button arrow, and then click *Eyedropper* at the drop-down gallery. The mouse pointer displays as an eyedropper. Position the tip of the eyedropper on the desired color and then click the mouse button. The color you click on is applied to the selected object. As you move the eyedropper, a live preview box displays above and to the right of the eyedropper. Use this live preview box to make sure you are pointing to the desired color. To pick a color outside the slide pane, hold down the Ctrl key, hold down the left mouse button, and then drag outside the slide pane. Position the tip of the eyedropper on the desired color and then release the mouse button and the Ctrl key. The *Eyedropper* option is also available with the Shape Fill, Shape Outline, and Font Color buttons on the HOME tab as well as with buttons on other tabs that apply color.

Customizing Placeholders at the Format Shape Task Pane

With options in the Format Shape task pane, apply shape options to a placeholder or apply text options to the text within a placeholder. The SHAPE OPTIONS tab of the Format Shape task pane displays three icons: Fill & Line, Effects, and Size & Properties, each with different options for formatting a placeholder. After clicking an icon, you may need to display (expand) the formatting options within the icons. For example, click *FILL* with the Fill & Line icon selected on the SHAPE OPTIONS tab to display options for applying a fill to a placeholder, as shown in Figure 3.7. The TEXT OPTIONS tab of the Format Shape task pane displays three icons: Text Fill & Outline, Text Effects, and Textbox, each with different options for formatting text within a placeholder. Display the Format Shape task pane by clicking the Drawing group task pane launcher on the HOME tab.

Align text in a placeholder with options at the Format Shape task pane with the Size & Properties icon selected. Scroll down the task pane list box to display the *TEXT BOX* section. With options in this section, you can align text in a placeholder as well as change text direction, autofit contents, and change internal margins.

When you apply formatting to a placeholder, you may need to move text within the placeholder. You can do this with the margin measurements in the Format Shape task pane. Display the margin measurements by clicking the Size & Properties icon and then scrolling down the task pane list box to the *TEXT BOX* section. Use the *Left margin*, *Right margin*, *Top margin*, and *Bottom margin* measurement boxes to specify internal margins for text inside a placeholder.

Figure 3.7 Format Shape Task Pane with SHAPE OPTIONS Tab Selected

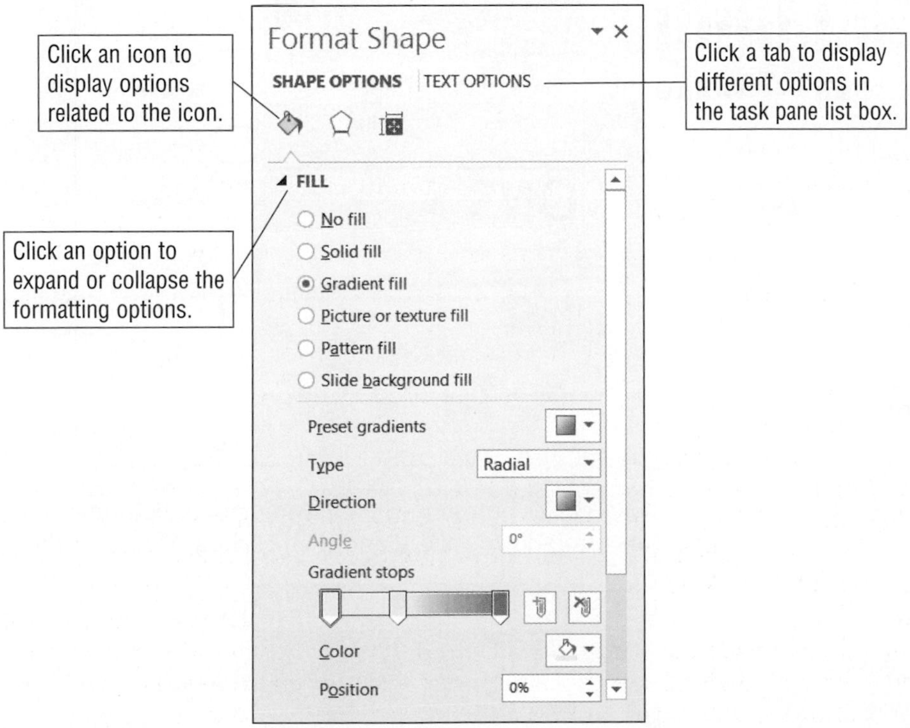

1. With **P-C3-P2-ColorPres.pptx** open, customize the title placeholder in Slide 1 by completing the following steps:
   a. If necessary, make Slide 1 active.
   b. Click in the title to select the placeholder.
   c. If necessary, click the HOME tab.
   d. Click the Quick Styles button in the Drawing group.
   e. Click the *Subtle Effect - Purple, Accent 6* option at the drop-down gallery (last column, fourth row).
   f. Click the Shape Outline button arrow in the Drawing group and then click *Purple, Accent 6, Darker 50%* (last column, last row in the *Theme Colors* section).
   g. Click the Shape Outline button arrow, point to *Weight*, and then click *3 pt* at the side menu.
   h. Click the Shape Effects button, point to *Bevel*, and then click *Cool Slant* at the side menu (fourth column, first row in the *Bevel* section).

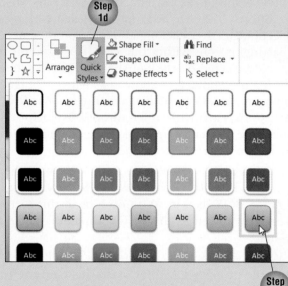

Step 1d

Step 1e

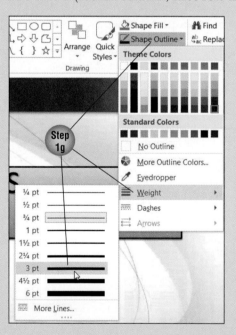

Step 1g

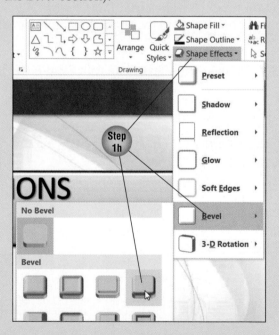

Step 1h

   i. Change the fill color by clicking the Quick Styles button in the Drawing group, pointing to *Other Theme Fills* at the bottom of the drop-down gallery, and then clicking *Style 6* at the side menu (second column, second row).

2. Change the alignment of the text within the placeholder by completing the following steps:
   a. With the title placeholder selected, click the Drawing group task pane launcher.
   b. At the Format Shape task pane with the SHAPE OPTIONS tab selected, click the Size & Properties icon.
   c. Click *TEXT BOX* to display the list of options.
   d. Click the down-pointing arrow at the right of the *Vertical alignment* option and then click *Middle* at the drop-down list.
   e. Click the up-pointing arrow at the right side of the *Left margin* measurement box until *0.5"* displays in the measurement box.
3. Close the Format Shape task pane by clicking the Close button in the upper right corner of the task pane.
4. Customize the subtitle placeholder by completing the following steps:
   a. Click in the subtitle text to select the placeholder.
   b. Click the Shape Fill button arrow in the Drawing group, point to *Texture*, and then click *Blue tissue paper* at the drop-down gallery (first column, fifth row).
   c. Click the Shape Effects button, point to *Bevel*, and then click *Cool Slant* at the side menu (fourth column, first row in the *Bevel* section).
5. You decide the texture fill does not match the theme of the presentation. Change the subtitle placeholder fill by completing the following steps:
   a. With the subtitle placeholder selected, click the Drawing group task pane launcher.
   b. Make sure the SHAPE OPTIONS tab is selected, click the Fill & Line icon, and then click *FILL* to display the list of options options.
   c. Click *Gradient fill*.
   d. Click the Preset gradients button and then click *Light Gradient, Accent 6* (sixth column, first row).
6. At the Format Shape task pane, click the Size & Properties icon, make sure the *TEXT BOX* options display, click the down-pointing arrow at the ride of the *Vertical alignment* option, and then click *Middle* at the drop-down list.

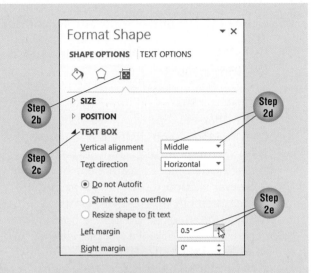

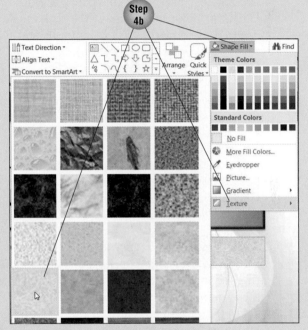

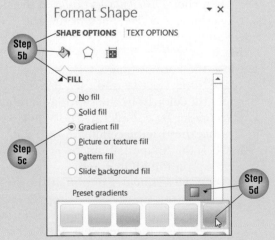

7. Click the up-pointing arrow at the right side of the *Left margin* measurement box until *0.5″* displays in the measurement box.

8. Make Slide 3 active and then change the spacing after paragraphs by completing the following steps:
   a. Select the bulleted text.
   b. Click the Paragraph group dialog box launcher.
   c. At the Paragraph dialog box, click twice on the up-pointing arrow at the right side of the *After* measurement box in the *Spacing* section to display *12 pt* in the measurement box.
   d. Click OK to close the dialog box.

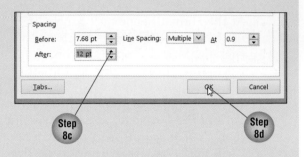

Step 8c

Step 8d

9. Customize and arrange the placeholder by completing the following steps:
   a. With the bulleted text placeholder selected and the Format Shape task pane open, click the Fill & Line icon, make sure the *FILL* options display, and then click *Solid fill*.
   b. Click the Color button and then click *Purple, Accent 6, Lighter 80%* (last column, second row in the *Theme Colors* section).
   c. Click the Effects icon and then click *SHADOW* to display the list of options.
   d. Click the Presets button and then click *Offset Diagonal Bottom Right* (first column, first row in *Outer* section).
   e. Click the Color button and then click *Purple, Accent 6, Darker 50%* (last column, bottom row in *Theme Colors* section).
   f. Click the up-pointing arrow at the right of the *Distance* measurement box until *15 pt* displays.
   g. Click the Size & Properties icon, make sure the *TEXT BOX* options display, and then change the left, top, and bottom measurements to 0.2 inches.
   h. Click the Arrange button in the Drawing group on the HOME tab, point to *Align* in the drop-down list, and then click *Distribute Vertically* in the side menu.

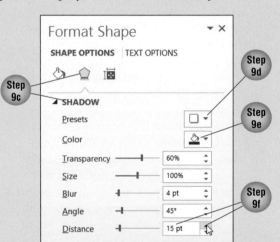

Step 9c

Step 9d

Step 9e

Step 9f

10. Make Slide 2 active, click in the bulleted text, and then customize and arrange the placeholder by completing the steps in Step 9.

11. Close the Format Shape task pane.

12. Make Slide 1 active and then use the eyedropper to apply fill color from the subtitle placeholder to the title placeholder by completing the following steps:
    a. Click the title placeholder.
    b. Click the Shape Fill button arrow in the Drawing group on the HOME tab.
    c. Click the *Eyedropper* option at the drop-down gallery.
    d. Position the tip of the eyedropper on the purple color below the word *Publications* in the subtitle placeholder and then click the left mouse button.

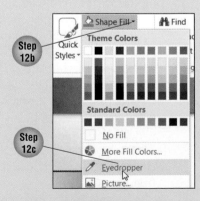

Step 12b

Step 12c

Step 12d

13. Run the presentation.
14. Print the presentation as a handout with six slides printed horizontally per page.
15. Save **P-C3-P2-ColorPres.pptx**.

Changing Page Setup ■■■■■■■■■■■■■■■■■■■■■■■■

Control page setup and the orientation of slides with options in the Slide Size dialog box, as shown in Figure 3.8. Display the Slide Size dialog box by clicking the Slide Size button in the Customize group on the DESIGN tab and then clicking *Custom Slide Size* at the drop-down list. With options in the dialog box, change slide orientation, specify how you want the slides sized, change the slide size ratio, and change the starting slide number. By default, slides are sized for an on-screen show with a widescreen 16:9 ratio. If you change a widescreen size (16:9) presentation to a standard size (4:3) presentation, you will need to maximize the size of the content to fit in the new slide size or scale down the slide content to ensure that all content fits on the new slide. Click the down-pointing arrow at the right side of the *Slides sized for* option box and a drop-down list displays with options for changing the slide size ratio and choosing other paper sizes. You can also change the orientation of notes, handouts, and outline pages.

Slide Size

Figure 3.8 Slide Size Dialog Box

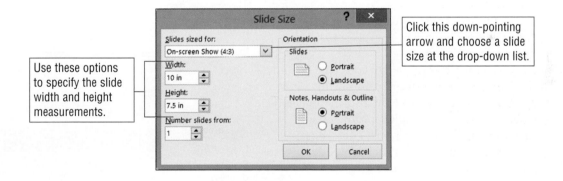

Use these options to specify the slide width and height measurements.

Click this down-pointing arrow and choose a slide size at the drop-down list.

| Project 2d | **Changing Orientation and Page Setup** | **Part 4 of 4** |

1. With **P-C3-P2-ColorPres.pptx** open, change the slide size by completing the following steps:
   a. Click the DESIGN tab.
   b. Click the Slide Size button in the Customize group and then click *Standard (4:3)* at the drop-down list.
   c. At the Microsoft PowerPoint dialog box, click the Ensure Fit button.

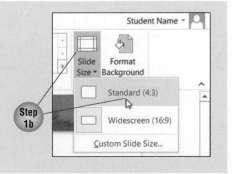

Step 1b

2. Run the presentation and notice how the slides appear in the standard size.
3. Change the slide orientation by completing the following steps:
   a. Click the Slide Size button in the Customize group and then click *Custom Slide Size* at the drop-down list.
   b. At the Slide Size dialog box, click the *Portrait* option in the *Slides* section, and then click OK.
   c. Click the Ensure Fit button at the Microsoft PowerPoint dialog box.
4. Run the presentation and notice how the slides appear in portrait orientation.
5. After running the presentation, change the page setup by completing the following steps:
   a. Click the Slide Size button and then click *Custom Slide Size* at the drop-down list.
   b. At the Slide Size dialog box, click the *Landscape* option in the Slides section.
   c. Click the down-pointing arrow at the right side of the *Slides sized for* option box and then click *On-screen Show (16:10)*. (Notice that the slide height changed from *10* to *6.25* in the *Height* measurement box.)
   d. Click OK.
   e. Click the Maximize button at the Microsoft PowerPoint dialog box.
6. Run the presentation.
7. Specify slide width and height and change slide numbering by completing the following steps:
   a. Click the Slide Size button and then click *Custom Slide Size* at the drop-down list.
   b. At the Slide Size dialog box, click the down-pointing arrow at the right side of the *Width* measurement box until *9 in* displays in the box.
   c. Click the down-pointing arrow at the right side of the *Height* measurement box until *6 in* displays in the box.
   d. Click the up-pointing arrow to the right of the *Number slides from* measurement box until *6* displays.
   e. Click OK.
   f. Click the Ensure Fit button at the Microsoft PowerPoint dialog box.
8. Notice the slide numbering in the slide thumbnails pane begins with Slide 6.
9. Run the presentation.
10. Save and then close **P-C3-P2-ColorPres.pptx**.

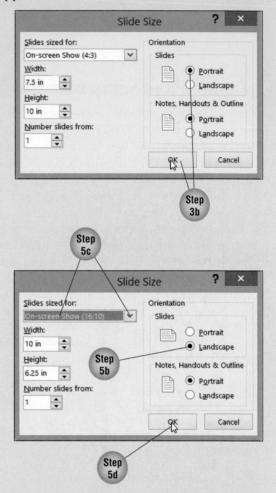

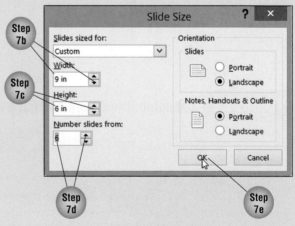

Project ▨ **Modify the Theme and Slide Background of a**   **1 Part**
               Network Presentation

You will open a network presentation, apply a design theme, and then change the
theme colors and fonts. You will also apply and customize a background style.

Modifying Theme Colors and Fonts ■■■■■■■■■■■■■■■

A design theme is a set of formatting choices that includes a color theme (a set of
colors), a font theme (heading and text fonts), and an effects theme (a set of lines
and fill effects). Click the More button located to the right of the Variants group
on the DESIGN tab to display options for changing design theme colors, fonts,
and effects.

A theme contains specific color formatting you can change with color options.
Display color options by clicking the More button at the right side of the Variants
group. At the drop-down menu that displays, point to the *Colors* option and a
drop-down gallery displays with named color schemes. Each theme applies specific
fonts, which you can change with options from the Fonts option in the More
drop-down list in the Variants group. Point to this option and a drop-down gallery
displays with font choices. Each font group in the drop-down gallery contains two
choices. The first choice in the group is the font that is applied to slide titles and
the second choice is the font that is applied to slide subtitles and text. If you are
formatting a presentation that contains graphic elements such as illustrations,
pictures, clip art, or text boxes, you can specify theme effects at the Effects option
drop-down gallery in the Variants group.

HINT

Themes are shared
across Office programs
such as PowerPoint,
Word, and Excel.

Customizing Slide Backgrounds ■■■■■■■■■■■■■■■

Format a slide background with background styles or with options at the Format
Background task pane. Display background styles by clicking the More button in
the Variants group on the DESIGN tab and then pointing to the *Background Styles*
option. Apply a background style by clicking an option at the side menu.

Click the Format Background button in the Customize group on the DESIGN
tab to display the Format Background task pane, as shown in Figure 3.9. With
options in the Format Background task pane you can apply fill, effects, or a
picture to a slide background. Apply the desired slide background to all slides in
the presentation by clicking the Apply to All button located toward the bottom
of the task pane. If you make changes to the slide background, you can reset
the background to the default by clicking the Reset Background button located
toward the bottom of the Format Background task pane.

Some of the design themes provided by PowerPoint contain a background
graphic. You can remove this graphic from a slide by clicking the *Hide background
graphics* check box in the *FILL* section of the Format Background task pane with
the Fill icon selected and then clicking the Apply to All button.

▼ **Quick Steps**

**Change a Slide
Background**
1. Click DESIGN tab.
2. Click Format
   Background button.
3. Make desired changes
   at Format Background
   task pane.

Format
Background

Figure 3.9 Format Background Task Pane

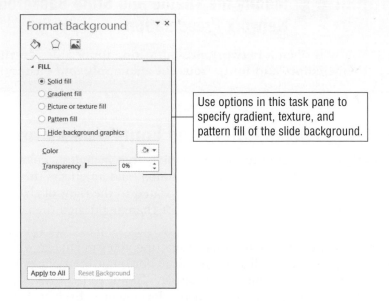

Use options in this task pane to specify gradient, texture, and pattern fill of the slide background.

Project 3 Customizing Theme Colors, Theme Fonts, and Slide Background Part 1 of 1

1. Open **NetworkPres.pptx** and then save the presentation with Save As and name it **P-C3-P3-NetworkPres.pptx**.
2. Apply a design theme by completing the following steps:
   a. Click the DESIGN tab.
   b. Click the More button at the right side of the design theme thumbnails and then click *Dividend* at the drop-down gallery.
3. Change the theme colors by clicking the More button located to the right of the Variants group thumbnails, pointing to *Colors*, scrolling down the color option list, and then clicking *Marquee* at the side menu.

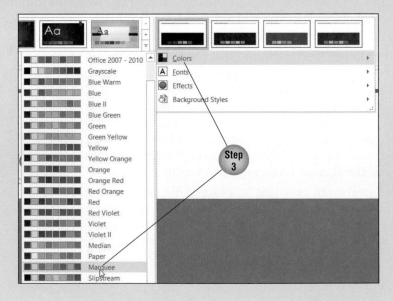

4. Change the theme fonts by clicking the More button in the Variants group, pointing to *Fonts*, scrolling down the font list, and then clicking *Calibri-Cambria* at the side menu.

5. Change the background style by clicking the More button in the Variants group, pointing to *Background Styles*, and then clicking *Style 5* at the side menu (first column, second row).

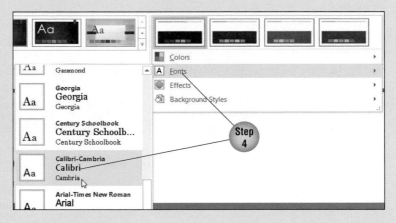

6. With Slide 1 active, run the presentation and notice the formatting applied by the design theme, theme colors, theme fonts, and background style.

7. Make sure Slide 1 is active and then apply and customize the background style of all slides by completing the following steps:
   a. Click the DESIGN tab.
   b. Click the Format Background button in the Customize group.
   c. At the Format Background task pane with the Fill icon selected and the *FILL* options displayed, click the *Picture or texture fill* option.
   d. Click the Texture button (located below the Online button) and then click the *Stationery* option (first column, bottom row).
   e. Click the up-pointing arrow at the right of the *Transparency* measurement box until *25%* displays.
   f. Click the Apply to All button located near the bottom of the task pane.
   g. Close the Format Background task pane.

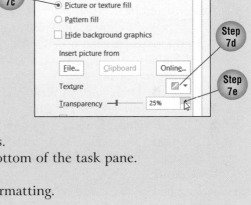

8. Run the presentation and notice the background formatting.

9. Apply an artistic effect to all slides in the presentation by completing the following steps:
   a. Make Slide 2 active.
   b. Click the Format Background button in the Customize group on the DESIGN tab.
   c. Click the Effects icon in the Format Background task pane.
   d. Click the Artistic Effects option button and then click the *Paint Brush* option (third column, second row).
   e. Click the Apply to All button located toward the bottom of the task pane.

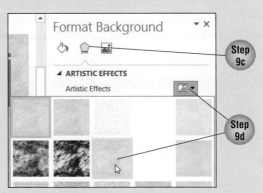

10. Run the presentation and notice the artistic effect applied to all slides in the presentation.

11. Change the background to a gradient fill rather than an artistic effect by completing the following steps:
    a. Click the Fill icon in the Format Background task pane.
    b. Click the *Gradient fill* option.
    c. Click the Preset gradients button and then click *Light Gradient - Accent 2* (second column, first row).
    d. Click the down-pointing arrow to the right of the *Type* option box and then click *Radial* at the drop-down list.
    e. Click the Direction button and then click the *From Bottom Left Corner* option (second option from the left).
    f. Select the *0%* in the *Position* measurement box, type **25**, and then press Enter.
    g. Click the Apply to All button.

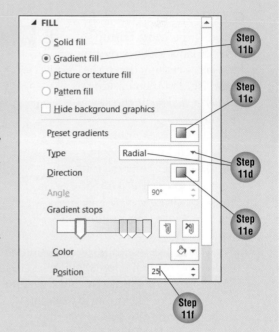

12. Look at the slides in the slide thumbnails pane and notice the gradient fill applied to all slides.
13. Apply a pattern fill to Slide 1 by completing the following steps:
    a. If necessary, click Slide 1 in the slide thumbnails pane.
    b. At the Format Background task pane, click the *Pattern fill* option.
    c. Click the *Divot* pattern fill in the *Pattern* section (first column, seventh row).
    d. Click the Background button and then click the *Green, Accent 2, Lighter 80%* option (sixth column, second row in the *Theme Colors* section).

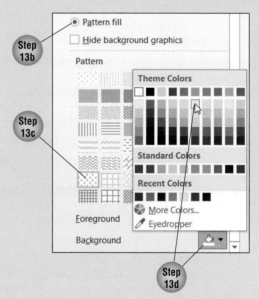

14. After viewing the pattern fill in the slide pane, reset the slide background of Slide 1 to the gradient fill background by clicking the Reset Background button located toward the bottom of the Format Background task pane.
15. Close the Format Background task pane.
16. Run the presentation and notice the background formatting.
17. Print the presentation as a handout with six slides printed horizontally per page.
18. Save and then close **P-C3-P3-NetworkPres.pptx**.

<table>
<tr><td>

Project 4   Create and Apply Custom Themes to Presentations

</td><td>

4 Parts

</td></tr>
</table>

You will create custom theme colors and custom theme fonts and then save the changes as a custom theme. You will then apply the custom theme to a job search presentation and a resume writing presentation.

Creating Custom Themes ■■■■■■■■■■■■■■■■■■■■

If the default themes, theme colors, and theme fonts do not provide the formatting you desire for your presentation, you can create your own custom theme colors, custom theme fonts, and a custom theme. A theme you create will display in the *Custom* section of the Themes drop-down gallery. To create a custom theme, change the theme colors, theme fonts, and/or theme effects.

Click the More button in the Variants group on the DESIGN tab and the options at the drop-down list display a visual representation of the current theme. If you change the theme colors, the colors are reflected in the small color squares on the *Colors* option. If you change the theme fonts, the *A* on the *Fonts* option reflects the change.

▼ **Quick Steps**

Create Custom Theme Colors
1. Click DESIGN tab.
2. Click More button in Variants group.
3. Point to *Colors*.
4. Click *Customize Colors*.
5. Change to desired background, accent, and hyperlink colors.
6. Type name for custom theme colors.
7. Click Save button.

Creating Custom Theme Colors

To create custom theme colors, click the DESIGN tab, click the More button located to the right of the Variants group, point to the *Colors* option at the drop-down list, and then click *Customize Colors* at the side menu. This displays the Create New Theme Colors dialog box, similar to the one shown in Figure 3.10. Theme colors contain four text and background colors, six accent colors, and two hyperlink colors, as shown in the *Themes color* section of the dialog box. Change a color in the option box by clicking the color button at the right side of the color option and then clicking the desired color at the color palette. If you make changes to colors at the Create New Theme Colors dialog box and then decide you do not

Figure 3.10 Create New Theme Colors Dialog Box

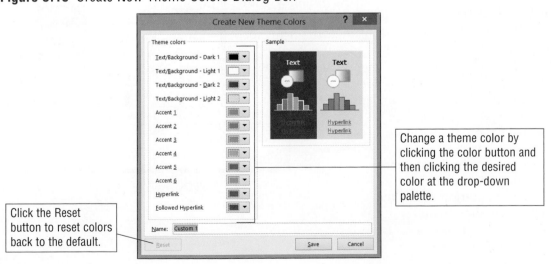

Change a theme color by clicking the color button and then clicking the desired color at the drop-down palette.

Click the Reset button to reset colors back to the default.

like the color changes, click the Reset button located in the lower left corner of the dialog box.

After you have made all desired changes to colors, click in the *Name* text box, type a name for the custom theme colors, and then click the Save button. This saves the custom theme colors and applies the color changes to the currently open presentation.

When you create custom theme colors, apply the theme to a presentation by clicking the More button in the Variants group on the DESIGN tab, pointing to the *Colors* option, and then clicking the custom theme colors that display toward the top of the drop-down gallery in the *Custom* section.

Project 4a   Creating Custom Theme Colors   Part 1 of 4

Note: If you are running PowerPoint 2013 on a computer connected to a network in a public environment such as a school, you may need to complete all four parts of Project 4 during the same session. Network system software may delete your custom themes when you close PowerPoint. Check with your instructor.

1. At a blank presentation, click the DESIGN tab, click the More button at the right side of the theme thumbnails in the Themes group, and then click Wisp at the drop-down gallery.
2. Click the third thumbnail in the Variants group (light blue color).
3. Create custom theme colors by completing the following steps:
   a. Click the More button in the Variants group, point to the *Colors* option, and then click the *Customize Colors* option at the side menu.
   b. At the Create New Theme Colors dialog box, click the color button that displays at the right side of the *Text/Background - Dark 2* option and then click the *Dark Blue, Accent 3, Darker 25%* option (seventh column, fifth row in the Theme Colors section).
   c. Click the color button that displays at the right side of the *Text/Background - Light 2* option and then click the *Purple, Accent 4, Lighter 80%* option (eighth column, second row in the Theme Colors section).
   d. Click the color button that displays at the right side of the *Accent 1* option and then click the *Purple, Accent 4, Darker 50%* option (eighth column, last row in the Theme Colors section).
4. Save the custom colors by completing the following steps:
   a. Select the current text in the *Name* text box.
   b. Type your first and last names.
   c. Click the Save button.
5. Save the presentation and name it **P-C3-P4-CustomTheme**.

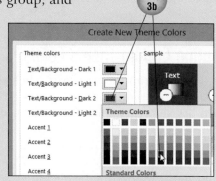

Step 3b

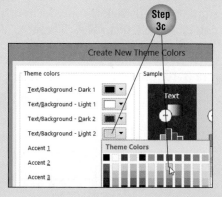

Step 3c

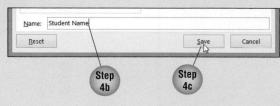

Step 4b   Step 4c

Creating Custom Theme Fonts

To create custom theme fonts, click the DESIGN tab, click the More button in the Variants group, point to the *Fonts* option, and then click *Customize Fonts* at the side menu. This displays the Create New Theme Fonts dialog box similar to the one shown in Figure 3.11. At this dialog box, choose a heading font and body font. Type the name of the custom theme fonts in the *Name* box and then click the Save button.

▼ Quick Steps

Create Custom Fonts
1. Click DESIGN tab.
2. Click More button in Variants group.
3. Point to *Fonts*.
4. Click *Customize Fonts*.
5. Choose desired fonts.
6. Type name for custom theme fonts.
7. Click Save button.

Figure 3.11 Create New Theme Fonts Dialog Box

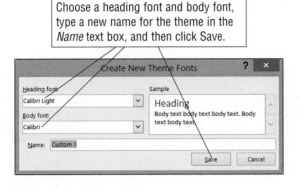

Choose a heading font and body font, type a new name for the theme in the *Name* text box, and then click Save.

Project 4b **Creating Custom Theme Fonts** Part 2 of 4

1. With **P-C3-P4-CustomTheme.pptx** open, create custom theme fonts by completing the following steps:
   a. If necessary, click the DESIGN tab.
   b. Click the More button in the Variants group, point to the *Fonts* option, and then click the *Customize Fonts* option at the drop-down gallery.
   c. At the Create New Theme Fonts dialog box, click the down-pointing arrow at the right side of the *Heading font* option box, scroll up the drop-down list, and then click *Candara*.
   d. Click the down-pointing arrow at the right side of the *Body font* option box, scroll down the drop-down list, and then click *Constantia*.
2. Save the custom theme fonts by completing the following steps:
   a. Select the current text in the *Name* text box.
   b. Type your first and last names.
   c. Click the Save button.
3. Save **P-C3-P4-CustomTheme.pptx**.

▼ Quick Steps

Save a Custom Theme
1. Click DESIGN tab.
2. Click More button in Themes group.
3. Click *Save Current Theme*.
4. Type name for custom theme.
5. Click Save button.

Saving a Custom Theme

When you have customized theme colors and fonts, you can save these as a custom theme. To do this, click the More button at the right side of the Themes group on the DESIGN tab and then click *Save Current Theme*. This displays the Save Current Theme dialog box with many of the same options as the Save As dialog box. Type a name for your custom theme in the *File name* text box and then click the Save button. To apply a custom theme, click the More button in the Themes group, and then click the desired theme in the *Custom* section of the drop-down gallery.

Project 4c | **Saving and Applying a Custom Theme** | **Part 3 of 4**

1. With **P-C3-P4-CustomTheme.pptx** open, save the custom theme colors and fonts as a custom theme by completing the following steps:
   a. If necessary, click the DESIGN tab.
   b. Click the More button at the right side of the theme thumbnails in the Themes group.
   c. Click the *Save Current Theme* option that displays at the bottom of the drop-down gallery.
   d. At the Save Current Theme dialog box, type **C3** and then type your last name in the *File name* text box.
   e. Click the Save button.

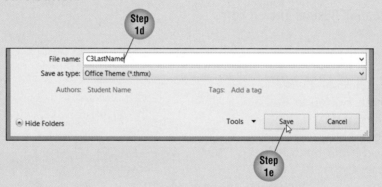

2. Close **P-C3-P4-CustomTheme.pptx**.
3. Open **JobSearch.pptx** and then save the presentation with Save As and name it **P-C3-P4-JobSearch**.
4. Apply your custom theme by completing the following steps:
   a. Click the DESIGN tab.
   b. Click the More button that displays at the right side of the theme thumbnails.
   c. Click the custom theme that begins with *C3* followed by your last name. (The theme will display in the *Custom* section of the drop-down gallery.)
5. Run the presentation and notice how the slides display with the custom theme applied.
6. Print Slide 1 of the presentation.
7. Save and then close **P-C3-P4-JobSearch.pptx**.

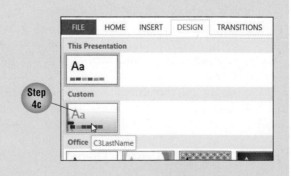

8. Open **ResumePres.pptx** and then save the presentation with Save As and name it **P-C3-P4-ResumePres**.
9. Apply your custom theme (the theme that displays beginning with *C3* followed by your last name).
10. Run the presentation.
11. Print Slide 1 of the presentation.
12. Save and then close **P-C3-P4-ResumePres.pptx**.

Editing Custom Themes

You can edit the custom theme colors and custom theme fonts. To edit the custom theme colors, click the More button in the Variants group on the DESIGN tab and then point to the *Colors* option. At the side menu of custom and built-in themes, right-click your custom theme and then click *Edit* at the shortcut menu. This displays the Edit Theme Colors dialog box that contains the same options as the Create New Theme Colors dialog box shown in Figure 3.10 on page 109. Make the desired changes to theme colors and then click the Save button.

To edit custom theme fonts, click the More button in the Variants group on the DESIGN tab, point to the *Fonts* option, right-click your custom theme fonts, and then click *Edit* at the shortcut menu. This displays the Edit Theme Fonts dialog box that contains the same options as the Create New Theme Fonts dialog box shown in Figure 3.11 on page 111. Make the desired changes and then click the Save button.

Deleting Custom Themes

You can delete custom theme colors from the *Colors* option side menu, delete custom theme fonts from the Fonts option side menu, and delete custom themes from the Themes drop-down gallery or the Save Current Theme dialog box. To delete custom theme colors, click the More button in the Variants group, point to the *Colors* option, right-click the theme you want to delete, and then click *Delete* at the shortcut menu. At the message asking if you want to delete the theme colors, click Yes. Complete similar steps to delete custom theme fonts.

Delete a custom theme by clicking the More button at the right side of the Themes group on the DESIGN tab, right-clicking the custom theme, and then clicking *Delete* at the shortcut menu. A custom theme can also be deleted at the Save Current Theme dialog box. To display this dialog box, click the More button at the right side of the Themes group on the DESIGN tab and then click *Save Current Theme* at the drop-down gallery. At the dialog box, click the custom theme file name, click the Organize button on the toolbar, and then click *Delete* at the drop-down list. At the message asking if you are sure you want to send the theme to the Recycle Bin, click Yes.

▼ **Quick Steps**

Edit Custom Theme Colors
1. Click DESIGN tab.
2. Click More button in Variants group.
3. Point to *Colors* option.
4. Right-click desired custom theme.
5. Click *Edit*.
6. Make desired changes.
7. Click Save button.

Edit Custom Theme Fonts
1. Click DESIGN tab.
2. Click More button in Variants group.
3. Point to *Fonts* option.
4. Right-click desired custom theme.
5. Click *Edit*.
6. Make desired changes.
7. Click Save button.

Delete Custom Theme Colors
1. Click DESIGN tab.
2. Click More button in Variants group.
3. Point to *Colors* option.
4. Right-click desired custom theme.
5. Click *Delete*.
6. Click Yes.

Delete Custom Theme Fonts
1. Click DESIGN tab.
2. Click More button in Variants group.
3. Point to *Fonts* option.
4. Right-click desired custom theme.
5. Click *Delete*.
6. Click Yes.

Delete Custom Theme
1. Click DESIGN tab.
2. Click More button in Themes group.
3. Right-click desired custom theme.
4. Click *Delete*.
5. Click Yes.

1. At a blank presentation, delete the custom theme colors by completing the following steps:
   a. Click the DESIGN tab.
   b. Click the More button in the Variants group and then point to the *Colors* option.
   c. Right-click the custom theme colors named with your first and last names.
   d. Click *Delete* at the shortcut menu.
   e. At the message asking if you want to delete the theme colors, click Yes.

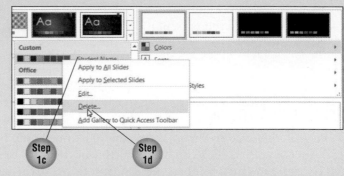

2. Complete steps similar to those in Step 1 to delete the custom theme fonts you created named with your first and last names.
3. Delete the custom theme by completing the following steps:
   a. Click the More button that displays at the right side of the theme thumbnails.
   b. Right-click the custom theme that begins with *C3* followed by your last name.
   c. Click *Delete* at the shortcut menu.
   d. At the message asking if you want to delete the theme, click Yes.
4. Close the presentation without saving it.

Chapter Summary

- The Font group on the HOME tab contains buttons for applying character formatting to text in slides.

- Design themes apply a font to text in slides. Change this default font with the Font and Font Size buttons in the Font group.

- Some buttons, such as the Font and Font Size buttons, contain the live preview feature, which allows you to see how the formatting affects your text without having to return to the presentation.

- You can also apply character formatting with options at the Font dialog box. Display this dialog box by clicking the Font group dialog box launcher.

- Select text in a slide and the Mini toolbar displays above the selected text. Apply formatting with buttons on this toolbar.

- Use the Format Painter feature to apply formatting to more than one location in a slide or slides.

- The Paragraph group on the HOME tab contains a number of buttons for applying paragraph formatting to text in slides.

- Customize paragraph formatting with options at the Paragraph dialog box with the Indents and Spacing tab selected. Display this dialog box by clicking the Paragraph group dialog box launcher or by clicking the Line Spacing button in the Paragraph group and then clicking *Line Spacing Options* at the drop-down list.

- Use the Add or Remove Columns button in the Paragraph group or options at the Columns dialog box to format selected text into columns. Display the Columns dialog box by clicking the Add or Remove Columns button and then clicking *More Columns* at the drop-down list.

- Use the Text Direction button or options at the Format Shape task pane to rotate or stack text in a slide. Display the Format Shape task pane by clicking the Drawing group task pane launcher on the HOME tab.

- Use the Align Text button or options at the Format Shape task pane to vertically align text in a slide.

- The SHAPE OPTIONS tab of the Format Shape task pane displays four icons: Fill & Line, Effects, Size & Properties, and Picture, each with different options for formatting a placeholder.

- Customize bullets with options at the Bullets and Numbering dialog box with the Bulleted tab selected. Display this dialog box by clicking the Bullets button arrow and then clicking *Bullets and Numbering* at the drop-down list.

- Customize numbering with options at the Bullets and Numbering dialog box with the Numbered tab selected. Display this dialog box by clicking the Numbering button arrow and then clicking *Bullets and Numbering* at the drop-down list.

- Click the Quick Styles button in the Drawing group on the HOME tab to apply formatting to a placeholder. The Drawing group also contains the Shape Fill, Shape Outline, and Shape Effects buttons for customizing a placeholder and the Arrange button for arranging slide elements.

- Click the Slide Size button and then click *Custom Slide Size* at the drop-down list to display the Slide Size dialog box. Use options in this dialog box to change the slide size and ratio, the start slide number, and the orientation of slides and notes, handouts, and outline pages.

- Use the Format Background task pane to customize the background of slides. Display the task pane by clicking the Format Background button in the Customize group on the DESIGN tab.

- Create custom theme colors with options at the Create New Theme Colors dialog box. Display this dialog box by clicking the More button in the Variants group on the DESIGN tab, pointing to the *Colors* option, and then clicking *Customize Colors* at the drop-down gallery.

- Create custom theme fonts with options at the Create New Theme Fonts dialog box. Display this dialog box by clicking the More button in the Variants group on the DESIGN tab, pointing to the *Fonts* option, and then clicking *Customize Fonts* at the drop-down gallery.

- Save a custom theme at the Save Current Theme dialog box. Display this dialog box by clicking the More button at the right side of the Themes group on the DESIGN tab and then clicking *Save Current Theme*.
- Edit custom theme colors with options at the Edit Theme Colors dialog box and edit custom theme fonts with options at the Edit Theme Fonts dialog box.
- Delete custom theme colors by clicking the More button in the Variants group, pointing to the *Colors* option, right-clicking the custom theme, and then clicking the *Delete* option.
- Delete custom theme fonts by clicking the More button in the Variants group, pointing to the *Fonts* option, right-clicking the custom theme, and then clicking the *Delete* option.
- Delete a custom theme by clicking the More button in the Themes group, right-clicking the custom theme, and then clicking *Delete* at the short cut menu. A custom theme also can be deleted at the Save Current Theme dialog box. Display this dialog box by clicking the Themes button and then clicking *Save Current Theme* at the drop-down gallery.

Commands Review

FEATURE	RIBBON TAB, GROUP	BUTTON, OPTION	KEYBOARD SHORTCUT
Bullets and Numbering dialog box with Bulleted tab selected	HOME, Paragraph	, *Bullets and Numbering*	
Bullets and Numbering dialog box with Numbered tab selected	HOME, Paragraph	, *Bullets and Numbering*	
Columns dialog box	HOME, Paragraph	, *More Columns*	
Create New Theme Colors dialog box	DESIGN, Variants	, *Colors, Customize Colors*	
Create New Theme Fonts dialog box	DESIGN, Variants	, *Fonts, Customize Fonts*	
Font dialog box	HOME, Font		Ctrl + Shift + F
Format Background task pane	DESIGN, Customize		
Format Painter	HOME, Clipboard		
Format Shape task pane	HOME, Drawing		
Paragraph dialog box	HOME, Paragraph		
Save Current Theme dialog box	DESIGN, Themes	, *Save Current Theme*	
slide size	DESIGN, Customize		

Concepts Check

Completion: In the space provided at the right, indicate the correct term, symbol, or command.

1. The Font button drop-down gallery is an example of this feature, which allows you to see how formatting will affect your text before you actually apply it. _____

2. Click this button to clear character formatting from selected text. _____

3. Click this to display the Font dialog box. _____

4. Select text in a slide and this displays above the selected text. _____

5. The Format Painter button is located in this group on the HOME tab. _____

6. Press this key to move text to the next tab stop (level). _____

7. Use options at this dialog box to change text alignment, indentation, and spacing. _____

8. Click this button in the Paragraph group and a drop-down list displays with options for rotating and stacking text. _____

9. Use the Align Text button or options at this task pane with the Size & Properties icon selected to vertically align text in a slide. _____

10. Customize numbering with options at the Bullets and Numbering dialog box with this tab selected. _____

11. The Quick Styles button is located in this group on the HOME tab. _____

12. Click this button to apply an outline to a placeholder. _____

13. Change slide orientation with options in this dialog box. _____

14. Click this button in the Customize group on the DESIGN tab to display the Format Background task pane. _____

15. Create custom theme colors with options at this dialog box. _____

16. Save a custom theme at this dialog box. _____

Skills Check Assess Your Performance

Assessment

1 CREATE, FORMAT, AND MODIFY A BENEFITS PRESENTATION

1. At a blank presentation, create the slides shown in Figure 3.12.
2. Apply the Facet design theme and then apply the blue variant.
3. Make Slide 1 active and then make the following changes:
   a. Select the title *BENEFITS PROGRAM*, change the font to Candara and the font size to 60 points, apply the Turquoise, Accent 1, Darker 50% font color, and apply italic formatting.
   b. Select the subtitle *Changes to Plans*, change the font to Candara and the font size to 32 points, apply the Turquoise, Accent 1 font color, and apply bold and shadow formatting.
   c. Click the title placeholder and then click the Center button in the Paragraph group.
   d. Center the subtitle in the placeholder.
4. Make Slide 2 active and then make the following changes:
   a. Select the title *INTRODUCTION*, change the font to Candara and the font size to 44 points, apply the Turquoise, Accent 1, Darker 50% font color, and apply shadow formatting.
   b. Using Format Painter, apply the title formatting to the titles in the remaining slides.
5. Center-align and middle-align the titles in Slides 2 through 5.
6. Make Slide 2 active, select the bulleted text, and then change the line spacing to double spacing (2.0).
7. Make Slide 3 active, select the bulleted text, and then change the line spacing to double spacing (2.0).
8. Make Slide 4 active, select the bulleted text, and then change the line spacing to 1.5.
9. Make Slide 5 active, select the bulleted text, and then change the spacing after paragraphs to *18 pt.* **Hint: Do this at the Paragraph dialog box.**
10. Make Slide 2 active and then select the text in the content placeholder. Display the Bullets and Numbering dialog box with the Numbered tab selected, choose the *1. 2. 3.* option, change the size to 90%, apply the Turquoise, Accent 1, Darker 50% color, and then close the dialog box.
11. Make Slide 3 active and then select the text in the content placeholder. Display the Bullets and Numbering dialog box with the Numbered tab selected, choose the *1. 2. 3.* option, change the size to 90%, apply the Turquoise, Accent 1, Darker 50% color, change the starting number to 5, and then close the dialog box.
12. Make Slide 4 active, select the text in the content placeholder, and then change the bullets to *Hollow Square Bullets*.
13. Make Slide 5 active, select the text in the content placeholder, and then change the bullets to *Hollow Square Bullets*.
14. Save the presentation and name it **P-C3-A1-Benefits**.
15. Print the presentation as a handout with six slides printed horizontally per page.
16. Apply the Organic design theme.

Figure 3.12 Assessment 1

Slide 1 Title   = BENEFITS PROGRAM
         Subtitle = Changes to Plans

Slide 2 Title   = INTRODUCTION
         Content = • Changes made for 2015
                     • Description of eligibility
                     • Instructions for enrolling new members
                     • Overview of medical and dental coverage

Slide 3 Title   = INTRODUCTION
         Content = • Expanded enrollment forms
                     • Glossary defining terms
                     • Telephone directory
                     • Pamphlet with commonly asked questions

Slide 4 Title   = WHAT'S NEW
         Content = • New medical plans
                       ○ Plan 2015
                       ○ Premier Plan
                     • Changes in monthly contributions
                     • Paying with pretax dollars
                     • Contributions toward spouse's coverage

Slide 5 Title   = COST SHARING
         Content = • Increased deductible
                     • New coinsurance amount
                     • Higher coinsurance amount for retail prescription drugs
                     • Co-payment for mail-order medicines
                     • New stop loss limit

17. Apply a transition and sound of your choosing to each slide.
18. Run the presentation.
19. Print the presentation as a handout with six slides printed horizontally per page.
20. Save and then close **P-C3-A1-Benefits.pptx**.

Assessment

2 FORMAT AND MODIFY A PERENNIALS PRESENTATION

1. Open **PerennialsPres.pptx** and then save the presentation with Save As and name it **P-C3-A2-PerennialsPres**.
2. Make Slide 3 active, format the bulleted text into two columns, and change the line spacing to double spacing (2.0). Make sure each column contains four bulleted items. With the bulleted items selected, display the Paragraph dialog box, change the *By* option (in the *Indentation* section) to 0.4, and then close the dialog box.

3. Make Slide 2 active, click anywhere in the bulleted text, click the Drawing group task pane launcher and then make the following changes at the Format Shape task pane:
   a. With the Fill & Line icon selected, click *FILL* to expand the options, click the *Gradient fill* option, change *Type* to Rectangular, and then change *Color* to Green, Accent 1, Lighter 60% (fifth column, third row in the *Theme Colors* section).
   b. Click the Effects icon, click the SHADOW option, click the Presets button, and then click the *Offset Right* option (first column, second row).
   c. Click the Size & Properties icon and then click *TEXT BOX* to expand the options.
   d. Change the left margin measurement to 1 inch and the top margin to 0.4 inch.
   e. Close the task pane.
4. Make Slide 1 active, click the subtitle placeholder, and then apply the following shape and outline fill:
   a. Click the Shape Fill button arrow on the HOME tab and then click the *Eyedropper* option.
   b. Point the eyedropper to the light green border at the top of the slide and then click the left mouse button.
   c. Click the Shape Outline button arrow and then click the *Eyedropper* option.
   d. Position the tip of the eyedropper on a yellow colored flower in the Greenspace Architects logo and then click the left mouse button.
5. Make Slide 2 active, click the DESIGN tab, click the Format Background button, and then apply the following formatting:
   a. At the Format Background task pane with the Fill icon selected, click the *Solid fill* option.
   b. Click the Color button and then click the *Aqua, Accent 5, Lighter 80%* option (ninth column, second row in the *Theme Colors* section).
   c. Click the Apply to All button.
   d. Close the task pane.
6. Print the presentation with six slides printed horizontally per page.
7. Add a transition and sound of your choosing to all slides in the presentation.
8. Run the presentation.
9. Save and then close **P-C3-A2-PerennialsPres.pptx**.

Assessment

3 CREATE AND APPLY A CUSTOM THEME TO A TRAVEL PRESENTATION  Grade It

1. At a blank presentation, apply the Parallax design theme.
2. Create custom theme colors named with your first and last names that changes the following colors:
   a. At the Create New Theme Colors dialog box, change the *Text/Background - Light 2* option to *Red, Accent 4, Lighter 80%* (eighth column, second row in the *Theme Colors* section).
   b. Change the *Accent 1* option to *Red, Accent 4, Darker 50%* (eighth column, bottom row in the *Theme Colors* section).
3. Create custom theme fonts named with your first and last names that applies the following fonts:
   a. At the Create New Theme Fonts dialog box, change the Heading font to *Copperplate Gothic Bold*.
   b. Change the Body font to *Rockwell*.

4. Save the current theme as a custom theme named with your first and last names. ***Hint: Do this at the Save Current Theme dialog box.***

5. Close the presentation without saving it.

6. Open **TravelEngland.pptx** and then save the presentation with Save As and name it **P-C3-A3-TravelEngland**.

7. Apply the custom theme named with your first and last names.

8. Improve the visual display of the bulleted text in Slides 2 and 3 by increasing the spacing between items and positioning the bulleted item placeholders attractively in the slides.

9. Make Slide 4 active, increase the spacing between bulleted items and then format the text into two columns. Make sure that each column contains three bulleted items. Consider decreasing the size of the placeholder.

10. Format the bulleted text in Slides 5 and 6 into two columns with four bulleted items in each column. Consider decreasing the size of the placeholder.

11. Print the presentation as a handout with six slides printed horizontally per page.

12. Add a transition and sound of your choosing to all slides in the presentation.

13. Run the presentation.

14. Save and then close **P-C3-A3-TravelEngland.pptx**.

15. Display a blank presentation and then delete the custom theme colors, custom theme fonts, and custom theme you created for this assessment.

16. Close the presentation without saving it.

Assessment

4 PREPARE A PRESENTATION ON ONLINE SHOPPING

1. Open Microsoft Word and then open the document **OnlineShopping.docx** that is located in the PC3 folder on your storage medium.

2. Print the document by clicking the FILE tab, clicking the *Print* option, and then clicking the Print button at the Print backstage area.

3. Close **OnlineShopping.docx** and then close Word.

4. At a blank PowerPoint presentation, use the information you printed to create a presentation on online shopping with the following specifications:
   a. Create a slide with the title of your presentation. Type your name as the subtitle.
   b. Create slides that summarize the information you printed. (You determine the number of slides in the presentation. Make sure the slides are not crowded with too much information.)
   c. Apply a design theme of your choosing.
   d. Apply a transition and sound of your choosing to all slides.

5. Save the presentation and name it **P-C3-A4-OnlineShopping**.

6. Run the presentation.

7. Print the presentation as a handout with six slides printed horizontally per page.

8. Close **P-C3-A4-OnlineShopping.pptx**.

Visual Benchmark Demonstrate Your Proficiency

FORMAT A PRESENTATION ON HOME SAFETY

1. Open **HomeSafety.pptx** and then save the presentation with Save As and name it **P-C3-VB-HomeSafety**.
2. Format the presentation so the slides appear as shown in Figure 3.13 with the following specifications.
   a. Apply the Facet design theme and the blue variant color.
   b. Delete and rearrange slides as shown in the figure.
   c. Apply the Parchment texture slide background and change the slide background transparency to 50% for all slides in the presentation. ***Hint: Apply these options using the Format Background task pane.***
   d. Change the font size of the title in Slide 1 to 60 points, apply bold formatting, apply the Blue, Accent 2, Darker 25% font color, and center-align the title.
   e. Change the font size of the subtitle in Slide 1 to 28 points, apply italics, change the font color to Turquoise, Accent 1, Darker 25%, and center-align the subtitle.
   f. Change the font size of the titles in Slides 2 through 6 to 48 points and the font color to Turquoise, Accent 1, Darker 50%.
   g. Change the line spacing, spacing after, column formatting, and bullet styles so your slides display in a manner similar to the slides in Figure 3.13.
   h. Select the bulleted text placeholder in Slide 6, display the Format Shape task pane, select the *Solid fill* option, and then change the color to Turquoise, Accent 1, Lighter 80%. Display the Format Shape task pane with the TEXT OPTIONS tab selected and the Textbox icon selected, then change the left margin to 1 inch and the top margin to 0.2 inch.
3. Print the presentation as a handout with six slides printed horizontally per page.
4. Save and then close the presentation.

Figure 3.13 Visual Benchmark

Case Study   Apply Your Skills

Part 1

You are the assistant to Gina Coletti, manager of La Dolce Vita, an Italian restaurant. She has been working on a new lunch menu and wants to present the new menu at the upcoming staff meeting. She has asked you to prepare a presentation she can use at the meeting. Open the Word document named **LunchMenu.docx** and then print the document. Close the document and then close Word. In PowerPoint, display the New backstage area, search for the *Fresh food presentation* design theme template at Office.com, and then download the template that contains the vegetables on the title slide. Create a presentation with the design theme template you downlaoded with the information you printed. Make any formatting changes to improve the visual appearance of the presentation. Save the presentation and name it **P-C3-CS-LunchMenu**.

Part 2

Ms. Coletti has looked over the presentation and has asked you to apply color and font formatting consistent with other restaurant publications. With **P-C3-CS-LunchMenu.pptx** open, create custom theme colors that change the *Text/Background - Light 1* color to *Gold, Accent 2, Lighter 80%* and the *Accent 3* color to *Blue*. Create custom theme fonts that apply Monotype Corsiva as the heading font and Garamond as the body font. Save the custom theme and name it *LaDolceVita* followed by your initials. Add a transition and sound to all slides in the presentation. Print the presentation as a handout with six slides printed horizontally per page. Save and then close **P-C3-CS-LunchMenu.pptx**.

Part 3

Ms. Coletti needs further information for the meeting. She wants you to use the Internet to search for two companies that print restaurant menus, two companies that design restaurant menus, and the names of two restaurant menu design software programs. Prepare a presentation with the information you find on the Internet using the design theme template you downloaded in part 1. Make any formatting changes to improve the visual appeal of each slide. Add a transition and sound to each slide in the presentation. Save the presentation and name it **P-C3-CS-RestMenus.pptx**. Print the presentation as a handout with six slides printed horizontally per page.

Part 4

When running **P-C3-CS-RestMenus.pptx**, Ms. Coletti would like to link to a couple of the sites you list in the presentation. Use PowerPoint's Help feature to learn how to insert a hyperlink in a slide to a web page or website. Create at least two hyperlinks between sites you list in the presentation and the web page or website. Print the slide(s) containing the hyperlinks. Save and then close **P-C3-CS-RestMenus.pptx**.

MICROSOFT®
POWERPOINT®

Inserting Elements in Slides

PERFORMANCE OBJECTIVES

Upon successful completion of Chapter 4, you will be able to:

- Insert, format, select, and align a text box
- Set tabs in a text box
- Insert, format, and copy shapes
- Display rulers, gridlines, and guides
- Group and ungroup objects
- Insert, crop, size, move, and format a picture
- Insert a picture as a slide background
- Insert, size, scale, rotate, and position a clip art image
- Create and insert a screenshot
- Create and format WordArt text
- Insert objects such as a header, footer, date, slide number, and symbol

Tutorials

4.1 Displaying Gridlines; Inserting a Text Box; Copying and Rotating Shapes

4.2 Formatting a Text Box

4.3 Drawing and Customizing Shapes

4.4 Grouping/Ungrouping Objects

4.5 Inserting and Formatting Images

4.6 Inserting and Formatting Clip Art Images

4.7 Creating and Inserting Screenshots

4.8 Inserting and Formatting WordArt

4.9 Inserting Headers and Footers

A presentation consisting only of text slides may have important information in it that will be overlooked by the audience because a slide contains too much text. Adding visual elements, where appropriate, can help deliver the message to your audience by adding interest and impact to the information. In this chapter, you will learn how to create visual elements on slides such as text boxes, shapes, pictures, clip art images, screenshots, and WordArt text. These elements will make the delivery of your presentation a dynamic experience for your audience. The model answer for this chapter's project appears on the following page.

Note: Before beginning the project, copy to your storage medium the PC4 subfolder from the PowerPoint folder on the CD that accompanies this textbook and then make PC4 the active folder.

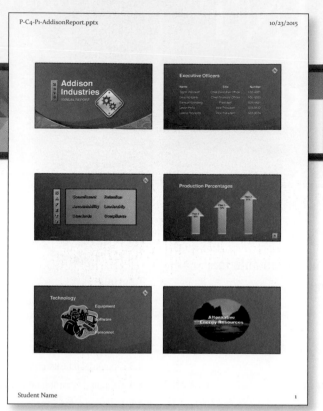

Project 1 Create a Company Presentation Containing Text Boxes, Shapes, and Images   P-C4-P1-AddisonReport.pptx

Project ⬛1 Create a Company Presentation Containing Text Boxes, Shapes, and Images   **14 Parts**

You will create a company presentation that includes slides with text boxes, a slide with tabbed text in a text box, slides with shapes and text, slides with pictures, and slides with clip art images. You will also insert elements in slides such as slide numbers, headers, footers, the date, and symbols.

Inserting and Formatting Text Boxes ⬛⬛⬛⬛⬛⬛⬛⬛⬛⬛⬛⬛

Many slide layouts contain placeholders for entering text and other elements in a document. Along with placeholders, you can insert and format a text box. To insert a text box in a slide, click the INSERT tab, click the Text Box button in the Text group, and the mouse pointer displays as a thin, down-pointing arrow. Using the mouse, drag in the slide to create the text box. You can also click in the desired location and a small text box is inserted in the slide.

Formatting a Text Box

When you insert a text box in the document, the HOME tab displays. Use options in the Drawing group to format the text box by applying a Quick Style or adding a shape fill, outline, or effect. Format a text box in a manner similar to formatting a placeholder. You can also apply formatting to a text box with options on the DRAWING TOOLS FORMAT tab. Click this tab and the ribbon displays, as shown in Figure 4.1. The Shape Styles group contains the same options as the Drawing group on the HOME tab. With other options on the tab, apply WordArt formatting to text and arrange and size the text box.

Move a text box in the same way you move a placeholder. Click the text box to select it, position the mouse pointer on the text box border until the pointer displays with a four-headed arrow attached, and then drag the text box to the desired position. Change the size of a selected text box using the sizing handles that display around the box. You can also use the *Shape Height* and *Shape Width* measurement boxes in the Size group on the DRAWING TOOLS FORMAT tab to specify the text box height and width.

As you learned in Chapter 3, PowerPoint provides a task pane with a variety of options for formatting a placeholder. The same task pane is available with options for formatting and customizing a text box. Click the Shape Styles task pane launcher and the Format Shape task pane displays at the right side of the screen with options for formatting the text box fill, effects, and size; options for formatting a picture in the text box; and options for formatting text in a text box. Click the WordArt Styles task pane launcher and the Format Shape task pane displays text formatting options. Click the Size task pane launcher and the Format Shape task pane displays size and position options.

You can apply the same formatting to text in a text box that you apply to text in a placeholder. For example, use the buttons in the Paragraph group on the HOME tab to align text horizontally and vertically in a text box, change text direction, set text in columns, and set internal margins for the text in the text box.

HINT
Use a text box to place text anywhere in a slide. Text in inserted text boxes does not appear in the Outline view.

HINT
To select an object that is behind another object, select the top object and then press the Tab key to cycle through and select the other objects.

Selecting Multiple Objects

You can select multiple text boxes and other objects in a slide and then apply formatting or align and arrange the objects in the slide. To select all objects in a slide, click the Select button in the Editing group on the HOME tab and then click *Select All* at the drop-down list. Or, select all objects in a slide with the keyboard shortcut Ctrl + A. To select specific text boxes or objects in a slide, click the first object, hold down the Shift key, and then click each of the other desired objects.

▼ **Quick Steps**

Select All Text Boxes
1. Click Select button.
2. Click *Select All.*
OR
Press Ctrl + A.

Select

Aligning Text Boxes

Use the Align button in the Arrange group on the DRAWING TOOLS FORMAT tab to align the edge of multiple objects in a slide. Click the Align button and a drop-down list of alignment options displays including options for aligning objects vertically and horizontally and distributing objects.

Align

Figure 4.1 DRAWING TOOLS FORMAT Tab

1. Open **AddisonReport.pptx** and then save the presentation with Save As and name it **P-C4-P1-AddisonReport**.
2. Insert a new slide with the Blank layout by completing the following steps:
   a. Click the New Slide button arrow in the Slides group on the HOME tab.
   b. Click *Blank* at the drop-down list.
3. Insert and format the *Safety* text box shown in Figure 4.2 (on page 131) by completing the following steps:
   a. Click the INSERT tab.
   b. Click the Text Box button in the Text group.
   c. Click anywhere in the slide. (This inserts a small, selected text box in the slide.)
   d. Type **Safety**.
   e. Select the text and then change the font to Copperplate Gothic Bold and the font size to 36 points.
   f. Click the Text Direction button in the Paragraph group on the HOME tab and then click *Stacked* at the drop-down list.
   g. Click the DRAWING TOOLS FORMAT tab.
   h. Click the More button that displays at the right side of the style thumbnails in the Shape Styles group and then click the *Moderate Effect - Aqua, Accent 5* option (sixth column, fifth row).

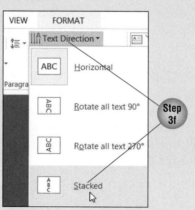

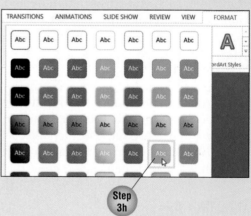

   i. Click the Shape Outline button arrow in the Shape Styles group and then click the *Blue* color (eighth option in the *Standard Colors* section).
   j. Click the Shape Outline button arrow, point to *Weight*, and then click the *1½ pt* option.
   k. Click the Shape Effects button, point to *Bevel*, and then click the *Circle* option (first option in the *Bevel* section).
   l. Click the More button at the right side of the WordArt style thumbnails in the WordArt Styles group and then click the *Fill - White, Text 1, Outline - Background 1, Hard Shadow - Background 1* option (first column, third row).
   m. Click in the *Shape Height* measurement box, type 4, and then press Enter.
   n. Drag the text box so it is positioned as shown in Figure 4.2 (located on page 131).

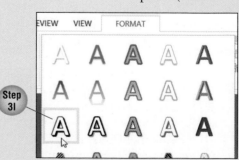

4. Insert and size the other text box shown in Figure 4.2 by completing the following steps:
   a. Click the INSERT tab.
   b. Click the Text Box button in the Text group.
   c. Drag in the slide to create a text box. (Drag to the approximate width of the text box in Figure 4.2.)
   d. Type the text shown in the text box in Figure 4.2 in a single column. Type the text in the first column and then type the text in the second column. (Your text will display as shown at the right in one column, in a smaller font, and with different line spacing than in Figure 4.2.)

   e. Select the text and then change the font size to 32 points.
   f. Click the Line Spacing button in the Paragraph group and then click *2.0* at the drop-down list. (The text will flow off the slide.)
   g. Click the Add or Remove Columns button in the Paragraph group and then click *Two Columns* at the drop-down list. (The text in the slide will not display in two columns until you complete steps 7k and 7l.)
5. Click the DRAWING TOOLS FORMAT tab.
6. Apply a WordArt style by completing the following steps:
   a. Click the More button at the right side of the WordArt style thumbnails in the WordArt Styles group.
   b. Click the *Fill - White, Text 1, Outline - Background 1, Hard Shadow - Background 1* option (first column, third row).
7. Change the height, width, and internal margin measurements of the text box and turn off Autofit in the Format Shape task pane by completing the following steps:
   a. Click the Size group task pane launcher.
   b. At the Format Shape task pane, make sure the Size & Properties icon is selected.
   c. If necessary, click *TEXT BOX* in the task pane to display the text box options.
   d. If necessary, scroll down to the bottom of the task pane list box.
   e. Click the *Do not Autofit* option.
   f. Select the current measurement in the *Left margin* measurement box and then type **0.8**.
   g. Select the current measurement in the *Right margin* measurement box and then type **0**.
   h. Select the current measurement in the *Top margin* measurement box, type **0.2**, and then press Enter.
   i. Scroll up to the top of the task pane list box.
   j. If necessary, click *SIZE* to display the size options.
   k. Select the current measurement in the *Height* measurement box and then type **4**.
   l. Select the current measurement in the *Width* measurement box, type **8**, and then press Enter.

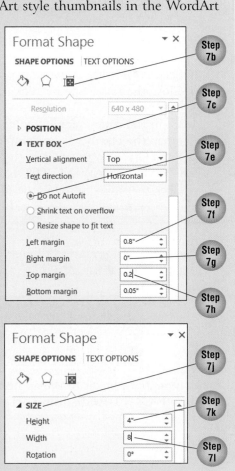

8. Apply fill formatting with options in the Format Shape task pane by completing the following steps:
   a. Click the Fill & Line icon in the task pane.
   b. Click *FILL* to display the fill options.
   c. Click the *Gradient fill* option. Notice the options available for customizing the gradient fill.
   d. Click the *Pattern fill* option and notice the pattern options that display.
   e. Click the *Picture or texture fill* option.
   f. Click the File button in the task pane.

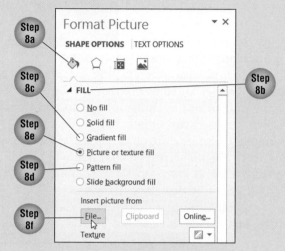

   g. At the Insert Picture dialog box, navigate to the PC4 folder on your storage medium and then double-click **Ship.jpg**.
   h. Select *0%* in the *Transparency* measurement box, type **10**, and then press Enter.
   i. Close the task pane by clicking the Close button located in the upper right corner of the task pane.
9. Click in the slide outside the text box.
10. Arrange the text boxes by completing the following steps:
    a. Press Ctrl + A to select both text boxes.
    b. Click the DRAWING TOOLS FORMAT tab.
    c. Click the Align button in the Arrange group and then click *Align Bottom* at the drop-down list.

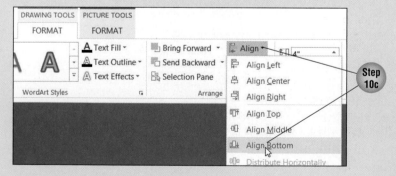

    d. Drag both boxes to the approximate location in the slide as shown in Figure 4.2.
11. Save **P-C4-P1-AddisonReport.pptx**.

12. Print only slide 2 by completing the following steps:
    a. Press Ctrl + P to display the Print backstage area.
    b. Click in the *Slides* text box in the *Settings* category and then type **2**.
    c. Click the Print button.
13. Select the text box containing the image of the ship.
14. Make sure the DRAWING TOOLS FORMAT tab is active.
15. Click the More button that displays at the right side of the style thumbnails in the Shape Styles group and then click the *Moderate Effect - Aqua, Accent 5* option (sixth column, fifth row).
16. Click the Shape Outline button arrow in the Shape Styles group and then click the *Blue* color (eighth option in the *Standard Colors* section).
17. Click the Shape Outline button arrow, point to *Weight*, and then click the *1½ pt* option.
18. Click the Shape Effects button, point to *Bevel*, and then click the *Circle* option (first option in the *Bevel* section).
19. Save **P-C4-P1-AddisonReport.pptx**.

Figure 4.2 Project 1a, Slide 2

You can display the Format Shape task pane using a shortcut menu. To do this, position the mouse pointer on the border of the text box until the pointer displays with a four-headed arrow attached and then click the right mouse button. At the shortcut menu, click the *Size and Position* option to display the Format Shape task pane with the Size & Properties icon active. Click the *Format Shape* option at the shortcut menu and the Format Shape task pane displays with the Fill & Line icon active. If you apply formatting to a text box and then want that formatting to be the default for other text boxes in the current presentation, click the *Set as Default Text Box* option at the shortcut menu.

1. With **P-C4-P1-AddisonReport.pptx** open, make sure Slide 2 is the active slide and then complete the following steps:
   a. Click the INSERT tab, click the Text Box button, and then click in the lower right corner of the slide.
   b. Type **Default text box**. (In the next step you will change the default text box. You will use the text box you just inserted to return to the original text box.)
2. Set as default the text box containing the word *SAFETY* by completing the following steps:
   a. Position the mouse pointer on the border of the text box containing the word *SAFETY* until the pointer displays with a four-headed arrow attached and then click the right mouse button.
   b. Click the *Set as Default Text Box* option at the shortcut menu.
3. Make Slide 1 active.
4. Insert a text box by clicking the INSERT tab, clicking the Text Box button, and then clicking between the company name and the left side of the slide.
5. Type **2016** in the text box.
6. Change the *Autofit* option, wrap text in the text box, and size the text box by completing the following steps:
   a. Position the mouse pointer on the border of the text box until the pointer displays with a four-headed arrow attached and then click the right mouse button.
   b. Click the *Size and Position* option at the shortcut menu.
   c. At the Format Shape task pane with the Size & Properties icon selected, click *TEXT BOX* to display the options, scroll to the bottom of the task pane list box, and then click in the *Wrap text in shape* check box to insert a check mark.
   d. Click the *Shrink text on overflow* option.
   e. Scroll up to the top of the task pane.
   f. Select the current measurement in the *Height* measurement box in the *SIZE* section and then type **2.4**.
   g. Select the current measurement in the *Width* measurement box, type **0.8**, and then press Enter.

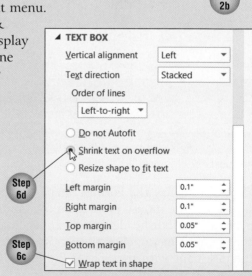

7. With the text box selected, change the shape of the text box by completing the following steps:

   a. Click the DRAWING TOOLS FORMAT tab to make the tab active.

   b. Click the Edit Shape button in the Insert Shapes group, point to *Change Shape*, and then click the *Bevel* option (last option, second row in the *Basic Shapes* section).

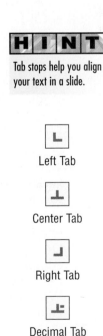

8. Precisely position the text box by completing the following steps:

   a. If necessary, scroll down the Format Shape task pane list box to the *POSITION* section and then click *POSITION* to display the options.

   b. Select the current measurement in the *Horizontal position* measurement box and then type **1.8**.

   c. Select the current measurement in the *Vertical position* measurement box, type **2**, and then press Enter.

9. Close the Format Shape task pane.

10. Return to the original text box by completing the following steps:

    a. Make Slide 2 active.

    b. Click in the text box containing the words *Default text box*.

    c. Position the mouse pointer on the border of the text box until the pointer displays with a four-headed arrow attached and then click the right mouse button.

    d. Click the *Set as Default Text Box* option at the shortcut menu.

    e. Press the Delete key to delete the text box.

11. Save **P-C4-P1-AddisonReport.pptx**.

Setting Tabs in a Text Box

Inside a text box you may want to align text in columns using tabs. A text box, by default, contains left alignment tabs that display as gray marks along the bottom of the horizontal ruler. (If the ruler is not visible, display the horizontal ruler as well as the vertical ruler by clicking the VIEW tab and then clicking the *Ruler* check box in the Show group to insert a check mark.) These default left alignment tabs can be changed to center, right, or decimal. To change to a different tab alignment, click the Alignment button located at the left side of the horizontal ruler. Display the desired tab alignment symbol and then click at the desired position on the horizontal ruler. When you set a tab on the horizontal ruler, any default tabs to the left of the new tab are deleted. Move tabs on the horizontal ruler by using the mouse to drag the tab to the desired position. To delete a tab, use the mouse to drag the tab off of the ruler.

You can also set tabs with options at the Tabs dialog box. To display this dialog box, click the Paragraph group dialog box launcher. At the Paragraph dialog box, click the Tabs button that displays in the lower left corner. At the Tabs dialog box, type a tab position in the *Tab stop position* measurement box, choose a tab alignment with options in the *Alignment* section, and then click the Set button. Clear a specific tab by typing the tab stop position in the *Tab stop position* measurement box and then clicking the Clear button. Clear all tabs from the horizontal ruler by clicking the Clear All button. When all desired changes are made, click OK to close the Tabs dialog box and then click OK to close the Paragraph dialog box.

HINT

Tab stops help you align your text in a slide.

L

Left Tab

⊥

Center Tab

⅃

Right Tab

⊥̇

Decimal Tab

1. With **P-C4-P1-AddisonReport.pptx** open, make Slide 1 active and then click the HOME tab.
2. Click the New Slide button arrow and then click the *Title Only* layout.
3. Click in the placeholder text *Click to add title* and then type **Executive Officers**.
4. Draw a text box by completing the following steps:
   a. Click the INSERT tab.
   b. Click the Text Box button in the Text group.
   c. Draw a text box in the slide that is approximately 10 inches wide and 0.5 inch tall.
5. Change tabs in the text box by completing the following steps:

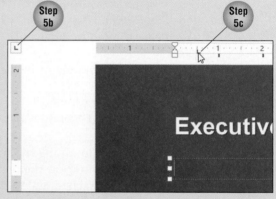

   a. Display the horizontal ruler by clicking the VIEW tab and then clicking the *Ruler* check box in the Show group to insert a check mark.
   b. With the insertion point inside the text box, check the Alignment button at the left side of the horizontal ruler and make sure the left tab symbol displays.
   c. Position the tip of the mouse pointer on the horizontal ruler below the 0.5-inch mark and then click the left mouse button.

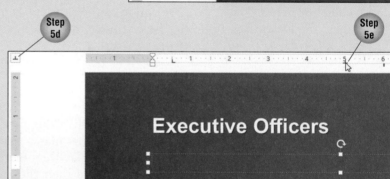

   d. Click once on the Alignment button to display the Center alignment symbol.
   e. Click immediately below the 5-inch mark on the horizontal ruler.
   f. Click once on the Alignment button to display the Right alignment symbol.
   g. Click on the horizontal ruler immediately below the 9.5-inch mark. (You may need to expand the size of the text box to set the tab at the 9.5-inch mark.)
6. Type the text in the text box as shown in the slide in Figure 4.3. Make sure you press the Tab key before typing text in the first column. (This moves the insertion point to the first tab, which is a left alignment tab.) Bold the three column headings—*Name*, *Title*, and *Number*.
7. When you are finished typing the text in the text box, press Ctrl + A to select all of the text in the text box.
8. Drag the left alignment marker on the horizontal ruler from the 0.5-inch mark to the 0.25-inch mark and then drag the center alignment marker on the horizontal ruler from the 5-inch mark on the ruler to the 5.5-inch mark.
9. With the text selected, click the Line Spacing button in the Paragraph group on the HOME tab and then click the *1.5* option.
10. Position the text box as shown in Figure 4.3.
11. Save **P-C4-P1-AddisonReport.pptx**.

Figure 4.3 Project 1c, Slide 2

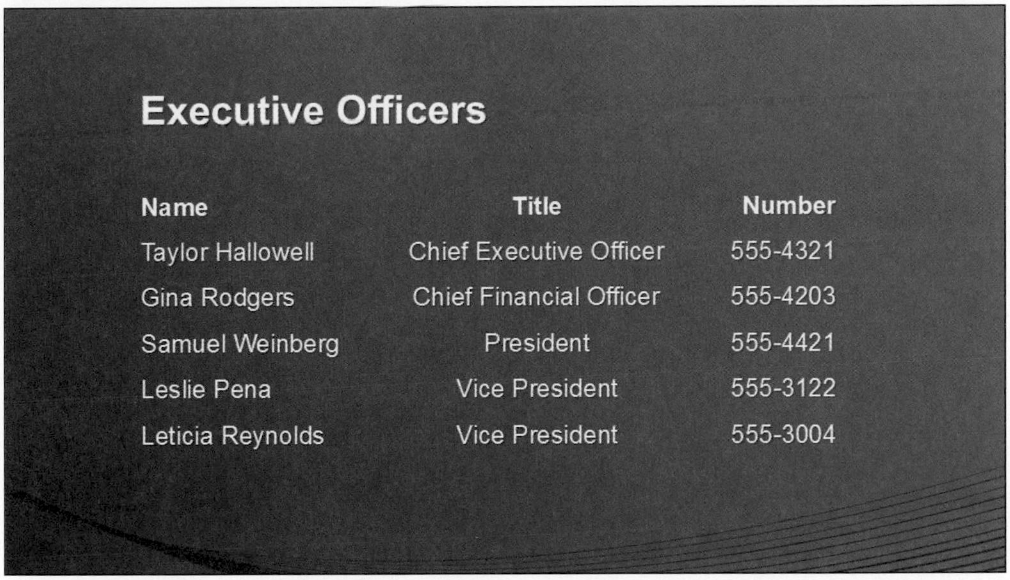

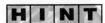

Executive Officers
Name
Title
Number
Taylor Hallowell
Chief Executive Officer
555-4321
Gina Rodgers
Chief Financial Officer
555-4203
Samuel Weinberg
President
555-4421
Leslie Pena
Vice President
555-3122
Leticia Reynolds
Vice President
555-3004

Inserting, Formatting, and Copying Shapes

You can draw shapes in a slide with shapes in the Drawing group or with the Shapes button in the Illustrations group on the INSERT tab. Use the Shapes button drop-down list to draw shapes including lines, basic shapes, block arrows, flow chart symbols, callouts, stars, and banners. Click a shape and the mouse pointer displays as crosshairs (plus sign). Click in the slide to insert the shape or position the crosshairs in the slide and then drag to create the shape. Apply formatting to a shape in a manner similar to formatting a text box. Format a shape with buttons in the Drawing group on the HOME tab, with buttons on the DRAWING TOOLS FORMAT tab, options in the Format Shape task pane, or with options at the shortcut menu. When drawing an enclosed object, you can maintain the proportions of the shape by holding down the Shift key while dragging with the mouse to create the shape.

If you draw and format a shape and decide that you want to use the same formatting for other shapes in the presentation, save the shape as the default. To do this, right-click the border of the shape and then click *Set as Default Shape*.

To copy a shape, select the shape and then click the Copy button in the Clipboard group on the HOME tab. Position the insertion point at the location where you want the copied image and then click the Paste button. You can also copy a selected shape by holding down the Ctrl key while dragging the shape to the desired location.

Quick Steps

Insert a Shape
1. Click INSERT tab.
2. Click Shapes button.
3. Click desired shape at drop-down list.
4. Click or drag in slide to create shape.

Shapes

HINT

Many shapes have an adjustment handle you can use to change the most prominent feature of the shape.

Quick Steps

Copy a Shape
1. Select desired shape.
2. Click Copy button.
3. Position insertion point at desired location.
4. Click Paste button.

OR

1. Select desired shape.
2. Hold down Ctrl key.
3. Drag shape to desired location.

Displaying Rulers, Gridlines, and Guides ■■■■■■■■■■

PowerPoint provides a number of features to help you position objects such as placeholders, text boxes, and shapes. You can display horizontal and vertical rulers, gridlines, and/or drawing guides and use Smart Guides as shown in Figure 4.4. Turn the horizontal and vertical rulers on and off with the *Ruler* check box in the Show group on the VIEW tab as you did in Project 1c. The Show group also contains a *Gridlines* check box. Insert a check mark in this check box and gridlines display in the active slide. Gridlines are intersecting lines that create a grid on the slide and are useful for aligning objects. You can also turn the display of gridlines on and off with the keyboard shortcut, Shift + F9.

Turn on drawing guides to help position objects on a slide. Drawing guides are horizontal and vertical dashed lines that display on the slide in the slide pane as shown in Figure 4.4. To turn on the drawing guides, display the Grid and Guides dialog box shown in Figure 4.5. Display this dialog box by clicking the Show group dialog box launcher on the VIEW tab. At the dialog box, insert a check mark in the *Display drawing guides on screen* check box. By default, the horizontal and vertical drawing guides intersect in the middle of the slide. You can move these guides by dragging the guide with the mouse. As you drag the guide, a measurement displays next to the mouse pointer. Drawing guides and gridlines display on the slide but do not print.

Figure 4.4 Rulers, Gridlines, Drawing Guides, and Smart Guides

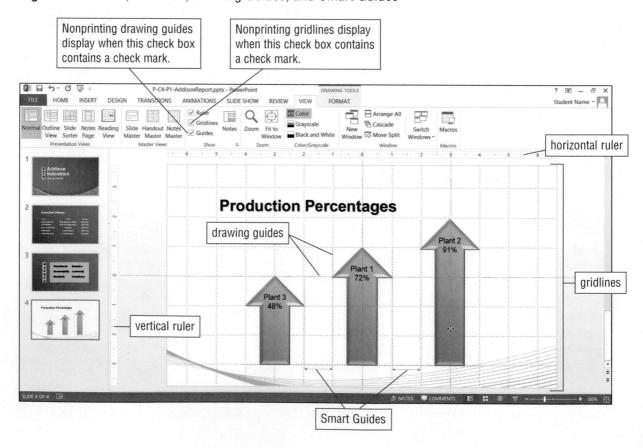

Figure 4.5 Grid and Guides Dialog Box

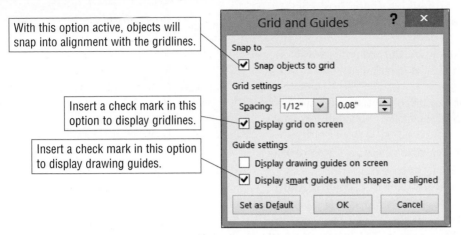

With this option active, objects will snap into alignment with the gridlines.

Insert a check mark in this option to display gridlines.

Insert a check mark in this option to display drawing guides.

PowerPoint includes Smart Guides, which appear when you move objects that are close together on a slide. Use these guides to help you align and evenly space the objects on the slide. Turn on gridlines with the *Gridlines* check box on the VIEW tab or by inserting a check mark in the *Display grid on screen* check box at the Grid and Guides dialog box. The horizontal and vertical spacing between the gridlines is 0.08 inch by default. You can change this measurement with the *Spacing* option at the Grid and Guides dialog box.

As you drag or draw an object on the slide, it is pulled into alignment with the nearest intersection of gridlines. This is because the *Snap objects to grid* option at the Grid and Guides dialog box is active by default. If you want to position an object precisely, turn off this option by removing the check mark from the *Snap objects to grid* check box or by holding down the Alt key while dragging an object. Smart Guides display when shapes are aligned. If you do not want Smart Guides to display, click the *Display smart guides when shapes are aligned* check box in the Grid and Guides dialog box to remove the check mark.

Project 1d **Drawing and Formatting Shapes** **Part 4 of 14**

1. With **P-C4-P1-AddisonReport.pptx** open, make Slide 3 active and then insert a new slide by clicking the New Slide button arrow in the Slides group on the HOME tab and then clicking the *White Background* layout at the drop-down list.
2. Turn on the display of gridlines by clicking the VIEW tab and then clicking *Gridlines* to insert a check mark in the check box.
3. Click in the title placeholder and then type **Production Percentages**.
4. Turn on the drawing guides and turn off the snap-to-grid feature by completing the following steps:
   a. Make sure the VIEW tab is active and then click the Show group dialog box launcher.

b. At the Grid and Guides dialog box, click the *Snap objects to grid* check box to remove the check mark.

c. Click the *Display drawing guides on screen* check box to insert a check mark.

d. Click OK.

5. Insert the left-most arrow in the slide, as shown in Figure 4.6 (on page 140), by completing the following steps:

a. Click outside the title placeholder to deselect it.

b. Click the INSERT tab.

c. Click the Shapes button in the Illustrations group and then click the *Up Arrow* shape (third column, first row in the *Block Arrows* section).

d. Position the crosshairs at the intersection of the horizontal drawing guide and the third vertical gridline from the left.

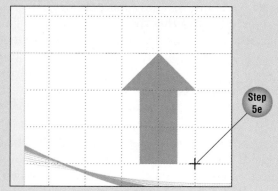

e. Hold down the left mouse button, drag down and to the right until the crosshairs are positioned on the intersection of the fifth vertical line from the left and the first horizontal line from the bottom, and then release the mouse button. (Your arrow should be the approximate size shown in Figure 4.6.)

f. With the arrow selected and the DRAWING TOOLS FORMAT tab active, click the Shape Fill button arrow in the Shape Styles group, and then click *Aqua, Accent 5* at the drop-down gallery (ninth column, first row in the *Theme Colors* section).

g. Click the Shape Outline button arrow and then click *Dark Blue* at the drop-down gallery (ninth option in the *Standard Colors* section).

h. Apply a shape style to the arrow by clicking the More button at the right side of the shape style thumbnails and then clicking the *Subtle Effect - Blue, Accent 1* option (second column, fourth row).

i. Click the Shape Effects button in the Shape Styles group, point to *Bevel*, and then click the *Soft Round* option (second column, second row in the *Bevel* section).

6. Insert text in the arrow by completing the following steps:

a. With the arrow selected, type **Plant 3**, press the Enter key, and then type 48%.

b. Click the HOME tab, click the Align Text button in the Paragraph group, and then click the *Top* option at the drop-down list.

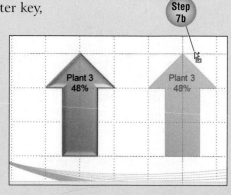

7. Copy the arrow by completing the following steps:

a. Position the mouse pointer on the border of the selected arrow until the mouse pointer displays with a four-headed arrow attached.

b. Hold down the Ctrl key and drag the arrow to the right so the tip of the arrow is positioned at the intersection of the horizontal and vertical drawing guides.

8. Move the vertical drawing guide and then copy the arrow by completing the following steps:

a. Click outside the arrow to deselect the arrow.

b. Position the mouse pointer on the vertical drawing guide, hold down the left mouse button, drag right until the mouse pointer displays with *3.00* and a right-pointing arrow in a box, and then release the mouse button.

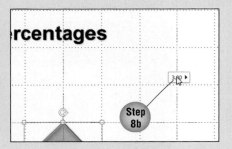

c. Click the arrow at the right, hold down the Ctrl key and then drag the arrow to the right so the tip of the arrow is positioned at the intersection of the horizontal and vertical drawing guides. Watch for the Smart Guides to display indicating that the arrows are aligned and evenly spaced (see image at the right).

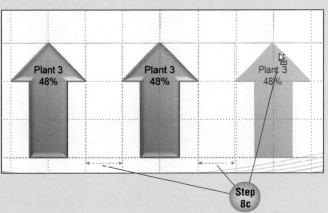

9. Increase the height of the middle arrow by completing the following steps:

a. Click the middle arrow to select it.

b. Using the mouse, drag the top middle sizing handle up to the next horizontal gridline.

c. Click the right arrow and then drag the top middle sizing handle up to the second horizontal gridline (see Figure 4.6).

d. Change the text in the middle arrow to *Plant 1 72%* and change the text in the arrow at the right to *Plant 2 91%* (see Figure 4.6).

10. Turn on the snap-to-grid feature and turn off the gridlines and drawing guides by completing the following steps:

a. Click the VIEW tab.

b. Click the Show group dialog box launcher.

c. At the Grid and Guides dialog box, click the *Snap objects to grid* check box to insert a check mark.

d. Click the *Display grid on screen* option to remove the check mark.

e. Click the *Display drawing guides on screen* check box to remove the check mark.

f. Click OK.

11 Change the slide layout by clicking the HOME tab, clicking the Layout button in the Slides group, and then clicking the *Title Only* layout.

12. Set the formatting of the arrow shape as the default by completing the following steps:

a. Click the first arrow shape.

b. Position the mouse pointer on the arrow shape border until the pointer displays with a four-headed arrow attached and then click the right mouse button.

c. Click the *Set as Default Shape* option at the shortcut menu.

13. Draw a shape by completing the following steps:

a. Click the INSERT tab, click the Shapes button, and then click the Bevel shape (first option, third row in the *Basic Shapes* section).

b. Click in the lower right corner of the slide.

c. Change the height and width of the shape to 0.6 inch.

d. Type **AI** in the shape.

e. Position the shape in the slide as shown in Figure 4.6.

14. Save **P-C4-P1-AddisonReport.pptx**.

Figure 4.6 Project 1d, Slide 4

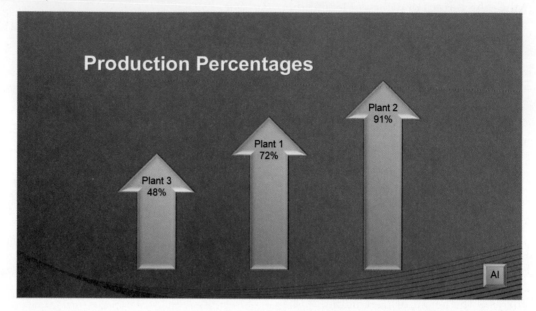

Merging Shapes ■■■■■■■■■■■■ ■■■■■■■■■■■■■ ■■■

Merge Shapes

Use the Merge Shapes button on the DRAWING TOOLS FORMAT tab to merge shapes to create custom shapes that are not available with the default shapes. To merge shapes, draw the shapes in the slide, select the shapes, and then click the Merge Shapes button in the Insert Shapes group on the DRAWING TOOLS FORMAT tab. At the drop-down list that displays, choose one of the options. The options include *Union*, *Combine*, *Fragment*, *Intersect*, and *Subtract*. Each option merges the cells in a different manner.

Project 1e | **Merging Shapes** | **Part 5 of 14**

1. With **P-C4-P1-AddisonReport.pptx** open, make Slide 4 active and then insert a slide from another presentation by completing the following steps:
   a. Make the HOME tab active.
   b. Click the New Slide button arrow and then click *Reuse Slides* at the drop-down list.
   c. At the Reuse Slides task pane, click the Browse button and then click *Browse File* at the drop-down list.
   d. At the Browse dialog box, navigate to the PC4 folder on your storage medium and then double-click *IEC.pptx*.
   e. Click the second slide thumbnail in the Reuse Slides task pane.
   f. Close the Reuse Slides task pane by clicking the Close button in the upper right corner of the task pane.

2. The slide you inserted contains a circle shape and four rectangle shapes already drawn for you. Merge the shapes to create an image for the International Energy Consortium by completing the following steps:

a. Click the slide in the slide pane and then press Ctrl + A to select all of the shapes in the slide.

b. Click the DRAWING TOOLS FORMAT tab.

c. Click the Merge Shapes button in the Insert Shapes group.

d. Hover your mouse over each option in the drop-down list, notice how the option merges the shapes in the slide, and then click the *Subtract* option. (This merges the shapes into one shape.)

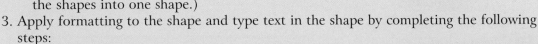

3. Apply formatting to the shape and type text in the shape by completing the following steps:

a. Click the Shape Fill button arrow in the Shape Styles group and then click the *White, Text 1* option (second column, first row in the *Theme Colors* section).

b. Click the Text Fill button arrow in the WordArt Styles group and then click the *Black, Background 1* option (first column, first row in the *Theme Colors* section).

c. Type the following in the shape pressing the Enter key to end the lines as shown:

International Energy
Consortium
Global Summit
March 10 to 12, 2016
Paris, France

d. Select the text you just typed and then change the font size to 20 points.

4. Save **P-C4-P1-AddisonReport.pptx**.

Grouping/Ungrouping Objects ■■■■■■■■■■■■■■■■■■■

If you want to apply the same formatting or make the same adjustments to the size or rotation of objects, group the objects. If you group objects and then apply formatting such as a shape fill, effect, or shape style, the formatting is applied to each object within the group. With objects grouped, you can apply formatting more quickly to objects in the slide. To group objects, select the objects you want included in the group by clicking each object while holding down the Shift key or draw a border around the objects you want to include. With the objects selected, click the DRAWING TOOLS FORMAT tab, click the Group button in the Arrange group, and then click *Group* at the drop-down list.

An individual object within a group can be formatted. To do this, click any object in the group and the group border displays around the objects. Click the individual object and then apply the desired formatting. If you no longer want objects grouped, click the group to select it, click the DRAWING TOOLS FORMAT tab, click the Group button in the Arrange group, and then click *Ungroup* at the drop-down list.

▼ **Quick Steps**

Group Objects
1. Select desired objects.
2. Click DRAWING TOOLS FORMAT tab.
3. Click Group button.
4. Click *Group* at drop-down list.

Group

Group objects so you can move, size, flip, or rotate objects at one time.

1. With **P-C4-P1-AddisonReport.pptx** open, make Slide 3 active.
2. Group the objects and apply formatting by completing the following steps:
   a. Using the mouse, draw a border around the two text boxes in the slide to select them.
   b. Click the DRAWING TOOLS FORMAT tab.
   c. Click the Group button in the Arrange group and then click *Group* at the drop-down list.

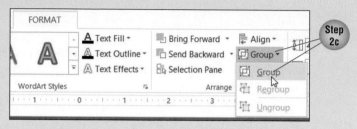

   d. Click the More button at the right side of the shape style thumbnails in the Shape Styles group and then click the *Subtle Effect - Blue, Accent 1* option at the drop-down gallery (second column, fourth row).
   e. Click the Shape Outline button arrow and then click the *Dark Blue* color (ninth color in the *Standard Colors* section).
   f. Click the Shape Outline button arrow, point to *Weight*, and then click *4½ pt*.
3. With the text boxes selected, ungroup the text boxes by clicking the Group button in the Arrange group and then clicking *Ungroup* at the drop-down list.
4. Click the text box containing the columns of text, click the More button at the right side of the WordArt style thumbnails, and then click the *Fill - White, Text 1, Outline - Background 1, Hard Shadow - Background 1* option (first column, third row).
5. Click Slide 1, click the text box containing *2016*, click the Quick Styles button in the Drawing group on the HOME tab, and then click the *Subtle Effect - Blue, Accent 1* option at the drop-down gallery (second column, fourth row).
6. Save **P-C4-P1-AddisonReport.pptx**.

Inserting an Image ■■■■■■■■■■■■■■■■■■■■■■■■

Insert an image such as a picture or clip art in a slide with buttons in the Images group on the INSERT tab. To insert a picture in a presentation, click the INSERT tab and then click the Pictures button in the Images group. At the Insert Picture dialog box, navigate to the folder containing the desired picture and then double-click the picture. Use buttons on the PICTURE TOOLS FORMAT tab to format and customize the picture.

Pictures

Insert a picture from your camera by downloading the picture to your computer and then copying the picture into PowerPoint.

Customizing and Formatting an Image

When you insert an image in a slide, the image is selected and the PICTURE TOOLS FORMAT tab is active as shown in Figure 4.7. Use buttons on this tab to apply formatting to the image. Use options in the Adjust group on the PICTURE TOOLS FORMAT tab to remove unwanted portions of the image, correct the brightness and contrast, change the image color, apply artistic effects, compress the size of the image file, change to a different image, and reset the image back to the original formatting.

Use buttons in the Picture Styles group to apply a predesigned style to the image, change the image border, or apply other effects to the image. With options in the Arrange group, you can position the image on the page, specify how text will wrap around it, align the image with other elements in the document, and rotate the image. Use options in the Size group to crop the image and change the size of the image.

Figure 4.7 PICTURE TOOLS FORMAT Tab

Sizing, Cropping, and Moving an Image

Change the size of an image with the *Shape Height* and *Shape Width* measurement boxes in the Size group on the PICTURE TOOLS FORMAT tab or with the sizing handles that display around the selected image. To change size with a sizing handle, position the mouse pointer on a sizing handle until the pointer turns into a double-headed arrow and then hold down the left mouse button. Drag the sizing handle in or out to decrease or increase the size of the image and then release the mouse button. Use the middle sizing handles at the left or right side of the image to make the image wider or thinner. Use the middle sizing handles at the top or bottom of the image to make the image taller or shorter. Use the sizing handles at the corners of the image to change both the width and height at the same time.

The Size group on the PICTURE TOOLS FORMAT tab contains a Crop button. Use this button to remove portions of an image. Click the Crop button and the mouse pointer displays with the crop tool attached, which is a black square with overlapping lines, and the image displays with cropping handles around the border. Drag a cropping handle to remove a portion of the image.

Crop

Move a selected image by dragging it to the desired location. Move the image by positioning the mouse pointer on the image border until the arrow pointer turns into a four-headed arrow. Hold down the left mouse button, drag the image to the desired position, and then release the mouse button. You can use the arrow keys on the keyboard to move the image in the desired direction. If you want to move the image in small increments (called *nudging*), hold down the Ctrl key while pressing an arrow key.

Use the rotation handle to rotate an image by positioning the mouse pointer on the white, round rotation handle until the pointer displays as a circular arrow. Hold down the left mouse button, drag in the desired direction, and then release the mouse button.

Arranging Images

Use the Bring Forward and Send Backward buttons in the Arrange group on the DRAWING TOOLS FORMAT tab or the PICTURE TOOLS FORMAT tab to layer one object on top of another. Click the Bring Forward button and the selected object is moved forward one layer. For example, if you have three objects layered on top of each other, selecting the object at the bottom of the layers and then clicking the Bring Forward button will move the object in front of the second object (but not the first object). If you want to move an object to the top layer, select the object, click the Bring Forward button arrow, and then click the *Bring to Front* option at the drop-down list. To move the selected object back one layer, click the Send Backward button. If you want to move the selected object behind all other objects, click the Send Backward button arrow and then click the *Send to Back* option at the drop-down list.

Bring
Forward

Send
Backward

1. With **P-C4-P1-AddisonReport.pptx** open, make Slide 4 active and click the INSERT tab.
2. Insert a new slide by clicking the New Slide button arrow in the Slides group and then clicking *Blank* at the drop-down list.
3. Insert a text box by completing the following steps:
   a. Click the Text Box button in the Text group on the INSERT tab.
   b. Click in the middle of the slide.
   c. Change the font to Arial Black and the font size to 36 points.
   d. Click the Center button in the Paragraph group.
   e. Type **Alternative**, press the Enter key, and then type **Energy Resources**.
   f. With the text box selected, click the DRAWING TOOLS FORMAT tab.
   g. Click the Align button in the Arrange group and then click *Distribute Horizontally* at the drop-down list.
   h. Click the Align button and then click *Distribute Vertically* at the drop-down list.
4. Insert a picture by completing the following steps:
   a. Click the INSERT tab.
   b. Click the Pictures button in the Images group.
   c. At the Insert Picture dialog box, navigate to the PC4 folder on your storage medium and then double-click *Mountain.jpg*.
5. You decide to insert a picture of the ocean rather than a mountain. Change the picture by completing the following steps:
   a. With the image of the mountain selected, click the Change Picture button in the Adjust group.
   b. At the Insert Pictures window that displays, click the Browse button located to the right of the *From a file* option.
   c. At the Insert Picture dialog box, make sure the PC4 folder on your storage medium is selected and then double-click *Ocean.jpg*.
6. Crop the picture and then crop the picture to a shape by completing the following steps:
   a. With the picture selected, click the Crop button in the Size group on the PICTURE TOOLS FORMAT tab.
   b. Position the mouse pointer (displays with the crop tool attached) on the cropping handle in the middle of the right side of the picture.
   c. Hold down the left mouse button and then drag to the left approximately 0.25 inch. (Use the guideline that displays on the horizontal ruler to crop the picture 0.25 inch.)
   d. Click the Crop button to turn off cropping.

e. Click the Crop button arrow, point to the *Crop to Shape* option at the drop-down list, and then click the Oval shape (first option) in the *Basic Shapes* section of the side menu.

7. Click in the *Shape Height* measurement box in the Size group, type **5**, and then press Enter.

8. Click the Send Backward button in the Arrange group. (This moves the picture behind the text in the text box.)

9. Align the picture by completing the following steps:

   a. Click the Align button in the Arrange group on the PICTURE TOOLS FORMAT tab and then click the *Distribute Horizontally* option.

   b. Click the Align button and then click the *Distribute Vertically* option.

10. Format the picture by completing the following steps:

   a. Click the Artistic Effects button in the Adjust group and then click the *Cutout* option (first column, bottom row).

   b. Click the Corrections button in the Adjust group and then click the *Soften: 25%* option (second option in the *Sharpen/Soften* section).

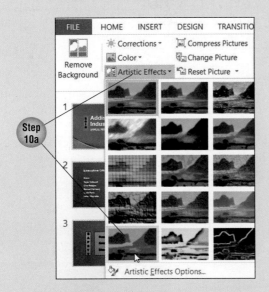

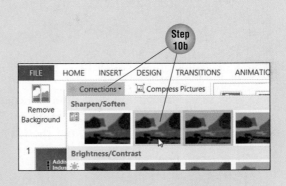

   c. Click the Picture Border button arrow in the Picture Styles group and then click the *Dark Blue* color (ninth option in the *Standard Colors* section).

11. After viewing the effects applied to the picture, reset the picture to the original effects by clicking the Reset Picture button arrow in the Adjust group and then clicking *Reset Picture* at the drop-down list.

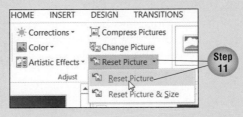

12. Format the picture by completing the following steps:
   a. Click the Corrections button in the Adjust group and then click the *Brightness: -20% Contrast: +40%* option (second column, bottom row in the *Brightness/Contrast* section).
   b. Click the Corrections button and then click the *Sharpen: 25%* option (fourth option in the *Sharpen/Soften* section).
   c. Click the More button that displays at the right side of the picture style thumbnails and then click the *Soft Edge Oval* option at the drop-down gallery (sixth column, third row).

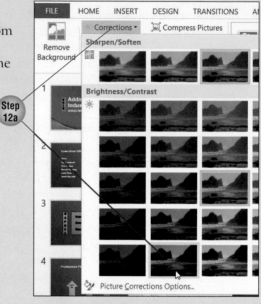

Step 12a

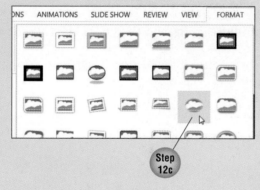

Step 12c

   d. Click the Compress Pictures button in the Adjust group. At the Compress Pictures dialog box, click OK.
13. Make Slide 6 active and then insert a new slide by clicking the HOME tab, clicking the New Slide button arrow in the Slides group, and then clicking *Title Only* at the drop-down list.
14. Click in the title placeholder and then type **Shipping Contracts**.
15. Insert a picture by completing the following steps:
   a. Click the INSERT tab and then click the Pictures button in the Images group.
   b. At the Insert Picture dialog box, make sure the PC4 folder on your storage medium is active and then double-click ***Ship.jpg***.
16. With the ship picture selected, remove some of the background by completing the following steps:
   a. Click the Remove Background button in the Adjust group on the PICTURE TOOLS FORMAT tab.
   b. Using the left middle sizing handle, drag the border to the left to include the back of the ship (see image at the right).
   c. Click the Mark Areas to Remove button in the Refine group on the BACKGROUND REMOVAL tab.
   d. Click anywhere in the water that displays below the ship. (This removes the water from the picture. If all of the water is not removed, you will need to click again in the remaining water.)

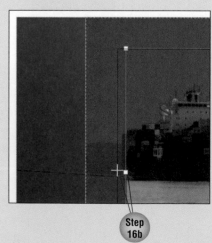

Step 16b

e. Using the right middle sizing handle, drag the border to the left so the border is near the front of the ship.

f. If part of the structure above the front of the ship has been removed, include it in the picture. To begin, click the Mark Areas to Keep button in the Refine group. (The mouse pointer displays as a pencil.)

g. Using the mouse, position the pencil at the top of the structure (as shown at the right), drag down to the top of the containers on the ship, and then release the mouse button.

Step 16g

h. Click the Keep Changes button in the Close group on the BACKGROUND REMOVAL tab.

17. Click the Corrections button in the Adjust group on the PICTURE TOOLS FORMAT tab and then click the *Brightness: +40% Contrast: +40%* option at the drop-down gallery (last column, bottom row in the *Brightness/Contrast* section).

18. Click the Corrections button in the Adjust group and then click the *Sharpen: 50%* option at the drop-down gallery (last option in the *Sharpen/Soften* section).

19. Drag the picture down to the middle of the slide.

20. Click outside the picture to deselect it.

21. Save **P-C4-P1-AddisonReport.pptx**.

Inserting a Picture as a Slide Background

A picture can be inserted as a slide background. To do this, click the DESIGN tab and then click the Format Background button in the Customize group. This displays the Format Background task pane with the Fill icon selected. Click the *Picture or texture fill* option in the FILL section of the task pane and then click the File button. At the Insert Picture dialog box, navigate to the desired folder and then double-click the picture. Click the Close button to close the Format Background task pane. If you want the picture background to display on all slides, click the Apply to All button at the Format Background task pane.

Use options in the Format Background task pane to apply formatting to the background picture. When you insert a picture in a slide, the Format Background task pane (with the Fill icon selected) includes options for hiding background graphics, applying a texture, changing the picture transparency, and offsetting the image on the slide either at the left, right, top, or bottom. Click the Effects icon and then click the Artistic Effects button and a drop-down palette of artistic options displays. Click the Picture icon and options display in the task pane for correcting the sharpness, softness, brightness, and contrast of the picture and for changing the picture color saturation and tone.

▼ **Quick Steps**

Insert a Picture as a Slide Background
1. Click DESIGN tab.
2. Click Format Background button.
3. Click *Picture or texture fill* option.
4. Click File button.
5. Navigate to desired folder.
6. Double-click desired picture.
7. Click Close button.

1. With **P-C4-P1-AddisonReport.pptx** open, make sure both Slide 7 and the HOME tab are active.
2. Click the New Slide button arrow in the Slides group and then click the *Title Only* layout at the drop-down list.
3. Insert a picture background on Slide 8 by completing the following steps:
    a. Click the DESIGN tab.
    b. Click the Format Background button in the Customize group.
    c. At the Format Background task pane, click the *Picture or texture fill* option in the FILL section.
    d. Click the File button in the task pane that displays below the text *Insert picture from*.
    e. At the Insert Picture dialog box, navigate to the PC4 folder on your storage medium and then double-click *EiffelTower.jpg*.
4. Apply formatting to the picture background by completing these steps:
    a. Click the *Hide background graphics* check box to insert a check mark.
    b. Select the current percentage in the *Transparency* measurement box, type **5**, and then press Enter.
    c. Select the current number in the *Offset top* measurement box, type **-50**, and then press Enter. (Decreasing the negative number displays more of the top of the Eiffel Tower.)
    d. Click the Effects icon in the task pane and then, if necessary, click ARTISTIC EFFECTS to display the formatting options.
    e. Click the Artistic Effects button and then click the *Glow Diffused* option (fourth column, second row).

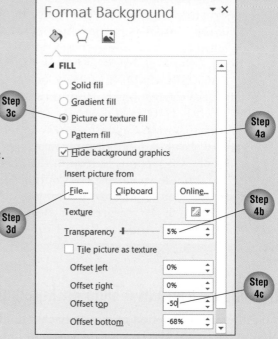

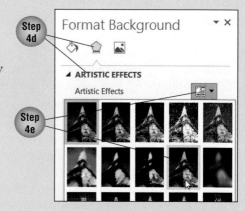

f. Click the Picture icon and, if necessary, expand the *PICTURE CORRECTIONS* section.

g. Select the current number in the *Contrast* text box, type **25**, and then press Enter.

h. If necessary, expand the *PICTURE COLOR* section.

i. Select the current number in the *Saturation* measurement box, type **80**, and then press Enter.

5. Remove the artistic effect by clicking the Effects icon, clicking the Artistic Effects button, and then clicking the *None* option (first option).

6. Close the Format Background task pane.

7. Click in the title placeholder, type **European**, press Enter, and then type **Division 2017**. Drag the placeholder so it is positioned attractively on the slide in the upper left corner.

8. Save **P-C4-P1-AddisonReport.pptx**.

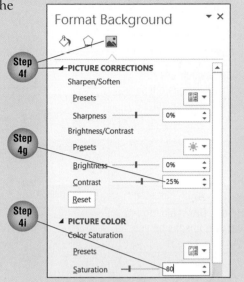

Inserting an Image from Office.com

Microsoft Office includes a gallery of media images you can insert in a slide, such as clip art images and photographs. To insert an image in a presentation, click the INSERT tab and then click the Online Pictures button in the Images group. This displays the Insert Pictures window, as shown in Figure 4.8 on the next page.

At the Insert Pictures window, click in the search text box to the right of Office.com Clip Art, type the search term or topic, and then press Enter. Images that match your search term or topic display in the window. To insert an image, click the desired image and then click the Insert button or double-click the image. This downloads the image from the Office.com website to your slide.

When you insert an image in a slide, the image is selected and the PICTURE TOOLS FORMAT tab is active. Use buttons on this tab to customize an image just as you customize a picture.

▼ **Quick Steps**

Insert Images from Office.com
1. Click INSERT tab.
2. Click Online Pictures button.
3. Type search word or topic.
4. Press Enter.
5. Double-click desired image.

Online Pictures

For additional clip art images, consider buying a commercial package of images.

Figure 4.8 Insert Pictures Window

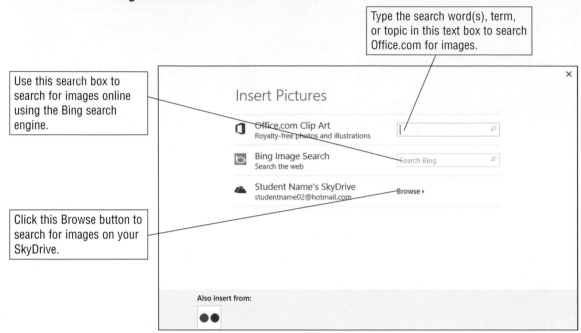

Type the search word(s), term, or topic in this text box to search Office.com for images.

Use this search box to search for images online using the Bing search engine.

Click this Browse button to search for images on your SkyDrive.

Sizing, Rotating, and Positioning Objects

Shape Height

Shape Width

PowerPoint provides a variety of methods for sizing and positioning an object such as a shape, text box, or image on a slide. As you learned earlier in this chapter, you can use the sizing handles that display around an object and use the *Shape Height* and *Shape Width* measurement boxes to increase or decrease the size of an object. You positioned shapes and text boxes by dragging the objects with the mouse. You also used options at the Format Shape task pane with the Size & Properties icon selected to size and position a shape and a text box. You can size and position an image in a similar manner using options at the Format Picture task pane with the Size & Properties icon selected. Display this task pane by selecting an image and then clicking the Size group task pane launcher location on the PICTURE TOOLS FORMAT tab.

Project 1i   **Inserting and Formatting a Clip Art Image**   **Part 9 of 14**

1. With **P-C4-P1-AddisonReport.pptx** open, make Slide 4 active.
2. Click the New Slide button arrow in the Slides group on the HOME tab and then click the *Two Content* layout at the drop-down list.
3. Click the placeholder text *Click to add title* and then type **Technology**.
4. Click the placeholder text *Click to add text* located at the right side of the slide.
5. Click the Bullets button in the Paragraph group to turn off bullets.
6. Change the font size to 32 points and turn on bold formatting.
7. Type **Equipment** and then press the Enter key twice.
8. Type **Software** and then press the Enter key twice.
9. Type **Personnel**.

10. Insert a clip art image by completing the following steps:
   a. Click the Online Pictures button that displays in the middle of the placeholder at the left side of the slide.
   b. At the Insert Pictures window, type **computer construction worker** in the search text box and then press Enter.

   c. Double-click the clip art image in the window as shown below and to the right.
11. Scale, rotate, and position the clip art image by completing the following steps:
   a. With the clip art image selected, click the Rotate button in the Arrange group on the PICTURE TOOLS FORMAT tab and then click *Flip Horizontal* at the drop-down list.
   b. Click the Size group task pane launcher.
   c. At the Format Picture task pane with the Size & Properties icon selected, if necessary, click *SIZE* to expand the options.
   d. Select the *0°* in the *Rotation* measurement box and then type **15**.
   e. Select the current percentage in the *Scale Height* measurement box and then type **225**.

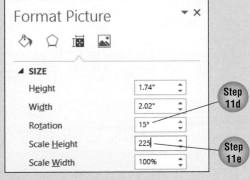

   f. Click *POSITION* to expand the options.
   g. Select the current measurement in the *Horizontal position* measurement box and then type **2.9**. (The image will slightly overlap the text.).
   h. Select the current measurement in the *Vertical position* measurement box, type **2**, and then press Enter.
   i. Close the Format Picture task pane.
12. Save **P-C4-P1-AddisonReport.pptx**.

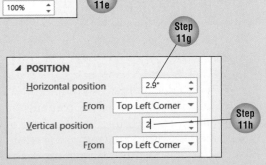

Copying Objects within and between Presentations

An object pasted to a different slide is positioned in the same location as the copied object.

Earlier in this chapter you learned how to copy shapes within a slide. You can also copy shapes as well as other objects to other slides within the same presentation or to slides in another presentation. To copy an object, select the object and then click the Copy button in the Clipboard group on the HOME tab. Make the desired slide active or open another presentation and display the desired slide and then click the Paste button in the Clipboard group. You can also copy an object by right-clicking the object and then clicking *Copy* at the shortcut menu. To paste the object, make the desired slide active, click the right mouse button, and then click *Paste* at the shortcut menu.

Project 1j **Copying an Object within and between Presentations** Part 10 of 14

1. With **P-C4-P1-AddisonReport.pptx** open, make Slide 1 active.
2. Open **Addison.pptx**.
3. Click the clip art image in Slide 1, click the Copy button in the Clipboard group, and then close **Addison.pptx**.
4. With **P-C4-P1-AddisonReport.pptx** open, click the Paste button. (This inserts the clip art image in Slide 1.)
5. With the clip art image selected, make Slide 2 active and then click the Paste button.
6. Decrease the size and position of the clip art by completing the following steps:
   a. Click the PICTURE TOOLS FORMAT tab.
   b. Click in the *Shape Height* measurement box, type **0.8**, and then press Enter.
   c. Drag the clip art image so that it is positioned in the upper right corner of the slide.
7. Copy the clip art image to other slides by completing the following steps:
   a. With the clip art image selected in Slide 2, click the HOME tab and then click the Copy button in the Clipboard group.
   b. Make Slide 3 active and then click the Paste button in the Clipboard group.
   c. Paste the clip art image to slides Slide 5 and 7.
8. Save **P-C4-P1-AddisonReport.pptx**.

Step 6b

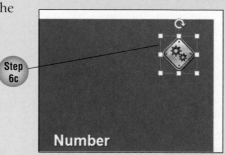

Step 6c

Number

Creating Screenshots ■■■■■■■■■■■■■■■■■■■■■■■■

Screenshot

The Images group on the INSERT tab contains a Screenshot button you can use to capture the contents or a portion of a screen as an image. This is useful for capturing information from a web page or from a file in another program. If you want to capture the entire screen, display the desired web page, or open the desired file from a program, make PowerPoint active, and then open a presentation. Click the INSERT tab, click the Screenshot button, and then click the desired screen thumbnail at the drop-down list. The currently active presentation does not display as a thumbnail at the drop-down list. Instead, any other file or program you have open displays. If you do not have another file or program open, the Windows desktop displays. When you click the desired thumbnail, the screenshot is inserted as an image in the active slide in the open presentation, the image is selected, and the PICTURE TOOLS FORMAT tab is active. Use buttons on this tab to customize the screenshot image.

In addition to making a screenshot of an entire screen, you can make a screenshot of a specific portion of the screen by clicking the *Screen Clipping* option at the Screenshot button drop-down list. When you click this option, the open web page, file, or Windows desktop displays in a dimmed manner and the mouse pointer displays as crosshairs. Using the mouse, draw a border around the specific area of the screen you want to capture. The specific area you identify is inserted in the active slide in the presentation as an image, the image is selected, and the PICTURE TOOLS FORMAT tab is active.

▼ **Quick Steps**

Insert a Screenshot
1. Open presentation.
2. Open another file.
3. Display desired information.
4. Make presentation active.
5. Click INSERT tab.
6. Click Screenshot button.
7. Click desired window at drop-down list.
OR
6. Click Screenshot button, *Screen Clipping*.
7. Drag to specify capture area.

Project 1k | **Inserting and Formatting a Screenshot** | **Part 11 of 14**

1. With **P-C4-P1-AddisonReport.pptx** open, make sure that no other programs are open.
2. Make Slide 9 active and then insert a new slide by clicking the New Slide button arrow in the Slides group on the HOME tab and then clicking the *Title Only* layout.
3. Click in the title placeholder and then type **Draft Invitation**.
4. Open Word and then open the document named **AddIndInvite.docx** from the PC4 folder on your storage medium.
5. Click the PowerPoint button on the Taskbar.
6. Insert a screenshot of the draft invitation in the Word document by completing the following steps:
   a. Click the INSERT tab.
   b. Click the Screenshot button in the Images group and then click *Screen Clipping* at the drop-down list.
   c. When the **AddIndInvite.docx** document displays in a dimmed manner, position the mouse crosshairs in the upper left corner of the invitation, hold down the left mouse button, drag down to the lower right corner of the invitation, and then release the mouse button.

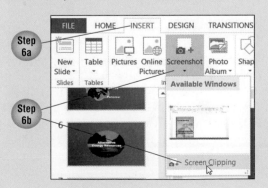

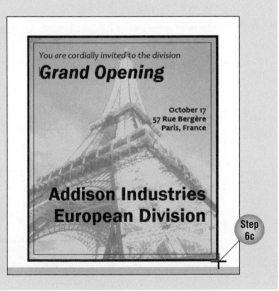

7. With the screenshot image inserted in the slide in the presentation, make the following changes:
   a. Click in the *Shape Width* measurement box in the Size group on the PICTURE TOOLS FORMAT tab, type 4.5, and then press Enter.
   b. Click the Corrections button in the Adjust group and then click the *Sharpen:25%* option (fourth option in the *Sharpen/Soften* section).
   c. Using the mouse, drag the screenshot image so it is centered on the slide.
8. Click outside the screenshot image to deselect it.
9. Save **P-C4-P1-AddisonReport.pptx**.
10. Click the Word button, close **AddIndInvite.docx**, and then close Word.

Creating and Formatting WordArt Text

▼ **Quick Steps**

Create WordArt Text
1. Click INSERT tab.
2. Click WordArt button.
3. Click desired WordArt style.
4. Type WordArt text.

WordArt

Text Fill   Text Outline

Use the WordArt feature to insert preformatted, decorative text in a slide and to modify text to conform to a variety of shapes. Consider using WordArt to create a company logo, letterhead, flier title, or heading. Insert WordArt in a slide by clicking the INSERT tab and then clicking the WordArt button in the Text group. This displays the WordArt drop-down list as shown in Figure 4.10. Click the desired WordArt style at this drop-down list and a text box is inserted in the slide containing the text *Your Text Here*. Type the desired WordArt text and then use the options in the DRAWING TOOLS FORMAT tab to customize the WordArt text.

When you insert WordArt text in a document, the DRAWING TOOLS FORMAT tab is active. Use options and buttons on this tab to format the WordArt text. Use the WordArt styles to apply predesigned formatting to the WordArt text. Customize the text with the Text Fill, Text Outline, and Text Effects buttons in the WordArt Styles group. Use the Text Fill button to change the fill color, the Text Outline button to change the text outline color, and the Text Effects button to apply a variety of text effects and shapes.

Figure 4.10 WordArt Drop-down List

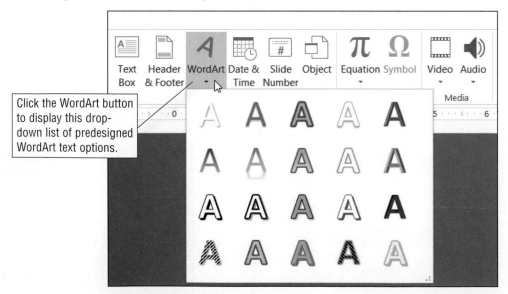

Click the Text Effects button and then point to *Transform* and a side menu displays with shaping and warping options as shown in Figure 4.11. Use these options to conform the WordArt text to a specific shape.

Text Effects

HINT

Use WordArt to create interesting text effects in slides.

HINT

Edit WordArt by double-clicking the WordArt text.

Figure 4.11 Text Effects *Transform* Side Menu

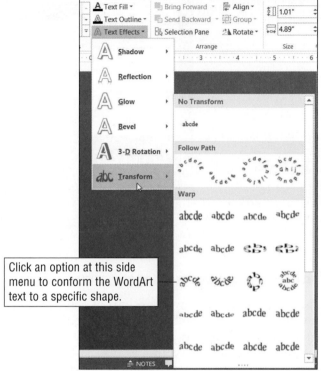

Click an option at this side menu to conform the WordArt text to a specific shape.

Project 1I   **Inserting and Formatting WordArt**   **Part 12 of 14**

1. With **P-C4-P1-AddisonReport.pptx** open, make sure Slide 10 is active and the HOME tab is active.
2. Click the New Slide button arrow in the Slides group and then click the *Blank* layout.
3. Click the INSERT tab.
4. Click the WordArt button in the Text group and then click the *Fill - White, Text 1, Outline - Background 1, Hard Shadow - Accent 1* option (second column, third row).
5. Type **Addison Industries**, press the Enter key, and then type **2016**.
6. Click the WordArt text border to change the border from a dashed line to a solid line. (This selects the text box.)

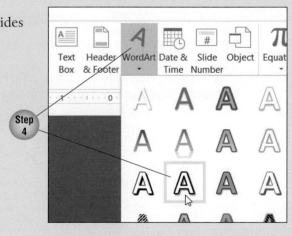

Step 4

Chapter 4 ■ Inserting Elements in Slides   **155**

7. Click the Text Outline button arrow in the WordArt Styles group and then click the *Dark Blue* color (ninth option in the *Standard Colors* section).
8. Click the Text Effects button, point to *Glow*, and then click *Blue, 11 pt glow, Accent color 1* at the side menu (first column, third row in the *Glow Variations* section).
9. Click the Text Effects button, point to *Transform*, and then click the *Triangle Up* option (third column, first row in the *Warp* section).
10. Click in the *Shape Height* measurement box, type 5, and then press Enter.
11. Click in the *Shape Width* measurement box, type 10, and then press Enter.
12. Click the Align button in the Arrange group and then click *Distribute Horizontally*.
13. Click the Align button and then click *Distribute Vertically*.
14. Save **P-C4-P1-AddisonReport.pptx**.

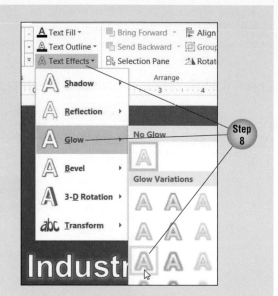

Inserting Symbols ■■■■■■■■■■■■■■■■■■■■■■■■

Ω
Symbol

Insert symbols in a slide in a presentation with options at the Symbol dialog box. Display this dialog box by clicking the Symbol button in the Symbols group on the INSERT tab. At the Symbol dialog box, choose a symbol font with the *Font* option in the dialog box, click the desired symbol in the list box, click the Insert button, and then click the Close button. The symbol is inserted in the slide at the location of the insertion point.

| **Project 1m** | Inserting Symbols in a Presentation | Part 13 of 14 |

1. With **P-C4-P1-AddisonReport.pptx** open, insert a symbol by completing the following steps:
   a. Make Slide 2 active.
   b. Click in the text box containing the names, titles, and telephone numbers. (This selects the text box.)
   c. Delete the *n* in *Pena* (the last name of the fourth person).
   d. Click the INSERT tab and then click the Symbol button in the Symbols group.

e. At the Symbol dialog box, click the down-pointing arrow at the right side of the *Font* option box, scroll down the drop-down list to the *Century Gothic* option, and then click the option.

f. Scroll down the symbol list box and then click the ñ symbol (located in approximately the ninth, tenth, or eleventh row).

g. Click the Insert button and then click the Close button.

2. Save **P-C4-P1-AddisonReport.pptx**.

Inserting Headers and Footers ■■■■■■■■■■■■■■■■■■

As you learned in Chapter 1, if you print a presentation as a handout or an outline, PowerPoint will automatically print the current date in the upper right corner of the page and the page number in the lower right corner. If you print the presentation as notes pages, PowerPoint will automatically print the page number when you print the individual slides. The date and page numbers are considered header and footer elements. You can modify existing header and footer elements or insert additional elements with options in the Header and Footer dialog box. Display the Header and Footer dialog box shown in Figure 4.12 by clicking the Header & Footer button in the Text group on the INSERT tab, clicking the Date & Time button in the Text group, or clicking the Slide Number button in the Text group. You can also display the Header and Footer dialog box by displaying the Print backstage area and then clicking the Edit Header & Footer hyperlink that displays below the galleries in the *Settings* category.

Header & Footer

Slide Number

The Header and Footer dialog box has two tabs, the Slide tab and the Notes and Handouts tab, and the options in the dialog box are similar with either tab selected. With options at the dialog box, you can insert the date and time, a header, a footer, and page numbers. If you insert the date and time in a presentation, you can choose the *Update automatically* option if you want the date and time updated each time the presentation is opened. Choose the date and time formatting by clicking the down-pointing arrow at the right side of the *Update automatically* option box and then choose the desired formatting at the drop-down list. If you choose the *Fixed* option, type the desired date and/or time in the *Fixed* text box. Type header text in the *Header* text box and type footer text in the *Footer* text box.

If you want to print the slide number on slides, insert a check mark in the *Slide number* check box in the Header and Footer dialog box with the Slide tab selected. If you want to include page numbers on handouts, notes pages, or outline pages, insert a check mark in the *Page number* check box in the Header and Footer dialog box with the Notes and Handouts tab selected. If you want all changes you make to the Header and Footer dialog box to apply to all slides or all handouts, notes pages, and outline pages, click the Apply to All button located in the lower right corner of the dialog box.

Figure 4.12 Header and Footer Dialog Box with the Notes and Handouts Tab Selected

Insert a check mark in this check box to insert the date and/or time.

If you want the date and/or time updated each time you open the presentation, click *Update automatically* and then choose the desired formatting at the drop-down list.

Text you type in the *Header* text box or *Footer* text box will print when you print the presentation as notes pages, handouts, or an outline.

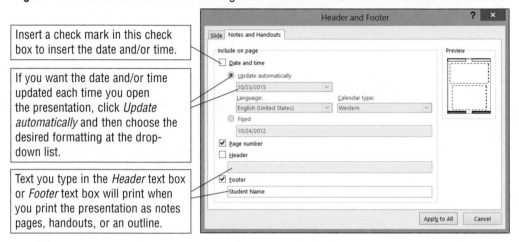

Project 1n **Inserting Headers and Footers** Part 14 of 14

1. With **P-C4-P1-AddisonReport.pptx** open, insert slide numbers on each slide in the presentation by completing the following steps:
   a. Make Slide 1 active.
   b. Click the INSERT tab.
   c. Click the Slide Number button in the Text group.
   d. At the Header and Footer dialog box with the Slide tab selected, click the *Slide number* check box to insert a check mark.
   e. Click the Apply to All button.
   f. Scroll through the slides and notice the slide number that displays in the lower right corner of each slide.
2. Insert your name as a footer that displays on each slide in the presentation by completing the following steps:
   a. Click the Header & Footer button in the Text group.

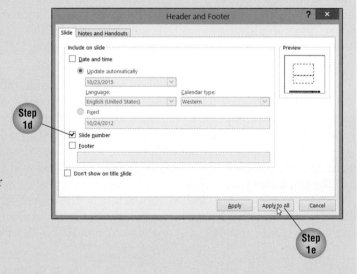

b. Click the *Footer* check box to insert a check mark, click in the *Footer* text box, and then type your first and last names.

c. Click the Apply to All button.

d. Run the presentation and notice that your name displays at the bottom left side of each slide.

3. You decide that you also want your name to print as a footer on handout pages. To do this, complete the following steps:

a. Click the Header & Footer button in the Text group.

b. At the Header and Footer dialog box, click the Notes and Handouts tab.

c. Click the *Footer* check box to insert a check mark, click in the *Footer* text box, and then type your first and last names.

d. Click the Apply to All button.

4. Insert the current date as a header that prints on handout pages by completing the following steps:

a. Click the Date & Time button in the Text group.

b. At the Header and Footer dialog box, click the Notes and Handouts tab.

c. Click the *Date and time* check box to insert a check mark.

d. Click the Apply to All button.

5. Insert the presentation name as a header that prints on handout pages by completing the following steps:

a. Click the FILE tab and then click the *Print* option.

b. At the Print backstage area, click the <u>Edit Header & Footer</u> hyperlink that displays below the galleries in the *Settings* category.

c. At the Header and Footer dialog box, click the Notes and Handouts tab.

d. Click the *Header* check box to insert a check mark, click in the *Header* text box, and then type **P-C4-P1-AddisonReport.pptx**.

e. Click the Apply to All button.

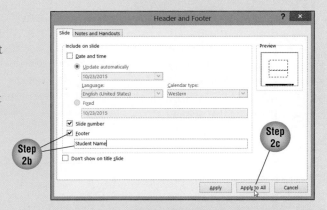

f. Click the second gallery in the *Settings* category and then click *6 Slides Horizontal* at the drop-down list. (If a number apears in the *Slides* text box, delete the number.)

g. Display the next handout page by clicking the Next Page button that displays toward the bottom of the Print backstage area.

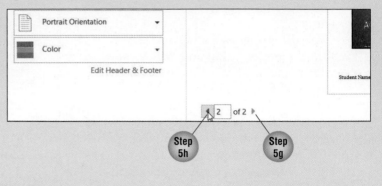

h. Click the Previous page button to display the first handout page.

i. Click the Print button to print the presentation as a handout with six slides printed horizontally per page.

6. Save and then close **P-C4-P1-AddisonReport.pptx**.

Chapter Summary

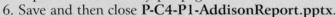

- Insert a text box in a slide using the Text Box button in the Text group on the INSERT tab. Format a text box with options in the Drawing group on the HOME tab, with options on the DRAWING TOOLS FORMAT tab, with options at the shortcut menu, or with options at the Format Shape task pane.

- Select all objects in a slide by clicking the Select button in the Editing group on the HOME tab and then clicking *Select All* or with the keyboard shortcut, Ctrl + A.

- Align selected objects with options from the Align button in the Arrange group on the DRAWING TOOLS FORMAT tab.

- Set tabs in a text box by clicking the Alignment button at the left side of the horizontal ruler until the desired symbol displays and then clicking on a specific location on the ruler. You can set a left, center, right, or decimal tab.

- Insert a shape in a slide with shapes in the Drawing group on the HOME tab or the Shapes button in the Illustrations group on the INSERT tab.

- With options in the Shapes button drop-down list, you can draw a line, basic shapes, block arrows, flow chart symbols, callouts, stars, and banners.

- Copy a shape by selecting the shape, clicking the Copy button in the Clipboard group, positioning the insertion point in the desired position, and then clicking the Paste button in the Clipboard group. You can also copy a shape by holding down the Ctrl key and then dragging the shape to the desired location.

- Turn the horizontal and vertical rulers on and off with the *Ruler* check box in the Show group on the VIEW tab and turn gridlines on and off with the *Gridlines* check box. You can also turn gridlines as well as drawing guides and the snap-to-grid feature on and off with options at the Grid and Guides dialog box.

- You can group objects and then apply the same formatting to all objects in the group. To group objects, select the objects, click the Group button in the Arrange group on the DRAWING TOOLS FORMAT tab, and then click *Group* at the drop-down list.

- Size images with the *Shape Height* and *Shape Width* measurement boxes on the PICTURE TOOLS FORMAT tab or with the sizing handles that display around a selected image.

- Use the Crop button in the Size group on the PICTURE TOOLS FORMAT tab to remove portions of an image.

- Move an image by dragging it to the new location. Move an image in small increments, called *nudging*, by holding down the Ctrl key while pressing an arrow key on the keyboard.

- Specify how you want to layer objects with the Bring Forward and Send Backward buttons in the Adjust group on the DRAWING TOOLS FORMAT tab or the PICTURE TOOLS FORMAT tab.

- Insert a picture in a slide with the Pictures button in the Images group on the INSERT tab.

- Insert a picture as a slide background with options at the Format Background task pane. Display this task pane by clicking the Format Background button in the Customize group on the DESIGN tab.

- Insert an image from Office.com with options at the Online Pictures window. Display this window by clicking the Online Pictures button in the Images group on the INSERT tab or clicking the Online Pictures button in a layout content placeholder.

- Size objects with options at the Format Shape or Format Picture task pane with the Size & Properties icon selected.

- Use the Screenshot button in the Images group on the INSERT tab to capture the contents of a screen or capture a portion of a screen.

- Use the WordArt feature to distort or modify text to conform to a variety of shapes. Insert WordArt with the WordArt button in the Text group on the INSERT tab. Format WordArt with options on the DRAWING TOOLS FORMAT tab.

- Insert symbols in a slide with options at the Symbol dialog box. Display this dialog box by clicking the Symbol button in the Symbols group on the INSERT tab.

- Click the Header & Footer button, the Date & Time button, or the Slide Number button located in the Text group on the INSERT tab to display the Header and Footer dialog box. You can also display the dialog box by clicking the Edit Header & Footer hyperlink at the Print backstage area.

Commands Review

FEATURE	RIBBON TAB, GROUP	BUTTON, OPTION	KEYBOARD SHORTCUT
date and time	INSERT, Text		
Format Background task pane	DESIGN, Customize		
Format Picture task pane	PICTURE TOOLS FORMAT, Picture Styles OR Size		
Grid and Guides dialog box	VIEW, Show		
gridlines	VIEW, Show	*Gridlines*	Shift + F9
header and footer	INSERT, Text		
Insert Picture dialog box	INSERT, Images		
Insert Pictures window	INSERT, Images		
rulers	VIEW, Show	*Ruler*	
screenshot	INSERT, Images		
shape	INSERT, Illustrations OR HOME, Drawing		
slide number	INSERT, Text		
Symbol dialog box	INSERT, Symbols		
text box	INSERT, Text		
WordArt	INSERT, Text		

Concepts Check

Test Your Knowledge

Completion: In the space provided at the right, indicate the correct term, symbol, or command.

1. The Text Box button is located in the Text group on this tab.

    _____

2. Use the sizing handles or these measurement boxes to change the size of a text box.

    _____

3. This is the keyboard shortcut to select all objects in a slide.

    _____

4. A text box, by default, contains tabs with this alignment.

    _____

5. The Illustrations group on this tab contains a Shapes button.

    _____

6. When dragging a shape to change the size, hold down this key to maintain the proportions of the shape.

    _____

7. Copy a shape by holding down this key while dragging the shape to the desired location.

    _____

8. Turn drawing guides on and off with options in this dialog box.

    _____

9. The Group button is located in this group on the DRAWING TOOLS FORMAT tab.

    _____

10. Click the Online Pictures button and this window displays.

    _____

11. Use this button in the Size group on the PICTURE TOOLS FORMAT tab to remove any unnecessary parts of an image.

    _____

12. With the Bring Forward button and this button in the Arrange group on the DRAWING TOOLS FORMAT tab or the PICTURE TOOLS FORMAT tab you can layer one object on top of another.

    _____

13. To capture a portion of a screen, click the Screenshot button in the Images group on the INSERT tab and then click this option at the drop-down list.

    _____

14. Use this feature to distort or modify text to conform to a variety of shapes.

    _____

15. The Symbol button is located in the Symbols group on this tab.

    _____

16. Click this hyperlink at the Print backstage area to display the Header and Footer dialog box.

    _____

Skills Check Assess Your Performance

Assessment

1 FORMAT AND ADD ENHANCEMENTS TO A TRAVEL PRESENTATION

1. Open **TravelEngland.pptx** and then save the presentation with Save As and name it **P-C4-A1-TravelEngland**.
2. Make Slide 8 active and then insert the slide shown in Figure 4.13 with the following specifications:
   a. Insert a new slide with the Title Only layout.
   b. Type the title *Travel England* as shown in the slide.
   c. Draw a text box in the slide and then type the text shown in Figure 4.13. Select and then change the text font size to 40 points and apply the Tan, Background 2, Darker 75% font color.
   d. Apply the Tan, Background 2, Darker 10% shape fill to the text box.
   e. Apply the Dark Teal, 8 pt glow, Accent color 4 shape effect (from the *Glow* side menu).
   f. Display the Format Shape task pane with the Size & Properties icon selected, change the height to 2.8 inches and the width 9 inches (in the *SIZE* section). Change the left, right, top, and bottom margins to 0.4 inch (in the *TEXT BOX* section). Close the Format Shape task pane.
   g. Distribute the text box horizontally and vertically on the slide. (Do this with the Align button on the DRAWING TOOLS FORMAT tab.)
3. Make Slide 2 active, select the text in the text box and then set a left tab at the 0.5-inch mark on the horizontal ruler, a center tab at the 6-inch mark, and a right tab at the 9.5-inch mark. Bold the headings in the first row.
4. Make Slide 6 active, select the picture, and then make the following changes:
   a. Use the Corrections button on the PICTURE TOOLS FORMAT tab to sharpen the image 25%.
   b. Display the Format Picture task pane with the Size & Properties icon selected.
   c. Change the scale height to 150%, the horizontal position to 5.5 inches, the vertical position to 2.2 inches, and then close the task pane.
5. Make Slide 4 active and then insert the picture named **Stonehenge.jpg** located in the PC4 folder on your storage medium with the following specifications:
   a. Crop the picture so it displays as shown in Figure 4.14.
   b. Send the picture behind the text.
   c. Size and move the picture so it displays as shown in Figure 4.14.
   d. Size and move the bulleted text placeholder so it displays as shown in the figure.
6. Make Slide 7 active and then insert a clip art image as shown in Figure 4.15 with the following specification:
   a. At the Insert Pictures window, search for *green umbrella* and then download the umbrella image shown in Figure 4.15.
   b. Flip the umbrella horizontally. (Do this with the Rotate button.)
   c. Correct the image to *Brightness: -40% Contrast: +20%*.
   d. Change the height of the image to 4 inches.
   e. Change the horizontal position to 6.8 inches and the vertical position to 2 inches at the Format Picture task pane with the Size & Properties icon selected.
7. Make Slide 8 active, display the Format Background task pane (use the Format Background button on the DESIGN tab), and insert the picture shown in Figure 4.16 with the following specifications:

    a. Insert the picture with the File button in the Format Background task pane with the Fill icon selected. The picture is named **BigBen.jpg** and is located in the PC4 folder on your storage medium.

    b. Click the Fill icon in the Format Background task pane and then change the *Offset top* option to -30% and the *Offset bottom* option to -125%.

    c. Display the Format Background task pane with the Picture icon selected.

    d. Change the sharpness to 25% and the contrast to 30%.

    e. Size and move the text in placeholders so the text is positioned as shown in Figure 4.16.

  8. Make Slide 9 active and then insert a new slide with the Title Only layout. Insert the title and insert and format a shape as shown in Figure 4.17 with the following specifications:

    a. Type the title *Travel Discounts!* as shown in Figure 4.17.

    b. Draw the shape shown in the slide using the Horizontal Scroll shape.

    c. Change the height of the shape to 5 inches and the width to 10 inches.

    d. Apply the Subtle Effect - Dark Teal, Accent 4 shape style to the shape.

    e. Type the text in the shape as shown in the figure. Change the font size for the text to 36 points; apply the Tan, Background 2, Darker 75% font color, and then turn on bold formatting.

    f. Distribute the shape horizontally and vertically on the slide.

  9. Apply the Peel Off transition to each slide.

10. Insert slide numbers on each slide.

11. Insert a footer for notes and handouts pages that prints your first and last names.

12. Run the presentation.

13. Print the presentation as a handout with six slides printed horizontally per page.

14. Save and then close **P-C4-A1-TravelEngland.pptx**.

Figure 4.13 Assessment 1, Step 2

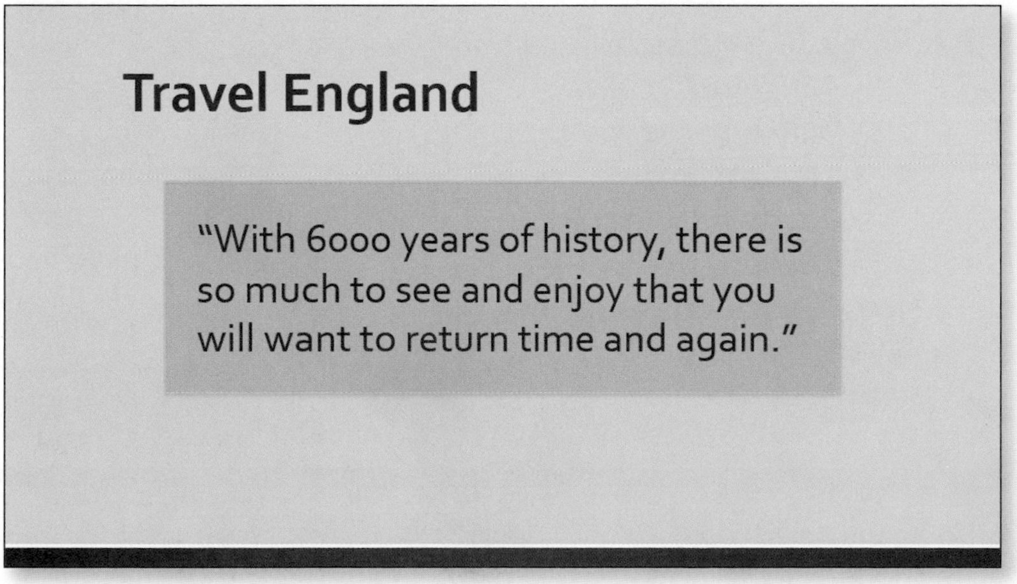

Figure 4.14 Assessment 1, Step 5

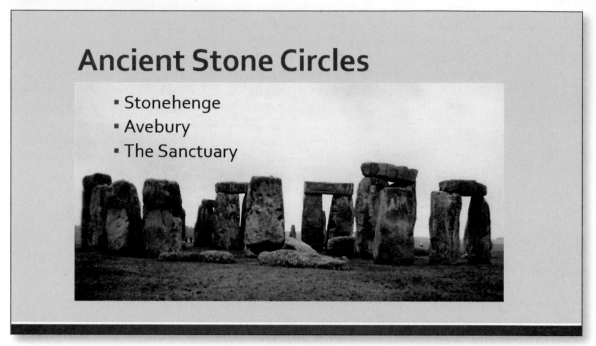

Figure 4.15 Assessment 1, Step 6

Figure 4.16 Assessment 1, Step 7

Figure 4.17 Assessment 1, Step 8

Assessment

2 FORMAT AND ADD ENHANCEMENTS TO A GARDENING PRESENTATION

1. Open **GreenspacePres.pptx** and then save the presentation with Save As and name it **P-C4-A2-GreenspacePres**.
2. Insert the slide shown in Figure 4.18 with the following specifications:
   a. Make Slide 2 active and then insert a new slide with the Blank layout.
   b. Insert the WordArt text using *Pattern Fill - Gold, Accent 3, Narrow Horizontal, Inner Shadow* (second column, bottom row).
   c. Change the shape of the WordArt to *Wave 1*. (The *Wave 1* option is the first option in the fifth row in *Warp* section of the Text Effects button Transform side menu.)
   d. Change the height of the WordArt to 4 inches and the width to 10 inches.
   e. Distribute the WordArt horizontally and vertically on the slide.
   f. Display the Format Background task pane. (Display this task pane by clicking the Format Background button on the DESIGN tab.) Insert a check mark in the *Hide background graphics* check box. Click the Preset gradients button, click the *Light Gradient - Accent 3* option (third column, first row), and then close the task pane.
3. Insert the slide shown in Figure 4.19 with the following specifications:
   a. Make Slide 8 active and then insert a new slide with the Title Only layout.
   b. Insert the title *English/French Translations* as shown in Figure 4.19.
   c. Insert a text box, change the font size to 28 points, set left tabs at the 1-inch and the 5.5-inch marks on the horizontal ruler, and then type the text shown in Figure 4.19 in columns. Bold the headings *English Name* and *French Name* and use the Symbol dialog box to insert the special symbols in the French names. Use the (normal text) font at the Symbol dialog box to insert the symbols.
   d. If necessary, move the text box so it is positioned as shown in Figure 4.19.
4. Make Slide 4 active and then make the following changes:
   a. Select the bulleted text and then change the line spacing to double spacing (2.0).
   b. With the bulleted text selected, set the bulleted text in two columns.
   c. Size the placeholder so four bulleted items display in each column.
5. Make Slide 5 active and then insert the clip art image shown in Figure 4.20 with the following specifications:
   a. Use the words *watering can gardening tools* to search for the image.
   b. Flip the image horizontally.
   c. Change the height of the image to 4 inches.
   d. Display the Format Picture task pane with the Size & Properties icon selected and then change the horizontal position to 6 inches and the vertical position to 2.2 inches.
6. Make Slide 9 active, insert a new slide with the Title Only layout, and then create the slide shown in Figure 4.21 with the following specifications:
   a. Insert the title *Gardening Magazines*.
   b. Create the top shape using the Bevel shape. Change the height of the shape to 1.1 inches and the width to 10 inches.
   c. Change the font size to 32 points and then type the text in the top shape. Insert the registered symbol at the Symbol dialog box with the (normal text) font selected.
   d. Select and then copy the shape two times. Use the guidelines and Smart Guides to help you align and position the shapes.

e. Change the text in the second and third shapes to match what you see in Figure 4.21.

f. Group the three shapes, apply the Dark Green, Text 2, Lighter 60% shape fill color, the Olive Green, Accent 1, Darker 50% shape outline, and the Dark Green, Text 2, Darker 25% text fill color.

7. With Slide 10 active, insert a new slide with the Title Only layout. Type **Gift Certificate** as the title and then insert a screenshot with the following specifications:

a. Open Word and then open the document named **GAGiftCert.docx** from the PC4 folder on your storage medium.

b. Click the PowerPoint button on the Taskbar and then use the *Screen Clipping* option from the Screenshot button drop-down list to capture only the gift certificate in the Word document.

c. With the gift certificate screenshot inserted in the slide, change the height to 3.5 inches and distribute the certificate horizontally and vertically on the slide.

d. Make Word active and then close Word.

8. Run the presentation.

9. Print the presentation as a handout with six slides printed horizontally per page.

10. Save **P-C4-A2-GreenspacePres.pptx**.

Figure 4.18 Assessment 2, Step 2

Figure 4.19 Assessment 2, Step 3

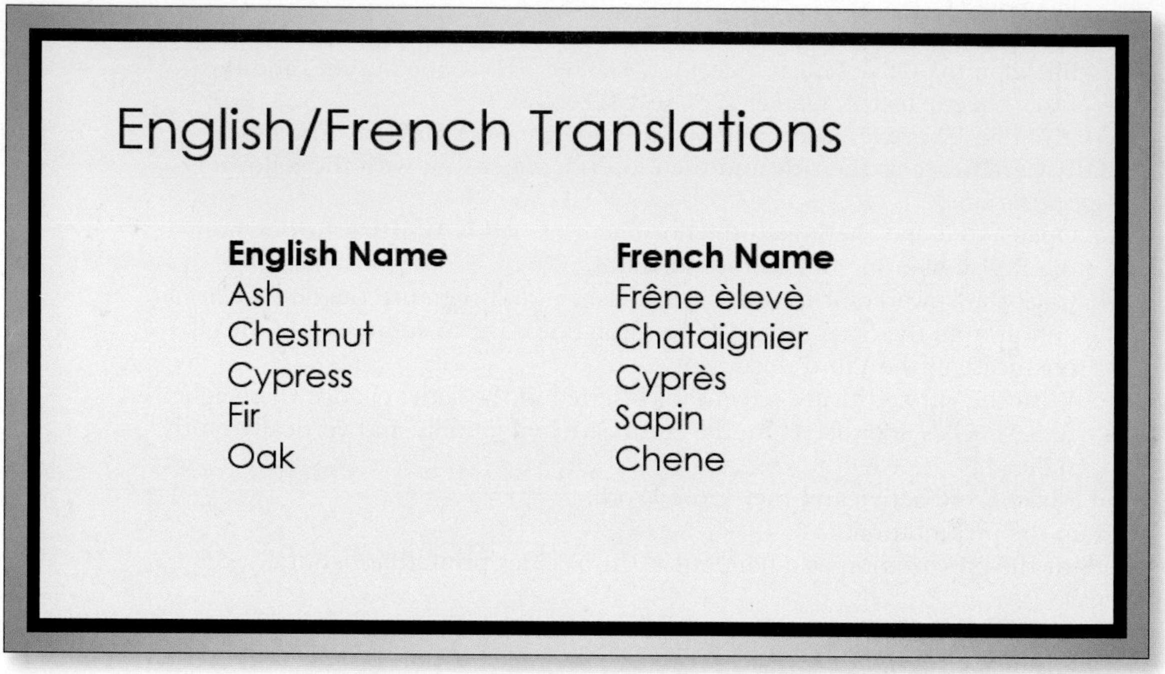

English/French Translations

English Name	**French Name**
Ash	Frêne èlevè
Chestnut	Chataignier
Cypress	Cyprès
Fir	Sapin
Oak	Chene

Figure 4.20 Assessment 2, Step 5

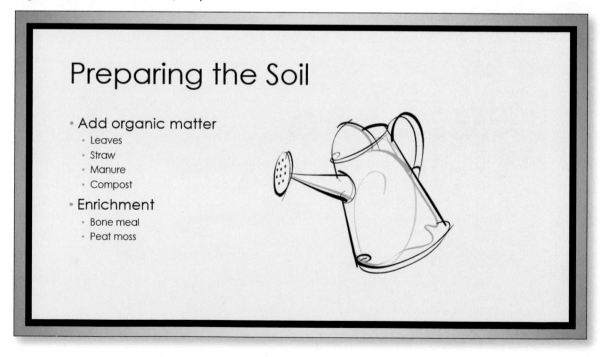

Preparing the Soil

- Add organic matter
  - Leaves
  - Straw
  - Manure
  - Compost
- Enrichment
  - Bone meal
  - Peat moss

Figure 4.21 Assessment 2, Step 6

Assessment

3

COPY A PICTURE FROM A WEBSITE TO A PRESENTATION

1. With **P-C4-A2-GreenspacePres.pptx** open, make Slide 6 active.
2. Use the Help feature to find information on copying a picture from a web page. (Begin by typing **insert a picture** in the PowerPoint Help window search text box, and then pressing Enter. Click the <u>Insert a picture</u> hyperlink and then click the <u>Insert a picture from the web</u> hyperlink.)
3. Using the information you learned about inserting a picture from a web page, use the *Bing Image Search* text box (at the Insert Pictures window) to search for a picture of flowers on the web and then insert the picture in Slide 6. Size and move the picture so it is positioned attractively in the slide. (Consider inserting at least one more picture of one of the flowers mentioned in the slide.)
4. Print only Slide 6.
5. Run the presentation.
6. Save and then close **P-C4-A2-GreenspacePres.pptx**.

Visual Benchmark   Demonstrate Your Proficiency

CREATING A STUDY ABROAD PRESENTATION

1. At a blank presentation, create the presentation shown in Figure 4.22 with the following specifications:
   a. Apply the Quotable design theme and choose the purple variant.
   b. In Slide 1, increase the font size for the subtitle to 36 points.
   c. In Slide 2, insert the WordArt using the *Pattern Fill – Purple, Accent 1, 50%, Hard Shadow - Accent 1* option. Apply the *Deflate* transform text effect and size and position the WordArt on the slide as shown in Figure 4.22.
   d. Change the line spacing to double spacing (2.0) for the bulleted text in Slides 3 and 4 and change the line spacing to one-and-a-half spacing (1.5) for the bulleted text in Slide 5.
   e. Use the words *apartment building* to search for the clip art image in Slide 4. The original color of the clip art image is dark pink. Change the color to *Purple, Accent color 1 Light*. (If this clip art image is not available, choose a similar image.) Size and position the image as shown in Figure 4.22.
   f. Insert the picture **Colosseum.jpg** in Slide 5. (This image is located in the PC4 folder on your storage medium.) Size and position the image as shown in Figure 4.22.
   g. In Slide 6, use the Bevel shape in the *Basic Shapes* section of the Shapes button drop-down list to create the shape. Change the font size to 20 points for the text in the shapes.
   h. Make any other changes to placeholders and other objects so your slides display similar to what you see in Figure 4.22.
2. Apply a transition and sound of your choosing to all slides in the presentation.
3. Save the presentation and name it **P-C4-VB-RomeStudy**.
4. Print the presentation as a handout with six slides printed horizontally per page.
5. Close **P-C4-VB-RomeStudy.pptx**.

Figure 4.22 Visual Benchmark

continues

Figure 4.22 Visual Benchmark—*continued*

Courses

○ Italian Language

○ Renaissance and Baroque Art History

○ Rome Through the Ages

○ Roman Mythology

○ Roman Archeology

Accommodations

○ Independent housing

○ Apartment with locals

○ Apartment with other foreigners

○ Host family

continues

Figure 4.22 Visual Benchmark—*continued*

Case Study   Apply Your Skills

Part 1

You work for Honoré Financial Services and the Office Manager, Jason Monroe, has asked you to prepare a presentation for a community workshop he will be conducting next week. Open the Word document named **HFS.docx** and then use the information in the document to create a presentation with the following specifications:

- Slide 1: Include the company name Honoré Financial Services (use the Symbol feature to create the é in Honoré) and the subtitle *Managing Your Money*.
- Slide 2: Insert the word *Budgeting* as WordArt.
- Slides 3, 4, and 5: Use the bulleted and numbered information to create these slides.
- Slide 6: Create a text box, set tabs, and then type the information in the *Managing Records* section that is set in columns.
- Slide 7: Create a shape and then insert the following slogan *"Retirement Planning Made Easy"*.
- Include at least one picture and one clip art in the presentation.

Apply a design theme of your choosing and add any additional features to improve the visual appearance of the presentation. Insert a transition and sound to each slide and then run the presentation. Save the presentation and name it **P-C4-CS-HFS.pptx**. Print the presentation as a handout with four slides printed horizontally per page.

Part 2

Mr. Monroe will be conducting a free workshop titled *Financial Planning for the College Student*. Create a slide in the **P-C4-CS-HFS.pptx** presentation (make it the last slide in the presentation) that includes a shape with text inside that includes information about the workshop. You determine the day, the time, and the location for the workshop. Print the slide.

Part 3

Mr. Monroe would like to post the information about the workshop in various locations in the community and wants to print a number of copies. You decide to copy the shape and then insert it in a blank Word document. In Word, change the orientation of the page to landscape, increase the size of the shape, and then drag the shape to the middle of the page. Save the Word document and name it **P-C4-CS-HFSWorkshop**. Print and then close **P-C4-CS-HFSWorkshop.docx**.

Part 4

Mr. Monroe has asked you to locate online finance and/or budgeting resources such as newsletters and magazines. He would like you to locate resources and then create a slide with hyperlinks to the resources. Locate at least two online resources and then insert this information with the hyperlinks in a new slide at the end of the **P-C4-CS-HFS.pptx** presentation. Print the slide and then save and close the presentation.

MICROSOFT® POWERPOINT® Performance Assessment

PowerPoint PU1

Note: Before beginning unit assessments, copy to your storage medium the PU1 folder from the PowerPoint folder on the CD that accompanies this textbook and then make PU1 the active folder.

Assessing Proficiency ▪▪▪▪▪▪▪▪▪▪▪▪▫▫▫

In this unit, you have learned to create, print, save, close, open, view, run, edit, and format a PowerPoint presentation. You have also learned how to add transitions and sound to presentations; rearrange slides; customize presentations by changing the design theme; and add visual appeal to slides by inserting text boxes, shapes, pictures, clip art, screenshots, and symbols.

Assessment 1 Prepare, Format, and Enhance a Conference Presentation

1. Create a presentation with the text shown in Figure U1.1 using the Quotable design theme. Use the appropriate slide layout for each slide. After creating the slides, complete a spelling check on the text in the slides.
2. Add a transition and sound of your choosing to all slides.
3. Save the presentation and name it **P-U1-A1-CSConf**.
4. Run the presentation.
5. Make Slide 1 active and then find all occurrences of *Area* and replace them with *Market*.
6. Make the following changes to Slide 2:
   a. Replace the text *Net income* with *Net income per common share*.
   b. Delete the text *Return on average equity*.
7. Make the following changes to Slide 4:
   a. Delete *Shopping*.
   b. Type **Business finance** between *Personal finance* and *Email*.
8. Rearrange the slides in the presentation so they are in the following order (only the slide titles are shown below):

   Slide 1 = CORNERSTONE SYSTEMS
   Slide 2 = Corporate Vision
   Slide 3 = Future Goals
   Slide 4 = Industrial Market
   Slide 5 = Consumer Market
   Slide 6 = Financial Review
9. Increase the line spacing to 1.5 for the bulleted text in Slides 2, 3, 5, and 6.
10. Make Slide 4 active, increase the line spacing to 2.0 for the bulleted text, and then format the bulleted text into two columns with three entries in each column. (You may need to decrease the size of the placeholder.)
11. Save and then run the presentation.

12. Print the presentation as a handout with six slides printed horizontally per page.
13. Display the Reuse Slides task pane, browse to the PU1 folder on your storage medium, and then double-click *CSMktRpt.pptx*.
14. Insert the *Department Reports* slide below Slide 4.
15. Insert the *Services* slide below Slide 2.
16. Close the Reuse Slides task pane.
17. Make Slide 8 active, select the bulleted text, and then create and apply a custom bullet using a dollar sign in a complementary color and set the size to 100%. (You can find a dollar sign in the normal text font in the Symbol dialog box.)
18. With Slide 8 active, insert a clip art image related to money or finances. Format, size, and then position the clip art attractively on the slide.
19. Move Slide 4 (*Future Goals*) to the end of the presentation.
20. Insert a new slide with the Title and Content layout at the end of the presentation with the following specifications:
    a. Insert *Future Goals* as the title.
    b. Type **International market** as the first bulleted item and then press Enter.
    c. Copy *Acquisitions*, *Production*, *Technology*, and *Marketing* from Slide 8 and paste them in the content area of the new slide below the first line of bulleted text. (When copied, the items should be preceded by a bullet. If a bullet displays on a blank line below the last text item, press the Backspace key twice.)
    d. Select the bulleted text and then change the line spacing to 1.5.
21. Make Slide 8 active, select the bulleted items, and then apply numbering.
22. Make Slide 9 active, select the bulleted items, apply numbering, and then change the beginning number to *6*.
23. With Slide 9 active, create a new slide with the Blank layout with the following specifications:
    a. Insert **Nightscape.jpg** as a background picture and hide the background graphics. *Hint: Do this with the Format Background button on the DESIGN tab.*
    b. Create a text box toward the top of the slide, change the font color to White, Text 1, increase the font size to 36 points, and then change the alignment to center.
    c. Type **National Sales Meeting**, press Enter, type **New York City**, press Enter, and then type **March 4 to 6, 2015**.
    d. Move and/or size the text box so the text is positioned centered above the buildings in the picture.
24. With Slide 10 active, insert a new slide with the Title Only layout. Type **Doubletree Guest Suites** as the title and then insert a screenshot with the following specifications:
    a. Open Word and then open **HotelMap.docx** from the PU1 folder on your storage medium.
    b. Click the PowerPoint button on the Taskbar and then use the *Screen Clipping* option from the Screenshot button drop-down list to capture only the map in the Word document.
    c. With the map screenshot inserted in the slide, apply the Sharpen: 25% correction. Size and position the map attractively on the slide.
25. Insert slide numbers on each slide.
26. Insert a footer for notes and handouts pages that prints your first and last names.
27. Save and then run the presentation.

28. Print the presentation as a handout with six slides printed horizontally per page.
29. Close **P-U1-A1-CSConf.pptx**.

Figure U1.1 Assessment 1

Slide 1	Title	=	CORNERSTONE SYSTEMS
	Subtitle	=	Executive Conference
Slide 2	Title	=	Financial Review
	Bullets	=	• Net revenues
			• Operating income
			• Net income
			• Return on average equity
			• Return on average asset
Slide 3	Title	=	Corporate Vision
	Bullets	=	• Expansion
			• Increased productivity
			• Consumer satisfaction
			• Employee satisfaction
			• Area visibility
Slide 4	Title	=	Consumer Area
	Bullets	=	• Travel
			• Shopping
			• Entertainment
			• Personal finance
			• Email
Slide 5	Title	=	Industrial Area
	Bullets	=	• Finance
			• Education
			• Government
			• Production
			• Manufacturing
			• Utilities
Slide 6	Title	=	Future Goals
	Bullets	=	• Domestic market
			• Acquisitions
			• Production
			• Technology
			• Marketing

Assessment 2 Format and Enhance a Kraft Artworks Presentation

1. Open **KAPres.pptx** and then save the presentation with Save As and name it **P-U1-A2-KAPres**.
2. With Slide 1 active, insert the text *Kraft Artworks* as WordArt and apply the following formatting:
   a. Transform the shape of the WordArt.
   b. Change the size so the WordArt better fills the slide.
   c. Change the text fill to a purple color.
   d. Apply any other formatting to improve the visual appearance of the WordArt.
3. Duplicate Slides 2 and 3.
4. Change the goal number in Slide 4 from *1* to *3* and change the goal text to *Conduct six art workshops at the Community Center.*
5. Change the goal number in Slide 5 from *2* to *4* and change the goal text to *Provide recycled material to public schools for art classes.*
6. With Slide 5 active, insert a new slide with the Title Only layout with the following specifications:
   a. Insert the title *Clients* and then format, size, and position the title in the same manner as the title in Slide 5.
   b. Insert a text box, change the font to Comic Sans MS and the font size to 20 points, apply the Lavender, Accent 1, Darker 50% font color and then type the following text in columns (you determine the tab settings):

School	Contact	Number
Logan Elementary School	Maya Jones	555-0882
Cedar Elementary School	George Ferraro	555-3211
Sunrise Elementary School	Avery Burns	555-3444
Hillside Middle School	Joanna Myers	555-2211
Douglas Middle School	Ray Murphy	555-8100

   c. Select all of the text in the text box and then change the line spacing to 1.5.
7. With Slide 6 active, insert a new slide with the Blank layout, hide the background graphic, and then create the slide shown in Figure U1.2 with the following specifications:
   a. Use the Explosion 1 shape (in the *Stars and Banners* section) to create the first shape.
   b. Apply the Light Green shape fill color and apply the Lavender, 18 pt glow, Accent color 2 glow effect.
   c. With the shape selected, change the font to 40-point Comic Sans MS with bold formatting and in the Lavender, Accent 1, Darker 50% font color and then type the text shown in Figure U1.2.
   d. Copy the shape twice and position the shapes as shown in Figure U1.2.
   e. Type the appropriate text in each shape as shown in Figure U1.2.
8. With Slide 7 active, insert a new slide with the Blank layout, hide the background graphic, and then create the slide shown in Figure U1.3 with the following specifications:
   a. Set the text in the two text boxes at the left and right sides of the slide in 54-point Comic Sans MS with bold formatting and in the Lavender, Accent 1, Darker 50% font color. Rotate, size, and position the two text boxes as shown in Figure U1.3.
   b. Use the Explosion 1 shape to create the shape in the middle of the slide.
   c. Apply the Light Green shape fill color, the Lavender, 18 pt glow, Accent color 2 glow effect, the Perspective Diagonal Upper Left shadow effect, the Lavender, Accent 1, Darker 50% shape outline color, and the 2¼ points shape outline weight.

d. Insert the text in the shape and then change the font to 28-point Comic Sans MS, apply bold formatting, and then apply the Lavender, Accent 1, Darker 50% font color. Change the alignment to *Center* and change the vertical alignment to *Middle*.

9. Create a footer that prints your first and last names and the current date on handout pages.

10. Print the presentation as a handout with four slides printed horizontally per page.

11. Save and then close **P-U1-A2-KAPres.pptx**.

Figure U1.2 Assessment 2, Slide 7

Figure U1.3 Assessment 2, Slide 8

Assessment 3 Create and Apply a Custom Theme to a Job Search Presentation

1. At a blank presentation, apply the Dividend design theme and the green variant (third option in the Variants group).
2. Create custom theme colors named with your first and last names that change the following colors:
   a. Change the Accent 1 color to *Brown, Accent 6, Darker 50%*.
   b. Change the Accent 2 color to *Olive Green, Accent 2, Darker 25%*.
   c. Change the Accent 3 color to *Orange, Accent 5, Darker 25%*.
3. Create custom theme fonts named with your first and last names that changes the heading font to Constantia and the body font to Cambria.
4. Save the current theme as a custom theme named with your first and last names. ***Hint: Do this at the Save Current Theme dialog box.***
5. Close the presentation without saving it.
6. Open **JobSearch.pptx** and then save the presentation with Save As and name it **P-U1-A3-JobSearch**.
7. Apply the custom theme named with your first and last names.
8. Insert a clip art image in Slide 5 related to telephone, people, or Internet. You determine the format, size, and position of the image.
9. Insert a clip art image in Slide 6 related to clock or time. You determine the format, size, and position of the image.
10. Improve the visual display of text in Slides 2, 3, 7, 8, and 9 by increasing the spacing between items and positioning the text placeholders attractively in the slides.
11. Insert the current date and slide number on all slides in the presentation.
12. Create the header *Job Search Seminar*, the footer *Employment Strategies*, and insert the date and page number for notes and handouts.
13. Add the speaker note *Distribute list of Internet employment sites.* to Slide 5.
14. Apply a transition and sound of your choosing to all slides in the presentation.
15. Save and then run the presentation.
16. Print the presentation as a handout with six slides printed horizontally per page.
17. Print Slide 5 as a notes page.
18. Change the slide size to *Standard (4:3)* and ensure the fit.
19. Scroll through each slide of the presentation and make any changes to placeholders and/or clip art images to improve the visual appearance of the slides.
20. Print the presentation as a handout with nine slides printed horizontally per page.
21. Save and then close **P-U1-A3-JobSearch.pptx**.

Assessment 4 Format and Enhance a Medical Plans Presentation

1. Open **MedicalPlans.pptx** and then save the presentation with Save As and name it **P-U1-A4-MedicalPlans**.
2. Apply a design theme of your choosing.
3. Create a new slide with a Blank layout between Slides 1 and 2 that contains a shape with the text *Medical Plans 2015 to 2016* inside the shape. You determine the format, position, and size of the shape and the formatting of the text.
4. Change the bullets in Slides 3, 4, and 5 to custom bullets (you determine the picture or symbol).
5. Insert a clip art image related to medicine in Slide 4. You determine the color, size, and position of the image.
6. Make Slide 5 active, and then apply the following formatting:
   a. Move the insertion point to the beginning of *Eugene* and then press the Enter key two times.
   b. Select all of the bulleted text and then change the line spacing to 2.0.
   c. With the bulleted text selected, format the text into two columns. (Make sure each column contains four entries.)
   d. Size and/or move the placeholder so the bulleted text displays attractively in the slide.
7. Apply any additional formatting or elements to improve the visual appearance of the slides.
8. Add a transition and sound of your choosing to the presentation.
9. Run the presentation.
10. Print the presentation as a handout with six slides printed horizontally per page.
11. Save and then close **P-U1-A4-MedicalPlans.pptx**.

Writing Activities ■■■■■■■■■■ ■■■■■■■■

The following activities provide you with the opportunity to practice your writing skills along with demonstrating an understanding of some of the important PowerPoint features you have mastered in this unit. Use correct spelling, grammar, and appropriate word choices.

Activity 1 Prepare and Format a Health Plan Presentation

Open Word and then open, print, and close **KLHPlan.docx**. Looking at the printout of this document, create a presentation in PowerPoint that presents the main points of the plan. (Use bullets in the presentation.) Add a transition and sound to the slides. Apply formatting and/or insert images to enhance the visual appearance of the presentation. Save the presentation and name it **P-U1-Act1-KLHPlan**. Run the presentation. Print the presentation as a handout with six slides printed horizontally per page. Save and then close **P-U1-Act1-KLHPlan.pptx**.

Activity 2 Prepare and Format a Presentation on Saving an Image as a JPG

At a blank presentation, use the Help feature to find information on inserting a picture or clip art image. *Hint: Display the PowerPoint Help window, type save image as a jpg, press Enter, and then click the Save a picture as a separate file hyperlink that displays in the window.* Print and read the information and then use the information to create a presentation that includes at least three slides (a title slide, a slide with the steps on saving an image in the JPG format, and a slide on the various file formats for saving an image). Format and add visual appeal to the presentation. With the presentation still open, open the **KLHPLogo.pptx** presentation. Group the image and the text and then save the grouped image as a JPG file named **KLHPLogo.jpg** in the PU1 folder on your storage medium. Close **KLHPLogo.pptx**. With your presentation open, insert the **KLHPLogo.jpg** file in the slide with the steps for saving in the JPG format. Size and position the logo attractively on the slide. Save the completed presentation and name it **P-U1-Act2-JPGPres**. Add a transition and sound of your choosing to each slide and then run the presentation. Print the presentation as a handout with four slides printed horizontally per page. Close **P-U1-Act2-JPGPres.pptx**.

Internet Research ■■■■■■■■■■ ■■■■■■■■■■

Analyze a Magazine Website

Make sure you are connected to the Internet and then explore the *Time®* magazine website at www.time.com. Explore the site to discover the following information:

- The different sections of the magazine
- The type of information presented in each section
- Details on how to subscribe

Use the information you found on the *Time* magazine website to create a PowerPoint presentation that presents the information in a clear, concise, and logical manner. Add formatting and enhancements to the presentation to make it more interesting. When the presentation is completed, save it and name it **P-U1-TimeMag**. Run, print, and then close the presentation.

MICROSOFT®
POWERPOINT®

Unit 2 ■ Customizing and Enhancing PowerPoint Presentations

MICROSOFT POWERPOINT

CHAPTER 5

Creating Tables, Charts, and SmartArt Graphics

PERFORMANCE OBJECTIVES

Upon successful completion of Chapter 5, you will be able to:

- Create and format a table
- Modify the design and layout of a table
- Insert an image in a table
- Create SmartArt graphics
- Modify the design and layout of SmartArt
- Convert text to a SmartArt graphic
- Create and format charts
- Modify the design and layout of charts
- Select and format chart elements
- Create, edit, and format a photo album

Tutorials

5.1 Creating a Table in a Slide

5.2 Inserting and Formatting an Excel Spreadsheet

5.3 Inserting and Formatting SmartArt

5.4 Converting Text and WordArt to a SmartArt Graphic; Converting a SmartArt Graphic to Text or Shape

5.5 Creating and Formatting Charts

5.6 Creating a Photo Album

If you want to present numbers and lists in a slide, consider inserting the information in a table. Use the Tables feature to create data in columns and rows in a manner similar to a spreadsheet. Display data in a slide in a more visual way by creating a SmartArt graphic. The SmartArt feature provides a number of predesigned graphics such as diagrams and organizational charts. You can create a SmartArt graphic and then modify the design and layout of the graphic.

While a table does an adequate job of representing data, create a chart from data to provide a more visual representation of the data. A chart is sometimes referred to as a *graph* and is a picture of numeric data. If you have Microsoft Excel installed on your computer, you can create a chart in a PowerPoint slide. If you do not have Excel installed on your computer, PowerPoint uses the Microsoft Graph feature to create your chart. Projects and assessments in this chapter assume that you have Excel installed on your computer.

You can create a photo album presentation to attractively display personal or business photographs. Use the Photo Album feature to insert pictures and then format the appearance of the pictures in the presentation. Model answers for this chapter's projects appear on the following page.

Note: Before beginning the projects, copy to your storage medium the PC5 folder from the PowerPoint folder on the CD that accompanies this textbook and then make PC5 the active folder.

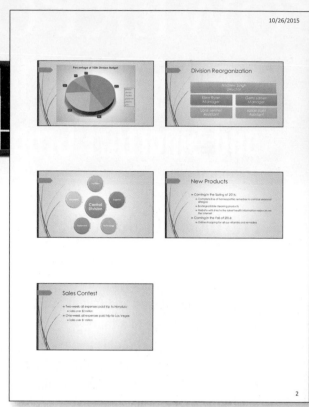

Project 1 Create a Company Sales Conference Presentation

P-C5-P1-Conference.pptx

Project 2 Create and Format a Travel Photo Album

P-C5-P2-Album.pptx

| Project | 1 | Create a Company Sales Conference Presentation | 14 Parts |

You will create a sales conference presentation for Nature's Way that includes a table, a column chart, a pie chart, and four SmartArt graphics.

Creating a Table ■■■■■■■■■■■■■■■■■■■■■■■■■■■■■■■

Use the Tables feature to create boxes of information called *cells*. A cell is the intersection between a row and a column. A cell can contain text, characters, numbers, data, graphics, or formulas. If you want to arrange the content of a slide in columns and rows, insert a new slide with a slide layout that includes a content placeholder. Click the Insert Table button in the content placeholder and the Insert Table dialog box displays. At the Insert Table dialog box, type the number of columns, press the Tab key, type the number of rows, and then press Enter or click OK. You can also insert a table using the Table button in the Tables group on the INSERT tab. Click the Table button, drag the mouse down and to the right to select the desired number of columns and rows, and then click the left mouse button.

When you create a table, the insertion point is located in the cell in the upper left corner of the table. Cells in a table contain a cell designation. Columns in a table are lettered from left to right, beginning with *A*. Rows in a table are numbered from top to bottom beginning with *1*. The cell in the upper left corner of the table is cell A1. The cell to the right of A1 is B1, the cell to the right of B1 is C1, and so on.

Entering Text in Cells

With the insertion point positioned in a cell, type or edit text. Move the insertion point to other cells by clicking in the desired cell. If you are using the keyboard, press the Tab key to move the insertion point to the next cell or press Shift + Tab to move the insertion point to the previous cell.

If the text you type does not fit on one line, it wraps to the next line within the same cell. If you press Enter in a cell, the insertion point is moved to the next line within the same cell. The cell vertically lengthens to accommodate the text, and all cells in that row also lengthen. Pressing the Tab key in a table causes the insertion point to move to the next cell. If you want to move the insertion point to a tab stop within a cell, press Ctrl + Tab. If the insertion point is located in the last cell of a table and you press the Tab key, PowerPoint adds another row to the table.

Selecting Cells

You can apply formatting to an entire table or to specific cells, rows, or columns in a table. To identify cells for formatting, select the specific cells using the mouse or the keyboard. Press the Tab key to select the next cell or press Shift + Tab to select the previous cell. Refer to Table 5.1 for additional methods for selecting in a table.

▼ Quick Steps

Insert a Table
1. Click Insert Table button in content placeholder.
2. Type number of columns.
3. Press Tab.
4. Type number of rows.
5. Click OK.
OR
1. Click INSERT tab.
2. Click Table button.
3. Drag in grid to desired number of columns and rows.

Table

Add a row to the bottom of a table by positioning the insertion point in the last cell and then pressing the Tab key.

You can move text to a different cell by selecting the text and then dragging the selected text to a different cell.

Table 5.1 Selecting in a Table

To select this	Do this
A cell	Position the mouse pointer at left side of the cell until pointer turns into a small, black, diagonally pointing arrow and then click the left mouse button.
A column	Position the mouse pointer outside the table at the top of the column until the pointer turns into a small, black, down-pointing arrow and then click the left mouse button. Drag to select multiple columns.
A row	Position the mouse pointer outside the table at the left edge of the row until the pointer turns into a small, black, right-pointing arrow and then click the left mouse button. Drag to select multiple rows.
All cells in a table	Drag to select all cells or press Ctrl + A.
Text within a cell	Position the mouse pointer at the beginning of the text and then hold down the left mouse button as you drag the mouse across the text. (When a cell is selected, the cell background color changes to gray. When text within a cell is selected, only those lines containing text are highlighted in gray.)

Project 1a Creating a Table Part 1 of 14

1. Open **Conference.pptx** and then save the presentation with Save As and name it **P-C5-P1-Conference**.
2. Make Slide 3 active.
3. Insert a table in the slide and enter text into the cells by completing the following steps:
   a. Click the Insert Table button located in the middle of the slide in the content placeholder.
   b. At the Insert Table dialog box, select the current number in the *Number of columns* measurement box and then type 2.
   c. Press the Tab key.
   d. Type 5 in the *Number of rows* measurement box.
   e. Click OK or press Enter.
   f. Type the text as displayed in the table below. Press the Tab key to move the insertion point to the next cell or press Shift + Tab to move the insertion point to the previous cell. Do not press Tab after typing the last cell entry.

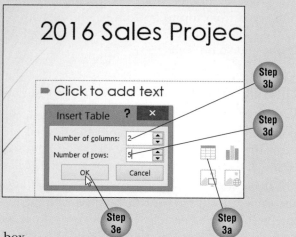

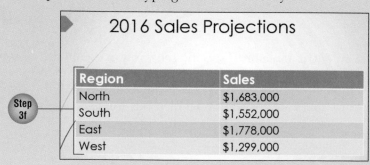

2016 Sales Projections

Region	Sales
North	$1,683,000
South	$1,552,000
East	$1,778,000
West	$1,299,000

4. Apply formatting to text in specific cells by completing the following steps:
  a. With the insertion point positioned in the table, press Ctrl + A to select all of the text in the table.
  b. Click the HOME tab and then change the font size to 32 points.
  c. Set the text below the headings in a smaller point size by positioning the mouse pointer at the left edge of the second row (to the left of the cell containing *North*) until the pointer turns into a small, black, right-pointing arrow. Hold down the left mouse button, drag down so the remaining rows are selected, and then change the font size to 28 points.
  d. Click outside the table to deselect it.
5. Save **P-C5-P1-Conference.pptx**.

Changing Table Design

When you create a table, the TABLE TOOLS DESIGN tab displays. This tab contains a number of options for enhancing the appearance of the table, as shown in Figure 5.1. With options in the Table Styles group, apply a predesigned style that applies color and border lines to a table. Maintain further control over the predesigned style formatting applied to columns and rows with options in the Table Style Options group. For example, if you want your first column to be formatted differently than the other columns in the table, insert a check mark in the *First Column* check box. Apply additional design formatting to cells in a table with the Shading, Borders, and Effects buttons in the Table Styles group and the options in the WordArt Styles group. Draw a table or draw additional rows and/or columns in a table by clicking the Draw Table button in the Draw Borders group. Click this button and the mouse pointer turns into a pencil. Drag in the table to create the desired columns and rows. Click the Eraser button and the mouse pointer turns into an eraser. Drag through the column and/or row lines you want to erase in the table.

Figure 5.1 TABLE TOOLS DESIGN Tab

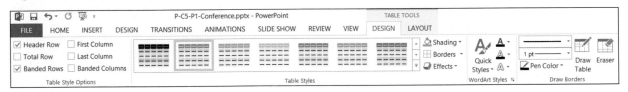

1. With **P-C5-P1-Conference.pptx** open, make sure Slide 3 is active, click in a cell in the table, and then click the TABLE TOOLS DESIGN tab.

2. Click the *First Column* check box in the Table Style Options group to insert a check mark. (This applies bold formatting to the text in the first column and applies darker shading to the cell.)

3. Click the More button that displays at the right side of the table style thumbnails and then click the *Themed Style 1 - Accent 1* thumbnail (second column, first row in the *Best Match for Document* section).

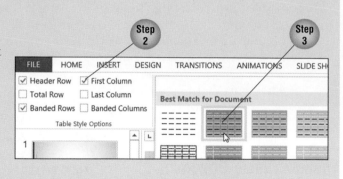

4. Select the first row of the table and then apply the following formatting:

   a. Click the Quick Styles button in the WordArt Styles group and then click the *Fill - White, Outline - Accent 2, Hard Shadow - Accent 2* option (fourth column, third row).

   b. Click the Text Fill button arrow in the WordArt Styles group and then click *Lime, Accent 3, Lighter 80%* (seventh column, second row in the *Theme Colors* section).

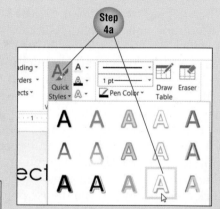

   c. Click the Text Outline button arrow in the WordArt Styles group and then click *Green, Accent 1, Lighter 80%* (fifth column, second row in the *Theme Colors* section).

5. Click the Pen Weight button arrow in the Draw Borders group and then click *2¼ pt*. (This activates the Draw Table button.)

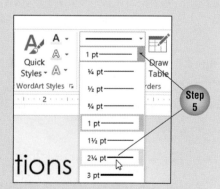

6. Click the Pen Color button in the Draw Borders group and then click *Green, Accent 1, Darker 25%* (fifth column, fifth row in the *Theme Colors* section).

7. Draw along the border that separates the two columns from the top of the first row to the bottom of the last row.

8. Draw along the border that separates the first row from the second row.

9. Click the Draw Table button to deactivate it.

10. Save **P-C5-P1-Conference.pptx**.

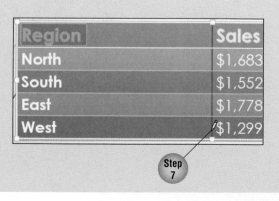

Changing Table Layout

To further customize a table, consider changing the table layout by inserting or deleting columns or rows and specifying cell alignments. Change the table layout with options on the TABLE TOOLS LAYOUT tab, shown in Figure 5.2. Use options and buttons on the tab to select specific cells, delete and insert rows and columns, merge and split cells, specify cell and table height and width, specify text alignment in cells, and arrange elements in a slide.

HINT
If you make a mistake while formatting a table, immediately click the Undo button on the Quick Access toolbar.

Figure 5.2 TABLE TOOLS LAYOUT Tab

| Project 1c | Modifying the Table Layout | Part 3 of 14 |

1. With **P-C5-P1-Conference.pptx** open, make sure Slide 3 is active.
2. Click in any cell in the table and then click the TABLE TOOLS LAYOUT tab.
3. Click in the cell containing the word *East*.
4. Click the Insert Above button in the Rows & Columns group.
5. Type **Central** in the new cell at the left, press the Tab key, and then type **$1,024,000** in the new cell at the right.
6. Click in the cell containing the word *Region*.
7. Click the Insert Left button in the Rows & Columns group.
8. Click the Merge Cells button in the Merge group.
9. Type **Sales Projections** in the new cell.
10. Click the Text Direction button in the Alignment group and then click *Rotate all text 270°* at the drop-down list.
11. Click the Center button in the Alignment group and then click the Center Vertically button in the Alignment group.
12. Click in the *Width* measurement box in the Cell Size group, type **1.2**, and then press Enter.

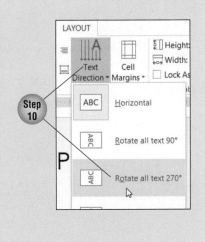

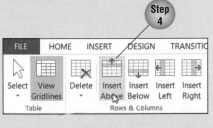

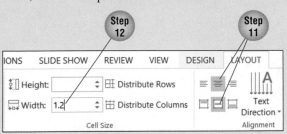

13. Click the TABLE TOOLS DESIGN tab.
14. Click the Borders button arrow in the Table Styles group and then click *Bottom Border* at the drop-down list.
15. Click in the cell containing the text *Sales* and then click the TABLE TOOLS LAYOUT tab.
16. Click in the *Height* measurement box in the Cell Size group and type **0.7**.
17. Click in the *Width* measurement box in the Cell Size group, type **2.5**, and then press Enter.
18. Click in the cell containing the text *Region*.
19. Click in the *Width* measurement box in the Cell Size group, type **4**, and then press Enter.
20. Click in the *Height* measurement box in the Table Size group, type **4.2**, and then press Enter.
21. Click the Select button in the Table group and then click *Select Table* at the drop-down list.
22. Click the Center button and then click the Center Vertically button in the Alignment group.
23. After looking at the text in cells, you decide that you want the text in the second column left-aligned. To do this, complete the following steps:
    a. Click in the cell containing the text *Region*.
    b. Click the Select button in the Table group and then click *Select Column* at the drop-down list.
    c. Click the Align Left button in the Alignment group.
    d. Click in any cell in the table.
24. Align the table by completing the following steps:
    a. Click the HOME tab.
    b. Click the Arrange button in the Drawing group, point to *Align*, and then click *Distribute Horizontally*.
    c. Click the Arrange button, point to *Align*, and then click *Distribute Vertically*.
    d. Looking at the table, you decide that it should be moved down in the slide. To do this, position the mouse pointer on the table border until the pointer displays with a four-headed arrow attached. Hold down the left mouse button, drag down approximately 0.5 inch, and then release the mouse button.
25. Insert a clip art image in the table by completing the following steps:
    a. Click the INSERT tab.
    b. Click the Online Pictures button in the Images group.

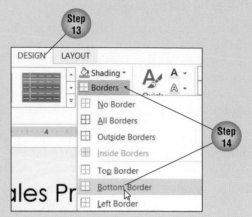

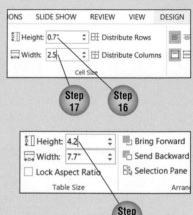

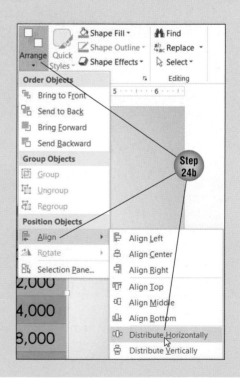

c. At the Insert Pictures window, type **flip chart sales** in the search text box and then press Enter.

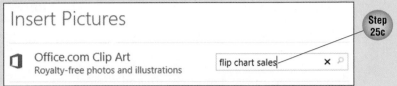

Step 25c

d. Double-click the image shown in Figure 5.3. (If this image is not available, choose a similar clip art image related to sales.)
e. With the image selected, click in the *Shape Height* measurement box in the Size group on the PICTURE TOOLS FORMAT tab, type 2.8, and then press Enter.
f. Drag the clip art image so it is positioned in the table as shown in Figure 5.3.
g. Click outside the clip art image to deselect it.

26. Save **P-C5-P1-Conference.pptx**.

Figure 5.3 Project 1c, Slide 3

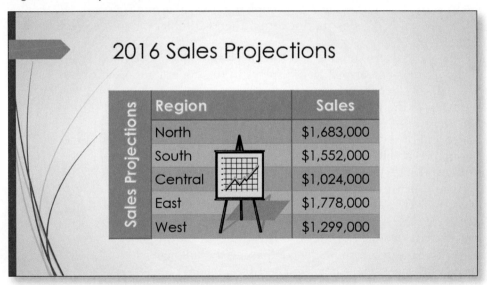

Inserting an Excel Spreadsheet

In addition to inserting a table in a slide, you can insert an Excel spreadsheet, which provides you with some Excel functions. To insert an Excel spreadsheet, click the INSERT tab, click the Table button in the Tables group, and then click the *Excel Spreadsheet* option at the drop-down list. This inserts a small worksheet in the slide with two columns and two rows visible. Increase the number of visible cells by dragging the sizing handles that display around the worksheet. Click outside the worksheet and the cells display as an object that you can format with options on the DRAWING TOOLS FORMAT tab. To format the worksheet with Excel options, double-click the worksheet and the ribbon displays with Excel tabs.

1. With **P-C5-P1-Conference.pptx** open, make sure Slide 3 is active and then insert a new slide with the Title Only layout.
2. Click the text *Click to add title* and then type **Projected Increase**.
3. Insert an Excel spreadsheet by clicking the INSERT tab, clicking the Table button in the Tables group, and then clicking *Excel Spreadsheet* at the drop-down list.

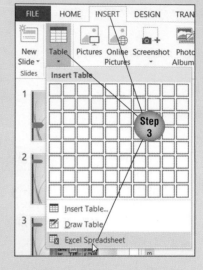

4. Increase the size of the worksheet by completing the following steps:
   a. Position the mouse pointer on the sizing handle (small black square) located in the lower right corner of the worksheet until the pointer displays as a black, diagonal, two-headed arrow.
   b. Hold down the left mouse button, drag down and to the right, and then release the mouse button. Continue dragging the sizing handles until columns A, B, and C and rows 1 through 6 are visible.
5. Copy a Word table into the Excel worksheet by completing the following steps:
   a. Open Word and then open **NWSalesInc.docx** from the PC5 folder on your storage medium.
   b. Hover your mouse pointer over the table and then click the table move handle (small square containing a four-headed arrow) that displays in the upper left corner of the table. (This selects all cells in the table.)
   c. Click the Copy button in the Clipboard group on the HOME tab.
   d. Click the PowerPoint button on the Taskbar.
   e. With Slide 4 active and the first cell in the worksheet active, click the Paste button in the Clipboard group on the HOME tab.
6. Size and position the worksheet object by completing the following steps:
   a. Click outside the worksheet to remove the Excel ribbon tabs.
   b. With the worksheet object selected, click the DRAWING TOOLS FORMAT tab.
   c. Click in the *Shape Width* measurement box, type **7**, and then press Enter.
   d. Using the mouse, drag the worksheet object so it is centered on the slide.
7. Format the worksheet and insert a formula by completing the following steps:
   a. Double-click in the worksheet. (This displays the Excel ribbon tabs.)
   b. Click in cell C2, type the formula **=B2*1.02**, and then press Enter.

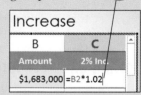

Step 7b

8. Copy the formula in C2 to cells C3 through C6 by completing the following steps:
   a. Position the mouse pointer (white plus symbol) in cell C2, hold down the left mouse button, drag down to cell C6, and then release the mouse button.
   b. Click the Fill button in the Editing group on the HOME tab and then click *Down* at the drop-down list.
   c. With cells C2 through C6 selected, click two times on the Decrease Decimal button in the Number group.
9. Click outside the worksheet to remove the Excel ribbon tabs.
10. Make the following changes to the table:
    a. Click the DRAWING TOOLS FORMAT tab.

Step 8b

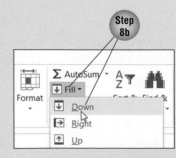

b. Click the Align button and then click *Distribute Horizontally* at the drop-down list.

c. Click the Align button and then click *Distribute Vertically* at the drop-down list.

11. Click the Word button on the Taskbar and then close Word.

12. Save **P-C5-P1-Conference.pptx**.

Drawing a Table

You can draw a table in a slide using the *Draw Table* option at the Table button drop-down list. When you click the Table button and then click the *Draw Table* option, the mouse pointer displays as a pen. Drag in the slide to create the table. Use buttons on the TABLE TOOLS DESIGN tab and TABLE TOOLS FORMAT tab to format the table.

Project 1e **Drawing a Table** **Part 5 of 14**

1. With **P-C5-P1-Conference.pptx** open, make sure Slide 4 is active.

2. Draw a table and then split the table into two columns and two rows by completing the following steps:

   a. Click the INSERT tab, click the Table button in the Tables group, and then click the *Draw Table* option at the drop-down list.

   b. Position the mouse pointer (displays as a pen) below the worksheet and then drag to create a table that is approximately 7 inches wide and 1 inch tall.

   c. Click the TABLE TOOLS LAYOUT tab and then click the Split Cells button in the Merge group.

   d. At the Split Cells dialog box, press the Tab key, type 2, and then click the OK button. (This splits the table into two columns and two rows.)

   e. Select the current measurement in the *Height* measurement box in the Table Size group and then type 1.

   f. Select the current measurement in the *Width* measurement box in the Table Size group, type 7, and then press Enter.

3. With the table selected, make the following formatting changes:

   a. Click the TABLE TOOLS DESIGN tab.

   b. Click the More button at the right side of the table style thumbnails and then click the *Themed Style 2 - Accent 1* thumbnail (second column, second row in the *Best Match for Document* section).

   c. Click the Effects button in the Table Styles group, point to *Cell Bevel*, and then click the *Relaxed Inset* option (second column, first row in the *Bevel* section).

   d. Click the HOME tab, click the Bold button, and then click the Center button.

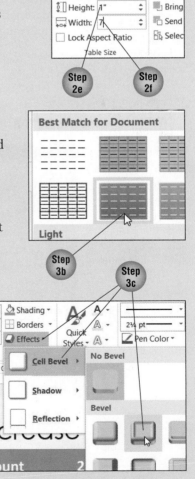

e. Click the Align Text button and then click *Middle* at the drop-down list.

f. Make sure the table is positioned evenly between the bottom of the top table and the bottom of the slide.

g. Click the Arrange button in the Drawing group, point to *Align*, and then click *Distribute Horizontally* at the side menu.

4. Type **Maximum** in the first cell in the table, press the Tab key, and then type **$1,813,360**.

5. Press the Tab key and then type **Minimum**.

6. Press the Tab key and then type **$1,044,480**.

7. Click outside the table to deselect it.

8. Save **P-C5-P1-Conference.pptx**.

▼ **Quick Steps**

Insert a SmartArt Graphic
1. Click Insert a SmartArt Graphic button in content placeholder.
2. Double-click desired diagram.
OR
1. Click INSERT tab.
2. Click SmartArt button.
3. Double-click desired diagram.

SmartArt

Creating SmartArt ■■■■■■■■■■■■■■■■■■■■■■■

Use the SmartArt feature to insert graphics such as diagrams and organizational charts in a slide. SmartArt offers a variety of predesigned graphics that are available at the Choose a SmartArt Graphic dialog box, shown in Figure 5.4. Display the Choose a SmartArt Graphic dialog box by clicking the Insert a SmartArt Graphic button that displays in a content placeholder or by clicking the INSERT tab and then clicking the SmartArt button in the Illustrations group. At the dialog box, *All* is selected in the left panel and all available predesigned graphics display in the middle panel.

Figure 5.4 Choose a SmartArt Graphic Dialog Box

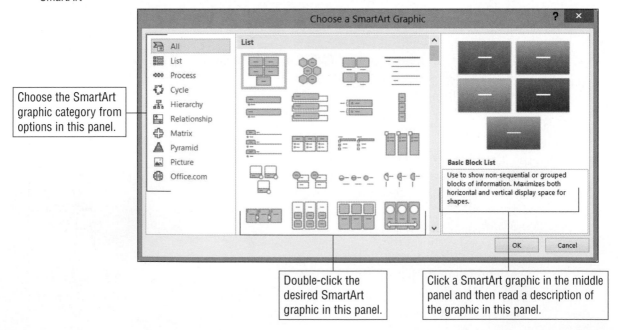

Choose the SmartArt graphic category from options in this panel.

Double-click the desired SmartArt graphic in this panel.

Click a SmartArt graphic in the middle panel and then read a description of the graphic in this panel.

Modifying SmartArt

Predesigned graphics display in the middle panel of the Choose a SmartArt Graphic dialog box. Use the scroll bar at the right side of the middle panel to scroll down the list of graphic choices. Click a graphic in the middle panel and the name of the graphic displays in the right panel along with a description of the graphic type. SmartArt includes graphics for presenting a list of data; showing data processes, cycles, and relationships; and presenting data in a matrix or pyramid. Double-click a graphic in the middle panel of the dialog box and the graphic is inserted in the slide.

When you double-click a graphic at the dialog box, the graphic is inserted in the slide and a text pane may display at the left side of the graphic. You can type text in the text pane or directly in the graphic. Apply design formatting to a graphic with options on the SMARTART TOOLS DESIGN tab, shown in Figure 5.5. This tab is active when the graphic is inserted and selected in the slide. Use options and buttons on this tab to change the graphic layout, apply a style to the graphic, and reset the graphic back to the original formatting.

HINT
Use SmartArt to communicate your message and ideas in a visual manner.

HINT
Limit the number of shapes and the amount of text to key points in a slide.

Figure 5.5 SMARTART TOOLS DESIGN Tab

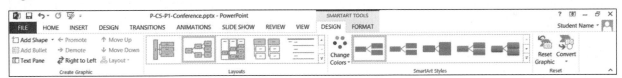

Project 1f   Inserting and Modifying a SmartArt Graphic   Part 6 of 14

1. With **P-C5-P1-Conference.pptx** open, make sure Slide 4 is active and then insert a new slide with the Title and Content layout.
2. Click in the title placeholder and then type **Division Reorganization**.
3. Click the Insert a SmartArt Graphic button located in the middle of the slide in the content placeholder.
4. At the Choose a SmartArt Graphic dialog box, click *Hierarchy* in the left panel of the dialog box.
5. Double-click the *Horizontal Hierarchy* option.
6. If a *Type your text here* pane displays at the left side of the organizational chart, close the pane by clicking the Text Pane button in the Create Graphic group.

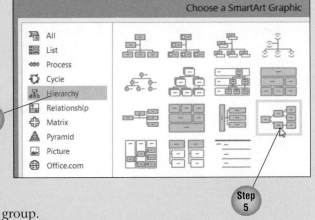

7. Delete one of the boxes in the organizational chart by clicking the border of the top box at the right side of the slide (the top box of the three stacked boxes) and then pressing the Delete key. (Make sure that the selection border that surrounds the box is a solid line and not a dashed line. If a dashed line displays, click the box border again. This should change it to a solid line.)

8. Click *[Text]* in the first box at the left, type **Andrew Singh**, press Shift + Enter, and then type **Director**. Click in each of the remaining boxes and type the text as shown below. (Press Shift + Enter after each name.)

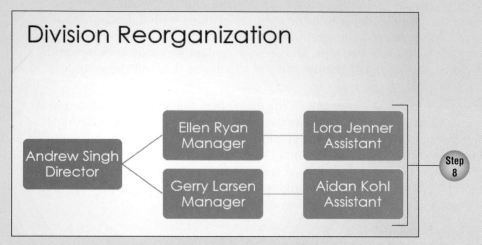

9. Click inside the SmartArt border but outside of any shape and then click the SMARTART TOOLS DESIGN tab.
10. Click the More button at the right side of the style thumbnails in the SmartArt Styles group and then click the *Polished* thumbnail (first column, first row in the *3-D* section).
11. Click the Change Colors button in the SmartArt Styles group and then click *Colorful Range - Accent Colors 3 to 4* (third option in the *Colorful* section).
12. Change the layout of the organizational chart by clicking the More button at the right side of the thumbnails in the Layouts group and then clicking *Table Hierarchy* at the drop-down list. Your slide should now look like the slide shown in Figure 5.6.

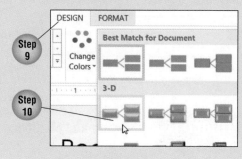

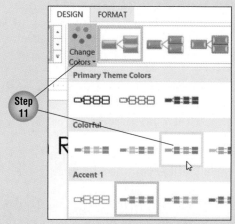

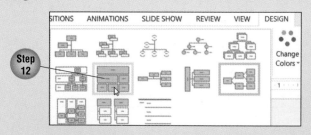

13. Save **P-C5-P1-Conference.pptx**.

Figure 5.6 Project 1f, Slide 5

Formatting SmartArt

Apply formatting to a SmartArt graphic with options on the SMARTART TOOLS FORMAT tab, shown in Figure 5.7. With options and buttons on this tab change the size and shape of objects in the graphic; apply shape styles and WordArt styles; change the shape fill, outline, and effects; and arrange and size the graphic. Move the graphic by positioning the arrow pointer on the graphic border until the pointer turns into a four-headed arrow, holding down the left mouse button, and then dragging the graphic to the desired location.

H I N T

Nudge selected shape(s) with the up, down, left, or right arrow keys on the keyboard.

Figure 5.7 SMARTART TOOLS FORMAT Tab

1. With **P-C5-P1-Conference.pptx** open, make Slide 1 active and then insert a new slide with the Blank layout.
2. Click the INSERT tab and then click the SmartArt button in the Illustrations group.
3. At the Choose a SmartArt Graphic dialog box, click *Relationship* in the left panel of the dialog box.
4. Double-click the *Basic Venn* option shown at the right. (You will need to scroll down the list to display this diagram.)

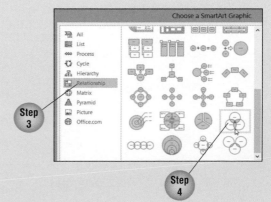

5. Click in the top shape and type **Health**.
6. Click in the shape at the left and type **Happiness**.
7. Click in the shape at the right and type **Harmony**.
8. Click inside the SmartArt border but outside of any shape.
9. Click the Change Colors button in the SmartArt Styles group and then click *Colorful Range - Accent Colors 3 to 4* (third option in the *Colorful* section).

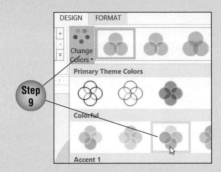

10. Click the More button at the right side of the thumbnails in the SmartArt Styles group and then click *Cartoon* at the drop-down gallery (third option in the *3-D* section).

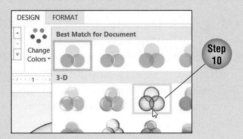

11. Click the SMARTART TOOLS FORMAT tab.
12. Click the More button at the right side of the WordArt Styles thumbnails and then click *Pattern Fill - Green, Accent 1, 50%, Hard Shadow - Accent 1* (third column, bottom row).
13. Click the Text Outline button arrow in the WordArt Styles group and then click *Green, Accent 1, Darker 50%* (fifth column, bottom row in the *Theme Colors* section).
14. Click in the *Shape Height* measurement box in the Size group and then type **6**.
15. Click in the *Shape Width* measurement box in the Size group, type **9**, and then press Enter.

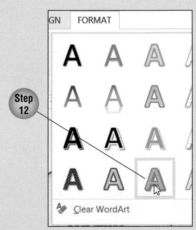

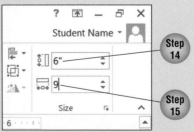

16. Save **P-C5-P1-Conference.pptx**.

Converting Text and WordArt to a SmartArt Graphic

To improve the visual display of text or WordArt and to create a professionally designed image, consider converting text or WordArt to a SmartArt graphic. To do this, select the placeholder containing the text or WordArt and then click the Convert to SmartArt Graphic button in the Paragraph group on the HOME tab. Click the desired SmartArt graphic at the drop-down gallery or click the *More SmartArt Graphics* option and then choose a SmartArt graphic at the Choose a SmartArt Graphic dialog box.

Convert to
SmartArt Graphic

Inserting Text in the Text Pane

Enter text in a SmartArt shape by clicking in the shape and then typing the text or by typing text in the Text pane. Display the Text pane by clicking the Text Pane button in the Create Graphic group on the SMARTART TOOLS DESIGN tab.

Text Pane

Project 1h   **Creating a SmartArt Graphic with Text and WordArt**   **Part 8 of 14**

1. With **P-C5-P1-Conference.pptx** open, make Slide 7 active. (This slide contains WordArt text.)
2. Click on any character in the WordArt text.
3. If necessary, click the HOME tab.
4. Click the Convert to SmartArt Graphic button in the Paragraph group.
5. Click the *More SmartArt Graphics* option that displays at the bottom of the drop-down gallery.
6. At the Choose a SmartArt Graphic dialog box, click *Cycle* in the left panel and then double-click *Diverging Radial* in the middle panel.

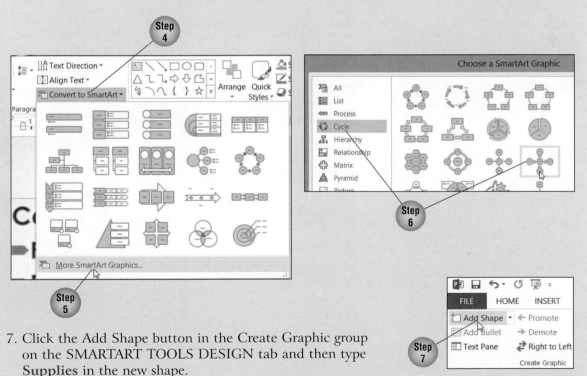

7. Click the Add Shape button in the Create Graphic group on the SMARTART TOOLS DESIGN tab and then type **Supplies** in the new shape.

8. Change the order of the text in the shapes at the left and right sides of the graphic by clicking the Right to Left button in the Create Graphic group.

9. Click the Change Colors button in the SmartArt Styles group and then click *Colorful - Accent Colors* (first option in the *Colorful* section).

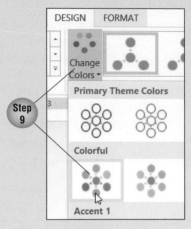

10. Click the More button at the right of the style thumbnails in the SmartArt Styles group and then click *Inset* (second option in the *3-D* section).

11. Click the SMARTART TOOLS FORMAT tab.

12. Click the middle circle (contains the text *Central Division*).

13. Click three times on the Larger button in the Shapes group.

14. Click inside the SmartArt border but outside of any shape.

15. Click in the *Shape Height* measurement box in the Size group and then type **6.6**.

16. Click in the *Shape Width* measurement box, type **8.2**, and then press Enter.

17. Click the HOME tab.

18. With the SmartArt graphic selected, click the Arrange button in the Drawing group, point to *Align*, and then click *Distribute Horizontally*.

19. Click the Arrange button, point to *Align*, and then click *Distribute Vertically*.

20. Click the Bold button in the Font group.

21. Make Slide 9 active.

22. Click in any character in the bulleted text and, if necessary, click the HOME tab.

23. Click the Convert to SmartArt Graphic button in the Paragraph group and then click *Vertical Block List* at the drop-down list (second column, first row).

24. Click the shape containing the text *Sales over $2 million* and then click the Demote button in the Create Graphic group on the SMARTART TOOLS DESIGN tab.

25. Click on any character in the text *One-week all expenses paid trip to Las Vegas* and then click the Promote button in the Create Graphic group.

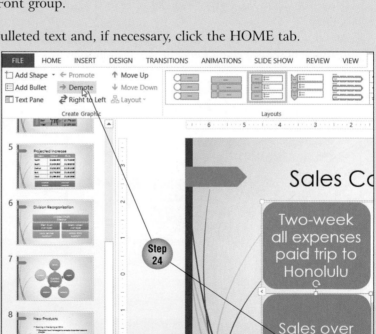

26. Click the Text Pane button in the Create Graphic group to display the *Type your text here* text pane.
27. Click immediately right of the *s* in *Vegas* in the text pane and then press the Enter key.
28. Press the Tab key and then type **Sales over $1 million**.
29. Close the text pane by clicking the Close button that displays in the upper right corner of the pane.
30. Click the More button that displays at the right side of the SmartArt Styles thumbnails and then click the *Inset* thumbnail (second column, first row in the *3-D* section).
31. Save **P-C5-P1-Conference.pptx**.
32. Print Slides 7 and 9.

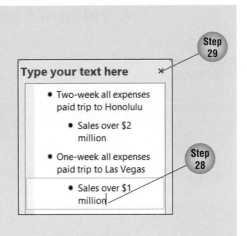

Converting a SmartArt Graphic to Text or Shapes

If you want to remove all formatting from a SmartArt graphic, click the Reset Graphic button in the Reset group on the SMARTART TOOLS DESIGN tab. With the Convert button, you can convert a SmartArt graphic to text or shapes. Click the Convert button and then click the *Convert to Text* option at the drop-down list to convert the SmartArt graphic to bulleted text. Click the *Convert to Shapes* option at the drop-down list to convert a SmartArt graphic to shapes. With the SmartArt graphic converted to shapes, you can move, resize, or delete a shape independently from the other shapes.

Reset Graphic

Convert

Project 1i **Converting SmartArt to Text and to Shapes** **Part 9 of 14**

1. With **P-C5-P1-Conference.pptx** open, make sure Slide 9 is active.
2. Click the SmartArt graphic to select it.
3. Click the SMARTART TOOLS DESIGN tab.
4. Click the Reset Graphic button in the Reset group.
5. With the SmartArt graphic still selected, click the Convert button in the Reset group and then click *Convert to Text* at the drop-down list.
6. Make Slide 7 active.
7. Click the SmartArt graphic to select it.
8. Click the SMARTART TOOLS DESIGN tab, click the Convert button in the Reset group, and then click *Convert to Shapes* at the drop-down list.
9. Select and then delete each of the arrows that points from the middle circle to each of the outer circles.
10. Save **P-C5-P1-Conference.pptx**.

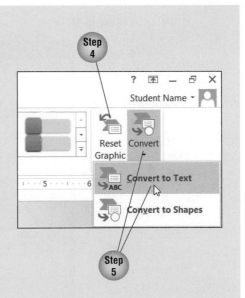

Creating a Chart ■■■■■■■■■■■■■■■■■■■■■■■■■■■■■■■

▼ **Quick Steps**

Insert a Chart
1. Click Insert Chart button in content placeholder.
2. Click desired chart style and type.
3. Enter data in Excel worksheet.
4. Close Excel.
OR
1. Click INSERT tab.
2. Click Chart button.
3. Click desired chart type and style.
4. Enter data in Excel worksheet.
5. Close Excel.

Chart

You can create a variety of charts including bar and column charts, pie charts, area charts, and much more. To create a chart, click the Insert Chart button in a content placeholder or click the INSERT tab and then click the Chart button in the Illustrations group. This displays the Insert Chart dialog box, as shown in Figure 5.9. At this dialog box, choose the desired chart type in the list at the left side, click the chart style, and then click OK. Table 5.2 describes the ten basic chart types you can create in PowerPoint.

When you click OK at the Insert Chart dialog box, a sample chart is inserted in your slide and Excel opens with sample data, as shown in Figure 5.10. Type the desired data in the Excel worksheet cells over the existing data. As you type data, the chart in the slide reflects the typed data. To type data in the Excel worksheet, click in the desired cell, type the data, and then press the Tab key to make the next cell active, press Shift + Tab to make the previous cell active, or press Enter to make the cell below active.

The sample worksheet contains a data range of four columns and five rows and the cells in the data range display with a light fill color. Excel uses the data in the range to create the chart in the slide. You are not limited to four columns and five rows. Simply type data in cells outside the data range and Excel will expand the data range and incorporate the new data in the chart. This is because the table AutoExpansion feature is on by default. If you type data in a cell outside the data range, an AutoCorrect Options button displays in the lower right corner of the cell when you move away from the cell. Use this button if you want to turn off AutoExpansion. If you do not insert data in all four columns and five rows, decrease the size of the data range. To do this, position the mouse pointer on the small, square, blue icon that displays in the lower right corner of cell E5 until the pointer displays as a diagonally pointing two-headed arrow and then drag up to decrease the number of rows in the range and/or drag left to decrease the number of columns.

Figure 5.9 Insert Chart Dialog Box

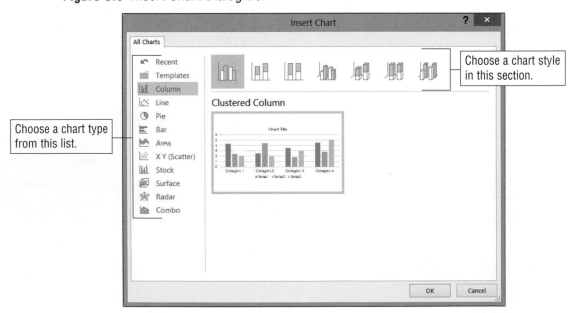

Once all data is entered in the worksheet, click the Close button that displays in the upper right corner of the screen. This closes the Excel window and displays the chart in the slide.

Table 5.2 Types of Charts

Type	Description
area	Emphasizes the magnitude of change, rather than time and the rate of change. It also shows the relationship of parts to a whole by displaying the sum of the plotted values.
bar	Shows individual figures at a specific time, or shows variations between components but not in relationship to the whole.
column	Compares separate (noncontinuous) items as they vary over time.
combo	Combines two or more chart types to make data easy to understand.
line	Shows trends and change over time at even intervals. It emphasizes the rate of change over time rather than the magnitude of change.
pie	Shows proportions and relationships of parts to the whole.
radar	Emphasizes differences and amounts of change over time and variations and trends. Each category has its own value axis radiating from the center point. Lines connect all values in the same series.
stock	Shows four values for a stock—open, high, low, and close.
surface	Shows trends in values across two dimensions in a continuous curve.
xy(scatter)	Either shows the relationships among numeric values in several data series or plots the interception points between x and y values. It shows uneven intervals of data and is commonly used in scientific data.

Figure 5.10 Sample Chart

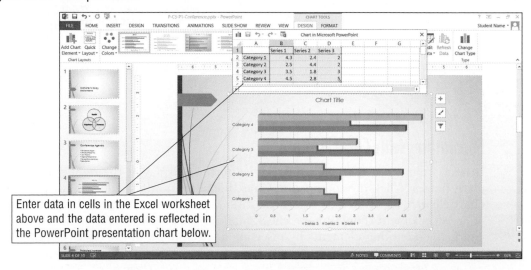

Enter data in cells in the Excel worksheet above and the data entered is reflected in the PowerPoint presentation chart below.

1. With **P-C5-P1-Conference.pptx** open, make Slide 3 active and then insert a new slide with the Blank layout.
2. Click the INSERT tab and then click the Chart button in the Illustrations group.
3. At the Insert Chart dialog box, click *Bar* in the left panel.
4. Double-click the *3-D Clustered Bar* option that displays at the top of the dialog box (fourth option).
5. In the Excel worksheet, position the mouse pointer in the bottom right corner of the cell D5 border until the mouse pointer displays as a diagonally pointing two-headed arrow. Hold down the left mouse button, drag to the left until the border displays at the right side of column C, and then release the mouse button.
6. Type the text in cells as shown below by completing the following steps:
   a. Click in cell B1 in the Excel worksheet, type **1st Half**, and then press the Tab key.
   b. With cell C1 active, type **2nd Half** and then press the Tab key.
   c. Click in cell A2, type **North**, and then press the Tab key.
   d. Type **$853,000** and then press the Tab key.
   e. Type **$970,000** and then press the Enter key.
   f. Continue typing the remaining data in cells as indicated at the right. (The data range will automatically expand to include row 6.)
7. Click the Close button that displays in the upper right corner of the Excel window.

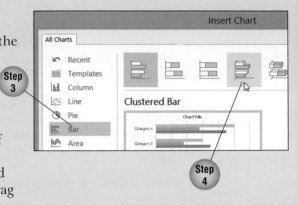

	A	B	C	D
1		Series 1	Series 2	Series 3
2	Category 1	4.3	2.4	2
3	Category 2	2.5	4.4	2
4	Category 3	3.5	1.8	3
5	Category 4	4.5	2.8	5

	A	B	C	D
1		1st Half	2nd Half	Series 3
2	North	$853,000	$970,000	2
3	South	$750,000	$910,000	2
4	Central	$720,000	$750,000	3
5	East	$880,000	$950,000	5
6	West	$830,000	$900,000	
7				

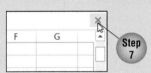

8. Save **P-C5-P1-Conference.pptx**.

Formatting with Chart Buttons

+

Chart Elements

When you insert a chart in a slide, three buttons display at the right side of the chart border. Click the top button, Chart Elements, and a side menu displays with chart elements such as axis title, chart title, data labels, data table, gridlines, and a legend. Elements containing a check mark in the check box are included in the chart. Include other elements by inserting a check mark in the check boxes for those elements you want in your chart.

Chart Styles

You can apply a variety of chart styles to your chart. Click the Chart Styles button that displays at the right side of the chart and a side menu gallery of styles displays. Scroll down the gallery, hover your mouse over an option, and the style formatting is applied to your chart. In this way you can scroll down the gallery and preview the style before you apply it to your chart. In addition to applying a chart style, use the Chart Styles button side menu gallery to change the chart colors. Click the Chart Styles button and then click the COLOR tab that displays to the right of the STYLE tab. Click the desired color option at the color palette that displays. Hover your mouse over a color option to view how the color change affects the elements in your chart.

Use the bottom button, Chart Filters, to isolate specific data in your chart. When you click the button, a side menu displays. Specify the series or categories you want to display in your chart. To do this, remove check marks from those elements that you do not want to appear in your chart. After removing the check marks, click the Apply button that displays toward the bottom of the side menu. Click the NAMES tab at the Chart Filters button side menu and options display for turning on/off the display of column and row names.

Chart Filters

Project 1k | **Creating a Chart** | **Part 11 of 14**

1. With **P-C5-P1-Conference.pptx** open, make sure Slide 4 is the active slide and that the chart in the slide is selected. (Make sure the chart is selected and not an element in the chart.)
2. Insert and remove chart elements by completing the following steps:
   a. Click the Chart Elements button that displays outside the upper right side of the chart.
   b. At the side menu that displays, click the *Chart Title* check box to remove the check mark.
   c. Click the *Data Table* check box to insert a check mark.
   d. Hover your mouse pointer over *Gridlines* in the Chart Elements button side menu and then click the right-pointing arrow that displays.
   e. At the other side menu that displays, click the *Primary Major Horizontal* check box to insert a check mark.
   f. Click the *Legend* check box to remove the check mark.
   g. Hover your mouse pointer over *Axis Titles* in the Chart Elements button side menu and then click the right-pointing arrow that displays.
   h. At the other side menu that displays, click the *Primary Vertical* check box to insert a check mark.
   i. With *Axis Title* selected in the rotated box at the left side of the chart, type **Region**.
3. Apply a different chart style by completing the following steps:
   a. Click the chart border to redisplay the chart buttons.
   b. Click the Chart Styles button that display to the right of the chart below the Chart Elements button.
   c. At the side menu gallery, click the *Style 3* option (third option in the gallery).

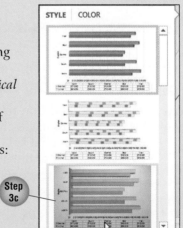

---

d. Click the COLOR tab at the top of the side menu and then click the *Color 2* option at the drop-down gallery (second row of color options in the *Colorful* section).

e. Click the Chart Styles button to remove the side menu.

4. Remove the horizontal axis title by completing these steps:
a. Click the Chart Elements button.
b. Hover your mouse pointer over Axes in the Chart Elements button side menu and then click the right-pointing arrow that displays.
c. At the other side menu that displays, click the *Primary Horizontal* check box to remove the check mark.
d. Click the Chart Elements button to remove the side menu.

5. Display only the North and South sales by completing the following steps:
a. Click the Chart Filters button that displays below the Chart Styles button.
b. Click the *Central* check box in the *CATEGORIES* section to remove the check mark.
c. Click the *East* check box in the *CATEGORIES* section to remove the check mark.
d. Click the *West* check box in the *CATEGORIES* section to remove the check mark.
e. Click the Apply button that displays toward the bottom of the side menu.
f. Click the Chart Filters button to remove the side menu.
g. After viewing only the *North* and *South* sales, redisplay the other regions by clicking the Chart Filters button, clicking the *Central*, *East*, and *West* check boxes, and then clicking the Apply button.
h. Click the Chart Filters button to remove the side menu.

6. Save **P-C5-P1-Conference.pptx**.

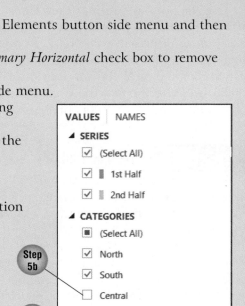

Changing Chart Design

Quick Steps

Change the Chart Type and Style
1. Make the chart active.
2. Click CHART TOOLS DESIGN tab.
3. Click Change Chart Type button.
4. Click desired chart type.
5. Click desired chart style.
6. Click OK.

Change Chart Type

In addition to the buttons that display outside the chart border, you can customize a chart with options on the CHART TOOLS DESIGN tab, shown in Figure 5.11. Use options on this tab to add a chart element, change the chart layout and colors, apply a chart style, select data and switch rows and columns, and change the chart type.

After you create a chart, you can change the chart type by clicking the Change Chart Type button in the Type group on the CHART TOOLS DESIGN tab. This displays the Change Chart Type dialog box. This dialog box contains the same options as the Insert Chart dialog box shown in Figure 5.9. At the Change Chart Type dialog box, click the desired chart type in the left panel and click the desired chart style in the right panel.

Figure 5.11 CHART TOOLS DESIGN Tab

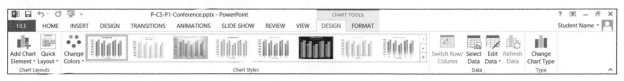

Use options in the Data group on the CHART TOOLS DESIGN tab to change the grouping of the data in the chart, select specific data, edit data, and refresh the data. When you create a chart, the cells in the Excel worksheet are linked to the chart in the slide. Click the Select Data button in the Data group and Excel opens and the Select Data Source dialog box displays. At the Select Data Source dialog box, click the Switch Row/Column button to change the grouping of the selected data. Filter data at the dialog box by removing the check mark from those items in the dialog box that you do not want to appear in the chart. If you need to edit data in the chart, click the Edit Data button and the Excel worksheet opens. Make the desired changes to cells in the Excel worksheet and then click the Close button.

Apply predesigned chart styles with options in the Chart Styles group and use the Change Colors button to change the color of the selected element or chart. Click the Quick Layout button in the Chart Layouts group to display a drop-down gallery of layout options and add an element to the chart with the Add Chart Element button.

Select Data

Switch Row/Column

Edit Data

Change Colors

Quick Layout

Project 1I   Changing the Chart Design   Part 12 of 14

1. With **P-C5-P1-Conference.pptx** open, make sure Slide 4 is active and the chart is selected. Click the CHART TOOLS DESIGN tab to make it active.
2. Looking at the chart, you decide that the bar chart was not the best choice for the data and decide to change to a column chart. Do this by completing the following steps:
   a. Click the Change Chart Type button in the Type group on the CHART TOOLS DESIGN tab.
   b. At the Change Chart Type dialog box, click the *Column* option in the left panel.
   c. Click the *3-D Clustered Column* option (fourth option at the top of the dialog box).
   d. Click OK to close the dialog box.
3. Change to a different layout by clicking the Quick Layout button in the Chart Layouts group and then clicking the *Layout 10* option (the last option).

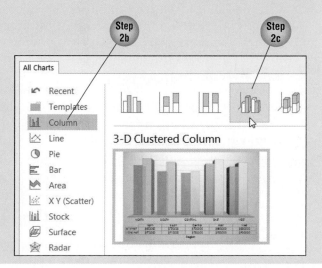

4. Click the Add Chart Element button in the Chart Layouts group, point to *Chart Title* at the drop-down list, and then click *Above Chart* at the side menu.
5. Type **2015 Regional Sales** as the chart title.
6. Click the chart border to deselect the chart title.
7. Click the *Style 1* thumbnail in the Chart Styles group (first thumbnail).
8. Select data and switch rows and columns by completing the following steps:
   a. Click the Select Data button in the Data group. (This opens Excel and displays the Select Data Source dialog box.)
   b. Click the Switch Row/Column button in the Select Data Source dialog box.

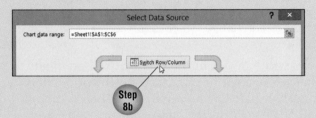

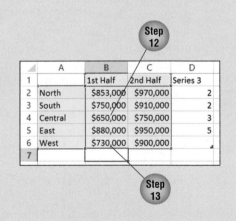

c. Click OK. (This switches the grouping of the data from *Region* to *Half Yearly Sales*.)
9. After viewing the chart, switch the rows and columns back to the original groupings by dragging the Excel window so the Switch Row/Column button is visible in the Data group on the CHART TOOLS DESIGN tab, clicking in the chart, and then clicking the Switch Row/Column button.
10. Close the Excel window by clicking the Close button that displays in the upper right corner of the Excel window.
11. Click the Edit Data button in the Data group.
12. Click in cell B4 (the cell containing the amount *$720,000*), type **650000**, and then press Enter. (When you press Enter, a dollar sign is automatically inserted in front of the number and a thousand separator comma is inserted.)
13. Click in cell B6 (the cell containing the amount *$830,000*), type **730000**, and then press Enter.
14. Click the Close button that displays in the upper right corner of the Excel window.
15. Save **P-C5-P1-Conference.pptx**.

Formatting a Chart and Chart Elements

Apply formatting to a chart or chart elements with options in the Drawing group on the HOME tab. Apply a predesigned style to a chart or chart element with the Quick Styles button. Use other buttons in the group to add fill and outline color and apply effects.

In addition to the buttons in the Drawing group on the HOME tab, you can format and customize a chart and chart elements with options on the CHART TOOLS FORMAT tab, as shown in Figure 5.12. To format or modify a specific element in a chart, select the element. Do this by clicking the element or by clicking the Chart Elements button in the Current Selection group and then clicking the element at the drop-down list. With the element selected, apply the desired formatting. Click the Format Selection button in the Current Selection group and a task pane displays with options for formatting the selected element. Insert shapes with options in the Insert Shapes group. Click a shape or click the More button and then click a shape at the drop-down list and then drag in the chart to create the shape. Click the Change Shape button if you want to change the shape to a different shape.

The Shape Styles group on the CHART TOOLS FORMAT tab contains predesigned styles you can apply to elements in the chart. Click the More button at the right side of the style thumbnails and a drop-down gallery displays of shape styles. Use the buttons that display at the right side of the Shape Styles group to apply fill, an outline, and an effect to a selected element. The WordArt Styles group contains predesigned styles you can apply to text in a chart. Use the buttons that display at the right side of the WordArt Styles group to apply fill color, an outline color, or an effect to text in a chart. Use options in the Arrange group to specify the layering, alignment, rotation, and size of a chart or chart element.

Additional formatting options are available at various task panes. Display a task pane by the clicking Format Selection button or by clicking a group task pane launcher. The Shape Styles, WordArt Styles, and Size groups on the CHART TOOLS FORMAT tab contain a task pane launcher. The task pane that opens at the right side of the screen depends on the chart or chart element selected.

HINT

Right-click text in a chart element to display the Mini toolbar.

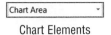
Chart Area

Chart Elements

Format Selection

HINT

Chart elements can be repositioned for easier viewing.

Figure 5.12 CHART TOOLS FORMAT Tab

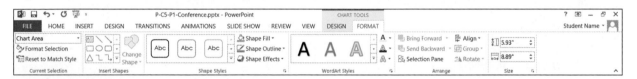

| Project 1m | Formatting a Chart and Chart Elements | Part 13 of 14 |

1. With **P-C5-P1-Conference.pptx** open, make sure Slide 4 is active and the chart is selected.
2. Reposition and format the legend by completing the following steps:
   a. Click the Chart Elements button that displays at the right side of the chart.
   b. Hover your mouse pointer over *Legend*, click the right-pointing arrow at the right side of *Legend* in the side menu, and then click the *Right* option at the other side menu.
   c. Click the Chart Elements button again to remove the side menu.
   d. Click the legend to select it.
   e. If necessary, click the HOME tab.

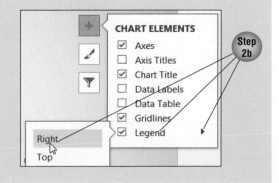

f. Click the Quick Styles button in the Drawing group and then click the *Subtle Effect - Lime, Accent 3* option (fourth column, fourth row).

g. Click the Shape Outline button arrow in the Drawing group and then click *Green, Accent 1, Darker 50%* (fifth column, bottom row in the *Theme Colors* section).

h. Increase the size of the legend by dragging down the bottom middle sizing handle about 0.25 inch.

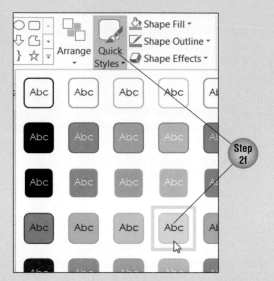

3. Format the title by completing the following steps:

a. Click the CHART TOOLS FORMAT tab.

b. Click the Chart Elements button arrow in the Current Selection group and then click *Chart Title* at the drop-down list.

c. Click the More button at the right side of the style thumbnails in the Shape Styles group and then click *Intense Effect - Green, Accent 1* (second column, bottom row).

d. Click the Shape Effects button, point to *Bevel*, and then click the *Cross* option (third column, first row in the *Bevel* section).

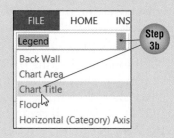

4. Customize the chart wall and floor by completing the following steps:

a. Click the Chart Elements button arrow in the Current Selection group and then click *Back Wall* at the drop-down list.

b. Click the Format Selection button in the Current Selection group. (This displays the Format Wall task pane.)

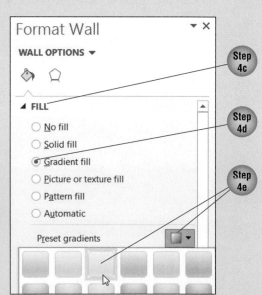

c. Click *FILL* to display the options.

d. Click the *Gradient fill* option in the Format Wall task pane with the Fill & Line icon selected.

e. Click the Preset gradients button and then click the *Light Gradient - Accent 3* option (third column, first row).

f. Click the Chart Elements button arrow and then click *Floor* at the drop-down list. (This displays the Format Floor task pane.)

g. Click the *Solid fill* option.

5. Customize the 1st Half data series by completing the following steps:

a. Click the Chart Elements button arrow and then click *Series "1st Half"* at the drop-down list.

b. Click the Effects icon in the Format Data Series task pane.

c. Click *3-D FORMAT* to display the options.

d. Click the Material button in the task pane.

e. At the gallery that displays, click the *Dark Edge* option (first option in the *Special Effect* section).

f. Click the Bottom bevel button and then click the *Hard Edge* option (third column, third row in the *Bevel* section).

6. Complete steps similar to those in Step 5a through 5f to format the *Series "2nd Half"* chart element.

7. Customize the chart by completing the following steps:

a. Click the Chart Elements button arrow and then click *Chart Area* at the drop-down list.

b. Click the Fill & Line icon and make sure fill options display in the Format Chart Area task pane. (If necessary, click *FILL* to expand the options.)

c. Click the *Picture or texture fill* option.

d. Click the Texture button (displays below the Online button)

e. Click the *Parchment* option (last column, third row).

f. Scroll down the task pane to the *BORDER* section and, if necessary, click *BORDER* to expand the options.

g. Click the *Solid line* option in the *BORDER* section.

h. Click the Size & Properties icon.

i. Click *SIZE* to display the options.

j. Select the current measurement in the *Height* measurement box and then type 6.

k. Select the current measurement in the *Width* measurement box, type 9, and then press Enter.

l. Click *POSITION* to display the options.

m. Select the current measurement in the *Horizontal position* measurement box and then type 2.5.

n. Select the current measurement in the *Vertical position* measurement box, type 0.8, and then press Enter.

o. Close the task pane by clicking the Close button in the upper right corner of the task pane.

8. Save **P-C5-P1-Conference.pptx**.

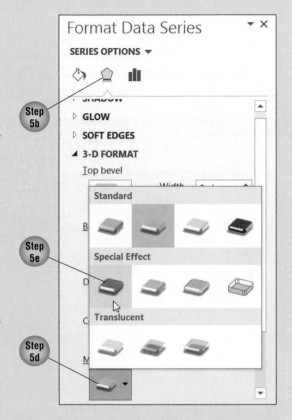

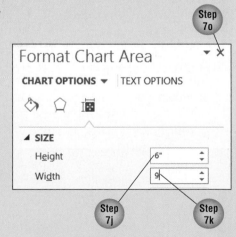

Another method for formatting a chart or chart elements is to use options at the shortcut menu. Some of the options on the shortcut menu vary depending on the chart or chart element selected. Some common options include deleting the element, editing data, rotating the element, and adding data labels. To display the shortcut menu, right-click the element or the chart. In addition to the shortcut menu, the Mini toolbar also displays. The Mini toolbar contains options for applying fill color and outline color.

Project 1n Creating and Formatting a Pie Chart   Part 14 of 14

1. With **P-C5-P1-Conference.pptx** open, make Slide 6 active and then insert a new slide with the Blank layout.
2. Click the INSERT tab and then click the Chart button in the Illustrations group.
3. At the Insert Chart dialog box, click *Pie* in the left panel.
4. Double-click the *3-D Pie* option at the top of the dialog box (second option).
5. Type the text in cells in the Excel worksheet as shown at the right.
6. When all data is entered, click the Close button that displays in the upper right corner of the Excel window.
7. Click the Chart Styles button that displays at the right side of the pie chart, click the *Style 3* chart style, and then click the Chart Styles button again to remove the side menu.

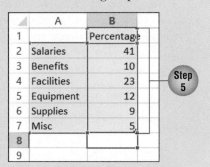

8. Move the data labels to the outside of the pie by completing the following steps:
   a. Click the Chart Elements button that displays at the right side of the chart.
   b. Hover your mouse pointer over the *Data Labels* option in the side menu and then click the right-pointing arrow that displays.
   c. Click the *Outside End* option.
   d. Click the Chart Elements button to remove the side menu.

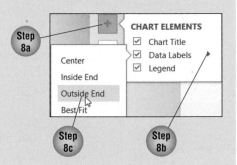

9. Apply formatting to the legend by completing the following steps:
   a. Hover your mouse just above the word *Salaries* in the legend until the mouse pointer displays with a four-headed arrow attached and then click the right mouse button.
   b. Click the Fill button on the Mini toolbar and then click *Tan, Background 2* (third column, first row in the *Theme Colors* section).
   c. Click the Outline button on the Mini toolbar and then click *Green, Accent 1, Darker 50%* (fifth column, bottom row in the *Theme Colors* section).
   d. Increase the size of the legend by dragging the bottom middle sizing handle down about 0.25 inch.

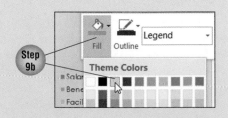

10. Edit the title by completing the following steps:
    a. Right-click the title *Percentage* and then click *Edit Text* in the shortcut menu.
    b. With the insertion point positioned in the title, press the End key to move the insertion point to the right of *Percentage*, press the spacebar, and then type **of 100k Division Budget**.
11. Click outside the title but inside the chart to select the chart.
12. Click the CHART TOOLS FORMAT tab.
13. Change the chart height to 6.5 inches and the chart width to 9 inches.
14. Click the Align button in the Arrange group and then click *Distribute Horizontally*.
15. Click the Align button in the Arrange group and then click *Distribute Vertically*.
16. Apply a transition and sound of your choosing to all slides in the presentation.
17. Save **P-C5-P1-Conference.pptx**.
18. Run the presentation.
19. Print the presentation as a handout with six slides printed horizontally per page.
20. Close **P-C5-P1-Conference.pptx**.

Project 2 Create and Format a Travel Photo Album   3 Parts

You will use the photo album feature to create a presentation containing travel photographs. You will also apply formatting and insert elements in the presentation.

Creating a Photo Album ■■■■■■■■■■■■■■■■■■■■■■■

With PowerPoint's photo album feature, you can create a presentation containing personal or business pictures. Customize and format the appearance of pictures by applying interesting layouts, frame shapes, and themes and insert elements such as captions and text boxes. To create a photo album, click the INSERT tab, click the Photo Album button arrow in the Images group, and then click *New Photo Album* at the drop-down list. This displays the Photo Album dialog box, as shown in Figure 5.14.

To insert pictures in the photo album, click the File/Disk button to display the Insert New Pictures dialog box. At this dialog box, navigate to the desired folder and then double-click the picture you want to insert in the album. This inserts the picture name in the *Pictures in album* list box in the dialog box and also displays the picture in the *Preview* section. As you insert pictures in the photo album, the picture names display in the *Pictures in album* list box in the order in which they will appear in the presentation. When you have inserted all of the desired pictures into the photo album, click the Create button. This creates the photo album as a presentation and displays the first slide. The photo album feature creates the first slide with the title *Photo Album* and the user's name.

▼ Quick Steps

Create a Photo Album
1. Click INSERT tab.
2. Click Photo Album button arrow.
3. Click *New Photo Album*.
4. Click File/Disk button.
5. Double-click desired picture.
6. Repeat Steps 4 and 5 for all desired pictures.
7. Make desired changes at Photo Album dialog box.
8. Click Create button.

Photo Album

Figure 5.14 Photo Album Dialog Box

Insert a picture by clicking this button and then double-clicking the picture at the Insert New Pictures dialog box.

Choose a picture and then preview it in this *Preview* box.

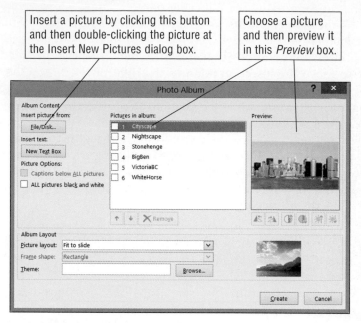

Project 2a   Creating a Travel Photo Album   Part 1 of 3

1. At a blank screen, click the INSERT tab, click the Photo Album button arrow in the Images group, and then click *New Photo Album* at the drop-down list.
2. At the Photo Album dialog box, click the File/Disk button.
3. At the Insert New Pictures dialog box, navigate to the PC5 folder on your storage medium and then double-click ***Cityscape.jpg***.
4. At the Photo Album dialog box, click the File/Disk button, and then double-click ***Nightscape.jpg*** at the Insert New Pictures dialog box.
5. Insert the following additional pictures: ***Stonehenge.jpg***, ***WhiteHorse.jpg***, ***BigBen.jpg***, and ***VictoriaBC.jpg***.
6. Click the Create button. (This opens a presentation with each image in a separate slide. The first slide contains the default text *Photo Album* followed by your name (or the user name for the computer).
7. Save the presentation and name it **P-C5-P2-Album.pptx**.
8. Run the presentation.

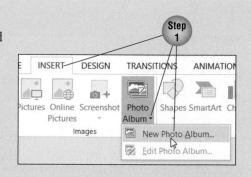

Step 1

Step 2

Step 6

Editing and Formatting a Photo Album

If you want to make changes to a photo album presentation, open the presentation, click the INSERT tab, click the Photo Album button arrow in the Images group, and then click *Edit Photo Album* at the drop-down list. This displays the Edit Photo Album dialog box, which contains the same options as the Photo Album dialog box.

Rearrange the order of slides in a photo album presentation by clicking the desired slide in the *Pictures in album* list box and then clicking the button containing the up-pointing arrow to move the slide up in the order or clicking the button containing the down-pointing arrow to move the slide down in the order. Remove a slide by clicking the desired slide in the list box and then clicking the Remove button. Use buttons below the *Preview* box in the Edit Photo Album dialog box, to rotate the picture in the slide and increase or decrease the contrast or brightness of the picture.

The *Picture layout* option in the Album Layout group has a default setting of *Fit to slide*. At this setting the picture in each slide will fill most of the slide. You can change this setting by clicking the *Picture layout* option box arrow. With options at the drop-down list, specify whether you want one picture, two pictures, or four pictures inserted into the slide. You can also specify that you want the pictures inserted with titles.

If you change the *Picture layout* option to something other than the default of *Fit to slide*, the *Frame shape* option becomes available. Click the *Frame shape* option box arrow and a drop-down list displays with framing options. You can choose a rounded, simple, or double frame, or a soft or shadow effect frame.

Apply a theme to the photo album presentation by clicking the Browse button located at the right side of the *Theme* option box and then double-clicking the desired theme in the Choose Theme dialog box. This dialog box contains the predesigned themes provided by PowerPoint.

If you want to include captions with the pictures, change the *Picture layout* to one, two, or four slides and then click the *Captions below ALL pictures* check box located in the *Picture Options* section of the Edit Photo Album dialog box. PowerPoint will insert below each picture a caption containing the name of the picture. You can edit the caption in the slide in the presentation. If you want to display all of the pictures in your photo album in black and white, click the *ALL pictures black and white* check box in the *Picture Options* section of the dialog box.

Click the New Text Box button in the Edit Photo Album dialog box and a new slide containing a text box is inserted in the presentation. You can edit the information in the text box in the presentation. Once all changes have been made to the photo album, click the Update button located toward the bottom right side of the dialog box.

▼ Quick Steps

Edit a Photo Album
1. Click INSERT tab.
2. Click Photo Album button arrow.
3. Click *Edit Photo Album*.
4. Make desired changes at Edit Photo Album dialog box.
5. Click Update button.

Project 2b   **Editing and Formatting a Photo Album**   **Part 2 of 3**

1. With **P-C5-P2-Album.pptx** open, make sure the INSERT tab is active, click the Photo Album button arrow in the Images group, and then click *Edit Photo Album* at the drop-down list.

2. At the Edit Photo Album dialog box, make the following changes:

a. Click the *ALL pictures black and white* check box to insert a check mark.

b. Click in the *VictoriaBC* check box in the *Pictures in album* list box and then click three times on the up-pointing arrow that displays below the list box. (This moves *VictoriaBC* so it is positioned between *Nightscape* and *Stonehenge*).

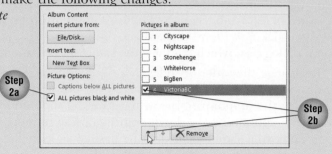

c. Click once on the Rotate button located below the *Preview* box (the first button from the left below the picture). Click three more times on the Rotate button to return the image to the original orientation.

d. Click the *VictoriaBC* check box in the *Pictures in album* list box to remove the check mark.

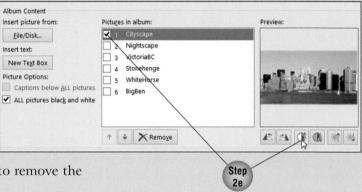

e. Click the *Cityscape* check box in the *Pictures in album* list box and then click twice on the Increase Contrast button located under the *Preview* box.

f. Click the *Cityscape* check box to remove the check mark.

g. Click the *Stonehenge* check box in the *Pictures in album* list box, click twice on the Increase Contrast button under the *Preview* box and then click twice on the Increase Brightness button (fifth button to the right of the Remove button).

h. Click the *Picture layout* option box arrow and then click *1 picture* at the drop-down list.

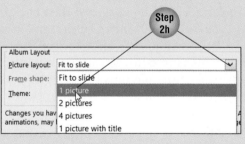

i. Click the *Frame shape* option box arrow and then click *Center Shadow Rectangle* at the drop-down list.

j. Click the Browse button located at the right side of the *Theme* option box. At the Choose Theme dialog box, double-click **Facet.thmx**.

k. Click the *Captions below ALL pictures* check box to insert a check mark.

l. Click the *Stonehenge* check box in the *Pictures in album* list box to remove the check mark and then click the *BigBen* check box in the *Pictures in album* list box to insert a check mark.

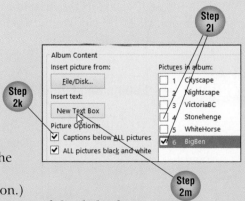

m. Click the New Text Box button that displays at the left side of the list box. (This inserts a new slide containing a text box at the end of the presentation.)

n. Click the Update button located in the lower right corner of the dialog box.

3. At the presentation, make the following formatting changes:
   a. Click the DESIGN tab.
   b. Click the blue variant in the Variants group (second variant).
4. With Slide 1 active, make the following changes:
   a. Select the text *Photo Album* and then type **Travel Album**.
   b. Select any text that displays after the word *by* and then type your first and last names.
   c. Click the INSERT tab and then click the Pictures button.
   d. At the Insert Picture dialog box, navigate to the PC5 folder on your storage medium and then double-click ***FCTLogo.jpg***.
   e. Click the Color button in the Adjust group on the PICTURE TOOLS FORMAT tab and then click *Set Transparent Color* at the drop-down list.
   f. Move the mouse pointer (pointer displays with a tool attached) to any white portion of the logo and then click the left mouse button. (This changes the white fill to transparent fill and allows the title to show through.)
   g. Change the height of the logo to 3.5 inches and then position the logo attractively in the slide.

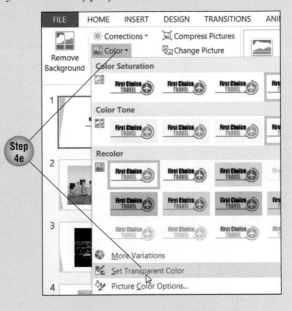

5. Make Slide 2 active and then edit the caption by completing the following steps:
   a. Click on any character in the caption *Cityscape*.
   b. Select *Cityscape* and then type **New York City Skyline**.

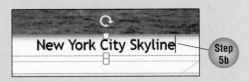

6. Complete steps similar to those in Step 5 to change the following captions:
   a. In Slide 3, change *Nightscape* to *New York City at Night*.
   b. In Slide 4, change *VictoriaBC* to *Victoria, British Columbia*.
   c. In Slide 5, change *Stonehenge* to *Stonehenge, Wiltshire County*.
   d. In Slide 6, change *WhiteHorse* to *White Horse, Wiltshire County*.
   e. In Slide 7, change *BigBen* to *Big Ben, London*.
7. Make Slide 8 active and then make the following changes:
   a. Select the text *Text Box* and then type **Call First Choice Travel at 213-555-4500 to book your next travel tour**.
   b. Select the text, change the font size to 48 points, apply the Blue font color, and center align the text.
   c. Change the width of the placeholder to 9 inches. (Do this with the *Shape Width* measurement box on the DRAWING TOOLS FORMAT tab.)
8. Apply a transition and sound of your choosing to all slides.
9. Run the presentation.
10. Save **P-C5-P2-Album.pptx**.

Formatting Pictures

If you format slides in the presentation instead of the Edit Photo Album dialog box, you may lose some of those changes if you subsequently display the Edit Photo Album dialog box, make changes, and then click the Update button. Consider making your initial editing and formatting changes at the Edit Photo Album dialog box and then make final editing and formatting changes in the presentation.

Since a picture in a slide in a photo album is an object, you can format it with options on the DRAWING TOOLS FORMAT tab and the PICTURE TOOLS FORMAT tab. With options on the DRAWING TOOLS FORMAT tab, insert shapes, apply a shape style to the picture and caption (if one is displayed), apply a WordArt style to caption text, and arrange and size the picture. Use options on the PICTURE TOOLS FORMAT tab to adjust the color of the picture, apply a picture style, and arrange and size the picture.

Project 2c   **Formatting Pictures in a Presentation**   **Part 3 of 3**

1. With **P-C5-P2-Album.pptx** open, make Slide 2 active.
2. Change the pictures back to color by completing the following steps:
   a. Click the INSERT tab.
   b. Click the Photo Album button arrow in the Images group and then click *Edit Photo Album* at the drop-down list.
   c. Click the *ALL pictures black and white* check box to remove the check mark.
   d. Click the Update button.
3. Format the picture in Slide 2 by completing the following steps:
   a. Click the picture to select it.
   b. Click the DRAWING TOOLS FORMAT tab.
   c. Click the More button at the right side of the thumbnails in the Shape Styles group and then click *Subtle Effect - Turquoise, Accent 1* (second column, fourth row).

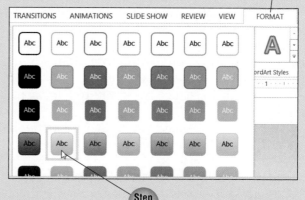

4. Apply the same style to the pictures in Slides 3 through 7 by making each slide active, clicking the picture, and then pressing F4. (Pressing F4 repeats the style formatting.)
5. Make Slide 2 active and then apply a WordArt style to the caption text by completing the following steps:
   a. With Slide 2 active, click the picture to select it.
   b. Click the DRAWING TOOLS FORMAT tab.
   c. Click the More button at the right side of the thumbnails in the WordArt Styles group and then click *Fill - Blue, Accent 2, Outline - Accent 2* (third column, first row).
6. Apply the same WordStyle style to the caption text in Slides 3 through 7 by making each slide active, clicking the picture, and then pressing F4.
7. Make Slide 8 active and then change the width of the placeholder to 9 inches.
8. Run the presentation.
9. Print the presentation as a handout with four slides horizontally per page.
10. Save and then close **P-C5-P2-Album.pptx**.

Chapter Summary

- With the Table button in the Tables group on the INSERT tab, you can create a table, insert an Excel spreadsheet, and draw a table in a slide.

- Change the table design with options and buttons on the TABLE TOOLS DESIGN tab. Change the table layout with options and buttons in the TABLE TOOLS LAYOUT tab.

- Use the SmartArt feature to insert predesigned graphics such as diagrams and organizational charts in a slide.

- Use options and buttons in the SMARTART TOOLS DESIGN tab to change the graphic layout, apply a style to the graphic, and reset the graphic back to the original formatting.

- Use options and buttons in the SMARTART TOOLS FORMAT tab to change the size and shapes of objects in the graphic; apply shape styles; change the shape fill, outline, and effects; and arrange and size the graphic.

- Insert text directly into a SmartArt graphic shape or at the Text pane. Display this pane by clicking the Text Pane button in the Create Graphic group on the SMARTART TOOLS DESIGN tab.

- You can convert text or WordArt to a SmartArt graphic and convert a SmartArt graphic to text or shapes.

- A chart is a visual presentation of data. You can create a variety of charts, as described in Table 5.2.

- To create a chart, display the Insert Chart dialog box by clicking the Insert Chart button in a content placeholder or clicking the Chart button in the Illustrations group on the INSERT tab.

- Enter chart data in an Excel worksheet. When entering data, press Tab to make the next cell active, press Shift + Tab to make the previous cell active, and press Enter to make the cell below active.

- Modify a chart design with options and buttons on the CHART TOOLS DESIGN tab.

- Cells in the Excel worksheet used to create a chart are linked to the chart in the slide. To edit chart data, click the Edit Data button on the CHART TOOLS DESIGN tab and then make changes to the text in the Excel worksheet.

- Customize the format of a chart and chart elements with options and buttons on the CHART TOOLS FORMAT tab. You can select the chart or a specific element, apply a style to a shape, apply a WordArt style to text, and arrange and size the chart.

- Use the Photo Album feature in the Images group on the INSERT tab to create a presentation containing pictures and then edit and format the pictures.

- At the Photo Album dialog box (or the Edit Photo Album dialog box), insert pictures and then use options to customize the photo album.

- Use options on the DRAWING TOOLS FORMAT tab and the PICTURE TOOLS FORMAT tab to format pictures in a photo album presentation.

Commands Review

FEATURE	RIBBON TAB, GROUP	BUTTON, OPTION	PLACEHOLDER BUTTON
Choose a SmartArt Graphic dialog box	INSERT, Illustrations	🖼	🖼
convert bulleted text to SmartArt	HOME, Paragraph	🖼	
create photo album	INSERT, Images	🖼, *New Photo Album*	
edit photo album	INSERT, Images	🖼, *Edit Photo Album*	
Insert Chart dialog box	INSERT, Illustrations	📊	📊
Insert Table dialog box	INSERT, Tables	▦, *Insert Table*	▦
Text pane	SMARTART TOOLS DESIGN, Create Graphic	▤	

Concepts Check   Test Your Knowledge

Completion: In the space provided at the right, indicate the correct term, symbol, or command.

1. This term refers to the intersection between a row and a column.

2. Display the Insert Table dialog box by clicking this button in a content placeholder.

3. Press this key on the keyboard to move the insertion point to the next cell.

4. Press these keys on the keyboard to select all cells in a table.

5. The Table Styles group is located on this tab.

6. Use options and buttons on this tab to delete and insert rows and columns and merge and split cells.

7. Click this button in a content placeholder to display the Choose a SmartArt Graphic dialog box.

8. When you insert a SmartArt graphic in a slide and the graphic is selected, this tab is active.

9. Create a SmartArt graphic with bulleted text by clicking in the text placeholder, clicking this button, and then clicking the desired SmartArt graphic at the drop-down gallery.

10. Click the Chart button in this group on the INSERT tab to display the Insert Chart dialog box.

_____

11. Insert a chart in a slide and this tab is active.

_____

12. To edit data in a chart, click the Edit Data button in this group on the CHART TOOLS DESIGN tab.

_____

13. This group on the CHART TOOLS FORMAT tab contains predesigned styles you can apply to elements in a chart.

_____

14. This group on the CHART TOOLS FORMAT tab contains predesigned styles you can apply to chart text.

_____

15. To create a photo album, click the INSERT tab, click the Photo Album button arrow, and then click this at the drop-down list.

_____

16. Click the down-pointing arrow at the right of this option in the Edit Photo Album dialog box to display a list of framing choices.

_____

17. To insert captions below pictures in a photo album, insert a check mark in this check box in the Edit Photo Album dialog box.

_____

Skills Check   Assess Your Performance

Assessment

1   CREATE AND FORMAT TABLES AND SMARTART IN A RESTAURANT PRESENTATION

1. Open **Dockside.pptx** and then save the presentation with Save As and name it **P-C5-A1-Dockside**.
2. Make Slide 6 active and then create the table shown in the slide in Figure 5.15 on page 227 with the following specifications:
   a. Create a table with three columns and six rows.
   b. Type the text in cells as shown in Figure 5.15.
   c. Apply the Medium Style 1 - Accent 2 style to the table (third column, first row in the *Medium* section).
   d. Select all of the text in the table, center the text vertically, change the font size to 20 points, and change the font color to *Turquoise, Accent 2, Darker 50%* (sixth column, bottom row in the *Theme Colors* section).
   e. Change the height of the table to 3.7 inches and the width to 9 inches.
   f. Center the text in the first row.
   g. Center the data in the third column.
   h. Horizontally distribute the table.

3. Make Slide 4 active and then create the table shown in the slide in Figure 5.16 with the following specifications:
   a. Create a table with four columns and three rows.
   b. Select the entire table, change the vertical alignment to center, and then change the font size to 28 points.
   c. Merge the cells in the first column, change the text direction to *Rotate all text 270°*, change the alignment to center, change the font size to 40 points, and then type **Lunch**.
   d. Merge the cells in the third column, change the text direction to *Rotate all text 270°*, change the alignment to center, change the font size to 40 points, and then type **Dinner**.
   e. Type the remaining text in cells as shown in Figure 5.16.
   f. Change the height of the table to 3 inches.
   g. Change the width of the first and third columns to 1.2 inches.
   h. Change the width of the second and fourth columns to 2.5 inches.
   i. Insert a check mark in the *Banded Columns* check box in the Table Style Options group on the TABLE TOOLS DESIGN tab and remove the check marks from the other check boxes in the group.
   j. Apply the Light Style 3 - Accent 2 style to the table.
   k. Select all of the text in the table and then change the font color to *Light Turquoise, Background 2, Darker 75%*.
   l. Distribute the table horizontally on the slide.
4. Make Slide 5 active and then create the SmartArt organizational chart shown in the slide in Figure 5.17 with the following specifications:
   a. Choose the Half Circle Organization Chart graphic at the Choose a SmartArt Graphic dialog box.
   b. Select and then delete the second box (select the text box) so your chart appears with the same number of boxes and in the same order as the organizational chart in Figure 5.17.
   c. Type the text in the boxes as shown in Figure 5.17 (Press Enter after typing each name.).
   d. Change the color to *Colorful Range - Accent Colors 3 to 4*.
   e. Apply the Polished SmartArt style.
   f. Change the text fill color to *Dark Teal, Text 2, Darker 25%*.
   g. Change the height of the organizational chart to 6.5 inches and change the width to 10 inches.
   h. Distribute the SmartArt organizational chart horizontally on the slide.
5. Make Slide 1 active and then format the title and create the SmartArt graphic shown in the slide in Figure 5.18 with the following specifications:
   a. Create the SmartArt graphic with the Linear Venn option located in the Relationship group.
   b. Type the text in the shapes as shown in Figure 5.18.
   c. Change the colors to *Colorful - Accent Colors*.
   d. Apply the Cartoon SmartArt style.
   e. Change the height of the graphic to 3 inches and the width to 9 inches.
   f. Align the SmartArt at the bottom of the slide. (Use the Align button in the Arrange group on the SMARTART TOOLS FORMAT tab.)
6. Make Slide 2 active, select the bulleted text placeholder, and then convert the bulleted text to a Basic Matrix SmartArt graphic as shown in the slide in Figure 5.19 with the following specifications:
   a. Change the colors to *Colorful - Accent Colors*.
   b. Apply the Cartoon SmartArt style.
   c. Change the height of the graphic to 4.5 inches.

7. Apply a transition and sound of your choosing to all slides in the presentation.
8. Run the presentation.
9. Print the presentation as a handout with six slides horizontally per page.
10. Save and then close **P-C5-A1-Dockside.pptx**.

Figure 5.15 Assessment 1, Slide 6

Figure 5.16 Assessment 1, Slide 4

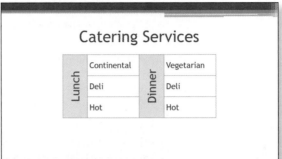

Figure 5.17 Assessment 1, Slide 5

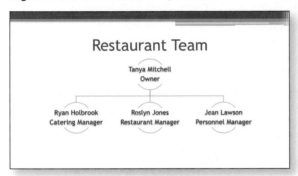

Figure 5.18 Assessment 1, Slide 1

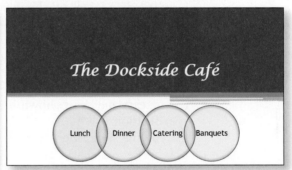

Figure 5.19 Assessment 1, Slide 2

Assessment

2 CREATE AND FORMAT CHARTS IN A MARKETING PRESENTATION

1. Open **MarketingPres.pptx** and save the presentation with Save As and name it **P-C5-A2-MarketingPres**.
2. Make Slide 2 active, insert a new slide with the Title and Content layout, and then create the chart shown in the slide in Figure 5.20 with the following specifications:
   a. Type the slide title as shown in Figure 5.20 on the next page.
   b. Use the pie chart *3-D Pie* option to create the chart.
   c. Type the following information in the Excel worksheet:

	Percentage
Salaries	47%
Equipment	18%
Supplies	4%
Production	21%
Distribution	10%

   d. Apply the Layout 7 chart layout using the Quick Layout button.
   e. Apply the Style 5 chart style.
   f. Move the legend to the right.
   g. Select the legend and then change the font size to 24 points.
   h. Insert data labels on the inside end.
   i. Select the data labels and then change the font size to 20 points.
3. Print Slide 3.
4. After looking at the slide, you realize that two of the percentages are incorrect. Edit the Excel data and change *47%* to *42%* and change *10%* to *15%*.
5. With Slide 3 active, insert a new slide with the Title and Content layout and then create the chart shown in the slide in Figure 5.21 with the following specifications:
   a. Type the slide title as shown in Figure 5.21.
   b. Use the line chart *Line with Markers* option to create the chart.
   c. Type the following information in the Excel worksheet:

	Revenues	Expenses
1st Qtr	$789,560	$670,500
2nd Qtr	$990,450	$765,000
3rd Qtr	$750,340	$780,000
4th Qtr	$980,400	$875,200

   d. Apply the Style 4 chart style.
   e. Add primary major vertical gridlines.
   f. Add a data table with legend keys.
   g. Remove the title and remove the legend.
   h. Select the chart area and then change the font size to 18 points.
   i. With the chart area still selected, display the Format Chart Area task pane and then specify a gradient fill of *Light Gradient - Accent 2*.
   j. Select the Revenues series and then change the weight of the line to 4 ½ points. (Do this with the Shape Outline button in the Shape Styles group on the CHART TOOLS FORMAT tab.)
   k. Select the Expenses series and then change the weight of the line to 4 ½ points.
6. Apply a transition and sound of your choosing to each slide in the presentation.

Figure 5.20 Assessment 2, Slide 3

Figure 5.21 Assessment 2, Slide 4

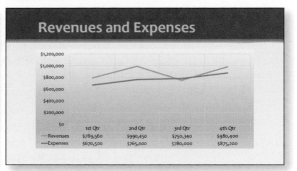

7. Run the presentation.
8. Print the presentation as a handout with six slides printed horizontally per page.
9. Save and then close **P-C5-A2-MarketingPres.pptx**.

Assessment

3 CREATE A SCENERY PHOTO ALBUM

1. At a blank screen, create a new photo album.
2. At the Photo Album dialog box, insert the following images:
   AlderSprings.jpg
   CrookedRiver.jpg
   Mountain.jpg
   Ocean.jpg
   Olympics.jpg
   River.jpg
3. Change the *Picture layout* option to *1 picture with title*.
4. Change the *Frame shape* option to *Simple Frame, White*.
5. Apply the Integral theme.
6. Click the Create button.
7. At the presentation, click the DESIGN tab and then click the fourth variant.
8. Insert the following titles in the specified slides:
   Slide 2 *Alder Springs, Oregon*
   Slide 3 *Crooked River, Oregon*
   Slide 4 *Mt. Rainier, Washington*
   Slide 5 *Pacific Ocean, Washington*
   Slide 6 *Olympic Mountains, Washington*
   Slide 7 *Salmon River, Idaho*
9. Make Slide 1 active, select any name that follows *by*, and then type your first and last names.
10. Save the presentation and name it **P-C5-A3-PhotoAlbum**.
11. Print the presentation as a handout with four slides printed horizontally per page.
12. Close **P-C5-A3-PhotoAlbum.pptx**.

Assessment

4 CREATE A SALES AREA CHART

1. Open **P-C5-A2-MarketingPres.pptx** and then save the presentation with Save As and name it **P-C5-A4-MarketingPres**.
2. Make Slide 4 active and then insert a new slide with the Title and Content layout.
3. Use Excel's Help feature to learn more about chart types and then create an area chart (use the *Area* chart type) with the data shown below. Apply design, layout, and/or formatting to improve the visual appearance of the chart. Type **Sales by Region** as the slide title.

	Region 1	Region 2	Region 3
Sales 2012	$650,300	$478,100	$225,500
Sales 2013	$623,100	$533,600	$210,000
Sales 2014	$725,600	$478,400	$296,500

4. Print Slide 5.
5. Save and then close **P-C5-A4-MarketingPres.pptx**.

Visual Benchmark   Demonstrate Your Proficiency

CREATE AND FORMAT A MEDICAL CENTER PRESENTATION

1. Open **RMCPres.pptx** and then save the presentation with Save As and name it **P-C5-VB-RMCPres**.
2. Create the presentation shown in Figure 5.22 with the following specifications:
   a. Create Slide 2 with the SmartArt Hierarchy relationship graphic and apply the Colorful Range - Accent Colors 2 to 3 colors to the graphic. (Press Enter after typing each title.)
   b. Create Slide 3 with the SmartArt Basic Radial relationship graphic and apply the Colorful - Accent Colors to the graphic.
   c. Create Slide 4 and insert the table as shown in Slide 5. Apply the Medium Style 2 - Accent 1 table style and apply other formatting so your table looks similar to the table in the figure.
   d. Use the information shown in the data table to create the 3-D Clustered Column chart as shown in Slide 5. Apply formatting so your chart looks similar to the chart in the figure. As the last formatting step, select the entire chart and change the font size to 16 points and apply the Black, Text 1 font color.
   e. Use the information shown in the legend and the data information at the outside end of each pie to create a 3-D pie chart as shown in Slide 6. Apply formatting so your pie chart looks similar to the chart in the figure. As the last formatting step, select the entire chart and change the font size to 16 points and apply the Black, Text 1 font color.
3. Apply a transition and sound of your choosing to all slides in the presentation.
4. Print the presentation as a handout with six slides printed horizontally per page.
5. Save and then close **P-C5-VB-RMCPres.pptx**.

Figure 5.22 Visual Benchmark

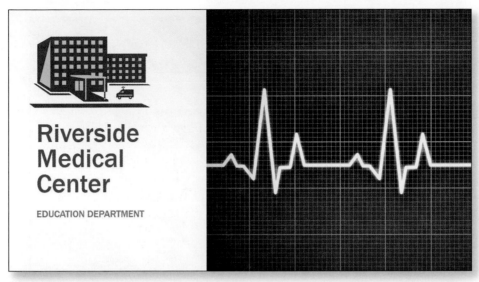

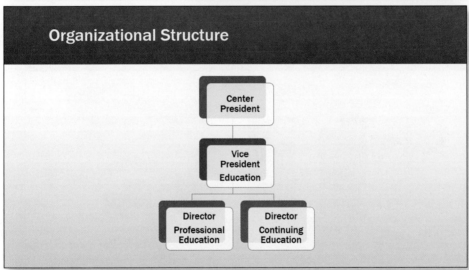

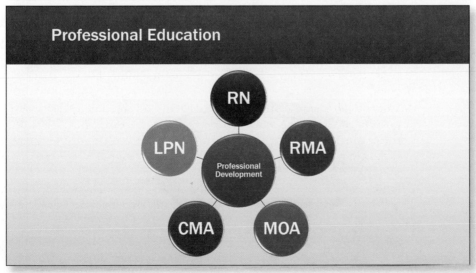

continues

Figure 5.22 Visual Benchmark—*continued*

Course Offerings

Course	Session 1	Session 2
AHA Basic Life Support	October 1	October 3
AHA First Aid	October 9	October 11
Basic Cardiac Care	October 15	October 17
Advanced Cardiac Life Support	October 30	November 1
Trauma Nursing Care	November 6	November 8
Emergency Pediatric Nursing Care	November 12	November 14

Current Enrollment

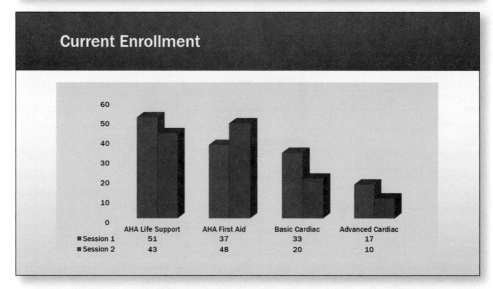

Education Budget Percentages

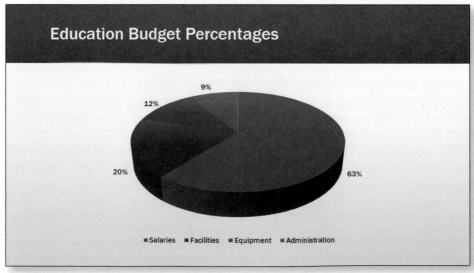

Case Study   Apply Your Skills

Part 1

You are an administrator for Terra Energy Corporation and you are responsible for preparing a presentation for a quarterly meeting. Open the Word document named **TerraEnergy.docx** and then use the information to prepare a presentation with the following specifications:

- Create the first slide with the company name and the subtitle *Quarterly Meeting*.
- Create a slide that presents the Executive Team information in a table.
- Create a slide that presents the phases information in a table (the three columns of text in the *Research and Development* section). Insert a column at the left side of the table that includes the text *New Product* rotated.
- Create a slide that presents the development team information in a SmartArt organizational chart.
- Create a slide that presents the revenues information in a chart (you determine the type of chart).
- Create a slide that presents the United States sales information in a chart (you determine the type of chart).

Apply a design theme of your choosing and add any additional features to improve the visual appearance of the presentation. Insert a transition and sound to each slide and then run the presentation. Save the presentation and name it **P-C5-CS-TECPres.pptx**. Print the presentation as a handout with four slides printed horizontally per page.

Part 2

Last year, a production project was completed and you want to display a graphic that illustrates the primary focus of the project. Create a new slide in the **P-C5-CS-TECPres.pptx** presentation and insert a *Funnel* SmartArt graphic (in the *Relationship* group) with the following information in the shapes inside the funnel (turn on the Text pane to type the information in the shapes):

> Updated Systems
> Safety Programs
> Market Expansion

Insert the information *Higher Profits* below the funnel. Apply formatting to the SmartArt graphic to improve the visual appeal. Print the slide and then save **P-C5-CS-TECPres.pptx**.

Part 3

You have created an Excel chart containing information on department costs. You decide to improve the appearance of the chart and then create a link from the presentation to the chart. Open Excel and then open **DepartmentCosts.xlsx**. Apply additional formatting to the pie chart to make it easy to read and understand the data. Save and then close the workbook and exit Excel. Create a new slide in the **P-C5-CS-TECPres.pptx** presentation that includes a hyperlink to the **DepartmentCosts.xlsx** workbook. Run the presentation and when the slide displays containing the hyperlinked text, click the hyperlink, view the chart in Excel, and then exit Excel. Print the presentation as a handout with four slides printed horizontally per page. Save and then close **P-C5-CS-TECPres.pptx**.

MICROSOFT
POWERPOINT®

Using Slide Masters and Action Buttons

PERFORMANCE OBJECTIVES

Upon successful completion of Chapter 6, you will be able to:

- Format slides in Slide Master view
- Apply themes and backgrounds in Slide Master view
- Delete placeholders and slide master layouts
- Insert elements in Slide Master view
- Create and rename a custom slide layout
- Insert a new slide master
- Save a presentation as a template
- Customize a handout in Handout Master view
- Customize notes pages in Notes Master view
- Change zoom, manage windows, and view presentations in color and grayscale
- Insert action buttons
- Insert hyperlinks

Tutorials

6.1 Formatting with a Slide Master
6.2 Working in Slide Master View
6.3 Saving a Presentation as a Template
6.4 Customizing a Handout and Notes Master
6.5 Using VIEW Tab Options
6.6 Inserting Action Buttons and Hyperlinks

If you make design or formatting changes and you want the changes to affect all slides in the presentation, consider making the changes in a slide master in the Slide Master view. Along with the Slide Master view, you can make changes to all pages in a handout with options in the Handout Master view and all notes pages in the Notes Master view. Insert action buttons in a presentation to connect to slides within the same presentation, connect to another presentation, connect to a website, or connect to another program. You can also connect to a website by inserting a hyperlink to the site. Model answers for this chapter's projects appear on the following pages.

PC6

Note: Before beginning the projects, copy to your storage medium the PC6 folder from the PowerPoint folder on the CD that accompanies this textbook and then make PC6 the active folder.

235

Project 1 Create a Travel Presentation and Apply Formatting in Slide Master View P-C6-P1-England.pptx

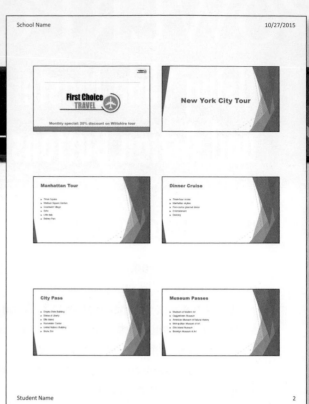

Project 2 Save a Template and Create a Travel Presentation with the Template P-C6-P2-ParisTour.pptx, Slides 2 and 4

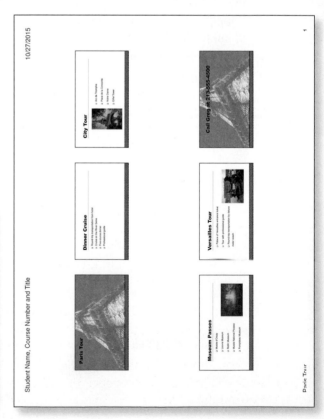

P-C6-P2-ParisTour.pptx

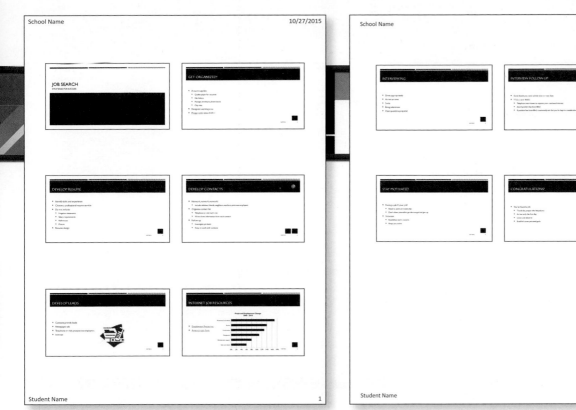

Project 3 Insert Action Buttons and Hyperlinks in a Job Search Presentation   P-C6-P3-JobSearch.pptx

---

<table>
<tr><td>Project 1</td><td>Create a Travel Presentation and Apply Formatting in Slide Master View</td><td>6 Parts</td></tr>
</table>

You will apply formatting to a blank presentation in Slide Master view, insert slides in the presentation, insert elements in Slide Master view, insert a custom slide layout, and insert a new slide master.

Customizing Slide Masters ■■■■■■■■■■■■■■■■■■■■■■

If you make changes to a slide and want the changes to affect multiple slides in the presentation, make the change in a slide master. Customize a slide master by changing the theme, theme colors, or theme fonts; inserting or changing the location of placeholders; applying a background style; and changing the page setup and slide orientation. If you know how you want to customize your slides, apply the formatting in Slide Master view before you create each slide.

If you edit the formatting of text in a slide in Normal view, that slide's link to the slide master is broken. Changes you make in Slide Master view will not affect the individually formatted slide. For this reason, make global formatting changes in Slide Master view before editing individual slides in a presentation.

To display Slide Master view, click the VIEW tab and then click the Slide Master button in the Master Views group. This activates the SLIDE MASTER tab, displays a blank slide master in the slide pane, and inserts slide master thumbnails

▼ Quick Steps

Display the Slide Master View
1. Click VIEW tab.
2. Click Slide Master button.

Slide Master

Figure 6.1 Slide Master View

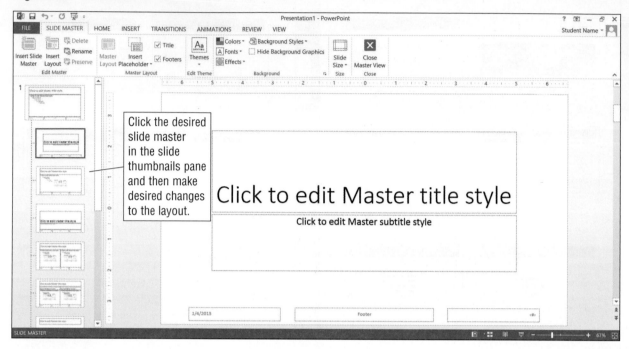

Click the desired slide master in the slide thumbnails pane and then make desired changes to the layout.

Click to edit Master title style

Click to edit Master subtitle style

HINT

Create a consistent look for your slides by customizing them in Slide Master view.

Close Master View

Themes

in the slide thumbnails pane. The largest thumbnail in the pane is the slide master, and the other thumbnails represent associated layouts. Position the mouse pointer on a slide thumbnail and the name of the thumbnail displays in a ScreenTip by the thumbnail along with information on what slides in the presentation use the slide master. Figure 6.1 shows a blank presentation in Slide Master view. To specify the slide master or layout you want to customize, click the desired thumbnail in the slide thumbnails pane. With the slide master layout displayed in the slide pane, make the desired changes and then click the Close Master View button.

Applying Themes to Slide Masters

Apply themes, theme colors, theme fonts, and theme effects to a slide master with buttons in the Edit Theme group on the SLIDE MASTER tab. Click the Themes button and a drop-down gallery displays with available predesigned themes as well as any custom themes you have created. Click the desired theme and the theme formatting is applied to the slide master. Complete similar steps to apply theme colors, theme fonts, and theme effects.

Project 1a Formatting a Slide Master   Part 1 of 6

1. Open a blank presentation.
2. Click the VIEW tab and then click the Slide Master button in the Master Views group.

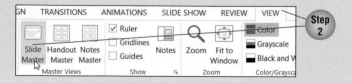

3. Scroll up the slide thumbnails pane and then click the top (and largest) slide master thumbnail in the slide thumbnails pane (Office Theme Slide Master). This displays the slide master layout in the slide pane.
4. Click the Themes button in the Edit Theme group on the SLIDE MASTER tab.
5. Click *Retrospect* at the drop-down gallery.
6. Click the Colors button in the Background group and then click *Blue* at the drop-down gallery.
7. Click the Fonts button in the Background group, scroll down the drop-down gallery, and then click the *Arial Black-Arial* option.

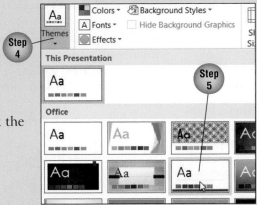

8. Change the font color for the title style by completing the following steps:
   a. Select the text *Click to edit Master title style* that displays in the slide master in the slide pane.
   b. Click the HOME tab.
   c. Click the Font Color button arrow in the Font group and then click *Black, Text 1* (second column first row in the *Theme Colors* section).
9. Change the font size and color and apply custom bullets by completing the following steps:
   a. Select the text *Click to edit Master text styles*.

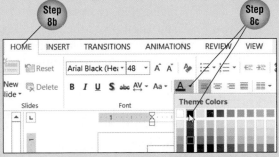

   b. With the HOME tab selected, click the Font Size button arrow and then click *24* at the drop-down gallery.
   c. Click the Font Color button arrow and then click the *Light Blue, Background 2, Darker 50%* option (third column, fourth row in the *Theme Colors* section).
   d. Click the Bullets button arrow in the Paragraph group and then click *Bullets and Numbering* at the drop-down gallery.
   e. At the Bullets and Numbering dialog box, click the *Hollow Square Bullets* option.
   f. Click the Color button and then click the *Light Blue, Background 2, Darker 50%* option (third column, fourth row in the *Theme Colors* section).
   g. Select *100* in the Size measurement box and then type **80**.
   h. Click OK to close the dialog box.
   i. Click the Paragraph group dialog box launcher.
   j. At the Paragraph dialog box, select the measurement in the *By* measurement box and then type **0.4**.
   k. Click OK to close the dialog box.

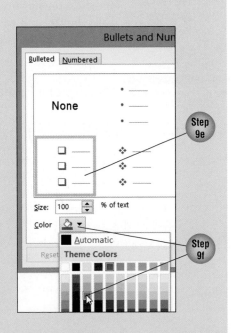

10. Click the SLIDE MASTER tab.
11. Click the Close Master View button.
12. Save the presentation and name it **P-C6-P1-TravelMaster.pptx**.

Applying and Formatting Backgrounds

In addition to the theme colors, fonts, and effects buttons the Background group on the SLIDE MASTER tab contains the Background Styles button and the *Hide Background Graphics* check box. If you want to change the background graphic for all slides, make the change at the slide master. To do this, display the presentation in Slide Master view and then click the desired slide master layout in the slide thumbnails pane. Click the Background Styles button and then click a background at the drop-down gallery. Or, click the *Format Background* option at the drop-down gallery and select the desired settings at the Format Background task pane. If you want to remove the background graphic for slides, click the *Hide Background Graphics* check box to insert a check mark.

▼ **Quick Steps**

Delete a Slide Master Layout
1. Display presentation in Slide Master view.
2. Click desired slide layout thumbnail.
3. Click Delete button.

Delete

H I N T

You can also delete a slide master layout by right-clicking the layout in the slide thumbnails pane and then clicking *Delete Layout* at the shortcut menu.

Deleting Placeholders

If you want to remove a placeholder for all slides in a presentation, consider deleting the placeholder in Slide Master view. To do this, display the presentation in Slide Master view, click the desired slide master layout in the slide thumbnails pane, click the placeholder border (make sure the border displays as a solid line), and then press the Delete key. You can also remove a title placeholder from a slide master by clicking the *Title* check box in the Master Layout group to remove the check mark. Remove footer placeholders by clicking the *Footer* check box to remove the check mark.

Deleting Slide Master Layouts

In Slide Master view, a slide master displays for each available layout. If you know that you will not be using a particular layout in the presentation, you can delete the slide master layout. To do this, display the presentation in Slide Master view, click the desired slide layout thumbnail in the slide thumbnails pane, and then click the Delete button in the Edit Master group.

Project 1b **Applying and Formatting Background Graphics**   **Part 2 of 6**

1. With **P-C6-P1-TravelMaster.pptx** open, click the VIEW tab and then click the Slide Master button in the Master Views group.
2. Apply a picture to the background of the title slide layout (the picture will appear only on slides with this layout) by completing the following steps:
   a. Make sure the second slide layout thumbnail (Title Slide Layout) is selected in the slide thumbnails pane.
   b. Select the text *Click to edit Master title style*, click the HOME tab, change the font size to 48 points, apply the Black, Text 1 font color (second column, first row in the *Theme Colors* section), and click the Center button in the Paragraph group.
   c. Click the SLIDE MASTER tab and then make sure the *Hide Background Graphics* check box in the Background group contains a check mark.

d. Click the Background Styles button in the Background group and then click *Format Background* at the drop-down list.

e. At the Format Background task pane, click the *Picture or texture fill* option.

f. Click the File button.

g. At the Insert Picture dialog box, navigate to the PC6 folder on your storage medium and then double-click *Stonehenge.jpg*.

h. Close the Format Background task pane.

i. Drag the master title placeholder so it is positioned above the stones and centered horizontally. (Make sure the bottom border of the placeholder is positioned above the stones.)

j. Delete the master subtitle placeholder by clicking the placeholder border (make sure the border displays as a solid line) and then pressing the Delete key.

k. Click the thin horizontal line that displays below the stones and then press the Delete key.

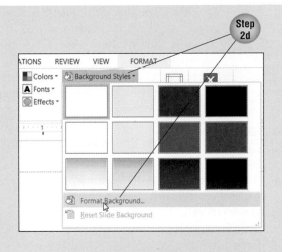

3. Delete slide layouts that you will not be using in the presentation by completing the following steps:

a. Click the fourth slide layout thumbnail (Section Header Layout) in the slide thumbnails pane.

b. Scroll down the pane until the last slide layout thumbnail is visible.

c. Hold down the Shift key and then click the last slide layout thumbnail.

d. Click the Delete button in the Edit Master group. (The slide thumbnails pane should now contain only one slide master and two associated layouts.)

4. Click the Close Master View button.

5. Delete the slide that currently displays in the slide pane. (This displays a gray background with the text *Click to add first slide*. The presentation does not contain any slides, just formatting.)

6. Save **P-C6-P1-TravelMaster.pptx**.

Inserting Slides in a Customized Presentation

If you customize slides in a presentation in Slide Master view, you can use the presentation formatting in other presentations. To do this, either save the formatted presentation as a template or save the presentation in the normal manner, open the presentation, save it with a new name, and then type text in slides. You can also insert slides into the current presentation using the Reuse Slides task pane. (You learned about this task pane in Chapter 2.) To use this task pane, click the HOME tab, click the New Slide button arrow, and then click *Reuse Slides* at the drop-down list. This displays the Reuse Slides task pane at the right side of the screen. Click the Browse button and then click the *Browse File* option at the drop-down list. At the Browse dialog box, navigate to the desired folder and then double-click the desired presentation. Insert slides into the current presentation by clicking the desired slide in the task pane.

Project 1c   **Inserting Slides in a Presentation**   **Part 3 of 6**

1. With **P-C6-P1-TravelMaster.pptx** open, save the presentation with Save As and name it **P-C6-P1-England**.
2. Make sure the HOME tab is active, click the New Slide button arrow, and then click *Title Slide* at the drop-down list.

3. Click the *Click to add title* text in the current slide and then type **Wiltshire, England**.
4. Insert slides into the current presentation from an existing presentation by completing the following steps:
   a. Click the New Slide button arrow and then click *Reuse Slides* at the drop-down list.
   b. Click the Browse button in the Reuse Slides task pane and then click *Browse File* at the drop-down list.
   c. At the Browse dialog box, navigate to the PC6 folder on your storage medium and then double-click *TravelEngland.pptx*.

   d. Click the *Wiltshire* slide in the Reuse Slides task pane. (This inserts the slide in the presentation and applies the custom formatting to the slide.)
   e. Click the *Ancient Stone Circles* slide in the Reuse Slides task pane.
   f. Click the *Ancient Wiltshire* slide in the Reuse Slides task pane.
   g. Click the *White Horses* slide in the Reuse Slides task pane.
   h. Click the Close button located in the upper right corner of the Reuse Slides task pane to close the task pane.
5. With Slide 5 active, format the bulleted text into two columns by completing the following steps:
   a. Click any character in the bulleted text.
   b. Move the insertion point so it is positioned immediately following *Marlborough*.
   c. Press the Enter key (to insert a blank line) and then click the Bullets button in the Paragraph group on the HOME tab to remove the bullet.
   d. Press Ctrl + A to select all of the bulleted text.
   e. Click the Line Spacing button in the Paragraph group and then click *2.0* at the drop-down list.
   f. Click the Add or Remove Columns button in the Paragraph group and then click *Two Columns* at the drop-down list.
6. With Slide 5 active, insert a new slide by completing the following steps:
   a. Click the New Slide button arrow and then click *Title Slide* at the drop-down list.
   b. Click in the text *Click to add title* and then type **Call Lucy at 213-555-4500**.
7. Save **P-C6-P1-England.pptx**.

Inserting Elements in a Slide Master

As you learned in Chapter 4, you can insert a header, footer, or the date and time that will print on every slide in the presentation. You can also insert these elements in a slide master. For example, to insert a header or footer in a slide master, display the presentation in Slide Master view, click the INSERT tab, and then click the Header & Footer button in the Text group. At the Header and Footer dialog box with the Slide tab selected, make the desired changes, click the Notes and Handouts tab, make the desired changes, and then click the Apply to All button. You can also insert additional elements in Slide Master view, such as a picture, clip art image, shape, SmartArt graphic, or chart. Insert any of these elements in Slide Master view just as you would in Normal view.

Project 1d   **Inserting Elements in Slide Master View**   **Part 4 of 6**

1. With **P-C6-P1-England.pptx** open, insert a header, a footer, and the date and time by completing the following steps:
   a. Click the View tab.
   b. Click the Slide Master button in the Master Views group.
   c. Click the slide master thumbnail (the top slide thumbnail in the slide thumbnails pane).
   d. Click the INSERT tab.
   e. Click the Header & Footer button in the Text group.
   f. At the Header and Footer dialog box with the Slide tab selected, click the *Date and time* check box to insert a check mark.
   g. Make sure the *Update automatically* option is selected. (With this option selected, the date and/or time will automatically update each time you open the presentation.)
   h. Click the *Slide number* check box to insert a check mark.
   i. Click the *Footer* check box to insert a check mark, click in the *Footer* text box, and then type your first and last names.
   j. Click the Notes and Handouts tab.
   k. Click the *Date and time* check box to insert a check mark.
   l. Make sure the *Update automatically* option is selected.
   m. Click the *Header* check box to insert a check mark, click in the *Header* text box, and then type the name of your school.
   n. Click the *Footer* check box to insert a check mark, click in the *Footer* text box, and then type your first and last names.
   o. Click the Apply to All button.

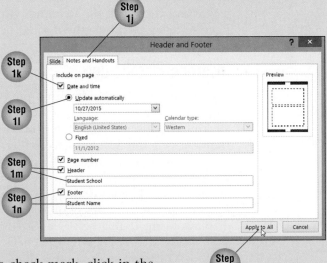

2. Insert the First Choice Travel logo in the upper right corner of the slide master by completing the following steps:

a. Click the Pictures button in the Images group.

b. At the Insert Picture dialog box, navigate to the PC6 folder on your storage medium and then double-click *FCTLogo.jpg*.

c. Click in the *Shape Height* measurement box in the Size group on the PICTURE TOOLS FORMAT tab, type **0.6**, and then press Enter.

d. Drag the logo so it is positioned in the upper right corner of the slide as shown at the right.

e. Click outside the logo to deselect it.

3. If necessary, click the SLIDE MASTER tab.

4. Click the Close Master View button.

5. Run the presentation and notice the logo and other elements in the slides.

6. Save **P-C6-P1-England.pptx**.

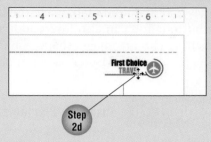

Creating and Renaming a Custom Slide Layout

Insert Layout

You can create your own custom slide layout in Slide Master view and then customize the layout by inserting or deleting elements and applying formatting to placeholders and text. To create a new slide layout, click the Insert Layout button in the Edit Master group on the SLIDE MASTER tab. This inserts in the slide pane a new slide containing a master title placeholder and footer placeholders. Customize the layout by inserting or deleting placeholders and applying formatting to placeholders.

PowerPoint automatically assigns the name *Custom Layout* to a slide layout you create. If you create another slide layout, PowerPoint will name it *1_Custom Layout*, and so on. Consider renaming your custom layout with a name that describes the layout. To rename a layout, make sure the desired slide layout is active and then click the Rename button in the Edit Master group. At the Rename Layout dialog box, type the desired name and then click the Rename button.

Rename

Inserting Placeholders

Insert Placeholder

Master Layout

You can insert placeholders in a predesigned slide layout or you can insert a custom slide layout and then insert placeholders. Insert a placeholder by clicking the Insert Placeholder button arrow in the Master Layout group and then clicking the desired placeholder option at the drop-down list. If you click the slide master, the Insert Placeholder button is dimmed. If you delete a placeholder from the slide master, you can reinsert the placeholder with options at the Master Layout dialog box. Display this dialog box by clicking the Master Layout button. Any placeholder that has been removed from the slide master displays in the dialog box as an active option with an empty check box. Reinsert the placeholder by clicking the check box to insert a check mark box and then clicking OK to close the dialog box.

Creating Custom Prompts

Some placeholders in a custom layout may contain generic text such as *Click to add Master title style* or *Click to edit Master text styles*. In Slide Master view, you can select this generic text and replace it with custom text. For example, you might want to insert text that describes what you want entered into the placeholder.

Project 1e **Inserting a Layout and Placeholder** **Part 5 of 6**

1. With **P-C6-P1-England.pptx** open, click the VIEW tab and then click the Slide Master button in the Master Views group.
2. Click the bottom slide layout thumbnail in the slide thumbnails pane.
3. Click the Insert Layout button in the Edit Master group. (This inserts in the slide pane a new slide with a master title placeholder, the logo, and the footer information.)
4. Remove the footer by clicking the *Footers* check box in the Master Layout group to remove the check mark.
5. Format and move the placeholder by completing the following steps:
   a. Select the text *Click to edit Master title style*.
   b. Click the HOME tab, change the font size to 28 points, apply the Light Blue, Background 2, Darker 50% font color (third column, fourth row in the *Theme Colors* section), and click the Center button in the Paragraph group.
   c. Move the placeholder so it is positioned along the bottom of the slide, just above the footer placeholder (as shown below).

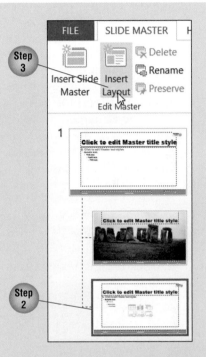

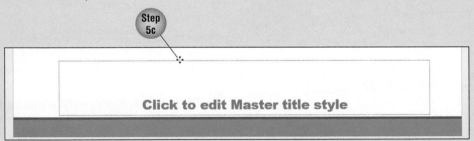

6. Click the SLIDE MASTER tab.
7. Insert a picture placeholder by completing the following steps:
   a. Click the Insert Placeholder button arrow.
   b. Click *Picture* at the drop-down list.
   c. Click in the slide to insert a placeholder.

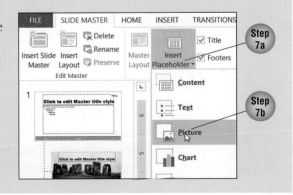

d. With the DRAWING TOOLS FORMAT tab active, click in the *Shape Height* measurement box and then type **3.5**.

e. Click in the *Shape Width* measurement box, type **7.5**, and then press Enter.

f. Drag the placeholder so it is positioned about 0.5 inch below the thin black line in the slide and centered horizontally. (The picture placeholder will overlap the title placeholder.)

g. Click anywhere in the word *Picture* in the placeholder. (This removes the word *Picture* and positions the insertion point in the placeholder.)

h. Type **Insert company logo** and then click outside of the placeholder.

8. Rename the custom slide layout by completing the following steps:

a. Click the Rename button in the Edit Master group on the SLIDE MASTER tab.

b. At the Rename Layout dialog box, select the text that displays in the *Layout name* text box and then type **Logo**.

c. Click the Rename button.

9. Click the Close Master View button.

10. Insert a slide using the new slide layout by completing the following steps:

a. Make Slide 6 active.

b. Click the New Slide button arrow.

c. Click *Logo* at the drop-down list.

d. Click the Pictures button in the slide.

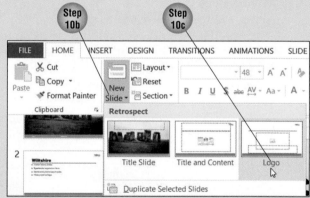

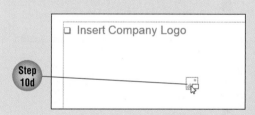

e. At the Insert Picture dialog box, navigate to the PC6 folder on your storage medium and then double-click *FCTLogo.jpg*.

f. Click in the text *Click to add title* and then type **Monthly special: 20% discount on Wiltshire tour**.

11. Save **P-C6-P1-England.pptx**.

Inserting a New Slide Master

A PowerPoint presentation can contain more than one slide master (and associated layouts). To insert a new slide master, display the presentation in Slide Master view and then click the Insert Slide Master button in the Edit Master group. This inserts a new slide master and all associated layouts below the existing slide master and layouts in the slide thumbnails pane. You can also insert a slide master and all associated layouts with a design theme applied. To do this, click below the existing

Insert Slide Master

slide master and associated layouts, click the Themes button in the Edit Theme group, and then click the desired theme at the drop-down gallery. A slide master containing the chosen design theme is inserted below the existing thumbnails.

Preserving Slide Masters

If you delete all of the slide layouts that follow a slide master, PowerPoint will automatically delete the slide master. You can protect a slide master from being deleted by preserving the master. To do this, click the desired slide master thumbnail and then click the Preserve button in the Edit Master group. If you insert a slide master using the Insert Slide Master button, the Preserve button is automatically active. When a slide master is preserved, a preservation icon displays below the slide number in the slide thumbnails pane.

Changing Page Setup

Click the Slide Size button in the Size group on the SLIDE MASTER tab and a drop-down list displays with options for choosing standard or widescreen size. In addition to these two options, the drop-down list also includes the *Custom Slide Size* option. Click this option and the Slide Size dialog box displays. This is the same dialog box you learned about in Chapter 3. The dialog box contains options for changing slide width, height, and numbering and applying slide orientation to slides, notes, handouts, and outline pages.

▼ **Quick Steps**

Preserve a Slide Master
1. Display presentation in Slide Master view.
2. Click desired slide master thumbnail.
3. Click Preserve button.

Preserve

Project 1f | **Applying a Second Slide Master** | **Part 6 of 6**

1. With **P-C6-P1-England.pptx** open, preserve the Retrospect slide master by completing the following steps:
   a. Click the VIEW tab and then click the Slide Master button in the Master Views group.
   b. Click the first slide master (Retrospect Slide Master) in the slide thumbnails pane.
   c. Click the Preserve button in the Edit Master group. (This inserts a preservation icon below the slide number in the slide thumbnails pane).
2. Insert a second slide master by completing the following steps:
   a. Click below the bottom slide layout in the slide thumbnails pane. (You want the second slide master and associated layouts to display below the original slide master and not take the place of the original.)
   b. Click the Themes button in the Edit Theme group and then click *Facet* at the drop-down gallery.
   c. Notice the slide master and associated layouts that display in the slide thumbnails pane below the original slide master and associated layouts and notice the preservation icon that displays below the second slide master.
   d. Click the new slide master (Facet Slide Master) in the slide thumbnails pane.

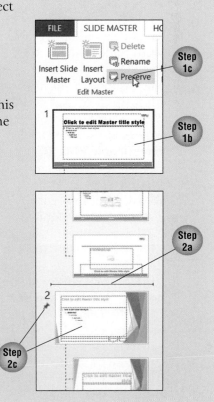

e. Click the Colors button in the Background group and then click *Blue* at the drop-down gallery.

f. Click the Fonts button and then click *Arial Black-Arial* at the drop-down gallery.

3. Click the first layout below the new slide master (Title Slide Layout) and then select and delete the master subtitle placeholder.

4. Click the third layout below the new slide master (Section Header Layout), scroll down to the bottom of the slide thumbnails pane, hold down the Shift key, click the bottom thumbnail, and then click the Delete button in the Edit Master group. (This deletes all but two of the layouts associated with the new slide master.)

5. Click the Close Master View button.

6. Insert a new slide by completing the following steps:

a. Make Slide 7 active.

b. Click the New Slide button arrow and then click *Title Slide* in the *Facet* section.

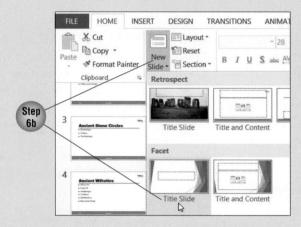

c. Click in the text *Click to add title* and then type **New York City Tour**.

7. Insert a new slide by completing the following steps:

a. With Slide 8 active, click the New Slide button. (This inserts a slide with the Facet Title and Content layout.)

b. Click the text *Click to add title* and then type **Manhattan Tour**.

c. Click the text *Click to add text* and then type the following bulleted text:

   Times Square
   Madison Square Garden
   Greenwich Village
   Soho
   Little Italy
   Battery Park

8. Insert slides using the Reuse Slides task pane by completing the following steps:

a. Click the New Slide button arrow and then click *Reuse Slides* at the drop-down list.

b. Click the Browse button in the Reuse Slides task pane and then click *Browse File* at the drop-down list.

c. At the Browse dialog box, navigate to the PC6 folder on your storage medium and then double-click ***FCTNewYork.pptx***.

d. Click the *Dinner Cruise* slide in the Reuse Slides task pane. (This inserts the slide in the presentation and applies the custom formatting to the slide.)

e. Click the *City Pass* slide in the Reuse Slides task pane.

f. Click the *Museum Passes* slide in the Reuse Slides task pane.

g. Click the Close button located in the upper right corner of the Reuse Slides task pane to close the task pane.

9. Assume that the presentation is going to be inserted into a larger presentation and that the starting slide will be Slide 12 (instead of Slide 1). Change the beginning slide number by completing the following steps:

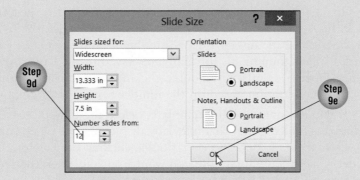

   a. Click the VIEW tab and then click the Slide Master button.
   b. Click the top slide master in the slide thumbnails pane.
   c. Click the Slide Size button in the Size group and then click *Custom Slide Size* at the drop-down list.
   d. At the Slide Size dialog box, select the current number in the *Number slides from* measurement box and then type **12**.
   e. Click OK to close the dialog box.

   f. Click the second slide master in the slide thumbnails pane (Facet Slide Master thumbnail).
   g. Click the INSERT tab and then click the Slide Number button in the Text group.
   h. At the Header and Footer dialog box, click the *Slide number* check box to insert a check mark and then click the Apply to All button.
   i. Click the SLIDE MASTER tab.
   j. Click the Close Master View button.
10. Make Slide 12 active (the first slide in the presentation) and then run the presentation.
11. Print the presentation as a handout with six slides horizontally per page.
12. Save and then close **P-C6-P1-England.pptx**.

Project 2 Save a Template and Create a Travel Presentation with the Template   **4 Parts**

You will save a travel presentation as a template and then use the template to create and format a travel presentation. You will insert elements in the presentation in Handout Master view and Notes Master view, change the presentation zoom, and view the presentation in grayscale and black and white.

Saving a Presentation as a Template ■■■■■■■■■■■■■■

▼ Quick Steps

Save a Presentation as a Template
1. Display Save As dialog box.
2. Click *Save as type* option.
3. Click *PowerPoint Template (*.potx).*
4. Type presentation name.
5. Click Save button.

Open a Presentation Based on a Template
1. Click FILE tab.
2. Click *New.*
3. Click *CUSTOM.*
4. Click *Custom Office Templates.*
5. Double-click template thumbnail.

If you create custom formatting to be used for future presentations, consider saving the presentation as a template. The advantage to saving your presentation as a template is that you cannot accidentally overwrite the presentation. Save a custom template in the Custom Office Templates folder in the Documents folder on the hard drive. Check to determine the default custom template folder location by displaying the PowerPoint Options dialog box with *Save* selected in the left panel. The *Default personal templates location* option should display the Custom Office Templates folder in the Documents folder as the default location. If this is not the default location, check with your instructor.

To save a presentation as a template, display the Save As dialog box, click the *Save as type* option button, and then click *PowerPoint Template (*.potx)* at the drop-down list. Type a name for the template in the *File name* text box and then click the Save button.

To create a presentation based on a template, click the FILE tab and then click the *New* option. At the New backstage area, click the *CUSTOM* option that displays above the design theme thumbnails and then click *Custom Office Templates.* This displays thumbnails for templates saved in the Custom Office Templates folder. Open a template by double-clicking the template thumbnail. PowerPoint opens a presentation based on the template, not the original template file.

If you no longer need a template, delete the template at the Custom Office Templates folder. Open this folder by displaying the Open dialog box, displaying the Documents folder, and then double-clicking the Custom Office Templates folder. Click the template file you want to delete, click the Organize button, and then click *Delete* at the drop-down list.

Project 2a	Saving a Presentation as a Template	Part 1 of 4

Note: If you are using PowerPoint 2013 in a school setting on a network system, you may need to complete Project 2a and 2b in the same day. Check with your instructor for any specific instructions.

1. Open **P-C6-P1-TravelMaster.pptx**.
2. Press F12 to display the Save As dialog box.
3. At the Save As dialog box, type **XXXTravelTemplate** in the *File name* text box. (Type your initials in place of the *XXX.*)
4. Click the *Save as type* option button and then click *PowerPoint Template (*.potx)* at the drop-down list.
5. Click the Save button.
6. Close the **XXXTravelTemplate.potx** template.

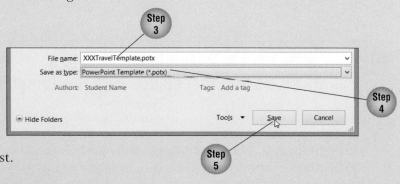

Step 3

File name: XXXTravelTemplate.potx

Save as type: PowerPoint Template (*.potx)

Authors: Student Name   Tags: Add a tag

Hide Folders   Tools ▼   Save   Cancel

Step 4

Step 5

7. Open the template and save it as a presentation by completing the following steps:
   a. Click the FILE tab and then click the *New* option.
   b. At the New backstage area, click the *CUSTOM* option (located above the template thumbnails) and then click *Custom Office Templates*.

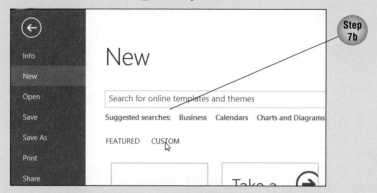

   c. Double-click the **XXXTravelTemplate.potx** template thumbnail.
8. Save the presentation with Save As and name it **P-C6-P2-ParisTour**.

Customizing the Handout Master ■■■■■■■■■■■■■■■■

As you learned in Chapter 1, you can choose to print a presentation as individual slides, handouts, notes pages, or an outline. If you print a presentation as handouts or an outline, PowerPoint will automatically print the current date in the upper right corner of the page and the page number in the lower right corner. Customize a handout with options in the Handout Master view. Display a presentation in Handout Master view by clicking the VIEW tab and then clicking the Handout Master button in the Master Views group. Use options on the HANDOUT MASTER tab to move, resize, and format header and footer placeholders, change page orientation, add or remove placeholders, and specify the number of slides you want printed on each page.

Handout Master

With buttons in the Page Setup group, change the handout orientation, display the Slide Size dialog box with options for changing the size and orientation of the handout page, and specify the number of slides you want printed on the handout page. By default, a handout will contain a header, footer, date, and page number placeholder. Remove any of these placeholders by removing the check mark before the placeholder option in the Placeholders group.

The Edit Theme group contains buttons for changing the theme color, font, and effects. Click the Themes button and the options in the drop-down gallery are dimmed, indicating that the themes are not available for the handout. If you apply a background style to the handout master, you can change theme colors by clicking the Colors button and then clicking the desired color theme at the drop-down gallery. Apply theme fonts by clicking the Fonts button and then clicking the desired font theme at the drop-down gallery.

Apply a background style to the handout page by clicking the Background Styles button in the Background group and then clicking one of the predesigned styles. You can also click the *Format Background* option and then make changes at the Format Background task pane. Remove any background graphics by clicking the *Hide Background Graphics* check box to insert a check mark.

Background Styles

1. With **P-C6-P2-ParisTour.pptx** open, click the New Slide button arrow in the Slides group on the HOME tab and then click *Reuse Slides* at the drop-down list.
2. In the Reuse Slides task pane, click the Browse button and then click the *Browse File* option at the drop-down list.
3. Navigate to the PC6 folder on your storage medium and then double-click *ParisTour.pptx*.
4. Insert the second, third, fourth, and fifth slides from the Reuse Slides task pane into the current presentation.
5. Close the Reuse Slides task pane.
6. Edit the Title Slide Layout in Slide Master view by completing the following steps:
   a. Click the VIEW tab and then click the Slide Master button.
   b. Click the second thumbnail in the slide thumbnails pane (Title Slide Layout).
   c. Click the Background Styles button in the Background group and then click *Format Background* at the drop-down list.
   d. At the Format Background task pane, click the File button (displays below the text *Insert picture from*).
   e. At the Insert Picture dialog box, navigate to the PC6 folder on your storage medium and then double-click *EiffelTower.jpg*.

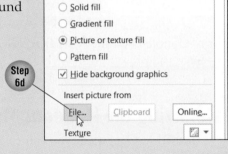

   f. Close the Format Background task pane.
   g. Select the text *Click to edit Master title style*, click the HOME tab, click the Font Color button arrow, and then click *Turquoise, Accent 2, Lighter 60%* (sixth column, third row in the *Theme Colors* section).
   h. Click the SLIDE MASTER tab.
   i. Click the Close Master View button.
   j. Make Slide 1 active, click in the text *Click to add title*, and then type **Paris Tour**.
   k. Size and move the text placeholder so *Paris Tour* displays in a blue area of the slide (not over the tower).
7. Make Slide 5 active and then create a new slide with the Title Slide layout. Type **Call Greg at 213-555-4500** in the title placeholder. (Leave the placeholder in the default location).
8. Save **P-C6-P2-ParisTour.pptx**.
9. Click the VIEW tab and then click the Handout Master button in the Master Views group.

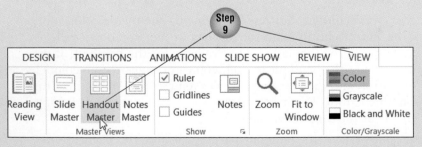

10. Click the Handout Orientation button in the Page Setup group and then click *Landscape* at the drop-down list.

11. Click in the Header placeholder on the page and then type your first and last names.
12. Click in the Footer placeholder and then type **Paris Tour**.
13. Click the Background Styles button and then click *Style 9* at the drop-down list (first column, third row).
14. Click the Colors button in the Background group and then click *Blue* at the drop-down list.
15. Click the Fonts button in the Background group, scroll down the drop-down gallery, and then click *Arial Black-Arial*.
16. Edit the header text by completing the following steps:
    a. Click in the header placeholder and then click any character in your name.
    b. Move the insertion point so it is positioned immediately right of the last character in your last name.
    c. Type a comma, press the spacebar, and then type your course number and title.
    d. Click in the handout page outside of any placeholder.
17. Click the Close Master View button.
18. Save **P-C6-P2-ParisTour.pptx**

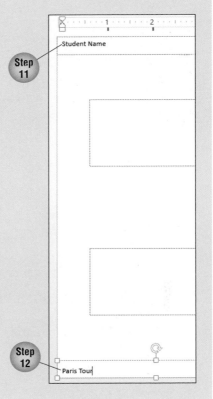

Step 11

Student Name

Step 12

Paris Tour

Customizing the Notes Master ■■■■■■■■■■■■■■■■■

You can insert notes in a presentation and then print the presentation as notes pages, with the notes printed below the slides. If you want to insert or format text or other elements as notes on all slides in a presentation, consider making the changes in the Notes Master view. Display this view by clicking the VIEW tab and then clicking the Notes Master button in the Master Views group. This displays a notes page along with the NOTES MASTER tab. Many of the buttons and options on this tab are the same as those on the HANDOUT MASTER tab.

Notes Master

Project 2c Customizing the Notes Master   Part 3 of 4

1. With **P-C6-P2-ParisTour.pptx** open, click the VIEW tab and then click the Notes Master button in the Master Views group.
2. Click the *Body* check box in the Placeholders group to remove the check mark.
3. Click the Fonts button in the Background group, scroll down the drop-down gallery, and then click *Arial Black-Arial*.
4. Click the INSERT tab.
5. Click the Text Box button in the Text group.
6. Click in the notes page below the slide.

Step 2

7. Type Visit www.first-choice.emcp.net for a listing of all upcoming tours.

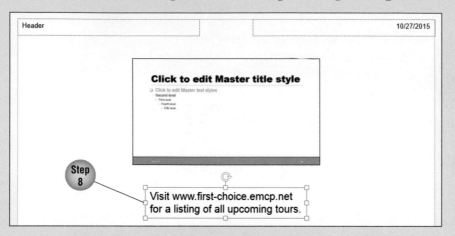

8. Size and position the text box below the slide as shown below.
9. Click the INSERT tab and then click the Pictures button in the Images group.
10. At the Insert Picture dialog box, navigate to the PC6 folder on your storage medium and then double-click *FCTLogo.jpg*.
11. Change the height of the logo to 0.5 inch. (This changes the width to 1 inch.)
12. Drag the logo so it is positioned below the text.
13. Click the NOTES MASTER tab and then click the Close Master View button.
14. Print Slides 2 and 4 as notes pages by completing the following steps:
    a. Display the Print backstage area.
    b. Click the second gallery in the *Settings* category and then click *Notes Pages* in the *Print Layout* section.
    c. Click in the *Slides* text box located below the first gallery in the *Settings* category and then type 2,4.
    d. Click the Print button.
15. Save **P-C6-P2-ParisTour.pptx**.

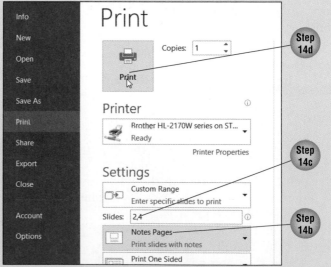

Using VIEW Tab Options ■■■■■■■■■■ ■■■■■■■■■■■

You have used buttons in the Presentation Views group and Master Views group on the VIEW tab to display your presentation in various views such as Normal, Slide Sorter, Slide Master, Handout Master, and Notes Master. In addition to viewing buttons, the VIEW tab includes options for showing or hiding the ruler and gridlines; displaying the Notes pane below the slide pane; zooming in or out in the slide; viewing the slide in color, grayscale, or black and white; and working with windows.

Changing the Zoom

Change the display size of the slide in the slide pane or the slides in the slide thumbnails pane with the Zoom button on the VIEW tab or with the Zoom slider bar located at the right side of the Status bar. Click the Zoom button on the VIEW tab and the Zoom dialog box displays. Use options in this dialog box to increase or decrease the display size of slides in the slide pane or slide thumbnails pane. To change the zoom with the Zoom slider bar, use the mouse to drag the slider bar button to the left to decrease the display size or to the right to increase the display size. Click the Zoom Out button (the minus symbol that displays at the left side of the Zoom slider bar) to decrease the display percentage or click the Zoom In button (the plus symbol that displays at the right side of the Zoom slider bar) to increase the display percentage. Click the percentage number that displays at the right side of the slider bar and the Zoom dialog box displays.

Zoom

Managing Windows

Use buttons in the Window group on the VIEW tab to work with presentation windows. Work in two locations in the same presentation by opening the presentation and then opening a new window with the same presentation. This is helpful if you want to view and edit slides in two different locations in the presentation. Open a new window by clicking the New Window button in the Window group.

New Window

If you have more than one presentation open, you can arrange them so a portion of each presentation displays. Click the Arrange All button in the Window group and each open presentation displays as a tile on the screen. Click the Cascade button in the Window group and the open presentations are displayed in a layered manner, with the title bar of each presentation visible.

Arrange All

Cascade

If you have more than one presentation open, you can switch presentations by clicking the Switch Windows button in the Window group. Click this button and a drop-down list with the names of the open presentations displays with a check mark in front of the active presentation. Make another presentation active by clicking the presentation name at the drop-down list.

Switch Windows

Increase or decrease the viewing area of each section of the presentation window with the Move Split button. Click this button and the mouse pointer displays as a four-headed arrow. Use the arrow keys on the keyboard to increase or decrease the viewing area of the slide pane and slide thumbnails pane. Click the left mouse button to deactivate the feature.

Move Split

Viewing in Color and Grayscale

Color

Grayscale

Black and White

By default, the slides in a presentation display in color. You can change the slides to grayscale or black and white with buttons in the Color/Grayscale group on the VIEW tab. Click the Grayscale button and the slides in the presentation display in grayscale and the GRAYSCALE tab becomes active. This tab contains a variety of options for changing the grayscale display, such as light grayscale, inverse grayscale, and gray or black with grayscale fill. Return to the color view by clicking the Back to Color View button on the GRAYSCALE tab. Click the Black and White button in the Color/Grayscale group and the slides in the presentation display in black and white and the BLACK AND WHITE tab becomes active. This tab contains many of the same options as the GRAYSCALE tab.

Project 2d **Viewing a Presentation**   **Part 4 of 4**

1. With **P-C6-P2-ParisTour.pptx** open, make Slide 1 active and then click the slide in the slide pane.
2. Click the VIEW tab.
3. Increase and decrease the zoom by completing the following steps:
   a. Click the Zoom button in the Zoom group.
   b. At the Zoom dialog box, click the *33%* option and then click OK.
   c. Click the Zoom button, click the *100%* option in the Zoom dialog box, and then click OK.
   d. Click the Slide 2 thumbnail in the slide thumbnails pane.
   e. Click the Zoom button, click the *66%* option in the Zoom dialog box, and then click OK. (Because the slide was active in the slide thumbnails pane, the percentage display changed for the thumbnails in the pane.)
   f. Position the mouse pointer on the Zoom slider bar button (located at the right side of the Status bar), drag the button to the right to increase the size of the slide in the slide pane, and then drag the slider bar to the left to decrease the size of the slide.
   g. Click the percentage number that displays at the right side of the Zoom slider bar. This displays the Zoom dialog box.
   h. Click the *100%* option in the Zoom dialog box and then click OK.
   i. Click the Fit to Window button in the Zoom group on the VIEW tab.
4. View the slides in grayscale by completing the following steps:
   a. Click the Grayscale button in the Color/Grayscale group on the VIEW tab.
   b. Click the slide in the slide pane.
   c. Click some of the buttons on the GRAYSCALE tab to display the slides in varying grayscale options.
   d. Click the Back To Color View button.
5. View the slides in black and white by completing the following steps:
   a. Click the VIEW tab and then click the Black and White button in the Color/Grayscale group.
   b. Click some of the buttons in the BLACK AND WHITE tab to display the slides in varying black and white options.
   c. Click the Back To Color View button.

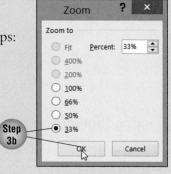

Step 3b

Step 4a

6. Open a new window and arrange the windows by completing the following steps:
   a. Click the VIEW tab and then click the New Window button in the Window group. (This opens the same presentation in another window. Notice that the name on the title bar displays followed by a colon and the number 2.)

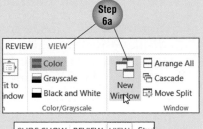

   b. Click the VIEW tab and then click the Arrange All button to arrange the two presentation in two side-by-side windows.
   c. Click the Window button in the window at the left side of the screen and then click the Cascade button at the drop-down list. (This arranges the two presentations with the presentations overlapping with the title bar for each presentation visible.)

   d. Click the Switch Windows button and then click the *P-C6-P2-ParisTour.pptx:1* option at the drop-down list.
   e. Click the Close button that displays in the upper right corner of the currently active presentation.
   f. Click the Maximize button that displays in the upper right corner of the presentation window. (The Maximize button displays immediately left of the Close button.)

7. Use the Move Split button by completing these steps:
   a. Click the Move Split button in the Window group. (The mouse displays as a four-headed arrow.)

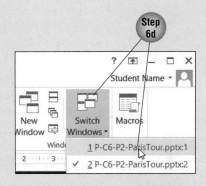

   b. Press the Right Arrow key on the keyboard several times and notice the slide thumbnails pane increasing in size.
   c. Press the Left Arrow key several times.
   d. Press the Up Arrow key several times and notice that the slide in the slide pane decreases in size and the notes pane displays.
   e. Press the Down Arrow key until the slide in the slide pane returns to the original size and the notes pane has closed.

8. With the VIEW tab active, click the Grayscale button in the Color/Grayscale group and then click the Light Grayscale button in the Change Selected Object group.

9. Print the presentation by completing the following steps:
   a. Display the Print backstage area.
   b. If any text displays in the *Slides* text box, select and then delete the text.
   c. If you are using a color printer, click the *Color* gallery that displays at the bottom of the *Settings* category and then click *Grayscale*. (Skip this step if you are using a black and white printer.)
   d. Click the second gallery in the *Settings* category and then click *6 Slides Horizontal* in the *Handouts* section.
   e. Click the Print button.

10. Click the Back To Color View button on the GRAYSCALE tab.
11. Make Slide 1 active and then run the presentation.
12. Save and then close **P-C6-P2-ParisTour.pptx**.

You will open a job search presentation and then insert action buttons that display the next slide, the first slide, a website, and another presentation. You will also create a hyperlink from text, a graphic image, and a chart in a slide to a website, a Word document, and another presentation.

Inserting Action Buttons ▪■▪■▪■▪▪▪■▪■▪▪▪■▪■▪■▪▪■▪▪

Action buttons are drawn objects on a slide that have a routine attached to them which is activated when the viewer or the presenter clicks the button. For example, you could include an action button that displays the next slide in the presentation, a file in another program, or a specific web page. Creating an action button is a two-step process. You draw the button using an Action Button shape in the Shapes button drop-down list and then you define the action that will take place with options in the Action Settings dialog box. Customize an action button in the same manner as customizing a drawn object. When the viewer or presenter moves the mouse over an action button during a presentation, the pointer changes to a hand with a finger pointing upward to indicate clicking will result in an action.

To display the available action buttons, click the INSERT tab and then click the Shapes button in the Illustrations group. Action buttons display at the bottom of the drop-down list. Hover the mouse pointer over a button and the name and the action it performs display in a ScreenTip above the button. The action attached to an action button occurs when you run the presentation and then click the button.

Project 3a | Inserting Action Buttons | Part 1 of 5

1. Open **JobSearch.pptx** and then save the presentation with the name **P-C6-P3-JobSearch**.
2. Make the following changes to the presentation:
   a. Apply the Dividend design theme.
   b. Click the INSERT tab and then click the Header & Footer button in the Text group.
   c. At the Header and Footer dialog box with the Slide tab selected, click the *Date and time* check box and make sure *Update automatically* is selected.
   d. Click the *Slide number* check box to insert a check mark.
   e. Click the Notes and Handouts tab.
   f. Click the *Date and time* check box and make sure *Update automatically* is selected.
   g. Click the *Header* check box to insert a check mark, click in the *Header* text box, and then type the name of your school.
   h. Click the *Footer* check box to insert a check mark, click in the *Footer* text box, and then type your first and last names.
   i. Click the Apply to All button.

3. Insert an action button in Slide 1 that will display the next slide by completing the following steps:
   a. Make sure Slide 1 is active.
   b. Click the INSERT tab and then click the Shapes button.
   c. Scroll down the drop-down list and then click the *Action Button: Forward or Next* button (second button in the *Action Buttons* group).
   d. Move the crosshair pointer to the lower right corner of the slide and then drag to create a button that is approximately 0.5 inch in height and width (see below).

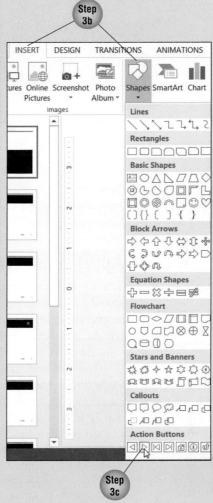

Step 3b

Step 3c

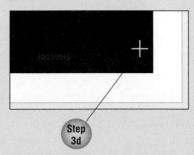

Step 3d

   e. At the Action Settings dialog box, click OK. (The default setting is *Hyperlink to Next Slide*.)
4. Insert an action button in Slide Master view that will display the next slide by completing the following steps:
   a. Display the presentation in Slide Master view.
   b. Click the top slide master thumbnail (*Dividend Slide Master*).
   c. Click the INSERT tab and then click the Shapes button.
   d. Scroll down the drop-down list and then click the *Action Button: Forward or Next* button (second button in the *Action Buttons* group).
   e. Move the crosshair pointer to the lower right corner of the slide master and then drag to create a button as shown at the right.

Step 4e

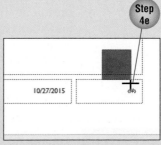

   f. At the Action Settings dialog box, click OK. (The default setting is *Hyperlink to Next Slide*.)
   g. Click the SLIDE MASTER tab and then click the Close Master View button.
5. Make Slide 1 active and then run the presentation, clicking the action button to advance slides. When you click the action button on the last slide (Slide 9) nothing happens because it is the last slide. Press the Esc key to end the presentation.
6. Change the action button on Slide 9 by completing the following steps:
   a. Make Slide 9 active.
   b. Click the INSERT tab and then click the Shapes button.

c. Scroll down the drop-down list and then click the *Action Button: Home* button (fifth button in the *Action Buttons* group).

d. Drag to create a button on top of the previous action button. (Make sure it completely covers the previous action button.)

e. At the Action Settings dialog box with the *Hyperlink to: First Slide* option selected, click OK.

f. Deselect the button.

7. Display Slide 1 in the slide pane and then run the presentation. Navigate through the slide show by clicking the action button. When you click the action button on the last slide, the first slide displays. End the slide show by pressing the Esc key.

8. Save **P-C6-P3-JobSearch.pptx**.

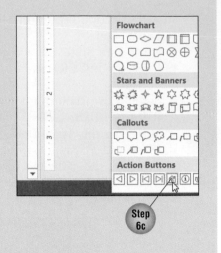

Step 6c

Applying an Action to an Object ■■■■■■■■■■■■■■■■■■

Action

The Links group on the INSERT tab contains an Action button you can use to specify an action to a selected object. To use this button, select the desired object in the slide, click the INSERT tab, and then click the Action button. This displays the Action Settings dialog box, which is the same dialog box that displays when you draw an action button in a slide.

You can specify that an action button or a selected object link to another PowerPoint presentation, another file, or a website. To link to another PowerPoint presentation, click the *Hyperlink to* option at the Action Settings dialog box, click the *Hyperlink to* option box arrow, and then click *Other PowerPoint Presentation* at the drop-down list. At the Hyperlink to Other PowerPoint Presentation dialog box, navigate to the desired folder, and then double-click the PowerPoint presentation. To link to another file, click the *Hyperlink to* option at the Action Settings dialog box, click the *Hyperlink to* option box arrow, and then click *Other File* at the drop-down list. At the Hyperlink to Other File dialog box, navigate to the desired folder and then double-click the file name. To link to a website, click the *Hyperlink to* option at the Action Settings dialog box, click the *Hyperlink to* option box arrow, and then click *URL* at the drop-down list. At the Hyperlink To URL dialog box, type the web address in the *URL* text box, and then click OK. Click OK to close the Action Settings dialog box. Other actions you can link to using the *Hyperlink to* drop-down list include *Next Slide*, *Previous Slide*, *First Slide*, *Last Slide*, *Last Slide Viewed*, *End Show*, *Custom Show*, *Slide*, and *Other File*.

Project 3b | Linking to Another Presentation and a Website | Part 2 of 5

1. With **P-C6-P3-JobSearch.pptx** open, add an action button that will link to another presentation by completing the following steps:

a. Make Slide 4 active.

b. Click the INSERT tab and then click the Shapes button in the Illustrations group.

c. Scroll down the drop-down list and then click *Action Button: Help* (second button shape from the right in the *Action Buttons* section).

d. Draw the action button to the left of the existing button located in the lower right corner of the slide.

e. At the Action Settings dialog box, click the *Hyperlink to* option.

f. Click the *Hyperlink to* option box arrow and then click *Other PowerPoint Presentation* at the drop-down list.

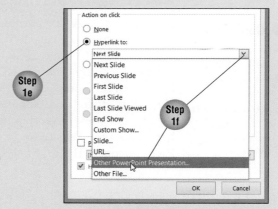

g. At the Hyperlink to Other PowerPoint Presentation dialog box, navigate to the PC6 folder on your storage medium and then double-click ***Contacts.pptx***.

h. At the Hyperlink to Slide dialog box, click OK.

i. Click OK to close the Action Settings dialog box.

2. Apply an action to the clip art image in Slide 5 that links to a website by completing the following steps:

a. Make Slide 5 active and then click the clip art image to select it.

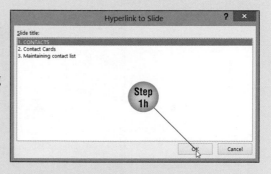

b. Click the INSERT tab and then click the Action button in the Links group.

c. At the Action Settings dialog box, click the *Hyperlink to* option.

d. Click the *Hyperlink to* option box arrow, and then click *URL* at the drop-down list.

e. At the Hyperlink to URL dialog box, type **www.usajobs.gov** in the *URL* text box and then click OK.

f. Click OK to close the Action Settings dialog box.

g. Click outside the clip art image to deselect it.

3. Run the presentation by completing the following steps:

a. Make sure you are connected to the Internet.

b. Make Slide 1 active.

c. Click the Slide Show button in the view area on the Status bar.

d. Navigate through the slide show to Slide 4.

e. Click the action button in Slide 4 containing the question mark. (This displays Slide 1 of **Contacts.pptx**.)

f. Navigate through the three slides in **Contacts.pptx**. Continue clicking the mouse button until you return to Slide 4 of **P-C6-P3-JobSearch.pptx**.

g. Display Slide 5 and then click the clip art image. (If you are connected to the Internet, the job site of the United States Federal Government displays.)

h. Search for information on a specific job title that interests you and then click a few links at the website.

i. When you have finished viewing the website, close your web browser.

j. Continue viewing the remainder of the presentation by clicking the action button in the lower right corner of each slide.

k. When Slide 1 displays, press the Esc key to end the presentation.

4. Save **P-C6-P3-JobSearch.pptx**.

Inserting Hyperlinks ■■■■■■■■■■■■■■■■■■■■■■■■■

▼ Quick Steps

Insert a Hyperlink
1. Click INSERT tab.
2. Click Hyperlink button.
3. Make desired changes at Insert Hyperlink dialog box.
4. Click OK.

In Project 3b, you created hyperlinks with options at the Action Settings dialog box. You can also create hyperlinks with options at the Insert Hyperlink dialog box shown in Figure 6.2. To display this dialog box, select a key word, phrase, or object in a slide, click the INSERT tab, and then click the Hyperlink button in the Links group or press Ctrl + K, which is the keyboard shortcut to display the Insert Hyperlink dialog box. You can link to a website, another presentation, a place in the current presentation, a new presentation, or to an email address. To insert a hyperlink to a website or an existing presentation, click the Existing File or Web Page button in the *Link to* group at the Insert Hyperlink dialog box.

Figure 6.2 Insert Hyperlink Dialog Box

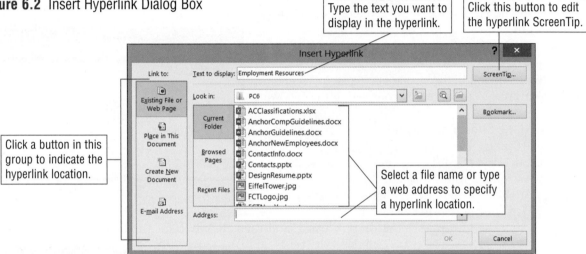

Type the text you want to display in the hyperlink.

Click this button to edit the hyperlink ScreenTip.

Click a button in this group to indicate the hyperlink location.

Select a file name or type a web address to specify a hyperlink location.

Project 3c **Inserting Hyperlinks to a Website**   Part 3 of 5

1. With **P-C6-P3-JobSearch.pptx** open, insert a new slide by completing the following steps:
   a. Make Slide 5 active.
   b. Click the HOME tab.
   c. Create a new slide with the Title and Content layout.
   d. Click the text *Click to add title* and then type **Internet Job Resources**.
   e. Click the text *Click to add text*, type **Employment Resources**, press Enter, and then type **America's Job Bank**.
2. Add a hyperlink to the Employment Resources site by completing the following steps:
   a. Select *Employment Resources* in Slide 6.
   b. Click the INSERT tab and then click the Hyperlink button in the Links group.
   c. At the Insert Hyperlink dialog box, type **www.employment-resources.com** in the *Address* text box. (PowerPoint automatically inserts *http://* at the beginning of the address.)
   d. Click OK to close the Insert Hyperlink dialog box.

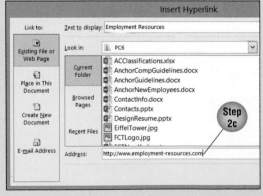

3. Add a hyperlink to the America's Job Bank website by completing the following steps:
   a. Select *America's Job Bank* in Slide 6.
   b. Click the Hyperlink button in the Links group.
   c. At the Insert Hyperlink dialog box, type **www.ajb.dni.us** in the *Address* text box.
   d. Click OK to close the Insert Hyperlink dialog box.
4. Save **P-C6-P3-JobSearch.pptx**.

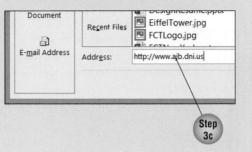

Step 3c

In addition to linking to a website, you can create a hyperlink to another location in the presentation with the Place in This Document button in the *Link to* group in the Insert Hyperlink dialog box. Click the slide you want to link to in the *Select a place in this document* list box. Use the Create New Document button in the Insert Hyperlink dialog box to create a hyperlink to a new presentation. When you click this button, you will be prompted to type a name for the new presentation and specify if you want to edit the new presentation now or later.

You can use a graphic such as a clip art image, picture, chart, or text box, to hyperlink to a file or website. To hyperlink with a graphic, select the graphic, click the INSERT tab, and then click the Hyperlink button or right-click the graphic and then click *Hyperlink* at the shortcut menu. At the Insert Hyperlink dialog box, specify what you want to link to and the text you want to display in the hyperlink.

You can insert a hyperlink to an email address at the Insert Hyperlink dialog box. To do this, click the E-Mail Address button in the *Link to* group, type the desired address in the *E-mail address* text box, and type a subject for the email in the *Subject* text box. Click in the *Text to display* text box and then type the text you want to display in the document. To use this feature, the email address you use must be set up in Outlook.

Navigate to a hyperlink by clicking the hyperlink in the slide. Hover the mouse over the hyperlink and a ScreenTip displays with the hyperlink. If you want specific information to display in the ScreenTip, click the ScreenTip button in the Insert Hyperlink dialog box, type the desired text in the Set Hyperlink ScreenTip dialog box, and then click OK.

HINT

Hyperlinks are active when running the presentation, not when creating it.

Project 3d | **Inserting Hyperlinks to a Website, to Another Presentation, and to a Word Document** | **Part 4 of 5**

1. With **P-C6-P3-JobSearch.pptx** open, make Slide 3 active.
2. Create a link to another presentation by completing the following steps:
   a. Move the insertion point immediately right of the word *Picture*, press the Enter key, press Shift + Tab, and then type **Resume design**.
   b. Select *Resume design*.
   c. Make sure the INSERT tab is active and then click the Hyperlink button in the Links group.

d. At the Insert Hyperlink dialog box, make sure the Existing File or Web Page button is selected.

e. Click the *Look in* option box arrow and then navigate to the PC6 folder on your storage medium.

f. Double-click ***DesignResume.pptx***.

3. Create a hyperlink from a graphic to a Word document by completing the following steps:

a. Make Slide 4 active.

b. Right-click the small clip art image that displays in the upper right corner of the slide and then click *Hyperlink* at the shortcut menu.

c. At the Insert Hyperlink dialog box, make sure the Existing File or Web Page button is selected.

d. Click the *Look in* option box arrow and then navigate to the PC6 folder on your storage medium.

e. Double-click ***ContactInfo.docx***.

4. Make Slide 6 active and then insert a chart by completing the following steps:

a. Press Ctrl + F12 to display the Open dialog box.

b. Navigate to the PC6 folder on your storage medium and then double-click ***USBLSChart.pptx***.

c. Select the chart.

d. Click the Copy button.

e. Click the PowerPoint button on the Taskbar and then click the thumbnail representing **P-C6-P3-JobSearch.pptx**.

f. Click the Paste button.

g. With the chart selected, drag the chart down so it is positioned attractively on the slide.

5. Create a hyperlink from the chart to the United States Bureau of Labor Statistics website by completing the following steps:

a. With the chart selected, click the Hyperlink button in the Links group on the INSERT tab.

b. At the Insert Hyperlink dialog box, make sure the Existing File or Web Page button is selected and then type **www.bls.gov** in the *Address* text box.

c. Click OK to close the Insert Hyperlink dialog box.

6. Hover the mouse pointer on the PowerPoint button on the Taskbar, click the thumbnail representing **USBLSChart.pptx**, and then close the presentation.

7. Run the presentation by completing the following steps:

a. Make sure you are connected to the Internet.

b. Make Slide 1 active.

c. Click the Slide Show button in the view area on the Status bar.

d. Navigate through the slides to Slide 3 and then click the Resume design hyperlink in the slide.

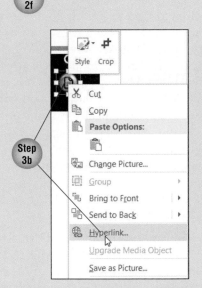

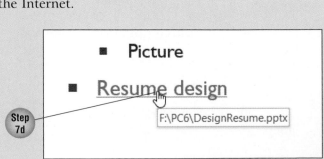

e. Run the **DesignResume.pptx** presentation that displays and then press the Esc key when the presentation has ended.

f. Click the mouse button to display Slide 4.

g. Display the Word document by clicking the small clip art image in the upper right corner of the slide.

h. Look at the information that displays in the Word document and then click the Close button located in the upper right corner of the Word window.

i. Continue running the presentation to Slide 6.

j. At Slide 6, click the <u>Employment Resources</u> hyperlink.

k. Scroll through the employment website and then close the web browser.

l. Click the <u>America's Job Bank</u> hyperlink.

m. Scroll through the America's Job Bank website and then close the web browser.

n. Click the chart.

o. Scroll through the Bureau of Labor Statistics website and then close the web browser.

p. Continue viewing the remainder of the presentation using the Action buttons. (When Slide 1 displays, press the Esc key to end the presentation.)

8. Save **P-C6-P3-JobSearch.pptx**.

You can modify or change hyperlink text or the hyperlink destination. To do this, right-click the hyperlink and then click *Edit Hyperlink* at the shortcut menu. At the Edit Hyperlink dialog box, make any desired changes and then close the dialog box. The Edit Hyperlink dialog box contains the same options as the Insert Hyperlink dialog box.

In addition to modifying the hyperlink, you can edit hyperlink text by making the desired editing changes. For example, you can apply a different font or font size, change the text color, and apply a text effect. Remove a hyperlink from a slide by right-clicking on the hyperlinked text and then clicking *Remove Hyperlink* at the shortcut menu.

Project 3e   Modifying, Editing, and Removing a Hyperlink   **Part 5 of 5**

1. With **P-C6-P3-JobSearch.pptx** open, make Slide 4 active and then modify the hyperlink in the clip art image by completing the following steps:

a. Position the mouse pointer on the small clip art image in the upper right corner of the slide, click the right mouse button, and then click *Edit Hyperlink* at the shortcut menu.

b. At the Edit Hyperlink dialog box, click the ScreenTip button located in the upper right corner of the dialog box.

c. At the Set Hyperlink ScreenTip dialog box, type **Click this image to display information on typing contact information.**

d. Click OK to close the Set Hyperlink ScreenTip dialog box.

e. Click OK to close the Edit Hyperlink dialog box.

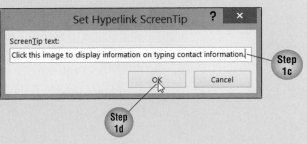

2. Make Slide 3 active and then remove the <u>Resume design</u> hyperlink by right-clicking the hyperlinked text (the text is dimmed and barely visible) and then clicking *Remove Hyperlink* at the shortcut menu.
3. Run the presentation and click the hyperlinks as they appear in slides.
4. Print the presentation as a handout with six slides horizontally per page.
5. Save and then close **P-C6-P3-JobSearch.pptx**.

Chapter Summary

- Display a presentation in Slide Master view by clicking the VIEW tab and then clicking the Slide Master button in the Master Views group. In Slide Master view, slide master thumbnails display in the slide thumbnails pane.

- Use buttons in the Background group on the SLIDE MASTER tab to change theme colors and fonts, apply a predesigned background style, display the Format Background task pane with options for applying background styles, and hide background graphics.

- Delete a placeholder by clicking in the placeholder, clicking the placeholder border, and then pressing the Delete key.

- Delete a slide master in Slide Master view by clicking the desired slide master thumbnail in the slide thumbnails pane and then clicking the Delete button in the Edit Master group.

- In Slide Master view, you can display the Header and Footer dialog box with the Slide tab selected and then insert the date and time, slide number, and/or a footer. At the Header and Footer dialog box with the Notes and Handouts tab selected, you can insert the date and time, a header, page numbers, and/or a footer.

- Create a custom slide layout by clicking the Insert Layout button in the Edit Master group on the SLIDE MASTER tab. Rename the custom slide layout with the Rename button in the Edit Master group.

- Insert placeholders in a slide layout or custom slide layout by clicking the Insert Placeholder button arrow in the Master Layout group and then clicking the desired placeholder at the drop-down list.

- In Slide Master view, create a custom prompt by selecting generic text in a placeholder and then typing the desired text.

- Click the Insert Slide Master button in Slide Master view to insert a new slide master and associated slide layouts. You can also insert a new slide master by applying a design theme using the Themes button in th Edit Theme group on the SLIDE MASTER tab.

- Save a presentation as a template by changing the *Save as type* option at the Save As dialog box to *PowerPoint Template (*.potx)*.

- Open a presentation based on a template by clicking the CUSTOM option at the New backstage area, clicking *Custom Office Templates*, and then double-clicking the desired template thumbnail.
- Customize a handout with options in the Handout Master view and customize notes pages with options in the Notes Master view.
- In addition to changing views, you can use buttons on the VIEW tab to show/hide the ruler and/or gridlines; change the zoom display; view slides in color, grayscale, or black and white; and work with multliple windows.
- Action buttons are drawn objects in a slide that have a routine attached, such as displaying the next slide, the first slide, a website, or another PowerPoint presentation.
- Create an action button by clicking the INSERT tab, clicking the Shapes button, clicking the desired button at the drop-down list, and then clicking or dragging in the slide to create the button.
- Apply an action to text or an object in a slide by selecting the text or object, clicking the INSERT tab, and then clicking the Action button.
- With options at the Insert Hyperlink dialog box, you can create a hyperlink to a web page, another presentation, a location within a presentation, a new presentation, or to an email. You can also create a hyperlink using a graphic.
- You can modify, edit, and remove hyperlinks.

Commands Review

FEATURE	RIBBON TAB, GROUP/OPTION	BUTTON	KEYBOARD SHORTCUT
action buttons	INSERT, Illustrations		
Action Settings dialog box	INSERT, Links		
Handout Master view	VIEW, Master Views		
Insert Hyperlink dialog box	INSERT, Links		Ctrl + K
New backstage area	FILE, *New*		
Notes Master view	VIEW, Master Views		
Slide Master view	VIEW, Master Views		

Concepts Check

Completion: In the space provided at the right, indicate the correct term, symbol, or command.

1. To display a presentation in Slide Master view, click this tab and then click the Slide Master button.

   _____

2. Click this button to close Slide Master view.

   _____

3. This group on the SLIDE MASTER tab contains buttons for applying theme colors and theme fonts.

   _____

4. This dialog box with the Slide tab selected contains options for inserting the date and time, a slide number, and a footer.

   _____

5. To create a new slide layout in Slide Master view, click this button in the Edit Master group.

   _____

6. To save a presentation as a template, choose this option at the *Save as type* option drop-down list in the Save As dialog box.

   _____

7. Change to this view to customize handouts.

   _____

8. Change to this view to customize notes pages.

   _____

9. The Zoom slider bar is located at the right side of this bar.

   _____

10. Click this button to display a drop-down list that includes action buttons.

    _____

11. Insert this action button in a slide to display the next slide in the presentation.

    _____

12. Insert this action button in a slide to display the first slide in the presentation.

    _____

13. This is the keyboard shortcut to display the Insert Hyperlink dialog box.

    _____

Skills Check   Assess Your Performance

Assessment

1 FORMAT A PRESENTATION IN SLIDE MASTER VIEW AND THEN SAVE THE PRESENTATION AS A TEMPLATE

Note: If you are using PowerPoint 2013 in a school setting on a network system, you may need to complete Assessments 1 and 2 in the same day. Check with your instructor for any specific instructions.

1. Open a blank presentation, click the VIEW tab, and then click the Slide Master button.
2. Click the top slide master thumbnail in the slide thumbnails pane.
3. Apply the Wood Type theme and apply the Yellow Orange theme colors.
4. Select the text *Click to edit Master text styles*, click the HOME tab and then change the font size to 24 points.
5. Select the text *Second level* in the slide master and then change the font size to 20 points.
6. Insert the **WELogo.jpg** image in the master slide, change the height of the logo to 0.5 inch, and then drag the logo to the upper right corner of the slide master.
7. Click the SLIDE MASTER tab.
8. Click the first slide layout below the slide master.
9. Click the *Footers* check box to remove the check mark in the Master Layout group to remove the footer and date placeholders.
10. Select and then delete the slide layouts from the third layout below the slide master (the *Section Header Layout*) to the last layout.
11. Preserve the slide master by clicking the top slide master in the slide thumbnails pane and then clicking the Preserve button in the Edit Master group.
12. Click the Close Master View button.
13. Save the presentation as a template and name the template **XXXPublicationTemplate** (use your initials in place of the *XXX*).
14. Close **XXXPublicationTemplate.potx**.

Assessment

2 USE A TEMPLATE TO CREATE A PUBLICATIONS PRESENTATION

1. Open a presentation based on the **XXXPublicationTemplate.potx** template presentation (where the XXX represents your initials). (To do this, display the New backstage area, click the CUSTOM option, click *Custom Office Templates*, and then double-click the *XXXPublicationTemplate.potx* template thumbnail.)
2. Save the presentation and name it **P-C6-A2-WEnterprises**.
3. Click the *CLICK TO ADD TITLE* text in the current slide and then type **Worldwide Enterprises**.
4. Click the *Click to add subtitle* text and then type **Company Publications**.
5. Display the Reuse Slides task pane, browse to the PC6 folder on your storage medium, and then double-click **Publications.pptx**.

6. Insert the second, third, fourth, and fifth slides from the Reuse Slides task pane into the current presentation and then close the task pane.
7. Insert a second slide master with the following specifications:
   a. Display the presentation in Slide Master view.
   b. Click in the slide thumbnails pane below the bottom slide layout.
   c. Apply the Frame theme.
   d. Click the Frame Slide Master thumbnail in the slide thumbnails pane and then apply the Yellow Orange theme colors.
   e. Apply the Style 9 background style.
8. Select and then delete slide layouts from the third layout (*Section Header Layout*) below the new slide master to the last layout.
9. Insert headers, footers, slide numbers, and dates with the following specifications:
   a. Click the INSERT tab, display the Header and Footer dialog box with the Slide tab selected, insert the date to update automatically, and insert slide numbers.
   b. Click the Notes and Handouts tab, insert the date to update automatically, insert a header that prints your first and last names, insert a footer that prints *Worldwide Enterprises*, and then click the Apply to All button.
10. Close Slide Master view.
11. Make Slide 5 active and then insert a new slide using the new Frame Title Slide layout and then type **Worldwide Enterprises** as the title and **Preparing the Company Newsletter** as the subtitle.
12. Insert the following text in slides using the Frame Title and Content layout:

    Slide 7   Preparing the Newsletter
    - Maintain consistent elements from issue to issue
    - Consider the following when designing the newsletter
        ◦ Focus
        ◦ Balance
        ◦ White space
        ◦ Directional flow

    Slide 8   Preparing the Newsletter
    - Choose paper size and weight
    - Determine margins
    - Specify column layout
    - Choose nameplate layout and format
    - Specify heading format
    - Determine newsletter colors

13. Insert a transition and sound of your choosing to all slides in the presentation.
14. Run the presentation.
15. Print the presentation as a handout with four slides printed horizontally per page.
16. Save and then close **P-C6-A2-WEnterprises.pptx**.

Assessment

3 INSERT ACTION BUTTONS IN A GARDENING PRESENTATION

1. Open **GAPres.pptx** and then save the presentation with the name **P-C6-A3-GAPres**.
2. Make Slide 1 active and then insert an action button in the lower right corner of the slide that displays the next slide.
3. Display the presentation in Slide Master view, click the top slide master in the slide thumbnails pane, create an action button in the lower right corner of the slide that displays the next slide, and then close Slide Master view.
4. Make Slide 8 active and then create an action button that displays the first slide in the presentation.
5. Make Slide 2 active, click the flowers clip art image, and then create a link to the presentation **MaintenancePres.pptx** (located in the PC6 folder on your storage medium). *Hint: Use the Action button in the Links group on the INSERT tab.*
6. Display Slide 8 and then make the following changes:
   a. Delete the text *Better Homes and Gardens®* and then type **Organic Gardening®**.
   b. Select *Organic Gardening®* and then create a hyperlink with the text to the website www.organicgardening.com.
7. Make sure you are connected to the Internet and then run the presentation beginning with Slide 1. Navigate through the slide show by clicking the next action button and display the connected presentation by clicking the clip art image in Slide 2. At Slide 8, click the <u>Organic Gardening®</u> hyperlink. Scroll through the website and click a few different hyperlinks that interest you. After viewing a few web pages in the magazine, close your web browser. When you click the action button on the last slide, the first slide displays. End the slide show by pressing the Esc key.
8. Print the presentation as a handout with four slides printed horizontally per page.
9. Save and then close **P-C6-A3-GAPres.pptx**.

Assessment

4 CREATE AN ACTION BUTTONS PRESENTATION

1. In this chapter, you learned to insert a number of action buttons in a slide. Experiment with the other action buttons (click the INSERT tab, click the Shapes button, and then point to the buttons in the *Action Buttons* section) and then prepare a PowerPoint presentation with the following specifications:
   a. The first slide should contain the title of your presentation.
   b. Choose four action buttons and then create one slide for each of the action buttons that includes the specific name as well as an explanation of the button.
   c. Apply a design theme of your choosing to the presentation.
2. Save the presentation and name it **P-C6-A4-ActionButtons**.
3. Print the presentation as a handout with six slides printed horizontally per page.
4. Close **P-C6-A4-ActionButtons.pptx**.

Visual Benchmark Demonstrate Your Proficiency

CREATE AND FORMAT A COMPANY BRANCH OFFICE PRESENTATION

1. Create the presentation shown in Figure 6.3 with the following specifications:
   a. Apply the Parallax design theme, the gray/orange variant, the Arial Black-Arial theme fonts and the Style 1 background style.
   b. In Slide 1, delete the title placeholder and insert the text shown in the figure in the subtitle placeholder. Insert **WELogo.jpg** and then size and position the logo as shown in the figure. Insert the Forward or Next action button in the lower right corner of the slide as shown in the figure.
   c. Display the presentation in Slide Master view and then click the top slide master thumbnail. Insert **WELogo.jpg**, change the height of the logo to 0.5 inch, and then position the logo in the upper right corner of the slide as shown in Figure 6.3. Select the text *Click to edit Master title style*, click the HOME tab, and then change the font color to *Orange, Accent 1, Darker 25%*. Insert the Forward or Next action button in the lower right corner of the slide master as shown in the figure and then close the Slide Master view.
   d. In Slide 4, create the 3-D clustered column chart as shown in the figure using the following numbers:

	>$25,000	>$50,000	>$100,000
Under 25	184	167	0
25 to 44	1,228	524	660
45 to 64	519	1,689	1,402
Over 64	818	831	476

   e. In Slide 5 (the *Top Public Employers* slide), insert the Information action button that links to the website www.clearwater-fl.com/gov and then size and position the action button as shown in the figure.
   f. In Slide 6, insert the clip art image of a hospital (use the search words *hospital* and *ambulance*), correct the color of the clip art image to *Brightness: -20% Contrast: +20%*, and then size and position the clip art as shown in the figure. Insert a Home action button over the Forward or Next action button.
   g. Change the line spacing in Slides 5 and 6 so your slides display similar to the slides in Figure 6.3.
2. Apply a transition and sound of your choosing to all slides in the presentation.
3. Save the presentation and name it **P-C6-VB-WEClearwater**.
4. Run the presentation.
5. Print the presentation as a handout with six slides printed horizontally per page.
6. Close **P-C6-VB-WEClearwater.pptx**.

Figure 6.3 Visual Benchmark

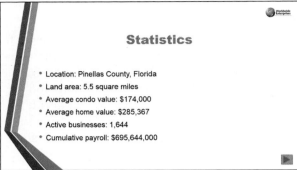

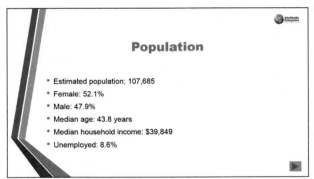

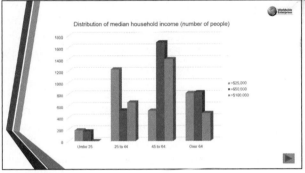

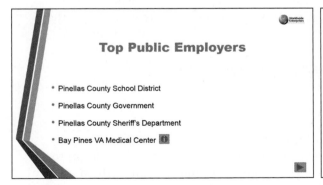

Case Study   Apply Your Skills

Part 1

You are the training manager for Anchor Corporation and one of your job responsibilities is conducting new employee orientations. You decide that a PowerPoint presentation will help you deliver information to new employees during the orientation. You know that you will be creating other PowerPoint presentations so you decide to create a template. Create a presentation template with attractive formatting that includes a design theme, theme colors, and theme fonts. Include an anchor clip art image in all of the slides. Apply any other formatting or design elements to increase the appeal of the presentation. Save the presentation as a template with the name **XXXAnchorTemplate** (insert your initials in place of the XXX) and then close the template.

Part 2

You have a document with notes about information on types of employment appointments, employee performance, and compensation. Open the Word document named **AnchorNewEmployees.docx** and then use the information to prepare a presentation using the **XXXAnchorTemplate.potx** template. Save the completed presentation with the name **P-C6-CS-AnchorEmp** and make sure it has the file extension *.pptx*. Apply a transition and sound to all slides in the presentation, print the presentation as a handout, and then close the presentation.

Part 3

Open the Word document named **AnchorGuidelines.docx** and then use the information in the document to prepare a presentation using the **XXXAnchorTemplate.potx** template. Save the completed presentation with the name **P-C6-CS-AnchorGuidelines** and make sure it contains the file extension *.pptx*. Apply a transition and sound to all slides in the presentation, print the presentation as a handout, and then close the presentation.

Part 4

During the new employee presentation you want to refer to a chart of employee classifications, so you decide to create a link to an Excel spreadsheet. Open the **P-C6-CS-AnchorEmp.pptx** presentation and then create a new slide that contains a hyperlink to the Excel workbook named **ACClassifications.xlsx**. Run the presentation, link to the Excel chart, and then continue running the remaining slides in the presentation. Print only the new slide and then save and close **P-C6-CS-AnchorEmp.pptx**.

Part 5

The information you used to create the **P-C6-CS-AnchorGuidelines.pptx** presentation was taken from a document that is part of a new employee handbook. You decide that you want to create a link in your presentation to the Word document to show employees the additional information in the document. Create a new slide in the **P-C6-CS-AnchorGuidelines.pptx** presentation that includes an action button that links to the Word document named **AnchorCompGuidelines.docx**. Include other action buttons for navigating in the presentation. Run the presentation, link to the Word document, and then continue running the remaining slides in the presentation. Print only the new slide and then save and close **P-C6-CS-AnchorGuidelines.pptx**.

MICROSOFT®
POWERPOINT®

CHAPTER 7

Applying Custom Animation and Setting Up Shows

PERFORMANCE OBJECTIVES

Upon successful completion of Chapter 7, you will be able to:

- **Apply animations**
- **Modify and remove animations**
- **Apply a build**
- **Animate shapes, images, SmartArt, and chart elements**
- **Draw motion paths**
- **Set up a slide show**
- **Set rehearse timings for slides**
- **Hide slides**
- **Create, run, edit, and print a custom show**
- **Insert and customize audio and video files**

Tutorials

7.1 Applying Animation to Objects and Text

7.2 Animating Shapes, Images, SmartArt, and Chart Elements

7.3 Setting Up a Slide Show

7.4 Applying Sound to Animations

7.5 Setting Timings for a Presentation

7.6 Creating and Running a Custom Show

7.7 Adding Audio and Video

7.8 Modifying Audio and Video Files

Animation, or movement, can add visual appeal and interest to your presentation when used appropriately. PowerPoint provides a number of animation effects you can apply to elements in a slide. In this chapter, you will learn how to apply animation effects as well as how to insert audio and video files to create dynamic presentations.

In some situations, you may want to prepare an automated presentation that runs on a continuous loop. You can customize a presentation to run continuously and set the time you want each slide to remain on the screen. You can also create a custom slide show to present only specific slides in a presentation. In this chapter, you will learn how to prepare automated presentations and how to create and edit custom slide shows. Model answers for this chapter's projects appear on the following pages.

PC7

Note: Before beginning the projects, copy to your storage medium the PC7 folder from the PowerPoint folder on the CD that accompanies this textbook and then make PC7 the active folder.

275

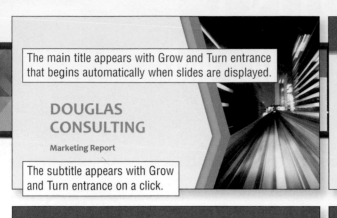

The main title appears with Grow and Turn entrance that begins automatically when slides are displayed.

DOUGLAS CONSULTING

Marketing Report

The subtitle appears with Grow and Turn entrance on a click.

Department Reports

Slide titles animate with Spiral In entrance on a click.

- Sales
- Public Relations
- Human Resources

Each bullet is animated with Zoom entrance and a chime sound on a click.

Current Projects

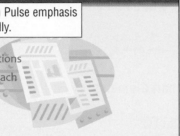

Clip art is animated with Pulse emphasis and appears automatically.

- Marketing Design
- Product Specifications
- Community Outreach

Services

- Project Management
- Research and Development
- Inventory Management
- Quality Control

Project 1 Apply Animation Effects to Elements in a Marketing Presentation

P-C7-P1-MarketingPres.pptx

ONLINE LEARNING

Clip art is animated with a motion path that begins automatically.

A GROWING TREND IN EDUCATION

Instructional Delivery Methods

▶ Traditional: Classroom environment only
▶ Hybrid: Classroom and online course site
▶ Internet: Online course site only

Each bullet is animated with Split entrance on a click; a pie chart displays when its bullet is clicked.

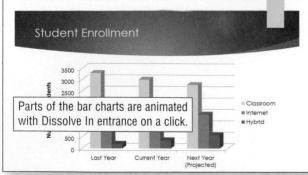

Student Enrollment

Parts of the bar charts are animated with Dissolve In entrance on a click.

Reasons for Growth

Convenient
- Accessible 24 hours a day
- No travel hassles
- No child care expenses

Addresses Multiple Learning Styles
- Audio/video clips
- Hands-on activities
- Student-controlled pace

The SmartArt shapes are animated with either Float In (Up) or Grow and Turn entrance on a click.

Project 2 Apply Custom Animation Effects to Elements in Slides in an Online Learning Presentation, Slides 1–4

P-C7-P2-OLLearning.pptx

Model Answers

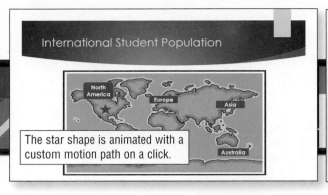

The star shape is animated with a custom motion path on a click.

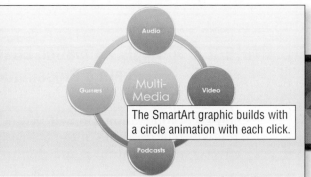

The SmartArt graphic builds with a circle animation with each click.

Each bullet is animated with Fly In entrance on a click and then dims.

▶ Electronic submission of assignments

▶ Evidence of online participation

▶ Peer evaluations

▶ Proctored exams

Project 2 Apply Custom Animation Effects to Elements in Slides in an Online Learning Presentation, Slides 5–9

P-C7-P2-OLLearning.pptx

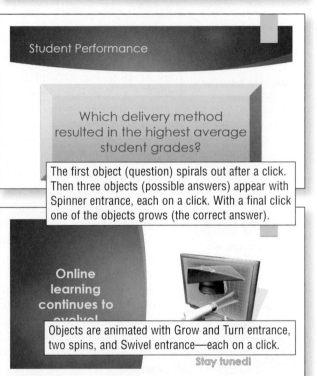

Student Performance

Which delivery method resulted in the highest average student grades?

The first object (question) spirals out after a click. Then three objects (possible answers) appear with Spinner entrance, each on a click. With a final click one of the objects grows (the correct answer).

Online learning continues to evolve!

Objects are animated with Grow and Turn entrance, two spins, and Swivel entrance—each on a click.

Stay tuned!

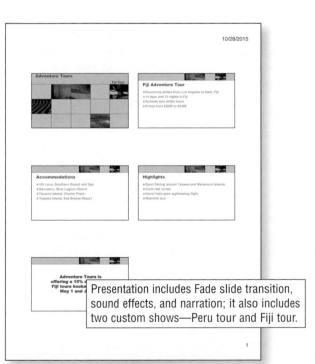

Presentation includes Fade slide transition, sound effects, and narration; it also includes two custom shows—Peru tour and Fiji tour.

Project 3 Prepare a Self-Running Adventure Presentation and Create Custom Shows

P-C7-P3-AdvTours-Custom.pptx

Video file inserted in slide that plays automatically. Video file deleted and then audio file inserted that plays throughout all slides as each slide advances automatically after five seconds.

Project 4 Insert Audio and Video Files in a Presentation

P-C7-P4-EcoTours.pptx

Project **1** Apply Animation Effects to Elements in a Marketing Presentation · 6 Parts

You will open a marketing presentation, apply animation effects to the title slide, and then apply animation effects in Slide Master view to the remaining slides. You will remove some of the animation effects and then apply custom animation effects, such as entrance and emphasis effects, to elements in slides.

Applying and Removing Animations

▼ Quick Steps

Apply an Animation
1. Click desired item.
2. Click ANIMATIONS tab.
3. Click More button in Animation group.
4. Click desired animation at drop-down gallery.

H I N T

You can animate text, objects, graphics, SmartArt diagrams, charts, hyperlinks, and sound.

Effects Options

Preview

Animate items such as text or objects in a slide to add visual interest to a presentation. PowerPoint includes a number of animations you can apply to items in a slide. These animations can be modified to fit your specific needs. For example, displaying items one at a time helps your audience focus on each topic or point as you present it, so you may want items to appear individually or in groups. You can control the direction that an item enters from and the rate of speed at which it enters. Try not to overwhelm your audience with too much animation. In general, you want them to remember the content of your presentation rather than the visual effects.

To animate an item, click the desired item, click the ANIMATIONS tab, click the More button at the right side of the animations in the Animation group, and then click the desired animation at the drop-down gallery. Once you have applied an animation, you can specify the animation effects with options in the Effect Options button drop-down gallery. Some of the animation effect options may include the direction from which you want the item to appear, and whether you want items such as bulleted text or SmartArt to appear as one object, all at once, or by paragraph. To apply effects to an animation, apply an animation to an item, click the Effect Options button located in the Animation group, and then click the desired effect at the drop-down gallery. (The appearance of this button changes depending on the selected effect.) Use options in the Timing group on the ANIMATIONS tab to specify when the animation needs to start on a slide, the duration of the animation, the delay between animations, and the order in which animations should appear on the slide.

If you want to see the animation in your slide without running the presentation, click the Preview button on the ANIMATIONS tab. Click this button and the animation effect you applied to the active slide displays on the slide in the slide pane. When you apply animation effects to items in a slide, an animation icon displays below the slide number in the slide thumbnails pane.

If you add or change an animation, PowerPoint will automatically preview the animation in the slide. If you want to turn off this feature, click the Preview button arrow and then click *AutoPreview* at the drop-down list to remove the check mark.

1. Open **MarketingPres.pptx** and save the presentation with the name **P-C7-P1-MarketingPres**.
2. Make sure Slide 1 is active and then apply animations to the title and subtitle by
   completing the following steps:
   a. Click anywhere in the title *DOUGLAS CONSULTING*.
   b. Click the ANIMATIONS tab.
   c. Click the *Fade* animation in the Animation group.

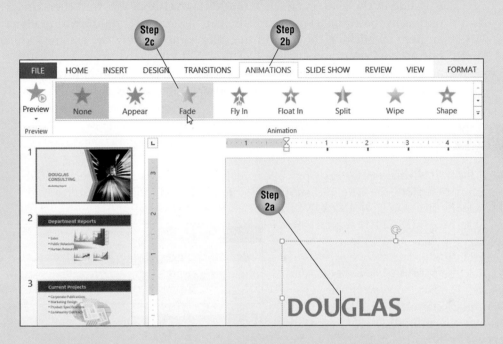

   d. Click anywhere in the subtitle *Marketing Report*.
   e. Click the *Fade* animation that displays in the
      Animation group.
   f. Click the Effect Options button in the Animation
      group and then click *All at Once* at the drop-down
      gallery.
   g. Click the Preview button on the ANIMATIONS tab
      to see the animation effects in the slide pane.

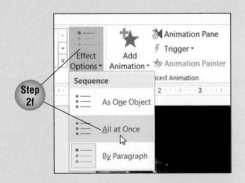

3. Apply animations to Slides 2 through 4 in Slide
   Master view by completing the following steps:
   a. Click the VIEW tab and then click the Slide
      Master button in the Master Views group.
   b. Click the third slide master layout in the slide
      thumbnails pane (Title and Content Layout).
   c. Click the text *Click to edit Master title style*.
   d. Click the ANIMATIONS tab and then click the *Fly In* animation that displays in the
      Animation group.
   e. Click the bulleted text *Click to edit Master text styles*.
   f. Click the *Fly In* animation that displays in the Animation group.
   g. Click the SLIDE MASTER tab and then click the Close Master View button.

4. Make Slide 1 active and then run the presentation. Click the mouse button to advance items in slides and to move to the next slide. Notice how the bulleted text in Slides 2 through 4 displays one item at a time.

5. Save **P-C7-P1-MarketingPres.pptx**.

▼ **Quick Steps**

Remove an Animation
1. Click desired item.
2. Click ANIMATIONS tab.
3. Click *None* option.

If you want to remove an animation effect from an item, click the item in the slide in the slide pane, click the ANIMATIONS tab, and then click the *None* option in the Animation group. You can also remove an animation effect from an item by clicking the item in the slide pane, clicking the assigned animation button, and then pressing the Delete key. If you want to apply a different animation to an item, make sure to delete any existing animations first. If you do not delete the first animation, both animations will be assigned to the item.

Project 1b   **Removing Animations**   **Part 2 of 6**

1. With **P-C7-P1-MarketingPres.pptx** open, make Slide 1 active and then remove the animation from the title and subtitle by completing the following steps:
   a. Click the title *DOUGLAS CONSULTING*.
   b. Click the ANIMATIONS tab.
   c. Click the *None* option in the Animation group.
   d. Click the subtitle *Marketing Report*.
   e. Click the *None* option in the Animation group.

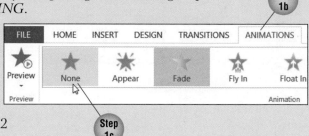

2. Remove the animation effects for Slides 2 through 4 by completing the following steps:
   a. Click the VIEW tab and then click the Slide Master button in the Master Views group.
   b. Click the third slide master layout in the slide thumbnails pane (Title and Content Layout).
   c. Click in the text *Click to edit Master title style*.
   d. Click the ANIMATIONS tab and then click the *None* option in the Animation group.
   e. Click in the text *Click to edit Master text styles*.
   f. Click the *None* option in the Animation group.
   g. Click the SLIDE MASTER tab and then click the Close Master View button.
3. Make Slide 1 active and then run the presentation.
4. Save **P-C7-P1-MarketingPres.pptx**.

Applying Animation Effects ■■■■■■■■■■■■■■■■■■■■

The Add Animation button in the Advanced Animation group on the ANIMATIONS tab provides four types of animation effects that can be applied to an item. You can apply an effect as an itcm enters the slide, as an item exits the slide, as emphasis to an item, and as a motion path that will cause an item to move in a specific pattern on, or even off, the slide.

To apply an entrance effect to an item, click the Add Animation button in the Advanced Animation group and then click the desired animation effect in the *Entrance* section of the drop-down gallery. Customize the entrance effect by clicking the Effect Options button in the Animation group and then clicking the desired entrance effect. Additional entrance effects are available at the Add Entrance Effect dialog box. Display this dialog box by clicking the Add Animation button and then clicking *More Entrance Effects* at the drop-down gallery. Complete similar steps to apply an emphasis effect and an exit effect. Display additional emphasis effects by clicking the Add Animation button and then clicking *More Emphasis Effects*. Display additional exit effects by clicking the Add Animation button and then clicking *More Exit Effects*.

Applying Animations with Animation Painter

If you apply an animation or animations to items in a slide and want to apply the same animation in more than one location in a slide or slides, use the Animation Painter. To use the Animation Painter, apply the desired animation to an item, position the insertion point anywhere in the animated item, and then double-click the Animation Painter button in the Advanced Animation group on the ANIMATIONS tab. Using the mouse, select or click on additional items to which you want the animation applied. After applying the animation in the desired locations, click the Animation Painter button to deactivate it. If you need to apply animation in only one other location, click the Animation Painter button once. The first time you click an item, the animation is applied and the Animation Painter is deactivated.

▼ **Quick Steps**

Apply an Animation Effect
1. Click desired item.
2. Click ANIMATIONS tab.
3. Click Add Animation button.
4. Click desired animation effect at drop-down gallery.

Apply Effects with Animation Painter
1. Click item, then apply desired animation effect.
2. Click item with animation effect.
3. Double-click Animation Painter button.
4. Click each item to which you want animation effect applied.
5. Click Animation Painter button to deactivate it.

Add Animation

Animation Painter

Project 1c   Applying Animation Effects   Part 3 of 6

1. With **P-C7-P1-MarktingPres.pptx** open, apply an animation effect to the title and subtitle in Slide 1 by completing the following steps:
   a. Make Slide 1 active.
   b. Click the title *DOUGLAS CONSULTING*.
   c. Click the ANIMATIONS tab.
   d. Click the Add Animation button in the Advanced Animation group and then click the *Wipe* animation in the *Entrance* section of the drop-down gallery.

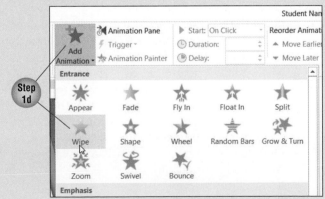

e. Click the Effect Options button in the Animation group and then click *From Top* at the drop-down gallery.

f. Click the subtitle *Marketing Report*.

g. Click the Add Animation button and then click the *Zoom* animation in the *Entrance* section.

2. Apply an animation effect to the titles in Slides 2 through 4 by completing the following steps:

a. Click the VIEW tab and then click the Slide Master button in the Master Views group.

b. Click the third slide master layout in the slide thumbnails pane (Title and Content Layout).

c. Click in the text *Click to edit Master title style*.

d. Click the ANIMATIONS tab, click the Add Animation button in the Advanced Animation group, and then click the *More Emphasis Effects* option at the drop-down gallery.

e. At the Add Emphasis Effect dialog box, click the *Grow With Color* option in the *Moderate* section.

f. Click OK to close the dialog box.

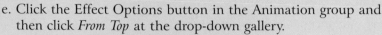

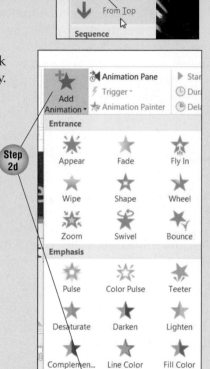

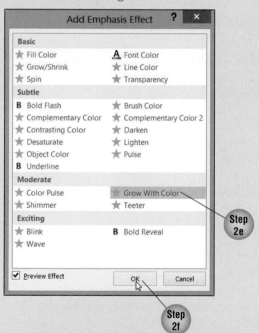

g. Click the SLIDE MASTER tab and then click the Close Master View button.

3. Use the Animation Painter to apply an animation effect to the bulleted text in Slides 2 through 4 by completing the following steps:

a. Make Slide 2 active.

b. Click anywhere in the bulleted text to make the placeholder active.

c. Click the ANIMATIONS tab, click the Add Animation button, and then click the *Split* animation in the *Entrance* section.

d. Click anywhere in the bulleted text.

e. Double-click the Animation Painter button in the Advanced Animation group.

f. Make Slide 3 active.

g. Click anywhere in the bulleted text. (The mouse pointer displays as an arrow with a paintbrush attached. The animations are applied to all four bulleted items.)

h. Make Slide 4 active and then click anywhere in the bulleted text.

i. Click the Animation Painter button to deactivate it.

4. Click the Preview button to view the animation effects.

5. Run the presentation by clicking the Start From Beginning button on the Quick Access toolbar. Click the mouse button to advance slide elements and to move to the next slide.

6. Save **P-C7-P1-MarketingPres.pptx**.

Modifying Animation Effects

When you apply an animation effect to an item, you can use options in the Timing group to modify the animation effect. Use the *Start* option box drop-down list to specify when you want the item inserted in the slide. Generally, items display in a slide when you click the mouse button. Click the *Start* option box arrow and then click *With Previous* or *With Next* at the drop-down list to make the item appear on the slide with the previous item or the next item.

Start

Use the *Duration* measurement box to specify the length of an animation. For example, click the up-pointing arrow at the right of the *Duration* measurement box to increase the length of time the animation displays on the slide and click the down-pointing arrow to decrease the length of time the animation displays. You can also select the current time in the *Duration* measurement box and then type the desired time.

Duration

The *Delay* measurement box allows you to tell an animation to play a certain number of seconds after the previous animation plays. Click the up-pointing arrow to increase this amount of time and click the down-pointing arrow to decrease this amount of time. You can also select the current time in the *Delay* measurement box and then type the desired time.

Delay

Reordering Items

When you apply an animation effect to an item, an animation number displays next to the item in the slide pane. This number indicates the order in which the item will appear in the slide. When more than one item displays in the slide, you can change the order with options in the *Reorder Animation* section of the Timing group on the ANIMATIONS tab. Click the Move Earlier button to move an item before another item or click the Move Later button to move an item after another item.

▼ **Quick Steps**

Reorder an Animation Item
1. Click item in slide.
2. Click Move Earlier button or Move Later button.

Move Earlier

Move Later

Project 1d Removing, Modifying, and Reordering Animation Effects   Part 4 of 6

1. With **P-C7-P1-MarketingPres.pptx** open, make Slide 1 active.
2. Modify the start setting for the animation effect you applied to the slide title by completing the following steps:
   a. Click anywhere in the title to activate the placeholder.

b. Click the down-pointing arrow at the right of the *Start* option box in the Timing group on the ANIMATIONS tab.

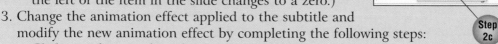

Step 2b

c. Click *With Previous* at the drop-down list. (At this setting, the title animation effect will begin as soon as the slide displays, without you having to click the mouse button. Notice that the number *1* located to the left of the item in the slide changes to a zero.)

Step 2c

3. Change the animation effect applied to the subtitle and modify the new animation effect by completing the following steps:

   a. Click anywhere in the subtitle *Marketing Report* in the slide.

   b. Click the More button at the right of the thumbnails in the Animation group and then click the *None* option in the drop-down gallery.

Step 3d

   c. Click the Add Animation button in the Advanced Animation group and then click the *Grow/Shrink* animation in the *Emphasis* section.

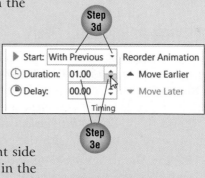

   d. Click the down-pointing arrow at the right side of the *Start* option box and then click *With Previous* at the drop-down list.

Step 3e

   e. Click four times on the down-pointing arrow at the right side of the *Duration* measurement box. (This displays *01.00* in the measurement box.)

4. Remove animations from slide titles in Slide Master view by completing the following steps:

   a. Click the VIEW tab and then click the Slide Master button in the Master Views group.

   b. Click the third slide master layout in the slide thumbnails pane (Title and Content Layout).

   c. Click in the text *Click to edit Master title style*.

   d. Click the ANIMATIONS tab.

   e. Click the More button at the right of the thumbnails in the Animation group and then click the *None* option in the Animation group.

   f. Click the SLIDE MASTER tab and then click the Close Master View button.

5. Remove animations from the bulleted text in Slides 2 through 4 by completing the following steps:

   a. Make Slide 2 active.

   b. Click in the bulleted text.

   c. Click the ANIMATIONS tab and then click the *None* option in the Animation group.

   d. Make Slide 3 active, click in the bulleted text, and then click the *None* option in the Animation group.

   e. Make Slide 4 active, click in the bulleted text, and then click the *None* option in the Animation group.

6. Make Slide 2 active and then apply and customize animation effects by completing the following steps:

   a. Click the title *Department Reports*.

   b. Click the Add Animation button in the Advanced Animation group and then click the *More Entrance Effects* option at the drop-down gallery.

Step 6c

   c. At the Add Entrance Effect dialog box, scroll down the list box and then click *Spiral In* in the *Exciting* section.

Step 6d

   d. Click OK to close the dialog box.

e. Click the bulleted text.

f. Click the Add Animation button and then click the *Zoom* animation in the *Entrance* section.

g. Click the clip art image.

h. Click the Add Animation button and then click the *Zoom* animation in the *Entrance* section.

7. Click the Preview button located at the left side of the ANIMATIONS tab to view the animation effects.

8. After viewing the animation effects, you decide that you want the clip art to animate before the bulleted text and you want the animation effects to begin with the previous animation (instead of with a mouse click). With Slide 2 active, complete the following steps:

   a. Click the clip art image. (The number 5 will display at the left of the clip art placeholder because the clip art is the fifth item to enter the slide.)

   b. Click the Move Earlier button in the *Reorder Animation* section of the Timing group. The number displayed to the left of the clip art image changes to 2 because you moved the clip art animation before the three bulleted items.)

   c. Click the down-pointing arrow at the right side of the *Start* option box in the Timing group and then click *With Previous* at the drop-down list.

   d. Click the title *Department Reports*.

   e. Click the down-pointing arrow at the right side of the *Start* option box in the Timing group and then click *With Previous* at the drop-down list.

9. Make Slide 3 active and then apply the same animation effects you applied in Slide 2. (Do this by completing steps similar to those in Steps 6a through 6h and Steps 8a through 8e.)

10. Make Slide 4 active and then apply the same animation effects you applied to Slide 2. (Do this by completing steps similar to those in Steps 6a through 6f and Steps 8d through 8e.)

11. Make Slide 1 active and then run the presentation.

12. Save **P-C7-P1-MarketingPres.pptx**.

Customizing Animation Effects at the Animation Pane

You can use the Animation Pane to customize and modify animation effects in a presentation. Display the Animation Pane, shown in Figure 7.1, by clicking the Animation Pane button in the Advanced Animation group on the ANIMATIONS tab. When you apply an animation to an item, the item name or description displays in the Animation Pane. Hover the mouse pointer over an item and a description of the animation effect applied to the item displays in a box below the item. If you click the down-pointing arrow at the right side of an item in the Animation Pane, a drop-down list displays with options for modifying or customizing the animation effect. For example, use options at the drop-down list to specify when you want the item to display on the slide, the delay and duration of the animation, and to remove an animation effect.

When you apply an effect to an item, the item name and/or description displays in the Animation Pane preceded by a number. This number indicates the order in which items will appear in the slide. When more than one item displays in the Animation Pane, you can change the order of an item by clicking the item and then clicking the Move Earlier button or the Move Later button located toward the top of the Animation Pane.

▼ Quick Steps

Reorder Animation Items
1. Click item in Animation Pane.
2. Click Move Earlier button or Move Later button.

Remove an Animation Effect
1. Click item in Animation Pane.
2. Click down-pointing arrow.
3. Click *Remove*.

Animation Pane

Figure 7.1 Animation Pane

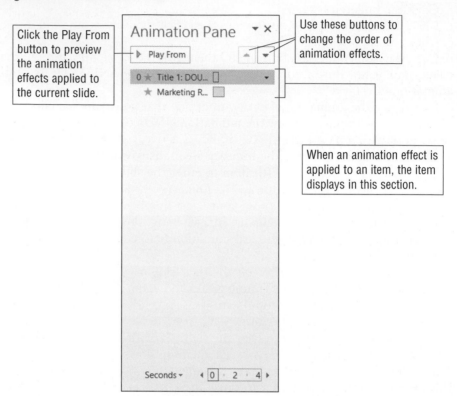

Figure 7.1 Animation Pane

Click the Play From button to preview the animation effects applied to the current slide.

Use these buttons to change the order of animation effects.

When an animation effect is applied to an item, the item displays in this section.

When you apply an animation effect or effects to a slide, you can play all the animations in the Animation Pane by clicking the Play All button at the top of the pane. (The name of the button varies depending on the contents of the Animation Pane and what is selected in the pane.) The animation effects display in the slide in the slide pane and a time indicator displays along the bottom of the Animation Pane with a vertical line indicating the progression of time (in seconds). You can also play only the selected animation effect in the Animation Pane by clicking the animation effect in the pane and then clicking the Play From button at the top of the pane.

Project 1e **Removing, Modifying, and Reordering Animation Effects in the Animation Pane**   Part 5 of 6

1. With **P-C7-P1-MarketingPres.pptx** open, make Slide 1 active.
2. Click in the title *DOUGLAS CONSULTING*, click the ANIMATIONS tab, and then click the *None* option in the Animation group.
3. With the title placeholder selected, click the Add Animation button in the Advanced Animation group and then click the *Grow & Turn* animation in the *Entrance* section.
4. Click twice on the down-pointing arrow at the right side of the *Duration* measurement box. (This displays *00.50* in the measurement box.)
5. Click in the subtitle *Marketing Report*, click the More button at the right of the animation thumbnails in the Animation group, and then click the *None* option.
6. With the subtitle placeholder selected, click the Add Animation button in the Advanced Animation group and then click the *Grow & Turn* animation in the *Entrance* section.
7. Click twice on the down-pointing arrow at the right side of the *Duration* measurement box. (This displays *00.50* in the measurement box.)

8. Modify the start setting for the slide title animation effect in the Animation Pane by completing the following steps:

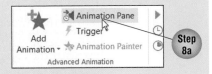

a. Click the Animation Pane button located in the Advanced Animation group on the ANIMATIONS tab. (This displays the Animation Pane at the right side of the screen.)

b. Click the Title 1 item that displays in the Animation Pane.

c. Click the down-pointing arrow at the right side of the item and then click *Start With Previous* at the drop-down list.

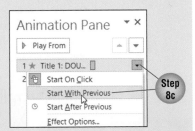

9. Remove animations from slides using the Animation Pane by completing the following steps:

a. Make Slide 2 active.

b. Click the Picture 3 item in the Animation Pane.

c. Click the down-pointing arrow at the right side of the item and then click *Remove* at the drop-down list.

d. Click the clip art image in the slide pane, click the Add Animation button in the Advanced Animation group, and then click the *Pulse* animation in the *Emphasis* section.

10. Make Slide 3 active and then complete steps similar to those in Steps 9b through 9d to remove the animation effect from the clip art image and add the *Pulse* emphasis effect.

11. With the Picture 3 image selected in the Animation Pane, click the Play From button located toward the top of the pane to view the animation effect applied to the clip art.

12. Play all animation effects applied to the slide by clicking anywhere in the blank area below the animation effects in the Animation Pane (this deselects the Picture 3 animation effect) and then click the Play All button (previously the Play From button) at the top of the pane.

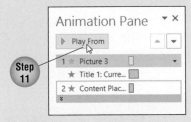

13. After viewing the animation effect, you decide that you want the clip art image to animate before the title and bulleted text and you want the animation effect to begin with the previous animation. With Slide 3 active, complete the following steps:

a. Click the Picture 3 item in the Animation Pane.

b. Click twice on the Move Earlier button located at the top of the Animation pane. (This moves the Picture 3 item above the Title 1 and the content placeholder items.)

c. Click the down-pointing arrow at the right side of the Picture 3 item and then click *Start With Previous* at the drop-down list.

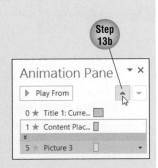

14. Reorder animation effects in Slide 2 to match the changes made to Slide 3.

15. Make Slide 1 active and then run the presentation.

16. Close the Animation Pane.

17. Save **P-C7-P1-MarketingPres.pptx**.

Applying Sound to Animations

Enhance an animation by applying a sound to the animation. To apply a sound, click the Animation Pane button to display the Animation Pane, click the desired animated item in the Animation Pane, click the down-pointing arrow at the right side of the item, and then click *Effect Options* at the drop-down list. At the effect options dialog box with the Effect tab selected, click the down-pointing arrow at the right side of the *Sound* option box and then click the desired sound at the drop-down list. The name of the dialog box will vary depending on the animation effect selected. You can also apply sound to an animation by clicking the desired animated item in the slide in the slide pane, clicking the Animation group dialog box launcher, and then choosing the desired sound effect at the dialog box that displays.

Applying a Build

You can group text (in a bulleted text placeholder) at the Effect Options dialog box by first, second, third, fourth, or fifth levels.

In Project 1a, you applied a build to bulleted text in a slide. A ***build*** displays important points on a slide one point at a time, keeping the audience's attention focused on the current point. You can further customize a build by causing a previous point to dim when the next point displays. To customize a build, click the Animation Pane button to display the Animation Pane, click the desired bulleted item in the Animation Pane, click the down-pointing arrow at the right side of the item, and then click *Effect Options* at the drop-down list. At the effect options dialog box with the Effect tab selected, choose a color option with the *After animation* option box.

Project 1f   Applying Sound and a Build to Animations   Part 6 of 6

1. With **P-C7-P1-MarketingPres.pptx** open, make Slide 2 active and then apply sound and a build to the bulleted text by completing the following steps:
   a. Click in the bulleted text.
   b. Open the Animation Pane by clicking the Animation Pane button in the Advanced Animation group on the ANIMATIONS tab.
   c. Click the down-pointing arrow at the right side of the Content Placeholder item in the Animation Pane and then click *Effect Options* at the drop-down list.
   d. At the Zoom dialog box, make sure the Effect tab is selected, click the down-pointing arrow at the right side of the *Sound* option box, scroll down the list box, and then click the *Chime* option.
   e. Click the down-pointing arrow at the right side of the *After animation* option box and then click the light gray color (last option).
   f. Click OK to close the dialog box.

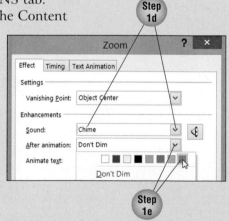

2. Click in the bulleted text in the slide.
3. Double-click the Animation Painter button.
4. Display Slide 3 and click anywhere in the bulleted text.
5. Display Slide 4 and click anywhere in the bulleted text.
6. Click the Animation Painter button to deactivate it.
7. Close the Animation Pane.
8. Make Slide 1 active and then run the presentation.
9. Save and then close **P-C7-P1-MarketingPres.pptx**.

You will open an online learning presentation and then apply animation effects to shapes, a clip art image, elements in SmartArt graphics, and elements in a chart. You will also draw a motion path in a slide.

Animating Shapes and Images

Animate individual shapes or images such as clip art images in a slide in the same way you animate a title or text content placeholder. You can select more than one shape and then apply the same animation effect to the shapes. To select more than one shape, click the first shape, hold down the Shift key, and then click any additional shapes.

Project 2a | **Animating Shapes and a Clip Art Image** | **Part 1 of 6**

1. Open **OLLearning.pptx** and then save the presentation with Save As and name it **P-C7-P2-OLLearning**.
2. Make Slide 8 active (this slide contains one large object with three smaller objects hidden behind it) and then animate objects and apply exit effects by completing the following steps:
   a. Click the ANIMATIONS tab and then click the Animation Pane button in the Advanced Animation group.
   b. Click the large shape in the slide.
   c. Click the Add Animation button in the Advanced Animation group and then click the *More Exit Effects* option at the drop-down gallery.
   d. At the Add Exit Effect dialog box, click the *Spiral Out* option in the *Exciting* section. (You will need to scroll down the list to display this option.) Watch the animation effect in the slide and then click OK.

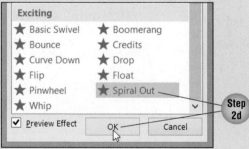

   e. Click the large object to select it and then drag it up the slide to display a portion of the three objects behind.
   f. Click the small object at the left, click the Add Animation button, and then click the *More Entrance Effects* option at the drop-down gallery.
   g. At the Add Entrance Effect dialog box, click *Spinner* in the *Moderate* section, and then click OK.
   h. Select the middle object, hold down the Shift key, and then click the object at the right. (This selects both objects.)
   i. Click the Add Animation button and then click the *More Entrance Effects* option at the drop-down gallery.

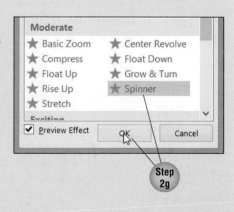

j. At the Add Entrance Effect dialog box, click *Spinner* in the *Moderate* section and then click OK. (Notice that the two objects are numbered *3* in the Animation Pane and are set to enter the slide at the same time. You will change this in the next step.)

k. Click the small object at the right, click the down-pointing arrow at the right of the *Start* option box in the Timing group, and then click *On Click* at the drop-down list.

l. Apply emphasis to the middle object by clicking the middle object, clicking the Add Animation button, and then clicking the *Grow/Shrink* option in the *Emphasis* section of the drop-down gallery.

m. Click the large object to select it and then reposition it over the three smaller objects.

n. Click the Preview button to play the animation effects in the slide.

3. Make Slide 9 active and apply and modify animation effects and change animation order by completing the following steps:

a. Click in the text *Online learning continues to evolve!* (this selects the text box), click the Add Animation button, and then click *Grow & Turn* in the *Entrance* section.

b. Click in the text *Stay tuned!* (this selects the text box), click the Add Animation button, and then click the *Swivel* option in the *Entrance* section.

c. Click the clip art image to select it.

d. Click the Add Animation button and then click the *Spin* animation in the *Emphasis* section.

e. Click the Effect Options button in the Animation group and then click *Two Spins* at the drop-down gallery.

f. Click the down-pointing arrow at the right side of the *Duration* measurement box until *01.00* displays.

g. Click once on the Move Earlier button in the Timing group. This moves the clip art image item in the list box above the *Stay tuned!* text box item.

h. Click the Preview button to play the animation effects in the slide.

4. Save **P-C7-P2-OLLearning.pptx**.

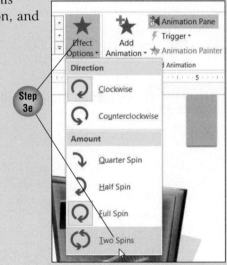

Step 3e

Animating a SmartArt Graphic

You can apply animation effects to a SmartArt graphic and specify whether you want the entire SmartArt graphic to display at once or the individual elements in the SmartArt graphic to display one at a time. Specify a sequence for displaying elements in a SmartArt graphic with the Effect Options button in the Animation group.

When you apply an animation effect to a SmartArt graphic, you can apply animations to individual elements in the graphic. To do this, click the Effect Options button and then click the *One by One* option at the drop-down list. Display the Animation Pane and then expand the list of SmartArt graphic objects by clicking the small double arrows that display in a gray shaded box below the item in the Animation Pane. Click the individual item in the Animation Pane to which you want to apply a different animation effect and then click the desired animation in the Animation group.

▼ **Quick Steps**

Animate a SmartArt Graphic
1. Click SmartArt graphic.
2. Apply animation effect.
3. Click Effect Options button.
4. Specify the desired sequence.

1. With **P-C7-P2-OLLearning.pptx** open, make Slide 4 active and then animate objects in the SmartArt graphic by completing the following steps:
   a. Click the shape in the SmartArt graphic containing the word *Convenient*. (Make sure white sizing handles display around the shape.)
   b. Make sure the ANIMATIONS tab is selected and then click the *Float In* animation in the Animation group.
   c. Click the Effect Options button in the Animation group and then click *One by One* at the drop-down gallery. (This will allow you to apply different effects to the objects in the SmartArt graphic.)
   d. Make sure the Animation Pane displays. (If not, click the Animation Pane button in the Advanced Animation group.)
   e. Expand the list of SmartArt graphic objects in the Animation Pane by clicking the small double arrows that display in a gray shaded box below the content placeholder item. (This expands the list to display four items.)
   f. Click the second item in the Animation Pane (the item that begins with the number *2*).
   g. Click the More button at the right side of the animations in the Animation group and then click the *Grow & Turn* animation in the *Entrance* section.
   h. Click the fourth item in the Animation Pane (the item that begins with the number *4*).
   i. Click the More button at the right side of the animations in the Animation group and then click the *Grow & Turn* animation in the *Entrance* section.
2. Click the Preview button on the ANIMATIONS tab to view the animation effects applied to the SmartArt graphic objects.
3. Make Slide 6 active and then apply animation effects by completing the following steps:
   a. Click the shape in the SmartArt graphic containing the text *Multi-Media*. (Make sure white sizing handles display around the shape.)
   b. Click the Add Animation button and then click the *More Entrance Effects* option.
   c. At the Add Entrance Effect dialog box, click the *Circle* option in the *Basic* section.
   d. Click OK to close the dialog box.
   e. Click the Effect Options button in the Animation group and then click *Out* in the *Direction* section of the drop-down list.
   f. Click the Effect Options button and then click *One by One* in the *Sequence* section of the drop-down list.
   g. Click the down-pointing arrow at the right of the *Duration* measurement box until *00.50* displays.
4. Click the Play Selected button located toward the top of the Animation Pane to view the animation effects applied to the SmartArt graphic objects.
5. Save **P-C7-P2-OLLearning.pptx**.

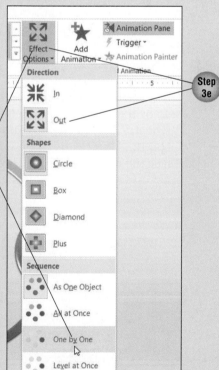

Animating a Chart

Like a SmartArt graphic, you can animate a chart or elements in a chart. Displaying data in a chart may have a more dramatic effect if the chart is animated. Bringing in one element at a time also allows you to discuss each piece of the data as it displays. Specify how you want the chart animated in the slide and how you want chart elements grouped. For example, group chart elements on one object or by series or category. Apply animation to elements in a chart in a manner similar to animating elements in a SmartArt graphic.

Project 2c Animating Elements in a Chart   **Part 3 of 6**

1. With **P-C7-P2-OLLearning.pptx** open, make Slide 3 active and then animate chart elements by completing the following steps:
    a. Click in the chart placeholder to select the chart. (Make sure you do not have a chart element selected and that the ANIMATIONS tab is selected.)
    b. Click the Add Animation button and then click the *More Entrance Effects* option.
    c. At the Add Entrance Effect dialog box, click the *Dissolve In* option in the *Basic* section.
    d. Click OK to close the dialog box.
    e. Make sure the Animation Pane displays and then click the down-pointing arrow at the right side of the Content Placeholder item in the list box.
    f. At the drop-down list that displays, click *Effect Options*.
    g. At the Dissolve In dialog box, click the down-pointing arrow at the right side of the *Sound* option box, scroll down the drop-down list, and then click the *Click* option.
    h. Click the Timing tab.
    i. Click the down-pointing arrow at the right side of the *Duration* option box and then click *1 seconds (Fast)* at the drop-down list.
    j. Click the Chart Animation tab.
    k. Click the down-pointing arrow at the right side of the *Group chart* option box and then click *By Category* at the drop-down list.

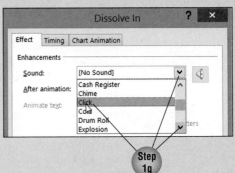

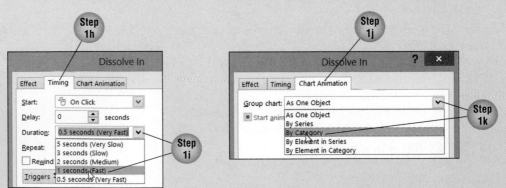

    l. Click OK to close the dialog box.

2. Make Slide 7 active and then apply a build animation effect to the bulleted text by completing the following steps:
   a. Click in the bulleted text.
   b. Click the *Fly In* animation in the Animation group on the ANIMATIONS tab.
   c. Click the Effect Options button and then click *From Right* at the drop-down gallery.
   d. Make sure the Animation Pane displays, click the down-pointing arrow at the right side of the Content Placeholder item in the pane, and then click *Effect Options* at the drop-down list.
   e. At the Fly In dialog box, make sure the Effect tab is selected, click the down-pointing arrow at the right side of the *After animation* option box, and then click the light green color (second from the right).
   f. Click OK to close the dialog box.
3. Save **P-C7-P2-OLLearning.pptx**.

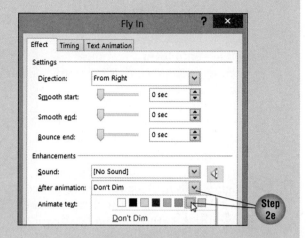

Creating a Motion Path

With options in the *Motion Paths* section of the Add Animation button drop-down gallery, you can specify a motion path. A **motion path** is a path you create for an object that specifies the movements of the object when you run the presentation. Click the Add Animation button in the Advanced Animation group, and a gallery of options for drawing a motion path in a specific direction can be found in the *Motion Paths* section. For example, if you want an item to move left in a line when running the presentation, click the Add Animation button in the Advanced Animation group and then click the *Lines* option in the *Motion Paths* section of the drop-down gallery. Click the Effect Options button in the Animation group and then click *Left* at the drop-down gallery. You can also apply a motion path by clicking the Add Animation button, clicking *More Motion Paths* at the drop-down gallery, and then clicking the desired motion path at the Add Motion Path dialog box.

To draw your own motion path, select the object in the slide you want to move in the slide, click the Add Animation button, and then click the *Custom Path* option in the *Motion Paths* section of the drop-down gallery. Using the mouse, drag in the slide to create the path. When the path is completed, double-click the mouse button.

▼ Quick Steps

Insert a Motion Path
1. Click desired item in slide.
2. Click ANIMATIONS tab.
3. Click Add Animation button.
4. Click desired path in *Motion Paths* section.

Draw a Motion Path
1. Click desired item in slide.
2. Click ANIMATIONS tab.
3. Click Add Animation button.
4. Click *Custom Path* in *Motion Paths* section.
5. Drag in slide to create path.
6. Double-click mouse button.

Project 2d Drawing a Motion Path   Part 4 of 6

1. With **P-C7-P2-OLLearning.pptx** open, make Slide 1 active and then apply a motion path to the clip art image by completing the following steps:
   a. Click the clip art image.
   b. Click the Add Animation button and then click the *More Motion Paths* option at the drop-down gallery.

c. At the Add Motion Path dialog box, scroll down the list box and then click the *Spiral Right* option in the *Lines Curves* section.

d. Click OK to close the dialog box.

e. Notice that a spiral line object displays in the slide and a dimmed copy of the clip art is selected. Hover the mouse pointer over the spiral line until the mouse pointer turns into a right-pointing arrow with a four-headed arrow attached and then drag the spiral line and dimmed copy of the clip art object so they are positioned over the original clip art (see the image above).

f. Click the down-pointing arrow at the right side of the *Start* option box in the Timing group and then click *With Previous* at the drop-down list.

g. Click the up-pointing arrow at the right side of the *Duration* measurement box in the Timing group until *03.00* displays in the measurement box.

h. Click the up-pointing arrow at the right side of the *Delay* measurement box in the Timing group until *01.00* displays in the measurement box.

i. Click outside the clip art to deselect it.

2. Make Slide 5 active and then animate the star on the map by completing the following steps:

a. Click the star object in the slide (located below the heading *North America*).

b. Click the Add Animation button, scroll down the drop-down gallery, and then click the *Custom Path* option in the *Motion Paths* section.

c. Position the mouse pointer (displays as crosshairs) on the star, hold down the left mouse button, drag a path through each of the five locations on the map ending back in the original location, and then double-click the left mouse button.

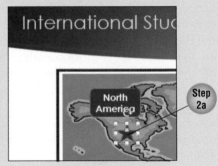

3. Run the presentation and click the mouse to advance slides and elements on slides as needed.

4. Save **P-C7-P2-OLLearning.pptx**.

Applying a Trigger

Use the Trigger button in the Advanced Animation group to make an animation effect occur by clicking an item on the slide during a slide show. A ***trigger*** creates a link between two items. For example, you can apply a trigger to a bulleted item that causes another item such as a picture or chart that provides additional information about the bulleted item to appear. When running the presentation, you hover the mouse over the item containing the trigger until the mouse pointer displays as a hand and then you click the mouse button. This displays the trigger item.

The advantage to applying a trigger to an item is that you can control whether or not the item displays when running the presentation. For example, suppose you created a presentation with product sales information and you wanted to provide additional specific sales data to one group but not another. When presenting to the group with whom you want to share the additional sales data, click the item to trigger the display of the data. When presenting to the other group, do not click the item and the sales data will remain hidden.

To insert a trigger, apply an animation effect to both items, display the Animation Pane, and then click the item to which you want to apply the trigger. Click the Trigger button in the Advanced Animation group, point to *On Click of*, and then click the item you want triggered at the side menu.

▼ Quick Steps

Apply a Trigger
1. Click desired object in slide.
2. Click ANIMATIONS tab.
3. Click Trigger button, point to *On Click of*, and then click trigger object.

Trigger

Project 2e   **Inserting Triggers**   **Part 5 of 6**

1. With **P-C7-P2-OLLearning.pptx** open, make Slide 2 active.
2. Apply animation effects to the text and charts by completing the following steps:
   a. Click anywhere in the bulleted text.
   b. Click the ANIMATIONS tab.
   c. Click the *Split* animation in the Animation group.
   d. Select the pie chart at the left. (To do this, click in the chart and then click within the chart border but not on a specific item in the chart. Make sure the chart is selected and not an individual chart element.)
   e. Click the *Split* animation in the Animation group.
   f. Select the middle pie chart and then click the *Split* animation. (Make sure you select the chart and not a chart element.)
   g. Select the pie chart at the right and then click the *Split* animation. (Make sure you select the chart and not a chart element.)
3. Make sure the Animation Pane displays.
4. Apply a trigger to the first bulleted item that, when clicked, will display the chart at the left by completing the following steps:
   a. Click the *Chart 5* item in the Animation Pane.
   b. Click the Trigger button in the Advanced Animation group, point to *On Click of*, and then click *Content Placeholder 2* at the side menu.
   c. Click the *Chart 6* item in the Animation Pane, click the Trigger button, point to *On Click of*, and then click *Content Placeholder 2* at the side menu.
   d. Click the *Chart 7* item in the Animation Pane, click the Trigger button, point to *On Click of*, and then click *Content Placeholder 2* at the side menu.
5. Close the Animation Pane.
6. Run the presentation by completing the following steps:
   a. Run the presentation from the beginning and when you get to Slide 2, click the mouse button until the first bulleted item displays (the item that begins with *Traditional*).

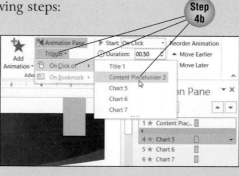

Step 4b

b. Hover your mouse over the
   bulleted text until the pointer
   turns into a hand and then click
   the left mouse button. (This
   displays the first chart.)

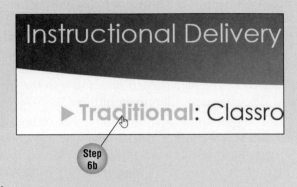

c. Position the mouse pointer
   anywhere in the white
   background of the slide and then
   click the left mouse button to
   display the second bulleted item
   (the item that begins with *Hybrid*).

d. Hover your mouse over the text in the second bulleted item until the pointer turns
   into a hand and then click the left mouse button. (This displays the middle chart.)

e. Position the mouse pointer anywhere in the white background of the slide and then
   click the left mouse button to display the third bulleted item (the item that begins
   with *Internet*).

f. Hover your mouse over the text in the third bulleted item until the pointer turns
   into a hand and then click the left mouse button. (This displays the third chart.)

g. Continue running the remaining slides in the presentation.

7. Save **P-C7-P2-OLLearning.pptx**.

8. Print the presentation as a handout with all nine slides printed horizontally on the
   page.

Setting Up a Slide Show ■■■■■■■■■■ ■■■■■■■■■■■

Set Up
Slide Show

Control how the presentation displays with options at the Set Up Show dialog
box, shown in Figure 7.2. With options at this dialog box, set slide presentation
options, specify how you want slides to advance, and set screen resolution.
Display the Set Up Show dialog box by clicking the SLIDE SHOW tab and then
clicking the Set Up Slide Show button in the Set Up group.

Figure 7.2 Set Up Show Dialog Box

Click this option to set
up the presentation
on a continuous loop.

Click this option to
show the presentation
without narration.

Click this option to show
the presentation without
animation effects.

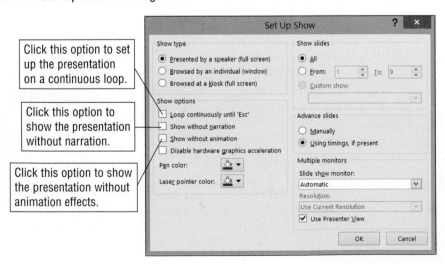

Running a Presentation without Animation

You can choose to run a presentation without the animations. To do this, display the Set Up Show dialog box, click the *Show without animation* check box to insert a check mark, and then click OK. Changes you make to the Set Up Show dialog box are saved with the presentation.

▼ **Quick Steps**

Run a Presentation without Animation
1. Click SLIDE SHOW tab.
2. Click Set Up Slide Show button.
3. Click *Show without animation*.
4. Click OK.

Project 2f   Running a Presentation without Animation   **Part 6 of 6**

1. With **P-C7-P2-OLLearning.pptx** open, specify that you want to run the presentation without animation by completing the following steps:
   a. Click the SLIDE SHOW tab.
   b. Click the Set Up Slide Show button in the Set Up group.
   c. At the Set Up Show dialog box, click the *Show without animation* check box to insert a check mark.
   d. Click OK to close the dialog box.
2. Run the presentation and notice that the animation effects do not play.
3. Specify that you want the presentation to run with animations by completing the following steps:
   a. Click the Set Up Slide Show button on the SLIDE SHOW tab.
   b. At the Set Up Show dialog box, click the *Show without animation* check box to remove the check mark and then click OK.
4. Save and then close **P-C7-P2-OLLearning.pptx**.

Set Up

Show type
- ● Presented by a speaker (full screen)
- ○ Browsed by an individual (window)
- ○ Browsed at a kiosk (full screen)

Show options
- ☐ Loop continuously until 'Esc'
- ☐ Show without narration
- ☑ Show without animation
- ☐ Disable hardware graphics acceleration

Pen color: [color icon] ▾

Step 1c

Project 3   **Prepare a Self-Running Adventure Presentation and Create Custom Shows**   **6 Parts**

You will open a travel tour presentation and then customize it to be an automated presentation set on a continuous loop. You will also hide slides and create and edit custom shows.

Setting Up a Presentation to Loop Continuously

In Chapter 1, you learned how to set automatic times for advancing slides. To advance a slide automatically, insert a check mark in the *After* check box in the Advance Slide section in the Timing group on the TRANSITIONS tab and then insert the desired number of seconds in the measurement box. If you want to be able to advance a slide before the specified amount of time has elapsed, leave the check mark in the *On Mouse Click* option. With this option active, you can let the slide advance after the specified number of seconds or you can click the left mouse button to advance the slide sooner. Remove the check mark from the *On Mouse Click* button if you do not want to advance slides with the mouse.

▼ **Quick Steps**

Loop a Presentation Continuously
1. Click SLIDE SHOW tab.
2. Click Set Up Slide Show button.
3. Click *Loop continuously until 'Esc'*.
4. Click OK.

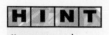 **HINT**
Use an automated presentation to communicate information without a presenter.

In some situations, such as at a trade show or convention, you may want to prepare an automated presentation. An automated presentation is set up on a continuous loop and does not require someone to advance the slides or restart the presentation. To design an automated presentation, display the Set Up Show dialog box and then insert a check mark in the *Loop continuously until 'Esc'* option. With this option active, the presentation will continue running until you press the Esc key.

Project 3a **Preparing a Self-Running Presentation** Part 1 of 6

1. Open **AdvTours.pptx** and then save the presentation with the name **P-C7-P3-AdvTours**.
2. Insert slides by completing the following steps:
   a. Click below the last slide thumbnail in the slide thumbnails pane.
   b. Make sure the HOME tab is selected, click the New Slide button arrow, and then click *Reuse Slides* at the drop-down list.
   c. At the Reuse Slides task pane, click the Browse button and then click *Browse File*.
   d. At the Browse dialog box, navigate to the PC7 folder on your storage medium and then double-click *PeruTour.pptx*.
   e. Click each slide in the Reuse Slides task pane in the order in which they display, beginning with the top slide.
   f. Close the Reuse Slides task pane.
3. Add transition and sound effects and specify a time for automatically advancing slides by completing the following steps:
   a. Click the TRANSITIONS tab.
   b. Click in the *After* check box in the Timing group to insert a check mark.
   c. Click the up-pointing arrow at the right side of the *After* measurement box until *00:05.00* displays.
   d. Click the *On Mouse Click* check box to remove the check mark.
   e. Click the *Fade* slide transition in the Transition to This Slide group.
   f. Click the down-pointing arrow at the right side of the *Sound* option box in the Timing group and then click *Breeze* at the drop-down list.
   g. Click the Apply To All button.

4. Set up the presentation to run continuously by completing the following steps:
   a. Click the SLIDE SHOW tab.
   b. Click the Set Up Slide Show button in the Set Up group.
   c. At the Set Up Show dialog box, click in the *Loop continuously until 'Esc'* check box to insert a check mark. (Make sure *All* is selected in the *Show slides* section and *Using timings, if present* is selected in the *Advance slides* section.)
   d. Click OK to close the dialog box.

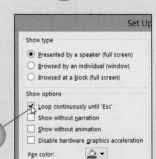

5. Click Slide 1 to select it and then run the presentation. (The slides will advance automatically after five seconds.)
6. After viewing the presentation, press the Esc key on the keyboard.
7. Save **P-C7-P3-AdvTours.pptx**.

Setting Automatic Times for Slides

Applying the same time to all slides is not very practical unless the same amount of text appears on every slide. In most cases, some slides should be left on the screen longer than others. Apply specific times to a slide with buttons on the Recording toolbar. Display this toolbar by clicking the SLIDE SHOW tab and then clicking the Rehearse Timings button in the Set Up group. This displays the first slide in the presentation in Slide Show view with the Recording toolbar located in the upper left corner of the slide. The buttons on the Recording toolbar are identified in Figure 7.3.

When the slide displays on the screen, the timer on the Recording toolbar begins. Click the Next button on the Recording toolbar when the slide has displayed for the appropriate amount of time. If you want to stop the timer, click the Pause button. Click the Resume Recording button to resume the timer. Use the Repeat button on the Recording toolbar if you get off track and want to reset the time for the current slide. Continue through the presentation until the slide show is complete. After the last slide, a message displays showing the total time for the presentation and asks if you want to record the new slide timings. At this message, click Yes to set the times for each slide recorded during the rehearsal. If you do not want to use the rehearsed timings when running a presentation, click the SLIDE SHOW tab and then click in the *Use Timings* check box to remove the check mark.

The times you apply to slides will display below each slide in the Slide Sorter view. The time that displays below the slide will generally be one second more than the time you applied to the slide. So, if you applied 5 seconds to Slide 1, *00.06* will display below the slide in Slide Sorter view.

If you need to edit the slide time for individual slides after you have recorded the times, you can do so with the *After* measurement box in the Advance Slide section in the Timing group on the TRANSITIONS tab. Make the slide active in the slide pane or click the slide in the Slide Sorter view and then click the up- or down-pointing arrows to change the slide duration to the desired time.

▼ Quick Steps

Set Automatic Times for Slides
1. Click SLIDE SHOW tab.
2. Click Rehearse Timings button.
3. Using Recording toolbar, specify time for each slide.
4. Click Yes.

Rehearse Timings

HINT

Enter a specific recording time by selecting the time in the *Slide Time* text box, typing the desired time, and then pressing Enter.

Figure 7.3 Recording Toolbar

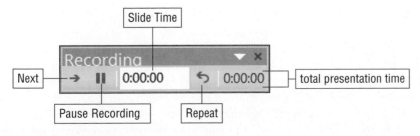

1. With **P-C7-P3-AdvTours.pptx** open, remove the automatic times for slides by completing the following steps:
   a. Click the SLIDE SHOW tab.
   b. Click the Set Up Slide Show button.
   c. At the Set Up Show dialog box, click the *Loop continuously until 'Esc'* check box to remove the check mark.
   d. Click OK to close the dialog box.
2. Set times for the slides to display during a slide show by completing the following steps:
   a. Make Slide 1 active.
   b. With the SLIDE SHOW tab active, click the Rehearse Timings button in the Set Up group.
   c. The first slide displays in Slide Show view and the Recording toolbar displays. Wait until the time displayed for the current slide reaches four seconds and then click Next. (If you miss the time, click the Repeat button to reset the clock back to zero for the current slide.)

   d. Set the times for remaining slides as follows:
      Slide 2 = 5 seconds
      Slide 3 = 6 seconds
      Slide 4 = 5 seconds
      Slide 5 = 6 seconds
      Slide 6 = 3 seconds
      Slide 7 = 6 seconds
      Slide 8 = 7 seconds
      Slide 9 = 7 seconds
   e. After the last slide displays, click Yes at the message asking if you want to record the new slide timings. (The slide times may display with one additional second for each.)
   f. If necessary, click the Normal button in the view area on the Status bar.
3. Click the Set Up Slide Show button to display the Set Up Show dialog box, click the *Loop continuously until 'Esc'* check box to insert a check mark, and then click OK to close the dialog box.
4. Run the presentation. (The slide show will start and run continuously.) Watch the presentation until it has started for the second time and then end the show by pressing the Esc key.
5. Save **P-C7-P3-AdvTours.pptx**.

Recording Narration

▼ **Quick Steps**

Record a Narration
1. Click SLIDE SHOW tab.
2. Click Record Slide Show button.
3. Click Start Recording button.
4. Narrate slides.

You can record narration with your presentation that will play when the presentation is running. To record narration you must have a microphone connected to your computer. To begin the narration, click the Record Slide Show button in the Set Up group on the SLIDE SHOW tab. At the Record Slide Show dialog box, click the Start Recording button. Your presentation begins and the first slide fills the screen. Begin your narration, clicking the mouse to advance each slide. When you have narrated all of the slides in the presentation, your presentation may display in Slide Sorter view.

Clicking the Record Slide Show button arrow displays a drop-down list with three options. Click the *Start Recording from Beginning* option to begin recording your narration with the first slide in the presentation or click the *Start Recording from Current Slide* option if you want to begin recording your narration with the currently active slide. Position your mouse on the third option, *Clear*, and a side menu displays with options for clearing the timing on the current slide or all slides and clearing the narration from the current slide or all slides.

Record Slide Show

When you click the Record Slide Show button on the SLIDE SHOW tab, the Record Slide Show dialog box displays. This dialog box contains two options: *Slide and animation timings* and *Narrations and laser pointer*. You can choose to record just the slide timings, just the narration, or both at the same time. With the *Slide and animation timings* option active (containing a check mark), PowerPoint will keep track of the timing for each slide. When you run the presentation, the slides will remain on the screen the number of seconds recorded. If you want to narrate a presentation but do not want slides timed, remove the check mark from the *Slide and animation timings* check box. With the *Narrations and laser pointer* option active (containing a check mark), you can record your narration and record laser pointer gestures you make with the mouse. To make laser pointer gestures, hold down the Ctrl key, hold down the left mouse button, and then drag in the slide.

The narration in a presentation plays by default when you run the presentation. You can run the presentation without the narration by displaying the Set Up Show dialog box and then clicking the *Show without narration* check box in the *Show options* section to insert a check mark.

Project 3c   Optional: Recording Narration   **Part 3 of 6**

This is an optional project. Before beginning the project, check with your instructor to determine if you have a microphone available for recording.

1. With **P-C7-P3-AdvTours.pptx** open, save the presentation and name it **P-C7-P3-AdvTours-NarrateSlide**.
2. Make Slide 9 active and then narrate the slide by completing the following steps:
   a. Click the SLIDE SHOW tab.
   b. Click the Record Slide Show button arrow in the Set Up group and then click *Start Recording from Current Slide* at the drop-down list.

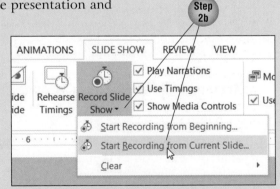

   c. At the Record Slide Show dialog box, make sure both options contain a check mark and then click the Start Recording button.
   d. Speak into the microphone the following text: Call Adventure Tours today to receive an additional ten percent savings when you book a Fiji or Peru tour.
   e. Press the Esc key to end the narration.
3. Make Slide 1 active and then run the presentation. If your computer has speakers, you will hear your narration when Slide 9 displays. After viewing the presentation at least once, press the Esc key to end it.
4. Save and then close **P-C7-P3-AdvTours-NarrateSlide.pptx**.

5. Open **P-C7-P3-AdvTours.pptx** and then save the presentation and name it **P-C7-P3-AdvTours-Narration**.

6. Remove the timings and the continuous loop option by completing the following steps:
   a. Click the SLIDE SHOW tab.
   b. Click the Record Slide Show button arrow, point to *Clear* at the drop-down list, and then click *Clear Timings on All Slides* at the side menu.
   c. Click the Set Up Slide Show button.
   d. At the Set Up Show dialog box, click the *Loop continuously until 'Esc'* check box to remove the check mark.
   e. Click OK to close the dialog box.

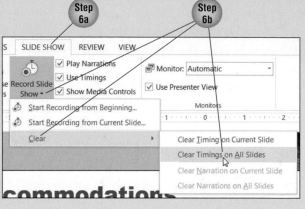

7. Make Slide 1 active and then record narration by completing the following steps:
   a. Click the Record Slide Show button in the Set Up group on the SLIDE SHOW tab.
   b. At the Record Slide Show dialog box, make sure both options contain a check mark and then click the Start Recording button.
   c. When the first slide displays, either read the information or provide your own narrative of the slide and then click the left mouse button. (You can also click the Next button on the Recording toolbar that displays in the upper left corner of the slide.)
   d. Continue narrating each slide (either using some of the information in the slides or creating your own narration). Try recording laser pointer gestures by holding down the Ctrl key, holding down the left mouse button, and then dragging in the slide.
   e. After you narrate the last slide (about accommodations for the Peru tour), the presentation may display in Slide Sorter view.

8. Make Slide 1 active and then run the presentation. If your computer has speakers, you will hear your narration as the presentation runs.

9. Run the presentation without narration by completing the following steps:
   a. Click the Set Up Slide Show button in the Set Up group on the SLIDE SHOW tab.
   b. At the Set Up Show dialog box, click the *Show without narration* check box to insert a check mark.
   c. Click OK.
   d. Run the presentation beginning with Slide 1. (The presentation will run automatically with the timing established when you were recording your narration but without the narration.)

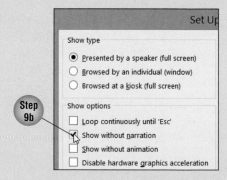

10. Save and then close **P-C7-P3-AdvTours-Narration.pptx**.

▼ Quick Steps

Hide a Slide
1. Make slide active.
2. Click SLIDE SHOW tab.
3. Click Hide Slide button.

Hiding Slides

A presentation you create may be presented to a number of different groups or departments. In some situations you may want to hide specific slides in a presentation depending on the audience. To hide a slide in a presentation, make the desired slide active, click the SLIDE SHOW tab, and then click the Hide Slide button in the Set

Up group. When a slide is hidden, a slash displays over the slide number in the slide thumbnails pane. and the slide in the slide thumbnails pane displays in a dimmed manner. The slide is visible in the slide thumbnails pane in Normal view and also in the Slide Sorter view. To remove the hidden icon and redisplay the slide when running a presentation, click the slide miniature in the slide thumbnails pane, click the SLIDE SHOW tab, and then click the Hide Slide button.

Hide Slide

Managing Monitors

If you have two monitors connected to your computer or are running PowerPoint on a laptop with dual-display capabilities, you can determine on which monitor to run the presentation with the *Monitor* option in the Monitors group on the SLIDE SHOW tab. By default, PowerPoint automatically chooses a monitor to display the slide show. Change the desired monitor for viewing the presentation by clicking the *Monitor* option box arrow and then clicking the monitor at the drop-down list.

Using Presenter View

Insert a check mark in the *Use Presenter View* check box in the Monitors group on the SLIDE SHOW tab if you are running PowerPoint on a computer with two monitors or on a laptop with dual-display capabilities. With this option active, you display your presentation in full-screen view on one monitor and display your presentation in a special speaker view on the other, similar to what is shown in Figure 7.4. If you have two monitors or a laptop with dual-display capabilities, try exploring Presenter View on your own using the information in the figure.

Figure 7.4 Presenter View

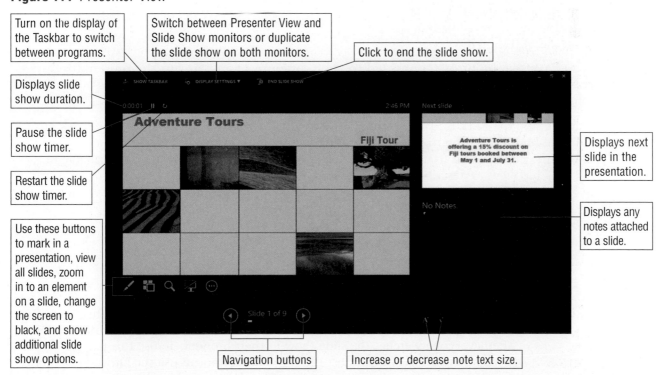

1. Open **P-C7-P3-AdvTours.pptx**.
2. Remove the continuous loop option and remove timings by completing the following steps:
   a. Click the SLIDE SHOW tab.
   b. Click the Set Up Slide Show button.
   c. At the Set Up Show dialog box, click the *Loop continuously until 'Esc'* check box to remove the check mark.
   d. Click OK to close the dialog box.
   e. Click the TRANSITIONS tab.
   f. Click the down-pointing arrow at the right side of the *After* measurement box until *00:00* displays in the box.
   g. Click the *After* check box to remove the check mark.
   h. Click the *On Mouse Click* option to insert a check mark.
   i. Click the Apply To All button.
3. Hide Slide 2 by completing the following steps:
   a. Click the Slide 2 thumbnail in the slide thumbnails pane.
   b. Click the SLIDE SHOW tab and then click the Hide Slide button in the Set Up group.
4. Run the presentation and notice that Slide 2 does not display (since it is hidden).
5. Unhide Slide 2 by clicking the Slide 2 thumbnail in the slide thumbnails pane and then clicking the Hide Slide button in the Set Up group on the SLIDE SHOW tab.

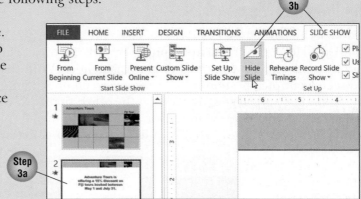

If you have two monitors connected to your computer, you can run the presentation in Presenter View. Complete these optional steps only if you have two monitors available with your computer.

6. Make sure the SLIDE SHOW tab is active and then click the *Use Presenter View* check box in the Monitors group to insert a check mark.
7. Run the presentation from Slide 1 and experiment with some of the options available in Presenter View, as described in Figure 7.4.
8. Make sure the SLIDE SHOW tab is active and then click the *Show Presenter View* check box to remove the check mark.
9. Save **P-C7-P3-AdvTours.pptx**.

Presenting a Presentation Online

With the Present Online feature, you can share a slide show with others over the Internet by sending a link to the people you want to view the presentation and then everyone watches the slide show in their browser. To use this feature, you need a network service to host the slide show. You can use the Office Presentation Service, which is available to anyone with a Windows Live ID, such as your

SkyDrive, and Microsoft Office 2013. You can view an online presentation in Internet Explorer, Firefox, and Safari.

To present a presentation online, click the Present Online button in the Start Slide Show group on the SLIDE SHOW tab. At the Present Online window that displays, click the CONNECT button, and, if necessary, enter your Windows Live ID user name and password. When PowerPoint has connected to your account and prepared your presentation, the Present Online window will display with a unique link PowerPoint created for your presentation. Click the Copy Link hyperlink in the Present Online window to copy the unique link, and then paste the link into an email you are sending to the people who will be viewing your presentation. If you have an Outlook account, you can also click the Send in Email hyperlink to open Outlook and paste the link in a message window.

After everyone has opened the presentation link in a web browser, click the START PRESENTATION button in the Present Online window. People viewing your presentation do not need to have PowerPoint installed on their computers to view the presentation since the presentation will display through their web browsers. When the slide show has ended, click the End Online Presentation button on the PRESENT ONLINE tab. At the message that displays asking if you want to end the online presentation, click the End Online Presentation button. The PRESENT ONLINE tab provides options for running the slide show, managing monitors, sharing the presentation through OneNote, and displaying the unique link to send to more people. You can also access the Present Online window by clicking the FILE tab, clicking the *Share* option, clicking *Present Online*, and then clicking the Present Online button.

You can enable the viewers of your presentation to download the presentation and view the slides on their own without watching it live with you. To do this, click the *Enable remote viewers to download the presentation* check box at the Present Online window before your click the CONNECT button.

▼ **Quick Steps**

Present Online
1. Click the SLIDE SHOW tab.
2. Click the Present Online button.
3. Click the CONNECT button.
4. If necessary, enter Windows Live ID user name and password.
5. Click Copy Link hyperlink.
6. Open email.
7. Paste link into email and send email.
8. Click START PRESENTATION button.

Present Online

Project 3e | **Optional: Presenting Online** | **Part 5 of 6**

To complete this project, you will need a Windows Live ID account. Depending on your system configuration and what services are available, these steps will vary.

1. With **P-C7-P3-AdvTours.pttx** open, click the SLIDE SHOW tab and then click the Present Online button in the Start Slide Show group.
2. At the Present Online window that displays, click the CONNECT button.
3. Type your user name and password into the Windows Security dialog box.
4. At the Present Online window with the unique link selected, click the Copy Link hyperlink.
5. Send the link to colleagues by opening the desired email account, pasting the link into a new message window, and then sending the email to the viewers. Or, if you are using Microsoft Outlook, click the Send in Email hyperlink and Microsoft Outlook opens in a new message window with the link inserted in the message. In Outlook, send the link to people you want to view the presentation.
6. When everyone has received the link, click the START PRESENTATION button at the Present Online window.
7. Run the presentation.
8. When the slide show has ended, press the Esc key and then click the End Online Presentation button on the PRESENT ONLINE tab.
9. At the message that displays telling you that all remote viewers will be disconnected if you continue, click the End Online Presentation button.

Create a Custom Show
1. Click SLIDE SHOW tab.
2. Click Custom Slide Show button.
3. Click *Custom Shows*.
4. Click New button.
5. Make desired changes at Define Custom Show dialog box.
6. Click OK.

Run a Custom Show
1. Click SLIDE SHOW tab.
2. Click Custom Slide Show button.
3. Click desired custom show.

Edit a Custom Show
1. Click SLIDE SHOW tab.
2. Click Custom Slide Show button.
3. Click *Custom Shows*.
4. Click desired custom show.
5. Click Edit button.
6. Make desired changes at Define Custom Show dialog box.
7. Click OK.

Print a Custom Show
1. Display Print backstage area.
2. Click first gallery in *Settings* category.
3. Click desired custom show at drop-down list.
4. Click Print button.

Custom
Slide Show

H I N T

Create custom shows to customize a presentation for a variety of audiences.

Creating a Custom Show ■■■■■■■■■■■■■■■■■■■■■■■■

A *custom slide show* is a presentation within a presentation. Creating a custom slide show might be useful in situations where you want to show only a select number of slides to a particular audience. To create a custom show, click the SLIDE SHOW tab, click the Custom Slide Show button in the Start Slide Show group, and then click *Custom Shows* at the drop-down list. At the Custom Shows dialog box, click the New button and the Define Custom Show dialog box displays, similar to what you see in Figure 7.5.

At the Define Custom Show dialog box, type a name for the custom presentation in the *Slide show name* text box. To insert a slide in the custom show, click the check box for the desired slide in the *Slides in presentation* list box to insert a check mark and then click the Add button. This inserts the slide in the *Slides in custom show* list box. Continue in this manner until all desired slides have been added to the custom show. You can also insert check marks in all the desired slide check boxes first and then click the Add button to add all the slides in the *Slides in custom show* list box at once. If you want to change the order of the slides in the *Slides in custom show* list box, click one of the arrow keys to move the selected slide up or down in the list box. When the desired slides have been inserted in the *Slides in custom show* list box and are arranged in the desired order, click OK. You can create more than one custom show in a presentation.

Running a Custom Show

To run a custom show within a presentation, click the Custom Slide Show button on the SLIDE SHOW tab and then click the desired custom show at the drop-down list. You can also choose a custom show by displaying the Set Up Show dialog box and then clicking the *Custom show* option. If the presentation contains more than one custom show, click the down-pointing arrow at the right of the *Custom show* option box and then click the show name at the drop-down list.

Figure 7.5 Define Custom Show Dialog Box

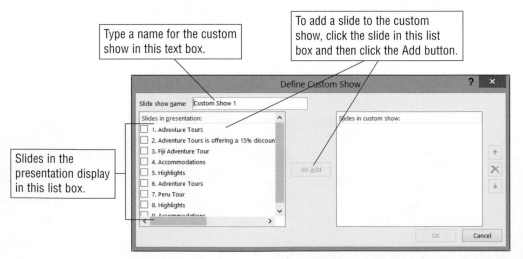

Editing a Custom Show

A custom show is saved with the presentation and can be edited. To edit a custom show, open the presentation, click the Custom Slide Show button on the SLIDE SHOW tab, and then click *Custom Shows* at the drop-down list. At the Custom Shows dialog box, click the custom show name you want to edit and then click the Edit button. At the Define Custom Show dialog box, make the desired changes to the custom show, such as adding or removing slides or changing the order of slides. When all changes have been made, click the OK button.

Printing a Custom Show

Print a custom show with options in the *Settings* category of the Print backstage area. To do this, click the FILE tab and then click the *Print* option to display the Print backstage area. Click the first gallery in the Settings category and then click the desired custom show in the *Custom Shows* section.

Project 3f   Creating, Editing, and Running Custom Shows   Part 6 of 6

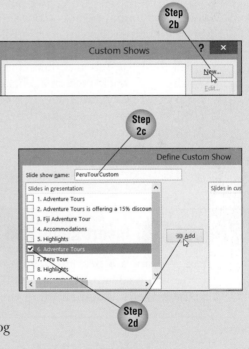

1. With **P-C7-P3-AdvTours.pptx** open, save the presentation and name it **P-C7-P3-AdvTours-Custom**.
2. Create two custom shows by completing the following steps:
   a. Click the SLIDE SHOW tab, click the Custom Slide Show button, and then click *Custom Shows* at the drop-down list.
   b. At the Custom Shows dialog box, click the New button.
   c. At the Define Custom Show dialog box, select the text in the *Slide show name* text box and then type **PeruTourCustom**.
   d. Click the Slide 6 check box in the *Slides in presentation* list box to insert a check mark and then click the Add button. (This adds the slide to the *Slides in custom show* list box.)
   e. Click the check boxes for Slides 7, 8, and 9 in the list box and then click the Add button.
   f. Click OK to close the Define Custom Show dialog box.
   g. At the Custom Shows dialog box, click the New button.
   h. At the Define Custom Show dialog box, select the text in the *Slide show name* text box and then type **FijiTourCustom**.
   i. Add Slides 1 through 5 to the *Slides in custom show* list box.
   j. Click OK to close the dialog box.
   k. Click the Close button to close the Custom Shows dialog box.
3. Run the *PeruTourCustom* custom show by completing the following steps:
   a. Click the Custom Slide Show button on the SLIDE SHOW tab and then click *PeruTourCustom* at the drop-down list.

b. Click the left mouse button to advance slides.
   c. Click the Custom Slide Show button, click *FijiTourCustom* at the drop-down list, and then view the presentation. (Click the left mouse button to advance the slides.)
4. Edit the FijiTourCustom custom slide show by completing the following steps:
   a. Click the Custom Slide Show button on the SLIDE SHOW tab and then click *Custom Shows* at the drop-down list.
   b. At the Custom Shows dialog box, click *FijiTourCustom* in the *Custom shows* list box and then click the Edit button.
   c. At the Define Custom Show dialog box, click Slide 2 in the *Slides in custom show* list box and then click the Down button at the right side of the list box three times. (This moves the slide to the bottom of the list.)
   d. Click OK to close the dialog box.
   e. Click the Close button to close the Custom Shows dialog box.

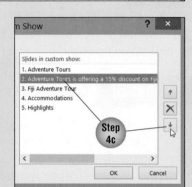

5. Run the FijiTourCustom custom show.
6. Print the FijiTourCustom custom show by completing the following steps:
   a. Click the FILE tab and then click the *Print* option.
   b. At the Print backstage area, click the first gallery in the *Settings* category and then click *FijiTourCustom* in the *Custom Shows* section.
   c. Click the second gallery in the *Settings* category and then click *6 Slides Horizontal* at the drop-down list.
   d. Click the Print button.
7. Save and then close **P-C7-P3-AdvTours-Custom.pptx**.

Project 4 Insert Audio and Video Files in a Presentation   4 Parts

You will open a presentation and then insert an audio file, video file, and clip art image with motion. You will also customize the audio and video files to play automatically when running the presentation.

Inserting Audio and Video Files ■■■■■■■■■■■■■■■

Adding audio and/or video files to a presentation will turn a slide show into a true multimedia experience for your audience. Including a variety of elements in a presentation will stimulate interest in your presentation and keep the audience motivated.

▼ **Quick Steps**

Insert an Audio File
1. Click INSERT tab.
2. Click Audio button.
3. Click *Audio on My PC*.
4. Double-click desired audio file.

Inserting an Audio File

To add an audio file to your presentation, click the INSERT tab, click the Audio button in the Media group, and then click *Audio on My PC* at the drop-down list. At the Insert Audio dialog box, navigate to the desired folder and then double-click the audio file.

You can search for and download audio files from Office.com. To do this, click the Audio button and then click *Online Audio* at the drop-down list. At the Insert Audio window, type a search word or topic and then press Enter. Double-click the desired audio to insert it in the slide. If you have an audio recording device attached to your computer, you can record audio for the presentation by clicking the Audio button and then clicking Record Audio at the drop-down list. At the Record Sound dialog box, name your audio, click the Record button, and then record your audio.

Audio

When you insert an audio file in a presentation, the AUDIO TOOLS FORMAT tab and the AUDIO TOOLS PLAYBACK tab display. Click the AUDIO TOOLS FORMAT tab and options similar to options on the PICTURE TOOLS FORMAT tab display. Click the AUDIO TOOLS PLAYBACK tab and options display for previewing the audio file, inserting a bookmark at a specific time in the audio file, specifying fade in and fade out times, and specifying how you want the audio file to play.

| Project 4a | Inserting an Audio File | Part 1 of 4 |

1. Open **EcoTours.pptx** and then save the presentation with Save As and name it **P-C7-P4-EcoTours**.
2. Insert an audio file that plays music at the end of the presentation by completing the following steps:
   a. Make Slide 8 active and then click the INSERT tab.
   b. Click the Audio button in the Media group, and then click *Audio on My PC* at the drop-down list.
   c. At the Insert Audio dialog box, navigate to the PC7 folder on your storage medium and then double-click *AudioFile-01.mid*.

   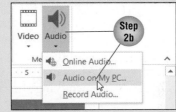

   d. With the AUDIO TOOLS PLAYBACK tab active, click the down-pointing arrow at the right side of the *Start* option box in the Audio Options group and then click *Automatically* at the drop-down list.
   e. Click the *Loop until Stopped* check box in the Audio Options group to insert a check mark.
   f. Click the *Hide During Show* check box to insert a check mark.

   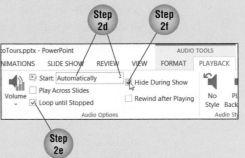

3. Click the Start from Beginning button on the Quick Access toolbar to run the presentation starting with Slide 1. When the last slide displays, listen to the audio file and then press the Esc key to return to the Normal view.
4. Save **P-C7-P4-EcoTours.pptx**.

Inserting a Video File

Inserting a video file in a presentation is a similar process to inserting an audio file. Click the Video button in the Media group on the INSERT tab and then click *Video on My PC* at the drop-down list to display the Insert Video dialog box. At this dialog box, navigate to the folder containing the video file and then double-click the file.

Quick Steps

Insert a Video File
1. Click INSERT tab.
2. Click Video button.
3. Click *Video on My PC*.
4. Double-click desired video file.

Video

You can also click the Video button and then click *Online Video* to display the Insert Video window. At this window, search for videos online using the *Bing Video Search* option, search for a video in your SkyDrive, or paste an embedded code into the *From a Video Embed Code* option to insert a video from a website. To embed code from a video you find online, locate and copy the embedded code of the desired video, paste the embedded code in the *From a Video Embed Code* section of the Insert Video window, and then click the Insert button. Another way to insert a video in a presentation is to click the Insert Video button in the content placeholder on a slide. This displays the Insert Video window with the additional option to browse for a file on your storage medium.

When you insert a video file in a presentation, the VIDEO TOOLS FORMAT tab and the VIDEO TOOLS PLAYBACK tab display. Click the VIDEO TOOLS FORMAT tab and options display for adjusting the video file color and frame, applying video styles, and arranging and sizing the video file. Click the VIDEO TOOLS PLAYBACK tab and options display that are similar to the options on the AUDIO TOOLS PLAYBACK tab. You can also apply formatting to a video with options in the Format Video task pane.

Optimizing and Compressing Audio and Video Files

If you insert a video in a presentation with an older file format, the Info backstage area may display an Optimize Compatibility button. Optimize compatibility of a video file to increase the likelihood that your video file will play on multiple devices.

Compress Media

If you insert an audio and/or video file in a presentation, consider compressing the file(s) to improve playback performance and save disk space. If a presentation contains audio and/or video files, the Info backstage area contains the Compress Media button. Click this button and a drop-down list displays with options for specifying the compressed quality of the video. Click the *Presentation Quality* option to save space and maintain the quality of the audio and/or video files. Click the *Internet Quality* option and the compressed video or audio files will be comparable to audio or video files streamed over the Internet. Choose the last option, *Low Quality*, to compress the audio or video files when space is limited such as when sending the presentation as an email attachment.

Showing and Hiding Media Controls

When a slide with an audio or video file displays during a slide show, media controls appear along the bottom of the audio icon or video window. Use these media controls to play the audio or video file, move to a specific location in the file, or change the audio level. The media controls display when you move the mouse pointer over the audio icon or video window. You can turn off the display of media controls by clicking the SLIDE SHOW tab and then clicking the *Show Media Controls* check box in the Set Up group to remove the check mark.

| **Project 4b** | **Inserting a Video File in a Presentation** | **Part 2 of 4** |

1. With **P-C7-P4-EcoTours.pptx** open, make Slide 8 active.
2. You will insert a video file in the slide that contains audio, so delete the audio file you inserted in Project 4a by clicking the audio file icon that displays in the middle of Slide 8 and then pressing the Delete key.

3. Insert a video file by completing the following steps:
   a. Click the INSERT tab
   b. Click the Video button in the Media group and then click *Video on My PC* at the drop-down list.
   c. At the Insert Video dialog box, navigate to the PC7 folder on your storage medium and then double-click the file named **Wildlife.wmv**.
   d. Click the Play button in the Preview group (on the left side of the VIDEO TOOLS FORMAT tab) to preview the video file. (The video plays for approximately 30 seconds.)
4. Format the video by completing the following steps:
   a. Make sure the video image is selected on the slide and the VIDEO TOOLS FORMAT tab is selected.
   b. Click the *Beveled Frame, Gradient* thumbnail in the Video Styles group (fourth option).
   c. Click the Video Shape button in the Video Styles group and then click *Rounded Rectangle* at the drop-down gallery (second option in the *Rectangles* section).
   d. Click the Poster Frame button in the Adjust group and then click *Image from File* at the drop-down list.
   e. At the Insert Pictures window, click the Browse button to the right of the *From a file* option, navigate to the PC7 folder on your storage medium, and then double-click **Olympics.jpg**.

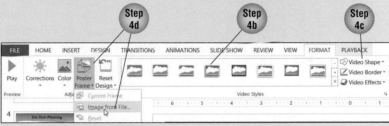

   f. Click the Corrections button in the Adjust group and then click *Brightness: 0% (Normal) Contrast: +20%* at the drop-down gallery (third column, fourth row).
   g. Click the Rotate button in the Arrange group and then click *Flip Horizontal* at the drop-down list.
   h. Click the Size group dialog box launcher to display the Format Video task pane.
   i. With the Size & Properties icon selected, make sure the *SIZE* options display.
   j. Select the current measurement in the *Height* measurement box and then type 4.9.
   k. Click *POSITION* to display the options.
   l. Select the current measurement in the *Horizontal position* measurement box and then type 2.3.
   m. Select the current measurement in the *Vertical position* measurement box and then type 1.8.
   n. Close the Format Video task pane.
   o. Click the VIDEO TOOLS PLAYBACK tab.
   p. Click the Volume button in the Video Options group and then click *Low* at the drop-down list.
   q. Click the *Loop until Stopped* check box in the Video Options group to insert a check mark.

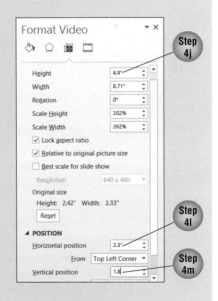

5. Make Slide 1 active and then run the presentation. When the slide containing the video file displays, move the mouse over the video file window and then click the play button located at the bottom left side of the window.

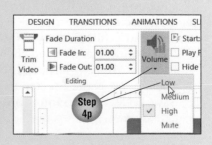

6. After viewing the video a couple of times, press the Esc key twice.
7. Specify that you want the video window to fill the slide, the video to automatically start when the slide displays, the video to play only once, and the display of media controls turned off by completing the following steps:
   a. Make sure Slide 8 is active, click the video file window, and then click the VIDEO TOOLS PLAYBACK tab.

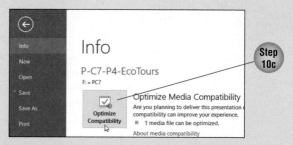

   b. Click the *Play Full Screen* check box in the Video Options group to insert a check mark and click the *Loop until Stopped* check box to remove the check mark.
   c. Click the down-pointing arrow at the right side of the *Start* option box in the Video Options group and then click *Automatically* at the drop-down list.
   d. Click the SLIDE SHOW tab.
   e. Click the *Show Media Controls* check box in the Set Up group to remove the check mark.
8. Make Slide 1 active and then run the presentation. When the slide displays containing the video, the video will automatically begin. When the video is finished playing, press the Esc key to return to Normal view.
9. Print Slide 8.
10. Compress the video file by completing the following steps:
    a. Make Slide 8 active and then click the video file window.
    b. Click the FILE tab.
    c. At the Info backstage area, click the Optimize Compatibility button.
    d. When the optimization is complete, click the Close button in the Optimize Media Compatibility dialog box.
    e. Click the Compress Media button and then click *Internet Quality* at the drop-down list.
    f. At the Compress Media dialog box, wait until the compression is complete (notice the progress bar along the bottom of the dialog box) and then notice the initial size of the video file and the number of megabytes saved by the compression.
    g. Click the Close button to close the dialog box and then click the Back button to return to the presentation.
11. Save **P-C7-P4-EcoTours.pptx**.

Complete these optional steps to insert a video from the Internet into a slide.

12. With Slide 8 active, insert a new slide with the Blank layout.
13. Click the INSERT tab, click the Video button in the Media group, and then click *Online Video* at the drop-down list.
14. Click in the *Bing Video Search* box, type **Antarctica wildlife**, and then press Enter.
15. At the search results window, double-click a video that interests you.
16. Size and position the video window in the slide to better fill the slide.
17. Make Slide 1 active and then run the presentation. When the slide with the video file you inserted displays, click the Play button in the video window. When the video is finished playing, press the Esc key to return to Normal view.
18. Save **P-C7-P4-EcoTours.pptx**.

Trimming a Video File

Use the Trim Video button on the VIDEO TOOLS PLAYBACK tab to trim the beginning and end of your video. This might be helpful in a situation where you want to remove a portion of the video that is not pertinent to the message in your presentation. You are limited to trimming a portion of the beginning of the video or the end.

To trim a video, insert the video file in the slide, click the VIDEO TOOLS PLAYBACK tab, and then click the Trim Video button in the Editing group. At the Trim Video dialog box, specify the time you want the video to start and/or the time you want the video to end. To trim the start of the video, you can insert a specific time in the *Start Time* text box or drag the green start point marker that displays on the slider bar below the video. You can zero in on a very specific starting point by clicking the Next Frame button or the Previous Frame button to move the display of the video a frame at a time. Complete similar steps to trim the ending of the video except use the red end point marker on the slider bar or insert the specific ending time in the *End Time* text box.

▼ **Quick Steps**

Trim a Video File
1. Insert video file.
2. Click VIDEO TOOLS PLAYBACK tab.
3. Click Trim Video button.
4. Specify start time and/or end time.
5. Click OK.

Trim Video

Project 4c Trimming a Video   Part 3 of 4

1. With **P-C7-P4-EcoTour.pptx** open, make Slide 8 active.
2. Trim out the first part of the video that shows the running horses by completing the following steps:
   a. Click the video to select it and then click the VIDEO TOOLS PLAYBACK tab.
   b. Click the Trim Video button in the Editing group.
   c. At the Trim Video dialog box, position the mouse pointer on the green start point marker on the slider bar until the pointer displays as a double-headed arrow pointing left and right. Hold down the left mouse button, drag the start point marker to approximately the *00:04.0* time and then release the mouse button.
   d. Click the Next Frame button until the first image of the birds displays and the horses have completely disappeared off the screen. (Depending on where you dragged the start point marker, you may need to click the Previous Frame button.)
   e. Click the OK button.

3. Click the up-pointing arrow at the right side of the *Fade In* measurement box in the Editing group until *01.00* displays and then click the up-pointing arrow at the right side of the *Fade Out* measurement box until *01.00* displays.
4. Run the presentation. Press the Esc key to return to Normal view.
5. Save **P-C7-P4-EcoTours.pptx**.

Playing an Audio File throughout a Presentation

Play in Background

In Project 4a, you inserted an audio file that played when a specific slide displayed. You can also insert an audio file in a presentation and have the audio play continually through all slides in the presentation. Generally you would add an audio file for the entire presentation when setting up an automated presentation. To specify that you want the audio file to play throughout the presentation, click the Play In Background button in the Audio Styles group on the AUDIO TOOLS PLAYBACK tab. When you click this button, the *Start* option box in the Audio Options group changes to *Automatically*, and check marks are inserted in the *Play Across Slides* check box, *Loop until Stopped* check box, and *Hide During Show* check box. To make the presentation automated, display the Set Up Show dialog box and then insert a check mark in the *Loop continuously until 'Esc'* check box.

Project 4d | **Playing an Audio File throughout a Presentation** | **Part 4 of 4**

1. With **P-C7-P4-EcoTours.pptx** open, make Slide 8 active and then make the following changes:
   a. Select and then delete the video file.
   b. Apply the Title Only slide layout.
   c. Type the title **Let the adventure begin!** and then change the font size to 54 points and the font color to Dark Blue.
   d. Distribute the title placeholder vertically on the slide.
2. Make Slide 1 active and then insert an audio file that plays throughout all files by completing the following steps:
   a. Click the INSERT tab, click the Audio button in the Media group, and then click *Audio on My PC* at the drop-down list.
   b. At the Insert Audio dialog box, navigate to the PC7 folder on your storage medium and then double-click *AudioFile-02.mid*.
   c. With the AUDIO TOOLS PLAYBACK tab active, click the Play in Background button in the Audio Styles group. (Notice that when you click the Play in Background button, the *Start* option box in the Audio Options group changes to *Automatically*, and a check mark is inserted in the *Play Across Slides* check box, *Loop until Stopped* check box, and *Hide During Show* check box.)
   d. Click the Volume button in the Audio Options group and then click *Medium* at the drop-down list.
3. Specify that you want slides to automatically advance after five seconds by completing the following steps:
   a. Click the TRANSITIONS tab.
   b. Click the up-pointing arrow at the right side of the *After* measurement box in the Timing group until *00:05.00* displays.
   c. Click in the *On Mouse Click* check box to remove the check mark.
   d. Click the Apply To All button.
4. Set up the presentation to run continuously by completing the following steps:
   a. Click the SLIDE SHOW tab.
   b. Click the Set Up Slide Show button.
   c. At the Set Up Show dialog box, click in the *Loop continuously until 'Esc'* check box to insert a check mark.
   d. Click OK to close the dialog box.

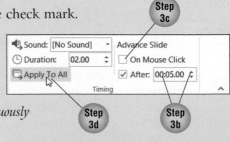

5. Make Slide 1 active and then run the presentation. When the presentation begins for the second time, press the Esc key to return to Normal view.
6. Save and then close **P-C7-P4-EcoTours.pptx**.

Chapter Summary

- Apply animation to an item in a slide with options in the Animation group on the ANIMATIONS tab. Specify animation effects with options from the Effect Options button drop-down gallery.

- Click the Preview button on the ANIMATIONS tab to view the animation effects without running the presentation.

- Remove an animation effect from an item in a slide by clicking the *None* option in the Animation group on the ANIMATIONS tab.

- The Add Animation button in the Advanced Animation group on the ANIMATIONS tab provides four types of animation effects—entrance, exit, emphasis, and motion paths.

- Use the Animation Painter, located in the Advanced Animation group on the ANIMATIONS tab, to apply the same animation to items in more than one location in a slide or slides.

- Use options in the Timing group on the ANIMATIONS tab to determine when an animation starts on a slide, the duration of the animation, the delay between animations, and the order in which animations appear on the slide.

- Use the Animation Pane to customize and modify animation effects. Display the pane by clicking the Animation Pane button in the Advanced Animation group on the ANIMATIONS tab.

- Apply a sound to an animation with the *Sound* option box at the effect options dialog box with the Effect tab selected. The name of the dialog box varies depending on the animation effect selected.

- A build displays important points on a slide one point at a time. You can apply a build that dims the previous bulleted point with the *After animation* option box at the effect options dialog box with the Effect tab selected.

- Specify a path you want an item to follow when it displays on the slide with options in the *Motion Paths* section of the Add Animation button drop-down gallery. To draw a motion path, choose the *Custom path* option at the drop-down gallery.

- Use the Trigger button in the Advanced Animation group to specify that you want to make an animation effect occur during a slide show by clicking an item on the slide.

- Customize a slide show with options in the Set Up Show dialog box.

- To prepare an automated presentation, insert a check mark in the *Loop continuously until 'Esc'* check box at the Set Up Show dialog box.

- To apply specific times to slides, click the Rehearse Timings button in the Set Up group on the SLIDE SHOW tab. Use buttons on the Recording toolbar to set, pause, or repeat times.

- To record narration for a presentation, click the Record Slide Show button in the Set Up group on the SLIDE SHOW tab and then click the Start Recording button at the Record Slide Show dialog box.

- Hide or unhide a slide in a presentation by clicking the Hide Slide button in the Set Up group on the SLIDE SHOW tab.

- Specify on which monitor to run the presentation with the *Monitor* option in the Monitors group on the SLIDE SHOW tab.

- If you are running PowerPoint on a computer with two monitors or on a laptop with dual-display capabilities, you can display your presentation in full-screen view on one monitor and display your presentation in a special speaker view on the other monitor.

- Use the Present Online feature to share a slide show with others over the Internet. Send a link to the people you want to view the presentation and then everyone can watch the slide show in their browsers.

- Create a custom slide show, which is a presentation within a presentation, with options in the Define Custom Show dialog box.

- To run a custom slide show, click the Custom Slide Show button in the Start Slide Show group on the SLIDE SHOW tab and then click the desired custom show at the drop-down list.

- Print a custom show at the Print backstage area by clicking the first gallery in the *Settings* category and then clicking the desired custom show in the *Custom Shows* section.

- Insert an audio file in a slide by clicking the Audio button in the Media group on the INSERT tab, and then clicking *Audio on My PC*. Use options on the AUDIO TOOLS FORMAT tab and the AUDIO TOOLS PLAYBACK tab to format and customize the audio file.

- Insert a video file in a slide by clicking the Video button in the Media group on the INSERT tab and then clicking *Video on My PC*. Use options on the VIDEO TOOLS FORMAT tab and the VIDEO TOOLS PLAYBACK tab to format and customize the video file.

- When a slide show runs, media controls display along the bottom of an audio icon or video window in a slide when you move the mouse over the icon or window. Turn on or off the display of these media controls with the *Show Media Controls* check box in the Set Up group on the SLIDE SHOW tab.

- Compress audio and video files to improve playback performance and save disk space. Compress audio and video files by clicking the FILE tab to display the Info backstage area, clicking the Compress Media button, and then clicking the desired compression.

- Use the Trim Video button on the VIDEO TOOLS PLAYBACK tab to trim the beginning and end of your video.

Commands Review

FEATURE	RIBBON TAB, GROUP/OPTION	BUTTON, OPTION
add animations	ANIMATIONS, Advanced Animation	
Animation Painter	ANIMATIONS, Advanced Animation	
Animation Pane	ANIMATIONS, Advanced Animation	
animations	ANIMATIONS, Animation	
compress audio and video files	FILE, *Info*	

FEATURE	RIBBON TAB, GROUP/OPTION	BUTTON, OPTION
Define Custom Show dialog box	SLIDE SHOW, Start Slide Show	, *Custom Shows, New*
hide/unhide slide	SLIDE SHOW, Set Up	
insert audio file	INSERT, Media	
insert video file	INSERT, Media	
optimize video files	FILE, *Info*	
present online	SLIDE SHOW, Start Slide Show	
Recording toolbar	SLIDE SHOW, Set Up	
Set Up Show dialog box	SLIDE SHOW, Set Up	
Trim Video dialog box	VIDEO TOOLS PLAYBACK, Editing	

Concepts Check   Test Your Knowledge   (SNAP)

Completion: In the space provided at the right, indicate the correct term, symbol, or command.

1. Once you have applied an animation, specify the animation effects with options in this button drop-down gallery.

2. Remove an animation effect from an item in a slide by clicking this option in the Animation group on the ANIMATIONS tab.

3. The Add Animation button in the Advanced Animation group on the ANIMATIONS tab provides four types of animation effects you can apply to an item—entrance, exit, motion paths, and this.

4. Use this feature if you apply an animation or animations to items in a slide and want to apply the same animation in more than one location in a slide or slides.

5. The *Duration* measurement box is located in this group on the ANIMATIONS tab.

6. Display the Animation Pane by clicking the Animation Pane button in this group on the ANIMATIONS tab.

7. This term refers to displaying important points one at a time in a slide when running a presentation.

8. To draw your own motion path in a slide, click the Add Animation button on the ANIMATIONS tab and then click this option in the *Motion Paths* section of the drop-down gallery. _____

9. The Hide Slide button is located on this tab. _____

10. Specify the slides you want included in a custom show with options at this dialog box. _____

11. The Audio and Video buttons are located in this group on the INSERT tab. _____

12. The Volume button for an audio file is located in the Audio Options group on this tab. _____

13. The Trim Video button is located on this tab. _____

Skills Check Assess Your Performance

Assessment

1 APPLY ANIMATION EFFECTS TO A TRAVEL PRESENTATION

1. Open **FCTCruise.pptx** and then save the presentation with Save As and name it **P-C7-A1-FCTCruise**.
2. With Slide 1 active, click the company logo and then apply the Fade entrance animation. *Hint: Click the ANIMATIONS tab*.
3. Click the subtitle *Vacation Cruise* and then apply the Fly In animation.
4. Display the presentation in Slide Master view, click the top slide master layout (Japanese Waves Slide Master) in the slide thumbnails pane, apply the Fade animation to the title style, and then close the Slide Master view.
5. Make Slide 2 active and then complete the following steps:
   a. Click in the bulleted text.
   b. Apply the Wipe entrance animation.
   c. Change the direction to *From Left*. *Hint: Change the direction with the Effect Options button*.
   d. Click in the bulleted text.
   e. Double-click the Animation Painter button.
   f. Make Slide 3 active and then click in the bulleted text.
   g. Make Slide 4 active and then click in the bulleted text.
   h. Make Slide 5 active and then click in the bulleted text.
   i. Click the Animation Painter button to deactivate it.
6. Make Slide 3 active and then insert a trigger by completing the following steps:
   a. Click the banner that displays toward the bottom of the slide and then apply the Wipe entrance animation and change the direction to *From Left*.
   b. Display the Animation Pane.
   c. Click the *Horizontal Scroll* item in the Animation Pane.
   d. Click the Trigger button, point to *On Click of*, and then click *Content Placeholder 2* at the side menu.
   e. Close the Animation Pane.

7. Run the presentation from the beginning and, when the third bulleted item displays in Slide 3, click the bulleted item to trigger the display of the banner.
8. Save and then close **P-C7-A1-FCTCruise.pptx**.

Assessment

2 APPLY ANIMATION EFFECTS TO AN EMPLOYEE ORIENTATION PRESENTATION

1. Open **GEOrientation.pptx** and then save the presentation with Save As and name it **P-C7-A2-GEOrientation**.
2. Make Slide 2 active and then apply the following animations to the SmartArt graphic:
   a. Apply the Blinds entrance animation effect. *Hint: You will need to click the More button at the right of the animations in the Animation group and then click* **More Entrance Effects**.
   b. Change the SmartArt animation so the sequence is *One by One* and change the direction to *Vertical*. *Hint: Do this with the Effect Options button.*
3. Make Slide 3 active and then apply the following animations to the organizational chart:
   a. Apply the Blinds entrance animation effect.
   b. Change the SmartArt animation so the sequence is *Level at Once*.
4. Make Slide 4 active and then apply the following animations to the bulleted text (click on any character in the bulleted text):
   a. Apply the Zoom entrance animation effect.
   b. Display the Animation Pane and then set the text to dim after animation to a dark blue color. *Hint: Click the down-pointing arrow at the right side of the content placeholder in the Animation Pane and then click* **Effect Options**.
5. Apply the following animations to the clip art image in Slide 4:
   a. Apply the Spin emphasis animation effect.
   b. Set the amount of spin for the clip art image to *Two Spins* and change the duration to *01.00*.
   c. Change the *Start* option to *With Previous*.
   d. Reorder the items in the Animation Pane so the clip art displays first when running the presentation.
6. Make Slide 5 active, select the SmartArt graphic, and then apply an entrance animation effect so the elements in the SmartArt graphic fade in one by one.
7. Make Slide 6 active and then apply the following animation effects to the images with the following specifications:
   a. Apply the Fly Out exit animation effect to the *Free Education* gift package, change the direction to *To Right*, and change the duration to *00.25*.
   b. Apply the Shape entrance animation effect to the diploma/books clip art image and change the duration to *01.00*.
   c. Move the *Free Education* gift package so the bulleted text underneath displays, apply the Grow & Turn entrance animation effect to the bulleted text, and then move the gift package back to the original location.
   d. Apply the Fly Out exit animation effect to the *Free Toys and Fitness* gift package, change the direction to *To Left*, and change the duration to *00.25*.
   e. Apply the Shape entrance animation effect to the notebook computer clip art image and change the duration to *01.00*.
   f. Move the *Free Toys and Fitness* gift package so the bulleted text underneath displays, apply the Grow & Turn entrance animation effect to the bulleted text, and then move the gift package back to the original location.

g. Close the Animation Pane.

8. Make Slide 1 active and then run the presentation.

9. Save **P-C7-A2-GEOrientation.pptx**.

10. Display the presentation in Slide Master view, click the top slide master layout in the slide thumbnails pane, apply an entrance animation effect of your choosing to the title, and then close Slide Master view.

11. Make Slide 1 active and then apply the following animation effects:
    a. Click the globe clip art image and then draw a motion path (using the *Custom Path* option) so the image will circle around the slide and return back to the original location.
    b. Apply the *Spiral In* entrance animation effect to the *New Employee Orientation* placeholder.

12. Run the presentation.

13. Print the presentation as a handout with nine slides printed horizontally per page.

14. Save and then close **P-C7-A2-GEOrientation.pptx**.

Assessment

3 APPLY ANIMATION EFFECTS, VIDEO, AND AUDIO TO A JOB SEARCH PRESENTATION

1. Open **JobSearch.pptx** and then save the presentation with Save As and name it **P-C7-A3-JobSearch**.

2. Apply the Wisp design theme and the blue-colored variant (third thumbnail) to the presentation.

3. Add appropriate clip art images to at least two slides.

4. Make Slide 10 active and then insert the video file named **Flight.mov** from the PC7 folder on your storage medium. Make the following changes to the video:
   a. Click the VIDEO TOOLS FORMAT tab and then change the height to 5 inches.
   b. Distribute the video horizontally on the slide.
   c. Click the VIDEO TOOLS PLAYBACK tab and then specify that you want the video to play automatically (do this with the *Start* option box), that you want the video to play full screen, and that you want the video to hide while not playing.
   d. Click the Trim Video button and then trim approximately the first nine seconds from the start of the video. Click OK to close the dialog box.

5. With Slide 10 active, insert the **AudioFile-03.mid** audio file in the slide (located in the PC7 folder on your storage medium) so it plays automatically, loops until stopped, and is hidden when running the presentation.

6. Compress the video file for Internet quality.

7. Run the presentation. After listening to the music for a period of time, end the presentation.

8. Print only Slide 10.

9. Create a custom show named *Interview* that contains Slides 1, 3, 6, 7, and 9.

10. Run the Interview custom show.

11. Print the Interview custom show as a handout with all slides printed horizontally on one page.

12. Edit the Interview custom show by removing Slide 2.

13. Print the Interview custom show again as a handout with all slides printed horizontally on one page.

14. Save and then close **P-C7-A3-JobSearch.pptx**.

Assessment

4 INSERT AN AUDIO FILE FROM OFFICE.COM

1. Open **JamaicaTour.pptx** and then save the presentation with Save As and name it **P-C7-A4-JamaicaTour**.
2. Click the INSERT tab, click the Audio button arrow, and then click *Online Audio*. (This displays the Insert Audio window.)
3. Type **Jamaica** in the Office.com Clip Art search box and then press Enter. Double-click *Jamaica Bounce (1 or 2)*. (If this audio file is not available, choose another audio file such as *Rainforest music*, *African song*, or a different audio file of your choosing.)
4. Set the audio file to start automatically, play across all slides, and hide when running the presentation.
5. Display the TRANSITIONS tab and specify that each slide should advance automatically after five seconds.
6. Set up the presentation to run on an endless loop. (Do this at the Set Up Show dialog box.)
7. Run the presentation.
8. Print the presentation as a handout with the six slides printed horizontally on the page.
9. Save and then close **P-C7-A4-JamaicaTour.pptx**.

Visual Benchmark Demonstrate Your Proficiency

CREATE AND FORMAT A MEDICAL CENTER PRESENTATION

1. Open **RMCPres.pptx** and then save the presentation with Save As and name it **P-C7-VB-RMCPres**.
2. Create the presentation shown in Figure 7.6 on pages 323–324 with the following specifications:
   a. Find the clip art image for Slide 2 (this is a caduceus symbol) by using the search words *caduceus healthcare*. Size and position the clip art as shown in the figure.
   b. Create the SmartArt in Slide 3 using the *Staggered Process* diagram (located in the *Process* section) and apply the *Colorful Range - Accent Colors 4 to 5* option to the diagram.
   c. Use the information shown in the legend and the data information shown above the bars to create a *Clustered Column* chart as shown in Slide 4. Increase the text size of all elements on the chart to 16 points.
   d. Use the Heart shape (located in the *Basic Shapes* section) to create the hearts in Slide 5. Apply the Subtle Effect - Red, Accent 1 shape style and change the shape outline weight to 4½ pt for all three shapes.
   e. Use the Frame shape (located in the *Basic Shapes* section) to create the shape in Slide 6.
3. Apply the following animation effects to items in slides:
   a. Display the presentation in Slide Master view, click the top slide master layout in the slide thumbnails pane (Medical Health 16x9 Slide Master), apply the Float In animation to the title style, and then close the Slide Master view.
   b. Make Slide 1 active and then apply an animation effect of your choosing to the subtitle.

c. Make Slide 2 active, apply an animation effect of your choosing to the clip art image, and then apply an animation effect to the bulleted text.

d. Make Slide 3 active, apply an animation effect of your choosing to the SmartArt, and then specify a sequence of *One by One*.

e. Make Slide 4 active, apply an animation effect of your choosing to the chart, and then specify a sequence of *By Category*.

f. Make Slide 5 active and then apply the *Shape* entrance animation effect to the heart at the left side of the slide. Using the Add Animation button, apply the *Pulse* emphasis animation effect. Click the same heart and then use the Animation Painter button to apply the entrance and emphasis animation effect to the middle heart and the heart at the right side of the slide.

g. Make Slide 6 active and then insert the **AudioFile-04.mid** audio file to play automatically, loop until stopped, and be hidden when running the presentation.

4. Run the presentation.

5. Print the presentation as a handout with six slides printed horizontally per page.

6. Save and then close **P-C7-VB-RMCPres.pptx**.

Case Study   Apply Your Skills

Part 1

You are a trainer in the Training Department at Summit Services. You are responsible for coordinating and conducting software training in the company. Your company hires contract employees and some of those employees work at home and need to have a computer available. You will be conducting a short training for contract employees on how to purchase a personal computer. Open the Word document named **PCBuyGuide.docx** and then use the information in the document to prepare your presentation. Make sure you keep the slides uncluttered and easy to read. Consider inserting clip art or other images in some of the slides. Insert custom animation effects to each slide in the presentation. Run the presentation and then make any necessary changes to the animation effects. Save the presentation and name it **P-C7-CS-PCBuyGuide**. Print the presentation as a handout.

Part 2

Some training sessions on purchasing a personal computer are only scheduled for 20 minutes. For these training sessions, you want to cover only the information about selecting computer hardware components. With the **P-C7-CS-PCBuyGuide.pptx** presentation open, create a custom show (you determine the name) that contains only the slides pertaining to selecting hardware components. Run the custom show and then print the custom show. Save **P-C7-CS-PCBuyGuide.pptx**.

Part 3

You would like to insert an audio file that plays at the end of the presentation and decide to find free audio files on the Internet. Log on to the Internet and then use a search engine to search for "free audio files for PowerPoint" or "free audio clips for PowerPoint." When you find a site, make sure that you can download and use the audio file without violating copyright laws. Download an audio file and then insert it in the last slide in your presentation. Set up the audio file to play after all of the elements display on the slide. Save and then close **P-C7-CS-PCBuyGuide.pptx**.

Figure 7.6 Visual Benchmark

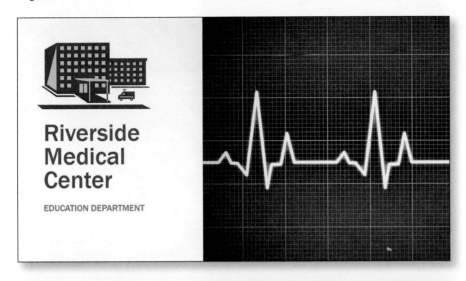

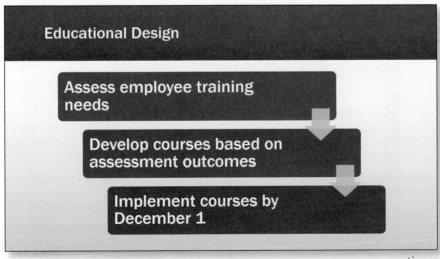

continues

Figure 7.6 Visual Benchmark—*continued*

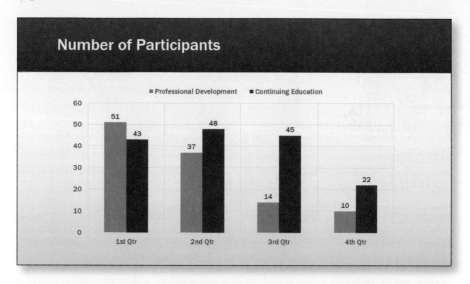

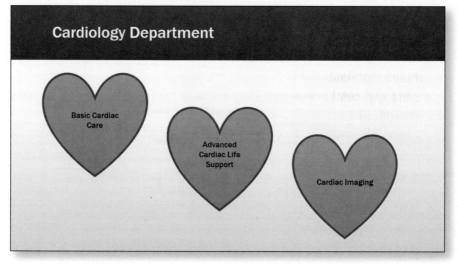

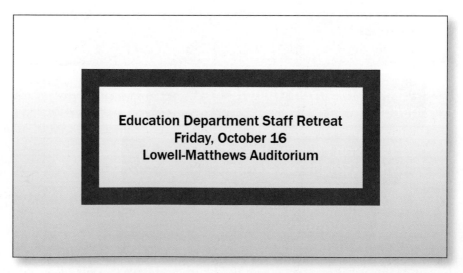

MICROSOFT® POWERPOINT®

Integrating, Sharing, and Protecting Presentations

PERFORMANCE OBJECTIVES

Upon successful completion of Chapter 8, you will be able to:

- Import a Word outline into a presentation
- Copy and paste data between programs and use the Clipboard
- Share presentations with others
- Export a presentation to Word
- Save a presentation in different file formats
- Embed and link objects
- Download templates
- Compare and combine presentations
- Insert, edit, and delete comments
- Manage presentation properties
- Protect a presentation
- Inspect a presentation and check for accessibility and compatibility issues
- Manage versions of presentations
- Customize PowerPoint options

Tutorials

8.1 Integrating with Word and Excel
8.2 Exporting Presentations
8.3 Saving a Presentation in a Different Format
8.4 Embedding and Linking Objects
8.5 Downloading and Applying a Design Template
8.6 Comparing and Combining Presentations; Inserting and Deleting Comments
8.7 Managing Presentation Information and Properties
8.8 Customizing PowerPoint Options

Share data between programs in the Microsoft Office suite by importing and exporting data, copying and pasting data, copying and embedding data, or copying and linking data. The method you choose depends on how you use the data and whether the data is static or dynamic. Use options in the Share backstage area to share a presentation online or as an email attachment and use options at the Export backstage area to create a video or handout of a presentation and save a presentation in a variety of file formats. If you use PowerPoint in a collaborative environment, you may want to insert comments in a presentation and then share the presentation with others. Use options in the Info backstage area to manage presentation properties, password protect a presentation, insert a digital signature, inspect a presentation, and manage versions. In this chapter, you will learn how to complete these tasks as well as how to download design templates from Office.com. Model answers for this chapter's projects appear on the following pages.

Note: Before beginning the projects, copy to your storage medium the PC8 subfolder from the PowerPoint folder on the CD that accompanies this textbook and then make PC8 the active folder.

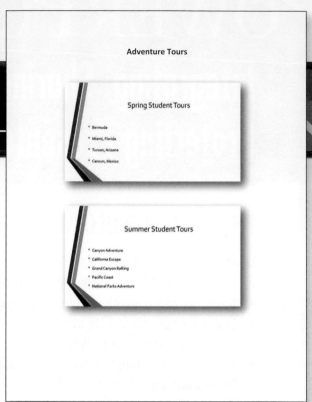

Project 1 Import a Word Outline, Save the Presentation in Different File Formats, and Copy and Paste Objects between Programs

P-C8-P1-ATTopFive.pptx

P-C8-P1-ATTours.docx

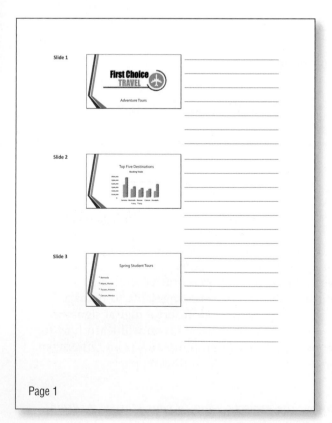

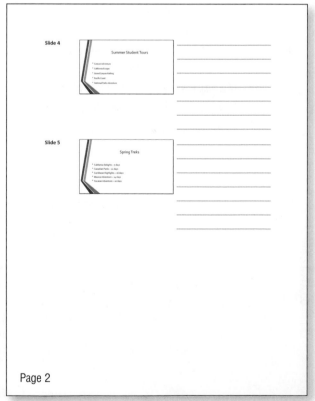

P-C8-P1-ATTopTours.docx

Model Answers

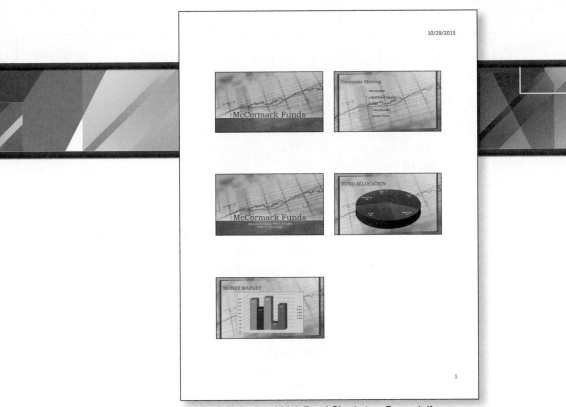

Project 2 Embed and Link Excel Charts to a Presentation

P-C8-P2-FundsPres.pptx

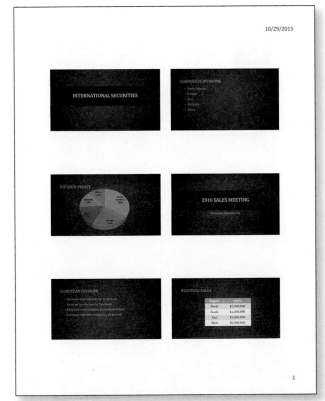
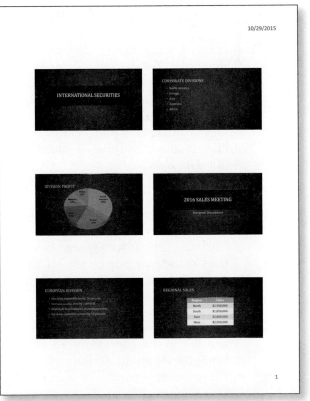

Project 3 Download and Apply a Design Template to a Presentation and Prepare a Presentation for Sharing

P-C8-P3-ISPres.pptx

Project **1** Import a Word Outline, Save the Presentation   **9 Parts**
in Different File Formats, and Copy and Paste
Objects between Programs

You will create a PowerPoint presentation using a Word document, save the presentation in different file formats, and then copy and paste an Excel chart and a Word table into slides in the presentation.

Importing a Word Outline ■■■■■■■■■■■■■■■■■■■■■■■

 Quick Steps

Import a Word Outline
1. Open blank presentation.
2. Click New Slide button arrow.
3. Click *Slides from Outline*.
4. Double-click desired document.

You can import a Word document containing text formatted as an outline with heading styles into a PowerPoint presentation. Text formatted with a Heading 1 style becomes the title of a new slide. Text formatted with a Heading 2 style becomes first-level text, paragraphs formatted with a Heading 3 style become second-level text, and so on. To import a Word outline, open a blank presentation, click the New Slide button arrow in the Slides group on the HOME tab, and then click *Slides from Outline* at the drop-down list. At the Insert Outline dialog box, navigate to the folder containing the Word document and then double-click the document. If text in the Word document does not have heading styles applied, PowerPoint creates an outline based on each paragraph of text in the document.

Project 1a Importing a Word Outline   **Part 1 of 9**

1. At a blank presentation, click the New Slide button arrow in the Slides group on the HOME tab and then click *Slides from Outline* at the drop-down list.
2. At the Insert Outline dialog box, navigate to the PC8 folder on your storage medium and then double-click *ATTopFive.docx*.
3. Click the DESIGN tab and then apply the Parallax design theme.
4. Change the background by completing these steps:
   a. Click the Format Background button in the Customize group on the DESIGN tab.
   b. At the Format Background task pane, click the *Solid fill* option.
   c. Click the Color button and then click the *White, Background 1* option (first column, first row in the *Theme Colors* section).
   d. Click the Apply to All button.
   e. Close the task pane.
5. Delete Slide 1.

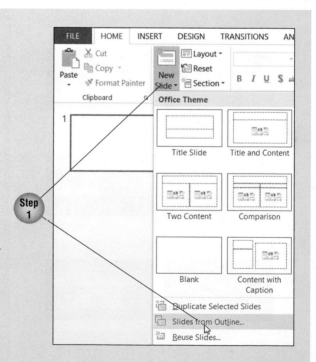

6. Format the new Slide 1 by completing the following steps:
   a. Change the slide layout by clicking the HOME tab, clicking the Layout button in the Slides group, and then clicking *Title Only* at the drop-down list.
   b. Drag the placeholder containing the text *Adventure Tours* toward the bottom of the slide and center it horizontally.
   c. Insert the **FCTLogo.jpg** located in the PC8 folder on your storage medium (do this with the Pictures button on the INSERT tab) and then increase the size of the logo so it fills a good portion of the white area of the slide.
7. Make Slide 2 active and then apply the Title Only layout.
8. Make Slide 3 active and then change the bulleted text line spacing to 2.0.
9. Make Slide 4 active and then change the bulleted text line spacing to 1.5.
10. Save the presentation and name it **P-C8-P1-ATTopFive**.

Copying and Pasting Data ■■■■■■■■■■■■■■■■■■■■■■■

Use the Copy and Paste buttons in the Clipboard group on the HOME tab to copy data such as text or an object from one program and then paste it into another program. For example, in Project 1b, you will copy an Excel chart and then paste it into a PowerPoint slide. You can move and size a copied object, such as a chart, like any other object.

| **Project 1b** | **Copying an Excel Chart to a PowerPoint Slide** | **Part 2 of 9** |

1. With **P-C8-P1-ATTopFive.pptx** open, make Slide 2 active.
2. Open Excel and then open **Top5Tours.xlsx**, located in the PC8 folder on your storage medium.
3. Click the chart to select it. (Make sure you select the chart and not just an element in the chart.)
4. Click the Copy button in the Clipboard group on the HOME tab.
5. Close **Top5Tours.xlsx** and then close Excel.
6. In PowerPoint, with Slide 2 active, click the Paste button in the Clipboard group on the HOME tab.
7. Move the chart so it is centered below the title *Top Five Destinations*.
8. Display Slide 1 in the slide pane and then run the presentation.
9. Print only Slide 2.
10. Save **P-C8-P1-ATTopFive.pptx**.

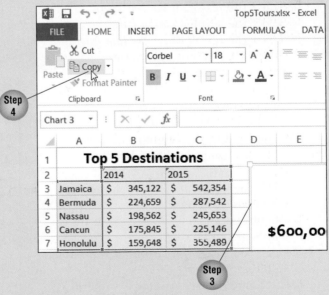

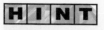
Use the Clipboard task pane to collect and paste multiple items. You can collect up to 24 different items and then paste them in various locations. Turn on the display of the Clipboard task pane by clicking the Clipboard group task pane launcher. The Clipboard task pane displays at the left side of the screen.

Select data or an object you want to copy and then click the Copy button in the Clipboard group. Continue selecting text or items and clicking the Copy button. To insert an item, position the insertion point in the desired location and then click the button in the Clipboard task pane representing the item. If the copied item is text, the first 50 characters display. When all desired items are inserted, click the Clear All button to remove any remaining items from the Clipboard task pane. If you want to paste all items from the Clipboard task pane at once, click the Paste All button.

Project 1c Collecting and Pasting Text Between a Document and a Presentation Part 3 of 9

1. With **P-C8-P1-ATTopFive.pptx** open, make Slide 4 active and then insert a new slide with the Title and Content layout.
2. Click the text *Click to add title* and then type **Spring Treks**.
3. Copy text from Word by completing the following steps:
   a. Open Word and then open **AdvTrek.docx**.
   b. Click the Clipboard group task pane launcher to display the Clipboard task pane.
   c. If any data displays in the Clipboard task pane, click the Clear All button located toward the top of the task pane.
   d. Select the text *Yucatan Adventure – 10 days* (including the paragraph mark following the text—consider turning on the display of nonprinting characters) and then click the Copy button in the Clipboard group.
   e. Select the text *Mexico Adventure – 14 days* and then click the Copy button.
   f. Select the text *Caribbean Highlights – 16 days* and then click the Copy button.
   g. Select the text *California Delights – 7 days* and then click the Copy button.
   h. Select the text *Canyon Adventure – 10 days* and then click the Copy button.
   i. Select the text *Canadian Parks – 12 days* and then click the Copy button.
   j. Select the text *Royal Canadian Adventure – 14 days* and then click the Copy button.
4. Click the PowerPoint button on the Taskbar and then paste items from the Clipboard task pane by completing the following steps:
   a. With Slide 5 active, click the text *Click to add text*.
   b. Click the Clipboard group task pane launcher to display the Clipboard task pane.
   c. Click the *California Delights* item in the Clipboard task pane.
   d. Click the *Canadian Parks* item in the Clipboard task pane.
   e. Click the *Caribbean Highlights* item in the Clipboard task pane.
   f. Click the *Mexico Adventure* item in the Clipboard task pane.
   g. Click the *Yucatan Adventure* item in the Clipboard task pane. (Press the Backspace key twice to remove the bullet below *Yucatan Adventure* and the blank line.)

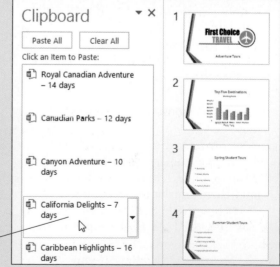

Step 4c

5. Clear the Clipboard task pane by clicking the Clear All button located in the upper right corner of the task pane.
6. Close the Clipboard task pane by clicking the Close button (contains an *X*) located in the upper right corner of the task pane.
7. Make Slide 1 the active slide and then run the presentation.
8. Print the presentation as a handout with all slides printed horizontally on one page. (Make sure the first gallery in the *Settings* category displays as *Print All Slides*.)
9. Save **P-C8-P1-ATTopFive.pptx**.
10. Make Word the active program, close the Clipboard task pane, close **AdvTrek.docx**, and then close Word.

Sharing Presentations ■■■■■■■■■■■■■■■■■■■■■■■■■■

PowerPoint provides a number of options for sharing presentations between programs, sites on the Internet, other computers, and as attachments. Options for sending and sharing presentations are available at the Share backstage area. Display this view by clicking the FILE tab and then clicking the *Share* option.

With the *Invite People* option at the Share backstage area, you can invite people to view your presentation. To use this feature, your PowerPoint presentation must be saved to your SkyDrive or a shared location such as a website or SharePoint library. (Microsoft SharePoint is a collection of products and software that includes a number of components. If your company or organization uses SharePoint, you can save a presentation in a library on your organization's SharePoint site so that you and your colleagues have a central location for accessing presentations.) If you have a PowerPoint presentation open from your SkyDrive folder (or other shared location), the Share backstage area with the *Invite People* option selected will display, as shown in Figure 8.1. If you have a presentation open that is not saved to your SkyDrive folder, the information at the right side of the backstage area will tell you to save your presentation. To do this, click the Save To Cloud button and, at the Save As backstage area, click your SkyDrive and then click the Browse button. At the Save As dialog box, navigate to your SkyDrive folder, and then click the Save button. In a few moments, the Share backstage area redisplays with the options shown in Figure 8.1.

When you click the *Invite People* option at the Share backstage area, options display for typing the names or email addresses of people you want to view and/or edit the presentation. Type more than one name or email address by separating the names or email addresses with a semicolon.

The option box to the right of the *Type names or e-mail addresses* text box contains the default setting *Can edit*. At this setting, the people you invite can edit the presentation. Change this option to *Can view* if you want the people you invite only to view the presentation. When all names or email addresses are entered, click the Share button. An email is sent to the email address(es) you typed and, in a few moments, the name or names display in the backstage area below the *Shared with* heading. Any time you open the presentation in the future and display the Share backstage area, the names you shared the presentation with will display below the *Shared with* heading. If you want to stop sharing the presentation with a person, right-click the person's name below the *Shared with* heading and then click *Remove User* at the shortcut menu.

Figure 8.1 Share Backstage Area with *Invite People* Option Selected

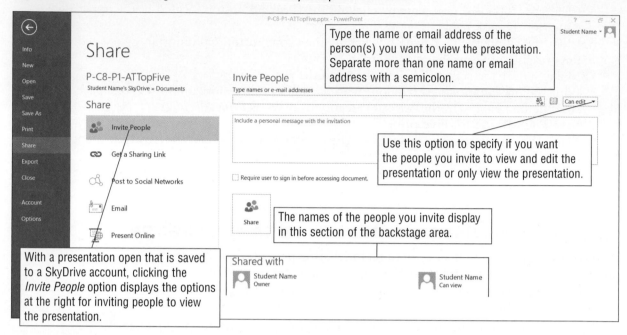

Project 1d | **Optional: Inviting People to View your Presentation** | **Part 4 of 9**

Note: To complete this project, you need to have a SkyDrive account.

1. With **P-C8-P1-ATTopFive.pptx** open, save the presentation to your SkyDrive folder and name it **P-C8-P1-ATTopFive-Shared**.
2. With the **P-C8-P1-ATTopFive-Shared.pptx** presentation open, click the FILE tab and then click the *Share* option.
3. At the Share backstage area, click in the *Type names or e-mail addresses* text box.
4. Type the email address for your instructor and/or the email address of a classmate or friend.
5. Click the down-pointing arrow at the right side of the option box containing the text *Can edit* and then click *Can view* at the drop-down list.
6. Click the Share button.
7. After a few moments, notice the name(s) that display below the *Shared with* heading in the Share backstage area.
8. Check with your instructor, classmate, and/or friend to see if they were able to open the email containing the link to your PowerPoint presentation.
9. Remove the name (or one of the names) that displays below the *Shared with* heading by right-clicking the name and then clicking *Remove User* at the shortcut menu.
10. If you have the **P-C8-P1-ATTopFive.pptx** presentation saved on a removable device, close the **P-C8-P1-ATTopFive-Shared.pptx** presentation saved to your SkyDrive and then reopen the **P-C8-P1-ATTopFive.pptx** presentation from your removable device.

If you open a presentation saved to your SkyDrive, the Share backstage area displays additional options including *Get a Sharing Link* and *Post to Social Networks*. Click *Get a Sharing Link* and options display for creating a link for viewing or for editing. Click the Create Link button that displays to the right of the *View Link* text box and a link displays for viewing the presentation. Click the Create Link button to the right of the *Edit Link* text box and a link displays in the text box for viewing and editing the presentation. If you want to paste a link for viewing your presentation without the ability to edit, select the link that displays in the *View Link* text box and then paste it in an email, instant message, social media site, and so on. If you want to paste a link for viewing and editing, click the Create Link button to the right of the *Edit Link* text box and then copy the link that displays.

Click the *Post to Social Networks* options to connect to and post your presentation to a social network such as Facebook or Twitter. Before being able to post, you must connect to the desired social network(s). If you are not connected, click the *Post to Social Networks* option and then click the <u>Click here to connect social networks</u> hyperlink.

Click the *Email* option at the Share backstage area and options display for sending a copy of the presentation as an attachment to an email, send a link to the presentation, attach a PDF or XPS copy of the open presentation to an email address, and send an email as an Internet fax.

To send the presentation as an attachment, you need to set up an Outlook email account. If you want to create an email that contains a link to the presentation, the presentation must be saved to your SkyDrive or a shared location such as a website or SharePoint library.

Click the Send as PDF button and your presentation is converted to the PDF format and attached to the email. The letters PDF stand for *portable document format*, which is a file format developed by Adobe Systems that captures all of the elements of a presentation as an electronic image. Click the Send as XPS button and your presentation is converted to the XPS format and attached to the email. The XPS format is a Microsoft file format for publishing content in an easily viewable format. The letters XPS stand for *XML paper specification*, and the letters XML stand for *extensible markup language*, which is a set of rules for encoding presentations electronically. Information displays to the right of both buttons providing a brief description of the format.

Click the Send as Internet Fax button to fax the current presentation without using a fax machine. To use this button, you must be signed up with a fax service provider. If you have not previously signed up for a service, you will be prompted to do so.

Click the *Present Online* option at the Share backstage area, to present your presentation through the Office Presentation Service. You learned how to do this in Chapter 7.

Use the *Publish Slides* option at the Share backstage area to save slides in a shared location such as a slide library or a SharePoint site so that other people have access to the presentation and can review or make changes to it.

Note: Before completing this optional project, check with your instructor to determine if you have Outlook set up as your email provider.

1. With **P-C8-P1-ATTopFive.pptx** open, click the FILE tab and then click the *Share* option.
2. At the Share backstage area, click the *Email* option and then click the Send as Attachment button.
3. At the Outlook window, type your instructor's email address in the *To* text box.
4. Click the Send button.

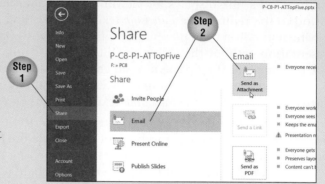

Exporting Presentations ■■■■■■■■■■■■■■■■■■■■■■■■■■■

The Export backstage area contains a number of options for saving and exporting a presentation. Options at the Export backstage area include saving a presentation in the PDF or XPS file format, creating a video of a presentation, packaging a presentation for a disc, creating handouts, and saving a presentation in a different file format.

Saving a Presentation in the PDF or XPS Formats

▼ Quick Steps

Save a Presentation in PDF/XPS Format
1. Open presentation.
2. Click FILE tab.
3. Click *Export* option.
4. Click *Create PDF/XPS Document* option.
5. Click Create PDF/XPS button.
6. At Publish as PDF or XPS dialog box, specify if you want to save in PDF or XPS format.
7. Click Publish button.

As you learned earlier, the portable document format (PDF) captures all of the elements of a presentation as an electronic image and the XPS format is used for publishing content in an easily viewable format. To save a presentation in PDF or XPS format, click the FILE tab, click the *Export* option, make sure the *Create PDF/XPS Document* option is selected, and then click the Create PDF/XPS button. This displays the Publish as PDF or XPS dialog box with the *PDF (*.pdf)* option selected in the *Save as type* option box. If you want to save the presentation in XPS format, click the *Save as type* option box and then click *XPS Document (*.xps)* at the drop-down list. At the Save As dialog box, type a name in the *File name* text box and then click the Publish button.

You can open a PDF file in Adobe Reader, Internet Explorer, Microsoft Word, and Windows Reader. You can open an XPS file in Internet Explorer, Windows Reader, and XPS Viewer. One method for opening a PDF or XPS file is to open File Explorer, navigate to the folder containing the file, right-click on the file, and then point to *Open with*. This displays a side menu with the programs you can choose to open the file.

Creating a Video of a Presentation

▼ Quick Steps

Save a Presentation as a Video
1. Open presentation.
2. Click FILE tab.
3. Click *Export* option.
4. Click *Create a Video* option.
5. Click Create Video button.

Create a video that incorporates all of a presentation's recorded timings and narrations and preserves animations and transitions using the *Create a Video* option. The information at the right side of the Export backstage area describes creating a video and provides a hyperlink to get help on burning a slide show video to a DVD or uploading it to the Web. Click the <u>Get help burning your slide show video to DVD or uploading it to the Web</u> hyperlink and information displays on burning your slide show video to disc and publishing your slide show video to YouTube.

Packaging a Presentation

Use the *Package Presentation for CD* option to copy a presentation and include all of the linked files, embedded items, and fonts. Click the *Package Presentation for CD* option and then click the Package for CD button and the Package for CD dialog box displays. At this dialog box, type a name for the CD and specify the files you want copied. You can copy the presentation to a CD or to a specific folder.

▼ **Quick Steps**

Package a Presentation for CD
1. Open presentation.
2. Click FILE tab.
3. Click *Export* option.
4. Click *Package Presentation for CD* option.
5. Click Package for CD button.
6. Click Copy to CD button or Copy to Folder button.

Project 1f | Saving a Presentation in PDF and XPS Formats, as a Video, and Packaged for a CD | Part 6 of 9

1. With **P-C8-P1-ATTopFive.pptx** open, save the presentation in PDF format by completing the following steps:
   a. Click the FILE tab and then click the *Export* option.
   b. Make sure the *Create PDF/XPS Document* option is selected.
   c. Click the Create PDF/XPS button.

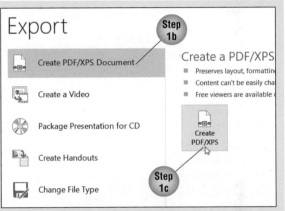

   d. At the Publish as PDF or XPS dialog box, make sure the *Save as type* option is set at *PDF (*.pdf)*, insert a check mark in the *Open file after publishing* check box and then click the Publish button. (In a few moments the presentation displays in PDF format in Adobe Reader.)
   e. Scroll through the presentation in Adobe Reader.
   f. Click the Close button located in the upper right corner of the window to close Adobe Reader.
2. Save the presentation in XPS format by completing the following steps:
   a. Click the FILE tab and then click the *Export* option.
   b. With the *Create PDF/XPS Document* option selected, click the Create PDF/XPS button.

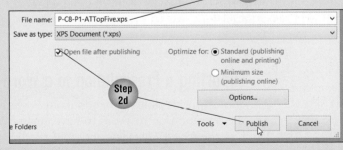

   c. At the Publish as PDF or XPS dialog box, click the *Save as type* option box and then click *XPS Document (*.xps)* at the drop-down list.
   d. Make sure the *Open file after publishing* check box contains a check mark and then click the Publish button. (In a few moments the presentation displays in the XPS Viewer.)
   e. Scroll through the presentation in the XPS Viewer.
   f. Close the XPS viewer by positioning the mouse pointer at the top of the screen (the pointer turns into a hand), dragging down to the bottom of the screen, and then releasing the mouse button.

3. Save **P-C8-P1-ATTopFive.pptx** as a video by completing the following steps:
   a. Click the FILE tab and then click the *Export* option.
   b. Click the *Create a Video* option.
   c. Click the Create Video button.
   d. At the Save As dialog box, click the Save button. (Saving as a video takes a minute or so. The Status bar displays the saving progress.)

Step 3b

Step 3c

Export

Create PDF/XPS Document

Create a Video

Package Presentation for CD

Create Handouts

Change File Type

Create a Video
Save your presentation as a video that you can burn to a disc, upload to the web, or email
- Incorporates all recorded timings, narrations, and laser pointer gestures
- Preserves animations, transitions, and media
- Get help burning your slide show video to DVD or uploading it to the web

Computer & HD Displays
For viewing on a computer monitor, projector, or high definition display (Large — 1280 x

Don't Use Recorded Timings and Narrations
No timings or narrations have been recorded

Seconds spent on each slide: 05.00

Create Video

4. When the video has been saved, play the video by completing the following steps:
   a. Click the File Explorer button on the Taskbar.
   b. Navigate to the PC8 folder on your storage medium and then double-click **P-C8-P1-ATTopFive.mp4**. (This opens the presentation video in a viewing window.)
   c. Watch the presentation video and, when it is finished, close the viewing window by using the mouse and dragging down from the top of the screen to the bottom.
   d. Close File Explorer.
5. With **P-C8-P1-ATTopFive.pptx** open, package the presentation by completing the following steps:
   a. Click the FILE tab and then click the *Export* option.
   b. Click the *Package Presentation for CD* option.
   c. Click the Package for CD button.
   d. At the Package for CD dialog box, select the text in the *Name the CD* text box and type **ATTopFiveforCD**.
   e. Click the Options button, at the Options dialog box make sure the Embedded TrueType fonts option includes a check mark, and then click OK.
   f. Click the Copy to Folder button.
   g. At the Copy to Folder dialog box, click the Browse button.
   h. Navigate to the PC8 folder on your storage medium.
   i. Click the Select button.
   j. At the Copy to Folder dialog box, click OK.
   k. At the message asking if you want to include linked files in the presentation, click the Yes button.
   l. When a window displays with the folder name and files, close the window by clicking the Close button in the upper right corner of the window.
   m. Close the Package for CD dialog box by clicking the Close button.

Copy to Folder

Copy files to a new folder with a name and location you specify.

Folder name: ATTopFiveforCD

Location: F:\PC8\

Browse...

☑ Open folder when complete

OK   Cancel

Step 5j

Exporting a Presentation to a Word Document

You can print slides as handouts in PowerPoint; however, you may prefer to export the presentation to Word to have greater control over the formatting of the handouts. Use the *Create Handouts* option at the Export backstage area to export a PowerPoint presentation to a Word document. Open the presentation, click the FILE tab, click the *Export* option, click the *Create Handouts* option, and then click the Create Handouts button. This displays the Send to Microsoft Word dialog box, shown in Figure 8.3. At this dialog box, select the page layout you want to use in Word and then click OK.

The first four-page layout options will export slides as they appear in PowerPoint with lines to the right or below the slides. The last option will export the text only as an outline. If you select the *Paste link* option, the Word document will be automatically updated whenever changes are made to the PowerPoint presentation.

Figure 8.3 Send to Microsoft Word Dialog Box

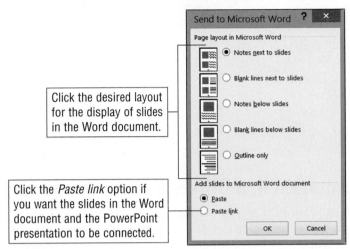

Click the desired layout for the display of slides in the Word document.

Click the *Paste link* option if you want the slides in the Word document and the PowerPoint presentation to be connected.

Project 1g Exporting a Presentation to Word   **Part 7 of 9**

1. Make sure **P-C8-P1-ATTopFive.pptx** is open, click the FILE tab, and then click the *Export* option.
2. At the Export backstage area, click the *Create Handouts* option.
3. Click the Create Handouts button.
4. At the Send to Microsoft Word dialog box, click the *Blank lines next to slides* option and then click OK.
5. Click the Word button on the Taskbar.
6. In Word, select the first column (the column that contains *Slide 1, Slide 2*, and so on) and then turn on bold formatting. (The presentation was inserted in a table in Word.)

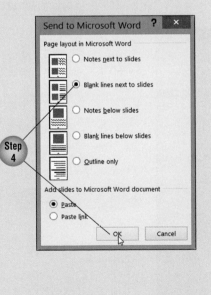

Step 4

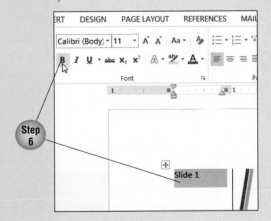

Step 6

Slide 1

7. Select the third column (contains the lines) and then apply the Red font color.
8. Save the document and name it **P-C8-P1-ATTopTours**.
9. Print and then close **P-C8-P1-ATTopTours.docx**.
10. Close Word.
11. In PowerPoint, export **P-C8-P1-ATTopFive.pptx** as an outline by completing the following steps:
    a. Click the FILE tab and then click the *Export* option.
    b. At the Export backstage area, click the *Create Handouts* option.
    c. Click the Create Handouts button.
    d. At the Send to Microsoft Word dialog box, click the *Outline only* option and then click OK.
    e. Click the Word button on the Taskbar.
    f. In Word, scroll through the document and then close Word without saving the document.
12. In PowerPoint, save **P-C8-P1-ATTopFive.pptx**.

Saving a Presentation in a Different Format ■■■■■■■■

When you save a presentation, it is automatically saved as a PowerPoint presentation with the .pptx file extension. If you need to share a presentation with someone who is using a different presentation program or a different version of PowerPoint, you may want to save the presentation in another format. At the Export backstage area, click the *Change File Type* option and the backstage area displays as shown in Figure 8.2.

Figure 8.2 Export Backstage Area with *Change File Type* Option Selected

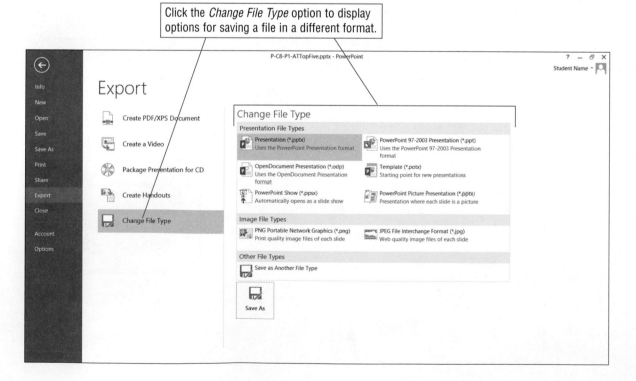

Click the *Change File Type* option to display options for saving a file in a different format.

With options in the *Presentation File Types* section, you can choose to
save a PowerPoint presentation with the default file format (.pptx) or to save
a presentation in a previous version of PowerPoint. Use the *OpenDocument
Presentation (*.odp)* option to save a presentation and make it available to open
in other applications. The OpenDocument format enables files to be exchanged,
retrieved, and edited with any OpenDocument-compliant software. Save a
presentation as a template if you want to use the presentation as a basis for
creating other presentations. (You learned how to do this at the Save As dialog box
in Chapter 6.) If you save a presentation in the PowerPoint Show (*.ppsx) format,
the presentation automatically starts when you open it. This might be useful, for
example, in a situation where you email a presentation to a colleague or client and
you want the presentation to automatically start when opened. When you save
a presentation using the *PowerPoint Picture Presentation* option, the contents of the
presentation are flattened to a single picture per slide. A presentation saved in this
format can be opened and viewed but not edited.

▼ **Quick Steps**

**Save a Presentation
in a Different
Format**
1. Click FILE tab.
2. Click *Export* option.
3. Click *Change File Type*
   option.
4. Click desired format.
5. Click Save As button.

Project 1h	**Saving a Presentation in Different Formats**	**Part 8 of 9**

1. Make sure that **P-C8-P1-ATTopFive.pptx** is open.
2. Save the presentation as a PowerPoint Show by completing the following steps:
   a. Click the FILE tab and then click the *Export* option.
   b. At the Export backstage area, click the *Change File Type* option.
   c. Click the *PowerPoint Show (*.ppsx)* option in the *Presentation File Types* section and then
      click the Save As button.

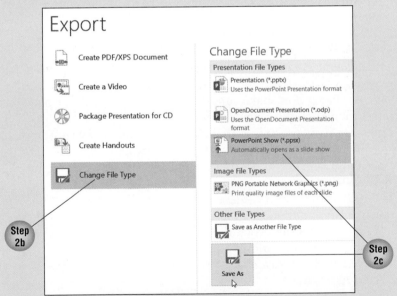

   d. At the Save As dialog box, click the Save button. (This saves the presentation with the
      file extension *.ppsx.*)
3. Close **P-C8-P1-ATTopFive.ppsx**.

4. Open the **P-C8-P1-ATTopFive.ppsx** file in File Explorer by completing the following steps:
   a. Click the File Explorer button (button containing yellow file folders) on the Taskbar.
   b. In File Explorer, double-click the drive representing your storage medium.
   c. Navigate to the PC8 folder on your storage medium and then double-click **P-C8-P1-ATTopFive.ppsx**. (This starts the presentation in Slide Show view.)
   d. Run the presentation.
   e. When the presentation has ended, click the left mouse button.
   f. Close File Explorer by clicking the File Explorer button on the Taskbar and then clicking the Close button located in the upper right corner of the window.
5. Open **P-C8-P1-ATTopFive.pptx** (make sure you open the file with the .pptx file extension) and then save the presentation in a previous version of PowerPoint by completing the following steps:
   a. Click the FILE tab and then click the *Export* option.
   b. Click the *Change File Type* option.
   c. Click *PowerPoint 97-2003 Presentation (*.ppt)* in the *Presentation File Types* section and then click the Save As button.
   d. At the Save As dialog box, type **P-C8-P1-ATTopFive-2003format** in the *File name* text box and then click the Save button.
   e. At the Microsoft PowerPoint Compatibility Checker dialog box, click the Continue button.
   f. At the presentation, notice that the file name at the top of the screen displays followed by the words *[Compatibility Mode]*.
6. Close **P-C8-P1-ATTopFive-2003format.ppt**.
7. Open **P-C8-P1-ATTopFive.pptx** (make sure you open the file with the .pptx file extension) and then save the presentation in OpenDocument Presentation format by completing the following steps:
   a. Click the FILE tab and then click the *Export* option.
   b. Click the *Change File Type* option.
   c. Click *OpenDocument Presentation (*.odp)* in the *Presentation File Types* section and then click the Save As button.
   d. At the Save As dialog box, make sure *P-C8-P1-ATTopFive.odp* displays in the *File name* text box and then click the Save button.
   e. When a message displays stating that the presentation may contain features that are not compatible with the format, click the Yes button.
   f. Run the presentation and notice that formatting remained the same.
8. Close **P-C8-P1-ATTopFive.odp**.
9. Open **P-C8-P1-ATTopFive.pptx** (make sure you open the file with the .pptx file extension) and then save the presentation as a picture presentation by completing the following steps:
   a. Click the FILE tab and then click the *Export* option.
   b. Click the *Change File Type* option.
   c. Click *PowerPoint Picture Presentation (*.pptx)* in the *Presentation File Types* section and then click the Save As button.
   d. At the Save As dialog box, type **P-C8-P1-ATTopFive-Picture** in the *File name* text box and then click the Save button.
   e. At a message telling you that a copy of the presentation has been saved, click OK.
   f. Close **P-C8-P1-ATTopFive.pptx**.
   g. Open **P-C8-P1-ATTopFive-Picture.pptx**.
   h. Click Slide 1 in the slide pane and notice how the entire slide is selected rather than a specific element in the slide. In this format you cannot edit a slide.
10. Close **P-C8-P1-ATTopFive-Picture.pptx**.

Save slides in a presentation as graphic images in PNG or JPEG format with options in the *Image File Types* section of the Export backstage area. Save slides as PNG images if you want print quality, and save slides as JPEG images if you are going to post the slide images to the Internet. To save a slide or all slides as graphic images, click either the *PNG Portable Network Graphics (*.png)* option or the *JPEG File Interchange Format (*.jpg)* option in the *Image File Types* section and then click the Save As button. At the Save As dialog box, type a name for the slide or presentation and then click the Save button. At the message that displays, click the All Slides button if you want every slide in the presentation saved as a graphic image or click the Just This One button if you want only the current slide saved as a graphic image. If you click the All Slides button, a message displays telling you that all slides in the presentation were saved as separate files in a folder. The name of the folder is the name that you type in the *File name* text box in the Save As dialog box.

Project 1i **Saving Slides as Graphic Images**   Part 9 of 9

1. Open **P-C8-P1-ATTopFive.pptx**.
2. Click the FILE tab and then click the *Export* option.
3. At the Export backstage area, click the *Change File Type* option.
4. Click the *PNG Portable Network Graphics (*.png)* option in the *Image File Types* section and then click the Save As button.
5. At the Save As dialog box, make sure **P-C8-P1-ATTopFive.png** displays in the *File name* text box and then click the Save button.
6. At the message that displays, click the All Slides button.
7. At the message telling you that each slide has been saved as a separate file in the P-C8-P1-ATTopFive.png folder, click OK.
8. Open Word.
9. At a blank document, change the font size to 18 points, turn on bold formatting, change the alignment to center, and then type **Adventure Tours**.
10. Press the Enter key twice and then insert one of the slides saved in PNG format by completing the following steps:
    a. Click the INSERT tab and then click the Pictures button in the Illustrations group.
    b. At the Insert Picture dialog box, navigate to the P-C8-P1-ATTopFive folder in the PC8 folder on your storage medium and then double-click **Slide3.PNG**.

11. Format the image in the document by completing the following steps:
    a. Click in the *Shape Height* measurement box in the Size group on the PICTURE TOOLS FORMAT tab, type **2.8**, and then press Enter.
    b. Click the *Drop Shadow Rectangle* option in the Picture Styles group (fourth thumbnail).
12. Press Ctrl + End to move the insertion point to the end of the document, press the Enter key, and then complete steps similar to those in Steps 10 and 11 to insert and format the image *Slide4.PNG* in the document.
13. Save the document and name it **P-C8-P1-ATTours**.
14. Print and then close **P-C8-P1-ATTours.docx**.
15. Close Word.
16. Capture an image of the Open dialog box and insert the image in a PowerPoint slide by completingthe following steps:
    a. Press Ctrl + N to display a new blank presentation.
    b. Click the Layout button in the Slides group on the HOME tab and then click *Blank* at the drop-down list.
    c. Press Ctrl + F12 to display the Open dialog box.
    d. At the Open dialog box, navigate to the PC8 folder on your storage medium.
    e. Click the option button that displays at the right side of the *File name* text box (option button that contains the text All PowerPoint Presentations) and then click *All Files (*.*)* at the drop-down list.
    f. Make sure all of your project files display. You may need to scroll down the list box to display the files.
    g. Hold down the Alt key and then press the Print Screen button on your keyboard. (This captures an image of the Open dialog box and not the entire screen.)
    h. Click the Cancel button to close the Open dialog box.
    i. Click the Paste button. (This inserts the image of the Open dialog box into the slide.)
17. Print the slide as a full page slide.
18. Close the presentation without saving it and then close **P-C8-P1-ATTopFive.pptx**.

Project 2 Embed and Link Excel Charts to a Presentation 3 Parts

You will open a company funds presentation and then copy an Excel pie chart and embed it in a PowerPoint slide. You will also copy and link an Excel column chart to a slide and then update the chart in Excel.

Embedding and Linking Objects ■■■■■■■■■■■■■■■■■■■

One of the reasons the Microsoft Office suite is used extensively in business is because it allows data from one program to be seamlessly integrated into another program. For example, a chart depicting sales projections created in Excel can easily be added to a slide in a PowerPoint presentation to the company board of directors on the new budget forecast.

Integration is the process of adding content from other sources to a file. Integrating content is different than simply copying and pasting it. While it makes sense to copy and paste objects from one application to another when the content is not likely to change, if the content is dynamic, the copy and paste method becomes problematic and inefficient. To illustrate this point, assume one of the outcomes from the presentation to the board of directors is a revision to the sales projections, which means that the chart originally created in Excel has to be updated to reflect the new projections. If the first version of the chart was copied and pasted into PowerPoint, it would need to be deleted and then the revised chart in Excel would need to be copied and pasted into the slide again. Both Excel and PowerPoint would need to be opened and edited to reflect this change in projection. In this case, copying and pasting the chart would not be efficient.

To eliminate the inefficiency of the copy and paste method, you can integrate objects between programs. An *object* can be text in a presentation, data in a table, a chart, a picture, a slide, or any combination of data that you would like to share between programs. The program that was used to create the object is called the *source* and the program the object is linked or embedded to is called the *destination*.

Embedding and linking are two methods you can use to integrate data in addition to the copy and paste method. When an object is embedded, the content in the object is stored in both the source and the destination programs. When you edit an embedded object in the destination program, the source program in which the program was created opens. If the content in the object is changed in the source program, the change is not reflected in the destination program and vice versa.

Linking inserts a code into the destination file connecting the destination to the name and location of the source object. The object itself is not stored within the destination file. When linking, if a change is made to the content in the source program, the destination program reflects the change automatically. Your decision to integrate data by embedding or linking will depend on whether the data is dynamic or static. If the data is dynamic, then linking the object is the most efficient method of integration.

HINT

Static data remains the same while dynamic data changes periodically or continually.

Embedding Objects

An object that is embedded is stored in both the source *and* the destination programs. The content of the object can be edited in *either* the source or the destination; however, a change made in one will not be reflected in the other. The difference between copying and pasting and copying and embedding is that embedded objects can be edited with the source program's editing tabs and options.

Since embedded objects are edited within the source program, the source program must reside on the computer when the presentation is opened for editing. If you are preparing a presentation that will be edited on another computer, you may want to check before embedding any objects to verify that the other computer has the same programs.

To embed an object, open both programs and both files. In the source program, click the desired object and then click the Copy button in the Clipboard group on the HOME tab. Click the button on the Taskbar representing the destination program file and then position the insertion point at the location where you want the object embedded. Click the Paste button arrow in the Clipboard group and then click *Paste Special* at the drop-down list. At the Paste Special dialog box, click the source of the object in the *As* list box and then click OK.

Edit an embedded object by double-clicking the object. This displays the object with the source program tabs and options. Make any desired changes and then click outside the object to exit the source program tabs and options. You can apply animation effects to an embedded object with the same techniques you learned in Chapter 7.

▼ **Quick Steps**

Embed an Object
1. Open source program.
2. Select desired object.
3. Click Copy button.
4. Open destination program.
5. Click Paste button arrow.
6. Click *Paste Special*.
7. Click source of object.
8. Click OK.

1. Open **FundsPres.pptx** and then save the presentation with Save As and name it **P-C8-P2-FundsPres**.
2. Open Excel and then open **Funds01.xlsx**, located in the PC8 folder on your storage medium.
3. Click the chart to select it. (Make sure the chart is selected and not an element in the chart.)
4. Click the Copy button in the Clipboard group on the HOME tab.
5. Click the PowerPoint button on the Taskbar.
6. Make Slide 4 active.
7. Click the Paste button arrow and then click *Paste Special* at the drop-down list.

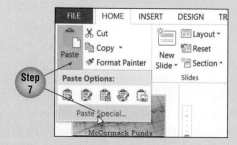

8. At the Paste Special dialog box, click *Microsoft Office Graphic Object* in the *As* list box and then click OK.

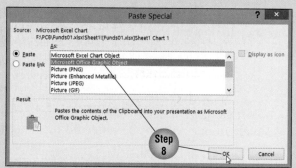

9. Click the CHART TOOLS FORMAT tab.
10. Change the height of the chart to 5.5 inches and change the width to 9 inches.

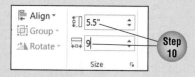

11. Center the pie chart in the slide below the title.
12. Save **P-C8-P2-FundsPres.pptx**.
13. Click the Excel button on the Taskbar, close the workbook, and then close Excel.

Linking Objects

Since linking does not increase the size of the file in the destination program, consider linking objects if file size is a consideration.

If the content of the object that you will integrate between programs is likely to change, then link the object from the source program to the destination program. Linking the object establishes a direct connection between the source and destination programs. The object is stored in the source program only. The destination program will have a code inserted into it that indicates the name and location of the source of the object. Whenever the presentation containing the link is opened, a message displays saying that the presentation contains links and the user is prompted to update the links.

To link an object, open both programs and open both program files. In the source program file, click the desired object and then click the Copy button in the Clipboard group on the HOME tab. Click the button on the Taskbar representing the destination program file and then position the insertion point in the desired location. Click the Paste button arrow in the Clipboard group on the HOME tab and then click *Paste Special* at the drop-down list. At the Paste Special dialog box, click the source program for the object in the *As* list box, click the *Paste link* option located at the left side of the *As* list box, and then click OK.

▼ **Quick Steps**

Link an Object
1. Open source program.
2. Select desired object.
3. Click Copy button.
4. Open destination program.
5. Click Paste button arrow.
6. Click *Paste Special*.
7. Click *Paste link* option.
8. Click OK.

Project 2b — Linking an Excel Chart to a Presentation — Part 2 of 3

1. With **P-C8-P2-FundsPres.pptx** open, open Excel and then open **Funds02.xlsx** located in the PC8 folder on your storage medium.
2. Save the workbook with Save As and name it **P-C8-P2-MMFunds**.
3. Copy and link the chart to a slide in the presentation by completing the following steps:
   a. Click the chart to select it.
   b. Click the Copy button in the Clipboard group on the HOME tab.
   c. Click the PowerPoint button on the Taskbar.
   d. Make Slide 5 active.
   e. Click the Paste button arrow and then click *Paste Special* at the drop-down list.
   f. At the Paste Special dialog box, click the *Paste link* option.
   g. Make sure *Microsoft Excel Chart Object* is selected in the *As* list box and then click OK.

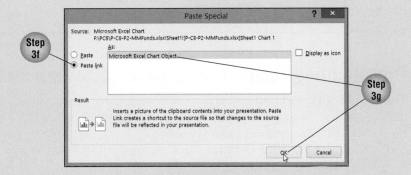

   h. Click the DRAWING TOOLS FORMAT tab, change the height of the chart to 5 inches, and then drag the chart so it is centered on the slide.
4. Click the Excel button on the Taskbar, close **P-C8-P2-MMFunds.xlsx**, and then close Excel.
5. Make Slide 1 active and then run the presentation.
6. Save and then close **P-C8-P2-FundsPres.pptx**.

Editing Linked Objects

Edit linked objects in the source program in which they were created. Open the document, workbook, or presentation containing the object; make the changes as required; and then save and close the file. If both the source and destination programs are open at the same time, the changed content is reflected immediately in both programs.

1. Open Excel and then open **P-C8-P2-MMFunds.xlsx**.
2. Make the following changes to data in the following cells:
   a. Cell B2: Change *13%* to *17%*.
   b. Cell B3: Change *9%* to *12%*.
   c. Cell B6: Change *10%* to *14%*.
3. Click the Save button on the Quick Access toolbar to save the edited workbook.
4. Close **P-C8-P2-MMFunds.xlsx** and then close Excel.
5. In PowerPoint, open **P-C8-P2-FundsPres.pptx**.
6. At the message telling you that the presentation contains links, click the Update Links button.
7. Make Slide 5 active and then notice the changes in the chart data.
8. Print the presentation as a handout with six slides printed horizontally per page.
9. Save and then close **P-C8-P2-FundsPres.pptx**.

	A	B
1		Percentage
2	2011	17%
3	2012	12%
4	2013	18%
5	2014	4%
6	2015	14%

Step 2a · Step 2b · Step 2c

Project 3   Download and Apply a Design Template to a Presentation and Prepare a Presentation for Sharing   10 Parts

You will download a design template from Office.com and apply the template to a company presentation. You will insert, edit, and delete comments in the presentation; modify the presentation properties; inspect the presentation; and encrypt the presentation with a password.

Downloading Templates ■■■■■■■■■■■■■■■■■■■■■■■■

▼ Quick Steps

Download a Template
1. Click FILE tab.
2. Click *New* option.
3. Click in search text box.
4. Type key word or phrase.
5. Press Enter.
6. Double-click desired template.

Thousands of PowerPoint templates are available for downloading at the New backstage area. To search for and download a template, click the FILE tab and then click the *New* option to display the New backstage area. Click in the search text box, type a keyword or phrase and then press the Enter key or click the Start searching button that displays at the right side of the search text box. PowerPoint searches the Office.com templates gallery and displays templates that match your key word or phrase. To download a template, double-click the template or click once on the template to display a download window. At this window, you can read information about the template and view additional template images by clicking the right- or left-pointing arrows that display below the template image. If you want to download the template, click the Create button.

When you download a template, the template opens with most templates containing predesigned slides. Use these slides to help you create your presentation or delete the predesigned slides and create your own using the template layouts. If you download a template, make some changes to the presentation, and decide you want to use it for future presentations, save the presentation as a template to the Custom Office Templates folder (as you learned in Chapter 6).

If you want the downloaded template (not a customized version of the template) available for future presentations, pin the template to the New backstage area. To do this, display the New backstage area, hover your mouse over the template you want to pin and then click the stick pin that displays. Complete the same steps to unpin a template from the New backstage area.

If you saved a customized template to the Custom Office Templates folder, you can apply the template to an existing presentation. To do this, open the presentation, click the DESIGN tab, click the More button at the right side of the design thumbnails, and then click the *Browse for Themes* option at the drop-down list. At the Choose Theme or Themed Document dialog box, navigate to the Custom Office Templates folder in the Documents folder on the computer's hard drive and then double-click the desired template in the dialog box Content pane.

| **Project 3a** | **Downloading and Applying a Design Template** | **Part 1 of 10** |

Note: Check with your instructor before downloading a design template. To download a template you must have access to the Internet and access to the hard drive. If you do not have access to the design template or cannot download it, open ISPres.pptx, save it with the name P-C8-P3-ISPres, apply a design theme of your choosing, and then continue with Step 16.

1. At a blank PowerPoint screen, click the FILE tab and then click the *New* option.
2. At the New backstage area, click one of the categories that displays below the search text box (such as *Business*, *Education*, and so on).
3. When templates display that match the category, scroll down the backstage list box and look at some of the templates.
4. Click the Home button that displays to the left of the search text box to return to the main New backstage area screen.
5. Click in the search text box, type **marketing plan**, and then press Enter.
6. Scroll down the backstage list box and view some of the templates.
7. Click in the search text box, type **red radial lines**, and then press Enter. (This displays the Red radial lines presentation (widescreen).)
8. Click the *Red radial lines presentation (widescreen)* template thumbnail.
9. At the template window, view some of the images for the template by clicking several times on the right-pointing arrow that displays below the template image.
10. Click the Create button. (This downloads the template and opens a presentation based on the template.)
11. Delete the sample slides in the presentation by completing the following steps:
    a. With the first slide selected in the slide thumbnails pane, scroll down the slide thumbnails pane to the last slide, hold down the Shift key, and then click the last slide. (This selects all of the slides in the presentation.)

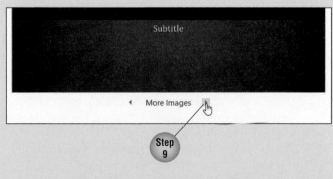

b. Press the Delete key. (When you press the Delete key, the slides are deleted and a gray screen displays with the text *Click to add first slide*.)

12. Save the presentation as a template to the Custom Office Templates folder by completing the following steps:

a. Press the F12 function key to display the Save As dialog box.

b. Click the *Save as type* option box and then click *PowerPoint Template (*.potx)* at the drop-down list. (Make sure the Custom Office Templates folder located in the Documents folder on the computer's hard drive is active.)

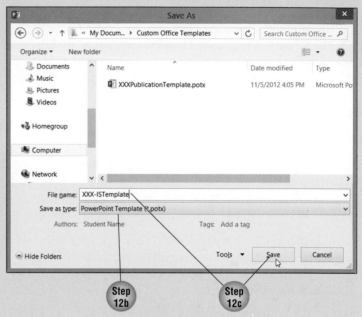

c. Click in the *File name* text box, type **XXX-ISTemplate** (type your initials in place of the *XXX*) and then click the Save button.

d. Close the **XXX-ISTemplate.potx** file.

13. Open the **ISPres.pptx** presentation from the PC8 folder on your storage medium.

14. Save the presentation with Save As and name it **P-C8-P3-ISPres**.

15. Apply the **XXX-ISTemplate.potx** template to the presentation by completing the following steps:

a. Click the DESIGN tab.

b. Click the More button at the right side of the design thumbnails.

c. Click the *Browse for Themes* option at the drop-down list.

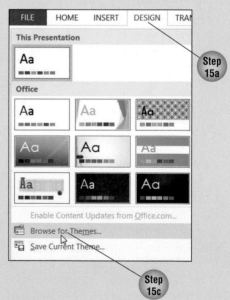

d. At the Choose Theme or Themed Document dialog box, double-click **XXX-ISTemplate.potx** (where your initials display in place of the *XXX*). (If the Custom Office Templates folder contents do not display in the Content pane of the Choose Theme or Themed Document dialog box, click the Documents folder located below the *Libraries* heading in the Navigation pane and then double-click the Custom Office Templates folder.)

16. Run the presentation.

17. Print the presentation as a handout with all nine slides printed horizontally on the page.

18. Save **P-C8-P3-ISPres.pptx**.

Comparing and Combining Presentations ■■■■■■■■■

Use the Compare button in the Compare group on the REVIEW tab to compare two PowerPoint presentations to determine the differences between the presentations. You have the options of combining all of the changes, accepting only specific changes, and rejecting some or all of the changes. To compare and combine presentations, open the first presentation, click the REVIEW tab, and then click the Compare button in the Compare group. This displays the Choose File to Merge with Current Presentation dialog box. At this dialog box, navigate to the folder containing the presentation you want to compare with the current presentation, click the presentation name in the Content pane, and then click the Merge button. (You can also double-click the presentation name.)

When you click the Merge button (or double-click the presentation name), a Reviewing task pane with the heading *Revisions* displays at the right side of the screen containing changes to slides and changes to the presentation. In addition, a revision mark displays in a slide indicating a difference between slides in the two presentations. If a difference occurs to the entire presentation, such as a difference between design themes, a revision mark displays at the left side of the screen near the top of the slide thumbnails pane. Click a revision mark to expand it to display a revision check box followed by information about the change.

If you want to accept the change, click the revision check box and then click the Accept button in the Compare group. You can also accept a change by clicking the Accept button arrow. When you click the Accept button arrow, a drop-down list displays with options to accept the current change, accept all changes to the current slide, or accept all changes to the presentation. If you do not want to accept the change, click the Reject button in the Compare group. Click the Reject button arrow and options display for rejecting the current change, rejecting all changes to the current slide, or rejecting all changes to the presentation.

Use the Previous and Next buttons in the Compare group to navigate to changes in the presentation. Click the Reviewing Pane button to turn on or off the display of the Reviewing task pane. When you have finished comparing the presentations, click the End Review button and the review ends and the accept or reject decisions you made are applied.

▼ Quick Steps

Comparing and Combining Presentations
1. Click REVIEW tab.
2. Click Compare button.
3. Navigate to folder containing presentation you want to compare with.
4. Click presentation.
5. Click Merge button.
6. Accept or reject changes.
7. Click End Review button.

Compare

Accept   Reject

Previous   Next

Reviewing   End
Pane   Review

Project 3b   **Comparing and Combining Presentations**   **Part 2 of 10**

1. With **P-C8-P3-ISPres.pptx** open, click the REVIEW tab and then click the Compare button in the Compare group.
2. At the Choose File to Merge with Current Presentation dialog box, navigate to the PC8 folder on your storage medium, click *ISSalesMeeting.pptx* in the Content pane, and then click the Merge button located toward the lower right corner of the dialog box.
3. Notice the Reviewing task pane (with the heading *Revisions*) that displays at the right side of the screen with the *DETAILS* option selected. This option contains a *Slide Changes* section and a *Presentation Changes* section. A message displays in the *Slide Changes* section indicating that the current slide (Slide 1) contains no changes. The *Presentation Changes* section indicates a change in the theme for Slides 1 through 9.

4. Click the revision check box that displays before the word *Theme* in the revision mark that displays near the top of the slide thumbnails pane. (When you insert a check mark in the check box, the design theme is removed from the presentation since the presentation to which you are comparing the current presentation does not include a design theme.)

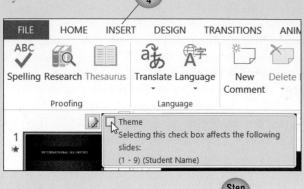

Step 4

5. You decide that you want the design theme to remain, so click the Reject button in the Compare group. (You could also click again the revision check box before the word *Theme* in the revision mark.)

Step 5

6. Click the Next button in the Compare group to display the next change.
7. Click the revision check box to the left of the text *All changes to Content Placeholder 2* located in the upper right corner of the slide in the slide pane.

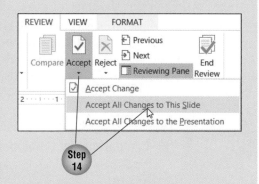

8. Click the Reject button to reject this change.
9. Click the Next button.
10. Click the revision check box to the left of the text *Table contents* located at the right side of the table in the slide. Notice the change to the amount for the West region.
11. Click the revision check box again to remove the check mark and then click the Accept button in the Compare group to accept the change.
12. Click the Next button.
13. Click the revision check box to the left of the text *All changes to Content Placeholder 2* located in the upper right corner of the content placeholder in the slide, notice the changes made to the slide, and then click the check box to remove the check mark.
14. Accept all changes by clicking the Accept button arrow and then clicking *Accept All Changes to This Slide* at the drop-down list.

Step 14

15. Click the Next button.
16. Click the Accept button to accept the changes to text in the content placeholder in Slide 9.
17. Click the Next button.
18. At the message that displays telling you that was the last change and asking if you want to continue reviewing from the beginning, click the Cancel button.
19. Click the End Review button in the Compare group.

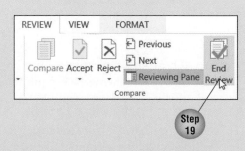

Step 19

20. At the message that displays asking if you are sure you want to end the review, click the Yes button.
21. Save **P-C8-P3-ISPres.pptx**.

Managing Comments ■■■■■■■■■■■■■■■■■■■■■■■■■■

If you are sending out a presentation for review and want to ask reviewers specific questions or provide information about slides in a presentation, insert a comment. To insert a comment, display the desired slide and then position the insertion point where you want the comment to appear or select an element in the slide. Click the REVIEW tab and then click the New Comment button in the Comments group. This displays an orange active icon at the location of the insertion point or next to the selected element and opens the Comments task pane with a text entry box in the pane. Type the desired comment in the text entry box and then click outside the text entry box, press the Tab key, or press the Enter key.

To insert another comment in the presentation, position the insertion point or select the desired element in the slide and then click the New button in the Comments task pane or click the New Comment button in the Comments group and then type the comment in the text entry box. To view a comment in a presentation, click the comment icon and then read the information in the Comments task pane.

To move between comments in a presentation, click the Next button or Previous button located toward the upper right corner of the Comments task pane. You can also click the Previous button or Next button in the Comments group on the REVIEW tab.

Other methods for displaying the Comments task pane include clicking the COMMENTS button on the Status bar or clicking the Show Comments button in the Comments group on the REVIEW tab. When the Comments task pane is open, the Show Comments button is active (displays with an orange background). Turn off the display of the Comments task pane by clicking the COMMENTS button on the Status bar, clicking the Show Comments button, or by clicking the Close button located in the upper right corner of the Comments task pane.

To print comments, display the Print backstage area and then click the second gallery in the *Settings* category. (This is the gallery containing the text *Full Page Slides*.) At the drop-down list that displays, make sure the *Print Comments and Ink Markup* check box contains a check mark. Comments print on a separate page after the presentation is printed.

▼ **Quick Steps**

Insert a Comment
1. Click REVIEW tab.
2. Click New Comment button.
3. Type comment text.

New Comment

Next   Previous

COMMENTS

Show Comments

| **Project 3c** | **Inserting Comments** | **Part 3 of 10** |

1. With **P-C8-P3-ISPres.pptx** open, make Slide 2 active and then insert a comment by completing the following steps:
   a. Position the insertion point immediately to the right of the word *Australia*.
   b. Click the REVIEW tab.
   c. Click the New Comment button in the Comments group.
   d. Type the following in the text entry box in the Comments task pane: **Include information on New Zealand branch.**
2. Make Slide 3 active and then insert a comment by completing the following steps:
   a. Click in the chart to select it. (Make sure you select the chart and not a chart element.)

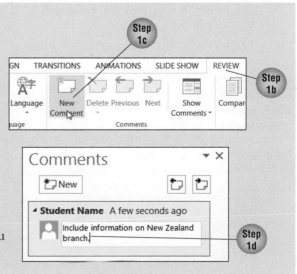

b. Click the New button in the Comments task pane.

c. Type the following in the text entry box: **Include a chart showing profit amounts.**

3. Make Slide 5 active, position the insertion point immediately to the right of the word *line* at the end of the third bulleted item, and then insert the comment **Provide detailed information on how this goal will be accomplished.**

4. Make Slide 8 active, position the insertion point immediately to the right of the words *Hong Kong* in the second bulleted item, and then insert the comment **Who will be managing the Hong Kong office?**

5. Click the Previous button in the Comments task pane to display the comment box in Slide 5.

6. Click the Previous button in the Comments group on the REVIEW tab to display the comment box in Slide 3.

7. Click the Next button in the Comments task pane to display the comment in Slide 5.

8. Click the Next button in the Comments group on the REVIEW tab to display the comment in Slide 8.

9. Click the Show Comments button in the Comments group on the REVIEW tab to turn off the display of the Comments task pane.

10. Print the presentation and the comments by completing the following steps:

a. Click the FILE tab and then click the *Print* option.

b. At the Print backstage area, click the second gallery in the *Settings* category, make sure the *Print Comments and Ink Markup* option contains a check mark, and then click the *9 Slides Vertical* option.

c. Click the Print button.

11. Make Slide 1 active and then run the presentation beginning with Slide 1.

12. Save **P-C8-P3-ISPres.pptx**.

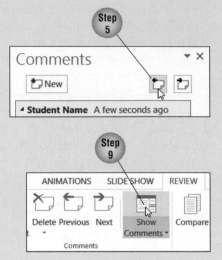

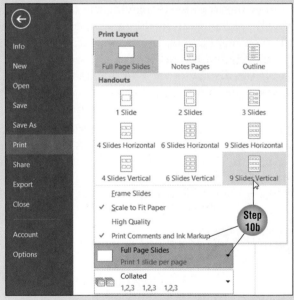

HINT

Move a comment in a slide by selecting the comment icon and then dragging it to the desired location.

Delete

To edit a comment, click the comment in the Comments task pane, click in the text entry box and then edit the comment. Reply to a comment by clicking the comment in the Comments task pane, clicking in the reply entry box and then typing your response. To delete a comment from a slide, click the comment icon and then click the Delete button in the Comments task pane or the Delete button in the Comments group on the REVIEW tab. You can also right-click the comment icon and then click *Delete Comment* at the shortcut menu. Delete all comments in a presentation by clicking the Delete button arrow in the Comments group and then clicking *Delete All Comments and Ink in This Presentation* at the drop-down list.

1. With **P-C8-P3-ISPres.pptx** open, make Slide 8 active and then edit the comment by
   completing the following steps:
   a. Click the comment icon that displays to
      the right of *Hong Kong*. (This displays the
      Comments task pane.)
   b. Click in the text entry box in the Comments
      task pane.
   c. Delete the text in the comment box and then
      type **Check with Sandy Cates to determine
      who will be appointed branch manager.**
2. Delete the comment in Slide 3 by completing the
   following steps:
   a. Click twice on the Previous button located
      toward the upper right corner of the Comments
      task pane to display Slide 3 and the comment
      in the slide.
   b. Click the Delete button (contains an X) that
      displays in the upper right corner of the
      comment box.
3. Close the Comments task pane.
4. Print the presentation as a handout with all
   nine slides printed horizontally on the page and
   make sure the comments print.
5. Save **P-C8-P3-ISPres.pptx**.

Managing Presentation Information ■■■■■■■■■■■■■■■

If you plan to distribute or share a presentation, you should check the
presentation information and decide if you want to insert presentation
properties in the presentation file, protect the presentation with a password,
check the compatibility of the presentation, or access versions of the
presentation. You can complete these tasks along with other tasks at the Info
backstage area shown in Figure 8.4. Display this backstage area by clicking the
FILE tab and then clicking the *Info* option.

Managing Presentation Properties

Each presentation you create has properties associated with it such as the
type and location of the presentation and when the presentation was created,
modified, and accessed. View and modify presentation properties at the Info
backstage area and at the document panel.

Property information about a presentation displays at the right side of
the Info backstage area. Add or update a presentation property by hovering
your mouse over the information that displays at the right of the property
(a rectangular box with a light orange border displays) and then typing the
desired information. In the *Related Dates* section, dates display for when the

Figure 8.4 Info Backstage Area

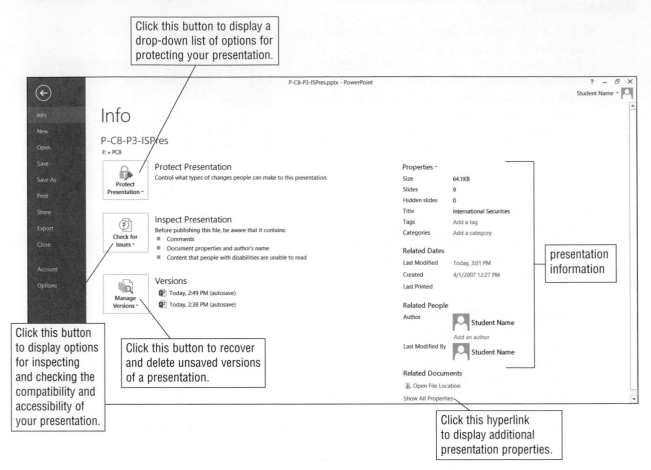

Click this button to display a drop-down list of options for protecting your presentation.

Click this button to display options for inspecting and checking the compatibility and accessibility of your presentation.

Click this button to recover and delete unsaved versions of a presentation.

presentation information

Click this hyperlink to display additional presentation properties.

presentation was created and when it was last modified and printed. The *Related People* section displays the name of the author of the presentation and also contains options for adding additional author names. Click the folder below the *Related Documents* section to display the folder contents where the current presentation is located.

Display additional presentation properties by clicking the <u>Show All Properties</u> hyperlink. You can also manage presentation properties at the document panel shown in Figure 8.5. Display this panel by clicking the Properties button that displays at the top of the property information and then clicking *Show Document Panel* at the drop-down list. Inserting text in some of the text boxes can help you organize and identify your presentations.

Figure 8.5 Document Panel

Document Properties ▼					Location: F:\PC8\P-C8-P3-ISPres.pptx	★ Required field ✕
Author:	Title:	Subject:	Keywords:	Category:	Status:	
Student Name	International Securities					
Comments:						

1. With **P-C8-P3-ISPres.pptx** open, click the FILE tab. (This displays the Info backstage area.)

2. At the Info backstage area, hover your mouse over the text *International Securities* that displays at the right of the *Title* property, click the left mouse button (this selects the text), and then type **IS Sales Meeting**.

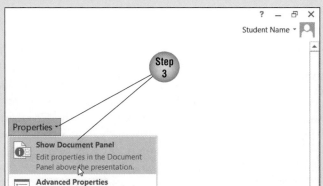

3. Display the document panel by clicking the Properties button that displays at the top of the property information and then click *Show Document Panel* at the drop-down list.

4. At the document panel, press the Tab key twice (this makes the *Subject* text box active) and then type **IS Corporate Sales Meeting**.

5. Press the Tab key and then type **International Securities, sales, divisions** in the *Keywords* text box.

6. Press the Tab key and then type **sales meeting** in the *Category* text box.

7. Press the Tab key twice and then type the following in the *Comments* text box: **This is a presentation prepared for the corporate sales meeting.**

8. Close the document panel by clicking the Close button located in the upper right corner of the panel.

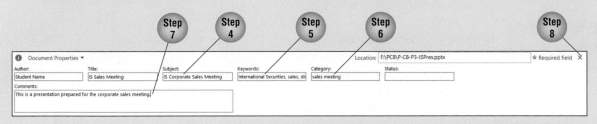

9. Save **P-C8-P3-ISPres.pptx**.

Protecting a Presentation

Click the Protect Presentation button in the middle panel at the Info backstage area and a drop-down list displays with the following options: *Mark as Final, Encrypt with Password, Restrict Access,* and *Add a Digital Signature.* Click the *Mark as Final* option to save the presentation as a read-only presentation. When you click this option, a message displays telling you that the presentation will be marked and then saved. At this message, click OK. This displays another message telling you that the presentation has been marked as final to indicate that editing is complete and

▼ **Quick Steps**

Mark a Presentation as Final
1. Click FILE tab.
2. Click Protect Presentation button.
3. Click *Mark as Final.*

Protect Presentation

that it is the final version of the presentation. The message further indicates that when a presentation is marked as final, the status property is set to "Final"; typing, editing commands, and proofing marks are turned off; and that the presentation can be identified by the Mark As Final icon, which displays toward the left side of the Status bar. At this message, click OK. After a presentation is marked as final, a message displays above the ruler indicating that the author has marked the presentation as final and includes an Edit Anyway button. Click this button to edit the presentation. When a presentation is marked as final an additional message displays to the right of the Protect Presentation button in the Info backstage area stating "This presentation has been marked as final to discourage editing."

Encrypting a Presentation

▼ **Quick Steps**

Encrypt a Presentation
1. Click FILE tab.
2. Click Protect Presentation button.
3. Click *Encrypt with Password.*
4. Type password, press Enter.
5. Type password again, press Enter.

Protect a presentation with a password by clicking the Protect Presentation button at the Info backstage area and then clicking the *Encrypt with Password* option at the drop-down list. At the Encrypt Document dialog box that displays, type your password in the text box (the text will display as round bullets) and then press the Enter key or click OK. At the Confirm Password dialog box, type your password again (the text will display as round bullets) and then press the Enter key or click OK. When you apply a password, the message *A password is required to open this document* displays to the right of the Protect Presentation button.

If you encrypt a presentation with a password, make sure you keep a copy of the password in a safe place because Microsoft cannot retrieve lost or forgotten passwords. If you do not remember your password you will not be able to open the presentation. You can change a password by removing the original password and then creating a new one. To remove a password, open the password-protected presentation, display the Encrypt Document dialog box, and then remove the password (round bullets) in the *Password* text box.

Project 3f | **Marking a Presentation as Final** | **Part 6 of 10**

1. With **P-C8-P3-ISPres.pptx** open, click the FILE tab.
2. At the Info backstage area, click the Protect Presentation button and then click *Mark as Final* at the drop-down list.
3. At the message telling you the presentation will be marked as final and saved, click OK.
4. At the next message that displays, click OK. (Notice the message that displays to the right of the Protect Presentation button.)
5. At the presentation, notice the message bar that displays above the ruler.
6. Close the presentation.

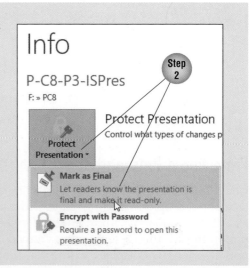

---

7. Open **P-C8-P3-ISPres.pptx**, click the Edit Anyway button on the yellow message bar, and then save the presentation.

8. Encrypt the presentation with a password by completing the following steps:
   a. Click the FILE tab, click the Protect Presentation button at the Info backstage area, and then click *Encrypt with Password* at the drop-down list.
   b. At the Encrypt Document dialog box, type your initials in uppercase letters. (Your text will display as round bullets.)
   c. Press the Enter key.
   d. At the Confirm Password dialog box, type your initials again in uppercase letters (your text will display as bullets) and then press the Enter key.

9. Click the Back button to return to the presentation.
10. Save and then close **P-C8-P3-ISPres.pptx**.
11. Open **P-C8-P3-ISPres.pptx**. At the Password dialog box, type your initials in uppercase letters and then press the Enter key.
12. Change the password by completing the following steps:
    a. Click the FILE tab.
    b. At the Info backstage area, click the Protect Presentation button and then click *Encrypt with Password* at the drop-down list.
    c. At the Encrypt Document dialog box, delete the round bullets in the *Password* text box, type your first name in lowercase letters, and then press Enter.
    d. At the Confirm Password dialog box, type your first name again in lowercase letters and then press the Enter key.
    e. Press the Esc key to return to the document.
13. Save and then close **P-C8-P3-ISPres.pptx**.
14. Open **P-C8-P3-ISPres.pptx**. At the Password dialog box, type your first name in lowercase letters and then press Enter.
15. Remove the password protection by completing the following steps:
    a. Click the FILE tab.
    b. At the Info backstage area, click the Protect Presentation button and then click *Encrypt with Password* at the drop-down list.
    c. At the Encrypt Document dialog box, delete the round bullets in the *Password* text box and then press the Enter key.
    d. Press the Esc key to return to the presentation.
16. Save **P-C8-P3-ISPres.pptx**.

Adding a Digital Signature

Add a *digital signature*, which is an electronic stamp that vouches for a presentation's authenticity, to a presentation to authenticate it and indicate that you agree with its contents. When you add a digital signature, the presentation is locked so that it cannot be edited or changed unless you remove the digital signature. Before adding

Quick Steps

Add a Digital Signature
1. Click FILE tab.
2. Click Protect Presentation button.
3. Click *Add a Digital Signature*.
4. Make desired changes at Sign dialog box.
5. Click OK.

Inspect a Presentation
1. Click FILE tab.
2. Click Check for Issues button.
3. Click *Inspect Document*.
4. Remove check marks from items you do not want to inspect.
5. Click Inspect button.
6. Click Close button.

Check for
Issues

a digital signature, you must obtain one from a commercial certification authority. Once you have obtained a commercial digital signature, add it to a presentation by clicking the Protect Presentation button at the Info backstage area and then clicking *Digital Signature* at the drop-down list.

Inspecting a Presentation

Use options from the Check for Issues button drop-down list at the Info backstage area to inspect a presentation for personal and hidden data and to check a presentation for compatibility and accessibility issues. When you click the Check for Issues button, a drop-down list displays with the options *Inspect Document*, *Check Accessibility*, and *Check Compatibility*.

PowerPoint includes a document inspector feature you can use to inspect your presentation for personal data, hidden data, and metadata. Metadata is data that describes other data, such as presentation properties. You may want to remove some personal or hidden data before you share a presentation with other people. To check your presentation for personal or hidden data, click the FILE tab, click the Check for Issues button at the Info backstage area, and then click the *Inspect Document* option at the drop-down list. This displays the Document Inspector dialog box.

By default, the document inspector checks all of the items listed in the dialog box. If you do not want the inspector to check a specific item in your presentation, remove the check mark preceding the item. For example, if you know your presentation contains comments and/or ink annotations, click the *Comments and Annotations* check box to remove the check mark. Click the Inspect button located toward the bottom of the dialog box, and the document inspector scans the presentation to identify information.

When the inspection is complete, the results display in the dialog box. A check mark before an option indicates that the inspector did not find the specific items. If an exclamation point is inserted before an option, the inspector found items and displays a list of the items. If you want to remove the found items, click the Remove All button that displays at the right of the desired option. Click the Reinspect button to ensure that the specific items were removed and then click the Close button.

Project 3g Inspecting a Presentation   Part 7 of 10

1. With **P-C8-P3-ISPres.pptx** open, click the FILE tab.
2. At the Info backstage area, click the Check for Issues button and then click *Inspect Document* at the drop-down list.

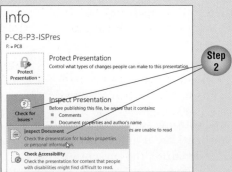

3. At the Document Inspector dialog box, you decide that you do not want to check the presentation for XML data, so click the *Custom XML Data* check box to remove the check mark.

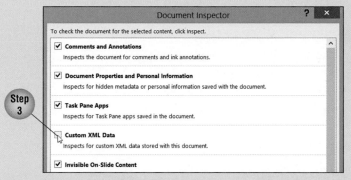

4. Click the Inspect button.
5. Read through the inspection results and then remove all comments by clicking the Remove All button that displays at the right side of the *Comments and Annotations* section.

6. Click the Close button to close the Document Inspector dialog box.
7. Click the Back button to return to the presentation.
8. Save **P-C8-P3-ISPres.pptx**.

Checking the Accessibility of a Presentation

PowerPoint includes the accessibility checker feature, which checks a presentation for content that a person with disabilities, such as a visual impairment, might find difficult to read. Check the accessibility of a presentation by clicking the Check for Issues button at the Info backstage area and then clicking *Check Accessibility*. The accessibility checker examines the presentation for the most common accessibility problems in PowerPoint presentations and groups them into three categories: errors—content that is unreadable to a person who is blind; warnings—content that is difficult to read; and tips—content that may or may not be difficult to read. The accessibility checker examines the presentation, closes the Info backstage area, and displays the Accessibility Checker task pane.

At the Accessibility Checker task pane, unreadable errors are grouped in the *ERRORS* section, content that is difficult to read is grouped in the *WARNINGS* section, and content that may or may not be difficult to read is grouped in the *TIPS* section. Select an issue in one of the sections and an explanation of how to fix the issue and why displays at the bottom of the task pane.

1. With **P-C8-P3-ISPres.pptx** open, click the FILE tab.
2. At the Info backstage area, click the Check for Issues button and then click *Check Accessibility* at the drop-down list.
3. Notice the Accessibility Checker task pane that displays at the right side of the screen. The task pane displays an *ERRORS* section. Click *Content Placeholder 7 (Slide 3)* in the *ERRORS* section and then read the information that displays toward the bottom of the task pane describing why you should fix the error and how to fix it.

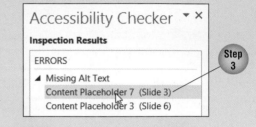

4. Add alternative text (which is a text-based representation of the chart) to the chart by completing the following steps:

   a. Make Slide 3 active, click the pie chart, right-click the chart border (mouse pointer displays with a four-headed arrow attached), and then click *Format Chart Area* at the shortcut menu.
   b. At the Format Chart Area task pane, click the Size & Properties icon.
   c. Click *ALT TEXT* to display the options.
   d. Click in the *Title* text box and then type **Division Profit Chart**.
   e. Click in the *Description* text box and then type **Profits: North America, 35%; Europe, 22%; Asia, 17%; Australia, 14%; and Africa, 12%**.
   f. Close the Format Chart Area task pane.
5. Click the remaining item in the Accessibility Checker task pane and then read the information that displays toward the bottom of the task pane.
6. Close the Accessibility Checker task pane by clicking the Close button located in the upper right corner of the task pane.
7. Save **P-C8-P3-ISPres.pptx**.

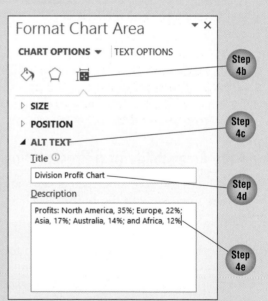

Checking the Compatibility of a Presentation

Use one of the Check for Issues button drop-down options, *Check Compatibility*, to check your presentation and identify elements that are either not supported or will act differently in previous versions of PowerPoint from PowerPoint 97 through PowerPoint 2003. To run the compatibility checker, open the desired presentation, click the Check for Issues button at the Info backstage area, and then click *Check Compatibility* at the drop-down list. This displays the Microsoft PowerPoint Compatibility Checker dialog box that displays a summary of the elements in the presentation that are not compatible with previous versions of PowerPoint and indicates what will happen when the presentation is saved and then opened in a previous version.

▼ **Quick Steps**

Check Compatibility
1. Click FILE tab.
2. Click Check for Issues button.
3. Click *Check Compatibility*.
4. Click OK.

Managing Versions

As you work in a presentation, PowerPoint automatically saves your presentation every 10 minutes. This automatic backup feature can be very helpful if you accidentally close your presentation without saving it, or if the power to your computer is disrupted. The automatically saved versions of a presentation are listed to the right of the Manage Versions button in the Info backstage area. Each autosaved presentation displays with *Today*, followed by the time and *(autosave)*. When you save and then close your presentation, the autosaved backup presentations are deleted.

Manage
Versions

To open an autosaved backup presentation, click the FILE tab to display the Info backstage area and then click the backup presentation you want to open at the right of the Manage Versions button. The presentation opens as a read-only presentation, and a yellow message bar displays with a Compare button and a Restore button. Click the Compare button and the autosave presentation is compared to the original presentation. You can then decide which changes you want to accept or reject. Click the Restore button and a message displays indicating that you are about to overwrite the last saved version with the selected version. At this message, click OK.

▼ **Quick Steps**

Open an Autosaved Backup Presentation
1. Click FILE tab.
2. Click presentation name at right of Manage Versions button.

When you save a presentation, the autosaved backup presentations are deleted. However, if you close a presentation after 10 minutes without saving it or if the power is disrupted, PowerPoint keeps the backup file in the *UnsavedFiles* folder on the hard drive. You can access this folder by clicking the Manage Versions button in the Info backstage area and then clicking *Recover Unsaved Presentations*. At the Open dialog box that displays, double-click the desired backup file you want to open. You can also display the *UnsavedFiles* folder by clicking the FILE tab, clicking the *Open* option, and then clicking the Recover Unsaved Presentations button that displays at the bottom of the Recent Presentations list.

1. With **P-C8-P3-ISPres.pptx** open, click the FILE tab.
2. Click the Check for Issues button and then click *Check Compatibility* at the drop-down list.
3. At the Microsoft PowerPoint Compatibility Checker dialog box, read the information that displays in the *Summary* list box.
4. Click OK to close the dialog box.
5. Click the FILE tab and then check to see if any versions of your presentation display to the right of the Manage Versions button. If so, click the version (or the first version, if more than one displays). This opens the autosave presentation as read-only.
6. Close the read-only presentation.
7. Click the FILE tab, click the Manage Versions button, and then click *Recover Unsaved Presentations* at the drop-down list.
8. At the Open dialog box, check to see if recovered presentation file names display along with the date and time and then click the Cancel button to close the Open dialog box.
9. Save the presentation.

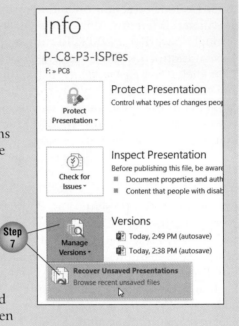

Customizing PowerPoint Options ■■■■■■■■■■■■■■■■

Customize PowerPoint with options at the PowerPoint Options dialog box, shown in Figure 8.6. Display this dialog box by clicking the FILE tab and then clicking *Options*. The panel at the left side of the dialog box contains a number of options you can select to customize specific features in PowerPoint. For example, click the *General* option in the left panel and options display for turning on or off the display of the Mini toolbar when text is selected, enabling or disabling live preview, and changing the user name and password.

Click the *Save* option at the PowerPoint Options dialog box and the dialog box displays with options for customizing how presentations are saved. You can change the format in which files are saved from the default of *PowerPoint Presentation* to a macro-enabled PowerPoint presentation, a 97-2003 presentation, a strict open XML presentation, or an OpenDocument presentation. With other options you can specify, by minutes, how often you want PowerPoint to automatically save a presentation, specify whether or not you want to save an autosaved version of a presentation if you close a presentation without first saving it, and specify a default location for saving presentations.

Click the *Proofing* option at the PowerPoint Options dialog box and the dialog box displays with options for customizing the spell checker, such as specifying what you want and do not want to be checked during a spelling check and creating a custom spell check dictionary. Click the AutoCorrect Options button and the AutoCorrect dialog box displays with options for changing how PowerPoint corrects and formats text as you type.

Figure 8.6 PowerPoint Options Dialog Box

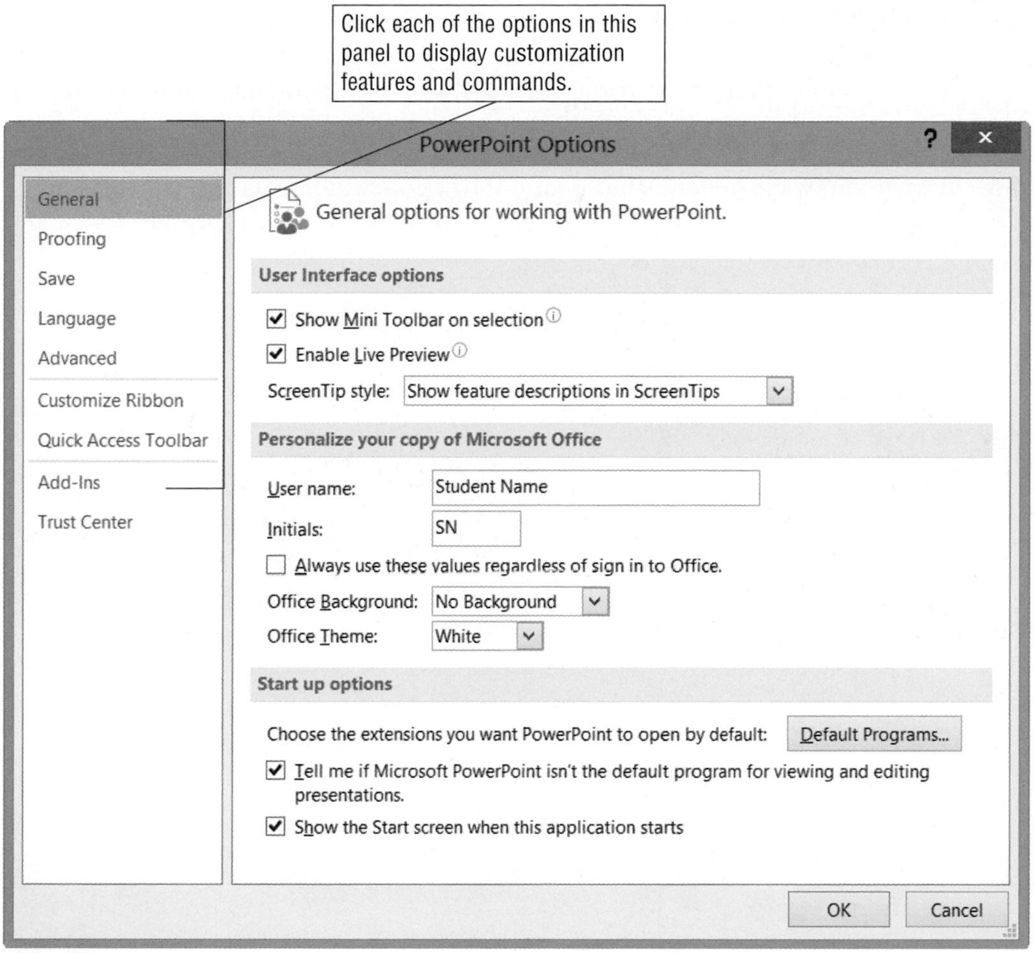

Click each of the options in this panel to display customization features and commands.

PowerPoint Options	? ×

General — General options for working with PowerPoint.

- General
- Proofing
- Save
- Language
- Advanced
- Customize Ribbon
- Quick Access Toolbar
- Add-Ins
- Trust Center

User Interface options

☑ Show Mini Toolbar on selection ⓘ
☑ Enable Live Preview ⓘ
ScreenTip style: [Show feature descriptions in ScreenTips ▾]

Personalize your copy of Microsoft Office

User name: [Student Name]
Initials: [SN]
☐ Always use these values regardless of sign in to Office.
Office Background: [No Background ▾]
Office Theme: [White ▾]

Start up options

Choose the extensions you want PowerPoint to open by default: [Default Programs...]
☑ Tell me if Microsoft PowerPoint isn't the default program for viewing and editing presentations.
☑ Show the Start screen when this application starts

[OK] [Cancel]

Project 3j **Customizing PowerPoint Options** Part 10 of 10

1. With **P-C8-P3-ISPres.pptx** open, insert new slides in the presentation by completing the following steps:
   a. Click below the bottom slide in the slide thumbnails pane.
   b. Click the New Slide button arrow and then click *Reuse Slides* at the drop-down list.
   c. At the Reuse Slides task pane, click the Browse button and then click *Browse File* at the drop-down list.
   d. At the Browse dialog box, navigate to the PC8 folder on your storage medium and then double-click *ISPresAfrica.pptx*.
   e. Click each of the three slides in the Reuse Slides task pane to insert the slides into the current presentation.
   f. Close the Reuse Slides task pane.
2. Make Slide 1 active.

3. Change PowerPoint options by completing the following steps:
   a. Click the FILE tab and then click *Options*.
   b. At the PowerPoint Options dialog box, click the *Save* option in the left panel.
   c. Click the down-pointing arrow at the right side of the measurement box containing *10* that is located to the right of the *Save AutoRecover information every* text until *1* displays in the measurement box.
   d. Specify that you want presentations saved in the 97-2003 format by clicking the down-pointing arrow at the right side of the *Save files in this format* option box and then clicking *PowerPoint Presentation 97-2003* at the drop-down list.

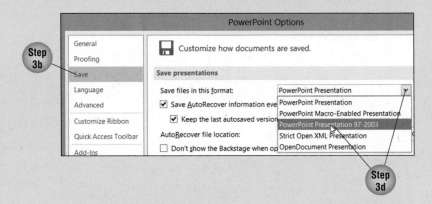

   e. Click the *Proofing* option in the left panel of the PowerPoint Options dialog box.
   f. Click the *Ignore words in UPPERCASE* check box to remove the check mark.
   g. Click the *Ignore words that contain numbers* check box to remove the check mark.

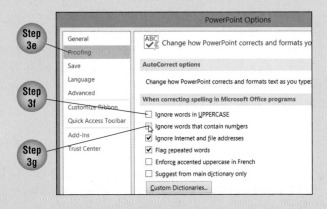

   h. Click OK to close the PowerPoint Options dialog box.

4. Complete a spelling check of the presentation and make changes as needed.
5. Move down the content placeholders on Slides 11 and 12 so they do not overlap the titles.
6. Save the presentation, print six slides horizontally per page, and then close the presentation.
7. Press Ctrl + N to open a new blank presentation.
8. Press F12 to display the Save As dialog box.
9. At the Save As dialog box, notice that the *Save as type* option is set at *PowerPoint 97-2003 Presentation (*.ppt)* because you changed the default format at the PowerPoint Options dialog box.
10. Click Cancel to close the dialog box.
11. Display the PowerPoint Options dialog box and then make the following changes:
    a. Click the *Save* option in the left panel.
    b. Change the number in the measurement box that is located to the right of the *Save AutoRecover information every* text to *10*.
    c. Click the down-pointing arrow at the right side of the *Save files in this format* option box and then click *PowerPoint Presentation* at the drop-down list.
    d. Click the *Proofing* option in the left panel of the PowerPoint Options dialog box.
    e. Click the *Ignore words in UPPERCASE* check box to insert a check mark.
    f. Click the *Ignore words that contain numbers* check box to insert a check mark.
    g. Click OK to close the PowerPoint Options dialog box.
    h. At the message that displays telling you that you are changing the default file format to Office Open XML and asking if you want to change this setting for all Microsoft Office applications, click the No button.
12. Close the blank presentation.

Chapter Summary

- Create a PowerPoint presentation by importing a Word document containing text with heading styles applied using the *Slides from Outline* option at the New Slides drop-down list.

- Use the Copy and Paste buttons in the Clipboard group to copy data from one program to another.

- Use the Clipboard task pane to collect and paste up to 24 items and paste the items into a presentation or other program files.

- With options at the Share backstage area, you can invite people to view and/or edit a presentation, send a presentation as an email attachment or in PDF or XPS format and as a fax, present a presentation online, and publish slides to a shared location.

- At the Export backstage area, create a PDF or XPS file with a presentation, create a video, package the presentation in a folder or on a CD, and create handouts.

- Click the *Change File Type* option at the Export backstage area and options display for saving a presentation in a different file format such as a previous version of PowerPoint, a PowerPoint show, an OpenDocument presentation, and as graphic images.

- An object created in one program in the Microsoft Office suite can be copied, linked, or embedded in another program in the suite. The program containing the original object is called the source program and the program the object is pasted to is called the destination program.

- An embedded object is stored in both the source and the destination programs. A linked object is stored in the source program only. Link an object if you want the contents in the destination program to reflect any changes made to the object stored in the source program.

- Download templates from the Office.com templates gallery at the New backstage area.

- If you download a template and then customize it, consider saving the template to the Custom Office Templates folder in the Documents folder on the computer's hard drive.

- Use the Compare button in the Compare group on the REVIEW tab to compare two presentations to determine the differences between the presentations. Use options in the Compare group to accept or reject differences and display the next or previous change.

- Insert, edit, and delete comments with buttons in the Comments group on the REVIEW tab.

- View and modify presentation properties at the Info backstage area and at the document panel. Display this panel by clicking the Properties button at the Info backstage area and then clicking *Show Document Panel* at the drop-down list.

- Use options from the Protect Presentation button drop-down list at the Info backstage area to mark a presentation as final, encrypt the presentation with a password, restrict access to the presentation, and add a digital signature.

- With options from the Check for Issues button drop-down list at the Info backstage area, you can inspect a document for personal and hidden data, check a presentation for content that a person with disabilities, such as a visual impairment, might find difficult to read, and check the compatibility of the presentation with previous versions of PowerPoint.

- PowerPoint automatically saves a presentation every 10 minutes. When you save a presentation, the autosave backup presentation(s) are deleted. Use the Manage Versions button at the Info backstage area to open an autosave backup presentation.

- Customize PowerPoint with options at the PowerPoint Options dialog box. Display this dialog box by clicking the FILE tab and then clicking *Options*.

Commands Review

FEATURE	RIBBON TAB, GROUP/OPTION	BUTTON, OPTION
Accessibility Checker task pane	FILE, *Info*	, *Check Accessibility*
Clipboard task pane	HOME, Clipboard	
compare presentations	REVIEW, Compare	
Document Inspector dialog box	FILE, *Info*	, *Inspect Document*
Encrypt Document dialog box	FILE, *Info*	, *Encrypt with Password*
Export backstage area	FILE, *Export*	
Insert Outline dialog box	HOME, Slides	, *Slides from Outline*
Microsoft PowerPoint Compatibility Checker dialog box	FILE, *Info*	, *Check Compatibility*
Package for CD dialog box	FILE, *Export*	
Paste Special dialog box	HOME, Clipboard	, *Paste Special*
Publish as PDF or XPS dialog box	FILE, *Export*	
Send to Microsoft Word dialog box	FILE, *Export*	
Share backstage area	FILE, *Share*	

Concepts Check   Test Your Knowledge

Completion: In the space provided at the right, indicate the correct term, symbol, or command.

1. Display the Insert Outline dialog box by clicking the New Slide button arrow and then clicking this option. _____

2. Use this task pane to collect and paste multiple items. _____

3. The *Invite People* option is available at this backstage area. _____

4. If you save the presentation in PDF format, the presentation opens in this. _____

5. With this option at the Export backstage area, you can export a PowerPoint presentation to a Word document. _____

6. A presentation you save as a PowerPoint show will display with this file extension. _____

7. With options in the *Image File Types* section of the Export backstage area with the *Change File Type* option selected, you can save slides in a presentation as graphic images as JPEG files or this type of file. _____

8. Do this to an object if you want the contents in the destination program to reflect any changes made to the object stored in the source program. _____

9. Download a template at this backstage area. _____

10. Click the Merge button at the Choose File to Merge with Current Presentation dialog box when comparing presentations and this task pane displays. _____

11. The New Comment button is located in the Comments group on this tab. _____

12. Display additional presentation properties at the Info backstage area by clicking this hyperlink. _____

13. Display the Encrypt Document dialog box by clicking the FILE tab, clicking the Protect Presentation button at the Info backstage area, and then clicking this option at the drop-down list. _____

14. Use this feature to inspect your presentation for personal data, hidden data, and metadata. _____

15. Use this feature to check a presentation for content that a person with a visual impairment might find difficult to read. _____

16. Use this button at the Info backstage area to open an autosaved backup presentation. _____

17. Customize PowerPoint with options at this dialog box. _____

Skills Check   Assess Your Performance

Assessment

1   COPY WORD AND EXCEL DATA INTO A SALES CONFERENCE PRESENTATION

1. Open **NWPres.pptx** and then save the presentation with Save As and name it **P-C8-A1-NWPres**.
2. Make Slide 2 active and then complete the following steps:
   a. Open Excel and then open the workbook named **SalesProj.xlsx** (located in the PC8 folder on your storage medium).
   b. Copy the chart and paste it into Slide 2.
   c. Resize the chart so it fills most of the slide below the title.
   d. Close the workbook and then close Excel.
3. Make Slide 4 active and then complete the following steps:
   a. Draw a text box in the slide.
   b. Open Word and then open the document named **HerbRemedies.docx**.
   c. Copy the first three terms and the paragraph below each term in the document to the text box in Slide 4.
   d. Move and/or resize the placeholder so it fills most of the slide below the title.
4. Make Slide 5 active and then complete the following steps:
   a. Draw a text box in the slide.
   b. Make active the **HerbRemedies.docx** Word document.
   c. Copy the last two terms and the paragraph below each term in the document and paste them into Slide 5 in the text box.
   d. Move and/or size the text box so it fills most of the slide below the title.
5. Make Word active, close **HerbRemedies.docx**, and then close Word.
6. With PowerPoint active, apply animation effects to each item on each slide.
7. Run the presentation.
8. Save **P-C8-A1-NWPres.pptx**.
9. Print the presentation as a handout with six slides printed horizontally per page.
10. Export the presentation to a Word document that prints blank lines next to slides.
11. Save the Word document and name it **P-C8-A1-NWPresHandout**.
12. Print and then close **P-C8-A1-NWPresHandout.docx** and then close Word.
13. In PowerPoint, close **P-C8-A1-NWPres.pptx**.

2 COPY AND LINK WORD AND EXCEL DATA INTO A COMMUNICATIONS PRESENTATION

1. Open **CommPres.pptx** and then save the presentation with Save As and name it **P-C8-A2-CommPres**.
2. Open Word and then open the document named **VerbalSkills.docx** (located in the PC8 folder on your storage medium).
3. Copy the table and embed it (use the Paste Special dialog box and click Microsoft Word Document Object in the *As* list box) into Slide 5.
4. Resize the table so it better fills the slide.
5. Make Word active, close the **VerbalSkills.docx** document, and then close Word.
6. Open Excel and then open the workbook named **NVCues.xlsx** (located in the PC8 folder on your storage medium).
7. Copy the chart and link it to Slide 6. Resize the chart so it fills a majority of the slide below the title.
8. Save and then close **P-C8-A2-CommPres.pptx**.
9. Make the following changes to the chart in **NVCues.xlsx**:
   a. Change the amount in B2 from *35%* to *38%*.
   b. Change the amount in B3 from *25%* to *22%*.
10. Save and then close **NVCues.xlsx** and then close Excel.
11. In PowerPoint, open **P-C8-A2-CommPres.pptx**. (At the message that displays when you open the presentation, click the Update Links button.)
12. Make Slide 2 active and then insert the following comment after the second bulleted item: **Ask Lauren to provide a specific communication example.**
13. Make Slide 4 active and then insert the following comment after the third bulleted item: **Insert a link here to the writing presentation prepared by Sylvia.**
14. Make Slide 8 active and then insert the following comment after the third bulleted item: **Distribute evaluation forms to audience.**
15. Run the presentation.
16. Save the presentation and then print the presentation as a handout with four slides printed horizontally per page and make sure the comments print.
17. Run the Document Inspector and remove comments.
18. Run the accessibility checker and then create the following alt text (right-click chart, click *Format Object*, click the Size & Properties icon at the Format Object task pane, click *ALT TEXT*) for the chart in Slide 6 with the title *Top Five Nonverbal Cues* and the description *Eye contact, 38%; Smiling, 22%; Posture, 15%; Position, 15%; Gestures, 10%.*
19. Close the Format Object task pane and the Accessibility Checker task pane.
20. Save and then close **P-C8-A2-CommPres.pptx**.

Assessment

3   SAVE A SALES CONFERENCE PRESENTATION IN VARIOUS FORMATS

1. Open **P-C8-A1-NWPres.pptx** and then save the presentation in the PowerPoint 97-2003 Presentation (*.ppt) file format and name the presentation **P-C8-A3-NWPres-2003format**. (At the compatibility checker dialog box, click Continue.)
2. Close **P-C8-A3-NWPres-2003format.ppt**.
3. Open **P-C8-A1-NWPres.pptx** and then save each slide in the presentation as a JPEG image file.
4. Close **P-C8-A1-NWPres.pptx** without saving the changes.
5. Open Word and at a blank document, complete the following steps:
   a. Change the font to Century Gothic, change the font size to 24 points, change the alignment to center, and then type **Nature's Way**.
   b. Press the Enter key and then insert the **Slide4.JPG** slide. (Use the Pictures button on the INSERT tab to insert this slide. The slide is located in the **P-C8-A1-NWPres** folder in the PC8 folder on your storage medium.)
   c. Change the height of the slide to 2.8 inches.
   d. Press Ctrl + End, press the Enter key, and then insert the **Slide5.JPG** slide.
   e. Change the height of the slide to 2.8 inches.
   f. Save the Word document and name it **P-C8-A3-Herbs**.
   g. Print and then close **P-C8-A3-Herbs.docx** and then close Word.
6. Open **P-C8-A1-NWPres.pptx** and then save the presentation in PDF file format. When the presentation displays in Adobe Reader, scroll through the presentation and then close Adobe Reader.
7. In PowerPoint, close **P-C8-A1-NWPres.pptx**.
8. Capture an image of the Open dialog box and insert the image in a PowerPoint slide by completing the following steps:
   a. Press Ctrl + N to display a new blank presentation.
   b. Click the Layout button in the Slides group on the HOME tab and then click the *Blank* layout at the drop-down list.
   c. Press Ctrl + F12 to display the Open dialog box.
   d. At the Open dialog box, make sure the PC8 folder on your storage medium is the active folder.
   e. Click the option box that displays to the right of the *File name* text box (option box that contains the text *All PowerPoint Presentations*) and then click *All Files (*.*)* at the drop-down list.
   f. Click the Change your view button arrow that displays below the search text box in the Open dialog box, and then click *List* at the drop-down list.
   g. Make sure that all of your project and assessment files display. You may need to resize the dialog box to display the files.
   h. Hold down the Alt key and then press the Print Screen button on your keyboard. (This captures an image of the Open dialog box.)
   i. Click the Cancel button to close the Open dialog box.
   j. Click the Paste button. (This inserts the image of the Open dialog box into the slide.)
9. Print the slide as a full page slide.
10. Close the presentation without saving it.

Assessment

4

DOWNLOAD AND FILL IN AN AWARD CERTIFICATE

1. Create the certificate shown in Figure 8.7 with the following specifications:
   a. In PowerPoint, display the New backstage area, click in the search text box, type **award certificate**, and then press Enter. Download the *Excellence award (with eagle)* template.
   b. Type the company name as shown in Figure 8.7, type your name in place of *Student Name*, type the current date in place of *Date*, and type the name and title of the president/CEO as shown in the figure.
2. Save the certificate and name it **P-C8-A4-Certificate**.
3. Print and then close **P-C8-A4-Certificate.pptx**.

Figure 8.7 Assessment 4

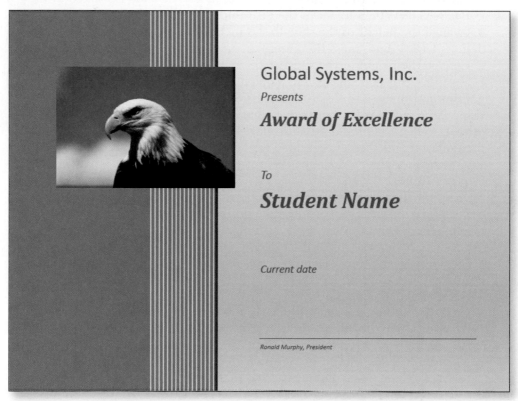

Visual Benchmark Demonstrate Your Proficiency

1 CREATE JPEG IMAGE FILES AND CREATE A WORD DOCUMENT

1. Open **FCTTours.pptx**, save all of the slides in the presentation in the JPEG graphic format, and then close **FCTTours.pptx** without saving the changes.
2. Open Word and, at a blank document, create the document shown in Figure 8.8 on the next page with the following specifications:
   a. Set the two lines of text in 24-point Calibri bold.
   b. Insert each slide and change the height of each slide to 2.5 inches, change the text wrapping to *Tight*, and size and position the slides as shown in Figure 8.8.
3. Save the completed Word document and name it **P-C8-VB1-FCTCovers**.
4. Print and then close **P-C8-VB1-FCTCovers.docx** and then close Word.

2 CREATE A TRAVEL COMPANY PRESENTATION

1. Create the presentation shown in Figure 8.9 on pages 375–376 with the following specifications:
   a. In PowerPoint, download the template named *Photo journal design template*.
   b. Delete all of the slides in the downloaded presentation.
   c. Use the **FCTQtrlyMtg.docx** Word outline document to create the slides in the presentation. ***Hint: Use the* Slides from Outline *option at the New Slide button drop-down list.***
   d. Insert a new slide at the beginning of the presentation using the Blank layout and then insert the **FCTLogo.jpg** image. (See the first slide in Figure 8.9.) Make the white background of the logo transparent. (Do this with the *Set Transparent Color* option from the Color button drop-down gallery on the PICTURE TOOLS FORMAT tab.) Size and position the logo as shown in Figure 8.9.
   e. Make Slide 5 active, apply the Title Only layout, and then copy and link the Excel chart in **Bookings.xlsx** to the slide. Size and position the chart as shown in Figure 8.9. (Close Excel after inserting the chart.)
2. Save the presentation and name it **P-C8-VB2-FCTQtrlyMtgPres**.
3. Print the presentation as a handout with six slides printed horizontally per page.
4. Close **P-C8-VB2-FCTQtrlyMtgPres.pptx**.
5. Open Excel, open **Bookings.xlsx**, and then make the following changes to the data in the specified cells:
   - C2: Change *45* to *52*
   - C3: Change *36* to *41*
   - C4: Change *24* to *33*
   - C5: Change *19* to *25*
6. After making the changes, save and then close **Bookings.xlsx** and then close Excel.
7. Open **P-C8-VB2-FCTQtrlyMtgPres.pptx** and update the links.
8. Print the presentation as a handout with six slides printed horizontally per page.
9. Save and then close **P-C8-VB2-FCTQtrlyMtgPres.pptx**.

Figure 8.8 Visual Benchmark 1

First Choice Travel

Proposed Tour Package Covers

Figure 8.9 Visual Benchmark 2

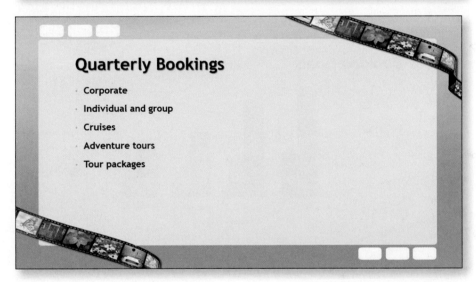

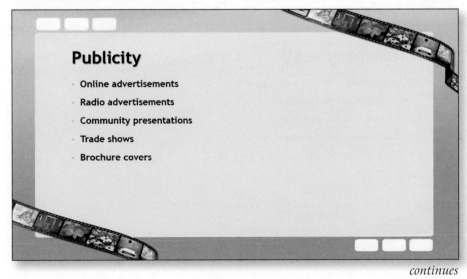

continues

Figure 8.9 Visual Benchmark 2—*continued*

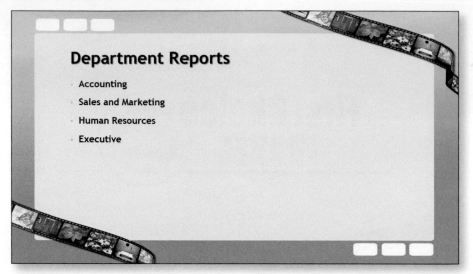

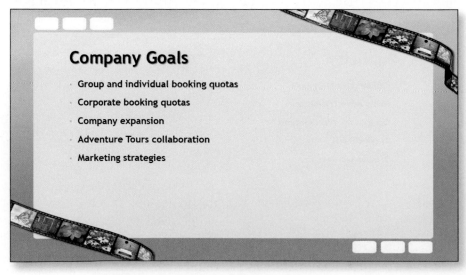

Case Study   Apply Your Skills

Part 1

You work for Rocky Mountain Family Medicine and are responsible for preparing education and training materials and publications for the center. You want to be able to insert the center logo in publications so you decide to save the logo as a graphic image. To do this, open the presentation (one slide) named **RMFMLogo.pptx** and then save the slide as a JPEG graphic image.

Part 2

You are responsible for presenting information on childhood diseases at an education class at a local community center. Open the Word document named **ChildDiseases.docx** and then use the information to create a presentation with the following specifications:

- Open the **RMFMDesign.pptx** presentation and then save the presentation with the name **P-C8-CS-RMFMDiseases**.
- Use the Title Only layout for the first slide, type an appropriate title for the presentation, and then insert the **RMFMLogo.jpg** graphic image in the first slide. Set transparent color to the background of the logo image. (Do this with the *Set Transparent Color* option in the Color button drop-down list on the PICTURE TOOLS FORMAT tab.) Size and position the logo attractively on the slide.
- Create additional slides with the information in the **ChildDiseases.docx** Word document.
- Apply any additional enhancements to improve the presentation.

Save and then run the presentation. Print the presentation as a handout with six slides printed horizontally per page and then close the presentation.

Part 3

You need to prepare a presentation for an upcoming education and training meeting. Open **RMFMDesign.pptx** and then save the presentation and name it **P-C8-CS-RMFMClasses**. Import the Word outline document named **RMFMOutline.docx** and then make the following changes:

- Create the first slide with the Title Only layout, insert the **RMFMLogo.jpg** graphic image, and then format, size, and position the logo in the same manner as the first slide in **P-C8-CS-RMFMDiseases.pptx**. Insert the title *Education and Training* in the title placeholder.
- Apply the Title Only layout to the *Community Contacts* slide and then copy the table from the Word document **RMFMContacts.docx** and paste it into the *Community Contacts* slide. Increase the size of the table so it better fills the slide.
- Apply the Title Only layout to the *Current Enrollment* slide and then copy the chart from the Excel workbook **RMFMEnroll.xlsx** and link it to the *Current Enrollment* slide.
- Apply any additional enhancements to improve the presentation.

Save and then run the presentation. Print the presentation as a handout with six slides printed horizontally per page and then close the presentation. You check the enrollments for classes and realize that more people have enrolled, so you need to update the numbers in the Excel workbook. Open **RMFMEnroll.xlsx** and then change *46* to *52*, *38* to *40*, and *24* to *27*. Save and then close the workbook. Open **P-C8-CS-RMFMClasses.pptx** and then update the links. Print only the *Current Enrollment* slide and then close the presentation.

Part 4

You decide that you want to include information on measles in the **P-C8-CS-RMFMDiseases.pptx** presentation on measles. Using the Internet, search for information such as symptoms, complications, transmission, and prevention. Include this information in new slides in the **P-C8-CS-RMFMDiseases.pptx** presentation. Run the presentation and then print only the new slides. Save and then close the presentation.

MICROSOFT®

POWERPOINT® Performance Assessment

Note: Before beginning unit assessments, copy to your storage medium the PU2 folder from the PowerPoint folder on the CD that accompanies this textbook and then make PU2 the active folder.

Assessing Proficiency ■■■■■■□□□□□□■■■■

In this unit you have learned to add visual elements to presentations such as tables, charts, and SmartArt graphics; create a photo album; apply formatting in Slide Master view; insert action buttons; apply custom animation effects; and set up slide shows. You also learned how to copy, embed, and link data between programs; how to insert comments; and how to protect and prepare a presentation.

Assessment 1 Save and Insert a Slide in JPEG Format, Format a Slide Master, Create a Table and SmartArt Graphics, and Insert Comments

1. Open **GreenDesignLogo.pptx**, save the only slide in the presentation as a JPEG graphic image, and then close **GreenDesignLogo.pptx**.
2. Open **GreenDesignPres.pptx** and then save the presentation with the name **P-U2-A1-GreenDesignPres**.
3. Display the presentation in Slide Master view and then make the following changes:
   a. Click the top slide master thumbnail.
   b. Select the text *Click to edit Master text styles* (in the bulleted section), change the font color to Tan, Background 2, Darker 75% (third column, fifth row), and change the font size to 28 points.
   c. Select the text *Second level*, apply the Green, Accent 1 font color (fifth column, first row), and then change the font size to 24 points.
   d. Close Slide Master view.
4. Make Slide 1 active and then make the following changes:
   a. Insert the **GreenDesignLogo.jpg** graphic image.
   b. Set transparent color for the logo background (the white background). (Do this with the *Set Transparent Color* option at the Color button drop-down gallery on the PICTURE TOOLS FORMAT tab.)
   c. Reduce the size of the logo and position it in the white space in the upper right corner of the slide above the water image.
5. Make Slide 6 active and then insert the following data in a table. You determine the formatting and positioning of the table and its data (next page):

Project	Contact	Completion Date
Moyer-Sylvan Complex	Barry MacDonald	07/31/2016
Waterfront Headquarters	Jasmine Jefferson	02/15/2017
Linden Square	Marion Van Horn	09/30/2017
Village Green	Parker Alderton	12/31/2017
Cedar Place Market	Gerry Halderman	03/31/2018

6. Make Slide 7 active and then insert the data from Figure U2.1 in a SmartArt organizational chart. You determine the organization and formatting of the chart.

7. Make Slide 5 active and then create a bar chart with the following data. Delete the chart title and chart legend. You determine the formatting and layout of the chart.

	Revenues
1st Qtr	$25,250,000
2nd Qtr	$34,000,000
3rd Qtr	$22,750,000
4th Qtr	$20,500,000

8. Make Slide 8 active and then insert a SmartArt graphic with the *Repeating Bending Process* graphic (found in the *Process* group) with the following information (insert the information in the slides from left to right). You determine the design and formatting of the SmartArt graphic.
   Mission Analysis
   Requirements Analysis
   Function Allocation
   Design
   Verification

9. Check each slide and make any changes that improve the visual appearance of the slide.

10. Make Slide 1 active and then run the presentation.

11. Make Slide 3 active, click in the slide title placeholder, and then position the insertion point immediately right of the slide title. Display the Comments pane and then insert the comment **Check with Marilyn about adding River View Mall to this list.**

12. Make Slide 4 active, click immediately right of the word *Australia* in the bulleted text, and then insert the comment **What happened to the plans to open an office in Sydney?**

13. Print the presentation as a handout with four slides printed horizontally per page and make sure the comments print.

14. Save and then close **P-U2-A1-GreenDesignPres.pptx**.

Figure U2.1 Assessment 1

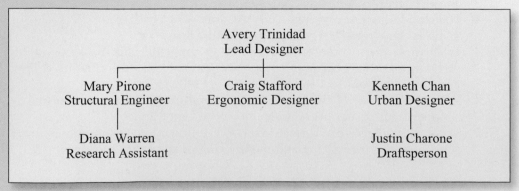

Assessment 2 Copy and Paste Data between Programs and Insert Action Buttons in a Travel Presentation

1. Open **NortonTravelPres.pptx** and then save the presentation with the name **P-U2-A2-NortonTravelPres**.
2. Make Slide 4 active and then create a new Slide 5 (with the Title Only layout) with the following specifications:
   a. Insert the title *Extreme Adventures* in the slide.
   b. Open Word and then open **NTExtremeAdventures.docx**.
   c. Display the Clipboard task pane. (Make sure the task pane is empty. If not, click the Clear All button.)
   d. Select and then copy *Small Groups*, the paragraph below it, and the blank line below the paragraph.
   e. Select and then copy *Comprehensive Itineraries*, the paragraph below it, and the blank line below the paragraph.
   f. Select and then copy *Custom Groups*, the paragraph below it, and the blank line below the paragraph.
   g. Select and then copy *Accommodations*, the paragraph below it, and the blank line below the paragraph.
   h. Display the **P-U2-A2-NortonTravelPres.pptx** presentation.
   i. Draw a text box below the title that is approximately 10 inches wide.
   j. Turn on the display of the Clipboard task pane.
   k. Paste the *Comprehensive Itineraries* item in the text box in the slide.
   l. Paste the *Small Groups* item in the text box.
   m. Paste the *Accommodations* item in the text box.
   n. Clear and then close the Clipboard.
   o. Make the **NTExtremeAdventures.docx** document active, close the Clipboard task pane, close the document, and then close Word.
3. Make Slide 1 active and then insert an action button with the following specifications:
   a. Use the *Action Button: Forward or Next* option to draw the button.
   b. Draw the button in the lower right corner of the slide and make it approximately one-half inch in size.
   c. Apply the Subtle Effect - Aqua, Accent 2 shape style.
4. Display the presentation in Slide Master view and then make the following changes:
   a. Click the top slide master thumbnail.
   b. Insert an action button in the lower right corner of the slide with the same specifications as those in Step 3.
   c. Close Slide Master view.
5. Run the presentation. (Use the action buttons to advance slides. At the last slide, press the Esc key.)
6. Create a footer that prints your first and last names at the bottom of each slide, create a footer for handouts that prints the presentation title *2016 Adventure Packages*, and insert the date in the upper right corner.
7. Print the presentation as a handout with six slides printed horizontally per page.
8. Save and then close **P-U2-A2-NortonTravelPres.pptx**.

Assessment 3 Save a Template Presentation and Copy, Embed, and Link Objects between Programs

1. Open **GSTemplate.pptx**.
2. Display the presentation in Slide Master view, insert **GSLogo.jpg** in the top slide master thumbnail (use the Picture button on the INSERT tab to insert the logo), change the height of the logo to one inch, and drag the logo to the lower right corner of the slide master, and then close Slide Master view.
3. Save the presentation as a template (to the Custom Office Templates folder) and name the presentation **XXXGSTemplate** (use your initials in place of the *XXX*).
4. Close **XXXGSTemplate.potx**.
5. Open **XXXGSTemplate.potx**. (To do this, display the New backstage area, click the CUSTOM option, and then double-click the *XXXGSTemplate. potx* thumbnail.)
6. Save the presentation and name it **P-U2-A3-GSMtg**.
7. Format the first slide with the following specifications:
   a. Change to the Blank layout.
   b. Use WordArt to create the text *Global Systems*. (You determine the shape and formatting of the WordArt text.)
8. Create the second slide with the following specifications:
   a. Choose the Title Slide layout.
   b. Type **2016 Sales Meeting** as the title.
   c. Type **European Division** as the subtitle.
9. Create the third slide with the following specifications:
   a. Choose the Title Only layout.
   b. Type **Regional Sales** as the title.
   c. Open Excel and then open **GSWorkbook01.xlsx**.
   d. Select cells A1 through D5 (the cells containing data) and then copy and embed the cells in Slide 3 as a Microsoft Excel Worksheet Object.
   e. Increase the size of the cells so they better fill the slide.
10. Create the fourth slide with the following specifications:
    a. Choose the Title and Content layout.
    b. Type **Company Goals** as the title.
    c. Type the following as the bulleted items:
       • **Increase product sales by 15 percent**
       • **Open a branch office in Spain**
       • **Hire one manager and two additional account managers**
       • **Decrease production costs by 6 percent**
11. Create the fifth slide with the following specifications:
    a. Choose the Title and Content layout.
    b. Type **Hiring Timeline** as the title.
    c. Create a table with two columns and five rows and then type the following text in the cells in the table. (You determine the formatting of the cells.)

Task	Date
Advertise positions	03/01/2016 to 04/30/2016
Review resumes	05/15/2016 to 06/01/2016
Conduct interviews	06/15/2016 to 07/15/2016
Hire personnel	08/01/2016

12. Create the sixth slide with the following specifications:
    a. Choose the Title Only layout.
    b. Type **Production Expenses** as the title.
    c. Make Excel the active program and then close **GSWorkbook01.xlsx**.
    d. Open **GSWorkbook02.xlsx**.
    e. Save the workbook with Save As and name it **GSExpensesWorkbook**.
    f. Copy and then link the pie chart in **GSExpensesWorkbook.xlsx** to Slide 6. Size and center the pie chart on the slide.
    g. Make Excel active, close **GSExpensesWorkbook.xlsx**, and then close Excel.
13. Run the presentation.
14. Create a footer for handouts that prints the presentation title *2016 Sales Meeting* and insert the date in the upper right corner.
15. Print the presentation as a handout with six slides printed horizontally per page.
16. Save and then close **P-U2-A3-GSMtg.pptx**.
17. Open Excel and then open **GSExpensesWorkbook.xlsx**.
18. Make the following changes:
    a. B2: Change *38% to 41%*
    b. B3: Change *35% to 32%*
    c. B4: Change *18% to 21%*
    d. B5: Change *9% to 6%*
19. Save, print, and close **GSExpensesWorkbook.xlsx** and then close Excel.
20. With PowerPoint the active program, open **P-U2-A3-GSMtg.pptx**. (At the message that displays, click the Update Links button.)
21. Display Slide 3, double-click the cells, and then make the following changes to the data in the embedded cells:
    a. C2: Change *2678450* to *2857300*
    b. C3: Change *1753405* to *1598970*
    c. C4: Change *1452540* to *1635400*
22. Run the presentation.
23. Print the presentation as a handout with six slides printed horizontally per page.
24. Save **P-U2-A3-GSMtg.pptx**.
25. Apply a transition and sound of your choosing to all slides in the presentation.
26. Use the Rehearse Timings feature to set the following times for the slides to display during a slide show (your actual time will display with an extra second for each slide):
    > Slide 1 = 3 seconds
    > Slide 2 = 3 seconds
    > Slide 3 = 6 seconds
    > Slide 4 = 5 seconds
    > Slide 5 = 6 seconds
    > Slide 6 = 5 seconds
27. Set up the slide show to run continuously.
28. Run the presentation beginning with Slide 1. Watch the slide show until the presentation has started for the second time and then end the show.
29. Save and then close the presentation.

Assessment 4 Apply Custom Animation Effects to a Travel Presentation

1. Open **NTAustralia.pptx** and then save the presentation with the name **P-U2-A4-NTAustralia**.
2. With Slide 1 active, apply a Fly In entrance animation effect to the subtitle *Australia Tour* that has the title fly in from the bottom.
3. Display the presentation in Slide Master view and then make the following changes:
    a. Click the third slide master thumbnail.
    b. Apply a Fly In entrance animation effect to the title that has the title fly in from the top.
    c. Apply a Fly In entrance animation effect to the bulleted text that has the text fly in from the left and then dims to a color of your choosing when the next bullet displays.
    d. Close Slide Master view.
4. Make Slide 5 active, select the sun shape that displays above *Sydney*, and then draw a freeform motion path from Sydney to Melbourne, Tasmania, Adelaide, Perth, Derby, Darwin, Cairns, and then back to Sydney. Change the duration to *04.00*.
5. Make Slide 6 active and then make the following changes:
    a. Click the bottom shape to select it. (You may want to move the top two shapes out of the way.)
    b. Apply the Grow & Turn entrance effect.
    c. Click the Add Animation button and then click the *Shrink & Turn* exit effect.
    d. Click the middle shape to select it and then apply the Grow & Turn entrance effect.
    e. Click the Add Animation button and then click the *Shrink & Turn* exit effect.
    f. Click the top shape to select it and then apply the Grow & Turn entrance effect.
    g. Position the shapes so they are stacked on top of each other so you do not see a portion of the shapes behind.
6. Save **P-U2-A4-NTAustralia.pptx**.
7. Make Slide 1 active, run the presentation, and then make sure the animation effects play correctly.
8. Print the presentation as a handout with all slides printed horizontally on one page.
9. Close **P-U2-A4-NTAustralia.pptx**.

Assessment 5 Inspect a Presentation and Save a Presentation in Different Formats

1. Open **P-U2-A1-GreenDesignPres.pptx** and then save the presentation with the name **P-U2-A5-GreenDesignPres**.
2. Inspect the presentation using the Document Inspector dialog box and remove comments from the presentation.
3. Run the compatibility checker. (Click OK at the Microsoft Compatibility Checker dialog box.)
4. Save the presentation in *PowerPoint 97-2003* format and name it **P-U2-A5-GreenDesignPres-2003format**. (Click the Continue button at the compatibility checker message.)
5. Close **P-U2-A5-GreenDesignPres-2003format.ppt**.

6. Open **P-U2-A5-GreenDesignPres.pptx** and then save the presentation as a PDF document.
7. View the presentation in Adobe Reader.
8. After viewing all of the slides, close Adobe Reader.
9. Close **P-U2-A5-GreenDesignPres.pptx** without saving the changes.
10. Capture an image of the Open dialog box and insert the image in a PowerPoint slide by completing the following steps:
    a. Press Ctrl + N to display a new blank presentation.
    b. Click the Layout button in the Slides group on the HOME tab and then click the *Blank* layout at the drop-down list.
    c. Press Ctrl + F12 to display the Open dialog box.
    d. At the Open dialog box, click the option button that displays to the right of the *File name* text box (option button that contains the text *All Power-Point Presentations*) and then click *All Files (*.*)* at the drop-down list.
    e. Scroll down the Open dialog box list box to display your assessment files.
    f. Hold down the Alt key and then press the Print Screen button on your keyboard. (This captures an image of your Open dialog box.)
    g. Click the Cancel button to close the Open dialog box.
    h. Click the Paste button. (This inserts the image of your Open dialog box into the slide.)
11. Print the slide as a full page slide.
12. Close the presentation without saving it.

Writing Activities ■■■■■■■■■■■■■■■■■■■

The following activities give you the opportunity to practice your writing skills along with demonstrating an understanding of some of the important PowerPoint features you have mastered in this unit. Use correct grammar, appropriate word choices, and clear sentence structure.

Activity 1 Prepare and Format a Travel Presentation

You work for Norton Travel and you are responsible for preparing a presentation on travel vacations. Open the Word document named **NTVacations.docx** and then print the document. Close the document and then close Word. Using the information in the document, prepare a PowerPoint presentation with the following specifications:

1. Create a presentation that presents the main points of the document.
2. Rehearse and set times for the slides to display during a slide show. You determine the number of seconds for each slide.
3. Insert a song into the first slide from the Insert Audio window (type **summer** in the search text box).
4. Set up the presentation to run continuously and the audio to play automatically across all slides and continuously as long as the presentation is running.
5. Run the presentation. (The slide show will start and run continuously.) Watch the presentation until it has started for the second time and then end the show by pressing the Esc key.
6. Save the presentation and name it **P-U2-Act1-NTVacations**.
7. Print the presentation as a handout with six slides printed horizontally per page.
8. Close **P-U2-Act1-NTVacations.pptx**.

Activity 2 Prepare and Format a Presentation on Media Files

Using PowerPoint's Help feature, learn more about audio and video file formats compatible with PowerPoint 2013. (Use the search terms *video and audio file formats*.) Using the information you find in the Help files, create a presentation with *at least* the following specifications:

- A slide containing the title of the presentation and your name
- Two slides that each contain information on compatible audio file formats, including the file extensions
- Two slides that each contain information on compatible video file formats, including the file extensions
- Optional: If you are connected to the Internet, search for websites where you can download free audio clips and then include this information in a slide with a hyperlink to the site.

Save the completed presentation and name it **P-U2-Act2-AudioVideo**. Run the presentation and then print the presentation as a handout with six slides printed horizontally per page. Close **P-U2-Act2-AudioVideo.pptx**.

Internet Research ■■■■■■■■■■■■■■■■■■■■

Presenting Office 2013

Make sure you are connected to the Internet and then explore the Microsoft website at www.microsoft.com. Browse the various categories and links on the website to familiarize yourself with how information is organized.

Create a PowerPoint presentation to deliver to someone who has just purchased Office 2013 and wants to know how to find more information about the software on the Microsoft website. Include tips on where to find product release information and technical support, as well as hyperlinks to other important pages. Add formatting and enhancements to make the presentation as dynamic as possible. Save the presentation and name it **P-U2-Int-Office2013**. Run the presentation and then print the presentation as a handout with four slides printed per page. Close **P-U2-Int-Office2013.pptx**.

Job Study ■■■■■■■■■■■■■■■■■■■■■■■■■■■■

Creating a Skills Presentation

You are preparing a presentation to give at your local job fair. Open the Word document **JobDescriptions.docx**, print the document, and then close the document and close Word. Use the information in the document to prepare slides that describe each job (do not include the starting salary). Using the Internet, locate information on two other jobs that interest you and then create a slide about the responsibilities of each job. Determine the starting salary for the two jobs and then use that information along with the starting salary information for the jobs in the Word document to create a chart that displays the salary amounts. Locate at least two online job search websites and then include their names in your presentation along with hyperlinks to the sites. Save the presentation and name it **P-U2-JobStudy**. Run the presentation and then print the presentation as a handout with six slides printed horizontally per page. Close **P-U2-JobStudy.pptx**.

Index